MW00532779

MULTICRISES

The MIT Press
Cambridge, Massachusetts, and London, England

MULTICRISES

SEA POWER AND GLOBAL POLITICS IN THE MISSILE AGE

JONATHAN TRUMBULL HOWE

Set in Linofilm Helvetica by Southern New England Typographic Service.
Printed by Publication Press, Inc.
Bound in the United States of America by The Maple Press Co.

ISBN 0262 08043 5 (hardcover)
Library of Congress catalog card number: 70–122258

The opinions or assertions in this book are the personal ones of the author and are not to be construed as official. They do not necessarily reflect the views of the Department of the Navy or the U.S. government.
JTH

To Robert Burgess Stewart and Uri Ra'anan

TABLES

FIGURES

PREFACE

As a new decade begins, one of the crucial issues of national security policy is the extent of American global responsibilities. In the following pages several aspects of American capability to meet its international obligations have been examined. Capability has been considered in a broad context of military, political, economic, psychological, and international elements. A primary objective has been to determine whether the United States is able to cope effectively with a second cold war crisis. In studying this question greater understanding has been gained of American decision making in a multicrisis involving the competing interests of the superpowers. A related objective has been to evaluate the effectiveness of conventional naval forces as instruments of foreign policy in the nuclear age.[1] Needless to say, the study does not attempt to examine every facet of these problems. But it has attempted to raise meaningful questions and provide some helpful insights relevant to the future conduct of American foreign policy.

The Middle East crisis of 1967 and the Quemoy crisis of 1958 have been selected for detailed analysis. Because these situations involved two of America's most sensitive and controversial global commitments, some of the evidence remains in classified form and therefore has not been available. There is, however, a wealth of public sources. In addition, the author has had the benefit of candid conversations and correspondence with a number of the principals in each crisis.

While there is a certain loss of perspective that accompanies a study of contemporary problems, there are some compensations for the researcher. In addition to providing relevant insights, there is also benefit derived from discussing the crises with decision makers before recollections become clouded by time. As has been discovered in this research, an important dimension of history is never properly documented. Telephone conversations and informal conferences at the height of a crisis provide an essential source for analysis that is absent in the dry verbiage of top secret briefing papers and intelligence assessments.

Analysis of Soviet intentions, as undertaken in this volume, is also an uncertain business that ultimately depends on an educated

[1]In singling out the political-military role of warships for evaluation, it is not meant to imply that other missions of the armed forces are less important or unrelated. There is no attempt to assess the relative value of the various diplomatic, political, economic, and military instruments of American foreign policy.

guess. However, the esoteric communications of the closed Communist society do provide revealing hints as to what transpires within the Kremlin walls.

The figures in Chapters 6, 11, and 12, used to summarize the evidence influencing capability factors and to show their interaction, are also subject to a number of qualifications and limitations. The main function is to illustrate, in a simplified form, an estimate of the relative influence of forces affecting capability. In many instances the judgments represented are, by necessity, highly speculative.

In undertaking this study I have been struck by the overwhelmingly generous and enthusiastic response of persons to whom I have addressed questions. Most of these individuals are enumerated in Appendix C, Sections 2.1 and 2.2.

A number of other authorities have been extremely helpful but do not desire attribution. The assistance of all these kind spirits is gratefully acknowledged. Most of the interview transcripts and letters, as well as interviews with various informed sources familiar with the crises, are on file at the Fletcher School of Law and Diplomacy. It is hoped they will provide a useful source of contemporary information for future scholars.

In preparing this manuscript I have benefited from the constructive suggestions of a number of persons. Professor Robert B. Stewart has provided exceedingly thorough and penetrating criticism. His objective and sound approach to American foreign policy has been presented in seminars that I have had the privilege of attending and many private consultations. Without his early recognition of the potential contribution of this study and encouragement during its preparation, it would not have been possible.

Professor Uri Ra'anan provided me with a wealth of insight concerning the Soviet Union and world politics in many hours of direct conversation as well as in his enlightening classes. I am grateful for his many helpful criticisms of this effort, enthusiastic encouragement, and most of all for his example of superior scholarship.

A number of other professors have read all or parts of this manuscript at some stage of preparation and offered useful criticisms. Professor Alexander F. Kiefer lent an element of practical insight into the workings of American policy as well as an important sense of perspective and proportion. Professor James Moceri devoted a number of hours to a thorough review and discussion of the Quemoy crisis, of which he has a firsthand knowledge. Professors Allan B. Cole and William E. Griffith have read the Quemoy section and provided useful criticism at stages in its development. It is a tribute to the Fletcher School of Law and Diplomacy that these experts in the field of international relations and many other members of the faculty readily devoted so many hours to productive consultations. I am also grateful to Geraldine Maciejewski of Winchester, Massachusetts, who typed the manuscript. I alone, of course, am responsible for the inadequacies, contents, and conclusions of this book, which was written prior to my assignment to the Office of the Assistant to the President for National Security Affairs.

Commander Jonathan T. Howe, USN
Washington, D.C.

I INTRODUCTION

1. HISTORICAL BACKGROUND

Following World War II the United States rapidly became a global power. For the first time it assumed permanent responsibilities beyond the historic regional limits of the Western Hemisphere. As the ambitions of the Soviet Union became apparent, there was a renewed awareness that American interests remained vitally linked to the security of the free world. In 1947 President Truman declared that American security was involved wherever aggression threatened the peace.[1] Shocked by Soviet subjugation of Eastern Europe and Russian-sponsored aggression in Korea, the United States formalized its intentions to withstand the threat in a series of mutual security treaties. Within the decade the United States made collective defense arrangements with forty-two nations. Figure 1.1 shows the countries with which the United States has defense treaties and other formal security arrangements. The rationale for these commitments was to give confidence to friends and to deter Communist aggression.

These formal commitments hardly defined the full scope of international responsibilities undertaken by the United States. Through executive agreements, declarations, presidential statements, and other means, officials of the government have identified American interests with the fate of many other nations. By unpublicized assurances and tacit acceptance of certain situations, global enterprises of private citizens, and actions of governmental agencies, the United States has become involved throughout the world. Government officials have continued to assert that the absence of a formal obligation does not grant "immunity to aggression."[2] In words reminiscent of those of President Truman, the Secretary of Defense testified in 1967 that "any threat to peace in any part of the world could, in some measure, become a threat to our own security and well be-

[1]President Truman has written that the Truman Doctrine, which was pronounced on March 12, 1947, was "the turning point in America's foreign policy, which now declared that wherever aggression, direct or indirect, threatened the peace, the security of the United States was involved." In sweeping language the doctrine stated that "it must be the policy of the United States to support free peoples who are resisting attempted subjugation by armed minorities or by outside pressures." Harry S. Truman, *Memoirs, Years of Trial and Hope* (Garden City, N.Y.: Doubleday and Co., 1956), p. 106.

[2]In 1966 Secretary of State Rusk warned that "No would-be aggressor should suppose that the absence of a defense treaty, congressional declaration, or U.S. military presence grants immunity to aggression." U.S., Congress, Senate, Preparedness Investigating Subcommittee of the Committee on Armed Services, *Worldwide Military Commitments*, 89th Cong., 2nd sess. (Washington, 1966), p. 9.

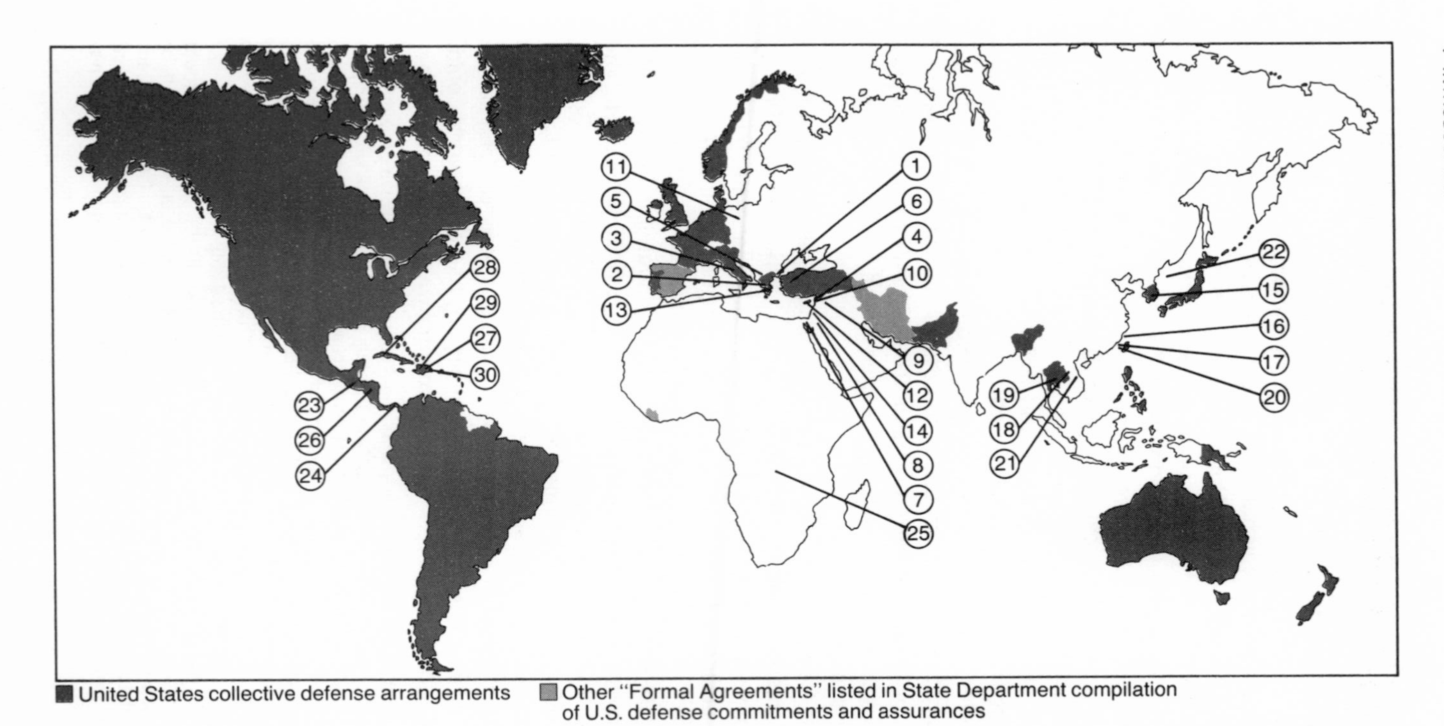

Figure 1.1 Locations of U.S. defense commitments contained in treaties and other formal assurances and cold war crises involving U.S. naval power

Multicrisis Situations

Far East	Mediterranean
1. Korean War (15)	Lebanon (4), Yugoslavia 1951 (5), Turkey 1953 (6)
2. Quemoy (17)	Lebanon (10)
3. Vietnam (21), *Pueblo* (22)	Greek coup (13), Arab-Israeli war (14)

Note: Numbers in parentheses and those circled on Figure 1.1 correspond to events listed in Tables 2.1 through 2.3 in the next chapter.

Countries with which the United States has collective defense arrangements:
Canada, Iceland, Norway, United Kingdom, Netherlands, Denmark, Belgium, Luxembourg, Portugal, France, Italy, Greece, Turkey, Federal Republic of Germany, Mexico, Cuba,* Haiti, Dominican Republic, Honduras, Guatemala, El Salvador, Nicaragua, Costa Rica, Panama, Colombia, Venezuela, Ecuador, Peru, Brazil, Bolivia, Paraguay, Chile, Argentina, Uruguay, Trinidad and Tobago, New Zealand, Australia, Phillippines, Japan, Republic of Korea, Thailand, Pakistan, Republic of China.

Other countries with which "Formal Agreements" exist:
Spain, Liberia, Iran.

*Although Cuba signed the Rio Pact, Resolution IV of the Final Act of the Eighth Meeting of Consultation of Ministers of Foreign Affairs of the American Republics, Punta del Este, signed January 31, 1962, excluded "the present Government of Cuba, which has officially identified itself as a Marxist-Leninist government" from participation in the inter-American system.

ing."[3] The most important determinant of danger to American security has been the degree of Russian involvement. United States security policy has been primarily a response to the aims of Soviet global strategy and, to a lesser extent, perceptions of Chinese intentions.

However, American assumption of a wide range of tacit and explicit responsibilities has not prevented a Russian effort to achieve hegemony in certain areas of the world. While there have been many changes in the tactics employed, challenges and the resulting conflicts have been an unvarying theme of the cold war. The acquisition of a "second strike" thermonuclear capability in the 1960s by the Soviet Union complicated the task of coping with Moscow's worldwide aspirations. The range of threats deterred by the possibility of massive retaliation has been narrowed. The McNamara doctrine of flexible response was fashioned to meet the wider challenges of the 1960s. In an attempt to expand Soviet influence, the USSR has exploited national liberation movements and the restive Third World, thus increasing the number of potential conflicts that might involve the interests of the United States. The threat is more subtle and, therefore, more difficult to meet.

The cost and complexity of dealing with a broader spectrum of threats has raised the widespread cry that the United States has "overcommitted" itself and can no longer afford to be the "world's policeman." The economic, military, political, and psychological strains of the protracted engagement in Southeast Asia have intensified this feeling; but the issue is much larger than the specific case of Vietnam. It concerns the whole cold war concept of collective security. Having experienced the benefits and burdens of global leadership, the United States has begun a critical reassessment of its role. Isolationist sentiment has revived, and the degree of American worldwide involvement has been seriously questioned. The debate concerns different perceptions of the interests of the United States and conflicting assessments of the limits of American power: congressional committees have expressed serious reservations about the extent of international obligations; foreign aid requests have been drastically reduced; and in the 1968 campaign both presidential candidates pledged a careful reappraisal of American commitments.

The assertion that the United States can no longer afford to play the role of "world policeman" needs careful analysis. During the

[3]Statement of Secretary of Defense Robert S. McNamara, in U.S. Congress, Senate, Committee on Armed Services and the Subcommittee on Dept. of Defense of the Committee on Appropriations, *Military Procurement Authorizations for Fiscal Year 1968*, 90th Cong., 1st sess. (Washington, 1967), p. 28.

past two decades this phrase has been used frequently by Soviet propagandists to convey American "protection of the ruling classes." However, the United States has been an anticolonial force. Its interventions against communism have not been in a policeman's role but in response to what in most cases was perceived to be an indirect challenge by Soviet power. The Vietnam war is a confrontation with the opposing camp. One can legitimately criticize an exaggerated perception of the Soviet threat or argue that it is not in the American interest to prevent a Pax Sovietica, but these criticisms must be distinguished from the misleading image of "global gendarme."

One could say that the United States has policed its own zones of influence. It has tried to impose itself between disputing friends, as in the case of Greece and Turkey and that of Israel and Jordan.[4] Those who have adopted the policeman image are usually not opposed to this limited peace-keeping role. Rather, these critics question the application of American power in civil wars or local disturbances that do not involve what they believe to be U.S. interests. America is accused of trying to single-handedly impose its sense of order on the world, but this country has directly involved itself in only about one-quarter of the world's major conflicts.[5] It has supported policing of international conflicts by the United Nations. Unfortunately, that organization was not designed to settle disputes between great powers and has been unable to cope with situations involving the conflicting interests of the United States and the Soviet Union.

A prominent issue of the foreign policy debate is whether net commitments are consistent with net capabilities. Repeatedly, the criticism has been made that the United States is overcommitted, but this is another imprecise phrase with a variety of connotations. While some feel that capabilities should not be the determinant of American interests, they argue that it is not in the American interest to be involved so extensively throughout the world. Others urge greater selectivity in commitments and identification of priorities because of limited American capacity. Critics of United States commitments frequently refer only to the formal legal obligations of the United States. However, security interests are not narrowly

[4]For example, during the 1967 Arab-Israeli confrontation the United States reputedly acted as an intermediary to transmit a message that Israel would not attack Jordan and urged Jordan not to participate in the attack against Israel.

[5]Of thirty-seven "International Political Crises and Critical Situations, 1961 to Mid-1966," the United States was involved in ten according to a list supplied by the Secretary of State to Congress. *Worldwide Military Commitments*, pp. 31, 32. In testimony the Secretary had recalled a figure of 6 out of 70 in which the United States was directly involved.

confined within the scope of formal defense treaties. For example, in the past the United States has made a military show of support for Tito of Yugoslavia and is deeply concerned with the fate of countries such as Israel and India with whom there are no alliances.

Others who assert that the United States is overcommitted refer to the possibility of American involvement in a number of "Vietnams" simultaneously. This is an unrealistic hypothesis. There are limitations to the number of conflicts that the Soviet Union can support at one time. On the other hand, it would be shortsighted to estimate military requirements only in terms of the power of major rivals. The substantial involvement of United States forces in Vietnam compared to only a light strain on China and the Soviet Union tends to disprove the thesis on which so much of defense planning in recent years has been predicated.[6] On a number of occasions "Kremlinologists" have been overly optimistic in their assessments of Russian intentions. The Czechoslovakian invasion of 1968 surprised many observers of Soviet affairs just as the act of planting offensive missiles in Cuba in 1962 astonished a number of experts. The traditional military inclination to put greater reliance on enemy capabilities, as opposed to perceptions of his intentions, may be overly conservative, but it does produce readiness to deal with the twists and turns in Soviet strategy.[7] The American penchant for rational explanations sometimes substitutes overly optimistic, wishful thinking for objective appraisals of Soviet policy.

A more plausible case of possible overcommitment is that of coping with a second threat while dealing with a preexisting crisis. It frequently is asserted that America is overcommitted without distinction as to where or when a second challenge occurs. To some critics of American involvement there is a necessity to define more clearly priorities because this country simply does not have the means to deal effectively with two situations at the same time. For others, the United States appears to have the potential but not the ready capability to cope with this type of challenge. Few understand the limits that are reached in such a multicrisis situation.

Since the Korean War the United States has maintained a ready capability to cope militarily with an isolated conflict of about the magnitude of that engagement. A number of simultaneous provo-

[6]See, for example, the statements of Secretary of Defense McNamara in *Military Procurement Authorizations for Fiscal Year 1968,* pp. 25, 72.
[7]There are, of course, limitations on resources that restrict the portion of the budget devoted to national security. In addition, intelligence estimates can be costly when made in the wrong direction. The "missile gap" of the late 1950s was based on predictions of potential to produce missiles, but the Soviets decided not to utilize the full extent of their potential.

cations of that magnitude might well be interpreted as equivalent to an outright missile attack on the United States. Between these limits there is a gray area in which America may be the most vulnerable. When involved in one limited war situation and challenged by a second one, U.S. security may be in greatest jeopardy. Two carefully limited conflicts at a time appear to be within the toleration levels of the superpowers without pushing them beyond the thermonuclear threshold.

During the last two decades there have been few periods without major crises. Potential conflicts involving the interests of the United States have existed at all times. It is on the level of intensity that major foreign policy dilemmas have been distinguished from everyday headaches. Numerous multicrises have developed. The locations of some major multiple challenges are displayed in Figure 1.1.[8] The Korean and Vietnamese wars appear to have produced a particularly inviting environment for second crisis tests.[9]

Vulnerability to further probes is apparently increased. The highest decision-making echelon tends to become "locked in" on the primary disturbance of the moment. Military capability is often reduced in the rest of the world. It is more economical and politically feasible to meet force requirements of an existing situation by diverting personnel and equipment from quiescent areas. In some instances it is the only way to meet an emergency shortage.

Limitations in such situations are not a new phenomenon. For example, the strain of the war in Vietnam has many parallels with the Korean War.[10] In 1961 President Kennedy reputedly was advised by the Joint Chiefs of Staff that he could not meet contingencies in both Laos and Cuba.[11] The criticism has been leveled that the United States shied away from threats to Israel in 1967[12] and could not respond to the *Pueblo* seizure in 1968 owing to its "overinvolvement" in Vietnam.

Because of these recent multicrisis situations a number of questions have been raised. What restraints are placed on American policy when dealing with a second crisis? How vulnerable is the United States in this situation? Does it tend to renege on its commitments or reinter-

[8]Only crises in which sea power had some specific role to play are shown.

[9]There were pressures in Yugoslavia, Turkey, and Lebanon that involved the United States during the Korean War. See Table 2.1.

[10]Robert Endicott Osgood, for example, asserted that the United States had "never fought a war more unpopular than the Korean War." *Limited War, The Challenge to American Strategy* (Chicago: The University of Chicago Press, 1957), p. 189.

[11]See William W. Kaufmann, *The McNamara Strategy* (New York: Harper and Row, 1964), p. 269.

[12]The validity of this accusation has been subjected to detailed evaluation in Part Two of this study.

pret its security interests at precisely the time that they are being most severely tested? What is the significance of adequate military capability and congressional and public opinion when dealing with a second crisis? How militarily and psychologically dependent on attitudes of allies does U.S. policy become?

In attempting to formulate answers to these questions, understanding of the multicrisis phenomenon should be increased. The influence of one crisis on a second challenge and vice versa should be clearer. The problems of translating American capacity into effective power during a second crisis should be more comprehensible. From such an understanding, better methods for dealing with the multicrises of the 1970s should become apparent.

Since there are actual cases available for examination, it is not necessary to make an analysis in hypothetical terms. In order to deal with the dynamics and complexities of the multicrisis, a model has been developed which evaluates those factors considered to be most relevant to a rational assessment of capability in any major crisis. The following factors have been considered: military (including the capabilities of the direct antagonists), economic, congressional and public opinion, the intentions of the Soviet Union, and dependence on allied support. By examining the relative changes that occur in these capability factors during various phases of a crisis, one can better understand the dynamics of a crisis and the changing importance of the various factors during the different phases. By assessing the influence of a prior commitment on each of the factors, the limitations that occur when a second crisis is faced become more obvious. The capability method does not completely explain the reasons for policy choices, but by observing the general trends of the factors, it becomes clearer why certain alternatives were accepted or rejected.

By restricting the cases examined to those in which naval ships were the primary instrument of military power, insight has been gained concerning the relevance of surface fleets in the missile age; however, many of the lessons derived from this examination apply to other components of the armed forces as well. In the final analysis it is overall military power of the country which is decisive. There is no guarantee that an enemy's response will be limited to a particular area of local conflict if weaknesses exist in other regions. Therefore, one should not examine the local forces in isolation. Instead, a conflict must be seen in its global context.

The multicrisis situation is one of the severest tests of conventional naval capabilities. The number of ships required depends on a complex mixture of military, political, and psychological elements. For example, if the will of the United States to engage in a second crisis is reduced, adequate forces may be available but possess little credible deterrent value.

The need for surface ships in the next decade has been seriously queried. One view is that the availability of units like the Sixth Fleet, deployed in the Mediterranean, and the Seventh Fleet, which patrols the coast of eastern Asia, tempts the government to become involved in situations it should avoid. Tensions are unwittingly exacerbated. Some congressmen, frustrated by their inability to check the executive, reason that by limiting the forces available for foreign deployment, the United States will be less likely to become embroiled abroad. Some authorities argue that the best approach to the increased Soviet presence in the Mediterranean is to let the USSR have the region, complete with its never-ending exasperations and headaches.

The United States Navy is faced with the problem of a large number of aging, obsolescent ships built during World War II. Appropriations for construction of vessels have been small in comparison to the number of ships nearing the end of their useful lives. Whether these ships should be replaced or whether competing defense systems should be procured is an important issue of national defense policy. With the increased costs of modernizing forces and the competition of domestic requirements for fiscal resources, there is a reluctance to invest in this type of appropriation.

The removal of ships from active service during 1968 and 1969 appears to indicate a tendency toward a contraction of naval surface forces. There will be a natural inclination toward retrenchment of existing force levels in the aftermath of the Vietnamese war; such a phenomenon usually occurs in postwar periods. In light of Soviet naval expansion and British withdrawal of forces, this possible trend in American naval policy has increased significance.

In many quarters the role played by the surface navy has not been fully appreciated. This is partly due to a failure to see those forces through the eyes of the Soviets. The political and military effectiveness of warships as instruments of U.S. policy during the earlier years of the cold war, at present, and in the foreseeable future needs careful evaluation. It is important to determine whether or not credible forces exist to cope with the multicrisis challenge, and if ships are likely to be effective instruments of national security policy in the 1970s.

In order to explore the limitations of the multicrisis situation and to evaluate the role of naval forces, two significant confrontations involving U.S. naval capabilities have been selected for analysis in depth. The first one is the Middle East crisis of 1967, while the United

States was deeply involved in Vietnam; the second situation is the Quemoy conflict of 1958, during a U.S. military commitment in Lebanon.

The 1967 Arab-Israeli conflict tested the current capability of the United States to cope with a multicrisis situation and the significance of naval power as an adjunct of foreign policy when faced with a Soviet naval presence during a crisis. The confrontation occurred at the time of a most difficult, exhausting prior involvement in Vietnam. It brought into sharp focus two diverging trends that have a significant bearing on the capability of the United States to cope with multicrisis situations involving the use of sea power—the expansion of Soviet naval power in the Mediterranean and the contraction of British forces east of Suez. For purposes of comparison and historical perspective, the Quemoy crisis of 1958 has also been analyzed. It developed while 15,000 American troops and elements of the Sixth Fleet were committed in Lebanon.

Both of these situations appear to be typical of the kind of crisis that the United States has faced so often in the post–World War II era—a limited conflict involving an indirect confrontation with the Soviet Union. War by proxy has been characteristic of Soviet probes. Both situations became difficult and complex foreign policy problems, replete with diverse factors and crosscurrents, and each occurred "in the wrong place at the wrong time." However, in these respects they were very typical problems.

After an examination of the general world context and American interests in the area of conflict, factors influencing U.S. policy choices during the buildup phase of each crisis have been analyzed. Special emphasis has been placed on this phase, for it is usually during the preliminary period that crucial policy determinations are made. In estimating the capability of the United States to cope with a multicrisis, the following questions have been examined:

1. What is the extent of Soviet national interests and intentions?
2. Does the United States have sufficient military capability to intervene without leaving itself exposed in other vital areas?
3. Will both the Congress and the general public support American intervention?
4. What economic factors complicate American policy?
5. What other factors are significant in approaching the particular problem, including the self-sufficiency of the nation requiring U.S. aid?
6. What assistance can be counted on from other allies, and what is its significance?

Of course, there are overlapping and interrelating factors involved with each of the questions. The success or failure of U.S. policy in terms of interests and commitments has been assessed, as well as the role played by naval forces. Because estimates of Soviet intentions heavily influence American decisions, Russian policy in each phase of the crisis has been examined. In addition, since Great Britain has shared many worldwide peace-keeping responsibilities with the United States, its policy has also been evaluated in determining the availability of allied support and American dependence on British backing. In examining the foreign policies of these three nations, emphasis has been placed on movements of naval vessels as indicators of actual intentions.

The validity of using the posture of forces as a tool for dissecting government intentions is among the underlying questions assessed in each of the cases. Observations have also been made concerning the usefulness of the United Nations in crisis situations, the limits of congressional bipartisanship, and evidence of different perceptions of the problem within the American bureaucracy.

An analysis similar to that of the buildup phase has been made of the period of intense hostilities. By analyzing each crisis in detail, phase by phase, an effort has been made to provide a clearer explanation of U.S. policy than has been available before. Comparison of the changes in capability factors has provided greater insight into the multicrisis phenomenon. A detailed comparison of 1958 and 1967 situations has added perspective.

In the pages that follow an attempt has been made to provide a clearer comprehension of the complications of a multicrisis situation and to add a dimension of understanding of the role that surface naval forces play in the present age. Chapter 2 examines the competing global interests of the United States and the Soviet Union and the role that naval power plays in defense of these interests. The multicrisis situation has been examined in Part Two, a study of the Middle East crisis of 1967; Part Three, an analysis of the Quemoy crisis of 1958; and Part Four, a comparison of the two crises. The effectiveness and adequacy of conventional naval power has also been evaluated in each of these parts. Analysis of the navy's role in the Middle East crisis of 1967 provides insight into the present value of surface ships, while the Quemoy study investigates the usefulness of fleets in the past. The assessment of Soviet naval expansion and British withdrawal in Part Four indicates the significance that fleets may have in future cold war operations.

By analysis of specific conflict situations of 1958 and 1967 and assessment of trends pertinent to the employment of naval power in the 1970s, a conclusion can be drawn about capability to cope with a multicrisis and whether or not the United States is overcommitted in such a situation. By focusing on two conflicts separated by nine years, the kinds of limitations encountered during concurrent crises have been more clearly revealed; remedies have become more apparent.

From this critical examination of actual cases we can arrive at a better understanding of broader problems related to achieving national security such as: the usefulness of mutual security arrangements, the value of primary and secondary deterrence systems, conditions under which the United States should intervene or stay out of local situations, the types of commitments America should make, and the relationship of local conflicts to global war. As a result of this analysis it should be possible to develop a sounder strategic foundation for future American policy and required force levels.

2. NAVAL POWER AND THE DEFENSE OF AMERICAN INTERESTS

2.1 COMPETING INTERESTS OF THE UNITED STATES AND THE SOVIET UNION

To understand the role of naval power in national security policy it is necessary to identify the competing interests of the United States and its major military, economic, and ideological rival, the Soviet Union. It is difficult to define precisely the global interests of the United States and Russia; they result from the dynamic interaction of internal and external variables. Since World War II both nations have actively sought to extend their influence throughout the world. As the Russians have striven for global hegemony, their ambitions have frequently conflicted with American goals. In some areas of the world it is almost a zero-sum game: a gain for one superpower is a loss for the other, although the gains and losses can seldom be measured in simple terms. The complex interrelationships in today's world are often expressed in terms of political and psychological influence rather than in particular pieces of real estate acquired.

For both nations survival is an essential precondition of global objectives. The Soviets have always maintained a healthy desire for self-preservation. The evolution of destructive weaponry has made avoidance of nuclear war a dominant element of national security policy. Effective deterrence no longer relies on strategic nuclear weapons alone. It includes the whole spectrum of military power required to meet a variety of threats and involves the total complex of elements that constitute strength and purpose for a nation.

A primary objective of U.S. policy during the cold war has been the containment of Soviet political and military expansion. Different interpretations of the nature of the threat have led to conflicting suggestions for effective strategy and tactics to meet it. Assessments of the Russian challenge range from the apocalyptic view of a spreading Red menace and the falling domino theory to beliefs that the Soviets are misunderstood and do not desire to dominate a hostile world. However, the free world will neither collapse with Moscow's next political military victory nor witness the rapid convergence of American and Soviet systems and interests. There is a tendency to confuse tactical shifts in Russian policy, resulting from complications like Chinese Communist hostility, as permanent changes in objectives.

Soviet foreign policy stems from a combination of pragmatic *raisons d'état* and a dynamic Communist ideology. The Russians have certain expansionist ambitions that predate Leninism, but Communist ideology has added a dynamic element that requires Soviet participation in the worldwide revolutionary movements. Moscow's strategies and tactics have varied radically; they are replete with twists and turns, zigs and zags, dynamic thrusts and strategic retreats. The Communists want to be where the action is and to stir it up where there is dormant opportunity. For Soviet leaders a stalemate is unacceptable, and it is inconceivable for them to accept the status quo for a long period of time. It was thus logical for the Soviets when confronted by a firm stance by NATO in Europe to turn south toward areas of the Third World like the Middle East and Africa.

The long reach of intercontinental weapons and the complex interaction of worldwide interests of the superpowers make geographical generalizations somewhat misleading. There is, however, some regional relationship to the intensity of national interests. While the United States officially rejects a spheres-of-interest concept, the definition of what is vital to American security seems to vary with the regions of the globe. Soviet security concerns appear to be directly proportional to distance from their frontiers. There is a tacit acceptance of some exercise of control by a superpower within its zone of dominance. In 1968 Moscow suppressed a Czechoslovakian challenge to the Russian concept of commonwealth without direct U.S. reprisals. The United States brought order to a disturbance in the Dominican Republic in 1965 without credible challenge from the Soviet Union. These two situations, however, were not entirely analogous. The Soviet Union has not been granted a carte blanche to act with impunity.

The United States has had a long-standing special interest in Latin America. In this region of the world American power predominates. A Communist regime in the Western Hemishpere can be as much a liability for the Soviet Union as a threat to the United States. Cuba, for example, has proved to be a costly investment for the Russians, and it is vulnerable if Washington should decide to impose a different order upon it. Moscow has not been without adventures in Latin America such as arms shipments to Guatemala in 1954 and placement of missiles in Cuba in 1962, but such episodes frequently have resulted in setbacks. Although the Russians are reluctant to promote Communist takeovers in Latin America or encourage

"Fidelist" movements, they do subscribe to the theory of Communist irreversibility. Once a nation has become Communist, even though it is only ninety miles off the coast of the United States, the Soviets will try to maintain it in the socialist commonwealth. Krushchev explained his withdrawal of Soviet offensive missiles from Cuba as justified by the concession of a U.S. guarantee not to invade Cuba.

The protection of Western Europe has been considered vital to American security during the cold war. In spite of strains in the Atlantic Alliance, the Soviet Union does not believe that it can successfully advance its frontiers in NATO nations. Moscow will undoubtedly continue to probe in vulnerable areas like Berlin. There is a remote possibility of a small territorial grab in an isolated country like Greece or Turkey presented as a *fait accompli*, but it is doubtful that the Soviets would take such risks. For the Russians survival is paramount, and they objectively estimate the strength of their opponents.

By way of contrast, Eastern Europe represents a vital sphere of interest for the Soviet Union. In the occupation of Czechoslovakia in 1968 Russia demonstrated that it intends to maintain a hold on its junior partners, and it is deeply concerned about the spread of Western influence into Eastern Europe. United States interest in these countries varies with their proximity to NATO and their changing political status in the Soviet bloc. The West has reluctantly acquiesced in Russian domination of the socialist commonwealth since World War II, but it would not necessarily accept Soviet invasion of countries like Yugoslavia and Romania.

In the northern Pacific American and Soviet territory is separated in places by only a few miles. The U.S. defense perimeter off the coast of Asia extends from Japan to Formosa and to the Philippines. The United States has made a stand on the continent of Northeast Asia in Korea, and this area has been a constant source of tension and conflict.

In the nonaligned southern regions of the world, the goals of the great powers are more ambiguous. The vital concerns of the United States are less clearly associated with Africa, the Middle East, and southern Asia. Therefore, there is greater opportunity for Soviet maneuvering and exploitation of unrest in the underdeveloped world. Because U.S. interests vary so widely within these regions, it is particularly misleading to generalize about them.

American concern in the nonaligned areas of the world often depends on the Soviet or Chinese threat. In various doctrines and treaties applying to these areas, U.S. obligations are defined in terms of a response to Russian Communist aggression.[1] Instability in these regions is a serious concern, but when it is believed that Moscow is the instigator or will be the ultimate benefactor, local conflicts become of much greater significance to U.S. national security. For example, the most immediate strategic concern of the United States in Africa is in the north on the southern flank of NATO and in the Horn, at the approaches to the Red Sea. These are areas of intensified Communist effort.[2]

Since 1954 the Soviets have utilized economic and political methods of penetration. Employment of more direct military means of obtaining leverage in the Third World is a recent innovation. Previously, Moscow apparently feared that such tactics would provide justification for direct intervention by the West. When conflicts do occur, the Soviets still prefer to fight them indirectly, by proxy.

Of course, Moscow is not responsible for every disturbance in these regions. It seldom instigates national liberation movements, but it frequently is dragged along in their wake. The Russians do not have a monolithic hold on their Communist comrades who frequently encourage revolutionary activities that become a dilemma for Soviet as well as U.S. policy. Sino-Soviet competition in the Third World complicates the problem. Particularly in Southeast Asia the Chinese are striving to achieve their own sphere of influence at the expense of the Russians and Americans. Communist gains are no longer automatically Russian gains.

The Middle East is of "special strategic significance" to the United States because of the position of the area as a political, economic, and military crossroads.[3] Greece, Turkey, and Iran form a defense perimeter against direct Soviet expansion, but it is indirect Soviet penetration that is the major concern. Moscow wants to dominate the strategic land bridge between Europe, Africa, and Asia and is trying to gain control of the region by achieving a protectorate relationship with certain Arab nations. Communist doctrine has been reinterpreted to explain ideological allegiance with certain non-

[1]In the SEATO treaty, for example, the United States has asserted that "its recognition of the effect of aggression and armed attack" applies "only to communist aggression." The Eisenhower Doctrine applies to "armed aggression from any country controlled by international communism." Text of the "Joint Resolution to Promote Peace and Stability in the Middle East."

[2]Statement of Secretary of Defense Robert S. McNamara in U.S., Congress, Senate, Committee on Armed Services and the Subcommittee on Department of Defense of the Committee on Appropriations, *Military Procurement Authorizations for Fiscal Year 1968*, 90th Cong., 1st sess. (Washington, 1967), p. 28.

[3]Ibid.

Communist leaders. Moscow has accorded a kind of honorary satellite status to Egypt and Syria. Military and economic assistance has been concentrated in Egypt, Syria, Algeria, and Iraq. Apparently the Soviet aim is to eliminate Western influence in the area and eventually establish the kind of relationship with Arab clients that they have with "junior partners" in Eastern Europe. Moscow's secondary objectives are to obtain guaranteed rights to Mediterranean ports and air fields and to have greater control of the oil resources of the region.

The United States has denied that it seeks a sphere of influence in Southeast Asia, but it has asserted that aggression in the area endangers American "peace and safety."[4] United States military efforts in Vietnam, Laos, and Thailand are indicative of a determination to back these security interests and to prevent subjugation of these areas by Russia, China, or North Vietnam.

Throughout the Third World the competing interests of the two superpowers vary from country to country and seemingly from day to day. It is in this area where there is the greatest opportunity for success of Soviet dynamics and the greatest probability of conflicts with interests of the United States.

2.2 THE SIGNIFICANCE OF U.S. NAVAL POWER IN THE COLD WAR[5]

United States fleets help guard the Atlantic approaches to Western Europe and NATO's southern flank in the Mediterranean. In addition, conventional sea power has been assigned a role in the defense of the island areas of Japan, Formosa, and the Philippines in the Pacific and support of U.S. commitments in the Korean and Indochinese peninsulas. The Navy has a major role in the direct defense of the Western Hemisphere. Figure 1.1 shows the locations of significant cold war crises involving the U.S. Navy.

Perhaps in the arena of the Third World U.S. naval forces have been most valuable, for where American interests are more ambiguous, the visible presence of American forces can be of critical significance. Mobile naval units can quickly be deployed to coastal areas of potential conflict and provide a stabilizing influence without entering the territorial waters of another nation. Since neither superpower is likely to risk a direct confrontation, it is extremely important

[4]Art. 4, Southeast Asia Collective Defense Treaty.

[5]No attempt has been made to provide a detailed presentation of the evidence for the assessments given in this introductory section. For a more detailed analysis see the author's two unpublished works, *The Influence of the Sixth Fleet on Soviet Foreign Policy* and *The Influence of The Seventh Fleet on Soviet Foreign Policy,* Department of Naval History, Washington, D.C.

to gain the initiative.[6] In cold war situations, naval vessels are chiefly instruments of political and psychological leverage.

Ships are symbols of the nation whose flag they fly and, therefore, exert an influence beyond that of their purely military capabilities. Of course, the *Pueblo* seizure demonstrated limits to the protection afforded by symbology not backed by credible power. Credibility also depends on the belief that warships will be committed under certain circumstances. Assessments of the Soviet naval presence in the Mediterranean frequently stress that the French and Italian navies are comparable numerically to the Soviet task force, but an Italian cruiser does not have the influence of a comparable Soviet vessel.

Although naval units gain much of their effectiveness because they represent the total power of their country, the amount of localized pressure that can be brought to bear frequently is decisive in a cold war confrontation. In the Mediterranean U.S. amphibious units have never been more than a token force. However, local forces must be strong enough to establish a beachhead until reinforcements arrive. It is quite possible that landing a single battalion of Marines would have stabilized the Lebanon situation in 1958, or one destroyer might have been sufficient to run the blockade of the Gulf of Aqaba in June 1967. However, conservative military planning that prepares for the worst conceivable contingencies is not likely to recommend such risks.

In the arena of the Third World visible power has special significance; ready forces make an impression. While nationalist leaders may be indifferent to other ideologies, they recognize the threat of modern warships from foreign nations. Intercontinental ballistic missiles buried in the ground and Polaris submarines cruising silently beneath the seas do not have this kind of impact in less developed nations. Power is primarily the ability to influence others, and deterrence depends upon the frame of reference of the one deterred. In the Western world some seriously question the value of surface ships in a missile age; those who live in the Third World usually do not. The conspiratorial mentality in some of these countries adds to the effectiveness of a display of power. The paranoiac outlook suspects the

[6]Such a confrontation would probably lead to a thermonuclear exchange; such a judgment, however, is speculative. Secretary McNamara said in testimony before Congress that "there is one possible contingency . . . which may require the large scale employment of our naval forces, and that is *a war at sea with the Soviet Union not involving any land battles.* Here, our global naval power would provide us with a unique advantage provided that the Soviet submarine threat can be contained. . . ." He went on to state that "the Soviet surface fleet, without aircraft carriers, would be ineffectual in challenging us for control of the seas." (Emphasis added.) *Military Procurement Authorizations for Fiscal Year 1968,* Statement of January 25, 1967, p. 79.

worst, thus increasing the deterrent value of a naval presence.

How great an influence U.S. naval capability has had on Soviet strategy is difficult to quantify. It has never been the only factor affecting Russian tactics which have been influenced by a complex variety of considerations of which sea power is but one of many elements. But the lack of comparable forces has undoubtedly influenced the selection of Soviet schemes for penetration. Historically, Russian territorial ambitions have been subordinated to Moscow's perception of the degree of risk involved. The Soviet Union has expanded territorially when it could be accomplished easily and with little danger. Moscow has been most cautious when faced with the possibility of determined resistance by another major power. Since 1948 it has expanded Russian influence, for the most part, by indirect methods.

It would be oversimplifying the problem to examine periods of Soviet restraint in areas patrolled by U.S. fleets and credit stability to the secondary deterrence value of U.S. naval forces. While failures of deterrence efforts are obvious, successes are difficult to prove. There are many complex determinants of Soviet policy, but some shows of force appear to have helped avert developing crises. Fleet operations near Indonesia in 1958, the Taiwan Straits in 1962, and Laos in 1963 were examples of displays of U.S. power intended to deter a potential Communist threat. Less publicized precautionary moves have been made frequently when there was only a hint of possible difficulty. In other instances, a small force has been used politically to demonstrate American firmness. For example, warships cruised the Black Sea during the following periods of tension: in 1946 over Iran, in 1960 and 1961 over Berlin, and in 1968 after the invasion of Czechoslovakia caused alarm throughout Europe.[7]

There are several methods by which the influence of American warships on Soviet strategic planning may be assessed. Content analysis of the Russian media, Soviet emulation of U.S. naval tactics, and Russian reactions in crisis situations provide indications of the degree of impact. The Russian propaganda campaign that has been waged against the U.S. Sixth and Seventh Fleets for the past two decades has been of an unvarying content. For years Soviet articles have described U.S. fleets as the "big stick" of the "world gendarme"—an image that now appears to have caught on with large segments of the American public. Stirring up resentment of American sea power is evidently intended to force its withdrawal. This is a major goal be-

[7]There have been periodic cruises in the Black Sea also for the purpose of asserting American rights to enter the sea under the Montreux Convention. This has been done more frequently since the increase of Soviet activity in the Mediterranean starting in 1964.

cause it would increase leverage and control for the Soviet Union in the important areas patrolled by American fleets. The Soviet media promote a "big bully" rather than a "paper tiger" image of American surface ships and reflects an underlying frustration as well as a resentful respect. Although the Soviets may not like this instrument of American policy, they respect its power. Their propaganda stresses deeds rather than words, and it interprets the movements of naval forces as the true indications of American intentions. Because this attitude prevails, it is easy for the United States to speak softly for the benefit of world opinion and yet project a tough, stern image for Soviet appraisals. A strictly neutral presence of U.S. forces becomes a credible threat in Soviet eyes because the USSR is more impressed by available means than by diplomatic assurances. By the quantity of references alone there appears to be a Russian preoccupation with the operations of U.S. naval units.[8]

Perhaps the best evidence of the influence of the American fleets has been the Soviet decision to imitate them. The Russians have been constructing a modern naval force and developing the oceangoing philosophy and operational experience essential to producing a credible surface navy. The deployment of helicopter carriers, oceangoing landing craft, missile cruisers, and an elite marine force indicates that the Soviets will have forces available in future limited conflicts. In recent years they have increased the numbers of politically oriented port calls, with modern Russian warships visiting countries of Africa, India, and the Middle East. In a cautious and circumspect manner Soviet task forces have appeared during recent tense situations like the Middle East war of 1967 and the *Pueblo* seizure in 1968. The increasing Russian naval presence has achieved certain political results and has reduced the influence of American vessels. However, the advantages would be substantially increased if U.S. fleets were recalled or became impotent as a result of Soviet bluffs.

Russian reactions during crises also provide insight into the influence of an American naval presence on Soviet policy. Since World War II there have been three major periods of activity in the Mediterranean area involving the United States and the Soviet Union which have attracted worldwide attention:

1. The years 1946–1948 when there was a crisis over evacuation of Iran, a threat to Turkey, and a civil war in Greece leading to proclamation of the Truman Doctrine.
2. The period June 1956–July 1958 during which the Suez, Jordan-

[8] Part of the motivation for these references, of course, is to increase foreign resentment about the U.S. presence.

ian, Syrian, Iraqi, and Lebanese crises occurred and the Eisenhower Doctrine was proclaimed.
3. The period beginning in April 1967 in which the Arab-Israeli war of June 1967 and its political aftermath has been the principal conflict. In each of these time frames the Sixth Fleet played a major role as an instrument of U.S. policy. (See Table 2.1 for a brief summary of significant cold war episodes involving the Sixth Fleet.)

During the first period America had a preponderance of power and applied it effectively to stem the Soviet offensive in that region of the world. When Stalin became convinced that the United States and Great Britain would utilize naval power in the Mediterranean in 1946, he decided to withdraw from thrusts in that area of the world. There were, of course, many factors involved in the Soviet decision not to continue pursuing interests in Iran, Turkey, and Greece—but one of them was the Sixth Fleet. The following remarks attributed to Stalin in early 1958 are indicative of his feeling about this demonstration of American power. Concerning the uprising in Greece he said,

What do you think, that Great Britain and the United States—the United States, the most powerful state in the world—will permit you

Table 2.1 Significant Cold War Episodes Involving the Sixth Fleet

1. March 1946	*Missouri* dispatched to Iran; steamed through the Bosporus in April
2. August–September 1946	Conflict in Greece; nucleus of permanent fleet formed in September 1946.
3. April 1948	Italian elections
4. June–December 1950	Lebanon
5. March–December 1951	Moves to bolster Tito in Yugoslavia
6. July 1953	Visits to Turkey in conjunction with Soviet pressure
7. October–November 1956	Suez crisis
8. April 1957	Jordanian crisis
9. September–October 1957	Syrian crisis
10. May–October 1958	Lebanon crisis
11. September 1960	Berlin crisis: U.S. carrier force increased
September 1961	Carrier and cruiser entered Black Sea
12. March 1964	Cyprus
13. April 1967	Greek coup
14. May–June 1967	Arab-Israeli war

to break their line of communications in the Mediterranean Sea! Nonsense, and we have no Navy. The uprising in Greece must be stopped, and as quickly as possible.[9]

The Lebanon landings in 1958, which occurred during the second major period of activity, demonstrated to the world that the Sixth Fleet was not just for show. The commitment of U.S. forces to action in the Middle East undoubtedly further enhanced its credibility as a limited war deterrent force in Soviet eyes. During the two months preceding the landings, when the situation in the Middle East was deteriorating, Soviet statements expressed concern about a possible U.S. invasion. However, the Russians made no overt military preparations to counteract possible U.S. intervention, and their propaganda campaign reflected a healthy respect for the power of the Sixth Fleet. The American fleet helped limit Russian options.

In response to the actual landings in July 1958, the Soviets hastily conducted exercises in the Black Sea areas, but they made no attempt to make a show of force in the Mediterranean. Reportedly, Khrushchev told Nasser that although exercises would be staged, they were only a bluff.[10] The Russians appeared to be powerless to counteract the U.S. move short of a full-scale war. Moscow did not threaten any specific retaliation; its carefully timed protest attempted to salvage some prestige, but it was clear that the Soviet Union did not desire to become involved militarily in the conflict. One of the numerous indications that the U.S. Navy was very much on the mind of Premier Khrushchev was the substantial portion of his initial message to President Eisenhower devoted to complaints about the commander of the Sixth Fleet.[11] The Soviets had been given an impressive demonstration of the flexibility of American power. It must have been obvious that their inability to influence the course of events lay in the inflexibility of their own military means.

The Kremlin's decision to improve surface naval forces contributed to the complications of the Arab-Israeli crisis of May and June 1967. The role of U.S. naval forces and their influence on the Soviet Union in that complex situation will be evaluated in Part Two.

The Sixth Fleet's presence has not stopped the spread of Soviet influence, but the fleet can help prevent Russian military intimidation of unaligned countries that are resisting Soviet penetration. The un-

[9]J. V. Stalin, as quoted in Milovan Djilas, *Conversations with Stalin*, translated by M. B. Petrovich (New York: Harcourt, Brace, 1962), p. 182.

[10]*Al Ahram* article by M. H. Haykal, January 22, 1965. Haykal's material is usually authoritative and frequently reflects the views of President Nasser.

[11]See N. S. Khrushchev's "Message to President Dwight D. Eisenhower of the United States, July 19, 1958," *New Times*, No. 30 Supplement (July 1958), pp. 7–9.

tamed force of nationalism in the Third World opposes all would-be foreign masters. If there had been no Sixth Fleet or the initiative to commit it during the last twenty years, the Mediterranean, instead of slowly changing from a Western lake to an international sea, might long ago have become a Soviet sea.

The Seventh Fleet is responsible for carrying out American policy in an area equivalent to one-fifth of the earth's surface and stretching from the Bering Sea in the north to Antarctica in the south. Among the Communist countries that border on the ocean area it patrols are the Soviet Union, North Korea, China, and North Vietnam. The major cold war conflicts involving the Seventh Fleet have been the Korean War, the Formosa Strait confrontation, and the war in Vietnam. They have occurred in widely separated regions patrolled by the Seventh Fleet. (See Table 2.2.) Although Communist nations were involved directly, Soviet participation has been by proxy, none of the disputes has been permanently settled, and there has been violence in Vietnam throughout most of the period. The Korean War did not bring permanent peace to that area of tension, and the possibility of another outbreak of fighting remains. Futhermore, the controversy between the Nationalists and Communist Chinese continues.

By briefly reviewing the Soviet response to U.S. naval activity during the Korean War, the Vietnamese war, and the *Pueblo* crisis, additional insight can be obtained concerning the influence of U.S. fleets on the Russians. A detailed evaluation of the role of naval forces in the Quemoy crisis of 1958 has been made in Part Three.

During the Korean War the Seventh Fleet operated effectively and unopposed against Soviet allies. Although the sea supply system was vulnerable to attack, there were few contacts with Soviet submarines.[12] Stalin had urged Mao to intervene, but for a variety of rea-

Table 2.2 Significant Cold War Episodes Involving the Seventh Fleet

15. June 1950-1952	Korean War
16. February 1955	Evacuation of the Tachen Islands
17. August–October 1958	Quemoy conflict
18. February–April 1961	Laotian crisis
19. May–July 1962	Landings in Thailand because of threat in Laos
20. June–July 1962	Chinese buildup opposite Formosa
21. August 1964–	The war in Vietnam
22. January 1968	The *Pueblo* seizure

[12]James A. Field, Jr., *History of United States Naval Operations Korea* (Washington, 1963), pp. 66, 395.

sons the Russians did not risk direct involvement in the fighting, even when their allies were being defeated. The Seventh Fleet was hard pressed to provide carrier air support and shore bombardment in Korea while guarding against the possibility of a Chinese invasion of Formosa, but it was equal to the task. The Soviets probably recognized that they could not successfully challenge U.S. sea power.

The Seventh Fleet also has complicated Soviet policy toward the Vietnamese war. One logical explanation for Moscow's decision to confine its response to war by proxy has been the U.S. naval power that has been concentrated in that remote region. Although the Soviets have benefited from U.S. involvement in Vietnam, they have lost prestige and credibility with other Communist nations by not making a firmer response to a U.S. war with a socialist country particularly during the bombing period. By contrast America has defended its ally from aggression. In response to U.S. initiatives against the North, Moscow carefully avoided commitments to specific actions other than arms supplies. The disproportionate sacrifice of the superpowers for their friends raises questions about Soviet willingness to protect communism at distant points.

In the Vietnam conflict the United States took three major steps of naval escalation: carrier raids following the attacks on U.S. destroyers in the Gulf of Tonkin in August 1964, initiation of bombing the North from U.S. aircraft carriers in February 1965, and commencement of shore bombardment and mining of the rivers in February 1967. These events presented the Soviets with serious dilemmas, and it might have been expected that they would have to respond directly in order to save face as the defenders of the Communist bloc. Although there are complex reasons for the absence of a direct Soviet military reaction to these moves, one purely military consideration is that Russia does not yet have the forces to challenge the U.S. Navy successfully in the waters of Southeast Asia. Even if it were possible to fight a limited war against the United States, Russia would have a most difficult task supplying its forces.

The Soviets have had to depend on U.S. acquiescence to seaborne supply of North Vietnam. The bitterness between the Soviet Union and China has forced increasing reliance on supply by sea, and the Russians realize that the Seventh Fleet could deny the sea routes to them. There appears to be a tacit tradeoff—the United States allowing the Soviets to supply North Vietnam and the Soviets avoiding supplying the offensive bombers and missiles necessary for heavy attacks on the South or the Seventh Fleet.

In spite of increasing worldwide naval operations and public boasts of Soviet admirals, there has been no credible challenge to the Seventh Fleet during the war in Vietnam. Although the Soviets claimed in 1968 to be operating elements of their fleet near Vietnam, Soviet combatant units have "never lingered or even appeared interested in operations being conducted by Seventh Fleet units"[13] in the area. One incident that may have been an effort to retaliate for increased U.S. naval pressure was the deliberate collisions of Soviet destroyers with the U.S.S. *Walker* in May 1967 in the Sea of Japan. The initial Soviet commentary complained of U.S. flights over ships "sailing to countries which are in great need of aid in the struggle against U.S. aggression" and that Seventh Fleet ships were "systematically shelling the DRV."[14] However, the Soviets quickly changed their explanation, apparently sensing the dangers of a possible direct confrontation over the issue. Instead of a bold Soviet response to increased Seventh Fleet activity in Vietnam, the collisions were subsequently depicted by the Russians as a deliberate provocation planned by the United States and an intentional violation of international law.

If there had been no strong U.S. fleet in the Pacific, the Soviet response in these situations might have been different. The Russians probably would have been more inclined to participate directly in some way in order to impress the Communist world, but under present circumstances they have not been ready to challenge the United States directly at sea in the waters surrounding Vietnam. One factor that seems to deter them from even feinting direct military support is their awareness that the United States is not bluffing and is determined to use its available power.

In the case of seizure of the *Pueblo,* it does not appear that Moscow provoked the North Korean action, which was a highly risky adventure even with American preoccupation in Vietnam. The Soviets played down the incident and did not initially declare themselves to be protectors of the Korean Communists. They evidently tried to disassociate themselves from the act and were probably not about to defend North Korea from American retaliation. Some nine days after the *Pueblo* capture, the Russians made a minor show of naval force, apparently convinced it was then safe to do so. However, their careful demonstration of support for a Communist nation confronted by an American task force was another significant sign that the Soviets may use shows of force more often in future crises.

[13]Information provided by Commander in Chief, Pacific Fleet, Intelligence Section in letter from Lt. Comdr. L. D. Hamilton, USN, to Lt. Comdr. J. T. Howe, USN, dated March 27, 1969. The claim had been made by Soviet Admiral Amelko in a *Pravda* article of April 27, 1968.

[14]Yakov Viktorov commentary, Moscow, in Turkish to Turkey, May 11, 1967.

The Seventh Fleet has had a substantial influence on Soviet strategy. It has reduced the options that rationally could be considered by the Russians. This is evident from the wide coverage given to its activities by the Soviet media, failure to respond with Russian forces to U.S. attacks on the Communist countries of North Vietnam and Korea, absence of direct support for aggressive initiatives of Communist nations in Asia, and by a beginning emulation of American naval tactics.

The First and Second Fleets protect the approaches to the United States and back up deployed naval forces. The Second Fleet has been involved in a number of crises in the Caribbean, particularly in the 1960s. (See Table 2.3.) The Cuban missile crisis of 1962 was perhaps the most dangerous showdown of the cold war. Three factors concerning the role of the U.S. Navy stand out. First, a quarantine was successfully conducted. Second, antisubmarine warfare forces demonstrated an ability to combat Soviet submarines in Caribbean waters. Finally, the fact that an invulnerable deterrent force was deployed beneath the seas in Polaris submarines helped restrict the choice of responses available to Moscow. The lessons of this demonstration of naval power were not lost on the Soviets. Shortly after this crisis Moscow began development of more mobile limited war forces.[15]

In summary, a study of Soviet reactions to the crises of the cold war indicates that the presence of U.S. fleets has had a significant influence on Soviet strategy and tactics. The study in depth of the Middle East and Quemoy crises will add further insight into the importance of this factor.

Table 2.3 Significant Cold War Episodes Involving the Second Fleet

23. May–June 1954	Guatemala
24. Spring 1959	Panama patrols
25. July 1960	U.N. Congo action
26. November 1960	Guatemala and Nicaragua, Castro invasion threat
27. June 1961	Dominican Republic
28. October–December 1962	Cuban missile crisis
29. Spring 1963	Dominican Republic versus Haiti
30. April 1965	Dominican Republic

[15] See the discussion of this point in Chapter 13.

II THE MIDDLE EAST CRISIS OF 1967

During April and early May of 1967 the number of incidents increased along the border between Israel and Syria. Israeli villages were shelled, and Tel Aviv retaliated with air raids against the Syria positions. On May 13, 1967, Egypt began to mass its Sinai army divisions on the desert border with Israel. Israel responded with full-scale mobilization.

The situation became a serious international crisis with the occur rence of two events in rapid succession. On May 18, 1967, the United Nations emergency force was ordered to begin withdrawal from the armistice line between Israel and the United Arab Republic in response to a request from Cairo. On May 22, 1967, President Gamal A. Nasser announced the closing of the Gulf of Aqaba to Israeli shipping. Israel had warned that such an act would be a *casus belli.*

By May 22, 1967, the Israeli government had decided that the Arab maneuvers were more than a repetition of the political and military demonstrations that had been made in the Sinai in 1960 following an Israeli retaliatory raid on Syria. What had been initially regarded in Tel Aviv as a political move to relieve alleged pressure on Syria became a serious threat as United Arab Republic strength in the Sinai area was more than doubled. When Israeli Foreign Minister Abba Eban arrived in Washington on May 25, 1967, Tel Aviv apparently had decided that an Arab attack was imminent.

Both the United States and Russia made some effort to cool the situation. Washington tried to generate interest in a multinational maritime force to assert free passage through the gulf, but there was little enthusiasm in the international community for such a peacekeeping effort. After several weeks of futile big power efforts, Israel attacked the surrounding Arab armies and obliterated then in a lightning six-day war. A cessation of hostilities was finally arranged after Israel had reached the Suez Canal, made substantial inroads into Jordan, and taken the Golan Heights from Syria.

Because Moscow was aligned with Egypt and Syria, and Washington was identified with Israel, the crisis became a significant great power confrontation. For the first time during a major international crisis Soviet and American warships operated in close proximity to each other. United States policy choices were made in an international atmosphere dominated by the draining involvement in Vietnam. As

Israeli forces continued to advance, the Russians found themselves in a serious predicament. This resulted in two dramatic showdowns between the United States and the USSR, one over a United Nations cease-fire resolution during the Israeli advance in Egypt and the other concerning the cessation of hostilities in Syria on the final day of the war.

3. GENERAL BACKGROUND

Before analyzing the American handling of the June 1967 Middle East crisis, it is important to examine the atmosphere in which various alternatives were considered; general trends of United States, Soviet, and British foreign policies; and the means available for implementing policy.

3.1 UNITED STATES POLICY

In the months prior to the crisis, Vietnam was the dominant issue of American foreign policy. There was growing war weariness, and congressmen were increasingly critical of America's apparent role as world policeman. The Senate Committee on Armed Services held hearings on *Worldwide Military Commitments* to determine whether the country was capable of responding to its obligations with the strain of Vietnam.[1] The Senate Foreign Relations Committee had collected testimony on *Conflicts Between United States Capabilities and Foreign Commitments*[2] and was planning to examine *U.S. Commitments to Foreign Powers* in an effort to reassert a measure of congressional authority over employment of the armed forces.[3] Anxiety that the United States might be overextended was expressed in hearings on military procurement,[4] Vietnam,[5] and the Atlantic Alliance.[6]

Senator Stuart Symington reflected a commonly held view in asserting he was not certain

[1]Hearings conducted August 25 and 30, 1966; and February 21 and 23; and March 1 and 2, 1967. U.S., Congress, Senate, Committee on Armed Services, Preparedness Investigating Subcommittee, *Worldwide Military Commitments,* 89th Cong., 2nd sess., 90th Cong., 1st sess. (Washington, 1966, 1967).

[2]U.S., Congress, Senate, Committee on Foreign Relations, *Conflicts Between U.S. Capabilities and Foreign Commitments,* 90th Cong., 1st sess. (Washington, 1967). Hearings conducted with Lt. Gen. James M. Gavin, USA (Ret.), February 21, 1967.

[3]U.S., Congress, Senate, Committee on Foreign Relations, *U.S. Commitments to Foreign Powers,* 90th Cong., 1st sess. (Washington, 1967). The decision to hold the hearings was made just prior to the Middle East crisis.

[4]See, for example, U.S., Congress, Senate, Committee on Armed Services and the Subcommittee on Department of Defense of the Committee on Appropriations, *Military Procurement Authorizations for Fiscal Year 1968,* 90th Cong., 1st sess., January 25–27, 30, 31, and February 1, 2, 1967 (Washington, 1967).

[5]See, for example, J. W. Fulbright, *The Vietnam Hearings* (New York: Random House, 1966).

[6]See, for example, U.S., Congress, Senate, Subcommittee on National Security and International Operations of the Committee on Government Operations, *The Atlantic Alliance,* 89th Cong., 2nd sess., April 27, May 5, 6, 19, 25, and June 16, 21, 1966 (Washington, 1966).

whether or not the United States is economically or politically overextended from the fiscal and monetary standpoint, but if military commitments are an important part of political and economic commitments, then this nation is overextended in all three categories.[7]

Other senators warned that we must distinguish between "what we were willing and what we are reasonably able to do";[8] that we needed to "establish proper national priorities";[9] and that we were "spread quite thin."[10] Congressmen expressed concern about faltering domestic programs, the international payments imbalance, and whether or not the United States could meet existing commitments. Underlying this apprehension was the dark specter of a second Vietnam. As Senator Mansfield, the majority leader and loyal administration supporter wrote: "we have so many commitments around the world, that if we were called upon to honor more than one of them at a time we might find ourselves in great difficulty."[11]

The rapid landing of troops in the Dominican Republic and the supply of military aircraft to the Congo seemed to accelerate anxiety about overcommitment.[12] Knowledgeable observers complained that Vietnam left us "very poorly prepared to face crises . . . in other areas of the world,"[13] fostered a disposition to avoid new commitments,"[14] and that our global role was "beyond our psychological resources."[15] As the Middle East crisis approached, strong congressional and domestic concern existed, and the Executive was painfully aware of it.

Public opinion surveys had shown a gradual increase of disapproval of the American role in Vietnam.[16] In mid-April 1967 those who dis-

[7]Statement of Senator Stuart Symington in *Worldwide Military Commitments,* p. 71. See also his statement on page 100.

[8]Statement of Senator John Stennis, Chairman, Preparedness Investigating Committee, in *Worldwide Military Commitments,* p. 2.

[9]Statement of Senator Henry M. Jackson in *Worldwide Military Commitments,* p. 51.

[10]Statement of Senator Howard W. Cannon in *Worldwide Military Commitments,* p. 107.

[11]Letter from Senator Mike Mansfield, to Lt. Comdr. J. T. Howe, USN, dated February 22, 1968.

[12]See, for example, comments of Senator Frank Carlson in *Commitments to Foreign Powers,* pp. 33, 34. See also *The Christian Science Monitor* article by J. N. Goodsell, "Dominican Move Roils U.S. Critics," April 30, 1965. Congressional criticism of the Dominican action was not necessarily reflected in public sentiment. See *The Washington Post* article by Louis Harris, July 5, 1965, p. A1, A14.

[13]Testimony of George F. Kennan in Fulbright, *The Vietnam Hearings,* p. 126.

[14]Herbert S. Dinerstein, *Intervention Against Communism* (Baltimore: The John Hopkins Press, 1967), p. 31.

[15]Henry A. Kissinger, "NATO: Evolution or Decline," Lecture contained in *The United States and The Atlantic Community (*Austin: University of Texas Press, 1967), p. 16.

[16]In August 1965 in answer to the question, "In view of the developments since

approved of the President's handling of his office almost outnumbered those who approved.[17] President Johnson watched the opinion polls closely. He frequently referred to them publicly and was reputed to carry the latest results in his back pocket.

In response to criticism of America's global role, the executive department asserted the country was not overextended. The Secretary of State's standard reply was, "I do not . . . think that we are overcommitted. I think there are very great dangers in our being undercommitted in areas where we have vital security and national interest. . . ."[18] Defense Secretary McNamara admitted we cannot meet forty-odd Vietnams simultaneously, but retorted "neither can our opponents."[19]

Critics addressed the problem of meeting additional crises with existing forces; the government counted on mobilization and help from allies in serious cases. Key questions were whether or not the country had the necessary relative capacity and if Americans were willing to take the strain of an additional commitment. The administration apparently felt the United States was not overcommitted because of the potential which stood behind ready forces.[20] Critics were not sure the will existed for translating American potential into effective power to carry out existing policies.

The administration's viewpoint was reflected in testimony of military leaders in early 1967. The heads of the Air Force and Marines

we entered the fighting in Vietnam do you think the United States made a mistake sending troops to fight in Vietnam?" 24 percent said "yes" and 61 percent said "no." In May 1967, 36 percent said "yes" and 50 percent said "no." Information taken from Gallup Polls in *The New York Times*, March 10, 1968. Louis Harris Polls, however, indicated that 70 percent favored the basic war policy. *The Washington Post*, March 25, 1968.

[17] At that time 45 percent approved and 44 percent disapproved. Figures taken from graph in *The Christian Science Monitor*, February 26, 1968, p. 3.

[18] Testimony of Secretary of State Dean Rusk in *Worldwide Military Commitments*, p. 107. The Secretary warned that "if those who would be our adversaries should ever suppose that our commitments are not worth anything, then we shall see dangers we have not yet dreamed of." Address of May 18, 1967, in Department of State *Bulletin*, Vol. LVI, No. 1459 (June 12, 1967), p. 874.

[19] Statement of Robert S. McNamara, Secretary of Defense, in *Military Procurement Authorizations for Fiscal Year 1968*, p. 72. The allusion to "forty odd Vietnams" referred, of course, to the forty-two nations with which the United States has collective defense arrangements.

[20] The Secretary of State, for example, stated that "behind our commitments stand not only the active forces in being but the potential of the United States, and that is very great indeed." *Worldwide Military Commitments*, p. 108. When asked about the readiness of the armed forces to meet another Vietnam, the Chairman of the Joint Chiefs of Staff replied, "I believe that we can meet our commitments . . . with both our Active and Reserve Forces." Statement of General Earle G. Wheeler, USA, in *Military Procurement Authorizations 1968*, p. 407.

felt mobilization would be necessary to meet a Vietnam-type crisis in some other area.[21] The Chief of Naval Operations admitted reduced Atlantic Fleet readiness.[22] The Commandant of the Marine Corps described shortages of helicopters and pilots, lower experience levels, and reduced battalion strength in the Mediterranean.[23]

Growing reluctance to consider utilization of tactical nuclear weapons in limited war situations had increased the importance of relative strength in conventional arms compared with earlier years of the cold war. Reservations were apparently due to improved Soviet capability, decreased public support, and heightened awareness of the difficulties of utilizing such weapons. The administration felt that a "fire break" must be preserved between conventional and nuclear weapons to prevent escalation of a local conflict to large-scale thermonuclear war.[24] Leaders doubted that tactical nuclear weapons could be used in limited war.[25] Decided disapproval of employing atomic weapons was also registered in opinion polls.[26] Resort to nuclear capability in meeting a second localized crisis was highly unlikely.

[21] Statements of General John P. McConnell, Chief of Staff, U.S. Air Force, *Worldwide Military Commitments,* pp. 201, 202; and General Wallace M. Greene, Jr., USMC, Commandant of the Marine Corps, p. 245. The Chief of Naval Operations felt existing forces could do the job if operated continuously in a manner similar to that of World War II naval operations. In heavily censored testimony that appears to have applied to the Middle East, Admiral McDonald admitted that such a conflict would be more difficult than the hypothetical one in the Caribbean being considered in the hearings. Testimony of Admiral David L. McDonald, USN, Chief of Naval Operations, in *Worldwide Military Commitments,* pp. 120, 133–135, and 152.

[22] Ibid., p. 119. He asserted that the major weakness was a shortage of experienced personnel.

[23] Testimony of General Green in *Worldwide Military Commitments,* pp. 247, 254, 264. A marine official was quoted as saying, "We are flat up against the stops now." *The New York Times* article by Hanson W. Baldwin, February 13, 1967, p. 4.

[24] See, for example, the article by Alain C. Enthoven, "American Deterrent Policy," Chap. 6 in Henry A. Kissinger, ed., *Problems of National Strategy,* (New York: Praeger, 1965), pp. 120, 124.

[25] Testimony of Secretary of State Rusk on May 3, 1967 in U.S., Congress, Senate, Combined Subcommittee of Foreign Relations and Armed Services Committees on the subject of U.S. troops in Europe, *US Troops in Europe*, 90th Cong., 1st sess. (Washington, 1967), p. 84. Secretary McNamara admitted the employment of tactical nuclear weapons "would present some extremely difficult and complex problems." Statement of Secretary of Defense McNamara in *Military Procurement Authorizations 1968,* p. 74.

[26] An examination of surveys from 1964 to 1968 indicates at least a 2-to-1 margin against the use of tactical nuclear weapons. Copies supplied by Miss Helene Klein, Louis Harris and Associates, letter of July 19, 1968, to Lt. Comdr. J. T. Howe, USN. In a poll during the Quemoy crisis of 1958, 42 percent favored and 41 percent opposed the use of tactical nuclear weapons in a war with China over Quemoy. Letter from Mr. George Gallup, Jr., July 6, 1968.

Soviet development of a credible second-strike missile capability had also increased the importance of conventional forces and lessened the significance of relative strength in thermonuclear weapons. However, in any confrontation with the Soviet Union, American strategic superiority provided additional confidence. Although there were allegations that the administration had not responded sufficiently to Soviet development of intercontinental missiles and defenses, the Defense Department was confident of superiority for the "close in period."[27]

Advocates of larger strategic forces were among the diverse groups complaining about the costs of Vietnam. The economic consequences of an escalated conflict in terms of sacrifices in other programs was a question of considerable controversy. The executive felt the economy was "strong enough" to permit "substantial progress" in meeting both domestic and international needs.[28] Secretary McNamara claimed that strain on the economy was not one of the many prices being paid as a result of the war.[29] In parrying complaints about defense spending, the administration argued that 10 percent of the Gross National Product was not too much.[30] A study on the impact of the war concluded in April 1967 that "the American economy could handle, with a minimum of dislocation or hardship, a far higher level" of defense spending.[31] However, there was growing concern that further military allocations would adversely affect domestic political stability and make an unpopular tax rise manda-

[27] Statement of Secretary of Defense McNamara in *Military Procurement Authorizations 1968,* p. 46.

[28] Letter from Secretary of State Rusk to Senator Stuart Symington dated August 30, 1966, as printed in *Worldwide Military Commitments,* pp. 38, 39.

[29] Secretary of Defense McNamara as quoted in U.S., Congress, Joint Economic Committee, *Economic Effect of Vietnam Spending,* 90th Cong., 1st sess. (Washington, 1967), p. 217.

[30] See, for example, testimony of Secretary of the Navy Paul H. Nitze in *Military Procurement Authorizations 1968,* p. 743. See also pp. 705, 706. In his annual report to Congress in February 1968, President Johnson reported that "Today the war in Vietnam is costing us 3 percent of our total production. That is a burden a wealthy people can bear. It represents less than one year's growth in our total output." President Lyndon B. Johnson, *Economic Report of the President,* February 1968 (Washington, 1968), p. 27.

[31] Report of Murray L. Weidenbaum in *Economic Effects of Vietnam Spending,* p. 218. See also the similar views of Gilbert Burck, p. 490, Arthur Okun, p. 545, and W. H. Chartener, p. 535. Even after the increased expenditures in late 1967, the President reported a healthy economy. He did, however, caution that certain restraints were required to keep it healthy. Johnson, *Economic Report of the President, 1968,* pp. 27, 28. Some Congressmen felt that this reasoning was unsound. See, for example, the statements of Senator Symington in *Economic Effect of Vietnam Spending,* pp. 17, 27, 28; and Senator Allen J. Ellender in *Military Procurement Authorizations 1968,* pp. 743, 744.

tory. While the administration was reluctant to increase defense expenditures, the state of the economy did not appear to preclude an additional military commitment.

The adverse balance of international payments was a serious economic problem. The deficit widened in the first two quarters of 1967. The war in Vietnam was a major contributor to the imbalance. "Extraordinary measures" had been taken to minimize its impact on the balance of payments,[32] but the percentage of deficit attributed to defense was increasing markedly.[33] Vietnam was costing a billion dollars in direct deficit in the balance and another billion in indirect adverse effects.[34] In any decision concerning further U.S. military involvement the effect on international payments was a serious consideration.

Preoccupation of key American policy makers with Vietnam may have contributed to the development of the Middle East crisis. Senator Javits charged that "neglect of the Middle East at the highest levels of our government . . . contributed to the outbreak of the war."[35] The former Deputy Chief of the U.S. mission in Cairo claimed that warnings of an impending crisis and the need to appoint an ambassador had gone unheeded.[36] However, Secretary of State Rusk has said in refutation that "from mid-April to mid-June I spent far more time on the Middle East than on Vietnam" and that an examination of his appointment books for the period would demonstrate the "predominant position of the Middle East in our actions and thinking."[37] By May 21, 1967, when an ambassador arrived in Egypt, the Middle East was unquestionably receiving considerable attention at the highest levels of government.

The concern existing in some circles that this nation might be overcommitted politically, militarily, economically, and psychologically undoubtedly was felt by the administration as it approached foreign policy decisions in May and June 1967. With expanding Vietnamese war costs and casualties, the United States was reluctant to become embroiled in another conflict.

[32]McNamara, *Military Procurement Authorizations 1968,* p. 37.

[33]See Table 26 in U.S., Council of Economic Advisers, *The Annual Report of the Council of Economic Advisers (*Washington, 1968), p. 167. Although progress had been made in reducing the adverse effects of all other defense costs, Vietnam expenditures had risen from 13 percent to 33 percent of the total defense deficit. Percentages computed using figures in Table 10, *Economic Effect of Vietnam Spending,* p. 217.

[34]These are estimates only. *Economic Effects of Vietnam Spending,* p. 59.

[35]Address by Senator Jacob K. Javits, "Confrontation in the Middle East," for release February 29, 1968, p. 3. Copy supplied by Senator Javits.

[36]See the account of David Nes's charges in *The Baltimore Sun*, June 14, 1967.

[37]Interview with former Secretary of State Dean Rusk, conducted April 9, 1969.

3.2 SPECIFIC FACTORS RELATING TO U.S. POLICY IN THE MIDDLE EAST

American policy toward the Middle East is as complex and contradictory as the diverse crosscurrents that exist both within and among the various nations of the region. United States interests in the area defy simple explanation. America's desire that peace be maintained has intensified as the region has gradually passed from a sphere of Western influence to an important arena of the cold war. The constant tensions and potential dangers resulting from the power struggle among Arab states and the Arab dispute with Israel have taken on a global cast.

Russian domination of the Middle East would mean more than loss of Western access to an important commercial and strategic area; it would be a major gain for the Soviet Union in its global quest for influence. Because of Soviet penetration it has become of increased importance to preserve American friendships in the area. Ideally, Washington would like to maintain good relations with all Mideast nations and prevent polarization of the region into East-West camps. The United States wants stability in the area, but as the number of Soviet-leaning regimes has grown, Western-oriented governments like Israel have become of increasing importance to the United States. Soviet military aid has been concentrated in Egypt, Syria, and Iraq, three countries that represent the greatest threat to Israel's security. The Arab-Israeli dispute has become identified with the conflicting global interests of the superpowers, and this has complicated the American quest for influence with Arab nations.

The American dilemma in an Arab-Israeli dispute is caused by its contradictory support of moderate Arab states as well as Israel. The United States has actively sought to strengthen its ties with oil-rich Arab nations such as Saudi Arabia, Kuwait, and Libya. It also has maintained a long-standing friendship with Israel's neighbors in Jordan and Lebanon. Although these nations, with the recent exception of Libya, presently lean toward the West, they share the antipathy of extreme Arab regimes toward Israel.

Israel does not always follow the American line; it is independently minded with its own interests and concerns. In the United Nations it has occasionally sided with the Soviet Union, but when threatened Israel depends on the West. In the eyes of Soviet and Arab leaders America is a staunch ally of Israel. Washington's relations with more "extreme" Arab governments have cooled as they moved closer to Moscow. In the years just prior to the 1967 crisis, relations with Cairo had gradually deteriorated. Aid agreements, for example, had lapsed because of angry congressional reactions to insults like Nasser's assertion that American food packages should be thrown into the Red

Sea. Although the positions of greatest strategic interest to the United States were controlled by Arab countries,[38] Israel alone maintained enough power to balance those countries leaning toward the Soviet Union.

Among the many other factors affecting American policy toward disputes between Israel and the Arabs, two are of some significance. The U.S. government must consider the economic consequences of Arab animosity and the domestic political effects of adopting a policy unfavorable to Israel. The United States is not itself greatly dependent on oil from the Middle East,[39] but the region is an important source for Western Europeans.[40] The most significant aspect of Arab oil is the revenue it provides on the positive side in the international balance of payments. In 1966 trade and investment in the Middle East and North Africa produced a net inflow to the United States of approximately $1.6 billion.[41] This was comparable to the net adverse effects of Vietnam spending. However, oil interests apparently are not a decisive influence on policy decisions during an international crisis.[42] Secretary Rusk has said that, since oil holdings are a very small percentage of GNP, "they really don't represent any sig-

[38]Non-Arab allies Turkey and Iran are excluded from this assessment.

[39]In 1966 the United States imported only one-fifth of its oil consumption, and two-thirds of this came from Venezuela. *The Times* (London) article by Joe Roeber, May 25, 1967, p. 25. The United States has tremendous oil reserves if the potential yield of shale oil using nuclear dynamite is considered. Recent discoveries of "one of the largest petroleum accumulations known to the world today" in Alaska greatly strengthens U.S. reserves. *The New York Times* article by William D. Smith, July 28, 1968, sec. 3, p. 1.

[40]Almost 80 percent of Western Europe's oil is supplied from the Middle East, Noel Mostert, "High Stakes Southeast of Suez," *The Reporter,* Vol. 38, No. 5 (March 7, 1968), p. 18. There are, of course, other markets to which Western Europe can turn, and it is not likely that Arab countries would cut off their major source of revenue for an extensive period.

[41]The net inflow is calculated to be $1.66 billion, the bulk of which arises from "production, refining, transportation, and sale of oil." See balance sheet in George Lenczowski (ed.), *United States Interests in the Middle East* (Washington: American Enterprise Institute, October 1968), p. 39. However, even in the unlikely case of a loss of all oil investments in Arab nations, the U.S. balance of payments would not be decreased by the full $1.66 billion.

[42]Interview with State Department officer familiar with the handling of the Arab-Israeli crisis of 1967, conducted December 10, 1968, and interview with Mr. Kermit Roosevelt, conducted February 20, 1968. At the same time American policy makers recognized that policies favorable to Israel may jeopardize American oil holdings in the Middle East. Townsend Hoopes, Deputy Assistant Secretary of Defense, wrote shortly after the crisis that in Libya and Saudi Arabia American oil companies "have substantial investments which would be jeopardized by any abrupt step taken against the Arab countries as a whole." Letter to Representative M. Rivers, Chairman, House Armed Services Committee, *The New York Times,* August 18, 1967.

nificant leverage."[43] While the United States was economically sensitive and somewhat vulnerable in 1967 to pressures from Arab nations,[44] it was not likely that this factor would be a predominant crisis influence. It did, however, increase the importance of maintaining stability in the area.

There are countering pressures in this country favorable to Israel. The Jewish population is a natural reservoir of Zionist support and a wealthy and articulate segment of American society. There also appears to be widespread sympathy for Israel among non-Jewish Americans. With an election year approaching, a realistic politician could not be insensitive to support for Israel. However, in spite of a wide base of sentiment for Israel, it is doubtful that it had more than a peripheral influence on the pragmatic considerations of decision makers during the crisis. An attempt to exert this pressure, which occurred in the buildup phase of the crisis, seems indicative of the weight of its influence. In response to a remark by President Johnson that the American people could not just give Israel a blank check, Israeli Ambassador Harman called prominent Jewish leaders in this country who in turn called President Johnson. Instead of being impressed or influenced by these tactics, the President was annoyed.[45] Nonetheless, President Johnson's deep personal admiration for Israel should not be underestimated. He was a strong opponent of American Suez policy in 1956 and 1957, and he frequently expressed warm regard for Israel.[46]

While it is difficult to formulate a quantitative judgment, and there are extreme opinions among informed observers and policy makers, it appears that neither American oil interests nor Israeli sentiment had a dominant influence in the 1967 crisis decisions. American policy makers were well aware of the concerns of various pressure groups, but as the Secretary of State has remarked, "they did not weigh upon us" and "simply did not play too much of a role in crisis considerations."[47]

In order to determine whether the United States hedged on its obligations, the American relationship to Israel must be assessed. The

[43]Rusk, interview.
[44]Interestingly, Moscow has attributed the June war to a conspiracy of the international oil consortium as "chief patron of *Israel*." (Emphasis added.) R. Andreasyan, "New Aspects of Middle East Countries' Oil Policy," *International Affairs,* No. 9 (September 1968), p. 28.
[45]Interview with an informed White House source, conducted March 6, 1969, Appendix B, question 9.
[46]Ibid.
[47]Rusk, interview.

extent of commitment is subject to diverse interpretations.[48] The United States has frequently indicated its deep sense of obligation to the continued existence of Israel, but assurances of Israel's territorial integrity had never been formalized in an agreement to provide armed forces. The situation was complicated because, in addition to the legal ambiguity, there was a strong sense of moral commitment. Although the United States does not have a formal alliance with Israel, there have been a number of official declarations and a congressional resolution applicable to Israel and her neighbors.

One of the most significant declarations was made by the United States, Britain, and France in 1950. It stated, in part:

> The three Governments, should they find that any of these states [i.e. the Arab states and Israel] was *preparing* to *violate frontiers* or armistice lines, would, consistent with their obligations as members of the United Nations, *immediately take action*, both within and *outside* the *United Nations*, to prevent such violation.[49] [Emphasis added.]

Some authorities, including the chairman of the Senate Foreign Relations Committee, felt this declaration no longer applied because it had been violated by the French and British in the Suez conflict of 1956.[50] However, the State Department had indicated by various statements that it still subscribed to the Tripartite Declaration. In the aftermath of the Suez crisis Secretary Dulles stated that the Tripartite agreement constituted "an expression of the United States policy."[51] Secretary Rusk testified on August 25, 1966, that the Tri-

[48] William R. Kintner has concluded that there "exists a de facto alliance between the United States and Israel." Address "U.S. Overseas Defense Commitments Now and In the 1970's," June 1968, Foreign Policy Research Institute of Pennsylvania. Senator J. W. Fulbright asserts "we are not bound . . . unless statements in Presidential press conferences are as binding upon the United States as treaties ratified by the Senate." U.S., Congress, Senate, Subcommittee on Separation of Powers of the Committee on the Judiciary, *Separation of Powers,* 90th Cong., 1st sess. Part 1 (Washington, 1967), p. 51.

[49] Tripartite Declaration Regarding Security in the Middle East, May 25, 1950, *Worldwide Military Commitments,* p. 25.

[50] It is not clear whether Senator Fulbright held this view prior to the 1967 crisis. In the hearings he conducted in August 1967 he stated that it is "extremely doubtful" that Great Britain and France still consider themselves bound by it, and that it is "now considered I think as superseded by subsequent events." *U.S. Commitments to Foreign Powers,* pp. 44, 45, and 256. This is also the view of Professor Ruhl J. Bartlett, who was questioned by the Senate Committee at the time. His opinion was confirmed in interview of July 25, 1968.

[51] Statement of Secretary of State John F. Dulles, in News Conference of February 5, 1957, U.S., Senate, Committee on Foreign Relations, *A Select Chronology and Background Documents Relating to the Middle East,* 90th Cong., 1st sess. (Washington, 1967), p. 87. President Eisenhower subsequently remarked that the Declaration made "in the context of the Israeli-Arab dispute" still applied. News conference of April 17, 1957, *Background Documents,* p. 112.

partite Declaration expressed our "opposition to the use of force or threat of force" in the Middle East.[52] The declaration has been listed in State Department compilations of "Defense Commitments and Assurances" submitted to Congress both prior to and following the 1967 crisis.[53]

Statements by Presidents Kennedy and Johnson expressing similar sentiments were also included in the compilations as "Official Declarations." President Kennedy had said:

In the event of aggression or *preparation for aggression* whether *direct or indirect*, we would support appropriate measures in the United Nations, *adopt other courses of action on our own to prevent or put a stop to such aggression*, which, of course has been the policy which the United States has followed for some time.[54] [Emphasis added.]

The reaffirmation of this statement in a toast to Israel's president by President Johnson in August 1966 was also listed as an "Official Declaration."[55] The Secretary of State had declared in August 1966 that presidential statements regarding our intentions in case of aggression "may be regarded as supplementing our treaty arrangements."[56] However, in answering a question concerning our commitment in the dispute between Israel and Syria at the time, he stressed "the central responsibility" of the United Nations.[57] Although official statements were broad and did not commit the United States to a specific course of action, they indicated a sense of obligation to take measures if the peace of the area were threatened.

The Joint Resolution of Congress of March 1957, known as the Eisenhower Doctrine, also stated the concern of the United States for the security of the Middle East. It reads, in part: "the United States regards as *vital* to the *national interest* and world peace the preservation of the independence and *integrity* of the nations of the Middle East."[58] (Emphasis added.) However, the use of American armed forces was specifically limited by congressional stipulations and

[52]Testimony of Secretary of State Dean Rusk in *Worldwide Military Commitments,* p. 26.

[53]See the compilations provided by the Department of State in *Worldwide Military Commitments,* August 19, 1966, pp. 24–26; *U.S. Commitments to Foreign Powers,* August 15, 1967, pp. 65–67.

[54]Reply by President Kennedy to a news conference question concerning the Middle East, May 8, 1963, *Worldwide Military Commitments,* p. 26.

[55]Remarks of President Johnson during exchange of toasts with President Shazar of Israel, August 2, 1966, *Worldwide Military Commitments,* p. 26.

[56]Testimony of Secretary of State Dean Rusk in *Worldwide Military Commitments,* p. 9.

[57]Ibid., p. 94.

[58]Joint Resolution to Promote Peace and Stability in the Middle East (The Eisenhower Doctrine), March 9, 1957, *Worldwide Military Commitments,* p. 25.

only applied to aggression from a country "controlled by international communism."[59]

Congressional approval was required prior to using force under the Eisenhower Doctrine, but there is more controversy as to the need for further authorization to act under the Tripartite Declaration.[60] One authority, while regarding the declaration as a "commitment of the President to ask the Congress for authority to act," doubted if the President actually would have done so.[61]

The commitment to free passage through the Gulf of Aqaba was more explicit. The basic policy of the United States had been delineated in an *aide-mémoire* of February 11, 1957, which said in a key passage: "the United States, on behalf of *vessels of United States registry* is prepared to *exercise the right of free* and innocent passage and to *join with others* to secure general recognition of this right."[62] (Emphasis added.) The *mémoire* was intended to provide Israel with some assurance as an inducement for withdrawal in the aftermath of the 1956 war,[63] and considerable pressure had been put on Israel to accept it as an adequate guarantee.[64] American policy was reaffirmed at several Dulles news conferences,[65] before the U.N. General Assembly,[66] and specifically to the Arab states.[67]

An important question was the willingness of the United States to exercise the right on behalf of Israel. The Secretary of State clarified the American position: "I do not think that the United States, in the *absence* at least of a treaty or *congressional action, has authority to*

[59] Ibid.

[60] See, for example, the conflicting opinions of Judge Albert Levitt and Professor W. Stull Holt in *U.S. Commitments to Foreign Powers,* pp. 257, 295.

[61] Testimony of Professor Rhul J. Bartlett in *U.S. Commitments to Foreign Powers,* p. 45. Amplified in interview of July 25, 1968.

[62] "Aide Mémoire from Secretary Dulles to Israeli Ambassador to the United States, Abba Eban, February 11, 1957," *Background Documents,* p. 90.

[63] The mémoire was intended to provide Israel with the "maximum assurance it can reasonably expect at this juncture, or that can be reconciled with fairness to others." "White House Statement on Withdrawal of Israeli Troops within Armistice Lines," February 17, 1957, *Background Documents,* p. 92.

[64] See President Eisenhower's speech of February 21, 1957, as an example of the public pressure being exerted by the United States on Israel. *The New York Times,* February 21, 1957.

[65] Secretary of State J. F. Dulles, "News Conference of March 5, 1957," p. 106; "News Conference of March 26, 1957," *Background Documents,* p. 110.

[66] "United States Support of United Nations Efforts to Secure Peaceful Conditions in the Armistice Areas of the Near East," statement by U.S. representative before the U.N. General Assembly, March 1, 1957, *Background Documents,* p. 100.

[67] "The United States Reply to the Arab States Representations Concerning the Suez Canal and the Gulf of Aqaba," statement delivered to the heads of mission of the Arab states at Washington, June 27, 1957, *Background Documents,* p. 95.

use force to defend the rights of ships of another registry."[68] (Emphasis added.) Washington did not commit itself publicly to act directly to assist Tel Aviv. It felt, however, that by maintaining American rights Israel would receive indirect benefits. Secretary Dulles added that

> . . . the United States, in acting on its own behalf and perhaps as I have suggested, in concert with other maritime powers, would, I think, be able to impress upon that body of water an international character the benefits of which would inure to all maritime states.[69]

Although congressional approval would be required to use force to assert Israel's rights, it was implied that authority existed for the United States to "exercise" its rights. The *mémoire* did not specify any timetable for diplomatic or military action if free passage was violated.

The implication was that direct actions to assert Israel's maritime rights would only be undertaken in cooperation with other nations. President Eisenhower had said in reference to free passage that Egyptian violation of its international obligations "should be dealt with firmly by the *society of nations.*"[70] Although it could be argued that the United States had tacitly agreed to guarantee Israeli rights in the Gulf of Aqaba, the public evidence indicates Washington had not agreed to act unilaterally on Tel Aviv's behalf. However, privately Secretary Dulles had made a strong assertion of what the United States would do in marginal notes on the copy given to Israel. The Johnson administration was evidently unaware of this pledge until it was brought to their attention several days after the official White House statement on the closing of the Gulf of Aqaba.[71]

If a crisis developed, Israel apparently did not expect the United States to do more than maintain free access through the Gulf of Aqaba and neutralize any Soviet interference. According to a senior Israeli official, his government did not expect military support but counted on the United States to deter Soviet action.[72] Prime Minister Levi Eshkol was asked on April 17, 1967, "If Israel were attacked in force

[68]Secretary of State J. F. Dulles in "News Conference of February 19, 1958," *Background Documents,* p. 95.

[69]Ibid.

[70](Emphasis added.) *The New York Times* text of address to the nation by President Eisenhower on February 20, 1957; February 21, 1957. In his speech to the United Nations, Ambassador Lodge stated that if violation of these obligations occurred, the United States would "consult with other members of the United Nations to consider appropriate action which they or the United Nations might take." Statement of U.S. representative before the U.N. General Assembly, March 1, 1957, *Background Documents,* p. 101.

[71]Interview with informed White House source, Appendix B, Question 1.

[72]Interview with Senior Israel Foreign Ministry Official, conducted October 24, 1968. There have been several other statements subsequent to the war indi-

by its neighbors, would you expect help from the United States and possibly Britain and France?" He answered:

Surely, we expect such help—but we would *rely primarily on our own Army*. . . . We get these promises when we ask the United States for arms and are told: 'Don't spend your money. We are here. The Sixth Fleet is here.' My reply to this advice is that the *Sixth Fleet might not be available fast enough for one reason or another, so Israel must be strong on its own*. This is why we spend so much money on arms proportionate to our population.[73] [Emphasis added.]

Israel felt its army could take care of itself. The Sixth Fleet was apparently expected to neutralize Soviet units.

In considering employment of force in the Middle East, the status of the Sixth Fleet was an important factor. The strong Mediterranean fleet consisted of some 50 ships, 25,000 men, and 200 aircraft. A small group consisting of a converted seaplane tender and two destroyers was maintained south of the Suez Canal in the Red Sea area. The major strike force was centered around two attack aircraft carriers. In addition, there was an amphibious capability to land a battalion of marines (approximately 2000 men). However, the fleet was operating at reduced strength, particularly in its amphibious and antisubmarine warfare capability. The following insight provided by the Assistant Commandant of the U.S. Marine Corps indicates the extent of the amphibious problem:

We had only the one battalion with the 6th Fleet at the time as I recall. . . . The Battalion was bobtailed—only two infantry companies, I believe, instead of the usual three, due to the pressures on the Second Division to supply Vietnam replacements. And, of course, there were no helos in the Med. at all—haven't been able to keep any there since the first year of the Vietnam war.[74]

Helicopters are essential for modern-day amphibious assault. There also was no antisubmarine warfare carrier in the Mediterranean.[75] The absence of a special hunter-killer group was a serious military shortcoming in light of Soviet submarine strength. In addition, a number of important radar systems were inoperative in both fleet

cating that Israel would expect the United States to come in its aid in case of a Soviet attack but would fight alone against the Arabs. See, for example, the statement of Israeli Deputy Premier Yigal Allon to Knesset, October 30, 1968, *Weekly News Bulletin*, October 29–November 4, 1968, Israeli Information Services. According to a House report, "Israelis believe that avoidance of Soviet intervention depends entirely on United States deterrence." U.S., Congress, House, Special Subcommittee on National Defense Posture of the Committee on Armed Services, *Review of the Vietnam Conflict and Its Impact on U.S. Military Commitments Abroad*, 90th Congress, 2nd sess. (Washington, 1968), p. 73. See, however, the comments of Secretary Rusk, Chapter 4, footnote 41.

[73] Prime Minister Levi Eshkol, "Troubles for Israel in Hostile Mid East," Interview in *U.S. News and World Report*, Vol. IXII, No. 16 (April 17, 1967).

[74] Letter from Lt. Gen. R. C. Mangrum, USMC (Ret.), to Lt. Comdr. J. T. Howe, USN.

[75] According to a Sixth Fleet information sheet, "Periodically, and in time of crisis, the Fleet is augmented by a special force known as the Anti-submarine

task forces.[76] In spite of these deficiencies, the Sixth Fleet remained the dominant naval force in the Mediterranean.

Any decision regarding the Middle East would include a number of diverse factors, but among them would certainly be desire to maintain good relations with all Mideast nations, determination to prevent Soviet domination of the region, the economic importance of the Arab world, American sympathy for Israel, previous declarations of policy and obligations to Israel, and the relative capability of the Sixth Fleet and other U.S. military forces to respond.

3.3 SOVIET FOREIGN POLICY

As the crisis developed, important American considerations were the general trend in Soviet policy, Russian interests in the Middle East, and their military means available for implementing policy in that region.

Moscow was concerned chiefly with the growing escalation of American participation in the war in Vietnam, the continuing hostility of the Communist Chinese, and the increasing pluralism in the socialist commonwealth. The Russian offensive in the Third World was fraught with difficulty and faced with a credibility gap because of seeming Soviet impotence to assist its radical associates. Events like the Cuban missile crisis of 1962 and overthrows of Ben Bella in Algeria, Nkrumah in Ghana, and Sukarno in Indonesia were reversals for Soviet policy and had given Moscow the reputation for being a fair-weather friend. Failure to make a firm response to American escalation of the war in Vietnam furthered this image, which was vigorously promoted in Chinese propaganda. The effects were being felt in Eastern Europe, the area of most vital interest to the Soviet Union. Some European Communists apparently doubted whether the Soviets would be willing to protect them.[77] Soviet articles also

force (Task Force 66). This hunter killer force consists of a carrier with a specialized air wing of anti-submarine aircraft including helicopters, accompanied by destroyers, carrying the most modern detection equipment and anti-submarine weapons. In wartime, Task Force 66 would seek out and destroy enemy submarines." U.S. Navy, *The United States Sixth Fleet,* Public Affairs Officer, Commander Sixth Fleet, January 1967, p. 1.

[76]The percentage of missile fire control and height-finder radars that were inoperative in each task group was deleted as classified information in *Vietnam Conflict and Its Impact,* p. 57. The report described the "marginal readiness" of the Sixth Fleet. Representative Porter Hardy remarked that the condition of the entire Mediterranean Fleet scared him half to death after studying its readiness firsthand. Testimony in U.S., Congress, House, Committee on Armed Forces, *Hearings on Military Posture and An Act (S.3293),* 90th Cong., 2nd sess. (Washington, 1968), p. 9446.

[77]This feeling was indicated in a Budapest newspaper poll. The public was asked if Hungary should do more for North Vietnam. Some 70 percent answered, "No, if we do the Americans will bomb us," which prompted the

reflected a concern that Washington had become more aggressive in the Third World and was actively pursuing a policy of "rollback" of Russian influence.[78] Moscow may have decided it would be valuable to demonstrate that the United States could be forced to look like a paper tiger in certain parts of the globe.

There may have been a hint of a second crisis in the April 1967 demand by Leonid Brezhnev that the U.S. Sixth Fleet be withdrawn from the Mediterranean.[79] If Moscow could score a limited political victory in a region of admitted U.S. military superiority because of the Sixth Fleet, some Soviet leaders may have felt faith would be restored in Soviet political ploys. Possibly, the deliberate bumping of an American destroyer on successive days in the Sea of Japan at the time of growing Middle East tension was part of an effort to demonstrate that U.S. naval strength was not invulernable.[80]

Moscow may have reasoned that the United States could be made to seem impotent while Russia furthered objectives in the Middle East. Support for Syria in border incidents involving Israel might cement relations with the pro-Soviet Ba'th regime, which had come to power in 1966. The Russians were still striving to establish a sphere of dominant influence in the Middle East. Moscow had a strong security interest in exercising greater control in the region contiguous to its southern borders. For the Soviets neutralization and eventual elimination of Western influence from the Middle East was a primary goal. In addition to continuing the momentum of the Communist movement, the Soviets appeared to have some underlying practical objectives for penetration into the region: the ability to exercise more leverage in dealing with Western Europe by regu-

editorial board to comment acidly that Hungarians appeared to have singularly little faith in the ability of their Soviet allies to protect them. Interviews with Professor Uri Ra'anan, conducted in 1968, 1969. For Professor Ra'anan's views on the role of sagging Soviet credibility in the 1967 Middle East crisis see the interview in *The Boston Sunday Globe*, July 2, 1967, p. 12. A somewhat similar thesis has been presented by Adam B. Ulam in his book *Expansion and Coexistence: History of Soviet Foreign Policy, 1917–1967* (New York: Prager, 1968), pp. 743–745.

[78] In one article, for example, the United States was said to have "sharply stepped up its opposition to the national liberation movement." Maj. N. Kuzin, "U.S. and Flexible Response Strategy," *Soviet Military Review*, No. 5 (May 1966), p. 55.

[79] Brezhnev, the General Secretary of the Communist Party, said in April 1967 at the Karlovy Vary Conference, "the time has come for the demand that the U.S. Sixth Fleet be withdrawn from the Mediterranean to ring out at full strength." *Pravda*, April 25, 1967, *Current Digest of the Soviet Press (CDSP)* Vol. XIX, May 17, 1967, p. 9.

[80] The incidents occurred on May 10 and 11, 1967.

lating the oil flow,[81] obtaining access to warm water ports,[82] and control of the strategic "junction of land, sea, and air communications between Europe, Asia, and Africa.[83]

By courting Arab nations rather than Israel, the Soviets were most likely to accomplish their objectives. Arabs occupy the valuable strategic areas,[84] own the rich oil resources, and are the dominant population of the region. Arab nationalism had a natural anticolonialist and anti-Western drift. The Israelis, on the other hand, were oriented to the West. The Arab-Israeli dispute, therefore, provided a ready-made issue by which the Soviets could improve their standing with Arab states by taking an anti-Israeli stand.

Although Khrushchev's policy of supporting national liberation movements had given the Soviets influence where it had practically none previously, the program had many frustrations. After an expensive aid program, Russia had been able to do little more than temporarily "vibrate in unison with certain Near Eastern regimes," and this phenomenon had brought no "tangible or permanent gains to the Soviet Union."[85] There was growing dissatisfaction with their inability to control developments in the Third World and to prevent Western intervention. The impression that the Russians would not intervene had given the West a great deal of freedom of action. Some Kremlin military leaders felt the only way to ensure direct control was to develop the means for intervention or at least for deterring the West.[86]

The hypothesis that any type of direct involvement would inevitably

[81] It would be self-defeating, of course, to separate the primary Middle Eastern source of wealth from its principal customer for any lengthy period of time, and there are other markets to which Europe can turn. Moscow has its own oil surplus, and it certainly did not want the economic burden of sustaining clients in the Middle East.

[82] Of course, since the Soviet navy was becoming self-sustaining, Russia's historic interest in ports for military purposes was becoming less significant.

[83] Seiful-Mulyukov, "Washington's Middle East Strategy," *New Times,* No. 23 (June 12, 1968), p. 8. The description of American interests in this article gives a fairly accurate description of Moscow's interests. The Soviet writer comments that "Supremacy here would give the United States the keys to Southern Europe, the Indian Ocean and North Africa, not to speak of the economic [oil] and trade [some 1500 cargo ships pass through the Mediterranean daily] advantages." Ibid., p. 8.

[84] This situation, however, has been altered somewhat because of territory occupied by Israel since the June war.

[85] Uri Ra'anan, "The USSR in the Near East: A Decade of Visissitudes," Chapter 12 of *Modernization of the Arab World,* T. H. Thompson and R. D. Reischauer, eds., (Princeton: Van Nostrand, 1966), p. 249.

[86] Uri Ra'anan, "Tactics in the Third World: Contradictions and Dangers," *Survey,* No. 57 (October 1965), p. 36. See also Marshall D. Shulman, *Beyond the Cold War* (New Haven: Yale University Press, 1966), p. 75.

lead to a nuclear exchange was no longer considered sacred by all military men. There were signs that Moscow had been reassessing the dangers of limited wars and was considering a more flexible policy.[87] The decision to construct a helicopter carrier in 1963 and a number of related developments indicates that Moscow may have been committed to obtaining additional policy options for some time.[88] The deployment of larger naval forces in the Mediterranean also indicated a swing in the Soviet leadership toward flexibility in foreign policy. However, the prevailing view apparently continued to be that military aid rather than direct force would be used in support of national liberation movements.[89] Definite currents of change toward a more flexible and aggressive policy for the Third World existed prior to the June war. While direct Soviet intervention was unlikely, it could not be discounted.

Publicity given to the buildup of Soviet naval forces in the Mediterranean following the crisis has obscured the fact that a marked change had occurred in Russian capabilities and operating philosophy prior to the events of May and June 1967.[90] Moscow had been maintaining a fleet of some ten surface ships, including the oilers and supply vessels necessary to sustain the force, in the Mediterranean since 1965. A small but modern amphibious capability had also been developed.[91] There were a few landing ships already in the

[87]There is quite a bit of evidence of this. See, for example, the contradictory statements on pages 286 and 288 of Y. D. Sokolovskii, *Soviet Military Strategy,* translated by Herbert S. Dinerstein, Leon Goure, Thomas W. Wolfe, published by Military Publishing House of the Ministry of Defense of the USSR, translation published for the Rand Corporation by Prentice-Hall (Englewood Cliffs, N.J., 1963). A call for further study of local war, by Col. I. Korotkov, is contained in "The Development of Soviet Military Theory in Postwar Years," *Voenno-Istoricheski Zurnal,* No. 4 (April 1964), p. 48.

[88]See Chapter 13 for a brief description of the expansion of the Soviet surface navy.

[89]The Soviets have made numerous claims of providing military assistance to various regimes, but "military" has always meant military equipment and not Soviet troops. See, for example, the claims in Col. U. Rzheshevsky, "Garthoff vs. Garthoff," *Soviet Military Review,* No. 9 (September 1967), p. 56. and Ye Zhukov, "The National Liberation Movement and Peaceful Co-existence," *Soviet Military Review,* No. 10 (October 1965), p. 9. When Premier Alexsi N. Kosygin was asked whether support of wars of national liberation should include military force, he ignored that part of the question. *The New York Times,* "Transcript of news conference . . . at U.N. by Premier Alexsi Kosygin," Question 21, June 26, 1967, p. 17.

[90]For example, Richard Nixon commented that *following* the Israeli victory the Soviet Union has "a naval presence in the Mediterranean which they have never had before." (Emphasis added.) "Nixon's Views in a Nutshell," *U.S. News and World Report,*" Vol. LXIV, No. 11 (March 11, 1968), p. 44.

[91]The Institute of Strategic Studies estimated that as of June 1967 there was a "small Marine Corps of perhaps 6000 men, units of which are stationed with all four fleets." *The Military Balance 1967–68 (*London: Institute for Strategic Studies 1967), p. 8.

Mediterranean at the time of the crisis, but these were not thought to have made any contribution during the war nor to have been a significant force.[92] Although the Soviet fleet was not yet a match for the Sixth Fleet, it was more imposing than popularly believed at the time. As the Deputy Commander of U.S. Naval Forces in Europe replied in answer to the question "Was their strength sufficient to be a formidable challenge to the Sixth Fleet?": "It was, and is, in two respects: up to ten or a dozen submarines,[93] and several ships equipped with surface-to-surface missiles whose effectiveness was demonstrated against an Israeli destroyer. . . . The Soviet strength was in no sense petty."[94] The U.S. Navy recognized the potential capability of the Soviet forces in the Mediterranean. Although the Russians had only a small force available for actual intervention, they had enough strength to present a formidable obstacle to the Sixth Fleet, even if they could not completely counterbalance its forces.

Of course, the local balance of conventional forces of the superpowers in only partially relevant since an actual attack on the Sixth Fleet would probably lead to a full-scale global exchange.[95] The Soviets appeared to be hoping to neutralize the Sixth Fleet, but it is doubtful that they would have risked a third world war if their bluff had been called. Although such reasoning remains speculative, it appears that Moscow decided that a carefully controlled low-risk crisis in the Middle East would bolster sagging Soviet prestige in Russia's existing spheres of influence.

3.4 BRITISH FOREIGN POLICY

Because Great Britain was already economically vulnerable and militarily overextended, it was most reluctant to assume any additional peace-keeping burdens. The British had reduced their defense budget and announced a gradual withdrawal of forces east of Suez. Although cutbacks of forces had not yet been carried out to any sig-

[92] Interview with Rear Adm. J. C. Wylie, USN, conducted December 22, 1967. It is possible, however, that the presence of these ships in a Levant port contributed to American concern about limited Soviet intervention during the crisis phase. See Chapter 5. An article by Thomas W. Wolfe, an American expert on Soviet military affairs, stated that the "Soviets dispatched . . . special landing vessels, to the Mediterranean in connection with the 1967 Arab-Israeli crisis," "Soviet Military Policy at the Fifty Year Mark," *Current History,* October 1967, p. 216. He has subsequently clarified that he meant the aftermath of the six-day war. Interview conducted December 9, 1968.

[93] Most U.S. newspaper and magazine estimates of Soviet submarine strength listed it as two to three submarines.

[94] Letter from Rear Adm. J. C. Wylie, USN, to Lt. Comdr. J. T. Howe, USN, dated December 7, 1967.

[95] This, of course, remains speculative. See Chapter 2, footnote 6.

nificant extent, the British public had been psychologically prepared, with some controversy, for contraction from international commitments.

The decision in late 1965 to decrease defense costs was primarily due to a large balance of payments deficit. Military expenditures accounted for 77 percent of the deficit.[96] The British pound had been in serious trouble since 1964. Subsequent devaluation in late 1967 indicated the precariousness of the situation during the crisis.[97] The earnings of British oil companies and exports to Arab countries provided an important source of revenue on the positive side of the balance of payments ledger. In addition, Arab countries were important members of the sterling block. The United Kingdom was sensitive to pressure on sterling because of the large liabilities owed to overseas holders.[98] Kuwait alone held almost as much sterling reserves as all of the Western European countries.[99] This financial situation made British opposition to unified Arab policies particularly difficult.

Although Great Britain has advantages in dealing with some areas, it also has distinct liabilities in addition to economic vulnerability. The British presence is accepted by a number of the rich oil-producing countries of southern Arabia. However, British dependence on Arabian oil makes it more difficult to take a stand against these countries. The United Kingdom receives 72 percent of its petroleum from Arab countries. Kuwait alone supplies 23 percent of British oil imports and Iraq 15 percent.[100] Britain also must overcome an anticolonial stigma and is a natural target for Arab nationalists. British influence in the region has declined sharply. Relations with Egypt had been severely strained over Yemen and officially broken over British action against Rhodesia.

London retained a deep concern for the fate of Israel but had been backing away from commitments to Tel Aviv as British interests in the Middle East became more dependent on Arab acceptance. Although the United Kingdom had been a party to the Tripartite Dec-

[96] *Economic Effect of Vietnam Spending*, p. 495.

[97] There was, of course, some direct contribution of the crisis itself to the strain on sterling which contributed to the devaluation of the pound. See D. C. Watt, "The Decision to Withdraw from the Gulf," *The Political Quarterly*, Vol. 39, No. 3 (July/September 1968), p. 312.

[98] British net liabilities were over four times reserves. As calculated from figures given in "Those Sterling Balances," *The Economist* Vol. CCXXII, No. 6440 (January 28, 1967), p. 336.

[99] Ibid., p. 336. Information extrapolated from graph. See also *The Times* article "Kuwait—Tiny Oil State With A Big Financial Stick," June 7, 1967, p. 26.

[100] "The Economic Fallout of the War," *The Economist*, Vol. CCXXIV, No. 6459 (June 10, 1967), p. 1104.

laration, the government explained that the situation had "entirely changed" and that it had no "special role in the Arab-Israeli dispute."[101] The Foreign Office described the status of the commitment to Israel in the following way:

In May 1963, Mr. Harold Macmillan, confirmed H. M. G.'s interest in peace and stability in the area but added 'I cannot say in advance what action we would take in a crisis since it is difficult to foresee the exact circumstances which might arise. We regard the United Nations as primarily responsible for the maintenance of peace in the area. If any threat to peace arises we would consult immediately with the United Nations, and would take whatever action we feel may be required.' This statement was endorsed by Mr. Wilson on 16 December 1964. Her Majesty's Government had no commitment to Israel beyond this general interest in the peace and stability of the area.[102]

This position had been reiterated in December 1966.[103] The United Nations was considered responsible for peace-keeping in the area. London, however, still stood by its policy toward the Gulf of Aqaba which had been proclaimed before the United Nations in 1957.

The Straits of Tiran must be regarded as an international waterway, through which the vessels of all nations have a right of passage. Her Majesty's Government *will assert* this right *on behalf* of all *British shipping*, and they are prepared to join with others to secure general recognition of this right.[104] [Emphasis added.]

The statement was similar to that made by the United States.

The British still had a patchwork of defense treaties with a number of small states of the Persian Gulf area including Kuwait. London was also concerned about possible expansion of the Yemen civil war, but British interests were clearly served by taking a neutral line in any dispute between Israel and the Arab states. London avowedly sought no political advantage and desired peace in the area,[105] but Britain depended on the United Nations to bring about the desired conditions.

British forces available for peace-keeping operations were relatively small and already actively employed. There were still some 40,000

[101] Explanation of government's position of December 19, 1966 as quoted by George Brown, Secretary of State for Foreign Affairs, statement of May 31, 1967, in the House of Commons, official text, British Information Services, Document T. 23, p. 6.

[102] Comments of the Foreign Office in answer to the question, "What was the extent of British commitment to the US and to Israel in connection with the crisis?" Letter from Mr. R. A. Lloyd Jones, Ministry of Defence, Letter D/DS5/36/57/20/68/B of April 9, 1968 to Lt. Comdr. J. T. Howe, USN.

[103] Brown, statement of May 31, 1967, p. 6.

[104] Ibid., pp. 4, 5.

[105] Speech by George Thomson, Minister of State for Foreign Affairs, repeating "Principles of British Policy in Middle East" pronounced in March 1967; House of Commons, July 6, 1967, text supplied by British Information Services, No. 33, p. 15.

troops in Singapore, where the United Kingdom had assisted the United States by defending Malaysia in its confrontation with Indonesia.[106] The Communists had initiated riots in Hong Kong on May Day, requiring a show of British force there. A conflict was developing between Kenya and Somalia which might involve the British in military aid to Kenya.[107] In addition, British frigates had been on continuous duty in the Mozambique Channel to enforce an embargo on shipments of oil to Rhodesia. British forces were involved all over the world and with not much reserve to fall back on if the situations deteriorated.

The British navy had only three aircraft carriers, two commando ships, and two assault ships to carry out its still substantial worldwide peace-keeping commitments. Although this was a small fleet relative to those of the superpowers, it compared favorably with the rest of the navies of the world. Aircraft carriers still could play a vital role in the Mediterranean, particularly since the U.S. carrier force was hard pressed in Vietnam and the Soviets had no attack aircraft carriers. Commando ships were also particularly important with U.S. amphibious shortages in the Mediterranean. The Royal Navy could be of some help in a Middle Eastern conflict. Whether it would be committed by the British in a crisis involving Israel remained to be seen.

[106] *Economic Effect of Vietnam Spending,* p. 90.
[107] "Kenya and Somalia Our Next War But Two?," *The Economist*, Vol. CCXXIII, No. 6457 (May 27, 1967), p. 900.

4. THE BUILDUP PHASE

MAY 23, 1967, TO JUNE 4, 1967

American policy choices during the buildup period can be better understood after examining a number of complex and interrelated factors, including the attitudes of the Soviet and British governments. The actions taken by each nation indicated how it intended to deal with the growing crisis.

4.1 UNITED STATES POLICY

Even before Nasser's announcement of a blockade of the Gulf of Aqaba on May 22, 1967 the United States had been busily engaged in diplomacy aimed at reducing tension in the Middle East. An important message from President Johnson indicating American willingness to try to calm the situation down had been sent prior to the blockade speech.

President Johnson's public statement of May 23, 1967, in response to the Egyptian move, set the tone for United States policy during the remainder of the buildup phase. Asserting that the United States earnestly supported "all efforts, *in and outside the United Nations . . .* to reduce tensions and to restore stability," he phrased the American commitment in the following way:

> To the leaders of all the nations of the Near East, I wish to say what three American Presidents have said before me—that the United States is *firmly committed* to the support of the political independence and territorial integrity of *all* the nations of that area. The United States strongly opposes aggression by anyone in the area, in any form, *overt or clandestine.*[1] [Emphasis added.]

This statement expressed elements of the Eisenhower Doctrine, the Tripartite Declaration, and previous presidential pledges. The message was a firm but restrained expression of concern and did not appear to back away from the spirit of past affirmations of commitment. It seemed to be the first step in fulfilling promises to take prompt action. As in previous official declarations it did not specify what would be done other than vigorous activity in the United Nations. In an allusion to the war in Vietnam it may have been intended to hint that the United States was prepared to act forcefully, if necessary, to oppose aggression.[2]

[1] "The Situation in The Middle East: Statement by President Johnson on May 23, 1967." U.S., Congress, Senate, Committee on Foreign Relations, *A Select Chronology and Background Documents Relating to the Middle East,* 90th Cong., 1st sess. (Washington, 1967), p. 136. Hereafter cited as *Background Documents.*

[2] The President said, "We have always opposed—and *we oppose in other parts of the world at this very moment*—the efforts of other nations to resolve their problems with their neighbors by the aggression route." [Emphasis added.] *Background Documents,* pp. 136, 137.

In discussing the "new and very grave dimension to the crisis," the "*purported* closing" of the gulf to *Israeli* shipping, the President appeared to take a strong stand. He declared that the right of "free, innocent passage . . . is a *vital* interest of the *entire* international community"[3] But his statement was actually weak when compared with the existing commitment to "exercise the right of free and innocent passage."[4] There were logical reasons for this approach. The extent of the blockade was not clear,[5] the public American obligation was to act on behalf of *U.S.* ships, and a hard line would have given the United Arab Republic no way to retreat gracefully from the announcement. The United States was already privately trying to work out a solution with Moscow and Cairo.

The President's overall position was reiterated by the U.S. representative to the United Nations. However, several statements in the United Nations appeared to soften the President's stand. On May 24 Ambassador Goldberg said the United States had made clear its "commitment to the solution of all problems of the area by *exclusively peaceful* means."[6] The President had emphasized interest in peace but had not limited the United States to "exclusively peaceful means." In a subsequent U.N. debate it was "necessary" to declare that the American "attitude" was not one of "partisanship."[7] This was probably in response to Arab charges that Washington was backing Israel, and it also reflected U.S. desire to retain the good will of both sides.

The Secretary of State indicated that the government hoped to avoid "unilateral action";[8] the White House announced that "all the em-

[3]Ibid., p. 136. (Emphasis added.)

[4]See Chapter 3, footnote 62.

[5]The day following the President's statement the announcement that other nations would be asked to stop for inspection was made, along with the claim that mines had been laid. Washington did, however, know not only that the guns that commanded the straits were occupied, but that in the days previous to the initial announcement Egyptian naval vessels had been observed moving south through the Suez Canal. *The New York Times,* May 22, 1967, p. 1. These moves may have indicated to the United States that Nasser meant business in his statement of May 22.

[6](Emphasis added.) "United Nations Debate on The Middle East Crisis," May 24, 1967, *Background Documents,* p. 138.

[7]Arthur J. Goldberg, "United Nations Debate on the Middle East Crisis," May 29, 1967, *Background Documents,* p. 147.

[8]Secretary Rusk had remarked to newsmen following an appearance before the Senate on June 1 that he did not "want to get into any question of unilateral action." He said, "It was a matter for the entire world community." *The Washington Post,* June 2, 1967, p. 19. In answer to the question "Was our decision not to undertake a unilateral action the result of congressional pressure or was this the government's independent view anyway?" Secretary Rusk said, "we pretty much agreed that nothing should be done." Interview with former Secretary of State Dean Rusk conducted April 9, 1969.

phasis is on a U.N. settlement."[9] Washington wanted the world community to solve the problem, but it seems inconceivable that the United States felt a solution could be achieved through the United Nations without Soviet cooperation. The message that seemed to be expressed by the President's official statement and its subsequent clarifications was that America wanted a peaceful solution, hoped to avoid accusations of playing favorites, was receptive to working with the Soviets, and was reluctant to take action outside the United Nations without the concurrence of allies. In short, Washington leaned toward a weaker rather than a stronger public interpretation of commitments to Tel Aviv.

Examining the factors influencing policy, it becomes easier to see why the United States took this position. Washington wanted to avoid a direct showdown with the Soviet Union which could jeopardize world peace. In some ways the situation was more serious than the war in Vietnam, because neither superpower had firm control of the third parties to whom they were linked.[10] The United States had begun to sound out the Soviet Union in mid-May. Reportedly, President Johnson urged Premier Kosygin to use Soviet influence to dampen the crisis,[11] and Ambassador Goldberg privately assured his Soviet counterpart in the United Nations that Washington was not colluding with Tel Aviv.[12] At least two direct conversations regarding methods for restraining the Arabs and Israelis were alleged to have occurred between Moscow and Washington.[13] That there were numerous dis-

[9]When asked if the White House saw a parallel between Vietnam and the Middle East, the press secretary, George Christian, said that "the White House position is to pursue the Middle Eastern matter as thoroughly as possible in the United Nations. We aren't drawing any parallels of any kind. All the emphasis is on a U.N. settlement." *The Washington Post* article by Carroll Kitpatrick "LBJ Cabinet Confer on Mideast," June 1, 1967, p. 2.

[10]The British particularly stressed this aspect of the crisis. See statements of Foreign Secretary George Brown, House of Commons, May 31, 1967, British Information Services, T.23, June 1, 1967; and Statement of Prime Minister Harold Wilson, House of Commons, May 31, 1967, B.I.S., No. T.24.

[11]*The New York Times,* May 21, 1967, p. 1. See also *The Sunday Times (*London) article by Henry Brandon, "Johnson Makes Secret Plea to Russia on Middle East," May 21, 1967, p. 1.

[12]*The New York Times* article, "U.S. Takes Leading Part in U.N. Talks to Ease Mideast Crisis," May 22, 1967, p. 7.

[13]This revelation was made following the crisis and appeared to reflect Soviet annoyance at Arab charges that the Soviets had let them down. It is probably a valid report, but it is incorrect in at least one instance. It specified that the conversations were held over the "hot line." A letter from the White House staff states that the hot line was not used prior to the outbreak of hostilities. Letter from Richard M. Moose to Lt. Comdr. J. T. Howe dated March 1, 1968. The statements of the "high Russian official" were made to the French newspaper *Le Nouvel Observateur,* "Pourquoi Moscou a lâché Nasser," No. 135 (June 14 to June 20, 1967).

cussions appears certain; what was said is less clear. An informed source commented, "we went to the Soviets and told them to call off their boys."[14] By examining speeches in the United Nations, Soviet activities during the period,[15] and reactions upon the outbreak of hostilities, a fairly accurate estimate can be made.

American statements of May 23 and 24 indicated deep concern about the implications of a direct confrontation of the superpowers. The President warned of a "miscalculation arising from a misunderstanding of the intentions and the actions of others."[16] He appeared to be warning the Soviets of the danger of not understanding the true intentions of the United States. Ambassador Goldberg emphasized in the United Nations that "Great powers have both interests and responsibilities in this matter—and the *greater the power the greater the responsibility*."[17] (Emphasis added.) This type of indirect reference to the Soviet Union seemed to disappear in subsequent statements,[18] probably because frequent private exchanges were in progress. But uncertainty about Soviet intentions remained. The uncertainty that existed when the war began indicates that positions on both sides had not been fully clarified.[19] Signs of some interest in preventing an outbreak of war could be discerned, but there was no logical reason for either side to reveal its various plans and little likelihood that any advance guarantees would be relied upon.

Defense Department recommendations regarding military capability were an important consideration. Pentagon officials were anxious to avoid an additional American military involvement. According to an admiral familiar with deliberations of the Joint Chiefs of Staff, "The overriding concern of the government was to avoid the involvement of the United States in a shooting war in the Mideast."[20] Correspondents sensed that defense leaders were "haunted by the prospect of a 'second Vietnam' in the Middle East for which they were

[14]Interview with an informed White House source concerning Middle East crisis of 1967, conducted March 6, 1969, Appendix B.2, Question 6.

[15]See Section 4.2 for an evaluation of Soviet policy.

[16]*Background Documents*, p. 136. This statement possibly was directed to Israel, Egypt, and Syria, but from the context it appeared to apply primarily to the Soviet Union.

[17]Statement of Arthur J. Goldberg during U.N. debate of May 24, 1967, *Background Documents*, p. 139.

[18]See, for example, the statement of Ambassador Goldberg to the United Nations on May 29, 1967, *Background Documents*, pp. 147–148.

[19]See Chapter 5 for description of messages exchanged at the outbreak of the crisis.

[20]Letter from Rear Adm. George C. Talley, Jr., Deputy Director, Strategic Plans and Policy Division, Chief of Naval Operations, to Lt. Comdr. J. T. Howe, USN, undated letter received April 10, 1969.

totally unprepared."[21] The Assistant Commandant of the Marine Corps recalled that "we were shying away from involvement as hard as we could because of our involvement in Vietnam."[22] He also speculated that "involved as we were . . . with SE Asia, no one was about to fire a shot elsewhere—unless, of course, the Russians started W.W. III."[23] Observers wrote of the strain on U.S. readiness in the Mediterranean because of Vietnam as evidenced by deficiencies in planes, pilots, experience levels, and inventories of supplies. It was predicted that the United States could not carry out sustained action for more than a limited period and that mobilization would be required for any protracted conflict.[24]

Although the Joint Chiefs of Staff had a "notable lack of enthusiasm for involving the U.S. in a conflict in the Mideast," their attitude was not based primarily on reduced capability because of Vietnam.[25] The Joint Chiefs of Staff simply saw no advantages for the United States in a military intervention in the Middle East. American forces in the area were superior to those of the Soviet Union. "Even with the war in Vietnam," the Joint Chiefs of Staff "had available sufficient forces to execute" its "Mideast Contingency Plan."[26] The Atlantic Fleet had an attack carrier and antisubmarine warfare carrier in "immediately deployable" readiness,[27] and within two weeks the United States "could have put into action four carrier task forces and a Marine Expeditionary Brigade."[28]

The United States could make an initial response in the Middle East, but would not have been able to sustain action there without mobilization because of the war in Vietnam.[29] The Sixth Fleet could have played a limited role without any preliminary reinforcement, but its effectiveness would have been small in any direct support of Israel. A key U.S. naval commander commented that he did not believe "any

[21] Theodore Draper, "Israel and World Politics," *Commentary,* Vol. 44, No. 2 (August 1967), p. 40.
[22] Letters from Lt. Gen. R. C. Mangrum, USMC (Ret.), to Lt. Comdr. J. T. Howe, USN.
[23] Ibid.
[24] See, for example, *The New York Times* article by Hanson W. Baldwin, "US Officers See a Mobilization in Any Big Mideast Intervention," May 25, 1967, p. 17; and *The New York Times* editorial "Military Reality in the Mideast," May 29, 1967.
[25] Talley, letter.
[26] Ibid.
[27] These were the U.S.S. *Roosevelt (*CVA 42) and U.S.S. *Wasp (*CVS18). Letter from Commander D. M. Cooney, USN, Headquarters of the Commander in Chief (CinC), U.S. Atlantic Fleet, dated April 17, 1969.
[28] Talley, letter.
[29] Ibid.

naval action could have altered the result of the action in the desert."[30] Because of the status of the military establishment, it would seem safe to assume that reserves would have been called if Washington had intended to prepare for a major intervention on behalf of Israel. Failure to do so was further evidence of Washington's hope to avoid involvement, if any doubts remained in Moscow, Cairo, and Tel Aviv. At the same time, the Sixth Fleet represented a credible deterrent to Soviet intervention.

Washington could seriously consider nonengagement as an acceptable solution because of its confidence in the ability of the outnumbered Israeli forces. It was considered an "article of faith" in the American intelligence community that Israel was capable of defeating the combined Arab armies.[31] The Joint Chiefs of Staff predicted an Israeli victory in less than a week if Israel struck first and only a few days longer if Israel absorbed the first blow. Reluctant to accept only one estimate, the President requested independent opinions of the State Department, the CIA, and Great Britain. These other estimates agreed closely with those of the Defense Department.[32] The Assistant Marine Corps Commandant stated that "we were well aware of mounting tension for some time, and after Egypt closed off Aqaba, we knew it would be only days, if not hours, before the *Israelis let them have it but good*."[33] (Emphasis added.)

Although the United States was confident of Israel's ability to triumph in a military engagement with its neighbors, the President urged Israel not to attack. The Israelis were told that "they would not be alone unless they chose to go it alone."[34] Israeli Foreign Minister Abba Eban was told by President Johnson on May 26, 1967 that the United States was hopeful about an international maritime force to break the blockade of the Gulf of Aqaba and that American unilateral action was out. Some key government officials expected Israel to forgo offensive action.

What Tel Aviv actually requested of Washington is not known for certain, but there are some excellent indications. A number of Israeli

[30]Letter from Rear Adm. J. C. Wylie, Deputy Commander, U.S. Naval Forces Europe, to Lt. Comdr. J. T. Howe, USN, dated December 7, 1967.

[31]Interview with Mr. George A. Carroll, Assistant for National Security Affairs to the Vice President of the United States, conducted December 6, 1968. It was publicly reported to be the view both of "military and non-military sources" shortly before the war that Israel could defeat the combined Arab forces. *The Washington Post,* June 2, 1967, p. A18.

[32]See interview with an informed White House source, conducted March 6, 1969, Appendix B.2, Question 4.

[33]Mangrum, letters.

[34]Interview with former Secretary of State Dean Rusk, conducted April 9, 1969.

officials conferred with the U.S. government during this period. The Israeli government apparently resolved to lay the groundwork for American political support before Israel achieved a military victory. Foreign Minister Abba Eban was determined to prevent a repetition of the 1956 situation "when a military victory was squandered because there was not sufficient political preparation."[35] For this reason Tel Aviv was apparently willing to adhere to what it interpreted as an American request to delay military retaliation for two weeks following the announcement of the Gulf of Aqaba blockade.[36] Premier Eshkol explained that "we were first asked to wait two days. Then we sent Mr. Abba Eban to the U.S.—and we were asked to wait a further fortnight."[37] Secretary Rusk, however, has stated that Israel "put the two week limit on" and that the United States expectation was for an "open ended agreement to forgo hostilities."[38] Foreign Minister Eban felt an essential distinction between 1956 and 1967 had been made when President Johnson allegedly told him during their May 26, 1967, meeting that "the American people and I believe that Israel is a victim of arbitrary lawlessness."[39]

Israel was confident of its military capability to defeat the Arabs,[40] and it probably expected Washington only to prevent Moscow's military intervention.[41] This, the Sixth Fleet could do without much strain. It could play a negative or neutralizing role with existing strength, but a decision to commit U.S. forces to positive action in support of Israel would have been a more difficult political decision. By simply operating uncommitted forces in the eastern Mediterranean the United States was performing an important service for Israel. The Soviets identified the American presence with support for Tel Aviv. As McGeorge Bundy has indicated, "Our role was to keep it

[35] *Ma'ariv* interview with Foreign Minister Abba Eban, Tel Aviv, February 7, 1969, p. 16. Although his comments were made more than a year after the events and in order to explain why Israel did not have to return to the status quo ante, they seem to be an accurate account, although such a judgment is speculative. Premier Levi Eshkol said on June 8, 1967, that waiting the three weeks before attacking "enhanced our political standing." *Jerusalem Post,* June 9, 1969.

[36] Theodore Draper cites some evidence for this assumption in *Israel and World Politics* (New York: Viking, 1968), pp. 90, 91.

[37] *The Jerusalem Post* quotation from speech June 8 of Israel Premier Levi Eshkol, June 9, 1967.

[38] Rusk, interview.

[39] This is Abba Eban's quotation of what President Johnson allegedly told him. *Ma'ariv* interview, February 7, 1969.

[40] Interview with senior Israel Foreign Ministry official conducted October 24, 1968.

[41] Ibid. According to Secretary of State Dean Rusk, Israel "never put it in those terms. There was never a discussion of that." Rusk, interview.

sufficiently controlled so that no other great power would become engaged."[42]

As diplomatic efforts proved futile, it became increasingly apparent that Israel would act on her own. Tel Aviv had asserted repeatedly that blockade of the Gulf of Aqaba would be a *casus belli,* and the Secretary General of the United Nations had warned this was the Israeli interpretation.[43] It was obvious Israel would not wait long to resort to arms; economically, it could not sustain full mobilization for more than a limited period.[44] As long as the Egyptian army was massed on its borders, Israel had to stay in full readiness. Growing pressure to act was being exerted by the Israeli population. The appointment of General Moshe Dayan as Defense Minister on June 1 indicated that military measures were imminent. Tel Aviv relieved Washington of any public embarrassment regarding its obligations when Dayan said on June 3, 1967, that he did not want "anyone else to fight for us."[45] Because of the impending U.S. visit of Egyptian Vice President Mohieddin on June 7, 1967, some American officials firmly believed that an Israeli offensive would be delayed at least that long, but the general impression in Washington seems to have been that time was short. As early as May 26, 1967, after meeting with Foreign Minister Eban, the following conversation occurred between President Johnson and a member of his staff:[46]

President Johnson: What do you think is going to happen?

Staff Member: They [Israel] are going to hit them [the Arabs].

[42]Letter from McGeorge Bundy to Lt. Comdr. J. T. Howe, USN, of April 3, 1968. Mr. Bundy wrote that this sentence was a correct interpretation of remarks he had made. He was appointed by the President to coordinate U.S. actions toward the Middle East upon the outbreak of the war.

[43]"Report by the United Nations Secretary General U Thant to the Security Council on the Middle East Crisis," *Background Documents,* p. 145. The date on Security Council Document S17906 is May 26, 1967.

[44]Israel had completed mobilization on May 21. On June 1 the Israeli Finance Minister warned that a prolonged crisis would seriously damage Israel's economy. *The New York Times,* June 2, 1967, p. 14. It has been claimed that although many people in the West felt Israel could not sustain full mobilization for more than a short period, privately experts in Tel Aviv felt that the economy could remain viable for six months. See Michael Howard and Robert Hunter, *Israel and the Arab World: The Crisis of 1967,* Adelphi Papers No. 41 (October 1967) (London: Institute for Strategic Studies, 1967), p. 28. This allegation was rebutted in interview with senior Israel Foreign Ministry official. Israel had used similar reasoning in the Suez crisis of 1956. The important point is whether finding an excuse or really in serious economic difficulty, Israel was creating the impression that she would act shortly. See also *The Times* (London), "Israel Is Having to Revise Her Economic Policies," June 3, 1967, p. 10; and *The Economist*, June 3, 1967, p. 1007.

[45]*The New York Times*, June 4, p. 1.

[46]Informed White House source, interview, Appendix B.2, Question 6.

President: Yes, they are going to hit them.

A key question affecting American political capability to support Israel was whether or not the President felt constrained to obtain congressional approval prior to taking action. The President explained to Israeli Foreign Minister Eban in their meeting on May 26, 1967, that he would have to go through Congress before acting, and for this reason unilateral action could not be considered. The Secretary of State, who conducted numerous briefings of Congress during this period, believed that the President would have sought congressional approval before committing U.S. forces to a maritime effort to test the blockade and before intervening militarily on behalf of Israel.[47] The President's apparent inclination to seek congressional approval of American initiatives increased the importance of sentiment among the legislators as a factor in assessing U.S. policy choices. However, the President evidently refused to tie his hands by assuring congressmen that he would consult them.[48]

Two predominant points of view were expressed by congressmen concerned about the Middle East situation.[49] One group felt the government might not do enough for Israel; the other was afraid it might do too much. However, in the period prior to the war there appeared to be uniform agreement that the United States must not take any *unilateral action.* As Senator Fulbright remarked, "In the days before the June War in the Middle East . . . strong and virtually *unanimous* sentiment was expressed in the Senate *against* any *unilateral* American military involvement in that part of the world."[50] (Emphasis added.) The Secretary of State concurred with this assessment of congressional sentiment.[51]

Senator Jacob Javits revealed that the Senate majority leader had commented during Foreign Relations Committee briefings, "there was no question of unilateral action in the Middle East at this point."[52] Instead of refuting this view, Senator Javits endorsed it

[47]Rusk, interview.

[48]See Chapter 6, footnote 1.

[49]"Interview with State Department Officer Familiar with the Handling of the Arab-Israeli crisis of 1967," conducted December 10, 1968. The official attended the congressional briefings. These points of view were reflected in statements on the floor of Congress. It is, of course, possible that there was a silent faction who would have opposed support for Israel with no war in Vietnam but found it politically astute to remain silent or identify with the "over-commitment sentiment."

[50]U.S., *Congressional Record*, 90th Cong., 1st sess., Vol. 113, No. 201 (December 8, 1967). Speech "The War and Its Effects."

[51]Rusk, interview.

[52]Senator Jacob Javits quoting Senator Mike Mansfield in U.S., *Congressional Record*, 90th Cong., 1st sess., Vol. 113, No. 82 (May 24, 1967). Senator Javits used the same words in a comment to the press following a meeting

with a slight change of emphasis: "The majority leader is absolutely right that *at this point* there is no question of *unilateral* action."[53] (Emphasis added.) His stress on "at this point" may indicate he expected U.S. intervention if Israel were endangered.[54]

It was significant that a senator, likely to express an extreme view,[55] had evidently accepted this limitation and in effect taken the government "off the hook" with Zionist advocates. Senator Javits has indicated that commitments to NATO allies were a significant factor keeping Washington from considering unilateral action,[56] but the United States has no requirement to obtain NATO permission until a "NATO war situation" has been declared.[57] However, Senator Javits also made the following comment:

> . . . It is difficult to ascertain whether the Congress would have favored direct U.S. military intervention on behalf of Israel last year without having in full hand the circumstances under which this may have been requested. For example, *there is always the factor of the posture of the Soviets*.[58] [Emphasis added.]

It is speculated that in briefings Senator Javits had been assured that Israel did not need any American help and that the Soviet Union would not be able to intervene. As long as Russia could be kept out of the situation, those who were particularly concerned about Israel's welfare could be confident. Without a Soviet threat there was little hope of rallying congressional support for an American initiative. In fact, a strong stand could be a tactical mistake. Senator Javits commented that such a stand "might have been used by the Soviets for its own purposes [*sic*] to worsen the situation."[59]

with Secretary of State Rusk on May 29. He used them in the order Senator Mansfield had. *The New York Times,* May 30, 1967, p. 2.

[53]Ibid. By "unilateral" he apparently meant action taken by the United States in conjunction with Israel but without the aid of other allies.

[54]Other senators expressed the sentiment that the United States could not allow Israel to be "driven into the sea." Remarks of Senator Joseph Clark, in U.S., *Congressional Record,* 90th Cong., 1st sess., Vol. 113, No. 81 (May 23, 1967), p. S7222.

[55]Senator Javits represents the state of New York with the most prominent and influential Jewish population in the country. He is a member of the Jewish faith himself and was up for reelection in 1968.

[56]Letter from Senator Jacob K. Javits, to Lt. Comdr. J. T. Howe, USN, dated November 25, 1968.

[57]Letter from Captain J. J. Nuss, USN, Executive Assistant to Commander, Allied Forces Southern Europe, to Lt. Comdr. J. T. Howe, USN, dated April 2, 1969. The United States, of course, as a matter of courtesy and practical necessity keeps its NATO allies informed of the dispostion of its forces which are designated for NATO employment in time of war. The Sixth Fleet remains under U.S. national command except in a NATO war situation.

[58]Javits, letter. This comment, however, was not a direct answer to the question of why the United States felt no unilateral action could be taken.

[59]Javits, letter.

The other group of congressmen stressed that there could be no unilateral action because of the strain of Vietnam. Senator Symington, for example, told the Senate he had "grave doubts about our once again pursuing any course on a unilateral basis."[60] He stressed the need for "extreme caution, . . . especially in view of our already deep involvement in Vietnam."[61] Other influential senators expressed similar sentiments.[62] Significantly, it was not publicly asserted that the United States had no commitment to Israel. There may have been private reservations expressed, however.[63] Senator Stennis said that "our nation has clear and specific commitments to this area."[64] Senators who had expressed alarm about overcommitment did not deny an American obligation to Israel, which was not one of the forty-three countries tied to the United States by formal security alliances. There was an interesting crossing of views of those who were "hawks" and "doves" on the Vietnam issue when it came to the Middle East. On the day before the war, for example, Senator Stennis, a leading hawk, continued to insist that the United States "must have help" prior to trying to force the blockade. At the same time, leading Vietnam critics Senators Wayne Morse and Edward Kennedy were urging that force be used to open the Gulf of Aqaba.[65] Throughout this period the consensus of the Senate

[60]U.S., *Congressional Record*, 90th Cong., 1st sess., Vol. 113, No. 81 (May 23, 1967), p. S7222.

[61]Ibid. He cited limitations in equipment and trained personnel.

[62]For example, Senator Stennis asserted categorically that "under no circumstances should there be unilateral action by us," and he referred to the "heavy drain on our military resources." U.S., *Congressional Record*, 90th Cong., 1st sess., Vol. 113, No. 81 (May 23, 1967), p. S7228. Senator Dirksen, the minority leader, said concerning a possible U.S. commitment in the Middle East, "The question is, how far does this country go? We are primarily committed to Vietnam. There can be no retreat there. We must finish the job there lest we lose face throughout the Far East." *The Sunday Times* (London) article by Frank Giles, May 28, 1967, p. 10. Senator Fulbright said that the Senate's attitude was due to the "extravagance and cost of Vietnam." Congressional Record, December 8, 1967.

[63]Senator Fulbright has stated that "in the days preceding the recent Arab-Israeli war there was a good deal of discussion of American responsibilities marked by a *prevailing assumption* that the United States was 'committed' to defend Israel against any act of aggression." He goes on to deny any such obligation. Statement of Senator Fulbright in *Separation of Powers*, p. 51. (Emphasis added.)

[64]*Congressional Record*, May 23, 1967, p. S7227. Senator Symington felt that a choice was needed between the Middle East and the Far East and said he favored the Middle East as meaning more to ourselves and our allies "politically, economically, and mutually." *Congressional Record*, May 23, 1967, p. S7222.

[65]As quoted in *The Washington Post* article by J. Y. Smith, "Congressional Worry for Israel Is Rising," June 5, 1967, p. 1, A12. Senator Eugene McCarthy commented on June 1 that "everyone knows our legal obligations . . . and

seemed to be that America must not become involved in the Middle East without the support of its Western European allies.

This attitude of Congress apparently reflected the sentiments of the American public. Although opinion was seemingly sympathetic to Israel, it did not favor active U.S. support. In a Gallup poll begun three days prior to the war,[66] a substantial percentage approved the President's handling of the situation.[67] An even larger group said their sympathies were with Israel. (See Table 4.1, Part D.) Respondents indicated their support stemmed from "feelings of close ties," the Communist powers, support of the Arabs, and an identification with the underdog.[68] But the sympathy was not convertible to concrete support under the existing circumstances (see Table 4.1, Part A), and there was not much encouragement for an American initiative.

Table 4.1 American and British Attitudes toward Middle East Crisis Expressed in Opinion Polls

A. Gallup poll June 11, 1967

"What would you like to see the U.S. Government do about this situation?"

Stay out of conflict	41%
Support Israel (aid, etc.)	16%
Negotiate for peace	14%
Work through United Nations	11%
Support Israel (send troops)	5%
Support Arab nations	less than .5%
Don't know	13%

B. Harris poll, June 10, 1967

"If you had to choose one, which course should the U.S. follow in the Middle East . . . ?"

Send supplies, not troops to Israel	10%
Work through United Nations	77%
Send U.S. troops to Israel	2%
Help Arabs	0%
Not sure	11%

our moral commitment is much clearer." *The Washington Post,* June 2, 1967, p. 1. According to Secretary Rusk, Senator Morse "wanted us to go through there [the Straits of Tiran] with all guns blazing." Rusk, interview.

[66]The poll was not completed until after hostilities had commenced, but George Gallup reported that there were only "minor differences in results" before and after the war began. George Gallup, "Johnson Wins Vote of Confidence on Handling of the Middle East Crisis," *The Gallup Report,* June 11, 1967. Copy provided by the American Institute of Public Opinion.

[67]Of those expressing an opinion, 47 percent approved the President's handling and 14 percent disapproved. *Gallup Report,* June 11, 1967.

[68]*Gallup Report,* June 11, 1967.

C. Harris poll, June 10, 1967

Question: Suppose the U.S. were asked to send troops and military supplies to back the Israeli government in the war in the Middle East. Would you favor or oppose our sending troops and supplies to Israel?

	% Favor	*% Opposed*	*% Not Sure*
Results: Nationwide	24	56	20
By Religion:			
Protestant	22	56	22
Catholic	23	60	17
Jewish	73	17	10

D. Gallup poll, June 11, 1967

"In this trouble, are your sympathies more with Israel or more with the Arab states?"

	U.S.	*G.B.*
Sympathies more with Israel	55%	50%
With Arab states	4%	5%
Neither, undecided	41%	45%

E. British Gallup poll, June 11, 1967

"What should Britain do . . . ?"

Work with other countries	41%
Leave them to fight it out	30%
Support Israel	16%
Support Israel (send troops)	3%
Support Arab nations	1%
Don't know	9%

Sources:
George Gallup, "Johnson Wins Vote of Confidence on Handling of Middle East Crisis," *The Gallup Report,* June 11, 1967. Copy provided by the American Institute of Public Opinion.
Harris information from *New York Post,* June 10, 1967. Copy provided by Louis Harris and Associates.

Although there was little empathy with Egypt and Syria, economic pressures were of some significance. On the weekend of May 27, 1967, Iraq and Saudi Arabia announced they would ban the supply of oil to states supporting Israeli "aggression."[69] More than half the oil being used by the United States in Vietnam was coming from the Persian Gulf,[70] but the need could be met from other sources. However, Kuwait threatened to freeze the Anglo-American oil concession in the event of Western support for Israel.[71] This was more potent economic pressure considering the balance of payments situation. Although the loss could be sustained for some time, it would be a

[69] *The Times* article by Nicholas Herbert, "Threat to West Over Oil," May 29, 1967, p. 3.
[70] U.S., Congress, House, Committee on Armed Services, *Military Posture and an Act (S.3293),* 90th Cong., 2nd sess. (Washington, 1968), p. 9880.
[71] *The Times,* May 29, 1967, p. 3.

heavy blow if followed by nationalization of the concession. Possible economic retaliation probably served as a restraining factor in contemplating actions such as testing the Gulf of Aqaba blockade.

While assessment of which factors were most influential is speculative, it is easier to discern what decisions were made. Examination of the state of preparations for forcing the gulf blockade and movements of American forces is revealing. The government evidently had ambivalent feelings about supporting the "British initiative"[72] to ensure free passage through the Gulf of Aqaba. Since U.S. flagships made little use of the passage, the effort was primarily a symbolic gesture. Washington was most interested in preserving access for Israel and secondarily concerned about the worldwide implications of the precedent in international law. Although the United States had obligated itself to assert the principle of innocent passage for U.S. ships, its primary motivation in 1967 was to prevent the outbreak of hostilities. Reopening the gulf was simply one of a number of efforts to forestall a war.

The issue became somewhat of a "red herring." Israel initially was enthusiastic about an international force to test the blockade, but by May 25, 1967, breaking the blockade became as unfavorable to Israel as it was to Egypt. It would have removed a convenient *casus belli* for Israel, whose major concern became the hostile armies massed near its borders.[73] The Secretary of State felt that because the action would deprive Israel of "an important *casus belli,*" it would help prevent a war.[74] Nasser apparently assured Western nations privately that he would let most goods pass, including oil.[75] There was legitimate doubt that the channel had even been mined.[76] Forcing the

[72] *The Times* article by Louis Heren, June 2, 1967. The effort appeared to be more of a joint effort, but it is interesting that the State Department spokesman claimed that it was a "British initiative."

[73] Comments of a senior Israel Foreign Ministry official in interview conducted October 24, 1968. However, the Israeli government evidently approved the maritime force concept subsequent to Eban's meeting with President Johnson on May 26, 1967. Department of State DPC 105, transcript of press and radio news briefing, June 2, 1967, p. 11. Supplied by letter from Mr. D. J. Simon, Records Services Division, Department of State, to Lt. Comdr. J. T. Howe, USN, dated April 17, 1969. Eshkol said, "They told us that 40 to 50 maritime powers would sign a guarantee for free passage . . . it really came down to a dozen and finally to only two countries, and then perhaps only one—Israel." *The Jerusalem Post,* Eshkol's speech of June 8, June 9, 1969.

[74] Rusk, interview.

[75] Israel Foreign Ministry official, interview.

[76] The captain of a West German freighter reported on May 25 that he saw no evidence of a blockade as he passed through the straits on the way to Jordan. *Background Documents,* p. 24. It was widely questioned how the straits could

blockade would have infuriated the Arab leader, caused a serious deterioration of American relations with Arab countries, and probably have meant economic retaliation. Only the Netherlands, Australia, and Great Britain indicated interest in participating in a multination force, and British support was no more than lukewarm.

Efforts were made to arrange a declaration of maritime nations and plans were prepared for various sanctions, including military action, to break the blockade. Progress was slow because of the lack of enthusiasm; however, plans for a declaration were "well along" by the time the war began,[77] and it was still considered to be a feasible course of action.[78] Apparently the declaration was to be proclaimed during the week of June 5, if the meeting with the Egyptian emissary on June 7, 1967, produced no results.[79] But the declaration would have been nothing more than an affirmation of the 1957 *aide-mémoire*.[80] It did not indicate what measures would be taken to assert the right of passage, and it did not establish that any action would be taken on behalf of Israel.

Arrangements for an international armada were even more indefinite. The Pentagon announced on several occasions that there was no plan to test the blockade,[81] and Secretary of State Rusk commented on June 1 that talk about an international blockade was just speculation at that point.[82] Plans for a military operation had been prepared but not delivered to fleet staffs.[83] On June 1 there were a few hints that naval action might be contemplated in about ten

be mined because of the configuration of the waterway. The Israelis found no mines following the war.

[77] Letter from Mr. Robert J. McCloskey, Deputy Assistant Secretary for Public Affairs, Department of State, to Lt. Comdr. J. T. Howe, USN, dated March 6, 1968.

[78] Rusk, interview.

[79] Eugene V. Rostow, "The Middle East Crisis and Beyond," Department of State *Bulletin*, Vol. LVIII, No. 1489 (January 8, 1968), p. 46.

[80] A description, allegedly of the declaration, was published in *The Washington Post* article by Chalmers M. Roberts. Theodore Draper has published what is reputed to be a "key paragraph" from the declaration in *Israel and World Politics*, p. 105. The passage is almost a carbon copy of the *aide-mémoire*. Secretary Rusk has agreed that the declaration was basically nothing more than a repetition of the *aide-mémoire*. Interview conducted April 9, 1969. "The draft document remains classified." Letter from Donald J. Simon, Chief, Records Services Division, Department of State, to Lt. Comdr. J. T. Howe, USN, dated April 17, 1969. (See Chapter 3, footnote 62.)

[81] The Pentagon announced on May 31 that no plan had been made by the United States to test the blockade. *The Washington Post*, June 1, 1967, p. 1. See also *The Times* article by Louis Heren, January 2, 1967, p. 1.

[82] *The Guardian* (Manchester) article by Richard Scott, June 2, 1967, p. 1. He evidently was referring to a force to maintain free passage.

[83] Interview with Rear Admiral J. C. Wylie.

days,[84] but these hints appeared to be very hollow amid talk that "time is desperately short."[85]

There was some question as to how much force would be necessary to ensure passage for a sustained period. American officials wanted a large maritime force. The need for air cover and the difficulties of operating in the Red Sea under attack led the Joint Chiefs of Staff to decide that even with British support south of Suez the existing forces were inadequate. In the words of an admiral familiar with Joint Chiefs of Staff deliberations, "Because of the lack of immediately available support for these forces in the Red Sea and the magnitude of the next step should these ships come under attack, the JCS did not recommend their employment in testing the blockade."[86] It was therefore unlikely that any action was contemplated in the near future. While the State Department had faith in the operation, the Defense Department appeared to be less than enthusiastic. In an atmosphere clouded by the Vietnam commitment, it was not likely that Washington would have acted to assert its maritime rights without substantial support from other nations. The effort to reopen the gulf appeared to be a slow-moving diplomatic attempt to help preserve peace, but by not testing the gulf blockade the United States probably increased the likelihood of war. Israel could not unilaterally assert its right of innocent passage through the gulf without going to war against Egypt. The multination maritime fleet concept seemed to be a futile gesture. In fourteen days of diplomatic activity, efforts to persuade Cairo to reopen the gulf and to organize maritime nations failed. As the war began, a final American decision to test the blockade still appeared to be days away.

The careful positioning of naval forces at some distance from the area of conflict seemed to reflect the President's concern that U.S. actions not be "misunderstood."[87] On the day Nasser announced the Gulf of Aqaba blockade two Sixth Fleet strike forces, led by the carriers *Saratoga* and *America*, were ordered toward the eastern Mediterranean. They rendezvoused on May 29 in the Sea of Crete and remained there throughout this period. (See Figure 4.1.) The

[84] This was first done by Geroge Ball, former Under Secretary of State, in a speech on June 1. *The Washington Post* article "Ball Sees More Intense Crisis Near," June 2, 1967, p. A16. An article on June 3 said that certain "officials" felt that the blockade would be tested in about ten days. *The Washington Post* article by Chalmers M. Roberts, June 3, 1967, p. 1.
[85] Statement of George Brown, British Secretary of State for Foreign Affairs, House of Commons debate, May 31, 1967, official text of speech supplied by the British Information Services, No. T.23, p.11.
[86] Talley, letter.
[87] See Section 4.1 for the President's statement of May 23, 1967.

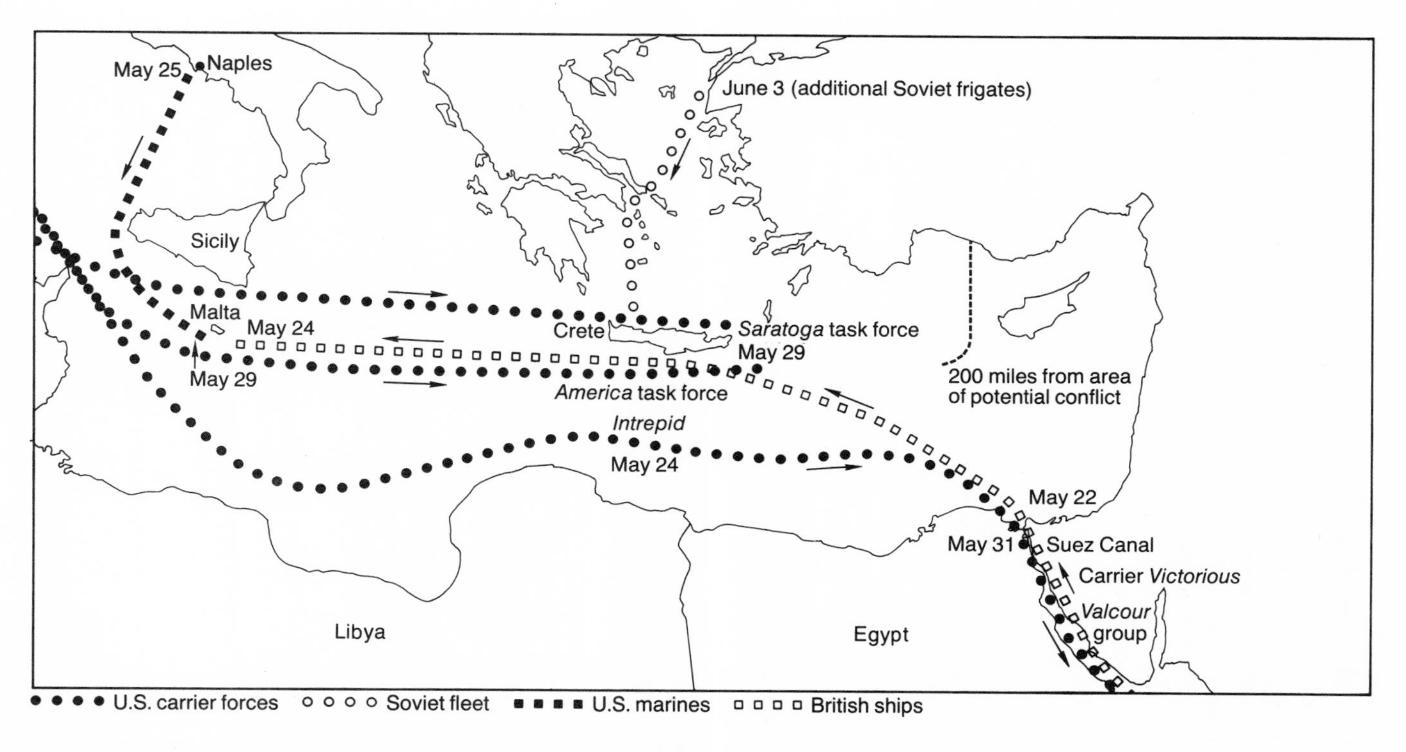

Figure 4.1 Movements of naval forces in Mediterranean during buildup phase

fleet commander announced that his options were open-ended and his orders were to "wait and see."[88] The moves were typical precautionary measures; they were not intended to influence directly the course of events during the buildup phase. At the same time, aircraft carriers were close enough for jets to reach the Middle East rapidly. The ships were ordered not to proceed farther east than Crete so intentions would be clear to the Soviets,[89] and there would "be no accusation of leaning on the Arabs—or the Israelis."[90]

The movements of marine amphibious forces, which would spearhead any use of American troops, clearly indicated Washington's desire to avoid military involvement. The Marine Battalion Landing Team in the Mediterranean remained on liberty in Naples until May 25, when it was moved toward Malta for a previously scheduled training exercise.[91] Although this placed the marines closer to the scene of possible conflict, they were still some 600 miles farther away from the trouble spot than the aircraft carriers. The press speculated that the troops might be heading for the Middle East, but on the day fighting began, the Marines were on "shore leave," and their officers estimated it would take "three days for the group to reach Egyptian or Israeli ports."[92] When asked if we were trying to tell the Russians something by sending the Marines on liberty, Admiral Wylie remarked, "Not only the Russians—but anyone in the world who wanted to look. Sending men on liberty is a good way to make your intentions known."[93] The message was meant for Cairo and Tel Aviv, as well as Moscow.

Several increases of American forces were made, but these were primarily of a defensive precautionary nature. The destroyer *Dyess* was sent through the Suez Canal on June 2 to join the small task force of two destroyers and a command ship already in the Red Sea. Antisubmarine forces previously scheduled to participate in a North Atlantic training exercise were ordered to the Mediterranean in early June. This was a defensive move to counter the Soviet submarine threat.

The movements of the *Intrepid*, a small attack aircraft carrier, might legitimately have been interpreted as threatening by the Arabs or the Soviets. The carrier had been passing through the Mediterranean on the way to Vietnam. Although its delay in the Mediterranean was

[88] *The New York Times*, Associated Press dispatch from the U.S.S. *America*, May 31, 1967, p. 18.
[89] Wylie, letter.
[90] Mangrum, letters.
[91] Ibid.
[92] *The New York Times*, June 6, 1967, p. 18.
[93] Wylie, interview.

attributed in the media to a possible beefing up of the Sixth Fleet, the *Intrepid* was actually waiting for permission to pass through the Suez Canal. It had been deliberately positioned off the eastern end of Libya to demonstrate that it was not part of an augmentation of the Sixth Fleet.[94] Its departure from the area on May 31, 1967, indicated either that hostilities in Southeast Asia had priority or that Washington saw no need for greater forces in the Mediterranean. The transit from the Mediterranean must have been an unmistakable sign to Moscow that Washington did not want to become involved militarily in the Middle East. It came after the announcement on May 30 that the Soviets were sending ten additional ships to the Mediterranean. The *Intrepid's* departure from the Gulf of Aqaba area should have reassured Nasser that no move against his blockade was imminent; in fact, it is doubtful that the *Intrepid* would have been cleared for passage if the Egyptian leader felt otherwise. Figure 4.1 shows the movements of various U.S. naval units in the Mediterranean during this phase.

4.2 SOVIET POLICY

During this period Soviet policy was characterized by qualified declaratory support for Egypt and Syria accompanied by cautious movements of naval forces. On May 23 Moscow cautioned that "peace and security" in the area adjacent to Soviet borders was a vital interest[95] and warned: "should anyone try to unleash aggression in the Near East, he would be met not only with the united strength of Arab countries, but also with *strong opposition to aggression* from the Soviet Union and all peace loving states."[96] (Emphasis added.) The government appeared to be asserting it would aid Arab nations if they were *attacked,*[97] while at the same time claiming it had no interest in kindling a military conflict.[98]

Assessment of the extent of Soviet precipitation of the crisis must

[94]Wylie, interview.

[95]Moscow Tass International Service in English, May 23, 1967. Soviet government statement on the situation in the Near East.

[96]Ibid. These statements were repeated verbatim in the speech before the United Nations on May 24 by Nikolai Fedorenko.

[97]This basic line was continued up to the outbreak of hostilities. For example, radio Moscow stated on May 28 that "he who starts unleashing aggression in the Near East" will meet with "decisive resistance to aggression on the part of the Soviet Union. . . ." Moscow Domestic Service in Russian, May 28, 1967, Observer's roundtable. A broadcast of May 31, 1967, warned of "resolute counteractions." Moscow in English to United Kingdom, Anatoliy Can Commentary.

[98]The official statement of May 23 said "the Peoples have no interest in the kindling of a military conflict in the Near East." Tass International Service. This thought was repeated in the United Nations statement as well as *Pravda,* May 29, 1967, p. 5. *CDSP,* Vol. 19, No. 22 (June 21, 1967).

remain somewhat speculative. It appears that the Russians promoted a mythical invasion threat to Syria and encouraged Nasser to mass his troops on Israel's border as a bluff.[99] When Nasser sent additional divisions to Sinai and closed the Straits of Tiran, Moscow apparently became alarmed and tried to restrain Nasser. In early May Moscow informed Nasser that Israeli troops were massed on the Syrian border and were going to attack on May 17.[100] The Soviet ambassador to Israel had been invited to visit the border but refused to do so.[101] On May 19 U.N. observers "confirmed the absence of troop concentrations and significant movements on both sides of the line."[102] Because of the terrain Israel would have had difficulty hiding a small unit, much less thirteen to eighteen brigades. But in the official Soviet statement of May 23 it was still claimed that the Israeli Knesset had approved military operations against Syria and that Israeli troops "moved to the frontiers of Syria" after being alerted.[103] It is possible that the Russians were misinformed, but it seems more likely that they deliberately tried to raise the level of

[99] In this regard, the statement of a "high Soviet official" following the crisis is of particular interest. He remarked, "Our intelligence services had taken very seriously the Israeli project to launch on May 15 a large raid on the interior of Syria in order to destroy the posts of the Palestine commandos and eventually to push on as far as Damascus in order to overthrow the Syrian government. Thus, it was with our full approval that Nasser massed his troops on the frontier of the Sinai in order to demonstrate to the Israelis that, in case of an offensive against Syria, that country would not be alone. Nasser considered that he would thus discourage Israel from launching this attack." *Le Nouvel Observateur.* "Pourquoi Moscou a lâché Nasser," No. 135 (June 14 to June 20, 1967).

[100] In a speech of May 22, 1967, Nasser stated that "on May 13 we received accurate information that Israel was concentrating on the Syrian border huge armed forces of about 11 to 13 brigades. . . . The decision made by Israel at this time was to carry out an aggression against Syria as of May 17." He implied that his source of information was not Syrian. *Background Documents,* p. 132. He subsequently asserted in two speeches following the war that an Egyptian parliamentary delegation on a visit to Moscow was informed that "invasion of Syria was imminent." "Nasser's Revolution Anniversary Speech at Cairo University," July 23, 1967, p. 327; "Nasser's resignation broadcast of June 9, 1967," p. 320. Texts in Walter Laqueur, *The Road to Jerusalem* (New York: Macmillan, 1968).

[101] When this fact was brought out in a subsequent U.N. debate by Abba Eban, Premier Alexei Kosygin "turned to Foreign Minister Gromyko and appeared to be questioning him on this point." Uri Ra'anan, interview in *The Boston Sunday Globe,* July 2, 1967, p. 2.

[102] Report by Secretary General, U.N. Security Council Document S/7896 of May 19, 1967, p. 2.

[103] Moscow Tass International Service in English, May 23, 1967. A subsequent observation claimed that U.S. circles were annoyed over the failure of their intelligence plans as a result of actions undertaken by the United Arab Republic and other Arab countries. Moscow Domestic Service in Russian, May 28, 1967.

tension. Their problem appeared to be how to control Nasser once they had aroused him.

Washington was annoyed that Moscow would not support U.N. resolutions concerning the crisis.[104] It is obvious from examining the transcripts of U.N. Security Council sessions in the weeks prior to the June war that the Soviet Union was not interested in talking about the Middle East situation. Evidently, the Russian U.N. delegate was equally aloof in private discussions. During the debates after the outbreak of fighting, American U.N. Ambassador Arthur Goldberg repeatedly charged that, when the United States had tried to interest the Soviet Union in a cooperative U.N. effort to dampen the crisis, the Russians accused the United States of "dramatizing the situation."[105] Concerning attempts to prevent warlike actions in the Middle East, Ambassador Goldberg responded on June 6, 1967:

> . . . when we joined in this effort, there were members of the Council who took the position that we were attempting to dramatize the situation, that everything was all right, that it was not necessary for the Council to take any action, that things were tranquil, that all we had to do was sit and let events happen.[106]

Privately, Moscow apparently made some attempts to restrain the Arabs after the crisis reached serious international proportions. The Soviets evidently asked the United States to "urge restraint upon the opposing sides in a private letter,"[107] and Nasser has claimed that on May 26 the Soviet government urged him not to fire the first shot.[108] Apparently Nasser received conflicting advice. The Soviet ambassador in Cairo was reportedly anything but a restraining influence,[109] and encouragement from this source may partially explain Nasser's bitterness toward the Soviets following his defeat. Secretary Rusk believes that "ten days or so before the war" the Soviets

[104] Rostow, "The Middle East Crisis," p. 46.

[105] The references to the Soviet Union were indirect but obvious. U.N., Security Council, Provisional Record of 1355th meeting, June 10, 1967, Document No. S/PV 1365.

[106] U.N., Security Council, Provisional Record of 1348th meeting, June 6, 1967, Document No. 1348.

[107] *The New York Times,* June 2, 1967, p. 1.

[108] He said, for example, in his speech of June 9, 1967, that on the night of the 26th, "the Soviet Ambassador asked to have an urgent meeting with me at 5:30 (as broadcast) after midnight. He informed me of an urgent request from the Soviet Government not to be the first to open fire." Text of "Nasser's resignation broadcast of 9 June 1967," in Laqueur, *Road to Jerusalem,* p. 321. A slightly different version appears in *The New York Times,* June 10, 1967, p. 12. Alexander Werth states that a "high foreign office official" of the USSR informed him that on June 3, 1967, Moscow warned Nasser against attacking Israel. Article "Year of Jubilee: The USSR at Fifty," *The Nation*, Vol. 205, No. 14 (October 30, 1967), p. 427.

[109] Informed White House source, interview. The ambassador was Dmitri Poxhdaev.

"were a restraining influence."[110] The Secretary of State recalls that Moscow had a "heavy hand in egging on the Arabs" and "only seemed to get worried once things were happening too fast."[111]

It had been claimed that Moscow thought the Arabs could win a war with Israel,[112] but it seems doubtful that their military advisers were not aware of the state of training in the Arab army and air force. Reportedly, a team of Soviet inspectors had been alarmed by conditions in the Egyptian Air Force prior to the war.[113] The attrition rate of Soviet supplied aircraft was close to 50 percent.[114] Many items of equipment provided had not been modified for desert warfare. Like most Soviet military aid, Moscow probably intended it more for show than for actual use.

Moscow's less than enthusiastic support for the Egyptian blockade of the Gulf of Aqaba also may have reflected a Soviet desire to keep the crisis controlled. The blockade was not initially given a wide play in the Soviet media,[115] and there have been some other indications that the Kremlin was surprised and embarrassed by the announcement. A "high Soviet official" has claimed that his government was not informed of the decision until after it was already taken.[116] Secretary of State Rusk stated categorically, "I know they did not approve of the blockade of Aqaba."[117]

Moscow may have tried to deter Cairo from resisting a Western effort to force the blockade. During the first days following Nasser's restriction on passage of strategic goods, Soviet reports of American forces ready to challenge the blockade were highly exagger-

[110]Rusk, interview.
[111]Ibid.
[112]See, for example, Bernard Lewis, "The Consequences of Defeat," *Foreign Affairs,* Vol. 46, No. 2 (January 1968), p. 324. It is possible that some Russians believed the Arabs, particularly the well-entrenched Syrians, might be able to hold the line. This may explain their initial reluctance to seek a cease-fire on the first day of fighting.
[113]Randolph S. and Winston S. Churchill, *The Six Day War* (Boston: Houghton Mifflin, 1967), p. 48.
[114]Interviews with Professor Uri Ra'anan, conducted during 1968 and 1969. This estimate applies to a few years earlier, but it is speculated that there had been little change in the interim.
[115]The Soviets did not, however, totally ignore the blockade. The prohibition for Israeli shipping and strategic cargo of all other countries was promptly reported but without comment. Tass International Service in English, May 23, 1967, and Moscow Domestic Service in Russian, 0500, May 24, 1967.
[116]Statement of "high Soviet official" in the French weekly *Le Nouvel Observateur,* "Pourquoi Moscou a lâché Nasser," No. 135 (June 14 to June 20, 1967), p. 16. Alexander Werth reported that a high Soviet Foreign Office official had told him the Soviets were "not informed of the closing of the Gulf of Aqaba by the Egyptians." "Year of Jubilee," p. 427. A Soviet article has claimed that the closing was "undertaken as a *temporary* measure." (Emphasis added.) I. Belyaev, "Ways of Ending the Middle East Crisis," *International Affairs,* No. 10 (October 1968), p. 26.
[117]Rusk, interview.

ated, perhaps deliberately. The U.S. "aircraft carrier" *Valcour*[118] was said to have been promised to Tel Aviv,[119] and "3500 marines aboard seven American carriers" were claimed to be rushing toward the area to back up Washington's threat concerning the Gulf Aqaba.[120] Moscow radio warned that *Egypt* regarded the waters as its own and *Cairo* would regard any intrusion as an act of aggression.[121] Moscow did not take a strong stand backing Nasser's action. The Soviets were apparently primarily concerned about the immediate dangers of the situation. In the long run, the international precedent of an Egyptian exercise of sovereignty over the waters would not bode well for Russian transit problems through the Dardanelles.[122]

A high Soviet official has claimed Nasser was informed that the Kremlin would undertake to neutralize the United States by matching any escalation by Washington. Russian support, however, would not go beyond that.[123] Based on what was said publicly prior to the fighting, this aid appears to be the *maximum* Moscow promised. The head of the Palestine Liberation Movement asserted that the Russians told him they would not intervene but merely keep the Sixth Fleet neutralized.[124] Nasser had publicly taken the Soviet Union "off the hook" on May 29 by declaring he would not request intervention by Moscow if the Sixth Fleet came to Israel's aid.[125] He asserted that "if the United States intervenes . . . we must defend our-

[118]The *Valcour,* an 1800 ton converted seaplane tender with one 5′ 38 gun, is hardly comparable to an aircraft carrier. The *America,* for example, is in the 80,000 ton class.
[119]Moscow Domestic Service in Russian, May 26, 1967.
[120]Moscow in Arabic to Arab World, May 26, 1967.
[121]Moscow in English to United Kingdom, June 4, 1967.
[122]By signing the Geneva Convention of 1958 the Soviets had legally committed themselves to the principle of free passage through the Straits of Tiran. Article 16.4 of the Convention on Territorial Seas reiterates the customary rule on innocent passage through straits. Moscow, however, subsequently has tried to justify Nasser's action under the Geneva Convention. The Soviet claim is that the threat to Syria amounted to a threat to the security of the United Arab Republic. I. Blishchenko, "International Law and the Middle East Crisis," *International Affairs,* No. 1 (January 1969), p. 29.
[123]Statement of "high Soviet official," "Pourquoi Moscou a lâché Nasser," No. 135 (June 14 to June 20, 1967), p. 16. In another section of the statement the official stated Moscow was pledged to protect Nasser against a possible American action but not one by Israel.
[124]Ahmed Shukairy, who made this statement on a CBS television report, headed the Palestine Liberation Organization segment of the unified Arab command. Interviews with Professor Uri Ra'anan, conducted during 1968. Theodore Draper reports that Shukairy said on May 21, 1967, in Cairo that he believed "the efforts of the Soviet Union" would be "directed in one direction—that is, the localization of the war in the Middle East and to prevent the United States from any military involvement."*Israel and World Politics,* p. 79.
[125]*The New York Times* article by Eric Pace, May 29, 1967. Nasser stated, "we will leave it to friendly countries to decide what action to take."

selves."[126] Evidently, he had no assurance from Moscow at that point. After the crisis Nasser claimed he had told Soviet President Podgorny that "Egypt did not want Russian soldiers to die for her—'we have enough heroes of our own.' "[127]

However, the Arab leader's tone had changed slightly upon the return of his war minister from a three-day trip to Moscow: "Badran relayed to me a message from Premier Kosygin saying that the Soviet Union stands with us in this battle and *will not allow any country to interfere*, so that the state of affairs prevailing before 1956 may be restored."[128] (Emphasis added.) This may have been sheer bluff. The fact that a trip to Moscow had been necessary would indicate signals were not clear between the two countries. Probably Moscow had agreed to attempt to counterbalance any moves by the Sixth Fleet so that a "fair" Arab-Israeli fight could occur. It is doubtful, however, that the Soviets committed themselves to take on the Sixth Fleet if bluffs proved to be insufficient.

The movements of Soviet ships also indicated a desire not to become involved in a confrontation with the United States. A small number of Russian warships was assigned to shadow the Sixth Fleet carriers, the *Intrepid*, and British naval vessels.[129] Other ships of the Soviet "Sixth Fleet" conducted routine exercises in the Ionian Sea between Sicily and Greece.[130] Any doubts that the Soviets had aggressive intentions should have been dispelled when on June 4 the only Soviet cruiser in the Mediterranean and ten other ships were sighted at anchor about one hundred miles northwest of Crete.[131] Either Moscow had no idea a war was imminent, which is not likely,[132] or it had no intention of trying to influence its outcome, even with Russian feints. Apparently, the limited objective was to try to offset the effect of a Sixth Fleet presence.

The transit of ten additional Soviet ships to the Mediterranean from the Black Sea beginning on May 31 probably was a response to

[126] Press conference of President Gamal Abdel Nasser in Presidential Palace, as reproduced in Draper, *Israel and World Politics*, p. 231.
[127] As quoted in Ernest Stock, *Israel on the Road to Sinai, 1949–1956, with a Sequel on the Six Day War, 1967* (Ithaca: Cornell University Press, 1967), p. 231.
[128] *The New York Times*, May 30, 1967, p. 3.
[129] The Soviets, evidently, were taking no chances on the *Intrepid*'s maneuvers. The Soviet cruiser and three destroyers were sighted following the carrier's movements before it passed through the Suez Canal. *The New York Times*, June 5, 1967, p. 4.
[130] Wylie, interview.
[131] *The New York Times*, June 6, 1967, p. 18.
[132] A definitive judgment would require examination of Soviet intelligence reports, but it is speculated that by June 4 the Russians were very uncertain that hostilities could still be prevented.

American naval movements. It appeared to be a minimum Soviet fulfillment of its alleged promise to Nasser to match any American escalation. Moscow's notification to the Turkish government on May 22 of the impending transits of the straits may have been a response to the ordering of Sixth Fleet carrier task forces toward the eastern Mediterranean. An eight-day period of notice which is stipulated by convention,[133] would explain the delay in beginning the movement of Russian ships through the Turkish straits.

Significantly, the first two ships of the ten were a tanker and a submarine supply vessel. The next group, consisting of three frigates and two auxiliaries, did not pass through the Bosporous until June 3.[134] Although the Soviet move was highly publicized in the Western press, Moscow could have increased the dramatic impact by adding a cruiser, a few submarines, or amphibious ships. The augmentation did not significantly alter the naval balance, but at the time the fleet of some thirty ships was the largest Russia had ever deployed into the Mediterranean.[135]

It is possible that the augmentation was nothing more than a routine replacement. The timing followed the pattern of previous Soviet rotations.[136] Because of the types of ships sent into the Mediterranean on May 31, it would appear that one major objective was to sustain the existing task force. However, the further augmentation of the force with destroyers while not withdrawing other warships indicates Moscow either intended to show more force at this time in the crisis or was enjoying the psychological impact the announcement had seemed to create. Of course, the consequences of exiting ships from the Mediterranean under the circumstances would have meant considerable loss of face with the Arabs. The move undoubtedly encouraged Nasser and slightly complicated Anglo-American attempts to arrange a joint naval force of maritime nations. Although Moscow probably meant to indicate that its augmentation was not a threat to the Sixth Fleet, the Soviet move increased American uncertainty about the sincerity of Russian claims to be

[133]Article 13 of the Montreux Convention.

[134]A destroyer made the passage on June 4 and a gunboat and minesweeper on June 5. *The New York Times,* May 31, June 4, 6, 1967.

[135]Admiral Thomas H. Moorer, USN, Chief of Naval Operations, Address at National Security Industrial Association 24th Annual Dinner, September 28, 1967, Washington, D.C., p. 7.

[136]This is the assessment of a former assistant naval attaché to Turkey. Robert W. Wells, "The Soviet Black Sea Fleet," U.S. Naval Institute *Proceedings,* Vol. 93, No. 9 (September 1967), pp. 136–139. *The Times* commented that "the strength of the Russian fleet at this time of year usually builds up to about 16 ships" and concluded that the augmentation raised the Soviet forces to the normal level for "summer exercises." *The Times* (London), June 5, 1967, p. 1.

trying to restrain the Arabs. Moscow may have been trying to capitalize on concern about involvement in American congressional circles. Because of the proximity in time of the Soviet request and the Egyptian announcement of a blockade, there may have been some link between these two events. The Russians may have been hoping a bluff would deter Western attempts to force the blockade and thus present Nasser with a bloodless triumph which would be credited to a new phenomenon—the Soviet naval presence in the Mediterranean. Moscow probably desired to avoid a confrontation with Washington and to prevent a major Arab-Israeli war but, seemingly was reluctant to abandon an opportunity to enhance its prestige by appearing to fulfill a pledge to Nasser.

Moscow's propaganda campaign was apparently intended to promote resentment of the "world gendarme"[137] in the Third World by capitalizing on Western naval moves, to ensure the Arabs were aware of the power realities, and to make it more difficult to generate Western support for an expedition to test the blockade. A motive may also have been to show that the powerful American fleet was nothing but a paper tiger. There were a number of assertions that the United States wanted a second front in the Middle East as part of its "global offensive" and to make up for "failure in one area by escalation in another."[138] The Pentagon was said to be boasting of its ability to cope with "several Vietnams in different areas of the world."[139] This was, of course, an obvious propaganda ploy to exploit European disapproval of U.S. Vietnam policy and give second thoughts to Arab and Israeli leaders. It also may have reflected a genuine Soviet concern that a very successful worldwide offensive was being conducted against them.

The call that had been sounded by Brezhnev for removal of the Sixth Fleet from the Mediterranean was repeated frequently and featured prominently.[140] The Sixth Fleet was said to have "aimed its

[137]See, for example, Tass International Service in English, May 25, 1967; Moscow Domestic Service in Russian, May 28, 1967; Tass International Service in English, May 30, 1967, Polyanov in *Izvestia*.
[138]Moscow in English to United Kingdom, June 2, 1967, Shakhov commentary. A May 29 *Izvestia* article asserted that the United States was "quite obviously conducting a Middle East escalation along the lines of its Vietnamese escalation." Moscow in English to United Kingdom, May 29, 1967.
[139]Moscow in English to United Kingdom, May 29, 1967. This was hardly the tone of statements coming from the Pentagon.
[140]See, for example, Moscow Radio in Arabic to Arab world, May 28, 1967; Moscow Tass International Service in English, May 26, 1967, Polyanov article in *Izvestia* on the front page; statement of World Peace Conference in Brussels, Moscow Tass International Service in English, June 3, 1967.

guns on the coasts of the Arab East." [141] This may have been part of a scheme to demonstrate the ineffectiveness of American power. However, the primary motivation probably was to lay responsibility for the tension on American fleet movements. A policy of raising worldwide animosity toward the United States would make it more difficult to maintain the Sixth Fleet in the Mediterranean. Removal of the Western presence was, of course, a long-range Soviet objective.

While the Kremlin may have hoped to score a political victory, it seems fairly certain that Moscow did not want a great power confrontation or an Arab-Israeli war. Moscow undoubtedly had difficulty controlling the Arabs, and this was one of the great dangers of the crisis. The Russians do not seem to be in favor of Israel's liquidation[142] and certainly not their own. When asked by irate Arabs how many successive blows they would tolerate from the United States, Soviet leaders reputedly responded, "What is your view of nuclear war?" [143]

The cautious movements of Soviet ships during the buildup phase and the absence of amphibious forces supports this analysis of Russian policy. Although Moscow may have tried to take advantage of the political situation, it did not want and was not prepared for open hostilities any more than Washington. The augmentation of Soviet ships appeared to be an attempt to fulfill an obligation to Egypt without presenting a serious challenge to the Sixth Fleet. The function of the Russian fleet seemed to be to track the Sixth Fleet, whose moves could provide the basis of progaganda exploitation or diplomatic counterbluffs and to add some legitimacy to possible future claims to have kept Washington from intervening.

American policy makers seemed to have concluded prior to the war that the Soviet attitude had changed to one of sincere interest in avoiding an Arab-Israeli conflict.[144] However, there was less confidence in what Moscow might do if the Arabs were defeated. The

[141]Moscow in Turkish to Turkey, May 31, 1967. See also Tass International Service in English, May 26, 1967, Domestic Service in Russian, May 28, 1967.
[142]See, for example, the remarks of Aleksei Kosygin, "A Rare Private Interview," Life, Vol. 64, No. 5 (February 2, 1968), p. 29. There are a number of reasons for Israel's continued existence as being advantageous to the Soviet Union. Among these are the problem for Communist leaders of the Jewish minority in Eastern Europe as well as Russia and the advantage of continued Arab-Israeli tension as a vehicle for increasing Soviet influence in the Arab world.
[143]Quoting President Boumédienne of Algeria in broadcast by M. H. Haykal, editor of *Al Ahram*, Cairo Radio, August 25, 1967 as reprinted in *Survival*, Vol. IX, No. 11 (November 1967), p. 359.
[144]Rusk, interview. Admiral Wylie, one of the chief naval planners in the situation, said "I am quite sure that they were even less anxious than we to have any of their own forces involved." Wylie, letter.

Russians had planted stories to the effect that they would not permit Syria to be taken over,[145] and there were conflicting indications of Soviet intentions. While professing interest in restraint and keeping their ship movements circumspect, Moscow had augmented its naval forces, procrastinated in the United Nations, encouraged Nasser to be aggressive, and supplied false information to Nasser concerning an Israeli threat. But the most disconcerting aspect of the Soviet posture to American analysts was that the Soviets themselves did not seem to be in agreement about what to do.[146]

4.3 BRITISH POLICY

Although the initial British reaction to the Egyptian blockade was cautious support of *U.N.* action to secure free passage,[147] the Prime Minister asserted on May 24 that Her Majesty's Government would "promote and support international actions" to keep the straits open to "ships of all nations."[148] He reaffirmed the 1957 British declaration which promised to assert the right of passage on behalf of British shipping.[149] His statement was much stronger on this point than President Johnson's, even though the United States had essentially the same 1957 commitment.[150] Evidently, Prime Minister Wilson felt that a forceful statement was the only way to prevent an immediate assault by Israel. He stated subsequently in the House of Commons that, had he not expressed strong concern, it was "very doubtful whether there would have been sufficient confidence last weekend to have averted what might have become a general conflagration."[151] He also had been urged by opposition party leaders on May 23 to assert British "rights" vigorously.[152] In Whitehall

[145] Informed White House source, interview, Appendix B, Question 4.
[146] Ibid.
[147] Foreign Office release of May 23, 1967, *The Times*, May 24, 1967, p. I.
[148] Information supplied by the British Foreign Office. Letter from R. A. Lloyd Jones, Ministry of Defence, to Lt. Comdr. Jonathan T. Howe, USN, dated April 9, 1968. Reports with slightly less information were carried in the British newspapers.
[149] The text of the British declaration which was reaffirmed is given in Section 3.4.
[150] See Section 4.1 for the U.S. statement.
[151] Speech by Prime Minister Harold Wilson, House of Commons, May 31, 1967. Text provided by British Information Services, Document T.24 of June 1, 1967, p. 8. In a similar vein, George Brown, the Secretary of State for Foreign Affairs, said in his speech that opened the debate, "only those of us who were involved deeply in the events of last weekend know how close we came to seeing acts of war from which the waves of destruction might have spread out to engulf us all. Through the efforts of several countries, including, I am proud to say, our own, this horror was averted." B.I.S. Document, T.23, June 1, 1967, p. 11.
[152] On May 23 opposition leaders made speeches urging a U.N. emergency session, support for the U.S. position, and visited the Prime Minister. Tory

Wilson's pledge was interpreted as meaning that Britain would act with other countries even if U.N. proposals failed[153] and that the Royal Navy would escort British merchant ships through the straits if necessary.[154]

There were no further official British statements until May 31 when a changed emphasis was expressed in a Commons "debate"[155] on the sensitive Middle East issue. Diplomatic efforts and U.N. action were stressed as the main means for solving the crisis.[156] In referring to Britain's role in securing a settlement, Prime Minister Wilson stated: "that role can best be fulfilled not on the basis of dramatic declarations but on patient diplomacy, seeking to influence others and as occasion offers to influence others to take initiatives which we might have felt it right to take ourselves."[157] London was no longer in a position to restate its forceful pledge of action or to provide the initiative for using force. Prime Minister Wilson cautioned that "our thoughts are best not said if we want to get the results which we want."[158] He stated the need to ensure that the straits *stayed open* and claimed that "overstating" the problem was making solution "more difficult."[159] He declined to specify what London would do if U.N. efforts or a declaration from maritime nations failed,[160] but it was obvious that many alternatives were contemplated prior to employment of British force.

The reason for de-emphasis of British action may have been implied in other references during the debate. Although Wilson supported Israel's "right to live," he stressed not "taking sides"[161] and Britian's interest in good relations with the Arab world. Foreign Minister

leader Heath declared in a speech on the evening of May 23 that Britain must show it has the "wherewithal to assert British rights." Churchill and Churchill, *The Six Day War*, p. 40.

[153] *The Guardian*, May 25, 1967, p. 9.

[154] *The Times*, May 25, 1967, p. 1.

[155] It was hardly a debate but seemed rather to be an opportunity for the Parliament to express a unified position. There were only minor differences in the position of the opposition party.

[156] This theme was frequently stressed in the speeches of Secretary of State for Foreign Affairs, George Brown, and Prime Minister Wilson. Brown, "Opening Statement, May 31," pp. 5, 8, 10, 11. Wilson, "Closing Statement, May 31," p. 5.

[157] Wilson, "Closing Statement, May 31," p. 2.

[158] Ibid.

[159] Ibid., p. 2, 4.

[160] Ibid., p. 8. Opposition leader Heath agreed it "would be wrong to press" Wilson, although Heath stated that the House looks to the government to insure the "declaration is implemented if necessary." Statement of Mr. Edward Heath, *Hansard Parliamentary Debates* (5th Series), Vol. 747, House of Commons, p. 116.

[161] Wilson, "Closing Statement, May 31," p. 10.

Brown cautioned that British actions had "to fit into the broader setting" of Middle East policy "as a whole" and that "trade-investment" was the principal interest.[162] Brown slipped several compliments to the United Arab Republic, recognizing Arab nationalism as "one of the most significant forces for change" and professing "his regard" for Nasser.[163]

Between May 24 and 31 the British apparently had been subjected to heavy Arab pressure against their vulnerable balance of payments and sterling reserve position. Public threats to British oil concessions from Iraq, Saudi Arabia, and Kuwait in the days prior to the debate may be indicative of more severe warnings made in private. Concern about the economic consequences of a unified Arab confederation may have been revealed in Prime Minister Wilson's observation that previously "deeply divided" Arab states had "suddenly made common cause . . . in new found unity directed against . . . Israel."[164] By May 27, 1967, all thirteen members of the Arab League had pledged their solidarity.

With an increasing possibility of Arab retaliation, the British became more reluctant to take the initiative or share the leadership in an international maritime force. In a Washington press conference on June 2 Prime Minister Wilson intimated that a maritime declaration would be forthcoming soon, but he was vague about Britain's willingness to use force and emphasized U.N. action.[165] He said subsequently that only if U.N. action and a multilateral declaration had failed would the United States and Great Britain "have been prepared to consider other means."[166] It was obvious the United Nations was getting nowhere. Privately, the British apparently were willing to participate if a large body of nations joined the effort.[167] The Royal Navy probably could have broken the blockade with the force poised south of Suez, but economic factors appeared to be a very effective deterrent.

There were other factors that disenchanted the British from risking involvement in the Middle East. One was the developing crisis in Nigeria, an important alternate source of oil. Biafra had seceded from Nigeria, and the one available British commando ship had sped

[162] Foreign Minister Brown argued that recognizing Israel's right to live could not be "attacked reasonably as 'taking sides in an Arab-Israel dispute,'" p. 7. Brown, "Opening Statement, May 31," p. 6.

[163] Ibid., pp. 7, 8.

[164] Wilson, "Closing Statement, May 31, 1967," p. 2.

[165] *The Guardian,* June 3, 1967, p. 1; *The Washington Post* article by Chalmers M. Roberts, June 3, 1967, p. 1.

[166] *The Guardian,* June 7, 1967, p. 2.

[167] Informed White House source, interview conducted March 6, 1969, Appendix B, Question 3.

off "presumably to cover the Nigerian situation."[168] British leaders were obviously concerned that the Middle East situation might escalate into a major war involving Great Britain. Although the Soviets were considered to be sincerely urging restraint,[169] it was felt that the great powers were not in control of the situation.[170] Prime Minister Wilson commented that a war in the region could escalate into a much wider conflict "in a matter of hours."[171]

British editorials reflected similar concern. *The Times* counseled that in such an "infinitely dangerous situation" as a clash in the area "the best thing that the rest of the world can do to start with is to stand aside." [172] Although it has been stated that during this period "public opinion rallied strongly to the cause of Israel,"[173] such an assessment must be carefully qualified. Newspaper and magazine commentaries were far from enthusiastic.[174] *The Economist*, for example, while conceding a moral commitment to Israel's preservation, said that shipping through the Gulf of Aqaba was "not a cause for which Israel's friends should fight Israel's fight for it."[175] While there apparently was considerable public sympathy for Israel, the British had no stomach for risking a military conflict in the Mideast. Public opinion polls taken at the outbreak of hostilities tended to confirm this hypothesis. (See Table 4.1, Parts D and E.)

British fleet movements complemented the changing policy. A force was rapidly assembled south of Suez to lend credibility to initial strong statements of maritime rights. On the day of Prime Minister Wilson's forceful declaration it was announced that the British aircraft carrier *Victorious* and her escort frigate, which were returning from the Far East, would be held at Malta.[176] The carrier

[168] *The Guardian*, June 3, 1967, p. 7. There was speculation that *Albion* might be sent to the Mediterranean, and the Soviets claimed it had been spotted there, but it apparently remained off Africa. British ships were reportedly standing by to evacuate British families from eastern Nigeria on June 4. *The Times*, June 5, 1967, p. 1. The Soviet claim was made in a broadcast to the United Kingdom on June 4, 1967.

[169] Prime Minister Wilson said, in reference to the visit of Foreign Secretary Brown to the Soviet Union, "I fully accept—indeed my Rt. Hon. Friend was given evidence of this on his visit to Moscow last week—the sincerity of the Soviet Union in desiring and urging restraint at this critical time". Wilson, "Closing Statement, May 31," p. 3.

[170] See, for example, the statements of Mr. Edward Heath in *Hansard Parliamentary Debates* (5th Series), Vol. 747, House of Commons, p. 115, and Prime Minister Wilson, "Closing Statement, May 31," p. 4.

[171] *The Washington Post*, June 3, 1967, p. 1.

[172] *The Times*, May 24, 1967, p. 11.

[173] Churchill and Churchill, *The Six Day War*, p. 40.

[174] See, for example, *The Guardian*, May 25, 1967.

[175] "Nasser Does It," *The Economist*, Vol. CCXXIII, No. 6457, p. 880.

[176] *The Guardian*, May 25, 1967, p. 1. Ships in Malta had been put on alert on May 23, 1967.

had passed through the Suez Canal on the day Nasser's blockade had been announced. By May 25 another British carrier rounding the southern tip of India heading for the Far East was ordered to return to the Red Sea area. She was sighted off Aden on May 31.[177] (See Figure 4.2.) The British thus had a carrier on either side of the Suez Canal.

Other naval forces were also sent to the region. By June 2, 1967, six frigates and a squadron of minesweepers had joined the carrier *Hermes* near Aden.[178] Militarily, Britain could have challenged the blockade with this force. Canadian destroyers were dispatched to the eastern Atlantic on May 26,[179] and frigates departed from England for the Mediterranean on May 29 and 31.

London's moves in the Mediterranean were precautionary, but they were useful to Washington. The presence of a British carrier and her escort augmented the Sixth Fleet, and subsequent additions matched the more highly publicized Soviet fleet escalation. By the types of ships sent, it did not appear that London was planning a military move with troops in support of Israel. However, the British buildup south of Suez obviously provided credibility to talk about a maritime task force.

The details of arrangements are classified, but provisions existed for a "cooperative effort."[180] It can be speculated that Britain would have joined the United States in any limited war at sea in the Mediterranean against the Soviet Union and would have provided a major contribution to any fleet designed to test the United Arab Republic blockade. Moscow obviously thought there was close Anglo-American cooperation and revealed this belief not only in broadcasts but also by trailing the British Mediterranean force headed by the *Victorious*.

During the first days of the phase the British seriously considered asserting the right of passage through the Gulf of Aqaba, apparently feeling this was the best way to avoid a dangerous war. Between May 24 and 30 there was a shift in policy, and any testing of the blockade was seemingly postponed to the indefinite future. The British adopted a "me too" attitude toward a multination maritime force. The most probable reason for this shift was economic pressure from

[177]It was reported she had been ordered to "stand by" on May 25. The *Hermes* was off Gan Island in the Maldive Islands at that time. *The Times*, May 26, 1967, p. 1.

[178]*The Times*, June 1, 1967, p. 1.

[179]The Canadian destroyers had reportedly been sent in case they should be "required in the Middle East." *The Times*, May 26, 1967, p. 10.

[180]Letter from Admiral John S. McCain, Jr., USN, Commander in Chief, U.S. Naval Forces Europe, to Lt. Comdr. J. T. Howe, USN, dated March 11, 1968.

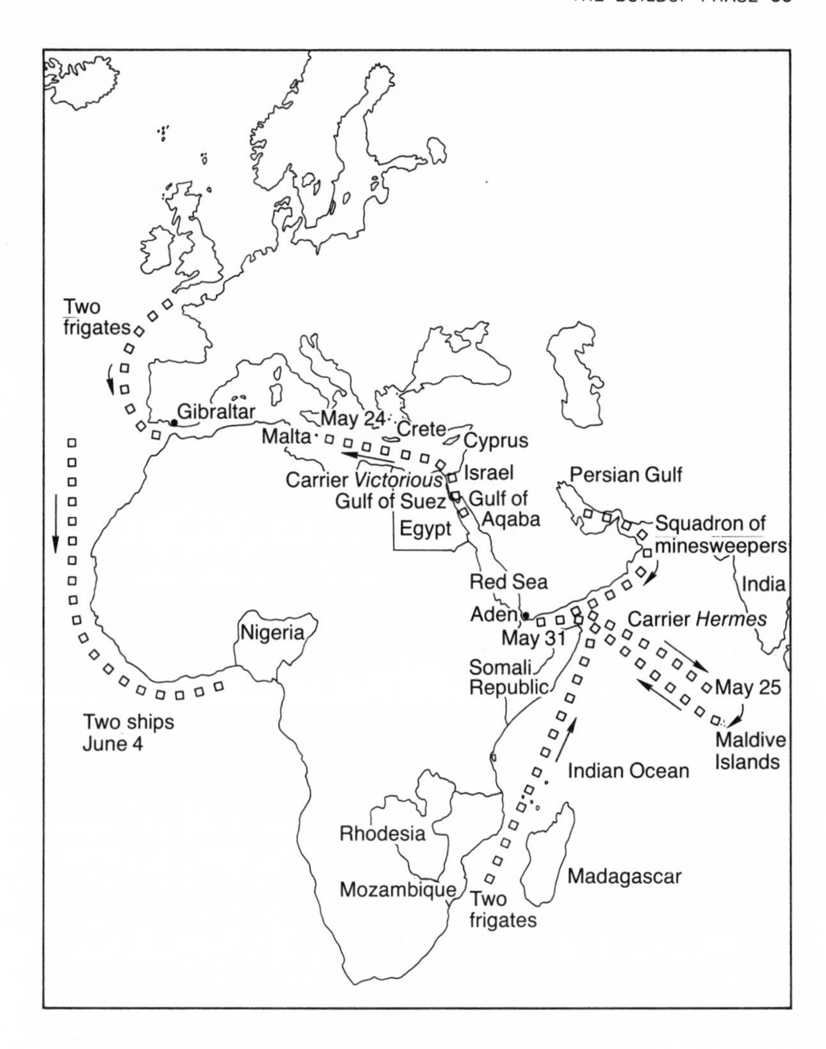

Figure 4.2 Movements of British forces during buildup phase

oil- and sterling-rich Arab countries. Apparently the British at no time entertained any idea of directly defending Israel.

4.4 UNITED STATES EVALUATION OF CAPABILITY

During this period Washington apparently decided that no active American military role should be played in the Middle East. The placement of military forces and the qualifications made on official statements indicate that no decision to provide military support for Israel had been made, and no more than a paper plan to force the Gulf of Aqaba blockade existed. By briefly reviewing the important factors affecting U.S. capability to cope with the situation, it is easier to understand why Washington leaned toward a passive role in approaching this multicrisis situation.

Tables 4.2 to 4.6 summarize the evidence related to each capability

Table 4.2 Estimate of Soviet Intentions

X NO SOVIET INTENTION TO INTERVENE

X Types of forces available in Mediterranean

X Employment and positioning of naval forces

X Estimates of Arab incompetence vis-à-vis Israel

X Belief that United States would intervene if Russia did

X Respect for power of Sixth Fleet

X Wilson statement concerning Soviet sincerity

X Characteristic Soviet avoidance of direct confrontation

X No direct threats concerning blockade

X Egyptian statements (Nasser, Shukairy)

X Diplomatic contacts and direct exchanges of letters

X Knowledge that Israel would go only so far owing to manpower limits (1956 precedent)

X Lack of cooperation in United Nations

X Public statements of support and propaganda

X Russian ambassador in Cairo not urging restraint

X Rumors Soviets would protect Syria

X Arms-aid buildup (although some of doubtful value)

X Augmentation of naval force

X False information concerning Israel on Syrian border

X SOVIET INTENT TO INTERVENE

factor. The distance of the "X" away from the dividing line is an estimate of relative weight and validity as evidence. For example, as seen in Table 4.2 the type of Soviet forces sent to the Mediterranean was the most solid evidence that Moscow did not intend to intervene in the crisis. Passing of false information to Egypt concerning the massing of the Israeli army on the Syrian border was probably the most important evidence tending to indicate that the Soviets might intervene. There was uncertainty concerning Soviet intentions during the buildup phase. Although the weight of evidence seemed to lean toward nonintervention, Washington could not take this factor for granted. It had to consider Soviet intervention a distinct possibility and be prepared for it.

A second important factor was the Defense Department estimate of its capability to intervene short of nuclear war. (See Table 4.3.) With-

Table 4.3 Defense Estimates of U.S. Capability to Intervene

X CAPABILITY		
X Backup attack, antisubmarine carriers available	X Ability to respond for limited time with available forces (ships and aircraft)	X Confidence that Israel could control land and air except against Soviets
	X Four carrier task forces and Marine force that could be assembled within two weeks	X Joint Chiefs of Staff assessment of sufficient forces to execute Mideast Contingency Plan.
X Vietnam requirements for carriers (*Intrepid*)		
X Inability of available forces to change outcome of desert war		
X Statements in *Worldwide Military Commitments* hearings		
		X Estimate of Assistant Commandant of the Marine Corps
X Reduced marine capability in Mediterranean (helicopters, reduced companies, inexperience)		X Reduced naval capability (pilot shortages, no antisubmarine warfare task force, reduced Atlantic fleet backup because of Vietnam)
X Limited size of naval force south of Suez and difficulty in rapidly or covertly reinforcing; Joint Chiefs of Staff belief it was not strong enough to use, even augmented by British		
X LACK OF CAPABILITY		

out at least calling the ready reserves and augmentation of U.S. forces in the area, the Defense Department would have been extremely reluctant to intervene in an Arab-Israeli war. However, it was capable of making Soviet intervention most difficult. Israel's local military capability, of course, made the need for U.S. forces, except to neutralize the presence of the Soviets, remote.

Another factor of importance was the estimate of domestic support for a U.S. initiative related to the crisis. (See Table 4.4.) It appears that Congress and the general public though generally sympathetic opposed a U.S. initiative in support of Israel.

Economic consequences of any decision also had to be carefully evaluated. (See Table 4.5.) Economically, it appears that the United States had nothing to gain and quite a bit to lose by making an overt

Table 4.4 Estimate of Congressional and Public Attitude

X DESIRE TO GIVE ISRAEL MILITARY BACKING		
		X Importance of Jewish vote (election year approaching)
	X Congressional feeling that area more important and commitment more binding than Vietnam	
		X President Johnson strong Israeli sympathizer; belief that United States had strong obligation to Israel
		X Possible anti-Semitism
	X Sympathy for Israel not translated into support for military initiative	
X Need for unpopular military mobilization		
		X General discouragement with Vietnam war and fear of another limited war experience
	X Senator Javits's action taking administration off the hook politically by his "no unilateral action" statement	
X Overriding congressional feeling of United States overcommitment		
	X Virtually unanimous feeling against unilateral action	
X OPPOSITION TO BACKING ISRAEL		

Table 4.5 Concern about Economic Effects

X SERIOUS ECONOMIC EFFECTS

X Threats to U.S. companies and balance of payments factor

X Heavy cost and balance of payment drain of Vietnam (cost of still another crisis)

X Unified front of Arabs

X Loss of oil supplies for Vietnam

X Feeling that economy was overextended

X Possibility of Suez Canal closure

X "Guns and butter" view; ability of healthy economy to meet crisis requirements

X NO ECONOMIC PROBLEMS FROM ADDITIONAL CRISIS

Table 4.6 Dependence on British Support

X NEED FOR BRITISH COOPERATION

X Insistence by Congress that there be no unilateral involvement by United States

X Necessary British forces available south of Suez

X Because of world policeman image, psychological need for British help (domestic and world opinion)

X Existence of cooperative military planning

X Numerous Anglo-American and Anglo-Soviet consultations (Wilson, Thomson visits to United States).

X Feeling that United States has strength by itself (to match Soviets and to intervene)

X NO NEED FOR BRITISH COOPERATION

---

show of support for Israel. This was particularly true in the face of a unified Arab front.

Whether there was British support was a factor of particular importance in this situation. (See Table 4.6.) The apparent unusually heavy dependence on British support was as much psychological as it was military.

The combination of relatively unfavorable capability factors, contradictory political aims in the Middle East, Israeli capability to defend itself against Arab opponents, and the dangers of a great power confrontation make it fairly easy to see why a logical American policy choice during the buildup phase was to keep well back from the Middle East situation.

5. THE CRISIS

JUNE 5, 1967, TO JUNE 10, 1967

The outbreak of fighting at 2 A.M. on June 5, 1967, added a new dimension of danger. Soviet intentions were put to the test. There were four significant periods of American uncertainty during this phase: (1) from the outbreak of fighting until Soviet and American views were clarified (2 A.M.–9 A.M., June 5, 1967); (2) showdown with the Soviet Union over the United Nations cease-fire resolution for the Egyptian front (6:40 A.M.–9 P.M., June 6, 1967); (3) the attack on the U.S.S. *Liberty* (8 A.M.–9 A.M., June 8, 1967); and (4) the confrontation with Moscow concerning cessation of hostilities on the Syrian front (8 A.M.–12:30 P.M., June 10, 1967).[1] Each of these events involved hot line exchanges between the United States and the Soviet Union. With the arrangement of a cease-fire shortly after noon on June 10, 1967, the June war came to an end, and a period of acute crisis for the United States had passed.

5.1 UNITED STATES POLICY

From the beginning of the war, the basic U.S. declaratory policy that had developed during the buildup phase was followed. President Johnson's statement of May 23, 1967,[2] was reiterated to the press and in the United Nations. The first White House release announced that the government would devote its "energies to bring about an end to the fighting" and appealed to "all parties to support the Security Council in bringing about an immediate cease-fire."[3]

At about 5:30 A.M. on June 5, following consultations between the Secretary of State and the President, a message was sent through normal channels by Secretary Rusk indicating that the United States was "astonished that fighting had commenced" and was "ready to do everything we could to end the fighting and help restore the peace."[4] At 7:05 A.M. the first White House press announcement was

[1] Unless otherwise indicated, all times are given in local Washington, D.C., time throughout this chapter. Israel time was 6 hours earlier; i.e., at 2 A.M. in Washington it was 8 A.M. in Tel Aviv and 6 A.M. GMT.

[2] See Section 4.1.

[3] White House Statement of June 5, 1967, read by George Christian, Department of State *Bulletin*, Vol. LVI, No. 1461 (June 26, 1967), p. 949.

[4] Interview with former Secretary of State Dean Rusk, conducted April 9, 1969. This quotation is not in answer to a specific question concerning the 5 A.M. message but rather to the question "What was our approach to the Soviets following the outbreak of the war?" It is not a quotation of the message itself or necessarily a summary of the message's contents.

released.[5] Anxiety as to what the Soviet Union might do was alleviated somewhat when Premier Kosygin used the hot line to comment on the dangerous situation and the need for both Russia and the United States to work for a cessation of the fighting.[6] The message was received at 8 A.M. on June 5, 1967, and represented the first use of the hot line in a crisis situation.[7] The clarification of a restrained Soviet position cleared the air for U.S. decision making. Resort to the hot line indicated serious Soviet concern that it might become embroiled in a confrontation with the United States. Moscow was evidently still somewhat unsure of Washington's policy.[8] The Johnson reply echoed Kosygin's position that the two nations should stay out of the fighting and try to encourage a cessation of hostilities.[9]

The United States was willing to work toward an immediate cease-fire resolution in the United Nations, but it found the Soviet Union strangely aloof. The Soviets apparently were not interested in talking. This was puzzling to the United States since the Egyptian Air Force had been virtually destroyed four hours before the Security Council was called into session. As Secretary Rusk commented, "We tried to get an immediate cease-fire. . . . If they had been willing to have an immediate cease-fire they could have gotten one. Israel would then not have moved into Jordan or Syria and probably

[5] The first U.S. statement on the situation was prepared and released prior to receipt of the Soviet hot line message. Letter from Mr. Harold H. Saunders of the National Security Council Staff, to Lt. Comdr. J. T. Howe, USN, dated July 17, 1968.

[6] There have been a number of conflicting accounts concerning the use of the hot line. Mr Richard M. Moose of the White House staff recommended the account in *Life* magazine by Hugh Sidey in the following manner, "the use of the hot line was fairly accurately described in this article." Hugh Sidey, "Over the Hot Line—the Middle East," in the column "The Presidency," *Life*, Vol. 62, No. 24 (June 16, 1967), p. 24b. In addition, the account given by Lester Velie in "The Week the Hot Line Burned," *Readers Digest* (August 1968), pp. 37–44, is considered to be reasonably accurate. References to the content of hot line message are based primarily on my own analysis, comparison of these and other articles, and other sources.

[7] Letter from Mr. Richard M. Moose, White House Staff, to Lt. Comdr. J. T. Howe, USN, dated March 1, 1968.

[8] It is conceivable, however, that the Soviets had read the U.S. press release and therefore were confident of what position the United States had taken. They could have been responding to a U.S. initiative rather than making the first gesture. They also probably had received the earlier message from Secretary Rusk.

[9] Sidey, "Over the Hot Line," p. 24b. A similar account is contained in *The Guardian* article by Richard Scott, "Success for Hot Line Diplomacy," June 10, 1967, p. 7. He states that in addition both leaders agreed to use their "limited power to restrain their friends in opposing camps."

Table 5.1 Clarification of U.S. and USSR Positions upon Outbreak of Fighting

Washington Time	War Situation	United States Position	United States-United Nations Activity	U.S. Ships	USSR Position	USSR-United Nations	USSR Ships
5:30 A.M. approx.	Destruction of Egyptian Air Force; Israel advance in Sinai; situation confused	Message from Secretary Rusk; astonishment at outbreak of fighting; readiness to work toward restoring peace		Normal routine			
7:05 A.M.	Israeli air success more certain	White House release prepared, appeal to all parties to bring about cease-fire; United States to devote energies to end fighting		"Conducting business as usual"; reduced number of flights; on alert			No unusual maneuvers.
8 A.M.					Hot line message, dangerous situation; United States and Russia must work to end hostilities		
8:47 A.M.		Hot line reply-agreement that United States and USSR should work to end the hostilities	United States push for cease-fire			Aloofness on cease-fire	

would only have been 50 miles or so into Egyptian territory."[10]

The posture of the Sixth Fleet reflected American interest in avoiding involvement. At the outbreak of hostilities the fleet reportedly was near Crete and planned to remain there.[11] The ships were put in an advanced state of readiness, and the number of fighter aircraft on alert to defend the carrier against surprise attack was doubled.[12] This was a prudent defensive precaution under the circumstances.[13] However, newsmen were initially restricted to reporting that the Sixth Fleet was "conducting business as usual" in order not to conflict with the "*neutral stance*" taken in official U.S. statements.[14] Ships and pilots had been ordered not to approach within two hundred miles of the area of conflict in order to "maintain a position of nonintervention."[15]

While the rapidity of Israeli battlefield success facilitated an American policy of watching passively, Washington had to keep Moscow convinced of staying out, impress interested Americans that Israel was not being abandoned, and minimize retaliation from Arabs looking for scapegoats to explain their debacle. Table 5.1 is a summary of the clarification of U.S. and USSR positions upon the outbreak of fighting.

A domestic stir was caused when a State Department spokesman commented at a midday briefing on June 5 that the United States was "neutral in thought, word, and deed"; this was interpreted in some circles as a formal declaration of neutrality and an attempt by the United States to "disassociate itself from the crisis."[16] But such inferences were not intended. Spokesman McCloskey replied to the allegation that his statement was an unfortunate *faux pas*[17] by giving the full context of the press conference exchange. Part of it went as follows:

Question: . . . the U.S. position in the U.N. has been stated as being neutral. Would you reaffirm that?

Answer: Indeed, I would; I would be more than happy to. We

[10] Rusk, interview.

[11] Rear Admiral L. R. Geis announced that "for the time being we will continue doing just what we've been doing for the last several days." *The New York Times* article by Neil Sheehan aboard U.S.S. *America*, June 5, 6, 1967, p. 18.

[12] *The New York Times* article by Neil Sheehan, June 7, 1967, p. 17.

[13] Interview with Rear Adm. J. C. Wylie, Jr., conducted December 22, 1967.

[14] *The New York Times,* June 7, 1967, p. 17. (Emphasis added.)

[15] *The New York Times,* June 8, 1967, p. 14. This particular restriction had been in effect before the fighting commenced.

[16] *The Washington Post* article by Carroll Killpatric and Murray Marder, "US Asserts Non-Control Stand on War," June 6, 1967, p. A8.

[17] Theodore Draper, *Israel and World Politics* (New York: Viking, 1968), pp. 11.

have tried to steer an even-handed course through this. Our position *is* neutral in thought, word, and deed.[18] [Mr. McCloskey's emphasis.]

He stated that "even-handed course" was the essential point, and that "The phrase 'in thought, word and deed' was added for emphasis only and was not, indeed, intended as a repudiation of our previous position in any way."[19] Although this remark was not intended to downgrade American concern for Israel, it was clear at the time that Tel Aviv needed no more than an "even-handed" approach.

Nonetheless, President Johnson was reputedly furious about the McCloskey statement and ordered Secretary Rusk to go to Congress and clarify the U.S. position.[20] The connotation of indifference to Israel's fate was a domestic political blunder as well as a misinterpretation of the American position internationally. In a subsequent news conference the Secretary of State reiterated the President's statement of May 23 and explained that "neutral" did not mean "indifferent."[21] Although the United States was not a "belligerent" and did not have "forces in the area," it was not "indifferent" and was "deeply concerned."[22] Military commanders were "very carefully" neutral.[23] But while the White House steered an "even-handed" course, it did so with full confidence that Israel's interests were being protected.

On June 6, 1967, an important test of will occurred concerning a cease-fire on the Egyptian front. In the early hours of that day Israel had managed to move behind the bulk of the Egyptian army, blocking their retreat and opening the Sinai to Israeli sweeps to the Suez Canal. The Soviet Union insisted in U.N. consultations on a cease-fire with withdrawal to the positions occupied on June 4, 1967.[24] At

[18] Letter from Mr. Robert J. McCloskey, Deputy Assistant Secretary for Public Affairs, to Lt. Comdr. J. T. Howe, USN, dated March 6, 1968.

[19] Ibid.

[20] Interview with an informed White House source, conducted March 6, 1969. See Appendix B, Question 14.

[21] Dean Rusk, Secretary of State, "News Briefing at the White House," June 5, 1967, Department of State *Bulletin,* Vol. LVI, No. 1461 (June 26, 1967), p. 950. Rusk's reiteration of the President's statement, however, was slightly toned down. He stated, for example, that the United States "is committed to the support of the independence and territorial integrity." President Johnson said "the US is *firmly* committed to the support of the political independence." (Emphasis added.) See Section 4.1.

[22] Ibid.

[23] Wylie, interview.

[24] It is not clear when the Soviets became interested in talking in the United Nations. The first official Soviet statement was released at 5:29 P.M. on June 5, 1967, and called for a "pullback beyond the truce line." It is speculated that the Soviets began to negotiate seriously about a cease-fire at about this point. Tass International Service in English, 2129 GMT, June 5, 1967.

6:40 A.M. Premier Kosygin sent a hot line message reportedly expressing concern that the war was spreading and called for a cease-fire and an Israeli withdrawal. As it happened, the Sixth Fleet carrier task forces had begun speeding at twenty knots in a southeasterly direction in order to vary their "position while still maintaining a neutral posture with respect to the Arab-Israeli war."[25] The ships were under orders to remain at least 200 miles from the area of conflict, and proceeded to a position about 100 miles southeast of Crete.[26] (See Figure 5.1.) Although this change of position was ordered on the initiative of local commanders, the movement represented a timely underlining of American determination. The White House took advantage of the repositioning as a means of showing the Russians, who were tailing the task forces, that the United States would not be intimidated although it earnestly sought a U.N. solution.

A Soviet Tass release at 7:38 A.M. complained that the United States was procrastinating on the withdrawal clause of a cease-fire resolution in order to facilitate further Israeli penetration into Arab territory. The U.S. delegation to the United Nations, Tass claimed, had modified its stand somewhat[27] and was now willing to consider reestablishment of the positions prior to the removal of United Nations emergency forces on May 19, 1967. The Russians were holding out for a return to positions as of June 4, 1967,[28] which in effect would restore the blockade of the Gulf of Aqaba, which had served as the Israeli *casus belli.* There is some evidence that the United States may have taken the position described in the Soviet account. Ap-

[25]Letter from Rear Admiral L. R. Geis, USN, Commander of the Sixth Fleet carrier task forces during the June war, to Lt. Comdr. J. T. Howe, USN, dated April 7, 1969.

[26]*The New York Times* article by Neil Sheehan aboard U.S.S. *America,* June 7, 1967; June 8, 1967, p. 14. Reconnaissance missions were flown on June 7, 1967, to "maintain surveillance over the movements of Soviet warships." *The New York Times,* June 7, 1967, p. 17. The exact time and duration of this movement is not yet clear.

[27]An earlier Tass dispatch from New York stated, "It was learned in well-informed circles of the Security Council that U.S. delegate Goldberg is strongly against the Security Council adopting a resolution that would provide for an immediate pullback of Israeli and Arab forces to the truce lines to position which they held before the outbreak of fighting." Tass in English, 1815 GMT, June 5, 1967. This commentary complained about American procrastination.

[28]Tass International Service in English, 1138 GMT, June 6, 1967. The dispatch said the "United States is proposing to reward the Israeli aggressors by returning United Nations forces to the Gaza Strip and Sinai and restoring the positions which Israel won by its complicity in the tripartite aggression against Egypt in 1956." According to another Soviet broadcast, the Soviets ostensibly wanted withdrawal without conditions. Moscow in Arabic to Arab world, 1230 GMT, June 6, 1967.

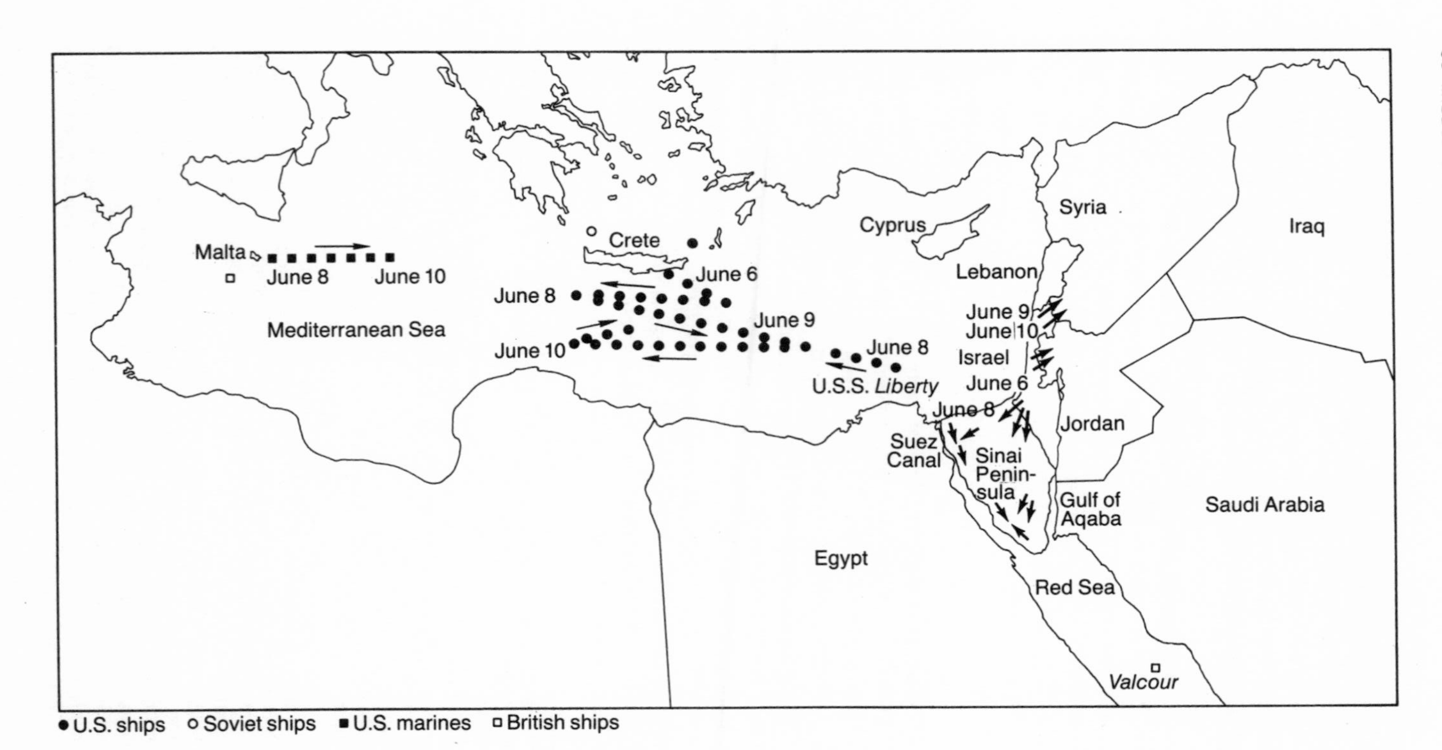

Figure 5.1 Movements of naval forces during the crisis phase

parently there was strong feeling in some parts of the government that Israel had rejected American advice not to attack and therefore should not be rewarded for its actions. It had not waited a fortnight or until the Arab emissary had come to Washington before attacking.

At the same time President Johnson was determined not to repeat what he considered to be errors in 1956 and 1957. He probably hoped that a long-term settlement could be worked out before Israel's withdrawal. This was consistent with the position he had taken as a senator during the Suez crisis a decade before.[29] Therefore, he was probably willing to support a cease-fire and withdrawal as long as there was some U.N. guarantee of free passage in the Straits of Tiran and prospects for a sustainable peace in the area. The withdrawal solution eventually adopted by the U.N. Security Council on November 22, 1967, included these provisions. The United States apparently was ready to support a qualified call for withdrawal. Because Israel was crushing the Arab resistance, the United States could afford to hold out while the Soviet Union came around to the American position.

A Soviet commentary released at 12:50 P.M. again complained that the United States was still procrastinating in order to allow Israel to advance. But there evidently was some difference of opinion and confusion about American tactics at that point. The observation was attributed to the "opinion of some observers."[30] The Soviet delegation to the United Nations apparently believed that the United States was stalling and holding out for a better arrangement. The Kremlin, however, seemed to be less convinced that Washington was being stubborn. Soviet Ambassador Fedorenko implied in private U.N. consultations that the United States would not accept a simple withdrawal. He claimed that

> The Soviet delegate was always of the opinion that the Security Council should also have taken a decision concerning the immediate withdrawal of the forces of the aggressor behind the Armistice lines. However, *because of the opposition of some members* of the Security Council, no agreement could be reached on this important problem.[31] [Emphasis added.]

[29] The Israeli Foreign Minister had left the meeting on May 26, 1967, with the impression that the 1956 experience was not going to be repeated.

[30] Tass International Service in English, June 6, 1967, 1650 GMT, Vishnevetakiy commentary in *Izvestia*.

[31] Statement of Soviet Ambassador N. T. Fedorenko during Security Council speech of June 6, 1967, U.N., Provisional Record of the 1348th Meeting, Document No. S/PV 1348, p. 27. This statement was made at approximately 7:45 P.M. on June 6, 1967.

At 6:20 P.M. Premier Kosygin reportedly sent another demand that the United States persuade Israel to withdraw and implied that if Washington did not, Moscow might. However, almost simultaneously with this strong message, and probably before it arrived, the Soviet U.N. delegation agreed to a cease-fire resolution without conditions. At 6:30 P.M. the Security Council was convened with the announcement that unanimous agreement had been reached in consultations.[32] After reluctantly accepting a cease-fire resolution with no withdrawal clause, Ambassador Fedorenko reiterated the official Soviet call for withdrawal issued during the evening of June 5.[33] Opportunely, the President interrupted nationwide television coverage of the Security Council proceedings to make a brief announcement just after Fedorenko had finished his speech. At 8 P.M. the President told the nation and the world that the cease-fire vote reflected

> *responsible concern for peace* on the part of *all* who voted for it. . . . We believe that a cease-fire is the necessary "first step," in the words of the resolution itself—a *first step* toward what we all must hope will be a *new time* of settled peace and progress for all the peoples of the Middle East.[34] [Emphasis added.]

Premier Kosygin had an answer to his hot line message.

Washington shared Moscow's concern for peace and desire for cease-fire, but it also shared Tel Aviv's view that a long-term solution to the Arab-Israeli problem should be worked out. The President's response via the hot line must have seemed anticlimactical in the Kremlin. It expressed America's hope for a United Nations solution to the problem.[35] By noon on June 7, 1967, the Sixth Fleet carriers had returned to a position about sixty miles south of the eastern end of Crete and were proceeding west. The Russian predicament was acidly summarized by the Iraqi Foreign Minister during the Security Council proceedings:

> The cease-fire resolution which the council adopted today is a *complete surrender to Israel*. I do not care what anybody says. That is a fact and it is very well known. For two days there have been negotiations to see whether a cease-fire resolution would be adopted that

[32] U.N., Security Council, Provisional Record of 1348th Meeting, Document No. 1348, p. 1.

[33] Fedorenko speech, Security Council, June 6, 1967, Document No. S/PV 1348, p. 27. The official statement appeared in *Pravda*, June 6, 1967, p. 1, Vol. XIX, No. 23 (June 28, 1967). This warning had been released by Tass International Service in English at 2120 GMT, June 5, 1967. It is speculated that Fedorenko's statement was very close to the content of the hot line warning. See footnote 24.

[34] "Statement by the President on the cease-fire vote of the United Nations Security Council, as Read for Radio and Television, June 6, 1967." Weekly compilation of *Presidential Documents*, Vol. 3, No. 23 (June 12, 1967), p. 836.

[35] Velie, "The Week the Hot Line Burned," p. 39.

> would be accompanied by a call for the withdrawal of forces back to the point from which hostilities started. This was not done because of the fact that certain States, and I mention the USA in particular, refused to go along with it.[36] [Emphasis added.]

Soviet sensitivity to embarrassing accusations that may have overstated the U.S. position was indicated by a correction made three hours after an initial Tass dispatch reported that the Iraqi official had attributed Soviet failure to obtain a withdrawal provision to U.S. resistance;[37] the reference to U.S. resistance was deleted. But the impression remained that the U.S. had gotten its way. Table 5.2 demonstrates the sequence and interaction of American and Soviet military and diplomatic maneuvering over the cease-fire resolution.

Shortly after the initial hot line message concerning the situation in Egypt, Moscow radio broadcast Arab charges that U.S. and British planes had participated in the Israeli attacks on Egypt. The Arabs had announced they had "real proof of interference" by American and British carrier aircraft "in military actions on the Israeli side."[38] Although the United States knew that the Soviets realized the truth, it denied the charges over the hot line.[39] This was probably conveniently tagged onto the response to Kosygin's earlier message concerning Israeli withdrawal. Washington also reacted sharply in public to Arab charges. Secretary Rusk branded the allegations as utterly false in a revealing statement: "We know that they and *some of their friends know where our carriers are.* We can only conclude that this was a malicious charge, known to be

[36]Statement of Iraqi Foreign Minister Adnan Al-Pachachi to the Security Council during speech of June 6, 1967. U.N., Provisional Record of 1348th Meeting, Document No. 1348, p. 52. His speech was made after the Soviet speech.

[37]Tass International Service in English, June 7, 1967, commented that "Adnan al Pachachi, the Foreign Minister of Iraq, said that the council should denounce the aggressor and demand the immediate and unconditional withdrawal of the aggressor's forces to positions occupied before 4 June. This has not been done, he said, because the US resisted the demand for the withdrawal of the forces, which did not suit Israel, which is seeking to retain control over the territories seized as a result of perfidious aggression." The Tass correction issued at 0938 GMT on June 7, 1967, simply reported that Pachachi had "insisted on an immediate cease-fire and unconditional withdrawal of the troops from the territory seized as a result of the perfidious aggression."

[38]Moscow Domestic Service in Russian, 1300 GMT, June 6, 1967. The Arabs subsequently claimed more specifically that "American fighter aircraft protected Israel while Israeli aircraft made attacks on the UAR." Radio Moscow in Finnish to Finland, 1630 GMT, June 6, 1967.

[39]The *Life* article referred to these as "a second flurry of exchanges" which "came when the U.A.R. made its wild charges that the U.S. and British planes had helped Israel. Over the hot line, Johnson and Kosiygin gave assurances that neither was getting involved in the shooting." Sidey, "Over the Hot Line," p. 24b.

Table 5.2 U.S.-Soviet Differences on U.N. Cease-Fire Resolution for Egyptian Front, June 5, 1967

Time	War Situation	U.S. Position	U.S.-U.N. Activity	U.S. Ships	USSR Position	USSR-U.N.	USSR Ships
6:40 A.M.	Israeli troops behind most of Egyptian Army; El Arish and Abu Agheila captured; Sinai wide open				Hot line—United States should support resolution calling on Israel to halt advance into Sinai and withdraw		
10:30 A.M. (approx.)	Hot line—support call for cease-fire and withdrawal that would not compromise Israeli position		United States holding out for cease-fire and withdrawal with guarantees	Sixth Fleet attack carriers moving at twenty knots toward Sinai but still two hundred miles back		Insistence on cease-fire with withdrawal clause to June 4, 1967 positions	Routine
5:30 P.M. (approx.)			Willingness to accept simple cease-fire			Reluctant acceptance of simple cease-fire without withdrawal	
6:20 P.M.	Israel advance in two directions in northern Sinai			Sixth Fleet repositioned nearer to area of conflict but two hundred miles back	Hot line—demanded United States halt Israelis and make them pull back		

Time	War Situation	U.S. Position	U.S.-U.N. Activity	U.S. Ships	USSR Position	USSR-U.N.	USSR Ships
6:30 P.M. U.N. meeting			Unanimous vote on simple cease-fire			Meeting called because USSR had agreed to cease-fire without conditions	
7:30 P.M. (approx.)						Fedorenko demand that Israel stop and pull back troops beyond truce line	
8:00 P.M. President's television speech		Cease-fire welcome as first step toward time of peace and progress; stated vote reflects responsible concern for peace by *all* who voted for it					
9 P.M.		Hot line answer—U.S. hope for U.N. solution		Back to area south of Crete on June 7			

false, and therefore obviously invented for some purpose not fully disclosed."[40] (Emphasis added.) The phrase "some of their friends" obviously referred to the Russians, who were able to supply precise information about U.S. carrier operations. Ambassador Goldberg invited U.N. observers to "interview air crews" and "look at logs" aboard the carriers.[41] The United States went out of its way to deny any complicity.[42]

Rusk theorized that the Arabs were "trying to create difficulties for Americans in the Near East."[43] Secretary Rusk's primary concern was that the false charge spreading through the Middle East would provide a "pretext for breaking relations and the long-range implications for our relations with Arab states were very severe."[44] Kuwait and Iraq announced cessation of all oil supplies to the United States and the United Kingdom.

The attack on the American communications ship *Liberty*[45] which occurred at 8 A.M. on June 8, 1967 brought a brief but significant third period of uncertainty. Because of the events of June 6 and 7 it is not so surprising that the Secretary of Defense first thought that the Russians had perpetrated the attack. Washington was still not fully assured that Moscow would not get involved. Secretary McNamara said subsequently in another context; "I thought the *Liberty* had been attacked by Soviet forces. Thank goodness, our carrier commanders did not launch immediately against the Soviet forces

[40]Dean Rusk, "News Briefing at the White House, June 6," *Department of State Bulletin,* Vol. LVI, No. 1461 (June 26, 1967), p. 951.

[41]Speech of Ambassador A. J. Goldberg to U.N. Security Council on June 6, 1967. U.N., Provisional Record of 1348th Meeting, Document No. S/PV 1348, pp. 8–10, 11. This speech was made shortly after the meeting convened at 6:30 P.M.

[42]The Navy invited foreign newsmen to come aboard the *America* following the Arab charges, and some twenty reporters took advantage of the opportunity. Ironically, an hour before the scheduled complete briefing on all carrier aircraft operations during the crisis period, carrier planes scrambled to go to the rescue of *Liberty*.

[43]Rusk, "News Briefing, June 6, 1967," p. 951.

[44]Rusk, interview.

[45]The *Liberty,* a lightly armed vessel designed for communications purposes, had been dispatched from North Africa. Although the Pentagon maintained throughout that *Liberty* had been sent to "provide additional communications to facilitate the evacuation of American citizens," it was widely speculated in the press that it had been sent to "monitor communications of the Egyptian and Israeli forces." *The New York Times,* June 29, 1967, p. 1. Robert Donovan stated "it was intercepting battle field messages from both Egyptian and Israeli forces in the Sinai battle, as well as unknown higher level messages between governments." Robert J. Donovan, *Israel's Fight for Survival* (New York: The New American Library, 1967), p. 142. Because of what has been released concerning the *Pueblo,* the latter explanation appears plausible.

who were operating in the Mediterranean at that time."[46] At least half an hour elapsed between the first reports to the Pentagon and the time that Secretary McNamara and the Joint Chiefs "concluded that a Soviet attack was unlikely."[47] The commander of the Sixth Fleet, however, did order carrier aircraft to go to *Liberty*'s rescue within minutes after receiving the initial report. The admiral, of course, had less reason to suspect a Soviet attack and more immediate verification of no Russian culpability than those aware of what had transpired over the hot line. Officers on the scene did not seriously consider that the Soviets had made the attack.[48]

President Johnson's concern about the "grave danger" of a "misunderstanding"[49] was seemingly reflected in his careful reaction. While still not sure who was responsible, "the President ordered U.S. planes to scramble and look for survivors."[50] He also "rushed a message to Kosygin explaining that the planes were not going to battle."[51] Reportedly, "while that was chattering out to Moscow, Israel admitted that it was responsible. Johnson, who was in the situation room, added this new information; Kosygin acknowledged immediately."[52] The White House subsequently explained that "our purpose was to prevent any misinterpretation of the movement

[46]Statement of Secretary of Defense Robert McNamara in answer to questions concerning U.S. reactions to the *Pueblo* seizure. "Sect. Rusk and Sect. of Defense McNamara Discuss Vietnam and Korea on 'Meet the Press,' " The Department of State *Bulletin,* Vol. LVIII, No. 1496 (February 26, 1968), p. 271.

[47]Testimony of Secretary of Defense Robert McNamara in U.S., Congress, Senate, Committee on Armed Services, *Authorization for Military Procurement, Research and Development, Fiscal Year 1969, and Reserve Strength,* 90th Cong., 2nd sess. (Washington, 1968), p. 47.

[48]This assumption is based on conversations with naval officers familiar with the Sixth Fleet operations.

[49]President's statement of May 23, 1967. See Section 4.1.

[50]Sidey, "Over the Hot Line," p. 24b.

[51]Ibid. The message was apparently dispatched at 11 A.M.

[52]Ibid. The real reasons for the attack are only speculative since the classified testimony of the investigation has not been released and no evidence was heard from the attacking nation. The U.S. Naval Court of Inquiry concluded the attack had been "unprovoked" and Israeli armed forces had "ample opportunity to identify *Liberty* correctly." *Liberty* was observed from the air on three separate occasions by Israeli aircraft, five hours, three hours, and two and one-half hours prior to the attack. The torpedo boats approached to within 2000 yards and were signaling to the *Liberty* prior to their attack. Summary of proceedings of U.S. Navy Court of Inquiry convened June 10, 1967. Copy supplied by U.S. Navy Office of Information, July 1968, pp. 1, 5. A likely explanation is that Israeli pilots initiating the attack were "tense, eager, and a little trigger happy." Wylie, interview. The pilots evidently decided to attack "without reference back to Headquarters." Interview with senior Israel Foreign Ministry official conducted October 24, 1968.

of our ships."[53] The carrier *America,* the cruiser *Little Rock,* and destroyers "went to the rescue of *Liberty.*"[54] A rendezvous between the *Liberty* and the destroyers was effected at 12:30 A.M. on June 9, 1967.[55] The ships then headed back toward Crete.

It was fortunate that the attack did not occur until the fourth day of the war during one of the periods of reduced U.S.-Soviet tension. At the time, a cease-fire was already in effect between Jordan and Israel, and the latter had expressed willingness to accept a cease-fire with Egypt. Cairo, however, still refused. Israel had taken Sharm el Sheikh, commanding the Straits of Tiran, controlled the access routes through the Sinai, and had reached the Suez Canal in the south. The *Liberty* did not arrive in its assigned area, fifteen miles north of the Sinai Peninsula, until the morning of June 8, 1967. By that time there was no logical reason for Moscow to assume Washington needed to intervene since the Egyptian military forces had been crushed. If the *Liberty* had been attacked on June 5, 1967, the chance of miscalculation in the confusion of the first clashes would have been greater. An attack on June 6 or 10 also would have produced a tenser situation.

It was on June 10, 1967, that the most serious Soviet-American confrontation occurred. In a few brief hours, the President perceived a threat of Soviet intervention and ordered an American initiative. On Friday, June 9, at 6 A.M. Israel had mounted its difficult assault on Syrian fortifications in the Golan Heights. Shortly after 3 P.M. Tel Aviv and Damascus had both accepted a U.N. cease-fire order. However, at 4:30 A.M. on June 10 a special U.N. Security Council session was called to hear Syrian charges that Israel had bombed Damascus and was heading for the Syrian capital city.[56] At

[53]Moose, letter. Most accounts indicated that the message concerned only carrier aircraft, which "were scrambling and speeding toward the damaged ship." See, for example, *The New York Times* article by William Beecher, "Israel in Error, Attacks U.S. Ship," June 8, 1967, p. 1. The attack occurred at 1403 local time. It was not until 1750 that the ship received word that escorts were on the way, and the rendezvous did not occur until the following morning. There is no mention of the actions of U.S. aircraft in the testimony. "Testimony before the U.S. Navy Court of Inquiry convened June 10, 1967 by Commanding Officer of U.S.S. *Liberty,*" pp. 9, 10. Unclassified transcript supplied by Department of Information, Navy Department, July 1968.

[54]Letter from Rear Adm. L. R. Geis, USN, to Lt. Comdr. J. T. Howe, USN, dated April 16, 1968. The *Liberty* was notified that ships were on the way at 11:50 A.M. The lengthy time to rendezvous indicated that the Sixth Fleet was at least 400 miles away.

[55]Transcript of the testimony of the commanding officer of U.S.S. *Liberty* before U.S. Navy Court of Inquiry convened on June 10, 1967, to inquire into the circumstances surrounding the attack on *Liberty,* p. 9.

[56]U.N., Security Document, Provisional Record of 1354th Meeting, Document No. S/PV 1354, June 10, 1967.

this point Israeli forces, which had halted during the night, had already scaled the Golan Heights at several other points. Major units were moving toward Quneitra and were only thirty-five miles from Damascus. With one ear to proceedings in the United Nations, Israel raced against time, hoping to encircle the Golan Heights and block the rear approaches. In the United Nations, Israel denied any intention of taking Damascus,[57] but the Soviets were apparently worried. The Soviet delegate to the United Nations repeated the official Soviet warning of the previous evening:

> At the present time it is necessary to take urgent and decisive measures to call a halt to the aggressor. If this is not done at once, the full weight of responsibility for the consequences will rest on the shoulders of those members of the Council who hinder the adoption of the necessary measures. We appeal to the Security Council to take severe immediate measures to curb the aggressors.[58]

The warning of June 9 that the Communist countries would do "all that is necessary to help the Arab peoples rebuff the aggressor" was not repeated.[59] However, at that time a note to Israel with similar language was being prepared. The Bulgarian representative charged that Israel sought a *coup d'état* of the Syrian government.[60] Reports were confused, and the United States insisted on confirmation of the various charges. The meeting was concluded before 8 A.M. to await additional information.

Around this time on June 10 the Kremlin had become anxious enough about the threat to Damascus to begin sending a stiff hot line message to the United States and a blunt warning to Israel. The Israeli ambassador was informed that Russia was breaking relations with Israel and was given a note which warned that "Unless Israel ceased military operations immediately, the Soviet Union jointly with other peace-loving states, will impose sanctions against

[57]Statement of Israeli ambassador to United Nations, ibid., p. 22. He said, "there is no foundation whatsoever for the allegations that Israel is planning to take Damascus." Israel also had apparently informed the United States privately that it had no such intention.

[58]Statement of Soviet U.N. Ambassador Fedorenko in U.N., Security Council, Provisional Record of 1354th Meeting, June 10, 1967, p. 21. This statement was repeated in a dispatch of 7:30 A.M. Moscow, Tass International Service in English, June 10, 1967.

[59]*Pravda,* June 10, 1967. The statement was released at 2205 GMT on June 9, 1967, by Tass International Service in English. It was read in its entirety by Fedorenko to the Security Council at the session beginning at 7:15 P.M. on June 9, 1967. U.N., Security Council, Provisional Record of 1353rd Meeting, June 9, 1967, p. 27. The translation of Fedorenko's remarks read: "will do everything necessary to help the peoples of the Arab countries to reject the aggressor resolutely." It was billed as the statement of Eastern European Communist party leaders. Rumania refused to sign.

[60]U.N., 1354th Meeting, June 10, 1967, p. 61.

Israel, with all the consequences arising therefrom."[61]

At 8:10 A.M. the U.N. Security Council was called back into session to hear a report received from U.N. observer General Bull that all strikes had been outside of Damascus in the area of the airport.[62] At 8:15 A.M. it was reported that Generals Dayan and Bull were meeting to work out arrangements for ending hostilities.[63] By 8:30 A.M. the last important Israeli objective, the road junction of Quneitra, had fallen.

However, Soviet Ambassador Fedorenko became increasingly belligerent. He repeated the warning in the note handed by the Soviet government to Israel and the warning concerning those who impair Security Council decisions. He added that if Israel was not stopped immediately, "this will create an extremely serious situation."[64] Fedorenko's statement probably seemed familiar to those gathered at 9:05 A.M. in the White House situation room to read the Soviet hot line warning. According to an informed White House source, the USSR

> . . . accused Israel of violating the ceasefire resolution at the U.N. [and] . . . stated that unless Israel unconditionally and immediately ceased operations against Syria, USSR foresaw confrontation and "grave catastrophe." USSR would take necessary actions including "*military*."[65] [Emphasis added.]

The President asked for a check of the translation and confirmation that the word was "military."

Intervention would not have been easy for the Soviet Union. The most likely possibility was a paratrooper landing or air transport of troops. Although less difficult to accomplish, a Soviet air strike or shore bombardment undoubtedly would have brought American counteraction. Soviet use of submarines or land-based missiles in such a situation was even more unlikely. Moscow probably felt its intervention had to be confined to Israeli forces on Syrian territory. However, this also might have meant American intervention. In any case, Israel had control of the air, and this made any Soviet intervention extremely hazardous.

While American decision makers felt Soviet intervention would have been most difficult,[66] there were other indications, probably

[61]*Pravda,* June 11, 1967, p. 1. *Current Digest of the Soviet Press* (*CDSP*), Vol. XIX, No. 23, p. 4. The text of the note was released at 8:16 A.M. Tass International Service in English, June 10, 1967.

[62]U.N., Security Council, Provisional Record of 1355th Meeting, June 10, 1967, Document No. S/PV 1355.

[63]Ibid.

[64]Ibid., p. 42.

[65]Informed White House source, letter.

[66]Secretary of State Rusk commented, "It was pretty complicated for them to bring forces to bear. We didn't think they would. It was a long way away

provided by intelligence sources, in addition to the threatening tone on the hot line that led the group in the White House basement to conclude that the Soviets might be seriously considering intervention.[67] Upon receipt of the hot line threat, the President remarked that he was not going to let the Russians get away with it. Turning to Secretary McNamara, the President asked where the Sixth Fleet was and learned that it was moving northwest in the vicinity of Crete. The President ordered Secretary McNamara to "Turn it around." McNamara called the National Military Command Center, and shortly thereafter the Sixth Fleet "turned full speed towards Syria."[68] It was anticipated that Moscow would understand the meaning of the ship movements instantly. At the same time, the President ensured that pressure was applied to Israel to cease fire.[69] President Johnson sent a bland hot line reply saying that "so far as we knew, Israel was preparing to observe the cease-fire."[70] The President apparently pointed out that the United States could not control Israel and that if Moscow had been more cooperative and responsive to U.S. diplomatic overtures in May, it would not have been in such a predicament. By the time major units of the Sixth Fleet were speeding toward the east, Israel and Syria were close to agreement on a cessation of hostilities. Around 10 A.M. the Israeli delegate reported that, as a result of the meeting with General Bull, Israel would agree to cease hostilities if Syria complied.[71] But moments later Ambassador Fedorenko charged that Israel had "repeatedly bombed Damascus."[72] Turning to Ambassador Goldberg, he warned: "it is the United States in the first instance which should *before it is too late,* take practical measures to call a halt to the criminal aggression which is fraught with very *ominous consequences.*"[73] (Emphasis added.)

The increasing severity of Ambassador Fedorenko's remarks was apparently also reflected in two additional hot line messages dur-

and they had no easy means of access with Turkey and Iran in the way. They might have flown in some paratroopers and it wouldn't have been too easy with Israel commanding the air." Rusk, interview.

[67]See, for example, interview with an informed White House source conducted March 6, 1969. Appendix B, Question 4.

[68]Informed White House source, letter.

[69]Velie, "The Week the Hot Line Burned," p. 42. Ambassador Goldberg remarked during the debate in the Security Council on June 10, 1969, that the United States had attempted to implement the cease-fire on Friday "by private diplomatic action." U.N., Document S/PV 1355, June 10, 1967, p. 82.

[70]This is not a direct quote of the message but rather a quote of the letter from an informed White House source.

[71]U.N., Security Council, 1355th meeting, p. 76.

[72]Ibid., p. 77.

[73]Ibid., p. 80.

ing the morning. However, at 10:12 A.M. General Bull had confirmed to the United Nations that Israel was prepared to cooperate on a cease-fire if Syria also agreed. The cease-fire was scheduled to go into effect at 12:30 P.M.[74] The U.N. meeting closed at 11:15 A.M. and shortly afterward word was received that both sides had agreed to a cease-fire at 12:30 P.M.[75] This in effect concluded the superpower confrontation. Soon thereafter the Sixth Fleet stopped its forward movement toward Syria. Table 5.3 is a summary of important exchanges during this brief cold war challenge.

In this short period the President demonstrated his confidence that the United States had the capability to counter Soviet military intervention. While it seems unlikely that the Soviets actually intended to intervene, the threat was very real to American decision makers clustered in the White House basement.

Understandably, members of Congress did not participate in the crucial decisions concerning confrontation with the Soviet Union. Congressmen continued to emphasize noninvolvement but not presumably because of fear of direct Soviet intervention. Not unexpectedly, certain congressmen urged the government to stand by Israel. But there was reference to the limitations imposed by Vietnam even by the most outspoken defenders of the Israeli cause. Senator Javits, for example, said that if Israel were in danger of liquidation, he could not "believe no matter what . . . *the other responsibilities and obligations* of our nation, that we will fail to meet this one squarely."[76] The Senate majority leader believed that "not even the combined forces of those who favored action in concert with other countries would command a majority."[77] Senator Mansfield subsequently explained the basis for his comments: "My colleagues on the Foreign Relations Committee and those I talked to on the Floor *seemed to be of one mind that there should be no action, either unilaterally or in concert with other powers,* in the mid-East *at that time, because of our being in*

[74]Ibid., p. 89.

[75]U.N., Security Council, Provisional Record of 1356th Meeting, June 10, 1967, Document No. S/PV 1356, p. 17.

[76](Emphasis added.) Statement of Senator Jacob Javits, U.S., *Congressional Record*, 90th Cong., 1st sess., Vol. 133, No. 87 (June 5, 1967), p. S7641. He also asserted that "we Americans have a great historic disposition as to what we do when justice is imperiled and *our means allow us to do something about it.*"

[77]*The Washington Post* article by J. Y. Smith, "Hill Leader Cautions on War Commitments," June 6, 1967, p. A6. This is a quotation of the article, but Senator Mansfield has agreed it was an accurate interpretation of his views. Letter from Senator Mike Mansfield to Lt. Comdr. J. T. Howe, USN, dated February 22, 1968.

Vietnam, and the cost it was taking of us in men and material."[78] (Emphasis added.) In the minds of congressmen, the Vietnam commitment was apparently an overriding concern. Although difficult to prove, the implication was that Congress might have felt differently without a war in Vietnam. Apparently, Secretary Rusk was warned that there would be no "backing in any unilateral US intervention."[79] Reportedly, none of the fifty-odd senators attending special briefings on June 5, 1967, "favored military action in the Middle East."[80] At the same time lawmakers favoring strong American action could comfort themselves with Israel's rapid demonstration of capability and President Johnson's refusal to guarantee Congress that he would not intervene without their consent.

Public opinion reacted similarly. Both the Gallup and Harris polls showed predominant sympathy for Israel,[81] but reported the margin against sending troops or supplies to Israel was more than two to one.[82] Subsequent polls obtained similar results.[83] Nonetheless, these surveys did not indicate what the response would be to Russian intervention. In such a case there probably would have been

[78]Mansfield, letter. On June 5, 1967, Senator Mansfield had commented that the "lack of support . . . was largely the result of the war in Vietnam." *The Washington Post,* June 6, 1967, p. A6.

[79]*The Washington Post* column by Rowland Evans and Robert Novak, "Uncle Sam Taken Off Hook," June 7, 1967, p. A23. *The New York Times* reported that "the dominant Congressional reaction today to the outbreak of hostilities between Israel and the Arab states was that the US should take no unilateral action." Article by E. W. Kenworthy, "Reaction in Congress US Must Not Act Alone," June 6, 1967, p. 18. Secretary Rusk recalled that the consensus of Congress seemed to be that there should be no unilateral action. Rusk, interview.

[80]Letter from Mr. Seth Tillman, Special Consultant, Senate Committee on Foreign Relations, to Lt. Comdr. J. T. Howe, USN, dated March 4, 1969.

[81]Harris found the percentage to be 41 percent to 1 percent and Gallup 55 percent to 4 percent. Harris information from *New York Post,* June 10, 1967, supplied by Louis Harris and Associates. See Table 4.1, Part D, for Gallup results.

[82]In a Harris poll, 56 percent opposed and 24 percent favored such an action. See Table 4.1, Part L. Other Harris questions and the Gallup poll, although offering more attractive alternatives, indicated there was little support for American intervention. See Table 4.1, Parts A and B.

[83]A Harris survey released on October 9, 1967, showed that Americans favored sending more aid to Israel by 42 to 36 percent, but only 22 percent favored "sending US troops to back Israel if war breaks out" while 59 percent were opposed to this action. *The Washington Post,* October 9, 1967. A Harris survey on July 10, 1967, showed that a large majority favored the Israeli view on Middle Eastern questions. For example, 88 percent felt that Israel should be guaranteed passage through the Gulf of Aqaba, while only 1 percent disagreed. *The Washington Post,* July 10, 1967. In a Gallup poll released on July 9, 1967, only "one American in seven" thought that Israel should be required to give back all lands seized during the war. *The Gallup Report,* July 9, 1967.

Table 5.3 U.S.-Soviet Confrontation over Cessation of Hostilities in Syria, June 10, 1967

Time/ Event	War Situation	U.S. Position	U.S.-U.N. Position	U.S. Ships	USSR Position	USSR-United Nations	USSR Ships
4:30 A.M. emergency Security Council meeting	Israel: troops holding areas of Golan Heights; several columns approaching road junction of Quneitra; confused reports of possible Israeli bombing of Damascus; Syrian charge Israeli forces heading for Damascus. Israeli forces thirty-five miles from Damascus		The need to straighten out the facts	Well back from conflict; position south of Crete		Urgent and decisive measures necessary to halt Israel; if not done, consequences rest on those who hinder adoption of necessary measures; Bulgaria charges Israel seeks *coup d'état*	
8 A.M.	Quneitra surrounded by Israeli forces; Golan Heights positions completely encircled				Relations broken with Israel, sanctions threatened in note to Israel		No unusual movements

Time/ Event	War Situation	U.S. Position	U.S.-U.N. Position	U.S. Ships	USSR Position	USSR-United Nations	USSR Ships
8:10 A.M. U.N. meeting resumed	Reports of air strikes outside of Damascus in airport vicinity						
8:15 A.M.	Generals Dayan and Bull meeting to arrange cessation of hostilities						
8:30 A.M. (approx.)	Fall of Quneitra to Israel					Warning that responsibility for serious situation will rest with those who hinder Security Council; Soviet note to Israel concerning sanctions read	
9:05 A.M. (approx.)					Strong Soviet hot line warning of confrontation, "grave catastrophe," and threatening "military" actions		

Time/ Event	War Situation	U.S. Position	U.S.-U.N. Position	U.S. Ships	USSR Position	USSR-United Nations	USSR Ships
9:30 A.M. (approx.)		Hot line—United States belief that Israel is preparing to observe cease-fire; U.S. can't control Israel; diplomacy should succeed		President tells Secretary of Defense to move Sixth Fleet toward Syria			
10 A.M. (approx.)	Sporadic fighting				Second hot line warning	Charge that Israel has repeatedly bombed Damascus; United States warned it must take action before too late; reference to "very ominous" consequences	
10:12 A.M.	Gen. Bull confirms Israel will accept cease-fire at 12:30 P.M., if Syria cooperates	Hot line reply—restrained but firm. Diplomatic solution					

Time/ Event	War Situation	U.S. Position	U.S.-U.N. Position	U.S. Ships	USSR Position	USSR-United Nations	USSR Ships
11:15 A.M.	Adjournment of U.N. meeting						
11:30 A.M. (approx.)	Word that both sides agree to cease fire				Hot line message		
12:30 P.M.	Cease-fire effected	U.S. hot line reply					
1:00 P.M.				High-speed movement to-ward Syria by sixth fleet ships stopped			

much greater support for American military action. In late 1967, for instance, a small majority still felt the United States had an obligation to "defend other Vietnams if they are threatened by *communism*."[84]

The rapid Israeli victory eased American policy decisions during the crisis. It was the Soviet Union that was in the weaker political and military positions and resorted to threats in an attempt to extricate itself.

5.2 SOVIET POLICY

Determining Soviet intentions was a vital American concern. Moscow's initiation of hot line exchanges and the inactivity of warships provided an early indication of Russian restraint, but Kremlin policy remained contradictory and ambiguous throughout the crisis.

In initial Soviet broadcasts to Arab countries, Moscow seemed to adopt an attitude that was consistent with both the official government pronouncement of May 23, 1967, and an attitude of aloofness in the United Nations. The Arabs were told that the "organizers" would have to face the "firm response to this aggression by the USSR"[85] and that "The Arab states are ready to reply to the imperialists and their forces . . . in a decisive and united form. The people of the Arab States are not alone in their just struggle against the imperialist adventure."[86] These statements may have reflected an initial hope that the Arabs would be able to hold their own against Israel.

By 5:29 P.M. when the first government statement following the outbreak of hostilities was released, the Soviet attitude had become much more restrained. Moscow's official pronouncements were very mild under the circumstances. The Soviet government demanded that Israel "pull back its troops beyond the truce line" and reserved the "right to take all steps that may be necessitated by the situation."[87] However, Moscow had clarified the kinds of measures it had in mind by referring in the preceding sentence to the duty of the United Nations to "promptly take measures necessary to *restore peace*."[88] A subsequent Soviet broadcast claimed

[84](Emphasis added.) Forty-four percent felt the US had an obligation; 39 percent said it did not. Forty-two percent favored defense of Thailand; 39 percent opposed this hypothetical situation. *The Boston Globe* article by Louis Harris, "Stop Communists the Majority Say," December 30, 1967.

[85]Moscow in French broadcast to Maghrib countries at 2000 GMT on June 5, 1967. This statement had been lifted from the basic Russian policy statement of May 23, 1967.

[86]Moscow in Arabic to Arab world, June 5, 1967, 1400 GMT.

[87]Tass International Service in English, 2129 GMT, June 5, 1967.

[88]Ibid. (Emphasis added.)

that Russia was *already* "seriously supporting the Arab countries regarding the armed aggression of Israel," which enjoys the support of the United States.[89] The Arab audience was reminded of Soviet help given in past cases of aggression, Suez and Lebanon. Moscow alleged that "in this fashion" it was "in practice" providing "support."[90] Soviet clients were being told not to hope for more than words of encouragement.

Although Israel was accused of aggression and demands were issued that military action be halted, serious Russian threats did not occur until after the military outcome was clear and Moscow had shifted its line in the United Nations to support a cease-fire resolution not stipulating an Israeli troop withdrawal. Why Moscow delayed accepting an American version of a cease-fire agreement remains a mystery. Russia, whose ally was being administered a smashing defeat, clearly had the most urgent interest. The war's outcome was obvious on the morning of June 5, and Jordan and Syria had not yet been invaded.

One plausible explanation of Soviet aloofness in the United Nations followed by insistence on an unconditional withdrawal clause is that Moscow felt the United Arab Republic could block an Israeli advance. Although the air war was decided in the first hours, there were fierce land battles near Israel's border throughout June 5. The Russians may have hoped that Egypt could at the same time carry out its battle plan and cut across the southern Negev. Such a move would have isolated the port of Eilat and linked Egypt with Jordan. Of course, even after Moscow realized the Egyptians were being badly mauled, it could anticipate charges of a sellout if it capitulated to U.S. demands concerning a cease-fire. A "high Soviet official" subsequently claimed that Nasser refused to follow Moscow's advice and insisted on an ill-fated counteroffensive.[91]

Soviet statements gradually became more strident. During the afternoon of June 7, 1967, Moscow threatened to break diplomatic relations with Israel and obtained U.N. approval of a reassertion of the cease-fire resolution.[92] Israel agreed to accept a cease-fire. The Soviet note to Israel asserted that the "Soviet Government

[89]Moscow in Persian to Iran, 1630 GMT, June 6, 1967.

[90]Ibid.

[91]*Le Nouvel Observateur,* "Pourquoi Moscow a lâché Nasser," No. 135 (June 14–June 20, 1967).

[92]The Soviet note to Israel was published by Tass International Service at 1:01 P.M. on June 7, 1967. The U.N. session, in which the note was quoted, began at 2:20 P.M. The resolution on a cease-fire was voted at about 2:30 P.M. to be effective at 4 P.M. Israel agreed to the cease-fire, but the Arab states refused.

will consider and implement other necessary measures stemming from Israel's aggressive policy."[93] On June 9 the Communist central committees promised a "resolute rebuff" if "Israel does not stop the aggression."[94] This was the prelude to strong warnings of June 10, 1967, concerning a cessation of hostilities in Syria. However, as early as May 23, 1967, Moscow had officially warned that aggression would be met with "strong opposition."[95]

Moscow's warnings reflected serious concern about Israel's penetration into Syria. Reportedly, a high Soviet foreign office official subsequently commented that "if the Israelis had captured Damascus, Soviet armed forces would have intervened *one way or another.*"[96] While it is unlikely that Tel Aviv ever envisaged a march to Damascus, Moscow was obviously apprehensive about the possibility. The fall of the Syrian capital would have drastic repercussions for the shaky Ba'th regime and represent a major loss of Soviet credibility with its allies throughout the world. It is speculated that Moscow's major concern was not the loss of Damascus itself but the Arab image of the Soviet Union because of its failure to act. A broadcast to the Arab world claimed the Soviet Union had provided extensive assistance and repeated several times the Soviet threat to impose sanctions on Israel. But, at the same time, it revealingly alluded to charges that the Soviet Union had not done enough: "The aim of the propaganda is clear: to drive a *wedge between the Soviet and Arab peoples* and to endeavor through this to weaken the forces of the Arabs in the struggle against the aggressors."[97] (Emphasis added.) Moscow may also have been worried about the embarrassing possibility that Russian military personnel might be captured.

It remains a mystery why the shelling of Israel from the Golan Heights of Syria was intensified on the fourth day of the war and

[93]*Pravda,* June 8, 1967, p. 1. *CDSP,* Vol. XIX, No. 23 (June 28, 1967). The warning was repeated in broadcasts in Arabic to Arab world, 1930 GMT, June 7, 1967, Boris Rykov commentary. This warning was added in a rebroadcast. The original commentary at 1600 GMT had not contained the warning.

[94]Tass International Service in English, June 9, 1967, 2205 GMT, "Statement by Central Committees of Communist and Workers Parties and Governments. . . ." Both Kosygin and Brezhnev attended.

[95]Soviet statement of May 23, 1967. This statement was reiterated on June 5, 1967. See Sections 4.2 and 5.2.

[96](Emphasis added.) This is Alexander Werth's account of what the official told him rather than a direct quotation. "Year of Jubilee: The USSR at Fifty," *The Nation,* Vol. 205, No. 14 (October 30, 1967), p. 427. Moscow apparently wanted to be credited with having such motives whether it actually had them during the crisis or not.

[97]Moscow in Arabic to the Arab world, June 10, 1967.

why Russian advisors had not been withdrawn to safer areas. Firing instructions in Russian were intercepted, and reportedly some Soviets were captured in Israel's sweep around the Syrian position.[98] Israel began its move against the Syrian artillery fortifications at 5:30 A.M. on June 9. Possibly Moscow felt that Tel Aviv could be deterred from attacking the heavily fortified positions. Instead, Israel was further provoked by the shelling. The Syrian artillery was dug into steep ridges and protected from air attack by overhanging cliffs and thick concrete bunkers. In making their assault, the Israelis had to bulldoze roads for their tanks. Moscow may still have hoped to salvage some prestige from the debacle by claiming to have protected Syria. If it considered the artillery positions to be impregnable, using Soviet advisors to direct the defense made sense; Moscow could claim that it helped hold off Israel. If the Soviet advisors had left at the first sign of a fight, it would have meant a great loss of face for Moscow throughout the Middle East. Although some preparations for intervention may have been in progress, Russia had little ready capacity available in the Mediterranean. The Soviets made no actual move to bolster their forces in Syria.

Movements of Soviet ships in the Mediterranean were circumspect throughout the crisis.[99] On the day the fighting began, Russian vessels not engaged in shadowing remained in their anchorages near the eastern shores of Crete and Cyprus.[100] By their deeds the Soviets indicated they were not going to become involved even though their huge investment in military equipment for the Arabs was being demolished. In the final hours of the crisis intervention may actually have been contemplated. However, as long as there was a possibility of American counteraction, it was unlikely Moscow actually intended to intervene.[101]

[98]Robert J. Donovan, *Israel's Fight for Survival* (New York: New American Library, 1967), p. 128.
[99]The only overt move reported was the systematic harassment of the *America*'s task group on June 8, 1967, by a Russian destroyer and patrol craft. Although Soviet warships had frequently tried to disrupt U.S. formations in the past, such tactics might seem inconsistent with the Soviet Navy's otherwise cautious conduct during the crisis. One logical explanation may be that the ships were trying to stop the task force from tracking a probable Soviet submarine contact that had been held since the previous day. *The New York Times* article by Neil Sheehan, "Russians Continue to Harrass 6th Fleet," June 8, aboard *America,* June 9, 1967, p. 1.
[100]Wylie, interview.
[101]There appears to be a difference in the author's interpretation of Soviet intentions and the apparent assessment of them by White House personnel at the time of the crisis. However, since the author has not viewed the intelligence reports held at the time, it is difficult to make a valid judgment on this issue.

Soviet treatment of U.S. policy and the various events involving the United States provides additional insight into their crisis tactics. Claims that the fighting was part of American global strategy and calls for withdrawal of the Sixth Fleet from the Mediterranean continued the propaganda theme of the buildup phase. However, during the actual crisis references to participation of American forces seemed to be de-emphasized. Most of the specific charges of American participation in the war were made after cessation of hostilities. Initially, there were, of course, numerous accusations that provocative maneuvers of the Sixth Fleet had encouraged Israel to resort to war.[102] For example, the Pentagon was accused of having "whipped up the Israeli general staff with a deliberate show of guns by the American Sixth Fleet."[103] At noon on June 6, 1967, during the confrontation over a cease-fire there did appear to be a significant reference to the movements of the Sixth Fleet. In complaining that the Western powers while "declaring neutrality in the war" were "in fact giving *active help* to Israel," a Soviet broadcast stated that "the U.S. Sixth Fleet has approached the coasts of the Arab countries and taken up a threatening position there."[104] A broadcast at 1:30 P.M. complained of the "conclusive maneuvers" of the Sixth Fleet.[105] These commentaries seemed to reflect Soviet recognition of the significance of the repositioning of the Sixth Fleet on June 6. By 6:30 P.M. that afternoon the Soviet Union had backed down on its cease-fire stand.

The Russians were circumspect in reporting Arab charges of Sixth Fleet participation in the Israeli attack. Moscow carefully attributed the allegations to Arab sources. The accusations were repeated only once over Moscow domestic radio and never in the English-language services.[106] The Russians obviously knew better from re-

[102]For example, the initial Soviet broadcasts concerning the war referred to the "threatening maneuvers" of the Sixth Fleet. Moscow Radio in English to the United Kingdom, 1200 GMT, June 5, 1967. Moscow Radio in Arabic to Arab world, 1400 GMT, June 5, 1967; Moscow Radio in French to Europe, 1730 GMT, June 6, 1967.

[103]*Izvestia* article by N. Polyanov, "The Cookstove of the Israeli Adventure," June 8, 1967, p. 5. This article may have been deliberately toned down in the Tass release summarizing the article in English. "Encouraged" is substituted for "whipped up," and "demonstration" is used for "deliberate show" in Tass International Service in English, 1713 GMT, June 7, 1967.

[104]Moscow in German to Germany, June 6, 1967. The broadcast stressed Arab gratitude for the resolute Soviet statement demanding withdrawal of the Israeli forces. (Emphasis added.)

[105]Moscow in French to Europe, June 6, 1967, Yurily Zhvedkov commentary.

[106]Jean Riollot, "The Middle East Crisis: The Soviet Role and Soviet Media Reactions Since the Outbreak of Hostilities," Radio Liberty Dispatch dated July 28, 1967, p. 1.

ports of ships trailing the Sixth Fleet carriers. As Admiral Wylie put it, 'after the initial Israeli air attacks were followed by Egyptian claims of U.S. involvement, we were able informally to refer the Egyptians to the Soviets for conclusive evidence that no U.S. aircraft had been flying in that area at that time."[107] The Israeli release on June 8, 1967, of a taped conversation alleged to have taken place between King Hussein and Nasser further indicated that the charges were perhaps a sham.[108] However, both Arab leaders may have been convinced that Israel had help because of the direction of the attack and the number of sorties flown by each Israeli pilot in rapid succession. The Soviets avoided a possible propaganda trap. It was probably not Moscow's intention to build up a false theme of practical U.S. aid for Israel, when the Russians did not intend to provide any for the Arabs.

The assault on the *Liberty* did not receive much coverage either. Initial reports commented that the attack had "created a very tense situation in Washington."[109] After the crisis Moscow implied that the *Liberty* was engaged in suspicious activities and speculated that the attack might have been staged in order to create "a provocative excuse for the interference of U.S. troops in the armed conflict."[110] By and large, Soviet references to the United States

[107]Wylie, letter. In a news report published on September 1, 1967, asserting that Nasser now admitted the United States had not intervened militarily, it was stated that within hours of the first accusations, "the Soviet Union—whose ships had been closely shadowing American vessels—had bluntly told the Egyptians that Moscow had positive evidence that the United States had not intervened in the war." *The New York Times* article by Hendrick Smith, "Envoys Say Nasser Now Concedes US Didn't Help Israel." September 16, 1967, p. 3.

[108]An excerpt from the tape read as follows:

Nasser: "Hello, will we say the US and England or just the US?"

Hussein: "The US and England."

Nasser: "Good. King Hussein will make an announcement and I will make an announcement. . . . and we will see to it that the Syrians make an announcement that American and British airplanes are taking part against us from their aircraft carriers." Conversation listed under June 8 in Susan Barnes, Arsene Eglis, and Olivia Gilliam, *Soviet News Media and the Middle East Crisis,* Radio Liberty Research Paper No. 16. See also *The Guardian,* "Tape of Arab Plotting," June 9, 1967. Nasser finally admitted that he was mistaken but not that the accusations were deliberately made knowing they were false. *The Christian Science Monitor,* "Nasser Shifts View on U.S. Air Cover," March 5, 1968. The tape was "submitted to a New York voice print analyst for verification." Donovan, *Israel's Fight for Survival,* p. 109.

[109]Tass International Service in English, 0828 GMT, June 9, 1967. An almost identical commentary appeared in *Izvestia,* June 10, 1967, p. 2.

[110]Moscow Domestic Service in Russian, June 14, 1967. Reports of suspicious activities were given in Moscow Radio, June 11, 1967, as reported in Radio Liberty Research Paper No. 16. This paper is misleading in its statement that there was no mention in *Pravda* or over Moscow radio until this broadcast of the *Liberty* incident.

from June 5, 1967, were cautious. While charging that the United States was responsible for Israeli aggression, the Soviet media tended away from accusations of direct participation.

In the aftermath of the crisis charges continued that the United States encouraged Israel to attack. Premier Kosygin declared to the United Nations that "with all certainty" Israel "enjoyed outside support," and that "statements" and "practical actions" were "direct encouragement to commit acts of aggression."[111] Among the examples Kosygin cited were a plan for establishing an international naval force and "the military demonstrations by the American Sixth Fleet off the coast of the Arab States."[112] In a series of magazine articles the United States was accused of having "pushed,"[113] "planned,"[114] and been "directly responsible"[115] for the Israeli aggression.[116] The Sixth Fleet's "provocative maneuvers"[117] were depicted as the main instrument for carrying out U.S. policy.[118]

In light of what happened during the crisis there is some truth in Moscow's conception of the Sixth Fleet's role. Soviet propaganda indicated the meaning of the fleet's presence, and crisis maneuvers had been understood all too well. The United States was claimed to have been "ready and threatening to swing its Mediterranean big stick."[119] One article stressed that Washington would not have al-

[111] *The New York Times,* "Text of Kosygin Address to General Assembly," June 20, 1967, p. 16.
[112] Ibid.
[113] Alexander Kushnir, "Truth About Israel's Aggression," *Soviet Military Review,* No. 8 (August 1967), p. 57. See also "Main Stages in Soviet Foreign Policy," *International Affairs,* No. 1 (January 1968), p. 55.
[114] G. Gerasimov, "Pentagon 1967," *International Affairs,* No. 7 (July 1967).
[115] "Aggression Against the Arab World," *New Times,* No. 24 (June 14, 1967), p. 2.
[116] In addition to the three articles cited in the preceding footnotes, a number of others follow a similar line. See, for example, A. Kafman, "US Big Stick in the Mediterranean," *International Affairs,* No. 8 (August 1967), p. 74; Vladimir Ukranistev, "Tool of Provocations and Aggressions," *Soviet Military Review,* No. 8 (August 1967), p. 58; Y. Bochkaryov, "The Forces Behind the Aggressor," *New Times,* No. 25 (June 21, 1967), A. Akimov, "US and British Armed Forces and the Middle East Crisis," *International Affairs,* No. 8 (August 1967), p. 105; O. Alexandrou, "Israel's Aggression," *Soviet Military Review,* No. 7 (July 1967), p. 57.
[117] Kushnir, "Truth About Israel's Aggression," p. 57.
[118] The articles listed in footnotes 115 and 116 use similar words.
[119] Kafman, "US Big Stick," p. 74. He also charged that the United States did not preclude using the Sixth Fleet, citing and totally distorting an article from *The New York Times* of May 25, 1967, by Hanson W. Baldwin. He also stated that the ships were moved "closer and closer to the shores . . ." and that "phantom fighters were ready at their catapults."

lowed Israel to be beaten,[120] indicating that American intentions were apparently clear to Moscow and perhaps offering an explanation for Soviet inaction.

The campaign following the crisis apparently attempted to capitalize on dislike of the United States and Israel in order to influence Arab states and make the United States as unwelcome as possible in the Mediterranean. Brezhnev's call for Sixth Fleet withdrawal was repeated in a number of articles.[121] In addition, Soviet comments may have reflected genuine concern that the United States was continuing a campaign of rollback. American action was cited as an example of the "stepup in the aggression of the US foreign policy line."[122]

Although the Soviet propaganda attacks were not surprising, the number of specific spurious accusations of U.S. participation is interesting. It was claimed that Sixth Fleet ships were concentrated in the "coastal waters of the Gaza area" since they knew the invasion would be in that direction.[123] The fleet also was falsely accused of jamming Egyptian radio networks.[124] In an article seven months after the crisis the Soviets charged that the Israeli battle plan had been corrected by NATO headquarters and that Israeli officers were trained in Vietnam.[125] Marine movements were also resurrected to show direct U.S. involvement. A battalion of marines was reputed to have been "sea-lifted to the Suez Canal area" during the crisis.[126] Another report had the "landing group" stationed in the "immediate vicinity of the Israeli coast, as a hint to America's wards that they would be given help in case of need.[127]

[120] Y. Bochkaryov, "The Forces Behind the Aggressor," *New Times*, No 25 (June 21, 1967).

[121] See, for example, Kafman, "US Big Stick," p. 75; and Valdimir Ukrain, "Tool of Provocations and Aggressions," *Soviet Military Review*, No. 8 (August 1967), p. 58.

[122] See, for example, L. Brezhnev, "Speech by CPSU General Secretary, 5 July at Kremlin reception for graduates of military academies," Moscow Domestic Service in Russian, July 5, 1967. See also N. T. Fedorenko, "Perfidity and Aggression," *New Times*, No. 26 (June 28, 1967), p. 3; and S. Astakhov, "More about the Secret Springs of the Israeli Aggression;" *International Affairs*, No. 10 (October 1967), p. 39.

[123] Kafman, "US Big Stick," p. 74.

[124] B. Teplinsky, "US Military Programme," *International Affairs*, No. 8 (August 1967), p. 50. Admiral Wylie confirmed that the charge was not true. Wylie, interview.

[125] I. Belyaev and Y. Primakov, "Lessons of the 1967 Middle East Crisis," *International Affairs*, No. 3 (March 1968), p. 41.

[126] A. Akimov, "US and British Armed Forces and the Middle East Crisis," *International Affairs*, No. 8 (August 1967), p. 105.

[127] Kafman, "US Big Stick," p. 74. Still another article described 3500 Marines heading out of Naples and another 1800 approaching Israel. Alexandrou, "Israel's Aggression," p. 57.

Throughout the war phase Moscow appeared not to be interested in a confrontation with the United States. While the Soviets manifested anxiety concerning the fate of Damascus, it seems doubtful that they actually planned to provide direct support for Syria or Egypt. In the aftermath of the crisis the Russians tried to salvage some propaganda gains by accusing the United States of directly aiding Israel. Moscow may also have been trying to retain some prestige for its clients as well as the USSR by associating U.S. power with Israeli success. However, prior to the cease-fire Moscow, for the most part, avoided leveling direct charges against the United States.

The Russians may have planned some sort of reprisal against Israel as a further warning if Damascus had been in danger of falling. Nonetheless although Moscow talked tough, Russian deeds were circumspect. It is not likely that the USSR actually was willing to risk war with the United States. If the crisis had continued for a few more hours, with American ships moving toward Syria, there would have been a clearer indication of Soviet intentions. However, Tel Aviv evidently never planned to go on to Damascus and, having achieved its military goals in Syria, was willing to end the hostilities.

Without examination of the exact text of Soviet hot line messages and review of all intelligence information available at the time, it is difficult to predict with confidence whether or not the Soviets would have intervened if Israel had marched toward Damascus. However, this was probably not the Soviet intention, although the United States had to take the hot line warnings seriously. The tone of Soviet public statements, the inactivity of their naval forces, and the media treatment of the crisis seemed to indicate that the Soviet Union was simply trying to retain as much credibility as possible with its clients in the face of a crushing defeat. If Soviet plans to intervene militarily were being hastily formulated, it is speculated that the continued movement of U.S. forces towards the area would have eventually caused cancellation. The next move contemplated by the Soviet Union probably was a "sanction" more severe than breaking diplomatic relations but not having the potentially dangerous consequences of a landing of Russian forces in Syria.

5.3 BRITISH POLICY

The stand taken by Great Britain was not surprising if one considers the evolution of its policy during the buildup phase. Britain was concerned primarily with protecting economic interests from Arab retaliation and hoped to avoid the appearance of taking sides.[128] The government immediately announced that British armed forces had been ordered to avoid involvement in the conflict.[129]

London was therefore highly incensed by Arab accusations that the United Kingdom's aircraft had helped Israel. In a speech to Commons, Prime Minister Wilson categorically denied the "monstrous story" and asserted that British aircraft carriers had been "1000 miles away."[130] Foreign Secretary Brown was extremely bitter about the persistence of the accusations. He called the stories a "downright lie" and charged the United Arab Republic with trying to excuse its military failures.[131] Arab governments were asked "not to disrupt commercial arrangements which are as much in their interest as ours."[132] But the Suez Canal had already been closed, Iraq had ceased pumping oil, and Kuwait had forbidden oil exports to British and American destinations.

Mr. Wilson avoided revealing what Britain would do if Israel were being defeated, but he stressed U.N. obligations as opposed to moral commitments to Israel.[133] He implied that military support for Israel was extremely remote. However, Israel's battlefield successes made the policy of impartiality more acceptable to those favoring stronger action on behalf of Israel.

Parliament supported the government's stand. The opposition leader endorsed the call for restraint since "so much" was "at

[128]In an official policy statement in Commons on June 5, 1967, Foreign Secretary Brown stated the "British concern is not to take sides." In reply to a question he stated that "national interests" and interests of peace necessitated "avoiding being thought to be taking sides on the merits of the issue." *The Times,* June 6, 1967, p. 7.

[129]Ibid.

[130]He was informing Parliament that the charges already had been denied. "Text of statement to the House of Commons by Prime Minister Harold Wilson," official text provided by British Information Services, T. 26, June 6, 1967, p. 2.

[131]"Text of a statement by Foreign Secretary George Brown in House of Commons on June 7, 1967," British Information Service, official text, No. T. 27, June 7, 1967, p. 2.

[132]"Statement by Harold Wilson, June 6, 1967," British Information Services, p. 1. Foreign Minister Brown warned, in a statement that appeared to reflect Britain's overriding economic concern, that the "action taken" had come at a time of "oil surplus," and that the Arabs might find they had "done their own economic interests much greater harm" than Britain's. "Statement by George Brown, June 7, 1967," British Information Services, official text, No. T. 27, June 7, 1967, p. 3.

[133]He seemed to dodge a question from the leader of the Liberal Party concerning the "continuing moral obligation for the future" of Israel. Question of Mr. Thorpe, *The Guardian,* June 7, 1967.

stake in this matter.[134] But there was not a clear consensus in Commons that Britain should stay out of the conflict if Israel were being defeated. *The Times* reported that "most of them add" that Britain could not "hold to that line if Israel were being militarily defeated."[135] *The Guardian* commented that while the government position had "pleased a majority of the Labour Party back benchers," their "current nightmare" was that they might have "to do something practical to protect Israel's 'right to live.' "[136]

Sympathy for Israel was widespread, but, as in the United States, the British public did not seem to favor active intervention. Polls indicated that sending troops to help Israel would be favored only as a last resort.[137] The influential *Times* editorialized that in spite of "commercial and political interests" Britain "even without the US" could not allow "the destruction of Israel."[138] *The Guardian,* on the other hand, emphasized the need to obtain a cease-fire.[139]

British fleet moves were in keeping with the professed desire to avoid involvement. The Royal Navy was reported to be "standing well back from the center of the fighting zone."[140] This typified the entire British policy, which appeared to manifest a desire to stand "well back." With more to lose than Washington by antagonizing the Arabs, London made every effort to appear neutral during this period. There was little inclination to become involved, but the United Kingdom might have acted militarily in concert with the United States if circumstances has demanded it.

5.4 EVALUATION OF U.S. CAPABILITY

Although the American role, as perceived by the President, probably changed little between the buildup and crisis, there were some important clarifications during the period between June 5, 1967, and June 10, 1967. American forces in the field and officials in the State Department had been very carefully neutral during the

[134]Statement of Mr. Edward Heath, *Hansard Parliamentary Debates,* House of Commons (5th Series), Vol. 747 (June 5, 1967), p. 642.
[135]*The Times,* June 6, 1967, p. 1.
[136]*The Guardian,* June 6, 1967, p. 1. Karl E. Meyer reported from London that the Labor Government was "divided on what course to follow with Cabinet debate reportedly revealing a 'hawk' vs. 'dove' division." *The Washington Post,* June 6, 1967, p. A6.
[137]The Gallup sampling was limited by the choices offered and did not necessarily indicate defense of Israel, if it was being defeated, would not be popular. Fifty-six percent were sympathetic to Israel, while 5 percent were sympathetic to Arab states. See Table 4.1, Parts D and E.
[138]*The Times* editorial, "The Aims of War," June 6, 1967.
[139]*The Guardian* editorial, "A War to be Stopped," June 6, 1967, p. 8.
[140]*The Times,* June 6, 1967, p. 10.

buildup phase. For many of them, unfamiliar with the details of the Soviet-American confrontations, U.S. policy appeared to remain carefully neutral throughout the crisis. The White House had vigorously joined in the effort to persuade Israel not to attack. Nonetheless, early in the war Israel's uncertainty about American backing began to be dispelled and the worst suspicions of Cairo, Damascus, and Moscow were confirmed.

Initially, confidence in Soviet interest in restraint was increased by timely Russian initiation of hot line exchanges, by the tone of Moscow's official statements, and above all by the circumspect conduct of their naval forces. However, seemingly unexplainable Soviet stalling in the United Nations provided an element of uncertainty about Moscow's intentions. During the difference over a cease-fire resolution on June 6, 1967, and the confrontation concerning halting the fighting in Syria on June 10, 1967, Washington was gravely concerned about Soviet intentions.

Defense estimates of U.S. capability to intervene effectively probably decreased even further because of the rapidity of a war largely confined to a land engagement. Increasingly, it became obvious that Israel needed no assistance in fighting restricted to Arab opponents. At the same time, the President demonstrated his belief that the United States was militarily capable of countering any Soviet intervention.

Although strong public sympathy for Israel was manifested during the fighting, there was little enthusiasm for intervention by U.S. forces in Israel's behalf. However, the President's concern about the interpretation of the expression "neutral in thought, word, and deed" indicated that the White House was sensitive to the domestic as well as international implications of American policy.

At the same time the careful wording of official U.S. pronouncements and the emphasis on neutrality seemingly reflected concern about the potentially damaging repercussions for Arab-American relations from the appearance of close association with Israel. Officials were obviously upset by false Arab accusations of Western participation in the initial Israeli air strikes. However, since circumspect U.S. conduct appeared to have little influence on the accusations by Arab leaders, careful consideration of political and economic implications became less important.

With the outbreak of fighting, the Gulf of Aqaba blockade question was upstaged. Consequently, dependence on the United Kingdom lessened. However, as the possibility of Soviet intervention increased, British naval power in the Mediterranean became more important. United Kingdom assistance would have been particularly valuable if American lives and property had been seriously threatened in the Arab states south of Suez. London's diplomatic support was also helpful but of less significance during this phase.

During the crisis it soon became apparent that predictions of Israel's military capability were correct and that American requirements would be limited to keeping the Soviets neutralized. The movement of ships[141] toward the eastern Mediterranean on June 6 and the decision to send American units toward Syria on June 10 indicated that Washington felt capable of matching an apparent Russian threat to intervene. From the beginning the United States expressed interest in a cease-fire. For the Soviet Union the need for a cease-fire became acute. Although U.S. capability factors had not changed significantly, it was clearer that decision makers felt American power was sufficient to deter Soviet intervention.

[141]Emphasis in this analysis has been concentrated on naval and marine forces, which were the primary military factors in this conflict. But there were also U.S. airborne units in Germany and some troops ready to be airlifted from the United States. Such movements, however, depend on available friendly air fields and air superiority. The British also had some troops on Cyprus and in Aden, as well as aircraft and forces in other parts of the region.

6. ANALYSIS AND CONCLUSIONS

The Middle East crisis of 1967 provided a most challenging problem for American foreign policy. Washington had to cope with a difficult crisis while being heavily burdened in Vietnam. The situation was further complicated by the proximity of Soviet warships to the U.S. Sixth Fleet and threats from Moscow to intervene in order to halt Israel's advance. Both superpowers considered the Mideast to be an area of vital interest, and each sought to prevent the dominance of the other in the region.

The crisis had many dynamic dimensions. The buildup phase could be viewed as a cut-and-dried affair in which little likelihood of outside intervention was anticipated. Seemingly, the superpowers tacitly agreed to attempt to restrain the antagonists and avoid direct involvement; however, elements of uncertainty and suspense existed in both phases of the crisis. There was give-and-take between Washington and Moscow and no firm agreement from either side to keep out.

Similar ambiguity existed domestically. Although there were numerous congressional briefings on the situation, the President was unwilling to assure Congress that he would seek its consent prior to taking military action.[1] The chairman of the Senate Foreign Relations Committee emerged from briefings on June 5, 1967, claiming he still had no conception of the President's policy.[2]

As it turned out, Congress had little influence on decisions made during two serious tests of will during the crisis phase. The United States held firm in the face of possible Soviet intervention. The first test involved the terms of the U.N. cease-fire resolution. The second test concerning Syria had certain limited analogies to the Cuban missile crisis. However, a firm agreement to cease hostilities came before the showdown reached its climax. Israel apparently never

[1]Senator J. W. Fulbright stated subsequent to the crisis that the administration's witness at a meeting on the crisis was "unwilling to answer either yes or no to the question of whether he was prepared to assure the committee that the President would not take the U.S. into war in the Middle East without the consent of Congress." Statement in U.S., Congress, Senate, Subcommittee on Separation of Powers of the Committee on the Judiciary, *Separation of Powers,* 90th Cong., 1st sess. (Washington, 1967), p. 49. Letter of Mr. Seth Tillman, who attended the meeting, to Lt. Comdr. J. T. Howe, USN, of March 4, 1969, also confirmed this was what the administration witness said.

[2]Statement of Senator J. W. Fulbright, *The Washington Post,* June 6, 1967.

intended to take Damascus, the major cause of Soviet anxiety. For Russia, the situation was also like a Korea in reverse. Territories of its allies were being invaded, but Moscow did not take military action to stop the aggressor. The United States was able to cope with its multicrisis situation; the Soviet Union was not.

6.1 CHANGES IN FACTORS AND THEIR INFLUENCE ON VARIOUS ALTERNATIVES

Factors affecting American capability varied in importance during the different phases of the crisis and according to the particular alternative being considered.

6.1.1 ESTIMATE OF SOVIET INTENTIONS TO INTERVENE Soviet professions of restraint during the buildup phase were substantiated by circumspect naval movements, but Soviet intentions were ambiguous. American concern over Moscow's objectives varied throughout the crisis. There was more uncertainty in the course of the crisis than in the buildup, but variations occurred almost daily during both phases. The atmosphere of uncertainty that grew out of the early days of the buildup continued through the confrontations over the Israeli advance on June 6 and June 10, 1967, although there was greater confidence that the problem could be localized in the week prior to the crisis and on the first and fourth days of the war. While the possibility of Russian intervention was remote, American policy makers could not afford to ignore any signs to the contrary such as Moscow's role in precipitating the crisis, Russian augmentation of naval forces just prior to the fighting, reluctance to cooperate in the United Nations even on the day fighting commenced, hot line trends, and indications of support for Damascus during the crisis.

It was unlikely that Moscow would have interfered with a Western attempt to restore free passage through the Gulf of Aqaba. Neither cautious Russian support of Nasser's initiative nor the realities of available power indicated that such a possibility was likely. The Soviets did not send credible intervention forces to the Mediterranean during the buildup phase. The possibility of some Soviet counteraction would have been slightly greater if the United States had elected to support Israel directly.

Once the war started and the Soviet Union made no military move to bolster the faltering Arabs, American confidence that Moscow did not intend to intervene was probably increased initially. Soviet threats, except possibly the final day's hot line transmissions, appeared to be mostly bluffs and political opportunism and an attempt to salvage what prestige was possible from the Arab debacle.

A factor of importance in Soviet calculations was assessment of American intentions. It was unlikely that Moscow would risk a direct military confrontation. Washington responded in restrained language to Soviet hot line threats but determined to make its resolve clear by movements of the Sixth Fleet. The hot line apparently was used by the Soviets primarily to emphasize Moscow's deep concern and to direct its warnings specifically to the President. Washington could not afford to discount the possibility of Russian intervention, particularly after the final hot line warning. Moscow apparently was deeply afraid that Damascus might fall, and the increasing intensity of its hot line warnings seemed to be a desperate effort to exert maximum pressure on the *United States* to halt Israel. Although such a judgment is speculative, it appears that Moscow did not intend to try stopping the Israeli advance by military intervention.

6.1.2 DEFENSE ESTIMATES OF U.S. CAPABILITY TO INTERVENE Military estimates were an important factor in American assessments of various alternatives. Reduced defense capability was a factor of some significance when considering a test of the Gulf of Aqaba blockade. It was a more restrictive element in contemplating intervention on behalf of Israel, but it was not the dominant consideration. As an Israeli victory became apparent, defense limitations became less relevant. The superpowers had to deal with the situation using the forces on hand. The Sixth Fleet more than balanced available Russian forces and would have made Soviet intervention by air or sea extremely hazardous.

6.1.3 CONGRESSIONAL AND PUBLIC OPINION There was little perceptible change in domestic attitude throughout the crisis. While sympathetic, most Americans apparently hoped Washington could remain clear of an additional obligation. This feeling may have helped persuade the President to forgo unilateral initiatives during the buildup period. However, in the unlikely case of a threat to Israel's survival, it is speculated that there would have been great pressure on the President to act in spite of some counterpressure. Whether sympathy for Israel could have been translated into popular backing for American intervention remains a moot point. The extent of domestic support became a much less significant factor during the rapid events of the crisis. The President did not consult with lawmakers and obviously was not deterred by possible negative opinion when making critical responses to what he perceived as serious Russian challenges. The President's own personal feeling of responsibility for Israel, his concept of American interests, and his view of the global Soviet challenge appeared to be the determining factors in actual crisis decisions. Congress's stress on avoiding unilateral action was most influential in the buildup period.

6.1.4 ECONOMIC EFFECTS Economic factors followed a similar pattern. While having some influence, at least on lower levels of government, in preliminary considerations of U.S. alternatives, economic consequences faded into the background during the actual conflict. While the political consequences of American actions on future relations with Arab countries were an important factor in policy choices, the possibility of economic retaliation was not a serious concern in deliberations at the highest decision-making level. Although intervention on behalf of Israel might have caused a severe deterioration of relations with "moderate" Arab nations, economic factors were of most relevance in contemplating a possible initiative to test Nasser's blockade by a multinational force. During the war concern over business investment was overridden by more important considerations.

6.1.5 DEPENDENCE ON THE BRITISH The psychological need for positive international support was the dominant factor restraining the United States from testing the blockade. Congressional emphasis on collective effort increased the importance of Britain's attitude. The United Kingdom was the only major allied government that seemed to share American concern about the Israeli predicament. However, British participation was of less importance when considering the possibility of a military show of support for Israel prior to the war. Once the fighting began the psychological need for British backing was further reduced. If the situation had developed into a prolonged military showdown with the Soviet Union, British forces probably would have been committed.

All of these factors were interrelated, which complicates deciding which had the most relative importance.[3] Two were of unusual significance during the buildup phase: the need for congressional backing and British cooperation. In response to criticism of previous initiatives, the President was apparently planning to seek congressional approval for any American military initiative.[4] Congressional aversion to unilateral commitments increased the

[3]There is, of course, a difference between what factors should have been considered and evaluated and what weight was actually assigned by decision makers at the time. There is evidence that all of these factors were considered at some level of the government. This analysis leans toward objective consideration of the factors as opposed to judgments as to which were actually given the greatest weight. However, both elements have been considered.

[4]It is felt that the President's refusal to commit himself to Congress was more in the nature of an executive-congressional power struggle. The Pres-

importance of British participation in any move.

6.1.6 ALTERNATIVES OF STRATEGY A logical hypothesis would be that defense limitations and other factors tending to restrain U.S. policy were simply a convenient excuse for not becoming embroiled in the Middle East. Direct involvement on behalf of either the Israelis or the Arabs would be replete with frustrations and disadvantages. It is possible that the United States would not have selected any of the alternatives given in Figures 6.1, 6.2, 6.3, and 6.4 and restricted itself to diplomatic actions even if limitations on capabilities had been minor. However, it is believed that American perceptions of its interests necessitated serious consideration of alternatives that might preserve peace in the area, safeguard Israel, and prevent increased Soviet influence.

This approach, by necessity, must be somewhat subjective. But it appears that the factors could be logically weighted in the following manner for alternative situations. The length of the vectors is an estimate of the relative importance that it is believed a factor had, and the direction of the vector indicates its effect on the decision for particular alternatives.

As shown in Figure 6.1, capability factors were not favorable for a unilateral initiative to force the blockade, particularly after the British became reluctant to share the leadership of the expedition.[5] Although the United States had a firm commitment dating back to 1957 concerning free passage for U.S. ships, the President's statement of May 23, 1967, had not reasserted it. In the

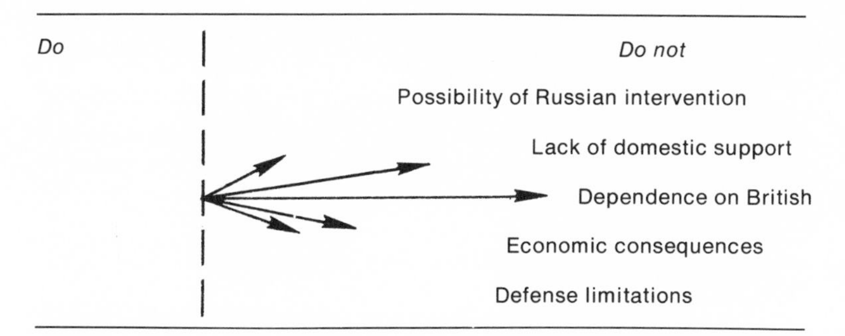

Figure 6.1 First alternative: use force to break the blockade

ident's failure to guarantee his actions in advance to the congressional leaders did not mean that their attitudes did not heavily influence his thinking. The President wanted freedom of action. Undoubtedly, his recognition of congressional sentiment made him even more wary of making guarantees to Congress.

[5]The British factor is shown following the apparent shift in policy in which the British became more reluctant to lead a military initiative.

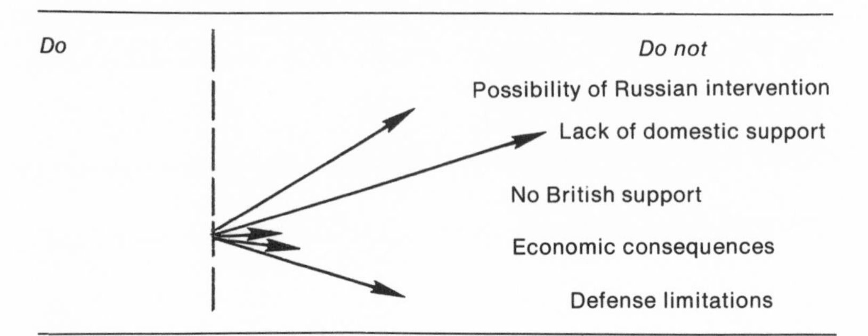

Figure 6.2 Second alternative: make a show of military support for Israel with intent to use force if necessary

two-week period prior to the war, Washington elected not to issue a unilateral declaration concerning maritime rights.

As shown in Figure 6.2, capability factors fell predominantly on the side of making a neutral rather than a pro-Israeli stand. However, the political realities of American interests in the Middle East rather than capability factors provided a predominant argument against a strong military demonstration on behalf of Israel prior to the outbreak of war. Such a show of force might have encouraged Israel to act; it certainly would have been interpreted that way in Arab capitals. Diplomatic efforts to mediate the dispute would have been more difficult, and the tendency would have been toward further internationalization rather than localization of the conflict.[6]

A more difficult consideration was the proper response to a possible Israeli defeat by the Arabs. There are a variety of opinions as to what Washington might have done.[7] Apparently, no final decision

[6]In answer to a question concerning a positive show of strength in the buildup period, the Secretary of State responded, "Who would we direct it against? Israel?" Interview with former Secretary of State Dean Rusk conducted April 9, 1969. The Joint Chiefs of Staff apparently felt that a show of force "would have been interpreted as being in support of one or the other of the sparring antagonists, would have heightened the chances of preemption by the weaker, would have led to more bellicose actions by the nation which felt itself supported and would have affected adversely our diplomatic negotiations to mediate. . . ." Letter from Rear Admiral George C. Talley, Jr., USN to Lt. Comdr. J. T. Howe, USN, undated letter received on April 10, 1969, 2.

[7]For example, Gen. Mangrum commented that, "we never would have been permitted to engage anywhere, no matter what happened to the Israelis," letters from Gen. Richard C. Mangrum, USMC, to Lt. Comdr. J. T. Howe, USN. On the other hand, an informed White House source was convinced the United States would have intervened. Interview with an informed White House source conducted March 6, 1969.

was made. McGeorge Bundy commented, "I think we honestly do not know what would have happened if the Israelis had been in danger of massive defeat, although obviously the arguments for a more active role in such a case would have been very much stronger."[8] On the basis of conversations with a number of policy makers it appears to be highly probable that the President would not have allowed a major defeat of Israel without an American response. Such a judgment is, of course, speculative. The firm belief that Israel would not be defeated made serious consideration of such an eventuality seem unrealistic.

With the marines and airplane troops a considerable distance away initial U.S. intervention in a quick war would have been limited to possible commitment of carrier air power to the side of Israel while neutralizing Soviet naval activity. Soviet intervention would have been less likely if a U.S. effort was confined to pushing Arabs back to Israeli borders. It is also probably safe to assume that any defeat of Israel on its home territory would not have been of the lightning variety of Israeli conquests in the Sinai desert.

On the estimate of capability shown in Figure 6.3, two vectors are given for each factor to indicate the relative changes between the buildup and crisis phases. It is speculated that the significant domestic opinion factor would have swung toward the *Aid Israel* side, and the extent of its swing would have depended on the de-

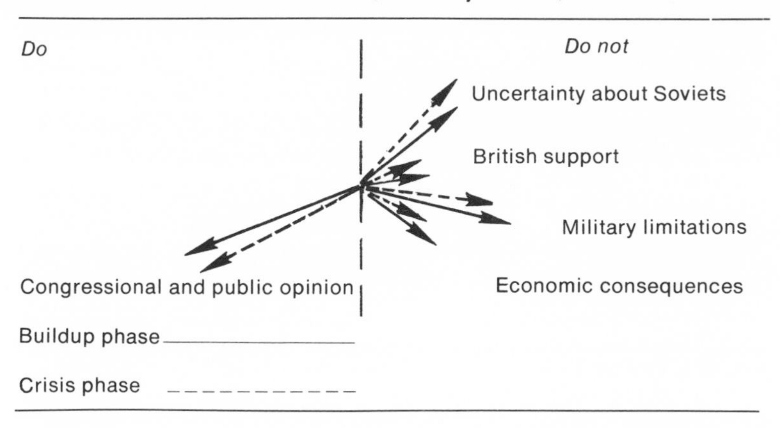

Figure 6.3 Third alternative: provide direct U.S. military aid if Israel is being defeated

[8]Letter from Mr. McGeorge Bundy to Lt. Comdr. J. T. Howe, USN, dated April 3, 1968.

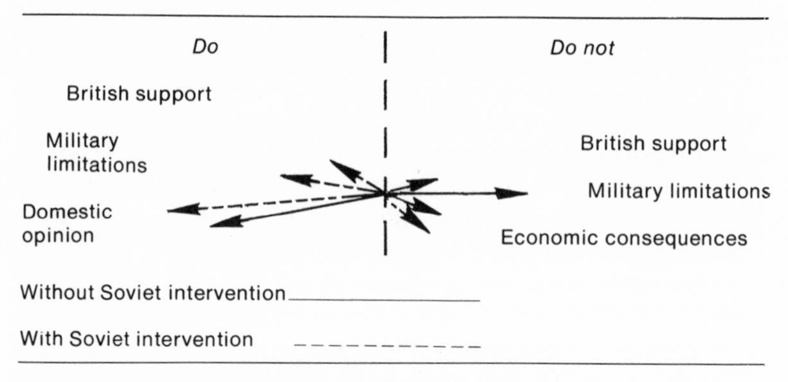

Figure 6.4 Fourth alternative: provide direct U.S. military aid if Israel is being defeated with Soviet intervention or direct aid

gree of Israeli defeat.[9] Overall capability would have been increasingly favorable to American action.

The more likely need for American action was in response to Soviet intervention since the Arabs were not likely to be successful without substantial help from Moscow. While it is doubtful that the United States assured Israel it would oppose an Arab invasion,[10] there is considerable evidence that Israel expected support only in case of Soviet intervention.

Washington wanted to avoid confrontation with Moscow, but it did not shy away from it. It could be argued that the President had an unrealistic conception of the power realities when he ordered the Sixth Fleet toward Syria. However, it is believed that the capability for countering a Soviet action would have been enhanced by firmer domestic support and more positive allied backing. Paradoxically, Russian intervention would have been a more severe military challenge but in some ways, easier to cope with. United States strategic and local superiority would predominate in a brief confrontation. The improved political context would have alleviated the problem of calling reserves and other steps to make up deficiencies for cop-

[9]This statement, however, must be carefully weighed against the results of public opinion polls following the outbreak of war. See also the counterargument in Section 6.2.3.

[10]Israel evidently did not request any military support from the United States. Interview with senior Israel Foreign Ministry official conducted October 24, 1968. However, James Reston wrote on May 24 that "the United States has quietly reassured the Israelis that it will oppose an Arab invasion of Israel." *The New York Times,* May 24, 1967, p. 46. He has since confirmed that the information came from "U.S. officials in the area" and that it seemed obvious that the "U.S. was attempting to balance the power in the area." Letter from James Reston, Associate Editor of *The New York Times,* to Lt. Comdr. J. T. Howe, USN, dated March 13, 1968.

ing over a longer period with a sustained Soviet intervention.

A Soviet move to intervene would have given the conflict a global cast. Instead of U.S. military power being engaged in a peripheral challenge, it would be concentrated on the main adversary. It is difficult to conceive of a direct clash between U.S. and USSR forces in the Middle East that would not rapidly escalate to World War III. If the Soviet Union actually intended to intervene on June 10, 1967, it probably planned to confine its move to a show of strength behind the battle lines. A likely U.S. response would have been landing forces in Israel. Moscow may have hoped the United States could be bluffed into passively allowing a Soviet intervention. The President's decision to demonstrate American resolve did not appear to be based on unrealistic assessments of capabilities.

6.2 INFLUENCE OF THE PREEXISTING INVOLVEMENT IN VIETNAM

Having examined possible U.S. positions, one can evaluate more precisely the effect that Vietnam had on American capability. As a general rule those in the executive department directly involved with Mideast crisis policy felt the war in Vietnam made little difference.[11] The supposition that the United States might not get embroiled because it was "bogged down" in Vietnam, according to McGeorge Bundy, was "just not applicable."[12] Most assertions of the deep influence of Vietnam on U.S. ability to deal with a second crisis came from those on the periphery of the policy process.[13] For example, Senator Robert Kennedy claimed that the Middle East war proved the United States "cannot meet its commitments elsewhere" because it is so "tied down" meeting "one commitment in Vietnam."[14] Impotence in the Middle East provided a convenient political issue for those advocating a change in Vietnam policy.

The actual influence of Vietnam seemed to lie somewhere be-

[11]For example, such a view was expressed in conversation with staff of the Chief of Naval Operations on April 7, 1968, and in an interview with a State Department officer familiar with the handling of the Arab-Israeli crisis of 1967, conducted December 10, 1968. See also, interview with an informed White House source conducted March 6, 1969, Appendix B, Question 7.
[12]This statement was confirmed by a letter from Mr. Bundy.
[13]Concerning the Middle East, Senator Jacob K. Javits has stated, "the dangers of the situation there, as well as our incapacity to act effectively, were briefly thrust upon the world's attention last May and June." Speech "Confrontation in the Middle East," February 29, 1968, p. 1. Copy provided by Senator Javits. See also the comments of Ernest Stock, *Israel on the Road to Sinai, 1949–1956 with a Sequel on the Six Day War, 1967* (Ithaca: Cornell University Press, 1967), p. 232.
[14]*The Christian Science Monitor* article by Saville R. Davis, "RFK on Vietnam," March 26, 1968, p. 1.

tween these diverse points of view. Those making critical decisions on a day-by-day basis may not have perceived certain limitations caused by the Vietnam experience. Critics of the U.S. policy during the crisis have seemingly based many of their conclusions on false assumptions of what actually happened. One can gain some understanding of the effect of Vietnam by comparing the relative weight that capability factors would have had and the changed framework in which alternatives would be selected without a Vietnam involvement.

6.2.1 ESTIMATE OF SOVIET INTENTIONS TO INTERVENE United States involvement in Vietnam probably had little influence on the Soviet approach to the Middle East crisis. Moscow may have believed it could demonstrate ability to support its clients in a limited incident without risking American counteraction. But the Soviets characteristically avoid direct military confrontation and more than one crisis at a time on different fronts. It seems inconceivable that Moscow sought another showdown in a remote area against locally superior American forces. The Soviet Union had not intervened directly in Vietnam even when a Communist nation was being assaulted by U.S. planes and warships. The psychological repercussions seemingly contributed to the unrest in Eastern Europe which finally necessitated Soviet intervention in Czechoslovakia.

On the other hand, the United States had again demonstrated in Vietnam that it would intervene in limited war situations. This probably increased the credibility of American resolve in the minds of Kremlin leaders. While the United States would have had some difficulty meeting immediate requirements in the Middle East, Sixth Fleet power exceeded that of Soviet warships in the Mediterranean and the United States retained worldwide strategic superiority. The Soviet media reflected concern that American responses to the Middle East situation were part of a global offensive. Russian commentaries did not speak disparagingly of American power. On the contrary, U.S. forces were to be feared precisely because they had become more aggressive and stronger as a result of the Vietnam war.

Although the Russians may have a greater interest in the Middle East stemming from its proximity to their borders and its strategic importance, it is speculated that Vietnam made the probability of direct Soviet military intervention slightly more remote.

6.2.2 DEFENSE ESTIMATES OF U.S. CAPABILITY TO INTERVENE The war in Vietnam made a significant difference in U.S. defense estimates. Authorities have claimed Washington's decision was not affected by Vietnam because the rapidity of the warfare meant that the decision had to be based on forces on the spot.[15] But this argument overlooks the important relationship between the buildup and crisis phases. With no war in Vietnam U.S. forces in the Mediterranean would have had additional capability (helicopters, numbers of marines and pilots, experience levels, and so on) and probably would have been positioned so that a more credible option was available to decision makers. Typically, U.S. forces would have been poised nearer the battle area. Therefore, defense estimates of capability would have been more confident even if limited to forces on the scene.

While the Sixth Fleet undoubtedly would have been stronger in a number of small ways with no war in Vietnam, whether it would have been positioned differently is more speculative. In answer to a question concerning possible Vietnam effects, Secretary Rusk said that the war had practically no influence on U.S. decisions. He reasoned that "we had no desire to get involved militarily."[16] However, the marines, who were eventually ordered toward Syria, might have been at sea in the vicinity of the carrier task forces instead of "on liberty" if the United States had not been involved in Vietnam. Washington could not avoid propaganda accusations that its forces were close to Arab shores even if the facts proved otherwise. Therefore, Vietnam appeared to reduce American readiness to deal with some possible developments. The war in Asia contributed to the fostering of an attitude of restraint, although the policy was based primarily on the complex American political problem in the Middle East.

At the same time, the United States obviously was not paralyzed by the requirements of Vietnam. Decisions in the critical phase demonstrated that the President felt he had the capability to cope with the only anticipated need for U.S. forces in the Middle East, prevention of Soviet intervention. The United States did not call reserves or supplement its forces because the President was confident that Israel could protect itself, except against the Soviet Union.

[15]McGeorge Bundy has commented that "if the Israelis had been in danger of losing, we would have had to act or not act with forces available on very short notice indeed." Bundy, letter. General Mangrum wrote, "I think it is purely speculation to ponder whether we might have acted differently had we not been involved in Vietnam. In view of the speed of the Mid-East action it seems unlikely that we would or could have acted much differently." Mangrum, letters.

[16]Rusk, interview.

6.2.3 CONGRESSIONAL AND PUBLIC OPINION Statements of lawmakers and public opinion surveys indicated that Vietnam was the principal reason for not supporting American intervention in the Middle East.[17] Involvement in Vietnam had a marked influence on the question of taking on an additional commitment. Although the crisis was relatively short, the public mood had unusual significance in the early stages. Instead of developing only as a reaction to specific events of the Near East crisis, domestic opinion was heavily influenced by the long engagement in Vietnam. Substantial sentiment against further involvement anywhere was well known to key decision makers. It was not necessary for opinion samples to be taken to realize that many Americans opposed intervention in the Middle East. Because of the Vietnam experience an Israeli defeat theoretically might have intensified American sentiment to avoid association with a losing cause. However, it is speculated that a reverse effect would have occurred. Without the atmosphere of war strain, the combination of Zionist political strength, natural American attachment for Israel, and U.S. strategic interests in the region probably would have generated greater support for a more active American role. There probably would have been much less outright opposition to involvement.

6.2.4 CONCERN ABOUT ECONOMIC EFFECTS The anticipated financial drain of another involvement partially contributed to congressional opposition to providing practical help for Israel. In addition, concerns about the adverse balance of payments and protection of oil supplies[18] were directly related to the Vietnam effort. If there had been no war in progress, economic factors would have been of even less significance.

6.2.5 DEPENDENCE ON BRITISH SUPPORT The war in Vietnam made British[19] involvement in any assertion of free passage through the Gulf of Aqaba mandatory for domestic, political, and psychological reasons. The relative strength of the Royal Navy in the area provided a ready force which would have taken time to duplicate. Even after fighting erupted, British Mediterranean strength was of more than negligible importance because of Vietnam. The presence of U.K. carrier task forces on either side of the canal as well as British

[17]Louis Harris stated, for example, "on the key issue of troop intervention if requested by the Israelis, public opinion registered a decisive opposition by better than 2 to 1. Many people feel that with heavy commitments in Vietnam the U.S. should move warily in becoming involved in another war." *New York Post,* "Harris Poll," June 10, 1967.

[18]As previously noted, oil for Vietnam could be transferred to other sources.

[19]Several other nations might have filled the role, but there were no eager candidates. Holland and Australia evidently were the most ready to help.

Mediterranean bases and air fields greatly strengthened Sixth Fleet forces. In contemplating intervention the Soviets had to consider the combined Anglo-American capability. The British presence, therefore, had a much greater significance because of heavy American naval involvement in the Pacific.

All of the factors had a close interrelationship. Public opinion, for example, was a very important element in considerations of defense capability, economic effects, and the need for allied support. The prior involvement in Vietnam appears to have had some influence on each of the important capability factors influencing policy decisions.

A comparison of the capability factors in the context of feasible alternatives with and without the Vietnamese war yields the results shown in Figures 6.5 and 6.6.[20] With no war in Vietnam, conditions

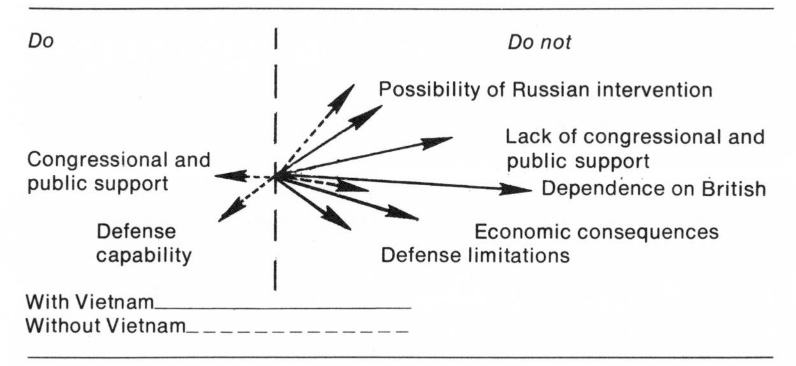

Figure 6.5 Effect of Vietnam on using force to break the blockade

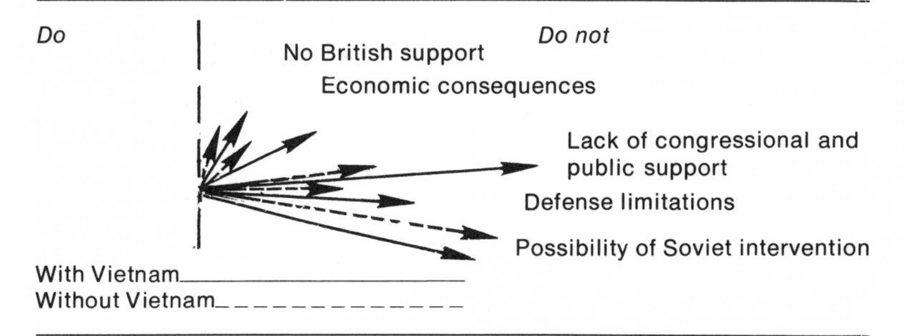

Figure 6.6 Effect of Vietnam on a show of military support for Israel with intent to use force if necessary

[20]These estimates are, of course, highly speculative. The estimates of relative change in each factor is more valid than the judgments as to absolute weights a factor should have in relation to the other factors. The Trends in Capability were of course just one aspect of any decision made in terms of U.S. interests.

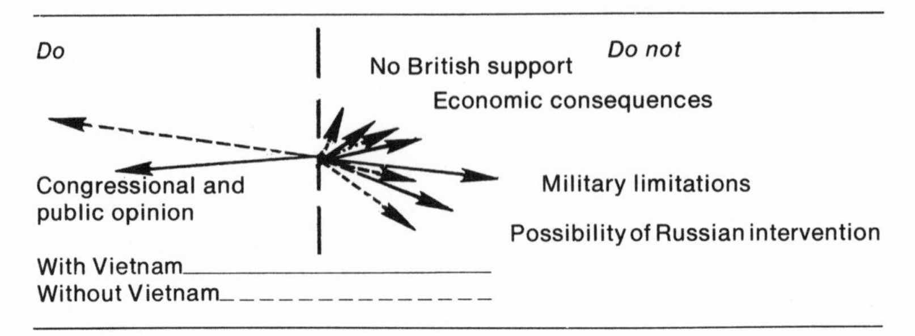

Figure 6.7 Effect of Vietnam on provision of direct U.S. military aid if Israel is being defeated

for asserting U.S. claims in the Straits of Tiran would have been much more favorable. It appears that estimated capabilities still tended to discourage a strong U.S. show of military support of Israel. The problem of possible Soviet intervention was the dominant restraint in considering this alternative without the war in Vietnam, particularly with Soviet naval forces close to the area. The Russians probably would have tried to duplicate American demonstrations for political purposes, thereby escalating U.S.–USSR tension. If the United States had sent troops to Israel, Russia might have sent "volunteers" to Syria and Egypt. United States maneuvers off Israel's coast might have evoked similar Soviet demonstrations.

With no Vietnamese war, it would have been easier to provide direct U.S. aid if Israel were losing, since the United States would have had a greater capability.

The Vietnamese war affected capability to undertake each of these three alternatives, but its most substantial effect was on the alternative of using force to break the blockade of the Gulf of Aqaba.

Insight can be gained by turning the question around and assessing the influence of the Middle East crisis on Vietnam. Few direct limitations or effects on Vietnamese policy seemed to result from the Middle East experience. Neither Soviet nor American involvement in Vietnam was radically changed by events in the Middle East. American war efforts were not reduced. The *Intrepid,* for example, passed through the Mediterranean area of tension en route to Vietnam. A longer crisis or actual superpower involvement in fighting would, of course, have increased the strain on both sides. The crisis did seem to stimulate domestic sentiment to scale down America's Asian commitment. Some influential Vietnam hawks and doves argued, somewhat inconsistently, that the crisis demonstrated American overcommitment and incapability to deal with more vital commitments. Oil transportation costs for the war in Vietnam were increased by the Middle East crisis, but this was a relatively insignificant factor. Overall, it did not appear that the Middle East crisis had a significant effect on American capability to cope with the war in Vietnam.

6.3 EFFECTIVENESS OF NAVAL FORCES AS INSTRUMENTS OF AMERICAN POLICY

It can be argued that the United States could have employed its forces more effectively, and, possibly, U.S. restraint contributed to the failure to maintain peace. However, warships played an important role; the fleet did not act in a peace-keeping capacity but rather as a strong second that made sure that outsiders did not interfere. Nevertheless, American forces were kept so far back from the scene of action that Moscow may have felt there was considerable scope for maneuver.

The crisis also demonstrated one of the limitations of naval shows of strength. The political ramifications of the Arab-Israeli dispute were so extensive that the United States did not want it to appear that it leaned toward either side. Therefore, naval movements close to the shores would result in a difficult political problem. The Joint Chiefs of Staff reasoned that such actions by naval force would have encouraged a preemptive attack from the favored side.[21] In other words, some officials argued that peace could be better maintained by assuming a neutral rather than a deterrent position. At the same time Moscow and Cairo felt Washington stood with Tel Aviv even without a formal alliance. Therefore, a tacit commitment backed by a restrained presence in the eastern Mediterranean was equally convincing. The Soviet commentators never tired of accusing the Sixth Fleet of threatening the Arab states during the buildup phase. It seems difficult to believe that the Soviets, aware of the power realities, would have seriously considered intervention in Egypt or Syria. It is possible that evidence to the contrary was only a deliberate Russian bluff or test of American determination. But when the United States rapidly changed its restrained posture during the second and sixth days of the war, the Soviets had visible evidence of where Washington stood. While it may seem that the American fleet was neutralized, it was really the weaker Soviet fleet that was unable to act. Because of confidence in Israeli capabilities, the consequences of not taking the initiative were relatively

[21] Talley, letter. Chapter 6, footnote 6.

minor for the United States. The local balance of U.S.–USSR forces did not provide a credible option for the Soviets. On the other hand, when the United States perceived two threats of possible Soviet intervention, it moved its forces toward the areas of conflict. The Soviets probably were impressed by these maneuvers.

In the final analysis the effectiveness of the Sixth Fleet is best indicated by contemplating the same circumstances without the presence of American forces. One can only speculate about the possibility of Soviet intervention in such a case. It might have strengthened the hand of those advocating a more aggressive Soviet policy.[22] Certainly, the Israelis feel that the American presence was a great help to them. Deputy Premier Yigal Allon has remarked that President Johnson "played a historic and courageous role in the Six-Day War, when he warned the Soviet Union that her military intervention would lead to a global confrontation."[23] The U.S. President used movements of the Sixth Fleet to emphasize his warning. While the Soviets could not have intervened effectively with the types of forces available for their use in the Mediterranean, their buildup might have been totally different with little possibility of American intervention. It seems safe to conclude that the number of options available to the Soviets was reduced by the American presence.

Because of the Soviet presence in the Mediterranean the impact of the Sixth Fleet during the buildup was diminished slightly, and American uncertainty about Soviet intentions was increased. Moreover, Russian ships may have raised false hopes among Egyptians that the USSR would prevent U.S. intervention under all circumstances. The presence of a Soviet force made it even more important that there be a counterbalancing U.S. force. A slightly stronger local American force seemed to close the option of intervention to Moscow. The very nearness of the superpowers' fleets to

[22]There was evidently no hawk-dove split in the case of the Middle East situation as there later was in the case of Czechoslovakia. Intervention was evidently not favored by any faction. However, if there had been less concern about American retaliation, there might have been a repetition of the Czech debate. There were differences in the Soviet approach. It seems inconceivable that the military miscalculated on the outcome of an Arab-Israeli war. Yet, the Russian ambassador in Cairo was evidently urging the Egyptians on. There also appeared to be differences between Moscow and U.N. Ambassador Fedorenko. Whether Soviet action can be partially explained as a limited ploy initially executed by the KGB or some other group is not yet clear. See the comments of informed White House source in interview conducted March 6, 1969, Appendix B, Question 4.

[23]Speech of Deputy Premier Yigal Allon to Israel's Knesset, October 30, 1968. *Weekly News Bulletin,* October 29–November 4, 1968, p. 3. Copy provided by Israel Information Service.

each other increased the dangers of a miscalculation. Careful fleet movements decreased their deterrent effect somewhat.

Overall, the American naval presence was very effective. The fact that there was only a remote chance of Russian intervention was partially attributable to the Kremlin's comprehension or interpretation of movements of American forces. Russia's threat to stop Israel may have been only bluff, but warship movements provided a way of convincing the Soviets that the United States was not bluffing. The Sixth Fleet appeared to have closed some options to the Kremlin.

6.4 ADEQUACY OF CONVENTIONAL NAVAL FORCES TO MEET THE DEMANDS OF THE MULTICRISIS

Whether American forces were adequate to meet the demands of two crises depends to some extent on perceptions of Soviet and Arab intentions and judgment of what the American role should have been. The potential employment of force in the second crisis was complicated by the Soviet naval presence and the strain on Mediterranean forces because of Vietnam. In assessing whether, under the circumstances, American forces were adequate, one must examine what options, if any, were closed by decreased capability to apply power locally.

Capability to break the Gulf of Aqaba blockade depended to some extent on available naval power. There were no Russian naval forces in the area to complicate that task. Several American destroyers might have been adequate. Although slightly inferior in firepower to Egyptian forces, these ships would have the psychological advantage of America's overall strength. However, the Joint Chiefs of Staff felt that a much larger force with substantial air cover was necessary.[24] To this extent U.S power was not adequate although Sixth Fleet carrier aircraft could have helped.

American caution during the buildup was to some degree a reflection of the Vietnam experience. The marines were three days from the Sinai, and the strike task forces were kept at least 200 miles away. Under other circumstances some American units might have been closer to the area of potential difficulty, if only as a precaution to safeguard American citizens. Washington's studied neutrality and noninvolvement seemed uncharacteristic of past reactions to potential challenges throughout the globe,[25] although the United

[24]Talley, letter. See, for example, interview with White House informed source, Appendix B, Question 3.

[25]In the Lebanon crisis of 1958 the United States had tripled the number of marine battalions available and made a substantial increase in the number

States generally approaches such situations with caution. A more typical American reaction would have been to build up its local forces, particularly in response to an augmentation by the Soviet Union, and then maintain the existing margin of superiority. In considerations of this type there seem to have been limitations on available American power. However, it was a combination of factors and not reduced military capability alone that made these alternatives seem undesirable.

Even if the United States had not been limited by political or capability factors, there is no guarantee that a greater show of naval strength would have altered the situation. Doubling American forces would not necessarily have had any impact on Israeli or Arab plans. It might have caused the Soviets to be more cautious, but they probably would have supplemented their naval task force in the Mediterranean anyway. Moscow already appeared to respect the existing power of the Sixth Fleet. The Soviet buildup of warships in early June apparently was politically rather than militarily oriented. The Kremlin may have reasoned that American restraint would make it safe to show support for Egypt and Syria in this manner. A larger number of U.S. warships would not necessarily have prevented a Soviet attempt to impress their allies. However, if the existing Sixth Fleet forces had made a more forceful demonstration of American backing of Israel, the Soviets might have decided to keep well clear of the situation.

In spite of reductions and equipment deficiencies the Sixth Fleet was more powerful than the Soviet force, but Russian power should not be underestimated. Russian missile ships and submarines were formidable, and American defense against missiles was questionable. The United States had no comparable surface-to-surface missile. The American antisubmarine task force was not in the Mediterranean when the crisis developed. Nevertheless, U.S. forces were stronger overall. Carrier movements were used to emphasize American will to employ them if necessary. If it had been felt that the *Intrepid* was needed to deter the Soviets, it would not have been sent on to Vietnam.

The Sixth Fleet proved adequate to carry out American policy. The specific limitations of the fleet's strength because of Vietnam did not prevent it from being an effective instrument of American power. However, the depletion of military capability throughout the

of ships in the area prior to the actual requirement to use them. In the Quemoy conflict of 1958 the United States doubled the number of ships of the Seventh Fleet and tripled the number of aircraft carriers. Of course, there is no precedent for direct U.S. military support of Israel.

world and reduced reserves seemed to impose more caution on American moves. This, of course, was also partially due to a new complication, the Soviet naval presence. However, the overriding reasons for American restraint were political, and when a military demonstration seemed needed, the President reacted quickly.

6.5 UNDERLYING QUESTIONS

The crisis provided some other insights related to underlying questions.[26]

6.5.1. ASSESSMENT OF THE VALUE OF ALLIANCES Both positive and negative aspects of alliance with Great Britain were demonstrated. The United Kingdom was carrying a demanding load throughout the world with its limited peace-keeping forces. The British presence both below the Suez Canal and in the Mediterranean proved valuable. It added credibility to talk of opening the Straits of Tiran, and it bolstered U.S. forces in the Mediterranean. But the crisis also demonstrated the frailty of big power alliances and the diversity of allied interests. Economic pressure apparently turned the British away from strong advocacy of a multinational force to break the blockade. However, British naval power added strength to the Western position in the Mediterranean and south of Suez.

Both positive and negative aspects were also demonstrated in the relationship with Tel Aviv. In many ways Israel provided an ideal alliance relationship. Because it is strong and self-sufficient in comparison to its neighbors, there is little likelihood that direct U.S. assistance would be needed in a purely local confrontation. With the existing balance of Arab-Israeli power, it is only a strong Soviet role that makes American intervention necessary. The Russian challenge can be viewed in a global rather than a regional context. The United States was better able to cope with the Soviet-sponsored scheme and avoid direct involvement because of Israel's relative local strength.

Another debatable point is whether America's ties to Israel increased the possibility of war with the Soviet Union. In attacking Egypt, Tel Aviv disregarded Washington's advice, and later in the war Israel appeared to try to accomplish its military objectives prior to complying with American requests that it adhere to U.N. cease-fire resolutions. The delays particularly antagonized the embarrassed Russians. However, the danger of alignment with Israel

[26]The observations that follow represent the author's views based on detailed study of this situation. Except in the case of Section 6.5.4, however, they are more in the nature of opinions than deductions based on intensive study of evidence.

should not be overstated. Tel Aviv expected Washington to deter Moscow only from intervening militarily. Israel agreed to a ceasefire prior to Egypt and agreed to halt hostilities in Syria before the Soviets could intervene. Moscow had encouraged Nasser to move his armies up near Israel's border, and Nasser had elected to provide the *casus belli*.

Israel, of course, has its own national interests. It is hardly a dependent state. It is difficult to control and obviously will not adhere to American injunctions if it considers Israeli concerns will be jeopardized. In this sense the dangers of a larger conflict are increased by the big power lineup in the Middle East. Ideally, the United States wants stability in the region; America seeks good relations with both sides and does not want to be excluded from Arab countries. United States strategic interests do not necessarily coincide with those of Israel. Certainly, in this case, the American goal of maintaining peace in the region was not achieved. But in a clash of interests promoted by the USSR, in which the local forces opted for one superpower or the other, the United States was in an advantageous position because of Israel's military capability.

6.5.2 TYPES OF COMMITMENTS The United States had no formal treaty with Israel, and yet it was deeply committed to the survival of that state. There is a case for establishing a formal alliance with Israel. If America's vital security interests are considered to be tied to the fate of Israel, then it can be argued that the United States should make its intentions to ensure Israel's safety clearer. Possibly, such an open arrangement would underline for Moscow the dangers of trying to capitalize on the Arab-Israeli dispute and convince extreme Arab nations that they cannot conquer Israel.

On the other hand, such an agreement would provide impetus for a similar Russian treaty with the Arabs and thus effectively increase Moscow's influence in the area. It would also make an appealing issue for further Soviet inroads in other Middle Eastern areas. Undoubtedly, Arab animosity toward the United States would be increased, reducing the possibility of continued U.S. access to the region. In addition, it would be more difficult for Washington or Moscow to avoid being drawn into a local dispute. There is no clear indication that Israel would necessarily want to tie its hands with the reciprocal obligations that are part of an alliance, although it apparently has broached the subject in the past. Certainly, a formal agreement is not needed to indicate to Cairo, Damascus, and Moscow where Washington stands in regard to Tel Aviv. But with a formal American obligation, there would be greater public support for

U.S. defensive activities and unilateral peace-keeping efforts.

6.5.3 RELATIONSHIP OF LOCAL CONFLICTS TO GLOBAL WAR While the superpowers managed to avoid escalation to global proportions, the crisis demonstrated the dangers of local conflict situations. In spite of hot line and other diplomatic exchanges and cautious movements of forces, doubt of intentions existed throughout. The possibility of escalation because of a misunderstanding was increased by the close proximity of rival forces. A primary example was the *Liberty* incident, in which American decision makers, although responding in a restrained way, thought initially that the attack might have been launched by the Soviets. The Soviet augmentation of naval forces with war in the Middle East imminent indicated an evolutionary step in Russian doctrine. There was apparently less concern that a local confrontation might rapidly escalate into a global exchange. Moscow was less cautious and seemed to have a more liberal interpretation of safe risks in the nuclear age.

The strategic nuclear power of the United States and the Soviet Union had very little influence except in encouraging greater caution. It is not likely that either country would have been willing to increase chances of a nuclear showdown for the sake of either the Arabs or the Israelis.

6.5.4 RELEVANCE OF SHIFTS OF FORCES AS INDICATORS OF POLICY Movements of naval forces were used to signal intentions. The United States did not intend to intervene with land forces and thus in the days prior to the war sent marines on liberty. The Soviets did not include amphibious forces in their augmentation of the Mediterranean fleet. Sixth Fleet carrier forces were kept within striking distance but well clear of the actual fighting. Soviet forces remained at anchor near the American ships. Washington took advantage of the proximity of Soviet forces to verify that it had not been involved in the destructive Israeli raid on Arab fields. Washington also used a show of force as an answer to Soviet threats of intervention in Egypt and Syria.

Since there were Soviet ships watching the American task forces, it was felt in Washington that a change in the fleet's position would be immediately reported to Moscow. The marines were sent back to sea and the Sixth Fleet task forces ordered to speed toward the area of conflict when Moscow became belligerent. Ship movements well back from the area of conflict were intended to make American resolve clear. Moscow apparently understood.

Soviet commentaries devoted much space to U.S. movements, indicating that the deeds of ships were more significant proof of

American intentions than the words of official statements or diplomatic conversations. A classic statement of the feeling that actions speak louder than words was contained in an *Izvestia* commentary allegedly showing

> . . . the hypocrisy of the American protestations that Washington is 'alarmed' by the development of events in the Near East. 'While American diplomacy is shedding crocodile tears about the hotbed of tension in the Eastern Mediterranean, the American military are getting up steam on their warships and putting Marines on board.'[27]

Washington could be reasonably sure that its military movements would be followed closely.

The United States and the Soviet Union attached great significance to warship movements as indicators of intentions, but the repositioning of the fleet was not always the result of master coordination from the White House basement. There are many forces at work in a crisis. The initial movements of the Sixth Fleet on June 6, 1967, resulted from a decision in the field not related to hot line warnings. At the same time, the White House was informed of the move and could have rapidly altered Sixth Fleet plans.

The Soviets also used their warship movements to indicate intentions not to intervene. Possibly, the augmentation of Soviet forces may have been misread by the Egyptians as a guarantee that the United States would be kept out of the situation. The Russians probably hoped to receive maximum credit for having deterred American intervention, but they apparently did not want a war. Although the increasing intensity of Russian hot line messages was of grave concern, Moscow's failure to back them with movements of forces was another sign that a military challenge remained remote.

The movements of British forces initially reflected London's enthusiasm for carrying out the declaration to keep the Straits of Tiran open. But by holding the force at Aden, London indicated that no decision to use them had been made. The augmentation of warships in the Mediterranean gave the impression that Britain stood with Washington in any conflict with the Soviet Union.

By looking at preliminary Royal Navy movements one can detect when the decision was made to consider seriously a blockade. The aircraft carrier *Hermes* departed from Aden for Singapore on the day Nasser's request for withdrawal of U.N. forces was announced.

[27]Moscow Tass International Service in English, May 26, 1967. Commentary on article by Polyanov. A Tass release of May 25 commented that "had Washington *and London* really been seeking relaxation of tension in the Middle East, *not only in words but also in deeds,* they would have first of all withdrawn from the Mediterranean all their naval forces." Moscow Tass International Service in English, May 25, 1967. (Emphasis added.)

The British carrier returning from the Far East passed through the Suez Canal, while the Gulf of Aqaba blockade was being made known. There had been some indications of Egyptian reinforcements south of Suez on the previous day. London, however, did not alert Mediterranean forces until the evening of May 23, 1967, and announced a strong position on May 24.

Although not conclusive, naval maneuvers did offer interesting indicators of the intentions of the various powers. The event versus naval movement tabulation in Table 6.1 helps to clarify the significance of these tactics and demonstrates which nations took the initiative at various stages of the crisis.

Table 6.1 The Interaction of Naval Movements and Crisis Events

Date/Event	Sequence of Naval Movements
1. May 18, 1967 UAR orders United Nations emergency force withdrawn from Egyptian territory	Departure of British aircraft carrier *Hermes* from Aden for Singapore
2. May 22, 1967 UAR announces Gulf of Aqaba blockade	Egyptian naval movements south through Suez in several days preceding announcement; U.S. Sixth Fleet carriers ordered toward eastern Mediterranean; passage for 10 ships through Dardanelles requested by Soviets; entry to Mediterranean of British aircraft carrier *Victorious* via Suez Canal
3. May 23, 1967	British forces alerted in Mediterranean
4. May 25, 1967	Departure of U.S. marine amphibious force from Naples, Italy; British carrier *Hermes* ordered back to Aden
5. May 29, 1967	Marines off coast of Malta
6. May 30, 1967	Soviet augmentation of Mediterranean force announced
7. May 31, 1967	Departure of U.S. carrier *Intrepid* from Mediterranean for Vietnam; British carrier *Hermes* at Aden

Date/Event	Sequence of Naval Movements
8. June 2, 1967	Entry of U.S.S. *Liberty* to Mediterranean en route to Sinai coast; American destroyer *Dyess* sent from Mediterranean through Suez Canal; U.S. ASW task force ordered to Mediterranean
9. June 5, 1967 Outbreak of war	U.S. Marines on liberty; most Soviet ships at anchor; entry of last Soviet augmenting forces to Mediterranean
10. June 6, 1967 U.N. cease-fire resolution difference	Sixth Fleet carrier task forces positioned closer to the area but still 200 miles away from the Sinai
11. June 7, 1967	Sixth Fleet task forces returned to position south of Crete
12. June 8, 1967 *Liberty* incident	*Liberty* arrival on station; *Liberty* attacked; Sixth Fleet aircraft and carrier *America* to rescue
13. June 8, 1967	Marines put to sea from Malta; subsequently proceed in easterly direction but still in Ionian Sea
14. June 10, 1967 Possibility of Soviet intervention	Sixth Fleet forces ordered to move to the east toward Syrian coast at high speed; movement terminated after four or five hours

6.5.5 USEFULNESS OF THE UNITED NATIONS IN CRISES Many aspects of the U.N. role in the crisis have not yet been examined. It is possible, for example, that the withdrawal of U.N. forces from Sharm el Sheikh was not anticipated by Cairo and Moscow. The Secretary General's rapid compliance with Egypt's request may have been an embarrassing development for Nasser which escalated the crisis. Attempts to control the situation in the United Nations were futile as long as the USSR did not wish to endorse publicly U.N. efforts to prevent hostilities. The Soviet Union was very uncooperative in the period prior to the fighting. If Moscow had been interested, the United States and USSR might have been able to convince Egypt to accept a return of the U.N. emergency force. This obviously was not part of the Soviet plan. Of course, given Nasser's ego and political precariousness, it was doubtful that he would have agreed. Even on the first day of the fighting the Soviets in the United Nations were clearly aloof. It was only after the power realities were clear that Moscow seemed willing to agree to a cease-fire acceptable to Washington and Tel Aviv. The United Nations served as a forum for exchanging opinions, but it became a vehicle for a cease-fire only when the great powers began to cooperate.

The United Nations was an important arena for diplomatic maneuvering. While there is no doubt that an international forum for the exchange of views among the involved nations was extremely important to working out a cease-fire, there appeared to be one minor disadvantage. The Soviet delegate apparently misrepresented the American view to his superiors and thus added to the confusion of the situation. Overall, however, there is no doubt that the United Nations was instrumental in working out a cessation of hostilities, even though it was impotent in preventing war in the first place.

6.5.6 LIMITS OF BIPARTISANSHIP The splits in Congress did not follow any particular party line. Since the President did not have to use American forces in the preliminary stages there was no test of partisanship. But differences on the Middle East, as on Vietnam, appeared to be based on the issue rather than on party politics and to that extent reflected a bipartisan spirit. The most persistent critics of the White House policy appeared to be in the President's party.

6.5.7 BUREAUCRATIC BIAS There has been no attempt to assess the motivations of various constituencies in the American bureaucracy in terms of blinders, infighting, power struggles, rigidities, and diverse perspectives. These factors had some influence, but they did not appear to be a major influence on the decisions made during the crisis. There was, however, a marked difference in the perception and interpretation of events by those involved in the decision-making process.[28] For instance, the viewpoints expressed by persons in the White House, Defense Department, State Department, and those directly involved with Sixth Fleet operations differed on a number of points. The State Department, for example, held out hope up to the time the shooting began that the Gulf of Aqaba blockade could be lifted through diplomatic and, if necessary, military pressures. The State Department appeared to be sincere in its surprise when the war began. The Defense Department appeared to be unconvinced about the desirability and feasibility of breaking the gulf blockade. Military leaders were quite certain that Israeli military action was imminent. The White House seemed to occupy the middle ground between these points of view. It held out hope for the success of the blockade-testing concept while appar-

[28]There has been no attempt to document all of the changes or discuss these implications in detail. The statements that follow should be treated more as impressions and observations. However, letters and interviews with military leaders, State Department officials, White House sources, and congressmen indicated the widely varying perspectives and the basis for many of the observations.

ently recognizing that efforts might not be rapid enough to forestall a war.

The Defense Department seemed to be more concerned than the State Department about the possibility of another engagement in addition to Vietnam. But even among the military, differences seemed to exist. Marine generals, for example, had stronger feelings about the military limitations than did naval admirals.

In considering American obligations to Israel, the State Department leaned toward a truly neutral stance and took a more detached view. In the White House neutrality appeared to be only a cover for an underlying strong sense of obligation to Israel. In Congress and the White House, America's commitment to Israel was viewed less dispassionately than in the Department of State. The slightly different interpretations may have affected the stand on such issues as the conditions for a cease-fire.

There were vastly different conceptions of Soviet intentions. The State Department and those operating the Sixth Fleet seemed to feel that the possibility of Soviet intervention was very remote; there was less confidence in the White House. This difference is probably explained by the flow of hot line warnings and intelligence reports into the White House situation room.

The degree of information available explains some of the differences, but in both phases of the crisis there is considerable evidence of various degrees of emphasis and weights of priorities in the agencies participating in the decision-making process.

6.7 CONCLUSIONS

American policy toward the buildup of tension in Middle East was one of active diplomacy but studied military inactivity. It is misleading to assume that no decision to intervene was not a decision. Restrained movements of forces in the buildup reflected Washington's desire to avoid involvement. Since a war was considered inevitable by many U.S. policy makers, failure to augment U.S. Mediterranean forces during the buildup phase seemed deliberately to foreclose any option for direct military initiatives in the local conflict or rapid American responses.

On the other hand, the President was determined to prevent the Soviet Union from intervening. The Sixth Fleet was used during the crisis phase to emphasize American resolve toward this narrower objective. In electing a passive military role in the period prior to June 5, 1967, Washington was convinced that Israel would triumph if war should come. The Kremlin, on the other hand, was in a dilemma; it could not be confident of an Arab victory. Therefore, with the American stand of seeming neutrality, the odds were against Moscow and its Arab friends.

Whether the American policy was a long-term gain or loss is not yet clear. One view is that greatly increased Arab dependence on Soviet economic and military aid has given Moscow additional leverage in the area. Moscow is especially influential while Israel remains in former Arab territory. In spite of the humiliating destruction of Soviet-trained and equipped allies, the Arab defeat has facilitated increased penetration into the Middle East. It has helped justify more frequent use of naval facilities in Arab countries and basing Soviet aircraft at Egyptian fields. Lack of air power is one of the major Russian deficiencies in combating American Mediterranean strength. However, the June war was not necessarily a prerequisite for increased Soviet access to these facilities. Egyptian ports were used prior to the war. The acquisition of bases is not a substantial advantage in a military sense since the Soviets have developed a more self-sustaining navy. It does increase the opportunity for exerting political influence. By contrast, Moroccan and Tunisian ports have been the only ones open to Sixth Fleet vessels since the June war.[29] The war has also weakened American popularity in Jordan and some other more Western-leaning Near Eastern governments.

On the other hand, when consequences of the June war are viewed in global as well as regional terms, it would seem that destruction of Arab forces hardly represented a net gain for the Russians. The Soviets lost rather than gained credibility with their Eastern European allies. The unrest that continued in Poland and especially Czechoslovakia can be partially attributed to the further loss of Soviet credibility occasioned by the June war.[30] Heavy eco-

[29]U.S., Congress, House, Special Subcommittee on National Defense Posture of the Committee on Armed Services, *Review of the Vietnam Conflict and Its Impact on U.S. Military Commitments Abroad* (Washington, 1968), pp. 59, 60. This, of course, symbolizes decreasing political influence rather than a serious military logistics problem.

[30]There is some evidence that Eastern Europeans were pleased by Israel's victory and the further loss of Soviet prestige. A Soviet article, for example, referred to celebrations of Israel's victory in Poland. K. Ivanov, "Israel, Zionism and International Imperialism," *International Affairs* (Moscow), No. 6 (June 1968), p. 19. A poll of Eastern Europeans visiting Paris revealed that 58 percent sympathized with Israel during the June war and only 12 percent with the Arabs. *The New York Times,* August 18, 1967. Of course, the Soviet invasion of Czechoslovakia, partially resulting from loss of credibility in Vietnam and the June war, bolstered the Soviet image of credibility in Eastern Europe.

nomic dependence by Arab nations is a dark specter for the Soviet Union. It is not anxious to repeat the costly Cuban experience. Moscow's loss of prestige was felt regionally as well as globally. The Arabs may have a new sense of the dangers of big power alignment and of following Russian advice. The Soviets were not able to bail them out of a costly defeat that was at least partially precipitated by misleading Russian advice. There is some evidence of honest Arab disillusionment with the Soviets for not backing their friends when they were in real trouble. Arabs have remarked bitterly that the United States would not have let Israel down. The closed Suez waterway provides a stark reminder of the debacle. The country identified with the United States can control passage through both the Suez Canal and the Gulf of Aqaba.

For Moscow the experience demonstrated the limits of control of volatile and uncompromising Middle Eastern regimes and the inherent dangers of being drawn into an escalated conflict. Since the war, the Soviet Union has more thoroughly infiltrated the ranks of the Egyptian army, but it is not certain that the motive is only to increase fighting capability. It appears to be an attempt to exercise greater control. The United Arab Republic government has seemingly surrendered some sovereignty, but it is not certain to what extent the highly nationalistic elements in these countries will tolerate Soviet incursions. A conclusive assessment of whether the war over the long run will result in a net gain or loss for Moscow is some years distant.

Evaluation of whether the war will result in a long-term gain for American policy to some extent obscures the success of Western-leaning forces in a most difficult situation. One has only to imagine a reversal of the results of the June war to put the Western situation in proper perspective. In the unlikely, hypothetical case of an Arab victory achieved through Soviet support and American neutrality, Soviet prestige would be enhanced at the expense of U.S. credibility, radical Arab regimes and their Soviet patrons would have greatly increased influence, and there would be no military equivalent or balance between West and East in the Middle East.

American policy enjoyed obvious short-term success. A major war involving the United States was avoided, and a friendly nation won a smashing victory against countries trained and supplied predominantly by the Soviets. The United States demonstrated the ability to handle effectively a crisis in addition to the war in Vietnam. But it is in the definition of success, that is, victory for a friend without U.S. involvement, that some of the limitations in the crisis are revealed. Since Israel was capable of defending itself and the United States had contradictory political objectives in the Middle East, tacit implication of American backing resulting from the presence of ships of the Sixth Fleet was a logical strategy and all that Israel expected. But a bloody war was not avoided, an explosive situation remained in the area, and the United States continued to be deeply embroiled in its major commitment to Vietnam.

A more aggressive U.S. stance, for example, forcing the blockade, may not have convinced Egypt and Syria to pull their armies back. Only removing the *casus belli* might not have prevented Israel's attack, but it would have made it much harder to justify. One reason Israel apparently delayed its assault was to ensure Washington's political support. Washington wanted Tel Aviv to give it time to persuade Nasser to pull his divisions back and to restore free passage through the Gulf of Aqaba. If Israel and Egypt had been only the victims of circumstance more forceful U.S. peace efforts might possibly have helped prevent a war. Of course, once Nasser's prestige was committed, the psychological obstacles to a deescalation were immense. There was some hope in Washington that Nasser could be persuaded to lift the blockade and that the maritime armada was a viable alternative. The aim was to reduce tension by eliminating Israel's *casus belli.* Considering the realities of Israeli politics, this confidence in a slow-moving diplomatic effort that in effect would weaken Israel's case for attacking the armies massed on the southern border seemed more representative of wishful thinking than realistic perception of the situation. A considerable group in Washington was convinced that Israel was going to take matters into its own hands. Confident of Israel's military success, some policy makers undoubtedly felt this was the only feasible resolution of the Arab-Israeli confrontation. Washington seemed powerless to prevent what seemed to be inevitable.

The multicrisis situation revealed some distinct limitations. Washington might not have adopted any different policy toward the crisis if there had been no war in Vietnam, but it had fewer policy options because of the influences of the prior involvement. Certainly, sentiment against playing the role of a world policeman would have been less strong. When faced with a second challenge the United States avoided asserting its international maritime claims unilaterally. It took great care to assume a neutral posture and to avoid commitments of U.S. military forces.

On the other hand, a case could be made that even with no Vietnamese commitment the United States would have acted as it did in

May and June 1967. The political realities of American interests in the Middle East were only slightly different because of Vietnam. Britain and other Western European nations probably would have been just as reluctant to form an international force. However, it is speculated that preparations for a test of the blockade would have progressed more quickly since Washington would have been less dependent on multinational support.

Possibly, without some preoccupation with Vietnam at the highest levels of government stronger diplomatic pressure would have been exerted in April and May. Perhaps, Nasser would have been convinced to avoid moving his army to Israel's borders if the United States had countered Moscow's diplomatic maneuvers. This, of course, is highly speculative.

It is in the overall framework of capability as well as in the influence on various alternatives in this particular situation that some of the limitations of dealing with multicrisis situations were revealed. One has only to envision a situation in which a country other than Israel was involved or a much stronger Soviet force was present to understand the increased vulnerability of the United States in this situation.

Fortunately, Washington was not put to the unhappy choice of becoming engaged or seeing Israel defeated. But very few other countries in the world with which the United States has commitments, either tacit or otherwise, have the unusual combination of military genius, equipment, and courage to match Israel's performance. In order to guarantee their survival other countries may require more from Washington than prevention of Soviet military intervention.

The Soviet naval presence added another element of caution to American actions. It increased Washington's uncertainty of Moscow's intentions and added credibility to the usual Soviet propaganda tirades in such situations. The possibility of Russian action, no matter how remote, had to be given more serious consideration because some limited naval means had been deployed in proximity to U.S. forces. There was, however, little doubt about the capabilities of the Sixth Fleet versus the Soviet warships, as the employment of the Sixth Fleet during the crisis confrontations demonstrated. American assessments of the predominance of its power vis-à-vis the Soviet Union in the local area appeared to be sound.

Strain to meet requirements in Vietnam, partially at the expense of readiness of forces, complicated considerations of displaying overwhelming power in the area of tension. The United States would have had, of course, much greater capacity if the reserves had been called and stringent domestic economic measures had been taken. This, however, was not necessarily politically acceptable under the circumstances. Partly as a result of the Vietnam situation and expense, the United States tried to meet its challenge in the Mideast by relying on ready forces. The weakening of units in the Mediterranean and Atlantic fleets to meet Vietnam's requirements made military leaders more reluctant to recommend active employment of the armed services. On the other hand, the Sixth Fleet provided an essential ingredient of Israel's military victory without having to fire a shot. There was little hesitation to employ force in the crisis confrontation.

Domestic opinion was more influential because the crisis developed in a climate created by the drawn-out struggle in Southeast Asia. There was fear of becoming stuck in another quagmire. Therefore, even though sentiment would normally be slow to be manifested with fast-moving events like those in May 1967, it developed with a negative bias not related to the specific second crisis. The President was obviously aware of concern about American commitments. Domestic opinion was a significant restraining influence during the buildup. But once the war occurred, the American response depended on the President's assessment of U.S. security interests. Potential public opposition did not preclude resolute action when a threat to Israel was perceived.

The economic drain of the Vietnam war intensified American reluctance to support the cost of another involvement and also increased vulnerability to balance of payments pressure. The economic capacity to handle a number of crises probably existed, but it was essential that the public was willing to tighten its belt in order to meet worldwide commitments. In spite of economic problems, they had practically no influence on considerations at the highest level of Washington decision making.

Because the United States was already involved in an unpopular war, there was greater dependence on British political, psychological, and even military support. This was particularly evident when considering evolutions that might have reduced the possibility of an Arab-Israeli war such as expeditiously assuring the rights of all nations of access through the Gulf of Aqaba. The predominant theme in Congress was avoidance of *unilateral* commitments.

From a technical point of view, the United States did not renege on any previous formal commitment to Israel.[31] American reluctance

[31] It could, however, be claimed that the United States did not adequately support commitments to the Arab nations of the Middle East after the fighting had commenced. It could be argued that the United States should have

to take unilateral action appeared to violate the spirit of the 1957 *aide-mèmoire* and private assurance evidently given by Secretary of State Dulles. But since Israel, at least during the latter stages of the buildup, was not anxious to have free passage guaranteed if United Arab Republic armies remained poised on its borders, it would appear that Washington fulfilled its written obligations to Tel Aviv.

Following the crisis there appears to have been a slight softening of the U.S. declaratory position that may be indicative of the heávy influences and complications of the June 1967 confrontation. In a prepared answer to a congressional question concerning U.S. commitments in the Middle East, the Department of State indicated that the policy was flexible and implied that some further congressional authority would be required prior to commitment of the armed forces. It claimed, for example, that statements of the President were statements of "policy and not a commitment" and that "use of armed forces in the Middle East can have especially serious consequences for international peace extending far beyond that area."[32] However, it is speculated that Israel's request that the United States "insulate the Middle East from global rivalry" has been granted,[33] meaning that the United States will protect Israel from direct Soviet attacks. Deputy Premier Allon has claimed to have "solid grounds"

been even more receptive to Soviet cease-fire proposals. It is doubtful that U.S. military forces would have intervened militarily to extricate Egypt from destruction. These judgments are, of course, speculative.

[32]The specific question was as follows: ". . . is the United States as a nation committed to supply American military or economic resources to protect the territorial integrity of these states?" And the answer supplied by the State Department was "President Johnson and his three predecessors have stated the United States interest and concern in supporting the political independence and territorial integrity of the countries of the Near East. This is a *statement of policy* and *not a commitment* to take particular actions in particular circumstances." (Emphasis added.) And the statement continued ". . . the use of armed force in the Middle East can have *especially serious consequences* for international peace *extending far beyond that area.*" (Emphasis added.) Letter from Assistant Secretary William B. Macomber, Jr., to Senator J. W. Fulbright, August 15, 1967, U.S., Congress, Senate, Commitment on Foreign Relations, *U.S. Commitments to Foreign Powers* 90th Cong., 1st sess. (Washington, 1967), pp. 50, 51. This same question and answer were quoted in a subsequent State Department letter answering a question concerning American commitment to Israel. Letter from Mr. Carl E. Bartch, Deputy Director of News, to Lt. Comdr. J. T. Howe, USN, dated December 4, 1968.

[33]Speech by Israel Foreign Minister Abba Eban of March 14, 1969, *The New York Times,* March 15, 1969, p. 10.

for asserting that Israel "will not be left to her own devices in the event of Soviet military intervention."[34]

During the 1967 crisis the United States demonstrated a capability to face successfully a second challenge. Throughout the crisis Washington had the capability to meet a Soviet challenge, and the President confidently used the Sixth Fleet to make the power realities clear to Moscow when a threat was perceived. It appears, however, that in spite of shrewd employment of existing resources, the June war policy was dependent to a considerable extent on good fortune and Israel's relative military superiority. An underlying cause of Washington's cautious approach during the buildup to the crisis was the war in Vietnam. The reduction in U.S. capabilities may have tempted Moscow to engage in a limited ploy. But the Soviets appeared to recognize the realities of American determination during the crisis confrontations.

Apparently, neither the United States nor the Soviet Union wanted a war to occur in the Middle East, but each nation found that it was unable to exert sufficient influence to deter the Arabs and Israelis from once again resorting to violence. In spite of a slight reduction in its capability and the presence of Soviet forces, the Sixth Fleet played an important role. If the crisis had been prolonged several more hours, fleet movements might have been decisive. The fleet might have played a stronger role in peace-keeping efforts with no Vietnam war. Nonetheless, it was more than adequate under the circumstances to meet crisis requirements.

The most serious limits of the second crisis seemed to be psychological. Undoubtedly, the experience of Vietnam fostered an inclination to avoid bold unilateral action. The United States was more dependent on its allies and sensitive to the climate of adverse domestic opinion. However, even this limitation can be exaggerated. The restrictions affected American initiatives. Domestic dissent did not preclude an American response to apparent Soviet challenges during the war. In spite of the limitations experienced, Washington coped effectively with the multicrisis challenge, but it did so with a reduced number of options. It is in the degree of effectiveness to preserve peace that some qualifications are necessary concerning American success.

[34]Speech by Deputy Prime Minister Allon, October 30, 1968, *Weekly News Bulletin*, October 29–November 4, 1968. Provided by Israel Information Service. See also *The New York Times*, October 31, 1968.

III THE QUEMOY CONFLICT OF 1958

During late July and early August 1958 there were an increasing number of signs of a threat to the Nationalist-occupied islands a few miles off the coast of mainland China. On August 23 the Chinese Communists began an intensive bombardment of the Quemoy and Matsu Islands. Heavy shelling combined with torpedo-boat attacks complicated reprovisioning of the offshore islands. The Chinese threatened imminent invasion.

On September 6, 1958, the first phase of the crisis ended with China's acceptance of an American offer to resume negotiations in Warsaw. During the second phase of the crisis the military situation improved gradually, and on October 5, 1958, Peking announced a seven-day cease-fire. Although sporadic dueling continued in the succeeding months, the threat of a major confrontation had passed.

The crisis presented a difficult dilemma. The offshore islands were hard to defend, and the U.S. commitment was ambiguous and politically controversial. American armed forces were involved in the Middle East (in Lebanon), and some policy makers suspected that Chiang Kai-shek wanted to exploit the situation to draw the United States into war with China. The dangers were intensified by possible Soviet acquiescence to Peking's scheme.

7. GENERAL BACKGROUND

Before examining the buildup phase it is important to consider relevant American problems in the summer of 1958, factors influencing U.S. relations with Nationalist China,[1] general trends of Soviet and British foreign policies, and the military capabilities of each nation for intervention in the Taiwan area.

7.1 UNITED STATES POLICY

As the crisis began to develop in the Formosa Strait, the United States was already committed in Lebanon, still recovering from the strategic implications of the Soviet space success with Sputnik, and concerned about the extent of anti-American sentiment throughout the world.

However, the Lebanon involvement did not necessarily create an environment hostile to additional commitments. The landings increased the credibility of U.S. limited war capabilities, and now American fleet strength could no longer be considered just as display. President Eisenhower's handling of the crisis had caused a sharp upswing in his popularity and had improved the outlook for Republican congressmen in the forthcoming elections.[2] While some concern was expressed about the "exposed position"[3] in the Middle East and the "serious inadequacies" demonstrated by the landings,[4] Congress had reacted by increasing defense appropriations.[5]

There was growing concern about the insufficiency of U.S. con-

[1]Reference to China or the Chinese without qualification means Communist-controlled China. Chiang Kai-shek's government on Formosa will normally be referred to as the Nationalists.

[2]See, for example, *The Washington Post* article by George Gallup, "Lebanon Gave Hypo to Ike's Popularity," August 17, 1958, p. E3, and *The New York Times* article by Arthur Krock, "Republican Outlook in Election Improves," August 3, 1958.

[3]Speech by Senator J. W. Fulbright "On the Brink of Disaster," in U.S., *Congressional Record,* 85th Cong., 2nd sess., vol. 104, part 13 (August 6, 1958), p. 16317.

[4]*The New York Times* editorial "More Billions for Defense," August 9, 1958, p. 12. John G. Norris observed, "Had fighting broken out the United States would have been hard pressed to reinforce and support them." *The Washington Post* article "Lebanon Bared U.S. Army Deficiencies," August 24, 1958, p. E1.

[5]In early August Congress appropriated the largest peacetime budget up to that time "under the double impact of the sputniks and the Middle East crisis." *The New York Times,* August 9, 1958, p. 12. Congress overruled cuts in the Army and Marines and voted $140 million above the budget for the airlift. *The Washington Post,* August 24, 1958, p. E1.

ventional forces.[6] In order to cope with the threat to Lebanon, 15,000 troops, three marine battalion landing teams, and the ships of the Sixth Fleet were tied down in the Middle East. Many of the Army troops had been taken from U.S. divisions in Germany, thus reducing NATO readiness. If there had been open fighting in Lebanon, the United States would have been hard pressed to cope with even a moderate struggle in the Formosa area.[7] Some military leaders felt that the range of threats which could be deterred by massive retaliation had narrowed considerably. As the Chief of Naval Operations warned Congress in June 1958, "the mutual capability to annihilate each other as we have seen is not a deterrent to Communist aggression by other means. It is in fact likely that the Communists will channel greater effort into the cold war. . . . Massive destruction will not prevent this type of creeping aggression."[8] Although the number of advocates of improved limited war capabilities was growing, this point of view was not yet prevalent in Washington.

While it was still generally believed that tactical weapons would compensate for disparities of conventional forces in a limited war,[9] there was growing concern about the implications of Soviet missile

[6]The Navy had joined the Army in stressing the need for greater limited war forces. Deficiencies had been exposed by the Gaither Committee and numerous congessional hearings.

[7]Admiral Arleigh A. Burke, for example, agreed with Senator Hubert Humphrey that "we were stretched pretty thin" in meeting the Quemoy situation and would have been hard pressed if there had been fighting in the Middle East." U.S., Congress, Senate, Subcommittee of the Committee on Foreign Relations, *Disarmament and Foreign Policy,* Part 2, 86th Cong. 1st sess. (Washington, 1959), pp. 106, 107.

[8]Statement of Admiral Arleigh A. Burke, USN, June 12, 1958, in U.S., Senate, Subcommittee of the Committee on Appropriations, *Department of Defense Appropriations, 1959,* 85th Cong., 2nd sess. (Washington, 1958), p. 143.

[9]The Secretary of Defense had asserted in 1957 that "tactical weapons, in a sense have now become conventional weapons," U.S., Congress, House, *United States Defense Policies in 1957,* 85th Cong., 2nd sess., House Document No. 436 (Washington, 1958), p. 9. In the 1958 version the House Report asserted, "we . . . have been rapidly replacing manpower with modern weapons, particularly tactical nuclear weapons, which we hope would give our force a parity with the numerically much larger Soviet ground forces." U.S., House, *United States Defense Policies in 1958,* House Document No. 227, 86th Cong. 1st sess. (Washington, 1959), p. 10. It should be noted that there had been some questions raised concerning the possibility of using such weapons in a controlled manner. The recently retired Commander of the Sixth Fleet, Admiral "Cat" Brown, commented in October 1958, that "I would not recommend the use of any atomic weapons no matter how small, when both sides have the power to destroy the world. . . . I have no faith in the so-called controlled use of atomic weapons." *Defense Policies in 1958,* p. 15.

developments. The Russian launching of Sputnik in November 1957 lent credibility to Moscow's claims of having intercontinental ballistic missiles with nuclear warheads. In June 1958 the United States was not sure where it stood vis-à-vis the Soviet Union concerning ICBMs.[10] However, in spite of anxiety about relative strategic deterrent strengths, most critics realized that the United States still had a margin of superiority because of its many bases and diversified means of delivery. Concern was focused on the period two years hence. Since neither side had yet developed an invulnerable second-strike capability, the United States maintained some deterrent advantage in strategic nuclear weapons, but the confusion of the "missile gap" period lessened the real advantage. Nevertheless, Khrushchev's cautious approach to the Lebanon landings undoubtedly increased American confidence in its ability to deter the Soviets as the Quemoy test approached.

It is possible that the Chinese undertook the Quemoy probe because of American preoccupation in Lebanon.[11] However, by August that crisis had passed its peak,[12] and it was clear that the United States would not become engaged in fighting in the Middle East. With troops still occupying Lebanon, the Defense Department was reluctant to become involved in another potential conflict situation. But, because of the limited scope of the Lebanon affair and the nature of defense requirements in the Formosa Strait area, the United States was not faced with serious military limitations. Troop shortages were not a significant factor in estimates of military capability to defend Taiwan or the offshore islands. The major brunt of any military effort there would be borne by forces of the Seventh Fleet, supplemented by Marine and Air Force planes.

The Seventh Fleet was a relatively strong naval force of two aircraft carriers, two cruisers, thirty-six destroyers, four submarines, and twenty amphibious and support ships. The fleet was vulnerable to submarine and air attack but considerably stronger than Sino-

[10]President Eisenhower stated at his June 18, 1958, news conference that "no one knows exactly how we stand with the Russians on the intercontinental missile." *Public Papers of the Presidents of the United States,* Dwight D. Eisenhower, 1958 (Washington, 1959), p. 486.

[11]The Commander in Chief in the Pacific testified following the crisis that "they probed in Taiwan because possibly they thought we were weak there and had mustered all our forces over in Lebanon." Testimony of Admiral H. D. Felt, USN, in U.S. Senate, Committee on Foreign Relations, *Mutual Security Act of 1959, Part 1,* 86th Cong. 1st sess. (Washington, 1959), p. 12.

[12]As early as July 19, 1959, it was obvious that the danger of war against the Soviet Union was extremely remote. See, for example, Khrushchev's letter to Eisenhower of July 19, 1958, *New Times,* Supplement, No. 30 (July 1958), pp. 5–7.

Soviet naval forces. Chinese fighters and bombers flying from airfields that had recently been put into operation in the vicinity of Quemoy posed the greatest threat, but American tactical nuclear weapons helped offset Chinese air strength.[13]

There were many trouble spots in the summer of 1958 where American forces might become involved. In May anti-American manifestations appeared in Algeria, Lebanon, Burma, Peru, Venezuela, and Canada. A civil war with Communist overtones in Indonesia was being monitored by Seventh Fleet ships. Anti-American riots were so severe during the Vice President's trip to Latin America that the President had ordered troops flown into Puerto Rico and Guantànamo Bay, Cuba. There had also been an insurrection in Panama in May, and Castro's revolution had begun in Cuba. In June the dispute between Greece and Turkey flared up again with serious implications for NATO defenses.

The unrest in Latin America and the Middle East produced some domestic criticism that America's position in the world was precarious and that U.S. foreign policy lacked direction.[14] There were predictions that additional opposition privately expressed by influential Democrats would come into the open as the need for unity during the Middle East crisis lessened.[15] With a congressional election approaching, Democrats were sensitive to potential accusations that they might be criticizing U.S. policy for electoral advantage and not providing support in a time of crisis.[16] The Senate authorized a thorough review of U.S. foreign policy on July 31, 1958.

[13]President Eisenhower had agreed with Secretary of State Dulles in March 1955 that "If we defend Quemoy and Matsu we'll have to use atomic weapons. They alone will be effective against mainland air fields." Dwight D. Eisenhower, *Mandate for Change, 1953–1956* (Garden City, N.Y.: Doubleday and Co., 1963), p. 476. The President had stated in a March 16, 1955, press conference that the United States would use tactical atomic weapons in a general war in Asia against a strictly military target. Hanson W. Baldwin has pointed out that the number of sorties necessary to "take out" the Chinese Communist airfields would be about seven if tactical nuclear weapons were used and about 7000 if conventional weapons were employed. "Limited War," *The Atlantic,* Vol. 203, No. 5 (May 1959), p. 42. Military doctrine at the time supported the use of nuclear weapons in limited war. This had been one of the important features of the "New New Look" approach to defense. See Samuel P. Huntington, *The Common Defense* (New York: Columbia University Press, 1961), pp. 105–106.

[14]See the speeches by Senator J. W. Fulbright in U.S., *Congressional Record,* 85th Cong., 2nd sess., vol. 104, pts. 9, 13, pp. 11844–11850 and pp. 16317–16320. See also the comments of Hanson W. Baldwin on the magnitude of U.S. commitments in *The New York Times,* August 3, 1958, p. E5.

[15]*The New York Times* article by James Reston, "Mood in Washington," August 7, 1958, p. 5.

[16]Richard P. Stebbins, *The United States in World Affairs 1958,* Council on Foreign Relations (New York: Harper and Bros., 1959), p. 122.

7.2 SPECIFIC FACTORS RELATING TO U.S. POLICY TOWARD NATIONALIST CHINA

To interpret U.S. policy during the Quemoy crisis, the extent of American interests and commitments to the Nationalists must first be assessed. The survival of the Republic of China was considered to be important to the United States as a "challenge to Communist influence in Asia" and as a vital link in the island chain off the Asian mainland which formed the "defense perimeter of the United States."[17] With American assistance the Nationalists maintained the second largest military force in the Far East. The $260 million annual American aid contribution provided almost two-thirds of the Nationalist budget.[18] As part of its hardening containment strategy toward Communist China in the aftermath of the Korean War and the struggle in Indochina, the United States had made a mutual defense pact with the Republic of China. The key article of the treaty specified that "Each party recognizes that an armed attack in the West Pacific Area directed against the territories of the parties would be dangerous to its own peace and safety and declares that it would act to meet the common danger in accordance with its constitutional processes."[19] The offshore islands occupied by the Nationalists had been deliberately omitted from the treaty perimeter, but the commitment to defend Taiwan and the Pescadores was clearly established. (See Figure 7.1.)

Another important agreement had been contained in an exchange of letters between Secretary of State Dulles and Foreign Minister Yeh on December 10, 1954. It was promised that the "use of force" from either Taiwan or the offshore islands would be a "matter of joint agreement."[20] President Eisenhower had interpreted this as an agreement "not to attack the mainland unilaterally."[21] In 1953 he had rescinded instructions to the Seventh Fleet to prevent a Na-

[17]Definition of U.S. interests concerning Republic of China in U.S., Congress, House, Committee on Foreign Affairs, *Mutual Security Act of 1958,* Vol. 2, 85th Cong., 2nd sess. (Washington, 1958), p. 1718.

[18]The figures, of course, varied from year to year. Total economic and military aid in fiscal year 1958 amounted to $261.9 million. The 1957 and 1959 figures are higher. Information supplied in letter from Office of the Director of Military Assistance, Department of Defense, to Lt. Comdr. J. T. Howe, USN, dated March 18, 1969.

[19]U.S., Senate, Committee on Foreign Relations, *Mutual Defense Treaty with the Republic of China,* 84th Congress, 1st sess., Executive Report No. 2 (Washington, 1955), p. 9. The meaning of "territories" was specified to be Taiwan and the Pescadores in the case of the Republic of China.

[20]U.S., Department of State, *American Foreign Policy 1950–1955,* Vol. 1 (Washington, 1957), pp. 947–949. The notes were kept secret for a month following their signing.

[21]Dwight D. Eisenhower, *Waging Peace 1956–1961* (Garden City, N.Y.: Doubleday and Co., 1965), p. 466.

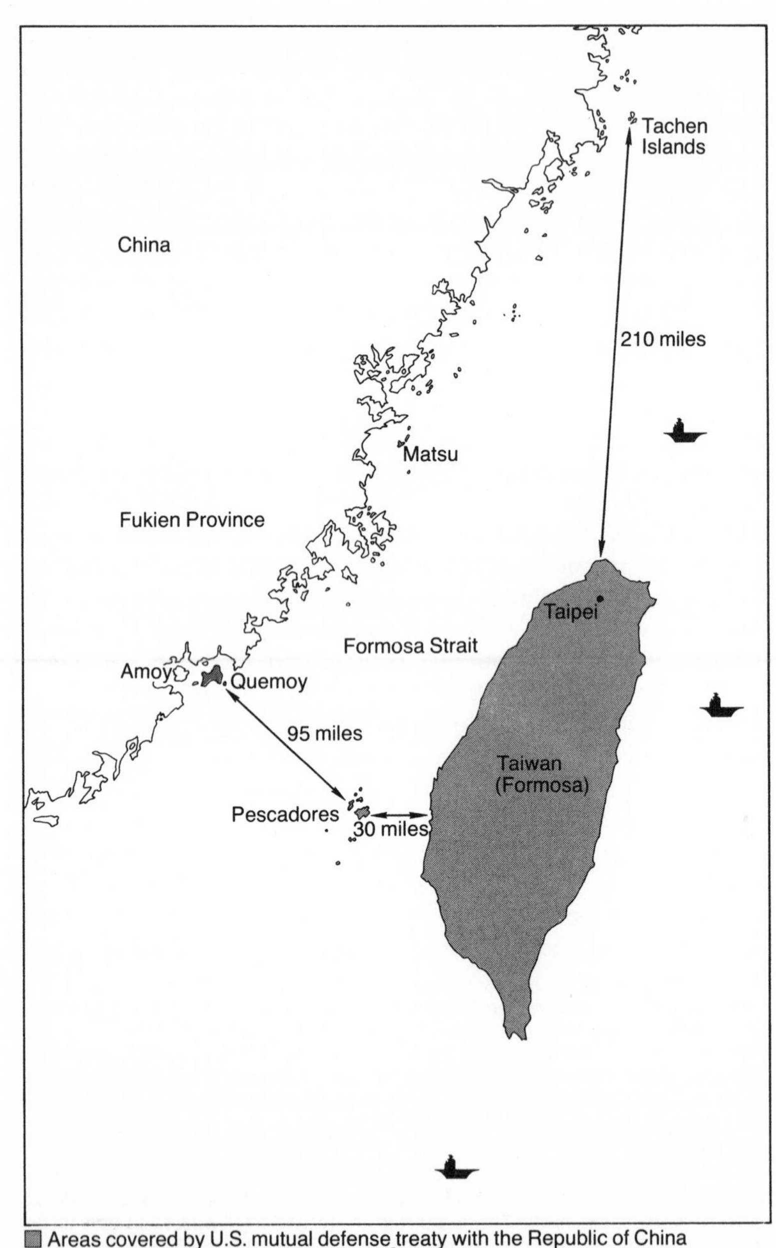

Figure 7.1 Territory covered by U.S. mutual defense treaty with Republic of China and general locations of Seventh Fleet task forces during Quemoy crisis

tionalist attack on the mainland.[22] The 1954 exchange obligated Chiang to consult Washington first. It was highly unlikely that Washington would agree to a Nationalist attempt to return to the mainland.

The commitment to defend the offshore islands was less specific and more controversial. Because of the Communist seizure of Ichiang Island on January 18, 1955, the President had asked Congress for authority to use American forces to defend other Nationalist-occupied islands if a threat to them was considered preliminary to an attack on Formosa. After considerable Senate debate, a resolution was passed with only three dissenting votes in each house. It authorized the President to

> . . . employ the armed forces of the United States, *as he deems necessary* for the specific purpose of securing and protecting Formosa and the Pescadores against armed attack, this authority to include the securing and *protecting* of *such related positions* and territories of that area now in friendly hands and the taking of such *other measures as he judges to be required* or appropriate in assuring the defense of Formosa and the Pescadores.[23] [Emphasis added.]

In essence Congress had presented the President a blank check to defend the offshore islands when he judged it was necessary to protect Formosa. Although it could be argued that Congress did not have the constitutional power to delegate its war powers to the President, the lawmakers' intent was clear. Permission to take "other measures" could have been interpreted as authority to launch a preventive war against the mainland, although the President disclaimed any such intention.[24] Amendment proposals limiting the authority granted to the President and excluding Quemoy[25]

[22]"The State of the Union," message to Congress of February 2, 1953, *American Foreign Policy, 1950–1955,* p. 60.

[23]Ibid., p. 12. The House had approved the resolution almost immediately with only three opposing votes.

[24]Senator Wayne Morse testified subsequently that he felt the proposals of Secretary of State Dulles and Admiral Radford in executive session "amounted to preventive war." U.S., Congress, Senate, Subcommittee on Separation of Powers of the Committee on the Judiciary, *Separation of Powers, Part 1,* 90th Cong., 1st sess. (Washington, 1967), p. 59. President Eisenhower subsequently commented that although neither he nor Secretary Dulles had ever recommended bombing the mainland of China, "under certain conditions—if they got too aggressive and arrogant—we had selected targets that we would hit. And we never talked about strategic bombing in the sense of going at great populated areas. There were just airfields and supporting points around the Quemoy and Matsu complex." Interview with General Eisenhower conducted on July 28, 1964, by Dr. P. A. Crowl of the Dulles Oral History Project, Princeton University, page 21 of the approved transcript.

[25]References to "Quemoy" are meant to include both the Big and Little Quemoy Islands.

and Matsu from the defense perimeter were defeated.[26]

The resolution was deliberately ambiguous to provide maximum flexibility. But the United States was not officially committed to defend the offshore islands unless Formosa was threatened. However, some private assurances may have been given to the Nationalists. It has been alleged that the United States made a secret commitment to defend Quemoy and Matsu when urging evacuation of the Tachen Islands in early 1955.[27] Another version is that "informal assurances" of "firm intentions" to defend the islands were given.[28] Chiang Kai-shek has asserted that Secretary Dulles "verbally promised us that, after our evacuation of the Tachen Islands, the United States of America would jointly defend Quemoy and Matsu."[29] However, one of the key policy makers during the 1955 crisis did not recall any "secret or private assurances" going beyond the public record.[30] The American ambassador to the Republic of China in 1958 has stated categorically that "we had no private agreement with Chiang to defend the islands."[31] Apparently, American officials intended that the informal assurances which

[26]Among those who voted in favor of a floor amendment to exclude Quemoy and Matsu were seven senators who were members of the Committee on Foreign Relations in 1958 during the second Quemoy crisis. Senator L. B. Johnson, who opposed the amendment, paired with Senator J. F. Kennedy, who wanted to restrict the authorization.

[27]Morton H. Halperin and Tang Tsou, "United States Policy Toward the Offshore Islands," *Public Policy,* vol. XV, 1966, Harvard Center for International Affairs reprint series, p. 125. The remarks of Senator Morse lend some credence to this view. During a January 26, 1955, Senate floor debate Morse quoted an article by Stewart Alsop which asserted, "In the end, the President decided on a curious compromise—the Tachens would be evacuated while war would be risked if necessary to defend Quemoy. . . ." U.S., *Congressional Record,* 84th Cong., 1st sess., vol. 101, pt. 1 (January 26, 1955), p. 743.

[28]Ambassador Karl Lott Rankin has written that the Nationalists hoped for "formal inclusion" of Quemoy and Matsu but "had to accept second best." *China Assignment* (Seattle: University of Washington Press, 1964), p. 221.

[29]Interview with Chiang Kai-shek and Mme. Chiang Kai-shek conducted on Taiwan on September 24, 1964, by Mr. Spencer Davis for Dulles Oral History Project, page 14 of the approved transcript. When asked if the "verbal assurance" was part of the military thinking of the two governments, Chiang replied, "Yes, there was an understanding on this point." It was understandable, of course, that Chiang would give informal assurances the most favorable interpretations for his point of view.

[30]Letter from Professor Robert R. Bowie, to Lt. Comdr. J. T. Howe, USN, dated August 16, 1968. Ambassador Rankin has also written that in presenting Chiang a message in May 1955, "we understand his position" with reference to the offshore islands, Chiang asked if it "meant that President Eisenhower would actually commit United States forces to help in the defense of Kinmen and Matsu," and the ambassador responded that he "thought not." Rankin, *China Assignment,* p. 229.

[31]Letter from Ambassador Everett F. Drumright to Lt. Comdr. J. T. Howe, USN, dated March 7, 1969.

were given apply only to the early 1955 situation and not necessarily permanently. President Eisenhower recounted that following a briefing in March 1955, Speaker of the House Sam Rayburn remarked, "he understood from it that if the Communists should attack Quemoy and Matsu, the United States would intervene." The President has written that he "quickly corrected this conclusion" by commenting, ". . . the tricky business is to determine whether or not an attack on Quemoy and Matsu, if made, is truly a local operation or a preliminary to a major effort against Formosa."[32] In order to provide maximum deterrent effect, the United States wanted to convince Peking that it would defend the islands. By 1958 it was felt the resolution had done just that.[33] At the same time Washington wanted Chiang Kai-shek to understand that the commitment was not automatic.

However, by acquiescing to Nationalist fortification and deployment of one-third of the army to the islands, the United States had put itself in a position in which defense of the offshore islands would most likely be found to be "appropriate in assuring the defense of Formosa." Tacitly Washington appeared to have assented to automatic defense of the islands. President Eisenhower had felt it was a mistake to place large troop concentrations on the islands and had sent a mission to convince Chiang to garrison the islands only as outposts.[34] But when Chiang remained adamant, the President sympathized.[35] United States military advisors assisted in fortifying the islands. In 1958 "our adopted policy" was "to assist in building them up to where they can defend the offshore islands."[36]

[32]Eisenhower, *Mandate for Change,* p. 480.
[33]For example, the Commander in Chief, Pacific, Admiral Felix Stump, testified in March 1958 that "the Communists are afraid because of that resolution we will act and act immediately to resist aggression and attack and I think particularly the good part of it is that the President of the United States has the right to determine whether or not an attack on the offshore islands constitutes an attack on Formosa and the Pescadores and I think that has prevented anything more than the usual shooting back and forth of artillery, with no attempt to take them." House, *Mutual Security Act of 1958,* p. 122. Secretary of State Dulles testified that the "blessing" of the Formosa resolution had been a "stabilizing effect" on the area, p. 224.
[34]Eisenhower, *Mandate for Change,* pp. 466, 481, 611, 612.
[35]The President wrote concerning the failure of the Radford-Robertson mission that "despite my disappointment, I could not help reflecting that if I had been in his position, I might well have made the same decision." Ibid., p. 482. Chiang Kai-shek has stated that the American government was in favor of the Nationalist decision to move troops from the Tachen Islands to Quemoy. Chiang Kai-shek, interview, p. 12. At that time, of course, Washington was anxious to persuade Chiang to evacuate the Tachen Islands.
[36]Testimony of Admiral Felix B. Stump, Commander in Chief, Pacific, on March 21, 1958, in U.S., Congress, Senate, Committee on Foreign Relations, *Mutual Security Act of 1958,* 85th Cong., 2nd sess. (Washington, 1958), p. 121.

The President summed up his dilemma in a letter to Winston Churchill in which he wrote,

Diplomatically it would indeed be a great relief to us if the line between the Nationalists and the Communists were actually the broad Strait of Formosa instead of the narrow Straits between Quemoy and Matsu and the Mainland. However, there are about 55,000 of the Nationalist troops on these coastal islands and the problem created thereby cannot, I fear, be resolved by our merely announcing a desire to transplant them to Formosa. We must not lose Chiang's Army and we must maintain its strength, efficiency, and morale.[37]

By 1958 some 150,000 first-line Nationalist troops were dug in a few miles off the mainland. The essential prerequisite for invoking the Formosa resolution appeared to have been established.

Concentration of troops on the offshore islands had increased Quemoy's military importance, but the overriding reasons for defending the islands were psychological. Chiang's primary concern was that in case of losing Quemoy his main forces would "lose their will to fight."[38] President Eisenhower concurred. He noted privately in 1955 that ". . . this retreat, and the coercion we would have to exert to bring it about, would so undermine the morale and the loyalty of the non-Communist forces on Formosa that they could not be counted on."[39] The Joint Chiefs of Staff had agreed in 1954 that "the offshore islands were not militarily necessary to the defense of Formosa" but that their loss would have "bad, possibly disastrous, psychological effects."[40] in 1958 the Commander in Chief in the Pacific reiterated a similar view that

. . . to abandon the offshore islands [deleted], would destroy the morale of the Chinese people and the Chinese military forces, which is a matter of fact. And, of course, an army is just as completely destroyed if you destroy its morale as if you defeat it in battle. For that reason the defense of the offshore islands are [*sic*] important because that is the way the Chinese feel about them.[41]

[37]This letter was written on February 19, 1955, to Winston Churchill. Eisenhower, *Mandate for Change,* p. 472.

[38]Eisenhower, *Mandate for Change,* p. 461.

[39]Letter of February 19, 1955, to Winston Churchill. Ibid., pp. 474, 475.

[40]Ibid., p. 463. President Eisenhower saw some military value in the positions as they made it much more difficult for the Communists to assemble an amphibious force for an invasion of Taiwan. Eisenhower, interview, page 23. General M. Ridgway, USA, Army Chief of Staff in 1955, did not agree that the islands should be defended. However, his successor seemingly concurred with the Joint Chiefs of Staff position. Letter from General Maxwell D. Taylor, USA (Ret.), to Lt. Comdr. J. T. Howe, USN, dated March 4, 1969.

[41]Testimony of Adm. Stump, *Mutual Security Act of 1958,* p. 121. In testimony following the 1958 crisis the new Commander in Chief, Pacific, Admiral H. D. Felt, USN, said in April 1959, "I think if we forced President Chiang

Why was Chiang insistent on concentrating troops on the islands in numbers that seemed to exceed the necessities of efficient defense? The motive may have been linked to his belief that he would eventually return to the mainland. Although to many Americans such a scheme seemed to be a totally unrealistic, romantic illusion, the hope of returning to the mainland was the lifeblood of Chiang's government and essential to the legitimacy of his office on Taiwan. The dream was an ingrained part of the mentality of the exile. By holding territory historically associated with the mainland, Chiang could genuinely claim to be occupying a small part of China.

The islands also provided Chiang with a base of operations for exploiting opportunities on the mainland. Chiang was realistic about his inability to invade China. Nonetheless, if widespread revolt or even a civil war in Fukien and neighboring provinces developed, he may have wanted to have a force ready to take advantage of the opportunity. However, the rugged landscape and heavy Chinese military fortifications opposite the offshore islands made that area of the coast far from ideal for an invasion. Chiang subsequently asserted that Quemoy was "completely unsuited as an offensive base."[42] The Nationalists probably would have launched any invasion direct from Taiwan to another point on the mainland.

It seems more likely that Chiang's primary aim in putting large numbers of troops on the offshore islands was to ensure American participation in their defense. President Eisenhower subsequently remarked, "We had the feeling that he wanted to reinforce them so heavily with personnel that it would be difficult, indeed, for us not to go right to their defense quickly, even if there were only a local attack."[43] Chiang may have hoped that American involvement would expand into operations against the mainland. The combination of large Nationalist forces on the islands commanding the entrances to Chinese ports, periodic raids against the mainland, harassment of Chinese shipping, and a major Nationalist propaganda operation undoubtedly was a sharp thorn in the Chinese side. The American government, however, was convinced that Chiang "would not give up an inch of territory in his possession."[44]

to give up these offshore islands, it would be disastrous. The free Asians would then lose confidence in the United States and be inclined to make accommodations with the Communists." *Mutual Security Act of 1959,* p. 19.

[42]*The Sunday Times* (London) report of interview with Chiang Kai-shek, October 5, 1958, p. 1.

[43]Eisenhower, interview, p. 31. It is possible that President Eisenhower did not feel this way until well into the crisis.

[44]Drumright, letter.

In the past, the Nationalists had successfully defended Quemoy. A Chinese invasion force of 15,000 men had reached the beaches in October 1949 but had been annihilated. Although a small island defended by a Nationalist garrison had been overrun by the Chinese in 1955, past history indicated that invasion of a heavily defended Quemoy was not as easy as it might appear from a glance at the geography.[45] (See Figure 7.2.)

While there were differences in 1958 because of the changing world situation, most problems related to defense of the offshore islands had been anticipated. There were many parallels between the 1954-1955 and 1958 offshore island crises. Key decision makers, such as the President, Secretary of State, Chairman of the Joint Chiefs,[46] and important congressional leaders, were the same. The position of close allies was known, and the President was aware that some domestic political opposition might be encountered, although his 1955 policy had been widely approved.

A number of pressure groups and prominent individuals were sympathetic to the cause of the Nationalists. However, the influence of the China lobby was declining, and there was not widespread pro-Nationalist sentiment among the general public. The interest group was small but not insignificant. The Assistant Secretary of State for Far Eastern Affairs advocated strong support for the Nationalists. Several members of the Committee of One Million were also prominent figures in the 1958 Quemoy crisis. Senator William Douglas and Acting Chairman Thomas E. Morgan of the House Foreign Affairs Committee were prominent Democrats. Nevertheless, it did not appear that the lobbies would have a direct influence on policy decisions.

Although Washington would not alter its policy toward recognition and was outspoken against the "two Chinas" solution,[47] it had tried in previous negotiations to arrange a mutual renunciation of force in the Formosa Strait area. But Peking had refused to discuss such

[45]The military commander responsible for coordinating military activities in the Taiwan area has commented, "I doubt very much that they could have captured them [the offshore islands] if they had tried. These islands are probably some of the most heavily defended pieces of real estate in the world, and the Communists had tried [twice], and each time took a terrible licking. Letter from Vice Adm. Roland N. Smoot, USN, to Lt. Comdr. J. T. Howe, USN, dated March 1, 1968.

[46]General N. Twining had served as the Chief of Staff, U.S. Air Force, during the 1954–1955 crisis.

[47]A strong statement defending the nonrecognition policy was made public on August 9 and sent to all U.S. embassies. See *The New York Times,* "Text of U.S. Policy Statement on Non-Recognition of Communist Regime in China," August 10, 1958, p. 30. See section 8.1.

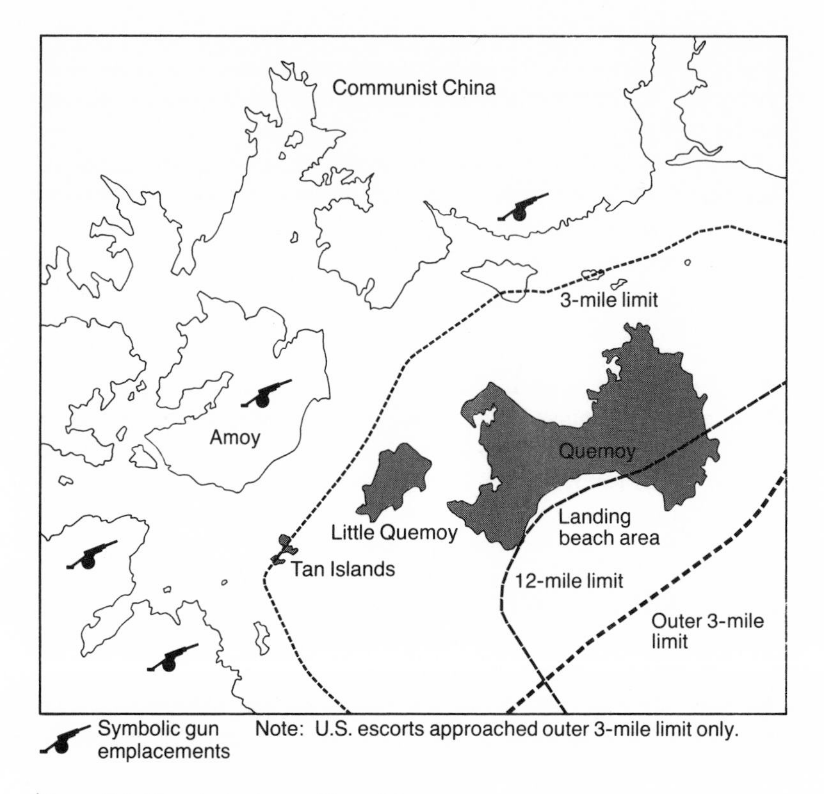

Figure 7.2 The strategic position of Quemoy

an arrangement. Seemingly in response to indications that a crisis might be developing, the United States attempted on July 28 to arrange the resumption of talks. However, these overtures were ignored.[48]

Threats and sporadic bombardments had occurred on numerous occasions since the 1955 crisis. In February of 1958, for example, Premier Chou En-lai had asserted that "Taiwan is an inalienable part of the Chinese territory. The Chinese people are determined to liberate Taiwan."[49] On July 17, there was a marked increase in Chinese propaganda calling for "liberation."[50] Significantly, Chinese military leaders had been gathered on May 27, 1958, for a conference that lasted eight weeks. Undoubtedly, the Quemoy strategy was discussed at that time. Chinese airfields in the Fukien Province were put into operation,[51] a railroad had been completed to the port of Amoy, and troop concentrations and general military activity in the area was increased. The United States had a number of indications that a crisis was developing.

7.3 SOVIET FOREIGN POLICY

To appreciate the extent of the American problem as the Quemoy crisis developed, one must consider the concerns of Russian policy makers, the state of Sino-Soviet relations, Washington's assessment of Moscow's motives, and the Russian capability to provide direct military support.

While actively pursuing a détente policy toward the West, Moscow hoped to weaken the position of the United States and its European allies and to continue an economic and political offensive in the Middle East and Africa. Internal dissension in Eastern Europe was a serious Russian concern, and Sino-Soviet relations had deteriorated markedly in the spring of 1958.

Although the extent of the Sino-Soviet rift was not widely recognized in the West, there were two important indications of a sharp turn for the worse. Harsh Chinese criticism of "Yugoslav" revisionism in April and May of 1958 was intended for the Soviet Union,[52]

[48]Kenneth T. Young, *Negotiating with the Chinese Communists: The United States Experience 1953–1967* (New York: McGraw-Hill Book Co., 1968), p. 140.

[49]*Defense Policies in 1958,* p. 30.

[50]*The Guardian* (Manchester) article by Victor Zorza, August 7, 1958, p. 5.

[51]MIGs were evidently moved into three airfields when the Lebanon landings occurred. Increasing air activity began about July 29. *The New York Times,* August 9 and August 12, 1958.

[52]Chinese criticisms of the Yugoslav "agentura" [agents for imperialism] were severe condemnations of the Russians. By this time Yugoslavia had become a surrogate for Soviet Union in Sino-Soviet esoteric polemics.

and Chinese authorities began to stress that China would have to develop its own military technology rather than depend on the Soviet Union.[53] In addition, Peking's emphasis on communes represented an ideological slap in the face as well as a hint of a Chinese alternative to the Soviet example for the Third World.[54]

The Chinese had already expressed reservations about the Soviet policy of "peaceful coexistence."[55] Peking feared that détente with the United States meant Chinese strategic ambitions in Asia would be relegated to a lower priority. Following the launching of the sputnik and Moscow's claims of missile superiority, Mao pressured Khrushchev to take greater advantage of the alleged alteration in the balance of power. He urged more militant support for national liberation movements and Chinese aspirations to "liberate" the Nationalist-held islands. Peking hoped to take advantage of Russia's mounting power to help achieve the eventual withdrawal of the United States from Asia. Moscow, well aware of the limits of these scientific breakthroughs, argued that its achievements made a policy of détente with the West even more feasible. The Kremlin was willing to make concessions for some Chinese goals in order to reestablish a firm alliance with Peking but not at the risk of a military confrontation with the United States.

Although the Soviet Union had verbally supported Chinese claims to the offshore islands, it was not clear to what extent Moscow would be willing to risk its own interests in order to foster Peking's ambitions. However, Moscow's cautious approach to the Lebanon landings provided some indication. The Soviets were extremely apprehensive about the entry of Western troops into a region of vital strategic importance, but their threats of retaliation were not convincing.[56] Chinese commentaries on the situation reflected disappointment with Russian restraint.

[53]See the evidence presented by Harold P. Ford in R. L. Garthoff, ed., *Sino-Soviet Military Relations* (New York: Praeger, 1966), pp. 102, 103.
[54]William E. Griffith, *The Sino-Soviet Rift* (Cambridge: The M.I.T. Press, 1964), p. 18.
[55]See, for example, the Chinese comments in the open letter of September 6, 1963, by the editorial departments of *People's Daily* and *Red Flag*. *Peking Review*, Vol. VI, No. 37 (September 13, 1963), pp. 6–23.
[56]The Soviets did not make their nuclear threats until it was clear that the United States had no intention of invading Iraq. Russian forces did not appear in the Mediterranean, and the Soviets responded weakly by holding "exercises" in the Transcaucasus and Turkestan military districts and staging a joint exercise with Bulgaria. The Soviet exercises were announced by the Soviet Home Service, July 17, 1958, although they did not at that time normally publicize military maneuvers. While no Russian ships were detected slipping into the Mediterranean early in the crisis, within weeks Soviet submarines and a tender were sent to a Soviet base in Albania. Statement of Office of Naval Intelligence in United States, Congress, House,

The Soviets preferred to conduct their political and economic offensive in an atmosphere of East-West stability. Khrushchev had labored persistently since the Hungarian uprising to arrange a summit conference, and he appeared to be seeking a permanent ban on the testing of nuclear weapons.[57] Soviet, British, and American experts on detection of nuclear testing had begun a conference in Geneva on July 2, 1958. It was just such détente tactics that antagonized the Chinese, who were becoming fearful of a Soviet-American deal at Peking's expense. They were especially concerned about nuclear weapons agreements, because Russians had promised in October 1957 to help develop Chinese nuclear technology.[58]

While the American government was receptive to peaceful Soviet overtures, it remained wary of Russian global ambitions. Secretary of State Dulles felt that the probability of war had decreased considerably,[59] but it was generally believed that Moscow would take advantage of any opportunity to increase its power in areas where no Western resistance was anticipated.[60] In facing the 1955 Quemoy crisis, President Eisenhower had assumed that Moscow would like to see the United States in a "debilitating war with Communist China."[61] However, in 1958, government officials thought that Khrushchev would not aid Mao either "militarily or logistically in an attempt to 'liberate' Taiwan" without first "being sure" of the American position.[62] Although believing that Peking received policy guidance from Moscow and that probes of weak spots by the Communists could be expected, Washington felt that the Soviets wanted

Special Subcommittee on Sea Power of Committee on Armed Forces, *Status of Naval Ships,* 91st Cong., 1st sess. (Washington, 1968), p. 244.

[57]The Soviet and U.S. media during the period prior to and during the Quemoy crisis devoted much attention to this question. For an account of Soviet objectives and maneuvers at this time see J. M. Mackintosh, *Strategy and Tactics of Soviet Foreign Policy* (New York: Oxford University Press, 1963), pp. 210–213, 237.

[58]For an authoritative summary of what is known to date about the agreement, see Walter C. Clemens, Jr., *The Arms Race and Sino-Soviet Relations* (Stanford: Hoover Institute, 1968), pp.16–24.

[59]See the statement of Secretary of State J. F. Dulles on June 6, 1958, in U.S., Congress, Senate, Committee on Foreign Relations, *Review of Foreign Policy, 1958, Part 2,* 85th Cong., 2nd sess. (Washington, 1958), p. 795.

[60]President Eisenhower, for example, warned in his State of the Union message that the Soviet threat to expand its power had become "increasingly serious" and reinforced by its industrial, military and scientific establishment. Message of January 9, 1958, *Public Papers of the President,* p. 3.

[61]Eisenhower, *Mandate for Change,* p. 469.

[62]For example, letter from Mr. Walter S. Robertson, Assistant Secretary for Far Eastern Affairs during both Quemoy crises, to Lt. Comdr. J. T. Howe, USN, dated December 12, 1968.

to expand their influence by peaceful means. Therefore, it was reasoned that a resolute American stand would deter direct Soviet involvement.

During most of Khrushchev's tenure, the belief that limited wars would lead to nuclear exchanges predominated in the Kremlin's policy. Khrushchev had written to British Prime Minister Macmillan at the height of the Lebanon crisis that "All talk of 'little' or 'local' wars is . . . only a naive illusion, and the hope that hostilities can be restricted a deception. . . ."[63] The Soviet leader had a disdain for conventional forces and, particularly, the surface navy. Even though the Russians possessed formidable forces, they lacked the psychological framework needed to employ them.

Moscow had little hope of challenging American naval power directly, but its fleet could not be disregarded. During the Suez crisis Soviet submarines had been active in the South China Sea,[64] and during 1958 there was a marked increase in operations away from home waters.[65] Since World War II Russia had built more warships than the rest of the world's navies combined and had become second in total tonnage.[66] There were concerns about the strength of the Soviet submarine fleet, rumors that Russia had built nuclear powered submarines, and predictions that a submerged missile-launching capability was imminent.[67] The Chief of Naval Operations described the buildup as "the most significant development in Soviet planned strategy since World War II."[68]

The Russians were estimated to have six cruisers, fifty destroyers, more than 100 submarines, and a limited amphibious capability[69] in their Pacific Fleet. Some 1100 naval aircraft helped compensate for the lack of aircraft carriers, but operations in the Taiwan area

[63]Message from N. S. Khrushchev to Harold Macmillan, July 19, 1958. *New Times* Supplement, No. 30 (July 1958), p. 9.

[64]In November 1956 Soviet naval forces were concentrated at Tsingtao, China, and a submarine barrier was established between the Gulf of Tonkin and the Spratly Islands. See Capt. Toshikazu Ohmal, "The New Position of Japan in the General Strategic Picture of the Far East," Chapter 13 in Comdr. M. G. Saunders, RN, ed., *The Soviet Navy* (New York: Praeger, 1958), p. 281.

[65]Testimony of Adm. Arleigh A. Burke, USN, in *Defense Appropriations 1959*, p. 142.

[66]*The Soviet Union and the NATO Powers: The Military Balance, 1959* (London: Institute for Strategic Studies, 1959). See also *United States Defense Policies in 1957*, p. 7.

[67]See, for example, the testimony in *Review of Foreign Policy, 1958*, p. 461, and *Mutual Security Act of 1958*, p. 109.

[68]Adm. Arleigh A. Burke, USN, as quoted in *The Soviet Navy*, p. 299.

[69]See, for example, J. Meister, "Soviet Sea Power Amphibious Assault," published in October 1957 issue of *The Navy* and reprinted in the *Military Review*, Vol. XXXVIII, No. 9 (December 1958), p. 109.

would require Chinese permission to use their fields. The Soviets regarded U.S. aircraft carriers, the main striking element of the Seventh Fleet, as vulnerable to submarines and already obsolete.[70] The Soviets obviously had some capability for naval operations in the Pacific, but their forces were considered to be inferior to the U.S. Pacific Fleet in the area. The Commander of the Seventh Fleet commented, "our naval strength was always far greater than the Soviets, *especially so in 1958.*"[71]

Chinese naval capability was almost insignificant. The Chinese owned twenty Russian-built submarines, but there had been little evidence of Chinese submarine operations.[72] Peking's counter to the Seventh Fleet was its fighter-bomber strength rather than its navy. However, even the Chinese air force lacked a nuclear capability.

In mid-1958 the Soviets were not interested in supporting the national aspirations of their Chinese comrades at the risk of a direct confrontation with the United States. Militarily, the Communists did not possess enough strength in either strategic nuclear weapons or local conventional forces to conduct a successful amphibious assault on the offshore islands in the face of determined U.S. resistance.

7.4 BRITISH FOREIGN POLICY

In approaching the Quemoy crisis, Washington did not anticipate much support from London. The limited British military resources were already heavily committed. The deployment of troops to the Middle East in conjunction with the American landings in Lebanon had not been limited to Jordan. British reinforcements had been sent to Libya, Bahrain, and Aden. Troops had also been dispatched to Cyprus to try to control the Greek-Turkish dispute. In order to provide the necessary manpower, the United Kingdom had scraped "the bottom of the barrel" at home and drastically weakened garrisons in places like Kenya and Gibraltar.[73]

[70]Marshal Malinovsky, the Soviet Defense Minister, stated that the submarine force was prepared "to drown any American aircraft carriers that appear in our waters" and that the U.S. Navy "does not seem to understand that carriers are already obsolete." As quoted in G. F. Elliot, *Victory Without War 1958–1961* (Annapolis: U.S. Naval Institute, 1958), p. 19.
[71](Emphasis added.) Letter from Vice Adm. Frederick N. Kivette, USN (Ret.), to Lt. Comdr. J. T. Howe, USN, dated March 5, 1968.
[72]Testimony of the CinC Pacific on March 2, 1958, in *Mutual Security Act of 1958*, p. 109.
[73]See, for example, *The Times* (London) editorial "Gambling on 1963," August 14, 1958.

The Royal Navy had also been concentrated near the coasts of the Middle East region. Of four operational aircraft carriers, two were in the Mediterranean and one was patrolling the Persian Gulf. A marine battalion had been sent to Libya, and ships had been rushed from the Far East and the south Atlantic to bolster the force south of Suez. From July through November 1958 these British forces were involved with the Middle East situation.[74]

British responsibilities in the Far East stretched from Aden to Hong Kong, but the forces available to support these interests were relatively small. The fleet based at Singapore normally consisted of a single cruiser and a number of destroyers, frigates, and smaller vessels. However, the bulk of this Far Eastern fleet had been dispatched to the Persian Gulf. Some light craft were assigned for local defense of Hong Kong, where tension was mounting due to Chinese pressure.

Any direct military contribution in the Far East would be relatively insignificant, but British forces were making an important addition to the global defense of the United States. Royal Navy squadrons in the Mediterranean and the Persian Gulf areas reduced the need for extra American warships that had been assigned to the Sixth Fleet.

There was also little likelihood of direct British political support for American defense of the Nationalists. Since the Korean armistices, Washington's and London's policies toward China had been on diverging courses. London had recognized China was "indifferent to the fate of Formosa," and favored seating China in the United Nations.[75] Peking appeared to be tacitly rewarding the British by limiting interference in Crown territories like Hong Kong, Malaya, and North Borneo. But the British were also paying a price in flexibility by depending on Peking's tacit approval in order to maintain these vulnerable positions.

London, therefore, had something tangible to lose if it took a pro-American stand on the Quemoy issue. The British were also genuinely concerned about the risks of being drawn into a major war. President Eisenhower had endeavored unsuccessfully during the 1955 crisis to convince the U.K. leadership of the soundness of America's Quemoy policy. Labor leader Clement Attlee had urged

[74]Rear Adm. H. G. Thrusfried, RN, ed., *Brassey's Annual: The Armed Forces Year Book* (New York: Macmillan, 1959), p. 298.

[75]G. F. Hudson, "British Relations with China," *Current History*, Vol. 33, No. 196 (December 1957), p. 330. *The Economist* commented in the August 23, 1958, issue that "American and British policies are as far apart as ever" over the policy of conciliating China. "Quemoy Again," August 23, 1958, p. 584.

neutralization of Formosa and getting "rid of Chiang."[76] Conservative Foreign Minister Anthony Eden had little enthusiasm for risking war and had proposed that the Nationalists withdraw from the offshore islands. And Prime Minister Churchill had counseled the United States to "disentangle" itself.[77]

The official British declaratory policy toward the Nationalist-occupied island was markedly different from that of the United States. In a prepared answer given in the House of Commons on February 4, 1955, Sir Anthony Eden had indicated that the *de jure* sovereignty over Formosa and the Pescadores was uncertain. But he diverged even further from the U.S. position in reference to the offshore islands when he stated, "The Nationalist held islands in close proximity to the coast of China are in a different category from Formosa and the Pescadores since they *undoubtedly form part of the territory* of the People's Republic of China." (Emphasis added.) He warned, however, against a Chinese attempt to assert the claim: "Any attempt by . . . China . . . to assert its authority over these islands by force would in the circumstances at present peculiar to the case, give rise to a situation endangering peace and security, which is properly a matter of international concern."[78] While not supporting the use of force to capture the islands, London felt that Peking had a legal right and a just claim to sovereignty.

Because of London's declared policy the United States had little reason to believe that British backing would be forthcoming in another offshore island crisis. However, their policy did not necessarily preclude support if the conflict expanded beyond Quemoy and Matsu. In 1955 President Eisenhower reportedly had commented in response to criticism of the allied attitude that "The question that bothers the British and French is the possibility of a general war starting over Quemoy and Matsu. They will support us in defending Formosa and they won't be lukewarm about it either."[79] There was concern in 1958 that the United States might be compelled to fight in the area without any allied support. In May Senator Russell Long

[76]Eisenhower, *Mandate for Change,* p. 464.

[77]Ibid., pp. 464, 472, 475.

[78]Written answers to questions, February 4, 1955, *Parliamentary Debates* (*Hansard*), House of Commons, Vol. 536 (January 25–February 16, 1955), p. 159. This statement was referred to when a similar question arose concerning British policy in February 1956. Oral Answers, February 15, 1956, *Parliamentary Debates (Hansard),* Vol. 548 (January 24–February 15, 1956), p. 2358.

[79]Sherman Adams, *Firsthand Report* (New York: Harper and Bros., 1961), p. 123. House Speaker Sam Rayburn had been the one who raised the question with the President.

asked whether anyone would support America in a fight over Formosa against the Russian-aided Chinese.[80] In the case of Quemoy and Matsu it was almost certain that the answer would be "no." What the British position would be if attacks included Formosa itself was a moot question. But in a major global war, Britain undoubtedly would respond.

It was not likely that Washington expected political or military help in a local war in the Formosa Strait. However, by deploying most of its mobile forces to the Middle East, London was providing the United States with significant military aid.

[80]Senator R. B. Long raised these questions to the Secretary of Defense in May 1958 hearings. *Mutual Security Act of 1958,* p. 38.

8. THE BUILDUP PHASE

AUGUST 4, 1958, TO AUGUST 22, 1958

Increasing tension in the Formosa Strait area became internationally significant on August 4 when it was revealed that Soviet Premier Khrushchev had just completed three days of secret discussions with the Chinese leader Mao Tse-tung. There was some speculation that the meeting was related to the military buildup in the Quemoy area.[1] The growing number of actual clashes between Nationalist and Chinese aircraft and ships and the increasing frequency of shelling portended an ominous development.[2] President Eisenhower was informed by intelligence sources on August 6 that the Chinese might try to seize the offshore islands,[3] and the Nationalists put their forces on alert.[4] To understand policy choices in this situation and estimates of U.S. capability to cope with the threat, it is necessary to consider a number of interrelated factors affecting American, Soviet, and British foreign policy.

8.1 UNITED STATES POLICY

During most of the buildup phase the U.S. government was deliberately silent. President Eisenhower explained that the idea of making a strong statement was carefully considered, and some thought it might deter a Chinese offensive. In the end, however, the idea was rejected because the predominant opinion was that it was more advantageous to keep the Chinese guessing. Officials thought that a definite commitment to defend certain islands would be an invitation to the Communists to attempt to take others.[5] In addition, Washington had the problem of restraining Chiang Kai-shek. The objective was to limit his aggressiveness without discouraging his determination to resist an attack.[6]

Although there was no official pronouncement, the United States seemingly tried to indicate a firm position by less direct methods. The State Department voiced concern about the deployment of jet

[1]See, for example, *The Guardian* article by Victor Zorza, "Khrushchev Talks With Mao," August 4, 1958, p. 1; and *The New York Times* article by Harry Schwartz, August 10, 1958, p. E3.
[2]Light shelling began on August 4 and lasted for three days. *The Guardian* (Manchester), "Growing Threat to Formosa," August 7, 1958, p. 5.
[3]Dwight D. Eisenhower, *Waging Peace, 1956–1961* (Garden City, N.Y.: Doubleday and Co., 1965), p. 292.
[4]*The New York Times*, August 7, 1958.
[5]Eisenhower, *Waging Peace*, p. 296. Eisenhower indicates that he felt that Secretary Dulles, who was out of the country, would have preferred a strong stand but that he (Eisenhower) went along with the Joint Chiefs.
[6]Ibid.

aircraft to the fields opposite the "offshore islands and Taiwan" and noted that propaganda broadcasts were "threatening to liberate Taiwan." According to the government, the Chinese buildup of air capability was designed to "raise the specter of war," and it was asserted that the situation was being watched closely.[7]

On August 9 an emphatic statement of U.S. policy on the nonrecognition of China was released.[8] The timing of this document and its underlying message seemed to be cautioning Peking that Washington would respond firmly to any major attack on Nationalist positions. The value of U.S. support was stressed. Although Washington was privately concerned that Chiang might someday invade the mainland, the Nationalist army had been advertised as a strong force which gave pause to Peking's expansionism. Chiang's "sizable military force" was depicted as a "significant deterrent to renewed Chinese Communist aggression."[9] It was asserted that Mao's regime "does not rule all China and there is a substantial force in being which contests its claim to do so."[10] This force, according to the memorandum, kept alive the hopes of Chinese who wanted to free their country. Communism in China was "not permanent," and "it one day will pass."[11] These statements were bound to antagonize Peking. Evidently, the purpose of this uncompromising approach[12] was to show that Washington was in no mood to change its policy and would not be intimidated by the Chinese military buildup.[13]

In a speech on August 19, 1958, the Secretary of State emphasized the need to maintain the "capacity and the will to retaliate against

[7]Text of State Department statement in *The Guardian* article by Victor Zorza, "Planes and Propaganda," August 9, 1958, p. 8.

[8]This statement was sent to all U.S. embassies. *The New York Times,* "Text of U.S. Policy Statement on Non-Recognition of Communist Regime in China," August 10, 1958, p. 30.

[9]"U.S. Policy on Nonrecognition of Communist China," Department of State *Bulletin,* Vol. XXXIX, No. 1002 (September 8, 1958), p. 387. Text of memorandum sent by Department of State to its missions abroad.

[10]Ibid., p. 388. It also stressed that the Chinese had "not completed their conquest of the country," p. 387.

[11]Ibid., p. 389. Secretary of State Dulles reputedly declared on August 10, "we will do all that we can to contribute to the passing away of this regime." Kenneth T. Young, *Negotiating with the Chinese Communists: The United States Experience 1953–1967* (New York: McGraw-Hill Book Co., 1968), p. 142.

[12]The claim was made, however, that "it is not an 'inflexible' policy that cannot be altered to meet changed conditions." Ibid., p. 385.

[13]The statement referred to frequent threats by the Chinese to seize Taiwan by force and asserted that attacks on the non-Communist world had "reached a level of intensity that has not been witnessed since the Korean War." Ibid., p. 386.

the Soviet Union" if it carries out threats of aggression and stated, in a reference to collective security pacts with "nearly fifty nations," that "an attack upon one is an attack upon all."[14] Agreements of this kind are contained in the NATO treaty and the Rio Pact, but such an automatic commitment does not exist in the defense treaty with the Republic of China.[15] The President took advantage of a press conference question to emphasize that the defense establishment was more than adequate and "the most powerful" it had ever been "in our whole history."[16] These indirect statements during the buildup phase, while not referring directly to the conflict in the Quemoy area, seemed calculated to indicate that the United States stood strongly and firmly behind the Nationalists.

In specific references to the situation there appeared to be some attempt to downgrade it as a potential crisis. "Private" remarks of State Department officials indicated that they were "concerned . . . but not alarmed." A statement had been issued "only because so many reporters had asked for official comment on reports from Taipei."[17] Reference was made to the "*usual* flow" of propaganda threats,[18] and officials declared that they had no confirmation of reports that the Communists were "preparing to invade Quemoy."[19] Officials thought that if the United States did not overreact, its national prestige might not become so deeply involved as to make a conflict inevitable.

The step-up of tension in the area was not an unusual phenomenon, and the tone of reports implied it might disappear. Most of the Chinese shells reportedly contained propaganda leaflets.[20] War-

[14]*The New York Times,* "Text of address to the Veterans of Foreign Wars" by Secretary of State John F. Dulles, August 19, 1958.

[15]Compare the provisions listed in the State Department compilation of commitments in U.S., Senate, Committee on Foreign Relations, 90th Cong. 1st sess., *U.S. Commitments to Foreign Powers* (Washington, 1967), pp. 52–60.

[16]*The Washington Post,* "Text of President's Press-Radio Conference," August 21, 1958, p. A8. He said in reference to indirect aggression by the Soviets, "we have got to keep on the job forever and forever with our own measures to make certain that these small countries and weaker countries do not fall one by one prey to their methods."

[17]*The New York Times* article "Red China Scored by US on Straits Jets," August 9, 1958.

[18]*The Guardian* (Manchester), August 9, 1958, p. 8. (Emphasis added.)

[19]*The New York Times* article "US Doubts Red Plan Attack," August 12, 1958, p. 9.

[20]During the year up to that time the Chinese were said to have fired 400 propaganda bursts over the islands compared with some 700 destructive shells. *The New York Times* article by Tillman Durdin, "Quemoy Visitor Finds Isle Calm," August 17, 1958.

ship engagements were described as a "frequent occurrence."[21] Invasion of Quemoy would require a "massive effort" for which preparations were not evident.[22] While it was true that sporadic shelling, naval and air duels, and propaganda attacks had been frequent in the past, the new and ominous factor was the buildup of Chinese air power and the increase in troop concentrations. A third airfield near the coast opposite the Formosa Strait was reported in operation on August 6 and a fourth field on August 18.[23] These developments and the Nationalist mobilization could not be ignored by U.S. policy makers. Apparently it was hoped that the situation would amount to just another nuisance.[24] The Commander in Chief in the Pacific made the following note stating, "Purpose of build-up obscure, of course. But it could mean assault on Taiwan."[25] While outwardly minimizing the conflict, the government was privately aware of the serious crisis potential of the developments.

An important factor in any American decision to defend Quemoy was the capability of Nationalists and Americans to hold the offshore island positions. Any estimate had first to consider the strategic balance between the United States and the Soviet Union and the probability of a direct Russian involvement.[26] But the most urgent military question concerned the threat of Chinese bombers within range of Taiwan. It was decided, as in 1955,[27] that tactical nuclear weapons would have to be used against the airfields if the Chinese made bomber attacks. President Eisenhower has written:

> We recognized, however, that to be successful we might face the necessity of using small yield atomic weapons against hostile airfields, for from vastly dispersed locations, enemy bombers could concentrate their lethality on the target area of Formosa, the Pescadores, and the offshore islands. This immense geographical advantage, extremely difficult if not impossible to eliminate with conventional weapons, would have to be offset by our sheer power.[28]

[21]*The New York Times,* August 11, 1958.

[22]*The New York Times* article by Tillman Durdin, August 17, 1958. It was reported that Nationalist headquarters stated there were no indications of any big amphibious buildup.

[23]*The New York Times* article "Red Build-up Reported," August 6, 1958, p. 8; article "Another Airfield in Use by Reds Near Taiwan," August 18, 1958, p. 7.

[24]See interview with official familiar with policy during Quemoy crisis of 1958, conducted January 31, 1969, Appendix B, Question 10.

[25]Letter from Admiral Harry D. Felt, USN (Ret.), to Lt. Comdr. J. T. Howe, USN, dated July 16, 1968.

[26]See Section 7.1 for a discussion of the strategic balance; for an estimate of Soviet motivations, see Section 7.3.

[27]See Section 7.1.

[28]Eisenhower, *Waging Peace,* p. 295. In a private memo of understanding between the President and the Secretary of State, dated September 4, 1958, the considerations for employment of nuclear weapons are discussed in de-

Although reports that Russia had given them the atom bomb had apparently been planted by the Chinese,[29] the Western intelligence community did not take the stories seriously.[30]

Of more immediate significance was whether the islands could be defended against an assault that remained localized. It would take a massive Chinese invasion to conquer the islands, but President Eisenhower felt that without U.S. intervention ". . . the Chicoms, by accepting heavy casualties, could take Quemoy by an amphibious assault supported by artillery and aerial bombardment."[31] He estimated that the assault could be staged "with little advance notice" and "once initiated might take from one to several days depending on the quality of the resistance."[32] With U.S. aid, however, it was apparently felt that the major islands could be held in spite of their vulnerable geographical position. (See Figure 7.1.) The Chief of Naval Operations at the time has written:

> I felt that Quemoy and Matsu could be defended by the Chinese Nationalists if they put their whole back into it and with the help of the 7th Fleet. Quite naturally I did not know for sure and so I was prepared to reinforce the 7th Fleet greatly, and we worked very hard also to insure that the Chinese Nationalists really put their own effort into it.[33]

tail. See Appendix 0, pp. 691–693 of *Waging Peace*. Admiral Burke testified that in the Quemoy situation, "we were prepared for the use of either conventional weapons or nuclear weapons" and that "when we went into Taiwan, the first reactions that our people had, were to prepare for a nuclear war." U.S., Senate, Subcommittee of the Committee on Foreign Relations, 86th Cong. 1st sess., *Disarmament and Foreign Policy* (Washington, 1959), pp. 83, 97. On September 27 the Secretary of the Air Force announced that the United States was prepared to use nuclear weapons in the defense of Quemoy. *The New York Times*, September 28, 1958.

[29]*The Sunday Times* (London) article by Richard Hughes, "China Has A-Bomb From Russia," August 10, 1958, p. 1. See also *The New York Times*, "Soviet A-Bomb Supply to Red China Reported," August 10, 1958, p. 2, and *The New York Times* article by A. M. Rosenthal from Warsaw, "Soviet Reported Planning to Send Chinese Atom Arms," August 18, 1958. However, on August 16 the Chinese called the atom bomb a "paper tiger" and said, "the people will destroy the bomb." They claimed that the Soviet Union, but not the Chinese, had nuclear weapons. *Red Flag* quoting Mao in *Peking Review*, Vol. 1, No. 25 (August 19, 1958), p. 10.

[30]See for example, interview with official familiar with policy during Quemoy crisis of 1958, conducted January 31, 1969, Appendix B, Question 6. Also letters from Lt. Gen. R. C. Mangrum, USMC, to Lt. Comdr. J. T. Howe, USN.

[31]Eisenhower, *Waging Peace*, p. 691. The Joint Chiefs in 1955, when faced with a similar problem, had agreed the Nationalists would need some U.S. aid. Dwight D. Eisenhower, *Mandate for Change, 1953–1956* (Garden City, N.Y.: Doubleday and Co., 1963), p. 473.

[32]Ibid.

[33]Letter from Adm. Arleigh A. Burke, USN (Ret.), to Lt. Comdr. J. T. Howe, USN, dated July 9, 1968.

Officers in the field were even more optimistic. The American coordinator of military operations in the Taiwan area doubted "very much" that China "could have captured them."[34]

Military planners also had to consider the limitations imposed by the Lebanon situation. However, U.S. capacity to react in the Far East had not been measurably affected because the "physical effects" of the Lebanon crisis were largely in the past and the United States had not been involved in fighting.[35] Therefore, commanders were confident that the Seventh Fleet was strong enough to defend the offshore islands.[36]

Although there probably was an agreement that the positions were not essential from a geographical and tactical point of view,[37] American leaders apparently believed that the islands should be defended for psychological reasons and because loss of one-third of the Nationalist army would have serious implications for defense of Formosa. Admiral Arleigh Burke has commented, "If I was asked once I was asked 100 times of what military importance is Quemoy and Matsu. Of course the answer was that they were not of great military importance. They were of tremendous psychological importance. . . . Quemoy and Matsu were just as important to the Republic of China as a man's wife is important to him. No more, no less."[38] President Eisenhower felt that loss of the islands by assault or surrender would have a serious impact upon the "authority and military capability" of the Nationalists and completely undermine Chiang's regime.[39] The American President believed that the surrender of Quemoy would eventually lead to "union with Communist China."[40] Although Chiang probably subtly stimulated these American fears, the likelihood of some sort of rapprochement between Taipei and Peking seemed remote.[41] Such a deal would violate the legalistic concept of authority held by both regimes. The Nationalists seemed to have no alternative to dependence on the

[34]Letter from Vice Adm. R. N. Smoot, USN, to Lt. Comdr. J. T. Howe, USN, dated March 1, 1968. Also letter from informed observer concerning the Quemoy crisis dated March 13, 1967.

[35]Burke, letter of July 9, 1968.

[36]Felt, letter.

[37]*The Economist,* for example, commented that "American military opinion is reported to be that Formosa could be more easily defended if "the offshore islands were given up." "Quemoy Again," *The Economist* (August 23, 1958), p. 583.

[38]Burke, letter of July 9, 1968.

[39]Eisenhower, *Waging Peace,* p. 692. "Memorandum Re Formosa Strait Situation" of September 4, 1958.

[40]Ibid.

[41]There apparently, however, has been some indirect communication between the two Chinese governments over the years.

United States. However, President Eisenhower evidently concluded that the loss of Quemoy would eventually have "catastrophic" consequences for the U.S. position in the Far East.[42] The defense establishment appears to have concluded that the offshore islands could and should be defended.

To evaluate whether the United States was capable of helping Chiang hold Quemoy it is necessary to assess congressional opinion. This is particularly difficult because of the absence of statements from senators and representatives concerning the developing crisis. The President's handling of the Lebanon crisis had met with general congressional approval even though the landings had been undertaken with questionable legal justification.[43] There did not appear to be a sense of impending crisis in Congress, which was working hard toward adjournment. Chairman Thomas Morgan's letter of August 22 expressed apprehension, but he was undoubtedly more concerned about too little being done to protect the Nationalists than the consequences of U.S. involvement.[44] The Committee on Foreign Relations, seven of whose members had voted to exclude Quemoy and Matsu from the Formosa resolution, apparently made some informal effort to influence policy formulation in the developing situation.[45] However, there are no records of formal consultations between the administration and the committee.[46] It is speculated that the lawmakers had little influence on policy during the buildup phase and that the President was not overly concerned by some anticipated opposition to his policy. The absence of critical congressional statements when it was evident that another crisis might develop indicated a tacit acceptance of the policy formulated in 1955.[47]

Public opinion also did not appear to have any significant negative influence on the government during this period. There were some indications of general concern about American foreign policy. As-

[42]Eisenhower, *Waging Peace,* p. 692.

[43]The President did not invoke the Eisenhower Doctrine but instead stressed preserving the "independence and integrity of Lebanon" and security for American residents. See U.S., Congress, House, 86th Cong., 2nd sess., *Joint Resolution to Promote Peace and Stability in the Middle East,* House Document No. 342 (Washington, 1960), p. 1.

[44]See Section 9.1, footnote 2.

[45]Letter from Senator Mike Mansfield to Lt. Comdr. J. T. Howe, USN, dated July 17, 1968. Because of the brevity of his answer, it is not certain to what extent or in what direction it was attempted to influence the policy.

[46]Letter from Seth Tillman, consultant for Committee on Foreign Relations, to Lt. Comdr. J. T. Howe, USN, dated March 4, 1969.

[47]Undoubtedly there was, however, some reluctance to speak out and perhaps weaken the U.S. stance, a sense of crisis loyalty.

sertions that the United States had become "overextended"[48] and considered itself the "fixer of the world"[49] continued. But few editorial comments pertained specifically to Quemoy. The President had no reason to believe that the defense of Quemoy would be unpopular, other than with a small minority.

The Nationalists sought a firm American pledge of support to defend the offshore islands. Taipei warned that an attack on Quemoy was likely because the world was focused on the Middle East and pushed the theme that the Soviets were behind the plot.[50] There is some evidence that Chiang was trying to lure the United States into a battle. For instance, the American military commander on Taiwan has asserted that ". . . the Chinese Nationalist ruling hierarchy, from the Gimo on down, welcomed the incident as being a possible opening for their one and everlasting objective: return to the mainland."[51] In order to pass judgment on Chiang's motivation it would be important to know whether his intelligence reports indicated the situation on the mainland provided an exploitable opportunity. Chiang apparently did hint of "*vast dissent* on the mainland."[52] While not all observers agreed on the extent of Chiang's ambitions in this situation, there was a general wariness about his possible motivations.[53] Washington was probably well informed of any changes in the tempo of provocative harassments of the mainland from the offshore islands. There were reportedly some 600 Central

[48]*The Guardian* (Manchester) article "Domestic Critics of Mr. Dulles," August 14, 1958, p. 7. It was reported that there was widespread dismay about foreign policy. One school of thought in the United States felt that commitments should be reduced and another that the country should be stronger and respond more rapidly, according to the article.

[49]*Wall Street Journal* editorials of August 20 and August 26 as quoted from D. F. Fleming, *The Cold War and Its Origins* (Garden City, N.Y.: Doubleday and Co., 1961), p. 937.

[50]See, for example, *The New York Times,* August 4, 1958, p. 4, and August 5, 1958, p. 6.

[51]Smoot, letter. This is also the theme of Tang Tsou in *The Embroilment Over Quemoy: Mao, Chiang, and Dulles,* International Study Paper No. 2 (Salt Lake City: University of Utah Press, 1959), pp. 15–24.

[52](Emphasis added.) The evidence, however, is not solid. This quotation is among some random notes of James Russell Wiggins dated November 18, 1958. He remarked that Ambassador Beam "Sees nothing to sustain Chiang's hints. . . ." "Notes on Conversations between James Russell Wiggins and John Foster Dulles," Princeton University Library. There was, however, some evidence of domestic discontent in China at the time. It is probably an exaggeration, however, to describe it as "vast."

[53]For example, Ambassador Drumright felt Chiang "would not have been adverse to a conflict between the Communists and the U.S., but I would say he was too sophisticated to try to exploit the crisis for the bigger purpose of return to the mainland." Letter from Ambassador Everett F. Drumright, to Lt. Comdr. J. T. Howe, USN, dated March 7, 1969.

Intelligence Agency personnel assigned to Formosa, in addition to U.S. military advisers. While one can only speculate about Chiang's intentions, American suspicions undoubtedly contributed to the restrained U.S. military movements during the buildup.

There also had been a "nagging doubt," probably a carry-over from the 1955 crisis, about "how loyal" Chiang's troops would be if attacked.[54] The will of the troops to resist was unknown. Some Nationalist officers, who were predominantly mainlanders, also shared these doubts about the fortitude of their troops, who were mostly native Taiwanese, in resisting an attack on Quemoy. Nationalist flyers were considered to be better pilots than their Chinese counterparts because of greater experience, but their aircraft were slightly inferior to the new MIGs appearing on the Chinese airfields.[55] American advisors were a little uncertain about how the Nationalists would perform in aerial combat. Some questions had also been raised about the aggressiveness of the Nationalist navy in its clashes with the Communists. Washington could not be sure that its ally would stand up under attack and, therefore, knew that a firmer American commitment might involve carrying on most of the fighting.

In contrast to the publicized buildup of U.S. forces in the Mediterranean prior to the Lebanon landings, there was no overt increase in the size of the Seventh Fleet and no major show of strength in the vicinity of the Formosa Strait in order to impress the Chinese with U.S. determination. The President had decided not to attempt to deter aggression with a strong declaratory and military stand. It was not desired to publicize the intentions of the United States or to aggravate the situation. The decision to commit U.S. forces remained tentative. When asked why we did not make a strong show of strength during this period, the Chief of Naval Operations said, "One of the essential ingredients to make a show of naval force effective is the willingness to use that force if the enemy does not cease and desist. You can't bluff these days."[56] Admiral Burke seemed to be implying there was not even a provisional decision to use American force to protect the offshore islands. The government's decision not to send forces to the area apparently reflected a high degree of uncertainty about Chinese intentions, Chiang's role in the crisis, and whether there was a legitimate threat to For-

[54]President Eisenhower described this as Dulles's reaction to his March 1955 trip to Formosa. Eisenhower added, "This disturbed me." Eisenhower, *Mandate for Change,* p. 476.
[55]See, for example, *The New York Times* article by Tillman Durdin, "Peiping Air Force More Combative," August 10, 1958, p. 28.
[56]Burke, letter, July 9, 1968.

mosa. Washington's reluctance probably raised legitimate doubts in Taipei about the firmness of the American commitment.

Such a tactic was militarily feasible because Chinese amphibious craft had not been moved into position for an assault and the Soviet navy remained in port. In addition, the major U.S. contribution in the initial phases would be its air power and ships which could rapidly be sent into the area. The strength of the Seventh Fleet was well known to the Russians and Chinese, and they probably did not need to be impressed with a show of force to know what they would face if the United States committed itself. There were reports of increased Seventh Fleet activity in the Strait, and some jets were flown into Formosa.[57] The Commander in Chief in the Pacific felt that the Seventh Fleet was ready to act,[58] but its public position was in keeping with the tendency to minimize the crisis. On the day the shelling began, half of the Seventh Fleet carrier-cruiser force was in dry dock in the Philippines.[59] The amphibious forces were in Singapore, nearly 2000 miles and about four days away from Formosa.[60] The marines had moved far away from the area of potential trouble, an indication that American troops were not expected to be utilized in initial stages of defense of the offshore islands. The U.S. Navy, which had been put on worldwide alert on May 19, 1958, because of the Lebanon situation, was given orders to restore normal operations on August 7.[61]

8.2 SOVIET POLICY

It is still not clear what advice Moscow gave Peking during the period preceding the shelling of Quemoy. Krushchev's sudden visit to Peking on July 31, 1958, probably was for the purpose of discussing the conflict as well as exchanging views on other problems disrupting Sino-Soviet relations. Undoubtedly, Mao had been aggravated by Krushchev's invitation to India and China's exclusion from a

[57]*The New York Times,* August 20, 1958, p. 5; *The Guardian* (Manchester), August 9, 1958, p. 8.

[58]Felt, letter.

[59]Franc Shor, "Pacific Fleet Force for Peace," *The National Geographic Magazine,* Vol. CXVI, No. 3 (September 1959), p. 316. One of two attack carriers and one of two cruisers, the flagship *Helena,* were docked there.

[60]Their presence in Singapore was attributed to a possible attempt to set up a U.S. force in the Indian Ocean, but this was denied by the President. *The Washington Post,* "Eisenhower Press Conference," August 21, 1958, p. A8. See also article by John G. Norris, *The Washington Post,* August 17, 1958, p. 1. The marines may have originally been intended to augment U.S. Middle East forces. Mangrum, letters.

[61]It was announced on August 13 that one of the marine battalions in the Middle East would reembark in ships, as a step toward deescalating the Middle East situation. *The New York Times,* August 13, 1958, p. 1.

five-power conference on the Middle East situation. In discussing the motives for the Peking meeting, the Soviet *New Times* editorialized, "In the present tense situation, when the Anglo-American aggression in the Middle East has brought the world to the brink of a war catastrophe, the Chinese and Soviet leaders *found it necessary* to meet for an *exchange of opinions*."[62] (Emphasis added.) Since that crisis was well beyond the critical stage, the statement may indicate that the primary purpose of the meeting was to iron out conflicts in their overall strategies. In the esoteric language of Communist communications, the phrase "exchange of opinions" usually indicates that serious differences exist.

In light of ensuing events it seems reasonably certain that Chinese ambitions concerning the offshore islands were discussed. It is less sure whether the Soviets tried to discourage such a venture entirely or gave it some grudging support. Since Defense Minister Malinovski accompanied Khrushchev, presumably military subjects were considered. According to one source, the Soviets proposed a "joint" defense scheme, including Russian bases on Chinese soil and "mixed" naval units equipped with nuclear-tipped missiles. The Soviets, however, would have controlled the trigger. Reportedly, the suggestion was discussed at the meeting and rejected by Mao, who was unwilling to have his defense and foreign policy handed over to virtual Russian control. The Soviets, in turn, seem to have utilized Mao's refusal as a convenient excuse to disassociate themselves from any plan to invade the offshore islands.[63] There are a number of substantive indications that some scheme for joint military operations was proposed and rejected in 1958.[64]

[62]"The Peking Meeting," *New Times*, No. 32 (August 1958), p. 1.
[63]This information is contained in an unpublished work of Mr. Fred Rendall, who had access to authoritative British Foreign Office material.
[64]The Secretary General of the Sino-Japanese Friendship Association allegedly claimed in 1964 that "Russia had tried to rule China in 1958 by proposing a joint Sino-Soviet fleet and the construction of a long-range navigational aid station on the Chinese mainland." BBC Summary of World Broadcasts, Part 3, FE/1488. Elizabeth Gurly Flynn, an American Communist who had attended the 1960 Moscow Communist conference, wrote that the Chinese would not cooperate in a scheme to build a "joint early warning radar station that would be used to defend Pacific waters." *Political Affairs*, Vol. XLII, No. 11 (November 1963), p. 30. Edward Crankshaw has alleged that the "scheme for establishing a unified Pacific naval command had broken down because of Moscow's fear that the Chinese might draw the Soviet Union into a war over Taiwan." "Khrushchev and China," *The Atlantic*, Vol. 207, No. 5 (May 1961), p. 46. He appears to have confused Moscow's motive. The Soviets wanted the scheme precisely to prevent their being drawn into an unwanted Formosa conflict. In the open polemics of 1963 the

There were other signs that the Soviets declined to give wholehearted support to Chinese plans. The official communiqué following the conference implied that differences had existed prior to the meeting and that many issues remained unresolved.[65] A Peking *People's Daily* editorial emphasized the basic Sino-Soviet disagreement on what constituted a safe risk. It may have reflected Chinese disappointment with Moscow's failure to support Peking's Taiwan ambitions as well as criticism of the Soviet response to Western intervention in the Middle East. It said,

The imperialists like to frighten the *nervous* with the choice between submission or war. *Their agents* frequently spread the nonsensical idea that peace can be achieved only by currying favor and *compromising* with the aggressors. *Some soft-hearted advocates of peace* even naively believe that in order to relax tension *at all costs* the *enemy must not be provoked* . . . .[66] [Emphasis added.]

The reference to "some soft-hearted advocates" obviously meant the Soviets. It is quite possible that Peking was also accusing Khrushchev's group of being "agents" of the West, the height of insult in Sino-Soviet polemics. This passage may imply that no Russian military backing had been obtained for aggression against the offshore islands. It is certainly evidence of sharply deteriorating Sino-Soviet relations.

Further manifestation of a serious disagreement was revealed in a Soviet editorial about the meeting which stated, "It is no secret that even now Washington is plotting and hoping for dissension in the socialist camp. The reactionaries would like nothing better than to see the Soviet Union and China part company. Vain hopes, they will never materialize."[67] This was an excellent example of affirmation by denial. If there was no serious disagreement, it would not have been necessary to find a conspiratorial explanation for it.

Chinese asserted that "in 1958 the leadership of the CPSU put forward unreasonable demands designed to bring China under military control. These unreasonable demands were rightly and firmly rejected by the Chinese government. . . ." "The Origin and Development of the Differences . . . ," Editorial Departments of *People's Daily* and *Red Flag,* September 6, 1963, reprinted in *Peking Review,* Vol. VI, No. 37 (September 13, 1963).

[65]The communiqué stated that "a number of important problems" were discussed and "complete agreement on the measures that should be taken" was reached. Soviet Home Service, August 5, 1958. The emphasis on full agreement seemed to indicate that there were differences prior to the meeting. (Omission of substantive statements indicated that numerous issues remained unresolved.) See *The Guardian* article by Victor Zorza, August 4, 1958, p. 1, and Donald S. Zagoria, *The Sino-Soviet Conflict 1956–61,* (Princeton: Princeton University Press, 1962), pp. 202, 206.

[66]Peking New China News Agency (NCNA) in English to Western and Northern Europe, August 8, 1958, *People's Daily* editorial of August 8.

[67]"The Peking Meeting," *New Times,* No. 32 (August 1958), p. 1.

Emphasis on unity of the two nations pervaded the Soviet media. Authoritative commentaries claimed that Sino-Soviet friendship was as "strong as steel"[68] and that the "whole socialist community" had never before "been so monolithic."[69] By overemphasizing solidarity the Soviets revealed the deep division that existed.

Moscow's accentuation of the "peaceful coexistence" theme following the meeting also was in marked contrast to the Chinese emphasis. The Russians stressed the importance of reducing international tension and achieving a nuclear test ban.[70] The American announcement on August 22, 1958, of a moratorium on nuclear testing and willingness to negotiate a test ban agreement undoubtedly intensified Chinese fears of a Russian deal at their expense.[71] In playing up the dangers of nuclear weapons Moscow may have been trying to explain to Peking why such support could not be offered. A Soviet broadcast on August 10 commented that "it was hard to imagine how a local conflict . . . , A bombs and H bombs being used, can be kept within bounds of a local war."[72] A Tass release complained that Nationalist raids were supported by the U.S. fleet "equipped with nuclear weapons,"[73] and it was asserted that the United States planned to arm the Nationalists with submarines equipped with "atomic guns."[74] The latter item may also have been indicative of "sour grapes" following a Chinese refusal of a multilateral force (MLF) arrangement. The Soviets appeared to be trying to convince Peking of the inadvisability of confrontation with the United States over Quemoy. This was most likely Krushchev's theme during the Peking meeting.

The absence of an authoritative declaration of support for a Chinese initiative, the fact that Peking's propaganda concerning Quemoy was not resumed until mid-August, and sparse coverage in

[68]Moscow Soviet Home Service, August 21, 1958, commentary on *Pravda* observer's article.

[69]Soviet European Service in Serbo-Croatian, August 4, 1958, Kuznenko commentary "Meeting in Interest of Peace and Socialism." There were numerous other commentaries stressing unity and "complete agreement" during this period.

[70]See, for example, Moscow Soviet Home Service, August 5, 1958, *Pravda* editorial, "The Forces of Peace and Socialism Will Score a Great Victory."

[71]A theory has been offered that the American announcement actually triggered the Chinese bombardment on August 23. While this is unlikely, it certainly contributed to Sino-Soviet suspicions. See Harold K. Jacobson and Eric Stein, *Diplomats, Scientists, and Politicians* (Ann Arbor: University of Michigan Press, 1966), pp. 95, 96.

[72]Soviet South Asian Service in English, August 10, 1958.

[73]Tass in Russian to Europe, August 8, 1958.

[74]*Sovetsky Flot,* August 7, 1958, as reported in *The New York Times,* August 8, 1958, p. 6.

the Soviet media also indicated that Moscow was less than enthusiastic about a Chinese adventure in the Quemoy area. It could be logically argued that Peking's dependence on Moscow was so great that China would not have attempted an offshore island probe without Soviet consent.[75] But because of what is now known about the Sino-Soviet dispute it appears that the Chinese could have undertaken such an adventure in the face of serious Russian disapproval. Militarily, Peking could not hope to prevail against a stern American reaction without the bluff of the Russian nuclear arsenal. This was a major cause of Sino-Soviet dissension at the time. Faced with a Soviet rejection of support for an invasion of Taiwan, Peking probably settled for a more limited scheme of carefully controlled probes to test U.S. resolve, beginning with the shelling and blockade. For this restricted undertaking they may have had some Soviet encouragement.

Subsequent polemics may reveal China's actual expectation as well as the limited scope of their plan. In 1963 an authoritative article asserted that "Although at the time the situation in the Taiwan Straits was tense, there was no possibility that a nuclear war would break out and *no need for the Soviet Union to support China* with its nuclear weapons." (Emphasis added.)[76] If a promise of nuclear backing had been broken, the Chinese would not have had any hesitation about revealing this in 1963.[77] The article went on to assert that "It was only when *they* were clear that this was the situation that the Soviets expressed their support for China." (Emphasis added.) This sentence may indicate that the Soviets were in doubt about Chinese intentions for some period during the crisis. Mao was obviously acting in an independent manner. The Russians have not denied the authenticity of these Chinese allegations. There have been other Chinese claims of a lack of Russian support for the conquest of Taiwan, but those do not necessarily refer to the 1958 crisis.[78]

[75]This was a prominent view in Washington at the time. See Section 8.2, footnote 85.

[76]"The Origin of the Differences," September 6, 1963, *Peking Review*, Vol. VI, No. 37 (September 13, 1963), p. 13.

[77]The absence of such claims lends credence to the theory that a Soviet scheme of nuclear aid in the form of an MLF had been rejected at the Peking meeting.

[78]See, for example, "Statement by the Spokesman of the Chinese Government: A Comment on the Soviet Government's Statement of 21 August," September 1, 1963, *Peking Review,* Vol. VI No. 36 (September 6, 1963); and *People's Daily* editorial, November 2, 1963, "The Truth About How the Leaders of the CPSU Have Allied Themselves with India against China," *Peking Review,* (November 22, 1963).

It is quite possible that the Chinese never planned a military invasion of Taiwan or Quemoy. If by siege tactics they could force the evacuation of the offshore islands, that alone would have been a major victory. Peking evidently recognized the risks of a direct invasion. The matter, therefore, may have been considered more of a political than a military problem. Possibly, Mao was simply trying to discredit the American-Nationalist alliance. A document of unknown date recovered in 1967 admonished a Chinese commander for rash acts and stated that ". . . all operational action against the Chiang bandits should be considered in an *overall way* from the *political and stratetic angle* and should be decided upon by the Central Committee according to the need of the *whole situation.*"[79] (Emphasis added.) It went on to assert that the struggle in the Formosa Strait is "mainly one against U.S. imperialism" and therefore "not simply a military but a political matter." It is not clear to what extent this document reflected Chinese thought in 1958. However, Chinese planning was probably conservative, especially while in doubt about Soviet help if China became too deeply involved. The statement implies a realization of the dangers of challenging the United States over Taiwan.

The absence of Soviet military maneuvers anywhere in the world also appeared to reflect a Russian desire to deemphasize the crisis and ensure that the conflict at most was restricted to a carefully controlled test of strength for limited goals. On August 7 the Soviets officially terminated the military maneuvers that had begun in the Black Sea area on July 19 in response to the Lebanon landings.[80] There were no significant Soviet naval moves during the weeks prior to the Quemoy crisis.

In contrast to the period prior to the Lebanon landings, there was a respite from Soviet propaganda and a noticeable absence of official Russian declarations on the subject of Quemoy. The reduced volume of references in the media seemed to reflect Moscow's disagreement with Peking on tactics to be employed toward Taiwan as well as an attempt to put any Chinese maneuvers in a highly localized context. Moscow made frequent comments about the Middle East during this period, indicating greater Soviet interest in that situation. There appeared to be no deliberate campaign to stir up a

[79]*The New York Times* dispatch by David Onancia, "Mao Sees Taiwan As Political Issue," February 14, 1967. The Soviets have claimed that Chinese Foreign Minister Chen I told a Japanese correspondent in April 1964 that China was in no hurry to solve the problem of Taiwan and other coastal islands. According to the account, he added that "it would probably take 20 or 30 years to settle this problem and China would wait patiently." Moscow Radio, Peace and Progress in Mandarin to China, June 11, 1970.

[80]This coincided with the American termination of a military alert.

pretext for supporting Chinese action. The dearth of U.S. statements gave the Soviets less material to work with and less of an obligation to respond, but this would not have precluded a campaign, if Moscow had felt one was in its interests.

References to the Seventh Fleet were relatively infrequent in comparison to Moscow's strenuous campaign against the Sixth Fleet prior to the Lebanon landings. But restraint during this period did not necessarily indicate that the Chinese were being discouraged from a limited initiative or that the Seventh Fleet was not as great an obstacle in Soviet strategic assessments. There was a less interested Third World audience to impress, and the Chinese were well aware of what the Seventh Fleet's presence had prevented them from doing in previous years. Since the Communists would be taking the initiative in this case, there was no logical way to deter the United States by protesting a challenge still in the future. Yet, it appeared that, while the United States was trying to minimize the impending crisis, the Soviets were hoping to avoid one entirely.

Although there is no definitive evidence, Moscow may have been willing to give some support to a limited probe of American policy toward the offshore islands. The Kremlin probably did not approve of an invasion of Quemoy and certainly was not ready to bolster the Chinese effort. Undoubtedly, U.S. strategic and conventional power was considered to be too powerful to confront directly. Thus, for a number of reasons major Communist naval forces were kept at home, and the engagement was planned to be very limited and strictly controlled.

American policy makers' opinion of Soviet intentions was not so optimistic. Although there was speculation in the press about a possible Sino-Soviet difference, it would not have been prudent for Washington to base its estimates on the contradictory evidence available at the time.[81] Key American leaders suspected the worst about the Soviets. President Eisenhower wrote that he was sure Khrushchev "would never fail to suggest dark and dangerous possibilities whenever he had the excuse."[82] The American president felt that a possible motivation was to divert attention from Lebanon and to show that "the Communists were still on the offensive."[83] However, his private papers indicated that Soviet participation was

[81]It is, of course, possible that intelligence sources knew what had taken place at the Peking meeting, but it is more likely that there was a large guess factor in intelligence estimates also. C. F. Rendall's information may mean that some idea of what had gone on was available through British sources.

[82]Eisenhower, *Waging Peace,* p. 292.

[83]Ibid. He also felt such a move might be to test Western unity in the Far East and "exploit apprehensions regarding Soviet advances in weaponry."

expected to be indirect.[84] Administration officials believed that at least a tacit Soviet "green light" was a prerequisite for a Chinese initiative.[85]

While it was considered the Soviets were probably behind the mounting tension, it was not felt that Moscow or Peking would press an attack against a determined American stand. President Eisenhower speculated, "If the ChiComs believe the US would actively intervene to throw back an assault, perhaps using nuclear weapons, it is probable there would be no attempt to take Quemoy by assault and the situation might quiet down, as in 1955."[86] American military leaders could not afford to base their preparations on political speculation, but the power realities made them optimistic about the risks involved. The Commander of the Seventh Fleet recollected, "We did, of course, give serious consideration to possible Soviet actions and were prepared for actions the Soviets might take. While we did not believe that they could take effective actions, nor that they would take any action, we were convinced that we could cope with anything they might attempt."[87] The Chief of Naval operations also "estimated that the Soviets would not be able to make any challenge" near Quemoy and Matsu, but "thought that they might take action in some other part of the world."[88] In viewing the possibility of Russian involvement, high American officials felt that the Soviets were behind the impending crisis but that the likelihood of direct Russian participation was remote.[89]

8.3 BRITISH POLICY

During this period the United States undoubtedly consulted its most important ally, but there was little public discussion of meetings

[84] Ibid., pp. 691–693.

[85] For example, Assistant Secretary of State Walter Robertson testified that the need for Soviet supplies "makes it impossible" for the Chinese "to embark upon a major military aggression in Asia without a green light from the Russians, because the Russians must be willing and able to supply them by that long line down through Siberia." U.S., Congress, Senate, Committee on Foreign Relations, *Mutual Security Act of 1959, Part 1,* 86th Cong., 1st sess. (Washington 1959), p. 390. A *New York Times* editorial on August 11, 1958, appeared to reflect the government's view at the time. "There can be no doubt that Peiping, with Moscow's approval, is again moving to heighten tension along the Taiwan Strait."

[86] Eisenhower, *Waging Peace,* p. 691.

[87] Letter from Vice Adm. Frederick N. Kivette, USN (Ret.), to Lt. Comdr. J. T. Howe, USN, dated March 5, 1968.

[88] Letter from Adm. Arleigh A. Burke, USN (Ret.), to Lt. Comdr. J. T. Howe, USN, dated March 15, 1968.

[89] See interview with an official familiar with policy during Quemoy crisis of 1958 conducted January 31, 1969, Appendix B, Question 6.

and practically no speculation in the media as to what the British role might be. British editorials had little sympathy for American policy toward the offshore islands, and Quemoy was depicted as a distant problem not likely to affect Great Britain.

Although American leaders did not feel British military or political support was an essential prerequisite for an effective stand,[90] London's diplomatic corroboration in the United Nations and military backing in an expanded conflict were desired. Even token British support would have been helpful psychologically in rallying domestic and world opinion. Great Britain continued to make significant military contributions in two trouble spots of vital interest to the United States. The British presence in Cyprus and the Middle East made it more difficult for the Soviet Union to exploit those situations.

Undoubtedly, the United States would welcome British assistance in the Taiwan area, but realistically it knew such help would not be forthcoming.

8.4 EVALUATION OF U.S. CAPABILITY

During the buildup phase of the crisis a clear-cut decision to defend the major offshore islands of Quemoy and Matsu had not been made, but such a determination seemed likely if a Chinese invasion occurred. President Eisenhower wrote,

> We assumed that under the circumstances of the moment, we would probably have to come to the aid of our ally, Chiang, no matter where an assault occurred. If the assault were directed toward Formosa, our assistance would be full-out. To save the offshore islands against a first phase attack limited initially to those islands alone, a lesser response would be required and would conform to the terms of the Formosa Resolution.[91]

Although reluctant to become involved, the United States was prepared to respond to a Chinese initiative.

A review of the important factors affecting the U.S. decision makes it easier to understand why Washington felt capable of commiting the United States even with the existing involvement in the Middle East. Tables 8.1 to 8.4 summarize the evidence affecting each factor. There is, of course, no clear line between the factors. They all have an important interrelationship. On the tables, the distance of the "X" away from the dividing line indicates its relative weight and importance as a piece of solid evidence. For example, in Table 8.1 the absence of Soviet military movements into the area was the most solid evidence that they had no intention of providing direct

[90] For example, the comments of the U.S. CinC Pacific. Felt, letter.
[91] Eisenhower, *Waging Peace,* p. 294.

Table 8.1 Estimate of Soviet Intentions

X NO SOVIET INTENTION TO INTERVENE DIRECTLY

X No Soviet movements of forces into area

X No significant military response to U.S. Lebanon landings

X Termination of military maneuvers in Black Sea area

X Absence of official Soviet statements of support

X Respect for power United States could bring to bear; lack of corresponding conventional mobility

X Characteristic avoidance of direct confrontation (as in Korea)

X Disagreement indicated in Sino-Soviet statements

X Rejection of MLF deal

X Sparse propaganda coverage; few pledges of support

X Possibility that increased Chinese activity following Peking meeting could indicate Soviet approval.

X Necessity of prestige to support ally

X Desire to appease China for sake of alliance

X SOVIET INTENT TO INTERVENE DIRECTLY

Table 8.2 Defense Estimates of U.S. Capability to Defend Quemoy

X CAPABILITY TO DEFEND QUEMOY

X Large naval power advantage

X Strategic superiority

X Tactical nuclear weapons use acceptable to President

X Need for U.S. air and naval strength rather than troops

X Opinion that islands could be defended (Burke, Felt, Smoot)

X Forces available to reinforce Seventh Fleet

X Lack of Chinese nuclear weapons

X Experienced Nationalist pilots

X Nationalist troops well entrenched on Quemoy (90,000)

X Possible Soviet ICBM superiority

X Questionable dependability of Nationalist forces under attack

X Offshore islands dominated by mainland gun emplacements

X Availability of strong Chinese bomber force

X LACK OF CAPABILITY TO DEFEND QUEMOY

military support for a Chinese probe. The evidence of a Sino-Soviet dispute from an analysis of statements was a more tenuous indication that the Soviets would not directly support a Chinese assault on Quemoy. It is not known what information intelligence sources contributed to the assessment, but most of the public evidence indicates that direct Soviet intervention was not likely. The estimates of indirect aid, of course, were more speculative. Washington did not overlook any possibility. It had to prepare for the worst, most remote eventualities.

A dominant factor in American estimates of capability was whether it was able to defend Quemoy and still meet other commitments. (See Table 8.2.) Although defense of the major offshore islands was a difficult military problem, the Defense Department had concluded that capture of the islands could be prevented.

It was important, of course, to ascertain the degree of domestic support for a decision to defend the islands. (See Table 8.3.) While there would always be some opposition, the President could anticipate that the majority of Congress and the public would back a decision to defend Quemoy.

The probability that British help would not be forthcoming did not appear to be a serious American concern. (See Table 8.4.) At this

Table 8.3 Estimate of Congressional and Public Attitude

X WILL SUPPORT DEFENSE OF QUEMOY

X Near unaminous approval of Formosa Resolution giving President mandate and legal authority to make judgment

X Middle East action approved (President's popularity rising)

X General public support for defense against Communist aggression

X Little editorial and other public criticism of Quemoy policy

X Unpublicized congressional concern

X No formal consultations

X Committee of One Million

X Concern about Soviet technology

X Small but influential group in 1955 tried to exclude Quemoy and Matsu from Formosa resolution

X Some quiet congressional opposition to Lebanon

X Some questioning of U.S. worldwide role

X WILL NOT SUPPORT DEFENSE OF QUEMOY

Table 8.4 Dependence on British Support

X BRITISH COOPERATION ESSENTIAL

X Would help allay domestic and world opinion
X Psychological value

X "Neither politically or militarily" necessary—CinC Pacific

X U.S. military capability without direct help

X BRITISH COOPERATION NOT ESSENTIAL

stage of the crisis, allied support was desirable rather than actually essential. In any case, British forces were aiding the United States by their efforts in connection with the Cyprus and Middle East problems.

Although the United States did not publicly discuss the developing crisis in the Formosa Strait and tried to avoid American involvement, its cautious and deliberately ambiguous policy was not based on lack of confidence in its capability to defend the offshore islands.

9. THE FIRST PHASE OF THE CRISIS

AUGUST 23, 1958, TO SEPTEMBER 6, 1958

With the beginning of intensive shelling of Quemoy on August 23, the situation became the center of worldwide attention. It is convenient to divide the crisis into two phases. The first extended to September 6, 1958, when the Chinese accepted an offer to negotiate the problem. Peking's consent meant the situation could probably be controlled. The first phase was slightly more serious because the intentions of the adversaries were not clear.

9.1 UNITED STATES POLICY

During this phase U.S. policy was a classic example of walking softly while carrying a big stick. Without issuing a direct warning, the United States attempted to demonstrate convincingly that it would respond to a Chinese assault. The main strategy continued to be keeping the enemy guessing.[1] Maintaining maximum flexibility while reassuring the Nationalists and deterring the Communists was not an easy task. Inherent contradictions made it undesirable to adopt a simple, clearly expressed policy. While there were some indications of domestic U.S. confusion, Peking and Moscow did not miss the significance of the massive U.S. naval and air buildup in the Taiwan area. The American declaratory position slowly evolved, and in the last few days of this phase it was affirmed that the United States would help prevent the capture of Quemoy.

Heavy shelling of Quemoy began at 5:30 A.M., Washington time, on August 23, 1958.[2] The United States responded on the same day by incorporating an implied warning to Peking in a widely publicized letter from Secretary of State Dulles to the Acting Chairman of the House Committee on Foreign Affairs.[3] The Secretary of State com-

[1]The President's press secretary commented on September 1, "the Chinese Communists have been trying to find out for years what we might do if they tried to take over Matsu and Quemoy on the way to Formosa. As far as I'm concerned they can keep guessing." *The New York Times,* "President Silent on . . . Islands," September 2, 1958, p. 6.

[2]It was 6:30 P.M. local time in Taipei.

[3]President Eisenhower commented that the letter was deliberately "well publicized." President Eisenhower also wrote that "Foster and I on August 23 *made use* of a letter from the Chairman of the House Foreign Affairs Committee to Secretary Dulles *as an excuse* for Foster to issue" the statement. (Emphasis added.) Dwight D. Eisenhower, *Waging Peace, 1956–1961* (Garden City, New York: Doubleday and Co., 1956), p. 296. It should be noted that Chairman Thomas E. Morgan was a prominent member of the

mented that "ties between these islands and Formosa have become closer and their independence has increased" over the last four years.[4] This was an obvious reference to the Formosa resolution, which authorized defense of the offshore islands only if related to assuring the defense of Formosa.[5] According to President Eisenhower, the "key statement" of the letter emphasized,

It would be highly hazardous for *anyone* to assume that if the Chinese Communists were to attempt to change this situation by attacking and seeking to conquer these islands that this act could be considered or *held to a 'limited operation.'* It would, I fear, constitute a threat to the peace of the area. Therefore, I hope and believe that it will not happen.[6] [Emphasis added.]

The reference to "anyone" was obviously meant for the Russians as well as the Chinese. The statement was replete with indications that the United States would determine that attacks on Quemoy and Matsu were related to defense of Formosa and therefore required U.S. defensive action. The apparent intent of the letter was to strengthen the U.S. commitment to the offshore islands as a response to the bombardment by hinting that the resolution was applicable. The message was also intended to allay Chiang's fears.[7]

In his press conference on August 27, 1958, President Eisenhower implied that he had not yet made a final decision to defend the offshore islands, but he did say, "we are not going to desert our responsibilities or the statements we have already made."[8] When asked to comment on Secretary of State Dulles's indication that the islands had become more important for the defense of Quemoy, the President answered, "Well, they have this increased importance: what we call the Nationalist Chinese have now deployed about a third of their forces to certain of these islands west of the Pescadores, and that makes a closer interlocking between the defense

Committee of One Million; therefore, it seems quite possible that the letter was prearranged, although no proof has been found to confirm this speculation. Chairman Morgan's letter was dated August 22, 1958, and expressed concern about the "build-up of air power . . . opposite . . . Quemoy and Matsu." U.S., Department of State, *American Foreign Policy, Current Documents, 1958* (Washington, 1962), p. 1144.

[4]Letter from the Secretary of State to the Acting Chairman of the House Committee on Foreign Affairs, August 23, 1958. *American Foreign Policy, 1958,* p. 1144.

[5]The resolution referred to the "securing and protection of such related positions . . . required or appropriate in assuring the defense of Formosa and the Pescadores." House Joint Resolution 159, January 29, 1955. U.S., Department of State, *American Foreign Policy, 1950–1955, Basic Documents, Vol. II* (Washington, 1957), p. 2487.

[6]Eisenhower, *Waging Peace,* p. 296.

[7]Ibid.

[8]*The Washington Post,* Eisenhower news conference, August 28, 1958, p. A14.

systems of the islands with Formosa than was the case before that."[9] He concluded, "there is a closer relationship than there was before." The President appeared to be preparing the public for a decision, that the defense of the offshore islands was essential to the security of Taiwan, in accordance with the Formosa resolution.

The resumption on August 27 of Chinese broadcasts announcing an "imminent invasion of Quemoy" and their determination to "liberate Taiwan"[10] made it easier for the administration to justify a firm stand by establishing that the threat was to Formosa as well as Quemoy. At the President's request the broadcasts were deliberately publicized.[11] The accompanying State Department commentary quoted Dulles's letter stating, "the *ties* between the offshore islands and Formosa *have become closer,*" and "their *interdependence has increased.*"[12] While U.S. government leaders apparently believed that Quemoy should not be allowed to fall, the relationship of the offshore islands to Formosa was not self-evident to the general public. There was no immediate or direct military threat of a Chinese assault on Formosa and little fear of an impending invasion on the island itself.[13] This made it difficult for the President to make a categorical commitment to defend Quemoy.

The statements of other high officials were used to underline U.S. determination. For instance, on August 28 the Secretary of the Army warned that if Russia and China "underestimate or misinterpret the statements of President Eisenhower or Secretary of State Dulles, they will be sorry for it."[14] On September 3, the Secretary of Defense remarked that "if the Chinese are wise they will be deterred,"[15] and the officer charged with coordination of U.S. and

[9]*The Washington Post,* August 28, 1958, p. A14. The President had referred to Dulles's letter to the chairman of the House Foreign Affairs Committee as "about the best thing that can be said at this moment."

[10]*The New York Times,* August 29, 1958, pp. 1, 3. Rebroadcast of the threats, originally made from local radio stations, by Peking gave them more authority.

[11]Eisenhower, *Waging Peace,* p. 298.

[12](Emphasis added.) *The New York Times,* August 29, 1958, p. 3.

[13]Letter from an informed observer concerning the Quemoy crisis of 1958, March 13, 1969; remarks of Mr. Joseph A. Yager, Economic Counselor of the U.S. Embassy on Taiwan during the crisis; letter of March 7, 1969; and comments of Professor James Moceri, Acting Public Affairs Officer of the U.S. Information Service (USIS) in Taiwan, interview conducted February 13, 1969. Chinese reluctance to employ their bomber force and their lack of an amphibious capability to assault the Nationalist stronghold made a military assault seem remote, in spite of propaganda statements.

[14]*The Washington Post* article by Chalmers M. Roberts, August 29, 1958 p. 1.

[15]*The Washington Post* article by J. G. Norris, "Red Chinese are Warned by McElroy," September 4, 1958.

Nationalist forces in the Taiwan area said "we will lick them."[16]

While it was desired to present a firm position to the Chinese, there seemed to be a continuing effort to play down the crisis. On the day that the shelling began, Secretary of State Dulles departed on a week's vacation,[17] and six days later the President left Washington for his scheduled vacation in Newport, Rhode Island.[18] At the State Department it was speculated that the Communist objective might well be diplomatic rather than military,[19] and the impression lingered that the ultimate decision as to whether or not to defend the islands had not been made.[20] The image the United States presented was as complex as the difficult problem it faced. It was not easy to find and maintain the right proportions of firmness and ambiguity which would deter the Communists, not overly encourage or discourage the Nationalists, offer the Chinese an excuse for backing down, and promote domestic support for the policy.

In order to assuage the fears of Chiang Kai-shek and to further warn Peking and Moscow, it was decided to clarify the U.S. position.[21] After consultations with the President, the Secretary of State made an official statement on September 4. He reiterated that "the securing and protecting of Quemoy and Matsu have become in-

[16] *The Washington Post,* September 4, 1958, p. 1.

[17] His departure for vacation was widely publicized. A picture of Dulles's airport departure was carried on the front page of *The New York Times,* August 24, 1958, p. 1.

[18] President Eisenhower's picture also was featured on the front page of *The New York Times* as he boarded the plane for vacation. *The New York Times,* August 30, 1958, p. 1. This crisis could easily be called the "Vacation Crisis." The Secretary of Defense was on vacation during part of this period. The British Prime Minister went on vacation in mid-September. Premier Khrushchev spent much of the time touring interior Russia and making speeches on domestic issues. He was reported to be on holiday in the Crimea on September 21. *The Guardian* (Manchester), September 22, 1958, p. 6. Kenneth T. Young reports that Mao and Liu Shao-chi spent the last ten days of September in the countryside "casually visiting various activities seemingly unconcerned with the zone of crisis." *Negotiating With the Chinese Communists: The United States Experience 1953–1967* (New York: McGraw-Hill Book Co., 1968), p. 174.

[19] *The New York Times* article by Russell Baker, "Capital Watches Far East Closely," August 26, 1958, p. 3. See also *The Washington Post* article by Rutherford Posts, August 26, 1958.

[20] President Eisenhower had said in his press conference of August 27, in reference to a possible decision, "you simply cannot make military decisions until after the event reaches you." *The Washington Post,* August 28, 1958, p. A14. When Secretary of State Dulles was asked on September 1 whether or not a decision had been made to defend the offshore islands, he responded, "that's a decision the President would have to make." *The Washington Post,* September 2, 1958, p. 1.

[21] Eisenhower, *Waging Peace,* p. 299.

creasingly related to the defense of Taiwan," and asserted that ". . . military dispositions have been made by the United States so that a Presidential determination, if made, would be followed by action both timely and effective."[22] Although it was claimed that the President had not yet found that using the armed forces was "required or appropriate,"[23] the implication was that American forces would be used if necessary to hold the offshore islands.

This view was reinforced by stronger statements attributed to the "briefing officer," who was subsequently identified as the Secretary of State.[24] The "briefing officer" said, "we would not, probably, wait until the situation was 'in extremis' " to act.[25] When asked whether "if we judged that the Chinese Nationalists could not hold these islands, . . . we would then go in with American fighting men," he replied, "that is in general the significance of this statement."[26] He was queried concerning the official statement as follows:

Question: Is it fair to interpret this as a very *stiff, blunt warning* to Peiping not to try to make an attack against Quemoy?
Answer: If I were on the Chinese Communist side, I would certainly think very hard before I went ahead in the face of this statement.[27] [Emphasis added.]

In a significant exchange concerning possible counterattacks against the mainland, the question was asked,

Question: Would the bombing of concentrations on the mainland be a part of the defense of Formosa?
Answer: It might become so if Formosa was attacked or immediately threatened from airfields on the mainland.[28]

He added that the answer applied to Quemoy as well. Secretary Dul-

[22]*The New York Times,* September 5, 1958, p. 2.
[23]The private memo of understanding between the President and Secretary of State did not commit the President to an explicit course of action, but the importance of the islands was stressed, and it was implicit that they would be defended. See Eisenhower, *Waging Peace,* pp. 691–693.
[24]*The New York Times,* September 10, 1958, p. 8. Secretary of State Dulles admitted this in answer to a question at his press conference. The transcript of the background briefing was not released, and automatic recording devices were turned off during the session. Where there are errors in newspaper reporting of the remarks, the correct version has been given using the transcript contained in the John Foster Dulles Papers, Princeton University Library.
[25]*The New York Times,* September 5, 1958, p. 2.
[26]Transcript of background briefing given by Secretary of State John Foster Dulles, September 4, 1958. The John Foster Dulles Papers. Secretary Dulles began his answer by saying "that is the indication of this thing," but he then corrected himself, saying he did not want to "add to or subtract from the precise language" approved by the President. He then went on to make the remark repeated in the text. *The Washington Post* gave a stronger version of the reply, "that was what the formal statement meant, and that was its significance." Article by Edward T. Folliard, September 5, 1958.
[27]*The Washington Post,* September 5, 1958, p. A4.
[28]*Ibid.*

les also stated categorically that the United States was not considering any evacuation of the islands.[29] Although five days passed before the Secretary of State admitted publicly that he was the "briefing officer," it would have been easy for the Communists to find out if they doubted the importance of the remarks that accompanied the official statement. The press interpreted the statement as declaring U.S. determination to repel any Communist attempt to invade Quemoy.[30] The President's avoidance of a public declaration committing the United States appeared to be a mere technicality for the purpose of minimizing the domestic reaction in the United States and hedging on any automatic commitment to Chiang. Lingering doubts were put to rest the following day when Senator H. Alexander Smith announced, after a meeting with Secretary Dulles, that the United States *"definitely"* had decided to use its forces to prevent capture of Quemoy.[31]

The government had obviously decided to take a stronger declaratory position.[32] But in the official statement of September 4, the door was held open for resumption of talks as "the only civilized and acceptable procedure."[33] Although Peking did not officially respond to the offer for two days, it gave an immediate indication of acceptance. The bombardment of the offshore islands was halted on September 4,[34] and on September 6 Chou En-lai announced that the Chinese government was prepared to resume ambassadorial talks since the United States had indicated a "desire to settle the

[29]He said in answer to a question on the subject, "No we are not." Transcript of background briefing, September 4, 1958. The John Foster Dulles Papers.

[30]See, for example, *The New York Times* article by Felix Belair, Jr., "US Decides to Use Force If Reds Invade Quemoy," September 5, 1958, p. 1; and *The Washington Post* article by Edward T. Folliard, "Eisenhower Warns US Will Fight to Save Quemoy from Red Chinese," September 5, 1958.

[31](Emphasis added.) *The New York Times* article by Jack Raymond, September 6, 1958, p. 1.

[32]It is interesting, however, that indications of American policy continued in the same basic pattern, altering it only in degree and emphasis. The official statement was still slightly ambiguous, the follow-up statements stronger and clearer, and the relationship between the defense of Quemoy and defense of Taiwan continued to be developed.

[33]*The New York Times,* September 5, 1958, p. 2.

[34]*The Washington Post* of September 5, 1958, reported that on the islands it was the "quietest day since August 23," p. 1. Chinese broadcasts later complained that "despite the fact that our guns have not fired a single shell at Quemoy since September 4," the Nationalists were bombarding the mainland. This indicated that the ceasing of bombardment was a deliberate move toward deescalation of the crisis. See *The Washington Post,* September 7, 1958, p. A10.

Sino-American dispute in the Taiwan area through peaceful negotiation."[35] The President felt that it was the first sign of a "lessening of the crisis."[36] But having learned a lesson in Korea and having gotten nowhere in previous negotiations concerning the offshore islands, Washington was under no illusions about the possibility of success for these negotiations. Nevertheless, Peking's acceptance did indicate it was willing to take a first step toward defusing the crisis.

In spite of the difficult problem of resupplying the offshore islands under siege, defense appraisals probably became more confident during this period. There was no Soviet military response. The Chinese did not employ their large bomber force, and there were no signs of preparation for a major amphibious assault. It therefore appeared that the situation would be confined to a very localized test. Although the Joint Chiefs evidently still believed the islands were not militarily essential to defense of Formosa, they favored a strong defense posture under the circumstances.[37] American military leaders, as well as the Nationalists, were pushing for permission to respond immediately to any major invasion attempt. As President Eisenhower recounted, "Throughout this whole period it seems that I was continually pressured—almost *hounded* by Chiang on one side and by our own military on the other requesting delegation of authority for *immediate action* to United States commanders on the spot in the case of attack on Formosa *or the offshore islands.*"[38] (Emphasis added.)

The most pressing military problem became resupplying of the islands, whose beaches were controlled by the Communist guns. (See Figure 7.2.) Since the islands were well stocked, the ability to reprovision was more important for the morale of the defenders, to demonstrate that a siege would not be effective, and to indicate American commitment to the defense of Quemoy. Reprovisioning was primarily a political issue. As the American military coordinator for the Taiwan area later quipped, "We were fairly certain from the start that the Communist Chinese would run out of ammunition

[35](Emphasis added.) *The New York Times,* "Text of Premier Chou's Statement on Taiwan Strait," September 7, 1958, p. 2.
[36]Eisenhower, *Waging Peace,* p. 300.
[37]See *The Washington Post* article by Chalmers M. Roberts, August 25, 1958, p. 1. See also *The Washington Post* editorial "Tail Wags Dog," August 25, 1958, p. A22. Both articles assert that the Joint Chiefs felt the islands were not militarily essential. However, Roberts points out that the Chiefs felt that evacuation was "politically impossible" under the circumstances.
[38]Eisenhower, *Waging Peace,* p. 299.

before the Nationalists would run out of food and other vital logistics."[39] Nationalist counterbattery fire, however, was reduced to conserve ammunition in case of invasion. Although the blockade was not broken during this period, the President and his military advisors were confident it could be.[40]

There were rumors of movements of Chinese naval and amphibious vessels,[41] but the absence of any significant buildup of these craft led officials to conclude that a Chinese invasion was not imminent.[42] At the same time, it was recognized that a fleet of junks could be rapidly assembled for an assault on the offshore islands.[43] However, lack of invasion craft, failure to use deep-penetration shells necessary to destroy Nationalist guns, and the avoidance of air raids against the islands indicated that the Chinese probe would be limited for the time being to interdiction.[44] The absence of large amphibious vessels made an invasion of Taiwan itself extremely remote, and by mid-September the weather alone would prevent such an effort.[45] Sacrifice of the element of surprise also indicated that a major assault was not contemplated. Surprise would have been an

[39]Letter from Vice Adm. Roland N. Smoot, USN, to Lt. Comdr. J. T. Howe, USN, dated March 1, 1969. A concurring firsthand opinion was contained in a letter from an informed observer concerning the Quemoy crisis of 1958 to Lt. Comdr. J. T. Howe, USN, dated March 13, 1969.

[40]President Eisenhower wrote, "The blockade of Quemoy had not been broken, but we were optimistic." *Waging Peace,* p. 299. Admiral Smoot, the Taiwan area coordinator, asserted that with combined efforts they would be able to overcome the interdiction of the offshore islands. *The Washington Post,* September 4, 1958, p. 1. Privately, there apparently was no doubt in Admiral Smoot's mind that the United States could "resupply in any quantity if the situation became desperate, which it never did." Smoot, letter.

[41]These reports came from Nationalist sources. See, for example, *The Washington Post* article by Al Kaff, August 28, 1958; *The Washington Post,* September 8, 1958, p. A5, and September 7, 1958, p. A10; *The New York Times,* August 31, 1958, p. 4.

[42]Interview with an official familiar with policy during the Quemoy crisis of 1958, conducted January 31, 1969, Appendix B, Question 1.

[43]Secretary of State Dulles in his background briefing of September 5 remarked that the "Chinese Reds had sufficient troops available and sufficient junks to transport them for a formidable assault against Quemoy." *The Washington Post,* September 5, 1958. Joseph Alsop quipped, "small craft are two-a-penny on the China Coast." *The Washington Post,* September 5, 1958, p. A13.

[44]After an initial strafing there were no more air attacks on the island during this period. It was noted on August 31 that they were not broadcasting their threats to their whole population. *The New York Times,* August 31, 1958, p. 16. This tactic, however, later changed. The Chinese did not start to use deep-penetration shells until well into the next phase of the crisis. See *The Washington Post* article "Reds Shift Aim to Guns on Quemoy," September 18, 1958. The article indicates deep-penetration shells were first fired on September 17.

[45]The Seventh Fleet Commander said, "I would say if we get through Sep-

essential element from a military point of view.[46] Instead, the United States had ample time to build up a major force in the area.

While the military coped with the immediate problems associated with defense of Quemoy, Washington continued to emphasize the commanding strength of the United States, undoubtedly to discourage the Russians. The fleet was said to have the "biggest striking power in history,"[47] and the Secretary of Defense again proclaimed the overall military superiority of the United States.[48] The Defense Department appeared to be confident that U.S. forces could hold the offshore islands and had sufficient strength to deter an expanded conflict.

Congressional opinion during this period had little negative influence on the administration's decision to make a clearer commitment to defend the offshore islands.[49] Intensification of the shelling had been reported just before Congress decided to adjourn.[50] By leaving Washington at a time of crisis, the lawmakers seemed to give the administration's policy a vote of confidence.[51] As James Reston observed on September 4, "the Congress is away and silent."[52] Senator Wayne Morse denounced defense of Quemoy as "aggression" on the part of the United States, but the reaction of this congressional maverick was not unexpected, and he was not joined by his colleagues.[53] A protest started to mount in response to the stronger U.S. position of September 4, but the impact of the first significant surge of criticism was blunted by reports on the

tember 15th Taiwan is not too threatened. The water gets too rough for invasion in the Strait." *The Washington Post,* September 8, 1958, p. A5.

[46]It had to be kept in mind, however, that the invasion of Ichiang Island in 1955 had followed a similar pattern.

[47]*The Washington Post* article "7th Fleet to be 'Mightiest ever!,' " September 1, 1958, p. A4.

[48]*The Washington Post* article "McElroy Sees No Gap In Defense," September 3, 1958, p. A4. Such statements were made throughout the crisis to reassure the public and to caution the Soviets.

[49]Letter from Senator Mike Mansfield, to Lt. Comdr. J. T. Howe, USN, dated July 17, 1968.

[50]Congress adjourned at 4:11 A.M. on August 24.

[51]Of course, it must be recognized that it would have taken a major calamity to keep Congress in session at that point. The November elections were imminent, and the session had already been extended several weeks beyond the target date for adjournment.

[52]*The New York Times* article by James Reston, "War Making Power," September 4, 1958, p. 4.

[53]Morse was one of the three senators who had voted against the 1955 Formosa resolution. His initial complaints were balanced by the comment of Senator Paul Douglas of Illinois the same day. Douglas, a Democrat, said defense of Quemoy was "up to President Eisenhower." *The New York Times* article by Russell Baker, August 26, 1958, p. 3.

same date that Peking had agreed to negotiations.[54]

Public reaction during this period was mixed and difficult to quantify.[55] Editorials appeared both attacking and defending the administration's approach. The influential *Washington Post,* for example, complained that the policy could lead to "war, probably nuclear, in the wrong place and at the wrong time over some wholly insignificant pieces of real estate"[56] and was "tragically unwise,"[57] and that policy initiative had been "abdicated" to the Chinese Nationalists.[58] But while condemning the circumstances that had led to the commitment, it concluded that "we are stuck for the moment."[59] When Secretary of State Dulles was asked if he realized some papers had editorialized that Quemoy was not worth one American life and that there might be a hostile reaction at home if U.S. forces were employed, he replied that the President took it "very much into account." But he pointed defensively to the almost unanimous congressional authorization of the Formosa resolution and concluded that the sentiment of the country, if adequately informed, would correspond with the sentiment on Capitol Hill.[60] His remark

[54]On September 5 Morse called for an emergency session of Congress, and Senator H. Humphrey felt the problem should be taken to the United Nations; but these comments were balanced by Senator Ives of New York, who said that sooner or later the Communist menace must be met head on, and Democratic whip of the House, Carl Albert of Oklahoma, warned that we must "meet them whenever they step across the line else there's no end to it." *The Guardian* (Manchester), September 6, 1958, p. 7. Significant protest was contained in articles on September 7. See, for example, *The New York Times,* "Democrats Lash Quemoy Policy," September 7, 1958, p. 13. It is possible that the dissenters saw the Chinese acceptance of negotiations as an opportunity to speak out without endangering the country since the crisis had eased somewhat. The Senate whip, Senator Mansfield, agreed in retrospect that Congress had had little influence on the executive in the period prior to September 4 when the administration took a strong stand in favor of defense of Quemoy.

[55]There were no major public opinion surveys related to the crisis taken during this period.

[56]*The Washington Post* editorial "Queasy Quemoys," August 26, 1958, p. A12. This editorial also complained that "the whole predicament is a prime example of the sort of hazardous commitment that strains American resources to little or no strategic purpose."

[57]*The Washington Post* editorial "Imminent War," August 29, 1958, p. A13.

[58]*The Washington Post* editorial "Tail Wags Dog," August 25, 1958, p. A22. An editorial on August 26 said, "it cannot be discounted that at least some of the current scene has been devised in Taipei to obtain more equipment and to increase American involvement."

[59]*The Washington Post* editorial "Queasy Quemoys," August 26, 1958, p. A12. Many of these sentiments were also shared by government policy makers.

[60]*The Washington Post,* September 5, 1958, p. A4. This remark was made in the background briefing on September 4, 1958.

may be another indication that any congressional misgivings which existed had not been regarded as significant.

The New York Times, on the other hand, endorsed the President's policy in a series of editorials. It observed that defense of the offshore islands was a "tactical problem to be met as it arises,"[61] and asserted that the problem was related to "what happens to freedom in the Far East" and not just to "what happens to three or four small islands."[62]

The general public apparently was not particularly alarmed by the situation.[63] Evidently there was little letter writing to the government or Congress and a dearth of statements by distinguished private citizens before September 4. Former President Truman declared that Formosa was the front line of America's defense and that it was up to the government to decide how to meet Chinese threats to seize the offshore islands.[64] During this phase of the crisis public opinion did not appear to have a very significant restraining influence.

One of the most difficult American problems was to strike the proper balance of restraint and encouragement in dealing with Chiang Kai-shek. When the bombardment intensified, he requested, in a "frantic letter" to President Eisenhower, a declaration of full U.S. military support for defense of the islands, convoys to the beaches of Quemoy, and approval to take more aggressive counteraction.[65] His exaggerated reports of damage from the artillery and his approach in general "puzzled" President Eisenhower.[66] The U.S. government could never totally dismiss the possibility that Chiang Kai-shek might like to see a war between the United States and China. As Vice Admiral R. N. Smoot, USN, the American coordinator of Taiwan military operations, asserted, "the big problem in our mutually supporting efforts . . . was to keep the

[61]*The New York Times* editorial "No Time for Jitters," August 29, 1958, p. 22. *The New York Times* of August 25, 1958, called for "resolution," which it felt was what Sectetary Dulles was doing in the situation.

[62]*The New York Times* editorial "Western Pacific Defense," September 2, 1958, p. 24.

[63]*The Sunday Times* (London) editorialized, "It is well realised by government officials, but hardly at all by the general public that this could bring war with China if President Eisenhower makes that fateful decision." "Eisenhower's Double Crisis," August 31, 1958, p. 17. See also *The Guardian* (Manchester) article by Alstair Cooke, "Americans Unaware of War Danger," September 6, 1958, p. 7.

[64]*The Washington Post* article "US Must Defend Formosa, Truman Says," September 3, 1958, p. A4.

[65]Eisenhower, *Waging Peace,* pp. 298, 299.

[66]Ibid.

Nationalist Chinese within the bounds of a strictly defensive effort."[67]

At the same time, Washington hoped to bolster the Nationalists enough to repulse any attack by themselves. It would save the administration much embarrassment if the Nationalists could do the job alone. The President reluctantly gave permission for the U.S. Navy to convoy relief ships as a result of the Chief of Naval Operation's (CNO's) assessment that the Nationalists could not assure resupply without U.S. aid.[68]

The American agreement had a deeper significance. While there was some military justification for surmounting the blockade, arguments that an immediate need for supplies existed, as previously noted, were spurious. Convoying was an important act of commitment to the Nationalists. American escorts began operations on September 4, 1958, the same day that Secretary of State Dulles indicated the United States would help defend the offshore islands. This first demonstration helped alleviate Chiang's anxiety about what Washington was actually willing to do for his country. Chiang subsequently remarked that during the "first two weeks of the bombardment" there had been no offer of help from the United States in defense of Quemoy, but that the United States *"finally came through* with an offer to convoy."[69] It seems likely that the Nationalists, who had the training and equipment to resupply on their own, were dragging their feet in order to obtain an American commitment.[70] If there was a scheme to embroil the United States in a conflict with China, the American agreement to convoy increased the likelihood.

Realizing that dangers might exist from allies as well as enemies, Washington was extremely cautious in its commitment. United States escorts accompanied Nationalist vessels only at night during this phase. American ships were limited to a line three miles seaward from the Nationalist-held islands. (See Figure 7.2.) This was just out of range of the major Chinese artillery concentrations. The President recognized that even with this safeguard there was ". . . a possibility of a deliberate or accidental hit by the Chicoms, which could have potential and unplanned reactions which might

[67]Smoot, letter.

[68]Eisenhower, *Waging Peace,* p. 299.

[69](Emphasis added.) Interview with Chiang Kai-shek and Mme. Chiang Kai-shek conducted on September 24, 1964, by Mr. Spencer Davis of the Dulles Oral History Project, Princeton University. Approved transcript, page 14.

[70]Smoot, letter. Also letter from an informed observer, March 13, 1969.

involve at least limited retaliation."[71] Since escort operations began at night on September 4,[72] the sudden Chinese announcement the same day,[73] that they now claimed a twelve-mile limit, instead of the usual three-mile limit, was not so surprising. Extension of the limit meant that if U.S. escort ships approached the Quemoy beaches, they would enter the territorial waters claimed by mainland China.[74]

Although the statements in the early part of the crisis were deliberately left flexible, the United States used the movement of its forces to affirm its intentions more definitely. The Seventh Fleet was ordered to sail for the Taiwan area as soon as reports arrived in Washington of intensified shelling, and U.S. armed forces in the area were put on alert. Additional ships were assigned to the Formosa Strait patrol force, and the Seventh Fleet was ordered to "show itself by supersonic fighter sweeps through the Formosa Straits."[75] Chinese complaints soon indicated that they had gotten the message.[76] In addition, a marine fighter squadron was ordered to move from Japan to Taiwan, and an Air Force squadron was deployed from the United States to Taiwan.[77]

An augmentation of the Seventh Fleet by dispatching an aircraft carrier from the Mediterranean and bringing another carrier and a heavy cruiser from the West Coast was announced.[78] The intent of

[71]Eisenhower, *Waging Peace,* p. 692.

[72]See *The Washington Post,* September 6, 1958, article by John G. Norris; and *The New York Times,* September 8, 1958, p. 1. Although President Eisenhower referred to commencement of escort operations on September 7, in the memo in his book dated September 4, it is stated that "US destroyers are cooperating with the Chinat sea supply operations within the limits of international waters, i.e., up to within three miles of Quemoy." *Waging Peace,* p. 692.

[73]Most accounts overlook the fact that the escort operations began on September 4 believing they began with the highly publicized daylight operations on September 7.

[74]See Figure 7.2. However, this distinction has only limited significance since the actual Chinese claim included the offshore islands, and Taiwan, as their territory.

[75]Letter from Adm. Harry D. Felt, USN (Ret.) to Lt. Comdr. J. T. Howe, July 16, 1968.

[76]Chinese newspapers on August 25 complained of "provocative reconnaissance flights near the mainland" by U.S. planes. *The Washington Post* article "US 'provocation' off Mainland Is Charged by Peking Newspapers," August 26, 1958.

[77]Felt, letter. The Air Force "super saber" jets touched down in Hawaii on August 31 on their way to Taiwan.

[78]The carrier *Essex* and four destroyers reached the northern end of the Suez Canal on August 27. *The New York Times* article by E. W. Kenworth, "Eisenhower Sees Increased Need to Guard Quemoy," August 28, 1958, p. 1. *The New York Times* article "Two More Ships Sent to 7th Fleet," August 30, 1958, p. 3. The other two ships were the *Midway* and the heavy cruiser *Los Angeles*.

this buildup of Seventh Fleet forces was to make a visible show of strength. As President Eisenhower wrote, "These movements were not secret; in fact, to insure that they were noticed, I instructed the Department of Defense to permit a few revealing words to reach the press. These would not escape the notice of the Communists."[79] It would be a number of days before the reinforcements could reach the area, but merely by embarking they had served an important purpose. On September 4 these two additional carriers were still en route. Nonetheless, by August 28 three attack carriers were deployed in a fan-shaped formation, one to the north, one to the east, and one to the south of Taiwan.[80] (See Figure 7.1.) Most of the Seventh Fleet, including an antisubmarine carrier, had arrived in the area. It was anticipated that the fleet would reach six aircraft carriers, three heavy cruisers, forty destroyers, and four submarines.[81] The United States was leaving no doubt about the power it had available. Admiral Burke recounted,

> As soon as the Quemoy incident started, I moved the 7th Fleet to the vicinity of Taiwan so that they would be ready. Again we began reinforcing the 7th Fleet and we made preparations so that if battle ensued the pipelines would be formed and would be filled and that we would commit enough military force to prevent not only the Communists from achieving their purposes but also to convince the Communists that if they started anything we would kick hell out of them.[82]

The marine amphibious units at anchor in Singapore harbor were ordered to sail on August 26, and it was announced that they would hold a combined landing exercise with the Nationalists in early September.[83] While U.S. diplomacy was offering to resume negotiations and professing an interest in preventing further conflict, Seventh Fleet movements were intended to convey a message of firm intentions to the Chinese and Soviets.

9.2 SOVIET POLICY

During the first days of the shelling, the lack of Russian announcements and movements indicated that their efforts on behalf of the

[79]Eisenhower, *Waging Peace,* p. 297.

[80]Capt. Edward F. Baldridge, USN, "Lebanon and Quemoy—The Navy's Role," U.S. Naval Institute *Proceedings,* Vol. 87, No. 2 (February 1961), p. 99.

[81]*The Washington Post,* August 30, 1958, p. 1.

[82]Letter from Adm. Arleigh Burke, USN (Ret.), to Lt. Comdr. J. T. Howe, USN, July 9, 1968.

[83]*The New York Times,* August 26, 1958, p. 3; "World Events," Entry for August 25, 1958, *New Times,* No. 35 (August 1958).

Chinese probe would be indirect. Moscow's coverage of events in the Taiwan area was relatively sparse, and the Soviet media did not begin to express serious concern until around August 26.[84] The first statement of a semiofficial nature was finally issued on August 31, 1958. On the day after the beginning of the intensive shelling a Khrushchev speech was published in which a significant statement was buried near the end stating,

Many are asking whether or not there will be war. Of course it is impossible to answer for the madmen in the imperialist world but it seems to me *at present there is no cloud from which a thunderstorm could break*. The imperialists are walking around the fence of the socialist countries like hungry wolves around a sheep pen but our fence is strong and we have a reliable defense.[85] [Emphasis added.]

Although the speech reputedly had been delivered on August 13, 1958, the delay in publication increased the significance of its release.[86] Khrushchev's remark, which was widely publicized in the Western press, may have been intended to reassure the United States as well as remind the Chinese that there were limits to Soviet support.

Even as late as August 27 a Soviet article referred to the "fictitious threat of aggression in the Far East" meant as a diversion from the "real" problem in the Middle East.[87] The Soviets apparently were annoyed that a problem of greater concern to them was being upstaged by a conflict initiated by Peking. Moscow's depiction of the Far Eastern threat as "fictitious" may have indicated foreknowledge that no serious aggression was intended. However, the follow-

[84]The attention given to the Seventh Fleet starting about August 26, 1958, indicated increased concern. Other writers have implied that there was a longer period before the Soviet press reported the seriousness of the developments. Evidently, these writers have overlooked some of the evidence. See, for example, John R. Thomas, "The Limits of Alliance: The Quemoy Crisis of 1958," Chapter 7 of *Sino-Soviet Military Relations,* R. L. Garthoff, ed., (New York: Praeger, 1966), p. 125.

[85]*Pravda* and *Izvestia,* August 24, 1958, pp. 1, 2, "Speech by Comrade N. S. Khrushchev at Formal Meeting of Smolensk Province Party Committee . . . ," *CDSP,* Vol. X, No. 34, p. 6.

[86]A delay in publication frequently signals a controversial point or a need to emphasize a particular issue. The speech was delivered after the Mao-Khrushchev Peking meeting. Khrushchev had been discussing the Middle East situation previous to this remark, but in a similar speech published on August 10, 1958, Khrushchev had declared in reference to the Middle East that "the threat of war in the area of the world remains very acute." Moscow Soviet Home Service, August 10, 1958, text of Khrushchev speech at Kubyshev.

[87]Moscow Soviet Home Service, August 27, 1958, *Izvestia* article by Vladimrov, "What Is Behind the Slander?"

ing day the Soviets reversed their explanation. The Quemoy developments were described as "far more serious than a mere diversion to detract attention" from the Middle East, and as a "brink of war" situation which could "explode at any moment."[88] Possibly, the publicized reinforcements of the Seventh Fleet caused the Russians to shift their tactics. Moscow's commentary referred to increases in U.S. naval strength and complained about the fleets of the "super gendarme" that were "scurrying from one ocean to another."[89]

Moscow's initial refusal to notice the Quemoy situation was now reversed. The Soviets made two direct statements of support for the Chinese effort, one on August 31 and the other on September 5.[90] Although both took a similar line, the latter was stronger, probably in response to the forceful stand taken by the United States in the Secretary of State's announcement of September 4. In a typical Soviet crisis reaction,[91] the September 5 editorial asserted, "The Soviet Union cannot remain inactive in the face of what is happening on the border or on the territory of its brave ally. The Soviet Union will not quietly watch U.S. military preparations in the Pacific whose waters also wash Soviet shores."[92]

The *Pravda* articles offered aid, but the form it would take was left ambiguous. It was implied that Moscow's help would consist of a propaganda campaign and military supplies rather than armed intervention. A distinction was made between support for a Chinese invasion and response to American aggression against China. It was warned that "he who threatens to *attack*" China "must not forget that he threatens the Soviet Union as well."[93] A strong pledge of aid in these circumstances was made:

The inspirers and organizers of the new military adventure in the Far East cannot count on the *retaliatory blow restricting* itself to the area of the offshore islands and the Taiwan Straits. They will re-

[88]Moscow Soviet European Service in English, August 28, 1958, Petr Zarin commentary.
[89]Ibid.
[90]Both were published as *Pravda* articles by "Observer" rather than as official government statements. However, this means is only slightly less authoritative than statements released as official declarations of the USSR.
[91]This kind of statement was made at least a dozen times in 1955, 1956, and 1957. It was repeated on several occasions prior to and following the Lebanon landings in official Soviet statements. See, for example, the Soviet statements of June 25, July 16, and July 18, 1958, and the *Pravda* statement of August 14, 1958.
[92]Tass in Russian to Europe, September 5, 1958. *Pravda* article by "Observer," "Military Adventure of U.S. Imperialists in Far East."
[93]*Pravda* article by "Observer," "Dangerous Playing with Fire," August 31, 1958, p. 4. *CDSP,* Vol. X, No. 35, p. 17. (Emphasis added.)

ceive such a devastating *counterblow* that an end will be put to U.S. imperialist aggression in the Far East.[94] [Emphasis added.]

Moscow offered aid to its ally in the unlikely circumstance of an American attack but put definite limits on support for a Chinese-initiated assault. The Kremlin, of course, could not be certain about the meaning of the buildup of American forces. The ambiguity of the American declaratory position may have been misinterpreted as an omen of U.S. offensive action. It is believed, however, that Moscow had confidence in American caution. The statements seemed to reflect some genuine Russian fear that American action in the Formosa Strait might lead to a global conflict. Since the Russians lacked mobile conventional power, the Red Army would have to be used in a border area to counter a test of strength. This seemed implicit in their warning of a spreading conflict. It is speculated, however, that Moscow would have been most reluctant to retaliate, except to a massive American assault on China.[95]

There was other evidence that the Russians were trying to limit their role in the crisis. The Soviets emphasized that the liberation of Taiwan was "an exclusively internal affair"[96] of the Chinese People's Republic and that China had "sufficient strength to counter the aggressors fully."[97] While giving lip service to Peking's desires, Moscow clearly indicated that the Chinese would be unaided in any assault on Quemoy. As a *Pravda* article put it, the Russians "*watch* the *efforts* of the *Chinese* people and *wish them success*."[98] The Russians were willing to cheer from the side lines.

Although tactically convenient because of military limitations, this Soviet position was not necessarily antagonistic to Peking. It would have violated the Chinese concept of their sovereignty to imply that the Taiwan problem was anything but an internal problem that the Chinese had the capability of handling. In referring to the internal

[94]*Pravda*, September 5, 1958. The previous article had warned that "any *aggression* of the U.S.A. in the Far East will inevitably increase international tension and result in the *spreading* of the *war to other areas,* with all the consequences that follow from this." (Emphasis added.) *Pravda,* August 31, 1958.

[95]Moscow must have known that such an assault was out of the question. It is possible that the initial Soviet response to an American attack on the Chinese mainland would have been to send "volunteers."

[96]See, for example, Moscow Soviet Home Service, September 1, 1958. Aleksandr Ter Gregoryan commentary.

[97]Tass in Russian to Europe, September 5, 1958, *Pravda* observer's article. The August 31 *Pravda* article had stated that provocative American actions were "bound to encounter resolute resistance from the *Chinese People's Republic*." (Emphasis added.)

[98](Emphasis added.) *Pravda* article by observer, September 5, 1958.

aspects of the crisis, the Soviets were justifying the Chinese claim and stating their view of the *de jure* situation. The implication was that the United States had no right to interfere in Peking's legitimate claim. The Sino-Soviet dispute pertaining to Chinese national aspirations centered on how much the Soviet Union was willing to do to keep the Taiwan issue an internal matter rather than an international crisis. The Russians were expected to prevent the United States from becoming involved, and the Kremlin may have felt that its warnings issued in broadcasts and newspapers were having that effect.

The Soviets seemed to be especially concerned that a crisis could involve the Soviet Union, against its will, in a world war. They had problems very similar to those of the Americans in dealing with a stubborn and unpredictable ally. In fact, the Soviet policy was practically a mirror image to that of the United States. Moscow also had to find the proper proportions of encouragement and discouragement in dealing with their Chinese comrades. The Kremlin was most reluctant to support an adventure initiated by its ally. By emphasizing the dangers of a world war, the probability of nuclear weapons employment, and the strength of the augmented Seventh Fleet, Moscow appeared to be warning both Washington and Peking that the situation was fraught with serious consequences that the Soviet Union wanted to avoid. A typical Russian commentary cautioned that "a little clash" might cause a "grave consequence beyond one's imagination." [99] Other articles predicted that the Americans probably would employ tactical nuclear weapons.[100] Although Moscow correctly anticipated secret U.S. planning, the Russian emphasis on nuclear dangers conveyed an anxiety that was disproportionate to the carefully worded American policy statements. Russia appeared to be seriously concerned about the consequences of American use of these weapons. Soviet preoccupation with the strenghtening of the Seventh Fleet was understandable since Washington issued subdued statements but emphasized its ship movements during this period. However, descriptions of the force exaggerated its strength.[101] The United States was said to be

[99]Moscow in Japanese, August 28, 1958, Alekseyev commentary. There are a number of similar comments. These apparently have been overlooked by authors like John R. Thomas, who asserts that the Soviets downgraded the possibility of world war during this phase. "Quemoy Crisis," pp. 125, 126.
[100]See, for example, Tass radioteletype in Russian to Europe, August 28 and September 4, 1958. See also the September 5 *Pravda* article by "observer" which is replete with references to tactical nuclear weapons.
[101]See, for example, Tass in English to the world, August 28, 1958, and Tass in Russian to Europe, September 4 and 5, 1958.

"in control of all Pacific routes to the Chinese shores with strong forces, equipped with atomic weapons." [102] The Russians obviously were worried about the implications of the American maneuvers and undoubtedly concerned that the United States might inadvertently be drawn into the conflict, thus complicating the Soviet position. Tass claimed that a plot had been uncovered in which Nationalist planes were to raid U.S. ships to justify intervention.[103] This appeared to be an attempt to increase American fears of being drawn into a conflict by Chiang, but it also reflected Soviet apprehension that Chiang might be successful in further involving the United States. The Russians may also have been trying to make their strategic predicament clear to the Chinese. Possibly, these statements were intended to offer an excuse for Soviet failure to support an ally facing a vigorous American demonstration of power. By stressing the inherent dangers Moscow seemed to be trying to put a damper on the activities of Peking and Washington.

The absence of Soviet military movements confirmed Moscow's desire to keep the affair limited and provide, at most, only indirect support. There was no show of Soviet naval power in the vicinity and no overt military maneuvers anywhere.[104]

There were also few signs that the Chinese were planning an immediate invasion. They appeared to be hoping to force evacuation of the islands rather than directly assaulting them. The Chief of Naval Operations recounted, ". . . although we had some indications that the Red Chinese Navy did go to sea, they never came around the Quemoy-Matsu area, and they didn't go to sea much either." [105] The inactivity of Soviet and Chinese naval elements indicated the limited nature of the probe as well as a tacit acceptance of the strength of the Seventh Fleet. No liberation of Taiwan could have been contemplated without first removing the U.S. Fleet.

In the absence of overt Soviet acts and official declarations of support, there was no widespread American fear of a direct clash with Russia. Since Washington did not know for certain how Moscow might react under various circumstances, the possibility that

[102]Soviet European Service in Greek, August 28, 1958, A. Druzhenin commentary. This remark was alleged to have come from an Associated Press military commentary.

[103]Tass in English to Europe, September 3, 1958. It is interesting that a similar plot was offered to explain the *Liberty* episode in the Middle East crisis. Moscow Domestic Service in Russian, June 14, 1967.

[104]Admiral Burke stated that he "thought that they might take action in some other part of the world. They did not take any action at all." Letter from Adm. Arleigh A. Burke, USN (Ret.), to Lt. Comdr. J. T. Howe, USN, dated March 15, 1968.

[105]Ibid.

the Russians would respond was seriously considered and weighed.[106] Because of the shelling, there was renewed speculation that the Peking meeting had harmonized Sino-Soviet planning. However, the consensus seemed to be that while the probe had a Soviet blessing, it would be kept limited.

Although conclusions concerning Soviet intentions during this phase must remain somewhat speculative, Moscow may have acquiesced initially to a carefully controlled Chinese probe restricted to siege tactics, anticipating that the Nationalists might evacuate the islands as they had the Tachen Islands in 1955. This approval was conceded probably to shore up the alliance rather than as a reflection of a Soviet desire to confront the United States. When it became clear after a few days that there would be a strong American reaction, the Russians expressed concern that the limited ploy might have serious worldwide repercussions. It is possible, of course, that the Chinese initiated the adventure unilaterally in an attempt to force the Soviets to commit themselves definitely.

Moscow was not interested in becoming involved directly and appeared to be trying to make this clear to Peking and Washington. When the Russians observed the rapid augmentation of the Seventh Fleet, they lapsed into a typical propaganda response to American demonstrations of naval strength. It is likely that there were mixed motivations for the propaganda campaign. Moscow probably wanted to convey an image of the United States as a super gendarme while playing on U.S. domestic fears of a land war in Asia. By confusing the issue it would be easier for Peking to retreat from the scheme. In light of American responses, the Kremlin may have been trying to convince Peking to dismiss any thoughts of expanding the conflict.

Since Khrushchev apparently was not willing to risk a clash with the United States over the offshore islands, the Seventh Fleet's activities limited Sino-Soviet options. If there were plans for a direct assault on Quemoy, they were probably canceled when the fleet's power was brought to bear, carrying with it the implication that the entire strength of the United States was behind it.

9.3 BRITISH POLICY

As the crisis intensified, the United States sought the support of its chief ally. Although British military assistance would provide an ad-

[106]See, for example, *The Washington Post,* "Remarks of 'high official' at Newport," September 5, 1958, p. A4, and "The Nation," *Time,* Vol. LXXII, No. 11 (September 15, 1958), p. 13.

ditional deterrent to the Communists, it was not essential. However, London's political and diplomatic backing would help counter hostile international and domestic opinion.

There were a number of consultations between the allies, but the British Foreign Office initially tended to minimize the crisis.[107] However, as shelling continued it announced that "H.M.G. fully share the concern . . . of the U.S. at any attempt to impose territorial changes by use of Force."[108] At the same time, London also indicated that its view of the legal status of the offshore islands had not changed.[109] In order to discourage the Chinese and Soviets, the British government adopted the domestically unpopular tactic of being vague about the extent of its commitment to the United States. But it privately counseled Washington that it could do little except in the diplomatic arena. Prime Minister Harold Macmillan, in a response to a letter sent at the President's behest, indicated he anticipated "rather negative attitudes."[110] He quoted Churchill's comment on the previous Quemoy crisis, "war to keep the coastal islands for Chiang would not be defensible" in Britain.[111]

British editorial opinion was decidedly opposed to any involvement. *The Guardian* was particularly outspoken, referring to the "dispair" of America's allies,[112] recognizing China's "indisputable claim" to Quemoy and Matsu,[113] and recommending that Washington "persuade the Nationalist to steal quietly away from the off-

[107]The Foreign Office said on August 30 that Britain saw no particular crisis in the Formosa dispute. *The Washington Post,* August 31, 1958, p. A4. See also *The New York Times,* August 24, 1958, p. 3. The Foreign Office announced on September 1 that "we are closely watching it and we are consulting about it with our American allies." *The Times,* September 2, 1958, Mr. R. A. Lloyd Jones of the Ministry of Defence has written that "HMG kept in closest touch with U.S. authorities." Letter of August 22, 1968, to Lt. Comdr. J. T. Howe, USN.

[108]*The Times,* September 6, 1958. On September 1 the Foreign Office commented that the "situation remains serious." *The Times,* September 2, 1958, p. 8.

[109]*The Washington Post* article "Britain Maintains Stand on Quemoys," September 6, 1958, p. A4.

[110]Eisenhower, *Waging Peace,* p. 300. Macmillan offered to approach the Soviets or the United Nations with the idea of a demilitarization of the islands. The British also appeared to believe that the Soviets were exerting the pressure indirectly.

[111]Ibid.

[112]*The Guardian* editorial "More Veiled Threats," September 5, 1958, p. 8. There were numerous similar comments. See, for example, *The Sunday Times* editorial "Quemoy and Formosa," August 31, 1958, p. 14.

[113]An editorial said, "the Chinese Communists have an indisputable claim to the offshore islands. Sooner or later the Communists were bound to eliminate such a *sharp thorn* in their side." *The Guardian*, "Hot Waters," August 29, 1958, p. 6. (Emphasis added.)

shore islands."[114] There were more realistic assessments of what was feasible in the American predicament, but they did not favor British involvement.[115] Observers predicted that the British public would not give support if the United States became deeply involved.[116]

London did dispatch a battalion of troops from Singapore to Hong Kong, and it was suggested that this was a gesture of support for the American policy.[117] However, the move probably was a response to the rising hostility of Chinese propaganda concerning Hong Kong.[118] Peking had accused the British of coordinating their efforts with those of the United States and Nationalists in the Taiwan area, and London may have felt that China had decided to discontinue their "special relationship" concerning Hong Kong. The British also announced that their Far East fleet would be "permanently reinforced by two aircraft carriers."[119] This statement undoubtedly was intended to convince China that Britain still had an interest in the Far East and had not necessarily abandoned the United States. The announcement was not news since it had been published in the 1958 defense plans.[120] Therefore, its timing had added meaning. Although not substantial, British military moves aided the United States in its stance on Quemoy.

Washington also sought the backing of its other allies. In the days just prior to the September 4 Newport conference, Secretary of State Dulles met with both SEATO and NATO ministers.[121] The letter to Prime Minister Macmillan was also drafted on September 4,

[114]*The Guardian* editorial "The Lull," September 1, 1958, p. 6.
[115]See, for example, "Offshore Squeeze," *The Economist* (September 6, 1958), p. 750; *The Times* editorial August 29, 1958, p. 9; *The Observer* (London) editorial "Too Many Brinks," August 31, 1958.
[116]Drew Middleton reported from London, "public support is almost nonexistent." *The New York Times,* September 4, 1958, p. 1. Warren Rodgers described the British action as "what amounts to a Bronx cheer." *The Washington Post,* August 31, 1958, p. A4.
[117]For example, *The Times* asked, "Is Britain doing in a smaller way with her Army what America is doing with her Navy and Air Force—Warning Communist China?" September 3, 1958, p. 10.
[118]A *Peking Review* editorial accused British military planes of intruding into China's air space to coordinate with the U.S. Nationalist efforts to "heighten tension in the Taiwan Straits." Vol. I, No. 27 (September 2, 1958), p. 3.
[119]*The New York Times* article "Britain to Bolster Her Fleet," August 26, 1958, p. 3.
[120]"Report on Defence, 1958," in *Brassey's Annual, The Armed Forces Year Book, 1958*, Rear Adm. H. G. Thrushfried, RN, ed. (New York: Macmillan, 1958), p. 311.
[121]Dulles had flown to Paris to consult with the NATO council. *The Washington Post,* September 4, 1958, p. 1.

1958. But negative responses did not deter the United States from taking a firm position.

9.4 EVALUATION OF U.S. CAPABILITY

During this period the Quemoy crisis was the number one American national security problem. It was the most acute phase of the crisis because Soviet, Chinese, Nationalist, and American intentions were all unknown. However, from Washington's point of view the most serious concerns were alleviated in the first few days because Peking did not then employ its sizable bomber force, and the Soviet Union played down the crisis. Although the groundwork had been laid during the buildup phase, hard decisions had to be made concerning the extent of American commitment. As the period progressed, the U.S., Soviet, and British policies became clearer. There were also some slight changes in American capability estimates.

The absence of Soviet military support combined with a fairly weak declaratory position seemed to indicate with greater assurance that the Russians did not intend to become involved directly. Soviet forces did not make a move either in the local area of conflict or near the borders of the Soviet Union. Rather than making official statements, Moscow voiced its policy through *Pravda* articles, and the propaganda campaign indicated Russian reluctance to become embroiled and its understanding of the dangers inherent in the situation. United States strength in the area was emphasized without counterclaims of similar Soviet capability or a reiteration of Chinese paper tiger descriptions of U.S. forces. Thus, there were a number of signs that gave Washington greater confidence that Soviet intervention was remote. Recognizing the power realities, as it appeared to, Moscow could only be embarrassed, as leader of the Communist world, by letting a situation develop in which its ally might become engaged in a battle with the United States.

Although resupplying the beleagured islands appeared to be a major challenge, American estimates of capability were probably even more optimistic than they had been in the buildup phase. The U.S. Navy was confident that the siege could be overcome with ingenuity and determination, and it had the sheer power of the Seventh Fleet to fall back on. China's failure to employ its bomber force combined with evidence that a major invasion was not imminent indicated that the probe was limited. Any action could probably be kept localized. The arrival of some augmenting forces shifted the military balance to an even more favorable condition.

Because the executive had anticipated there would be some negative domestic reaction, it was probably somewhat relieved when there was so little criticism. Congress had adjourned with the crisis intensifying, strategic nuclear concerns were quieted by the lack of Soviet threats, and the general public protest was light. The absence of a major Chinese attack could have raised questions about whether or not there was any serious threat to Formosa, but the critics did not seize on this issue. Editorials opposing policy were undoubtedly a concern, but there were also counterbalancing expressions of support. The failure of any significant public dissent to materialize up to September 4 probably gave the administration confidence that it could weather the storm without much difficulty. For this reason, congressional and public opinion appeared to have had little impact on policy, particularly on the firmer stand taken on September 4.[122]

Lack of British endorsement of the Quemoy policy was not particularly surprising. Actually the ambiguity of London's public position was encouraging for the United States. The reinforcement of the Hong Kong garrison indicated to Peking that Britain did not intend to be pushed around in the Far East just because it held a position contrary to U.S. policy toward the offshore islands. Pressure on Hong Kong had the influence of unifying the Anglo-American stance versus China and also underlined allied interdependency. But the military need in the Far East was chiefly that of Britain for American power. British forces sent to the Far East were token. On the other hand, Washington demonstrated a greater anxiety during this period to have the political support of its major ally, and in that sense the dependency on the British position appeared to have increased.

During this crucial phase of the crisis, the United States gradually hardened its declaratory stand. It was privately reluctant to make an irrevocable commitment, but its public demonstration of power had none of the aspects of gradualism. Whether the Chinese precipitated the conflict unilaterally or with Russian encouragement is not certain. Either way, it probably was not intended to be more than a limited probe. It became apparent that a military seizure of the major offshore islands would be at great cost, if not impossible. The probability of Soviet intervention was remote, particularly if the Chinese mainland was not attacked. Moreover, there was a prepon-

[122]The commencement of outspoken criticism of the policy began after, and partly as a result of, the statements of September 4. The impact of this criticism will be assessed in Chapter 10.

derance of U.S. military power available on the scene, which was backed by strategic nuclear superiority. Domestic dissidents had not mounted a significant protest, and support of Britain, while desirable, was not essential. All of these factors facilitated a decision to prevent conquest of Quemoy. The involvement in the Middle East reduced to some extent the capability of the United States to respond to the Quemoy crisis, but the effect was not serious enough to be a significant influence on assessment of U.S. capability to cope with the crisis during this period.

10. THE SECOND PHASE OF THE CRISIS

SEPTEMBER 7, 1958, TO OCTOBER 6, 1958

The second phase began with Chinese acceptance of negotiations and terminated with their announcement of a seven-day cease-fire beginning on October 6. Finding a solution to the Quemoy challenge continued to be a primary preoccupation of American policy makers. The more authoritative Soviet statements of support for China increased the importance of accurately assessing Moscow's motivations. The British position became increasingly significant as domestic criticism in the United States mounted. A number of U.S. troops and warships remained committed to the Lebanon situation.

10.1 UNITED STATES POLICY

The American declaratory position during this period reflected the difficulties of trying simultaneously to negotiate with an uncompromising enemy, remain firm as Soviet threats increased, solve the formidable resupply problem, control an intractable ally, and contend with rising domestic criticism. In view of the contradictory aspects of these objectives, the apparent modifications in the public position were understandable.

A number of significant U.S. policy statements were issued. While affirming American determination not to back down under the threat of force, most of them also indicated a desire to negotiate a realistic settlement. However, what seemed fair and reasonable to Washington was totally unacceptable to Peking. The general trend of public declarations implied increasing flexibility in the American position and a desire to make some concessions. But the apparent concessions were deceptive. Rather than making real modifications, the United States appeared to be trying to obtain Peking's approval of positions Washington had taken in 1955. Although it has been asserted that a "major switch" in policy occurred on September 30,[1] the change was not radical when compared with statements made prior to that date.

[1]Alexander De Conde, *A History of American Foreign Policy* (New York: Charles Scribner's Sons, 1963), p. 833. Kenneth T. Young called it a "dramatic shift" in *Negotiating with the Chinese Communists: The United States Experience, 1953–1967* (New York: McGraw-Hill Book Co., 1968), p. 186. Richard B. Stebbins asserts that policy was "redefined" in a "rather noticeable change of position" and that it appeared that the United States "had decided to back away from its previous stand." Council on Foreign Relations, *The United States in World Affairs, 1958* (New York: Harper and Brothers, 1959), pp. 325, 326.

During the early days of this phase there were two important definitions of the American position: Secretary of State Dulles's press conference of September 9 and President Eisenhower's speech to the nation two days later. On both occasions firm stands were moderated by broad hints of willingness to negotiate a permanent solution to the problem. The President asserted that the Formosa resolution applied, and there would be "no retreat in the face of armed aggression."[2] He warned that a "Western Pacific 'Munich' " would not appease the Communists.[3] Secretary Dulles made an analogy to Berlin as a "forward position which . . . could not be lost in the face of a frontal attack without consequences which are unacceptable to the United States."[4] The American commitment to defend the islands was clearly expressed.

At the same time, the American leaders alluded to possible concessions. Secretary of State Dulles implied there might be some concession made on previous positions[5] and remarked that renouncement of force in the area would "probably have *consequences.*"[6] The President was more explicit when he stated, "There are *measures that can be taken* to assure that these offshore islands will not be a *thorn in the side of peace.*"[7] (Emphasis added.) The implication was that the islands might be demilitarized and Nationalist raids and harassments curtailed.

The United States corroborated public hints with more specific offers in private negotiations with the Chinese at Warsaw. During the first several meetings, which began on September 15, the United States offered a withdrawal of forces in stages from the offshore islands. It may also have suggested that future sovereignty over the offshore islands was negotiable.[8]

[2]U.S., Department of State, *American Foreign Policy Current Documents 1958* (Washington: Government Printing Office, 1962), p. 1159.
[3]Ibid, p. 1157. The President stressed that conquest of Quemoy by the Chinese would not be the "end of the story."
[4]*The New York Times,* "State Department Transcript of Remarks Made by Dulles at his News Conference," September 10, 1958, p. 8, Question 43.
[5]He stated, for example, that "it might not be useful to repeat the ritual of the last three years" during the negotiations. Ibid., Question 44. He was also more conciliatory in the tone of his answer to questions that might provoke the Chinese than he had been on September 4, 1958. See, for example, his answer to the question of retaliation in case of a Chinese air attack. Question 30.
[6]Ibid., Question 45. (Emphasis added.) See also Question 41. He stated his hope that out of the Warsaw negotiations would come "as a minimum a modus vivendi." Question 22.
[7]Department of State, *American Foreign Policy, 1958,* p. 1160.
[8]Kenneth T. Young believes this to be the case. See *Negotiating with the Chinese,* pp. 166–168. According to one report the State Department out-

Few policy statements were made while the parties sounded each other out at Warsaw. But after several weeks Secretary of State Dulles made a speech that appeared to soften slightly the public position. While again stressing America would not "retreat in the face of armed force," he revealed that the position was "*otherwise flexible*."[9] He indicated just how "flexible" the policy had become by stating,

> . . . we would *find acceptable any arrangement* which on the one hand did not involve surrender to force or the threat of force; and on the other hand *eliminated* from the situation *features* that could *reasonably* be *regarded* as *provocative* or which, to use President Eisenhower's phrase, were 'a thorn on the side of peace.' [10] [Emphasis added.]

Washington was becoming more interested in eliminating a "thorn" in its own policy. This particular passage had been personally inserted by Secretary Dulles into a September 24 draft of the speech. It replaced an earlier version which stated that ". . . between fighting and give-away there are many intermediate possibilities. These we are *prepared to explore* in accordance with our United Nations charter obligation."[11] (Emphasis added.) In addition to indicating the Secretary of State's interest in the passage, the correction also illustrated the increased flexibility of the American position. Instead of being "prepared to explore" possibilities, the United States now found "acceptable any arrangement" that did not involve surrender to force. On September 9, Secretary Dulles had only hinted that an "*effective, dependable*, renunciation of force . . . *might* have further consequences."[12] The United States was apparently de-emphasizing the need for a cease-fire as a prerequisite for meaningful discussions. Another deletion from an earlier draft of Secretary Dulles's speech of September 25, 1958, was "President Eisenhower and I have made clear that, once there *were a cease*

lined a three-step plan for peaceful settlement of the crisis: (1) call a cease-fire, (2) demilitarize Quemoy and Matsu, and (3) appeal to the United Nations if no peaceful settlement can be arranged. *The Guardian* (Manchester) article by Max Freedman, "Three Stages to Peace," September 19, 1958, p. 1.

[9](Emphasis added.) *The New York Times*, "Secretary Dulles's Policy Speech to the Far East American Council of Commerce," text of speech delivered September 25, September 26, 1958, p. 3.

[10]Ibid.

[11]September 21, 1958, draft of Secretary Dulles's speech before the Far East America Council, p. 37. Secretary Dulles's correction had been made on the September 24, 1958, draft on page 28. The John Foster Dulles Papers, Category 1B, Princeton University Library.

[12](Emphasis added.) *The New York Times*, September 10, 1958, p. 8, Question 41.

fire, other matters could be discussed . . . . [13] (Emphasis added.)

In his speech the Secretary of State also intimated that the United States favored reduction of the Quemoy garrison by remarking that "any readjustment of Free-World positions that would add strength is desirable," and that Quemoy, like Berlin, was "militarily indefensible."[14] Washington seemed to be signaling that it was ready to curtail Nationalist activities which Peking considered threatening to the mainland and that the United States was seeking to dampen the crisis.

The Secretary's speech preluded his significant September 30 news conference. Although his remarks to the press again slightly softened the declaratory position, their significance has been exaggerated. The statements were neither "fundamental changes"[15] nor a "definite switch"[16] in policy, but rather a disclosure of a readiness to consider concessions hinted at throughout the period. The press conference appeared to bring the public position closer to the one taken in the secret talks with the Chinese.

The convergence of public and private positions may explain the disparity between policy makers, who do not recall a shift,[17] and observers, who felt a significant change had occurred. It is possible that because the declaratory position had been indefinite as the crisis developed, the Secretary of State felt it was necessary to clear up impressions both deliberately and inadvertently created. Secre-

[13]September 21, 1958, draft of speech. The passage as actually given in the speech said, "President Eisenhower and I have made clear that in these Warsaw talks we will not be a party to. . . ." *The New York Times,* September 26, 1958. The cease-fire stipulation had been dropped.

[14]Ibid. The press release had said "strength *and security*" and the latter two words had been penciled in on the September 24, 1958, draft of the speech. The John Foster Dulles Papers, Category 1B, Princeton University Library. Under Secretary of State Christian Herter continued this thesis on September 29, 1958, when he stated that the offshore islands "are not strategically defensible in the defense of Formosa." *The New York Times,* September 30, 1958, p. 5.

[15]Arthur Krock wrote that there had "been at least two fundamental changes." *The New York Times,* October 3, 1958.

[16]*The Washington Post* article by Marquis Childs, October 8, 1958. See also the editorial "Change in the Wind" in *The Washington Post,* October 1, 1958.

[17]See, for example, interview with an official familiar with policy during Quemoy crisis of 1958, conducted January 31, 1969, Appendix B, Question 5. Assistant Secretary Robertson and Admiral Felt did not recall a shift. Letters from Mr. Walter Spencer Robertson, to Lt. Comdr. J. T. Howe, USN, dated December 12, 1968, and Adm. Harry D. Felt, USN (Ret.), to Lt. Comdr. J. T. Howe, USN, dated July 16, 1968.

tary Dulles may have reasoned that the United States had created dangerous expectations in Chiang's mind, unnecessarily subjected the administration to domestic criticism, and perhaps given the Soviet Union too much cause for alarm. The remarks at the press conference also appeared to be an attempt to break the negotiating stalemate and allay public criticism by demonstrating the "reasonableness" of the private position.

In his remarks of September 30, Dulles put increased emphasis on the flexibility of American policy. He said, for example, that "if the situation we have to meet changes, our policies change with it."[18] In other comments he indicated what these "changes" might entail. Concerning the prerequisites for withdrawal, he stated, "If there were a cease-fire in the area which *seemed to be reasonably dependable,* I think it would be foolish to keep these large forces on these islands."[19] (Emphasis added.) A formal cease-fire was not required. Dulles reiterated that placing large troop concentrations on the islands was not a sound military judgment.[20] He again hinted that the American interest was narrow: ". . . if the United States believed that these islands could be *abandoned* without its having any adverse impact upon the potential defense of Formosa and the Treaty area, we would not be thinking of using any force there."[21] (Emphasis added.) These comments, however, represented a continuation of a theme rather than a sharp reversal of policy.

The Secretary's statements were, perhaps, more significant in what they did not stress. The importance of Quemoy in the defense of Formosa and the free world was hardly mentioned. And Dulles referred to Chinese intentions to go beyond Quemoy as "the problem we have to think about" instead of making a stronger declaration of determination to stop aggression.[22]

His comments indicated that the American position was pliable. Chiang was undoubtedly incensed when Dulles publicly admitted that he doubted if the Nationalists would reach the mainland "just by their own steam," that it had been "rather foolish" to put large forces on the offshore islands, and that the United States "did not have any legal commitment to defend the off-shore islands" and did

[18]*The New York Times,* "State Department Transcript of Remarks Made by Dulles at News Conference," October 1, 1958, p. 8.
[19]Ibid. Compare this with the position taken on September 9 concerning preconditions for a possible concession.
[20]See Appendix A for his specific remarks.
[21]Ibid.
[22]*The New York Times,* October 1, 1958, p. 8.

not want to make one.[23] While the reasons for such statements become clearer when the influence of relations with the Nationalists, the Soviet position, and rising domestic and world criticism are examined, these remarks were not substantial changes from previous American positions expressed in public or private. It is primarily in the timing and number rather than the content that a further softening of the U.S. stance was indicated.

Examination of American declarations prior to September 30 puts allegations that a major policy shift occurred on that date in proper perspective. It has been alleged that "for the first time since the beginning of the crisis Mr. Dulles now laid heavy emphasis on the fact that the United States had no legal commitment to defend the offshore islands."[24] Assertions on September 30 were the most categorical yet, but these disclaimers were no stronger than ones in 1955 and only slightly more explicit than those of September 9 and September 11, 1958.[25] On September 9 Secretary Dulles declared it had been clear from the beginning that the offshore islands were "not to be defended as such by the United States," and that if only Quemoy and Matsu were involved, "there would be no basis for action on the part of the United States."[26] The government had continually stressed that the relationship of the offshore islands to the protection of Taiwan was the key prerequisite of the Formosa resolution.[27] In informal remarks the day prior to the press conference, Secretary Dulles had stated his feelings that the President did not have the authority to "announce, without qualification, that come what may we would defend Quemoy and Matsu."[28]

The disavowal of any commitment to aid a Nationalist return to the mainland was reputed to be the "first time that the United States

[23]Ibid.
[24]Stebbins, *World Affairs, 1958,* p. 326.
[25]See Table A.1, Appendix A, statements 1, 3, 4, and 6.
[26]*The New York Times,* September 10, 1958, p. 8.
[27]See Table A.2, Appendix A.
[28]The Secretary of State had preceded this statement by commenting that "the Communists have so closely tied together, in their own statements, the off-shore islands and Formosa that it goes pretty far to resolve the problem and make it clear what we would do." Off-the-record remarks by Secretary Dulles before participants of Foreign Service Senior Officer Course, September 29, 1958. The John Foster Dulles Papers, Category 1B, Princeton University Library. There appears to be little inconsistency between these remarks and public statements. It is possible, of course, that the Secretary may have been just as careful with this audience considering the extent of alleged dissent within the State Department.

had said publicly that it would not support a war of reconquest."[29] While it was probably deflating for Chiang to have the myth exploded, it had been made clear in the treaty discussions that the purpose was defensive and that there could be no military operations without joint agreement.[30] This position had been reiterated in the Dulles speech of September 25. American assertions that the Communist regime was not permanent had suggested that any changes would result from internal unrest and not invasion.[31] On September 30 Dulles commented that even in case of internal revolt Chiang might not be invited to head a new mainland government.[32] But nonsupport for invasion was not a new concept. It was significant, however, that the Secretary of State publicly restated a position embarrassing to Chiang. Dulles's remarks were probably meant for a diverse audience: the Chinese Nationalists, as a warning of the limits of American support; the Chinese Communists, as an indication of willingness to disavow a policy that was a "sharp thorn"; the Soviets, to signal that their bluff of defending China if attacked would not be called; and the American public, to reassure them that Chiang would not drag the United States into war with China.

The comment that Chiang was "rather foolish" to put so many troops on the offshore islands has been cited as evidence of a policy shift.[33] But Washington had tried to avert such a buildup in 1955 and indicated in earlier crisis statements that it discouraged such a decision.[34] However, Dulles admitted, as he also had implied during his September 9 press conference that the United States had *acquiesced* because of strong Nationalist views. He reiterated that the United States could not always impose its will on an ally. Disapproval of Chiang's decision was more explicit on September 30, but it had been implied in earlier references. It was Dulles's choice of words that had such a devastating impact on the Nationalists, who found them offensive. On top of reluctant American support, Taipei

[29]De Conde, *American Foreign Policy,* p. 834. See also Young, *Negotiating with the Chinese,* p. 186.
[30]See U.S., Senate, Committee on Foreign Relations, *Mutual Defense Treaty with the Republic of China,* 84th Cong. 1st sess., Executive Report No. 2 (Washington, 1955), p. 4; and Table A.4, Appendix A, statement 1.
[31]Compare the positions taken in statements 1, 2, 3, and 4 of Table A.3 and statement 1 of Table A.4, Appendix A.
[32]*The New York Times,* October 1, 1958, p. 8.
[33]See De Conde, *American Foreign Policy,* p. 833; Stebbins, *World Affairs, 1958,* p. 326; and Arthur Krock in *The New York Times,* October 3, 1958, p. 3.
[34]See Table A.5, Appendix A, statements 1 and 2.

now felt it was being publicly insulted.[35] The phrase probably was simply an unfortunate choice of words, but the underlying implication of criticizing the ally may have been that the Secretary of State did not intend to be duped by possible Nationalist scheming.

The "reciprocal aspect of the renunciation of force" was also reputed to be a new feature.[36] But in light of previous statements this was not a change.[37] In the positions taken on September 30 the Secretary of State appeared to be showing U.S. intentions, rather than making a major shift in policy.[38] The public line had been softened somewhat, and emphasis was placed on American readiness to seek a solution to the problem. But most of what was said on September 30 had been implied all along.

Throughout this period the problem was not that the United States had a rigid policy. Washington was willing to consider a number of possibilities—but not the only one acceptable to Peking. The Chinese would accept no less than full sovereignty over the offshore islands. Peking felt its claim was legitimate, as did most of the international community, and it was inconceivable that China would settle for anything less. In addition, the sharpest thorn for Peking was Formosa. There was little probability that the Chinese would accept a solution that stopped with acquisition of Quemoy and Matsu.

President Eisenhower reiterated the more flexible line in the following days. He agreed it was not wise to have so many troops on the islands and was less emphatic about defending Quemoy.[39] In a public letter to the Chairman of the Senate Foreign Relations Committee, he wrote "Certainly there is always the *possibility* that it *may in certain contingencies, after taking account of all relevant facts, become necessary* or appropriate for the defense of Formosa

[35]Interview with Professor James Moceri, conducted February 13, 1969. Professor Moceri was Acting Public Affairs Officer of United States Information Service on Formosa during the crisis.
[36]This allegation was made at the press conference and denied by Dulles, who stated that renunciation of force had always been considered to be a reciprocal proposition. See, however, Kenneth Young's comment that this was a "significant" remark by Dulles. *Negotiating with the Chinese,* p. 186.
[37]See Table A.4, Appendix A, statements 1, 2, and 6.
[38]It is possible that Dulles's remarks were prompted by diplomatic feelers. According to Thomas J. Hamilton, "Authoritative sources" revealed that the Communists had sent word at that time that they were willing to negotiate an interim settlement of hostilities and that Dulles's conference was a response to these feelers. *The New York Times,* October 10, 1958, p. 1. See also Young, *Negotiating with the Chinese,* pp. 185, 186.
[39]Department of State, *American Foreign Policy, 1958,* p. 1169. Statement by President Eisenhower at his news conference on October 1, 1958.

and the Pescadores *also* to take measures to secure and protect the related positions of Quemoy and Matsu."[40] (Emphasis added.) The President's statement was indefinite and imprecise compared with his speech of September 11.[41] The indecisiveness was probably a reflection of the improved military situation and decreased likelihood of an invasion. Changing circumstances allowed the President to modify his language and thus alleviate domestic criticism.

After a tense week in which resupply techniques were developed, American military estimates of the situation became increasingly optimistic. It was alleged that the Commander in Chief in the Pacific had doubts about the wisdom of defending Quemoy. With the situation still tenuous, *The New York Times* reported that the Pacific commander questioned the wisdom of defending the offshore islands because of low stock of conventional weapons and doubts about the effectiveness of the Nationalist forces.[42] However, Admiral Felt says that the story was made up of "whole cloth" and that he supported the Quemoy policy from the beginning.[43] President Eisenhower, however, has written that only a few hours before his speech to the Nation on September 11, the Secretary of Defense informed him that "the Joint Chiefs of Staff now felt the Quemoy and Matsu Islands should be vacated (or lightly manned as outposts only)."[44] It is not certain that the Joint Chiefs "reversed themselves" or even modified their approach. It is possible that what the President perceived as a sharp change simply represented the first clarification of this particular Joint Chiefs' opinion in the President's mind.[45]

Apparently the 1955 military judgment that forces on the islands should be reduced was re-emphasized. Some military leaders may have indicated that once the Chinese had been deterred, it would be wise to attempt again to persuade Chiang to withdraw most of his troops. It is doubtful that the service chiefs urged the islands be evacuated under fire. Secretary Dulles remarked during his Sep-

[40]Ibid., p. 1171. Letter to Senator Theodore Green dated October 2, 1958.
[41]He had asserted then that the Formosa resolution applied to the "present situation."
[42]*The New York Times* article by Jack Raymond, "US Pacific Chief Said to Question Policy on Quemoy," September 11, 1958.
[43]Letter from Admiral H. D. Felt, USN (Ret.), to Lt. Comdr. J. T. Howe, USN, dated July 16, 1968.
[44]Dwight D. Eisenhower, *Waging Peace, 1956–1961,* (Garden City, N.Y.: Doubleday and Co., 1965), p. 300.
[45]See the answers to questions 3 and 4 of interview with an official familiar with policy during the Quemoy crisis of 1958 conducted January 31, 1969, Appendix B.

tember 30 conference that the military agreed it would not be wise to keep Nationalist troops on the islands if there were a cease-fire.[46] This position was corroborated by the negotiating terms offered at Warsaw and the increasing flexibility of the American declaratory position. At the same time, military leaders seemed to have continued to favor defense of the islands under the existing circumstances. Admiral Burke wrote, "I don't remember whether the Joint Chiefs reversed themselves or not. I never did because I felt Quemoy and Matsu should be defended from the beginning."[47] Several other military leaders have concurred that there probably was not a reversal of the Joint Chiefs' estimates.[48]

At the time the United States appeared to make slight concessions diplomatically, the military situation was considerably improved. The blockade had been broken on September 14 by using armored amphibious tractors (LVTs) to transport supplies from ship to shore. By September 29 it was widely publicized that the convoying problems were over.[49] Admiral Burke announced on October 5 that the islands could hold out for "10 years—forever!"[50] Among the first items delivered to the islands were eight-inch howitzers that were meant to provide more effective counterbattery fire. These weapons were installed by U.S. Marines.[51] Because the howitzers were capable of shooting a nuclear shell, the significance of the emplacement of these guns has been exaggerated.[52] The United States had no intention of providing nuclear weapons to the Nationalists.[53] But in order to take advantage of the possible sobering

[46]*The New York Times,* "State Department Transcript of Remarks Made by Dulles at News Conference," October 1, 1958, p. 8, Question 18.

[47]Admiral Burke was, of course, a member of the Joint Chiefs. Letter from Admiral Arleigh Burke, USN (Ret.), to Lt. Comdr. J. T. Howe, USN, dated July 9, 1968.

[48]Letter from General Maxwell P. Taylor, USA, to Lt. Comdr. J. T. Howe, USN, dated March 4, 1969. Felt, letter. Comments of Lt. Gen. R. C. Mangrum, USMC (Ret.), in letters to Lt. Comdr. J. T. Howe, USN.

[49]*The New York Times* article "Convoying Problem Over, Says Brucker," September 29, 1958, p. A7.

[50]*The Washington Post* article by Robert J. Donovan, "Burke Hits Pressure to Yield Strategic Isles," October 5, 1958.

[51]Letter from an informed observer concerning the Quemoy crisis of 1958, to Lt. Comdr. J. T. Howe, USN, dated March 13, 1969.

[52]The significance of the nuclear capability has been stressed by Hanson W. Baldwin and Robert W. Barnett. But they exaggerated the role played by these guns. See *The New York Times,* September 28, 1958, p. E3, and the Baldwin article "Limited War," *The Atlantic,* Vol. 203, No. 5 (May 1959), p. 41. See also Robert W. Barnett, unpublished study, *Quemoy: The Use and Consequence of Nuclear Deterrence,* Center for International Affairs, Harvard University, March 1960.

[53]Letter from Vice Adm. Roland N. Smoot, USN (Ret.), to Lt. Comdr. J. T. Howe, USN, dated March 1, 1969.

effect on the Chinese, American officials "neither confirmed or denied the presence of nuclear ordnance" on Quemoy.[54] The installation of these heavy guns on Quemoy apparently explains why the Chinese suddenly shifted to deep-penetration shells. Rather than being a portent of an impending invasion, the Chinese move had a logical defensive explanation. The more destructive shells were evidently first used the day after the eight-inch howitzers were landed on Quemoy.[55]

Another factor that significantly improved military estimates was the establishment of control of the air over the strait by Nationalist pilots. American officials were astonished by the ease with which the Nationalist aviators demonstrated their superiority. The Communist Chinese pilots proved to be inexperienced and froze in combat.[56] By September 20 Communist Chinese aviators appeared to be avoiding challenging the Nationalists. On September 24 an outnumbered group of Nationalist pilots fought their way out of a trap, aided by newly supplied sidewinder missiles, and routed 100 Chinese MIGs.[57]

Because strength of the Seventh Fleet continued to be increased, there was no doubt that the United States commanded the air and sea in the area. In addition, scheduled armed services manpower cuts were delayed to further indicate U.S. determination to hold Quemoy.[58] As the United States tended to soften its declaratory position toward the end of this phase, it was negotiating from strength. It was not likely the Chinese could mount a successful military challenge.

Although the military situation improved, congressional criticism increased. Democrats on the Foreign Relations Committee vigorously protested administration policies. Some senators called for a special session of Congress, and Chairman Green asserted that action in defense of Quemoy would be "at the wrong time, the wrong

[54]Letter from an informed observer, dated March 13, 1969.

[55]Deep-penetration shells were first used on September 17, 1958, according to *The Washington Post,* September 13, 1958. The eight-inch howitzer installation began on September 15 or 16. *The Washington Post,* September 21, 1958, p. A12.

[56]See interview with an official familiar with policy during Quemoy crisis of 1958, conducted January 31, 1969, Appendix B, Question 1.

[57]See the descriptions of these victories in Tang Tsou, *The Embroilment Over Quemoy: Mao, Chiang and Dulles* (Salt Lake City: University of Utah Press, 1959), pp. 23, 24, and *The Guardian* (Manchester) article "Sidewinders for Chiang," October 1, 1958, p. 9.

[58]In making the announcement, the Secretary of Defense said that the U.S. government "has made it clear we would resist an assault on the Quemoys by the Chinese Communists." *The Washington Post,* September 13, 1958.

place, on issues not of vital concern to our security, and without allies."[59] Although almost as many congressmen voiced support for the government's stand, the critics' messages were more frequently and widely publicized. Dissent, however, was not overwhelming. The Democrats were split on the issue, and *The Washington Post* complained of a "lamentable silence" from Congress.[60] Nevertheless, the President was obviously concerned about congressional criticism, and efforts were made to gain bipartisan support.[61] Government officials repeatedly referred to the unanimous congressional mandate given by the 1955 Formosa resolution. Pressure from the lawmakers probably contributed to the executive's decision to stress the flexibility of the American position.

Public opinion had a much greater influence during this phase as mail, editorials, polls, and statements of prominent figures reflected increasing opposition to the government's policy. While the public reaction was small in letter volume and divided, rather than predominantly negative, the dissent had an impact on policy makers. As Admiral Burke, the Chief of Naval Operations, wrote, ". . . the *difficult part* of the problem was in *convincing our own people* of the importance of the retention of Quemoy and Matsu by the Chinese Nationalists."[62] (Emphasis added.) When asked about how much weight should be given to the public reaction, the Secretary of State responded, ". . . public opinion is always important because obviously you cannot carry out effectively a public policy without the support of public opinion. The question is always present as to whether the public opinion is sound or not. Certainly you cannot allow your foreign policy to be dictated by public opinion."[63] Dulles evidently felt that misguided dissenters were complicating the conduct of U.S. policy.

The impact of the criticism was increased because there was heavy opposition within the government itself. Criticism could not just be attributed to misinformation or politics. Then Vice President Richard Nixon commented subsequently that during the crisis Sec-

[59]Letter from Senator T. F. Green to President Eisenhower quoted in *The New York Times,* October 1, 1958, p. 6.
[60]*The Washington Post* editorial, September 23, 1958, p. A20. See also *The Washington Post* article "Democrats Split Sharply Over Quemoy," September 16, 1958, p. A6. Lyndon Johnson, the majority leader, and House Speaker Rayburn remained neutral.
[61]See Eisenhower, *Waging Peace,* p. 301, and *The New York Times,* September 10, 1958, Dulles's answer No. 34, and September 29, 1958, p. 1.
[62]Burke, letter.
[63]*The New York Times,* October 1, 1958, p. 8. He had made a similar comment on September 9. *The New York Times,* September 10, 1958, p. 8.

retary Dulles "took on the whole foreign policy establishment" and that "the State Department was violently against him."[64] The Vice President's observations help explain the vehemence of his public reprimand of a "State Department official" who revealed that 80 percent of the mail was running against the Quemoy policy. He called it an act of "sabotage."[65] The Vice President also asserted that it was the "responsibility of a leader to lead public opinion—not just to follow it."[66] Key leaders apparently were determined to see the policy through, in spite of mounting opposition.

Although Senator Green predicted the American people would not support involvement in the defense of Quemoy,[67] many informed observers felt the public would rally behind the President in any war with China.[68] Eisenhower predicted the "American people would unite as one."[69] But this was not the real problem during the difficult diplomatic maneuvering. In trying to deter aggression, minimize concessions, and reassure an ally, the administration's major handicap was a dissenting public. The President warned that he believed disunity at home would encourage enemies and make conflict almost inevitable.[70]

Dissent was expressed in mail to the White House, State Department, and Congress, but the volume was relatively small. White House mail allegedly rose from "equally divided to two to one" in support of the President following his speech to the nation.[71] State Department mail, on the other hand, ran almost four to one against U.S. policy. This apparent contradiction might be explained by a swell of support for the President's refusal to back down accompanied by complaints to the State Department for getting into such a

[64]Interview with Richard Nixon conducted on March 5, 1965, by Dr. R. D. Challener. Dulles Oral History Project, Princeton University. Approved transcript, p. 33.
[65]He also asserted that foreign policy decisions cannot be based on "opinion polls." *The Washington Post*, September 28, 1958, p. 1. *The New York Times* subsequently claimed that the information had been provided by the State Department in response to routine request, September 29, 1958, p. 9.
[66]Ibid.
[67]Department of State, *American Foreign Policy, 1958*, p. 1170.
[68]See, for example, the views of Arthur Krock, *The New York Times,* October 3, 1958, p. 28; and Chalmers M. Roberts, *The Washington Post,* September 28, 1958.
[69]President's Letter of October 2, 1958, to Senator Green. Department of State, *American Foreign Policy,* 1958, p. 1172.
[70]Ibid.
[71]See *The New York Times,* September 13, 1958, p. 1, and *The Washington Post,* September 30, 1958, p. A6.

predicament.[72] Congressional mail was predominantly opposed to U.S. policy, although not by large ratios in the case of Republicans.[73] Although volume remained light,[74] mail increased substantially following the President's speech to the nation. In the next two weeks State Department letters increased from 300 to 5000.[75] This trend undoubtedly made an impression on government leaders.

Although editorial opinion remained divided, the amount of criticism increased as the crisis continued. Of editorial comments contained in some twenty-three major papers following the President's speech to the nation about half were critical. Reportedly, the State Department found "little support" in their survey of 100 newspapers during the crisis.[76] *The New York Times* reversed its editorial position of the previous phase. It urged reduction of the offshore garrisons and asserted that the islands were not worth war.[77] *The Washington Post*, while remaining critical, admitted there was probably "no alternative to standing firm in the circumstances."[78] Editorial opinion did not speak as a single voice, but among the dissenters were some very influential journals.[79]

Opinion polls were not necessarily meaningful. Few major surveys were conducted and questions did not bear directly on whether the United States should defend the offshore islands. A Gallup survey of September 26, 1958,[80] asked, "Would you like to see the U.S. work out a solution to this problem in the United Nations before we

[72]The President's mail also may have resulted from an organized effort to demonstrate support, although this is highly speculative.

[73]*The New York Times* article by Allen Drury, September 26, 1958. One report alleged that Senator Douglas's mail was 30 to 1 against U.S. policy and Senator Knowland's, 25 to 7. *The Guardian* (Manchester), September 25, 1958, p. 6.

[74]Congressmen who normally received 200 to 300 letters a day with Congress in session were averaging 15 to 30 a day. *The New York Times*, September 26, 1958. The volume was no greater than that received during the Suez, Lebanon, and Hungarian crisis. *The Washington Post* article by Don Irwin, September 28, 1958, p. 1.

[75]*The Guardian* (Manchester) article by Max Freedman, September 29, 1958, p. 1.

[76]*The New York Times* article by E. W. Kenworthy, October 5, 1958.

[77]See, for example, *The New York Times* editorials of Semptember 25 and 26, 1958.

[78]*The Washington Post* editorial, September 25, 1958, p. A16.

[79]*The New York Times, The Washington Post,* the *Christian Science Monitor,* and *The Wall Street Journal* were among the critical papers. Not unexpectedly, *The Reporter* and *The New Republic* were critical of government policy.

[80]"Overwhelming Public Support for UN Handling Quemoy Crisis" by George Gallup, September 26, 1958. Information provided by George Gallup, Jr., in letter of July 6, 1968.

get more involved in a military way in the fight over these two islands?" In response, 91 percent felt that the United Nations should try to handle the problem, 6 percent said the United Nations should not interfere, and 3 percent voiced no opinion. This result was interpreted by some as indicating a lack of public support for the administration's policy,[81] but the question was so worded that practically any American would vote yes during a crisis. It simply demonstrated that Americans preferred peace to war if there was a choice! A second question allowed more opportunity for meaningful dissent. It asked, "It has been suggested that Formosa be neutralized—that is, put under the protection of the United Nations. Do you think this is a good idea or a poor idea?" Of those questioned, 61 percent favored the idea, 19 percent opposed it, and 20 percent had no opinion. An informed person might possibly have understood that by recommending Formosa be put under U.N. protection he was disagreeing with the administration's professed determination to defend the offshore islands.[82] The poll indicated that the public wanted to avoid the risks of war if at all possible. But it was not necessarily a no confidence vote on the administration's policies.

Other polls reflected some public concern about the Quemoy predicament. Results of several newspaper surveys indicated public dissent may have ranged from 30 to 50 percent.[83] On the basis of surveys asking more general questions, Gallup reported that keeping the peace had become the most important concern of the American people, that the majority believed Democrats could best maintain peace, and that Eisenhower's popularity had dropped

[81]See, for example, *The Washington Post* editorial "Architects of Crisis," September 28, 1958, p. E4.

[82]The President of the American Institute of Public Opinion could not explain why a more pertinent question had not been asked. Letter from Mr. George Gallup, Jr., President Institute of Public Opinion, to Lt. Comdr. J. T. Howe, USN, dated July 18, 1968. A subsequent Gallup poll showed that 28 percent thought the United States should go to war for Taiwan and 32 percent opposed; 40 percent were undecided. A. T. Steele, *The American People and China* (New York: McGraw-Hill Book Co., 1966), p. 104.

[83]*The Economist* reported that an American newspaper poll had revealed that 40 percent of those questioned opposed the President's stand. "Islands of Doubt" (September 20, 1958), p. 935. A Trendex News poll following the President's speech to the nation indicated that 33 percent strongly opposed use of American force to defend Quemoy. *The Wall Street Journal* sampling of opinion found that little less than half the people interviewed disapproved of defense of Quemoy and Matsu. A small majority in both cases favored defense of Quemoy and Matsu. Marian D. Irish, "Public Opinion and American Foreign Policy: The Quemoy Crisis of 1958," *The Political Quarterly*, Vol. 31, No. 2 (April to June 1960), pp. 152, 155.

slightly.[84] While there was nothing conclusive about these polls, they may have been disconcerting to Republican leaders aware that congressional elections were approaching. The Republican defeat in the Maine election undoubtedly heightened the administration's concern, although the results were not attributed to the crisis.[85]

Notwithstanding claims of widespread domestic dissatisfaction with the Quemoy policy, the dissent was neither overwhelming nor seemingly a decisive influence. The attentive public was small and divided; the general public was confused and somewhat apathetic. Domestic opinion probably had little direct influence on crisis decisions. Top policy makers did not feel that it caused any substantive alterations.[86] Nonetheless, it did create an atmosphere that may have persuaded administration leaders to lean toward flexibility and increased their anxiety to find a solution. Although the Nationalists increasingly demonstrated an ability to cope militarily, they were an obdurate ally when it came to diplomatic maneuvering with Peking. The sneaking suspicion remained that Chiang was trying to lure the United States into his reconquest ambitions. The Secretary of Defense warned the President on September 11, 1958, that Chiang's refusal to reduce troop strength on the offshore islands reflected "his hope of promoting a fight . . . as a prelude to a . . . Nationalist invasion of the mainland."[87] On September 29 Under Secretary Herter reportedly spoke of the Nationalists' " pathological devotion" to the islands and described a chain of events beginning with attacks on mainland artillery positions and airfields and ending in war between the United States and Russia.[88] It was felt increasingly in Washington that Chiang was trying to exploit the situation

[84]*The Washington Post* articles by George Gallup, September 28, 1958, p. A2 and October 1, 1958, p. A15.

[85]*The Washington Post* article by George Gallup, October 5, 1958, p. E5, and article by Marquis Childs, September 8, 1958, p. A5.

[86]See, for example, the interview with official familiar with policy during Quemoy crisis of 1958 conducted January 31, 1969, Appendix B, Question 5. Vice President Richard Nixon recalled that in spite of the pressure, Secretary Dulles "stood firm in the crisis," Nixon, interview, p. 33.

[87]This is President Eisenhower's description of what the Secretary of State said. Eisenhower, *Waging Peace,* pp. 300, 301. A number of editorials at the time voiced a similar opinion. The theme, of course, made a convenient whipping boy for both American opponents of the policy and Communist propagandists looking for divisive issues. It apparently was the U.S. military estimate of the situation. Smoot, letter.

[88]*The New York Times* article by Kenneth Campbell, September 30, 1958, p. 5.

to embroil the U.S. militarily and that he would rather lose his nation than surrender the offshore islands.[89]

The Nationalists, who were understandably suspicious of negotiations, asserted they would not agree to a renunciation of force, and impatiently threatened to retaliate against mainland batteries and other installations. The United States, however, publicly rejected Chiang's requests for raids.[90] Chiang reacted angrily to Dulles's press conference of September 30. The Secretary of State sent a message to try to correct the "misinterpreting the misinterpretation."[91] While Chiang apparently was annoyed by Dulles's comment that the Nationalists were not likely to reconquer the mainland, there appears to have been some prior consultation. On the day of Dulles's conference a Nationalist spokesman told the United Nations that his country had no thought of trying to invade the mainland and could do so only if called on during a Hungarian-type uprising.[92] Therefore, there was seemingly little actual difference in American and Nationalist positions on this issue. While Chiang had certain frustrated ambitions, he was undoubtedly aware of American policy. At the same time the Nationalists understandably found comments that they were "rather foolish" to be particularly offensive.

Although the Nationalists were irascible and difficult to deal with, confidence increased during this period that they were a sturdy ally militarily. It was in American interests to further develop Nationalist capability to defend themselves and therefore lessen the possibility of direct American involvement. The supply of sidewinder air-to-air missiles to Nationalist pilots reflected this facet of U.S. policy. At the same time U.S. officials felt that a demonstration of Nationalist

[89]See, for example, interview with an official familiar with policy during Quemoy crisis of 1958, conducted January 31, 1969, Appendix B, Question 3.

[90]After a conference with the President on September 24, 1958, Secretary McElroy said he "doubted if the US was going along with Chiang's demands on bombing," *The Washington Post* article by J. G. Norris, "Plane Raid Out, McElroy Declares After Seeing Ike," September 25, 1958, p. 1. See also *The Washington Post,* September 13, 1958, p. A8.

[91]Dulles claimed that the problem had been caused by "an exaggerated idea of a shift of position on our part—misinterpreting the misinterpretation." The "misinterpretation" had been given by "the press out there." *The Washington Post* article by Chalmers M. Roberts, "Dulles Acts to Reduce Taipei Fears," October 3, 1958, p. 1. See also Chiang's statements in reaction to the Dulles press conference of September 30. *The New York Times* article by Greg MacGregor, October 2, 1958, p. 1.

[92]He added that such an "uprising of the people could not be caused artificially from the outside." *The New York Times* article by K. Teltseh, October 1, 1958, p. 13.

capability to do the job themselves would greatly enhance Taipei's prestige.[93] Where U.S. and Nationalist interests coincided, the alliance was extremely successful. However, the nagging concern remained that the United States could be trapped into serving only Nationalist interests either by inadvertency, Chinese irrationality, or Chiang's schemes.

Another difficult American problem of control was the convoy of Nationalist supply ships in daylight. The United States wanted to convince Peking that the siege would not be successful while at the same time to avoid the danger of a major conflict resulting from fire mistakenly directed at its ships.[94] Some precautions were taken. United States escorts continued not to approach closer than three miles to the offshore islands. The United States sought to avoid acts that could be construed as combat operations and to lessen material risk of coming under the fire of shore batteries.[95] Washington did not want to become involved in a war because of Chinese error. The Chinese reciprocated by carefully avoiding attacking U.S. vessels.

The United States made several other significant military moves to demonstrate determination. A joint landing exercise was conducted on Taiwan by Nationalist and American amphibious forces. But the key actors were the heavy combatants of the Seventh Fleet. Five attack carriers (with a sixth on the way) equipped with nuclear weapons, supported by an antisubmarine task force and three heavy cruisers, were accurately described as "the largest integrated naval force ever assembled in peacetime history."[96] The military buildup was no subtle hint; it was a blatant demonstration of power that complemented the restrained words and conciliatory tone of U.S. declaratory policy.

10.2 SOVIET POLICY

During this period Soviet declarations of support for the Chinese were more forceful, authoritative, and frequent. Whether a tougher

[93]Smoot, letter.

[94]The orders were reportedly, "if the Communists shoot, shoot back." Robert P. Martin, "With the Seventh Fleet." *U.S. News and World Report,* Vol. XLV, No. 12 (September 19, 1958), p. 32.

[95]*The New York Times,* September 10, 1958, p. 8, Question 19. Secretary Dulles explained that "there were two elements involved in the decision. One was that to conduct what might appear to be combat activities within the three-mile limit around Matsu and Quemoy might involve a decision or require a decision under the Joint Resolution. The other was that as a practical matter . . . our ships can operate on that basis without any material risk of coming under the fire of shore batteries."

[96]Statement of Seventh Fleet commander as quoted in "Rough Week in the Strait," *Time,* Vol. LXXII, No. 12 (September 22, 1958), p. 24.

line was adopted because Mao's agreement to talks in Warsaw had put the crisis in a slightly safer context or because of the firmer position of the United States is not clear. Probably both factors influenced Russian policy. If Moscow had been in doubt, it now could be more certain that Peking intended to keep the conflict limited. It also probably felt greater need to impress bloc and world opinion with a strong stand for its ally.

There were two important Soviet declarations on the situation: Khrushchev's letters to President Eisenhower of September 7 and 19. Both documents contained the blunt warning that "*An attack* on the People's Republic of China, which is a great friend, ally, and neighbor of our country, *is an attack on the Soviet Union*."[97] (Emphasis added.) This was an upgrading of a similar statement in the previous phase,[98] and it was repeated in numerous follow-up commentaries.[99] Accompanying these affirmations were indications that Khrushchev was very uncomfortable about the situation and did not intend to expand the hostilities. He could be reasonably sure that the United States would not deliberately launch an "attack" on China, but he may not have been as confident of Mao's or Chiang's intentions. In expressing the Soviet dilemma, he cautioned, "no one would be able to get out of the situation, neither you, nor we, should a war break out in the Far East."[100] And he concluded his first letter by disclaiming any aggressive intentions, stating "it fully depends on the further actions of the U.S. Government whether

[97]Tass in English to Europe, September 8, 1958, "Text of Khrushchev note to Eisenhower."

[98]The article of August 31, 1958, had warned that "he who threatens today to attack the Chinese People's Republic must not forget that he threatens the Soviet Union as well." *Pravda,* August 31, 1958, p. 4. Article by "Observer," *CDSP,* Vol. X, No. 35.

[99]For example, *Pravda* and *Izvestia* editorials of September 10, 1958, the statement of the Soviet Peace Committee on September 15, 1958, and the statement of Soviet Foreign Minister Gromyko on September 17 to the United Nations. See, Moscow Soviet Home Service, September 10, 1958, Tass in English to the World, September 15, 1958, and Tass in English to Europe, September 18, 1958. John R. Thomas has claimed that the Soviets "began quickly to scale down Khrushchev's warning" by using "would consider" rather than the more direct "an attack is an attack." While the Soviets used this and similar phrases like "will be" and "would be" in a number of commentaries, there does not appear to have been any attempt to reduce the impact of Khrushchev's warning. Perhaps the best evidence is contained in commentaries that used both phrases in the same article. This was the case in a broadcast of September 10, 1958 and the article "The World Gendarme's Policy," *International Affairs,* No. 10 (October 1958), p. 12.

[100]Tass in English to Europe, September 8, 1958, "Text of Khrushchev note to Eisenhower."

peace will prevail in the Far East."[101] The Russians were clearly hoping to avoid involvement. One indication that this was the intended interpretation was Moscow's publication of a commentary attributed to an Associated Press correspondent:

> ... Khrushchev's letter ... which was sent after Chou En-lai agreed to the resumption of talks on the ambassadorial level, *is aimed at reducing the immediate threat of war* for the sake of Taiwan ... together with an energetic warning that in case of an attack against China it will not be alone, the message of the head of the Soviet Government contains a frank appeal: *'Talks instead of war.'*[102] [Emphasis added.]

The most significant addition in the Russian leader's second letter was the intimation that Soviet nuclear capability might be employed.

> Those who harbor plans of an *atomic attack* on the Chinese ... should not forget that the other side too has atomic and hydrogen weapons and the appropriate means to deliver them, and if the Chinese People's Republic *falls victim to such an attack*, the aggressor will at once get a *rebuff* by the same *means*.[103] [Emphasis added.]

The statement was a strong one, but it came too late in the crisis (several days after talks had actually begun) to have much impact, and it was carefully qualified. Krushchev seemed to be warning that if the United States employed nuclear weapons in an attack against the Chinese, the Soviets would respond. The Soviet threat did not necessarily apply to American repulsion of a Chinese-initiated invasion. While it was well advertised that Seventh Fleet ships carried nuclear weapons, it is doubtful that the Russians had a similar capability in the area. Thus, the threat, by its timing and carefully worded content, could be regarded more as a propaganda ploy than as a serious warning. On the other hand, it may have reflected genuine concern about the continuing American military buildup in the region and the possibility that Moscow would have to respond in some way. Khrushchev may have been playing on the fears of Western Europeans and Americans sharing his concern. In past crises like Suez in 1956 and Lebanon in 1958, Khrushchev had made serious-sounding threats during the "safe" periods of crises, presumably in order to enhance his prestige as the guardian of

[101]Ibid. This was very similar to what Khrushchev had written in his letter of July 19, 1958, to President Eisenhower concerning Lebanon.
[102]Tass in Russian to Europe, September 9, 1958, L. Velechansky dispatch.
[103]Tass in English to Europe, September 19, 1958, "Text of Message from Khrushchev to Eisenhower." A similar claim to have atomic weapons was made in his July 19, 1958, letter to President Eisenhower concerning Lebanon. In that letter, however, he also claimed to have "intercontinental missiles." *New Times* supplement, No. 30 (July 1958), p. 7.

communism. It was not until after this phase of the crisis, when tension was further alleviated, that Khrushchev made his most direct threat.[104]

The late invocation of Soviet nuclear weapons probably annoyed the Chinese. However, although they have subsequently claimed that the Russians expressed support only when it was clear there was "no possibility of nuclear war," it is not at all certain that Peking ever thought it would get such backing. There were other signs of Peking's dissatisfaction over Moscow's caution, but these seemed to refer back to the planning stage of the crisis. For example, a Chinese *Red Flag* editorial released on September 16, 1958, asserted,

> The new war provocations of the American aggressor against our country are no indication of strength but merely a manifestation of the extreme weakness of the imperialist world. But up to now there are still *some people* who have failed to understand this really. *They often overestimate the strength of the enemy* and underestimate that of the people.[105] [Emphasis added.]

This comment reflected Peking's frustration with Russian "overestimates" of American strength and may have persuaded Khrushchev that he needed to make a more bellicose declaration in order to allay Chinese criticism. It can be surmised that the Russians had refused to risk a showdown with the United States. In his letter of September 19 to President Eisenhower, Khrushchev remarked that "full unanimity of views . . . on the main thing . . . was reaffirmed during . . . discussions in Peking."[106] But his broad definition of the "main thing"[107] did not necessarily apply to the strategy and tactics to be used in the case of Taiwan. His statement implied that while there might have been agreement on broad generalities, there were serious differences on many issues.

Other evidence of continuing differences was also manifested during this phase. Peking may have been annoyed by Moscow's frequent public statements about what China could do on its own. The overemphasis seemed to exceed the requirements of proper defer-

[104]He warned in November that "it must not be forgotten that in our age, the age of atomic energy and *intercontinental rockets,* any country which attempts to settle international disputes by force of arms *hazards its own existence* by so doing." (Emphasis added.) "Khrushchev!" *International Affairs,* No. 11 (November 1958), p. 4.

[105]*Red Flag* editorial, "The U.S. Aggressors Have Put Nooses Round Their Own Neck," *Peking Review,* Vol. 1, No. 29 (September 16, 1958), p. 10.

[106]Tass in English to Europe, September 19, 1958, "Text of September 19th Message from Khrushchev to Eisenhower."

[107]Khrushchev described the "main thing, that is in the means of a continuous fight against all forces of aggression and of support for the forces working for peace all over the world."

ence to Chinese nationalism. Peking may have been surprised to read that Moscow considered China to be "militarily superior" to the United States[108] and to possess "all the means to rebuff any aggressor."[109] There were numerous assertions that the Chinese would expel hostile armed forces without outside assistance. Such claims usually followed the Soviet demand that the Seventh Fleet and American troops go home.[110] The immense task of driving the Americans out seemingly was left to "People's China."

During this phase the Soviets continued to distinguish between China's effort to reconquer Taiwan and an American attack on the mainland. Moscow implied that it did not intend to assist a Chinese invasion and would respond only if the United States attacked China. Conquest of the island was considered to be an "internal matter."[111] Khrushchev underlined this concept in a long answer to a question allegedly from a Tass reporter:

> Does this contain the slightest hint that the USSR is . . . ready to take part in a civil war in China? No, we have stated and do state something quite different. The USSR will come to the help of the CPR if the latter is attacked from without; speaking more concretely, if the *United States attacks the CPR* . . . if the United States steps over this brink, the USSR will not stand aside.[112] [Emphasis added.]

But Khrushchev again disclaimed any intention of supporting a Chinese initiative by saying,

> But we have not interfered in and *do not intend to interfere* in the civil war which the Chinese people are waging against the Chiang Kai-shek clique . . . . The intention to get back their islands of Quemoy and Matsu and to free Taiwan and the Pescadores is an *internal affair* of the Chinese people.[113] [Emphasis added.]

[108] I. Yermashov, "China's Rode to Victory," *New Times,* No. 39 (September 1958), p. 5.

[109] "The World Gendarme's Policy," *International Affairs,* No. 10 (October 1958), p. 12.

[110] The theme was reiterated in both of Khrushchev's letters to President Eisenhower as well as in many other commentaries. See, for example, Soviet Home Service, September 21, 1958, and Soviet North American Service in English, September 30, 1958.

[111] See for example, V. Baryshinikov, "Background to the Taiwan Crisis," *New Times,* No. 38 (September 1958), p. 28.

[112] Tass in Russian to Europe, October 5, 1958. This distinction was emphasized in subsequent articles. See, for example, "Purely Internal Matter," *New Times,* No. 42 (October 1958), p. 1; and M. Ukraintsev, "American Adventurism in the Far East," *International Affairs,* No. 11 (November 1958), pp. 28, 29.

[113] Ibid. According to the Soviets, Mao sent a message on October 15, 1958, to the Communist Party of the Soviet Union Central Committee commenting that "we believe completely that if the Taiwan incident should lead to a war between China and the United States, the Soviet Union will certainly wholeheartedly support us." Moscow in Mandarin to China, April 28, 1970, ser-

While it was true, as Moscow was quick to point out, that the Chinese also emphasized that the Taiwan dispute was an internal affair, Peking seemingly would have liked more assurance the Soviets were willing to act as a counter to the Americans.[114]

Another example of carefully qualified backing was the Russian response to Peking's extension of its territorial waters to twelve miles. If Moscow had given unequivocal endorsement it might have been obligated to take some limited action against the United States or suffer a loss of prestige in case of an American violation. An intrusion into territorial waters could legitimately be construed to be an act of aggression. In keeping with its strategy of avoiding direct involvement, Moscow complained about American violations, but avoided a commitment to defend the new Chinese claim. The Soviets emphasized "respect" for rather than enforcement of the territorial limit, and they made it clear that the decision to claim a wider territorial sea emanated solely from Peking.[115]

Since the precondition for Russian intervention was limited to an unlikely American attack on the mainland, it was not surprising that there continued to be no Russian military movements in the area. The Soviet announcement of a month's maneuvers by the northern fleet with "various types of modern weapons" beginning on September 20, 1958, may have had some remote relationship to the crisis.[116] Possibly, the operation was meant to provide credibility for Khrushchev's warning that Russia had "appropriate means to deliver" atomic weapons.[117] However, if this was the intention there undoubtedly would have been greater publicity and the Soviet Pacific Fleet would have been assigned to conduct the tests.

Further insight into Soviet intentions can be gained by examining the thrust of their propaganda campaign. Although Russian commentaries lacked consistency, the themes were similar to those in the previous phase. There were many references to the dangers of

ies on "Glorious Chapters in the History of Soviet-Chinese Relations." The war was a precondition for Soviet consideration of involvement.

[114]See Soviet Home Service, September 14, 1958, *Pravda* observer's article, "Clumsy Attempts to Justify Aggression"; and "Premier Chou En Lai's Statement on the Situation in the Taiwan Straits Area," *Peking Review*, Vol. 1, No. 28 (September 8, 1958), p. 15.

[115]Tass in Russian to Europe, September 9, 1958; Moscow in German to Germany, September 8, 1958, G. Shakhov commentary.

[116]*The Times*, September 13, 1958, p. 5. Shipping was warned to avoid an area in the Arctic Ocean. Russian nuclear tests were held on September 30, 1958, north of the Arctic Circle. *The Times* (London), October 11, 1958, p. 6.

[117]Since the testing announcement came a week before Khrushchev's message to Eisenhower, it is unlikely that the test was directly linked to the message. See Section 10.2, footnote 103.

a world war. For example, in one article the observation that the United States was trying to dismiss the Quemoy situation as just another little war was preceded by the following commentary on the grave worldwide implications of local wars: ". . . in our time the methods of warfare and the alignment of international forces have changed so radically that every 'local' war is always fraught with the danger of developing into a world war."[118] This concept of expansion of local wars accurately reflected Soviet military doctrine and some genuine concern that the United States did not recognize the dangers.

In frequent references to the Seventh Fleet in the media and in official statements, Moscow seemed to offer an explanation for inaction while trying to discredit the United States in the eyes of Third World countries. In addition, a number of comments indicated the pressure the naval concentration had put on Russia as an ally of China. A *Pravda* article complained, for example, that "By their nature and scale these maneuvers *look like* open preparation for an invasion upon the territory of the Chinese People's Republic."[119] (Emphasis added.) Although the Russians undoubtedly were delighted with the disunity being expressed in the United States, they had frustrations of their own resulting from an inability to control an adventurous ally and to shake the image of a paper tiger unable to counter the American display of power with credible forces in the local area.

Another propaganda tactic also seemed to reflect the impotent position the Soviets found themselves in because of their lack of strategic mobility. The assertion was made repeatedly that the Chinese were not operating ships off American shores, and the United States was asked how it would feel if the Chinese operated off Long Island.[120] This was something Peking obviously had no power to do. The same type of underdog appeal was made six years later in response to the Tonkin Gulf raids from American carriers. But there was a significant difference. Russian ships were used in the anal-

[118]Maj. Gen. M. Millstein and Col. A. Slobodenko, "Limited War-Weapon of Unlimited Aggression," *New Times*, No. 40 (October 1958), p. 14.

[119]Soviet Home Service, September 10, 1958, *Pravda* article, "Put an End to the Policy of Provocation and Blackmail."

[120]See, for example, Soviet North American Service in English, September 12, 1958, Viktor Naimushin commentary; Soviet South Asian Service in English, October 5, 1958. Gromyko employed the same analogy in his September 17 address to the United Nation. *The New York Times*, September 18, 1958, p. 4. The analogy had also been invoked in the previous phase but less frequently. See, for example, Soviet Home Service, September 2, 1958. A. Leontyev commentary.

ogy.[121] The probable Soviet motive for these and similar remarks about the "excessively reinforced Seventh Fleet"[122] was to convey an image of the United States as a big bully "blackmailing" the weaker nations.[123]

During this period Moscow issued several strong warnings to the United States, but the contrast with the previous phase was not as sharp as most scholars have asserted. The Soviets seemed to express their frustration that an uncomfortable problem was not being solved. Stepped-up warnings appeared to be in response to moves or statements publicized in the American press, and thus requiring a face-saving response. The Russians very carefully qualified their threats. Moscow would respond only if China was attacked by the United States. Invasion of the offshore islands may have had Soviet sympathy, but it obviously did not have Russian military backing.

From the American point of view, of course, Soviet threats had to be taken seriously. Moscow's warnings were a mixed blessing. While raising the dark specter of world war, they also added validity to administration claims that the conquest of Quemoy and Matsu was part of a worldwide Communist plot. American public opinion generally favors standing firm in the face of Soviet threats. In countering arguments, advanced by both the Russians and domestic critics that this was strictly a civil war, the government emphasized the Soviet role in the Quemoy conflict. In his speech to the nation on September 11, for example, the President asserted that the Chinese and Soviets appeared to be "working hand in hand."[124] This theme was reiterated in other authoritative statements.[125] In answering Senator Green's critical letter, the President also made heavy use of the Soviet link:

The Chinese *and Soviet* Communist leaders assert . . . that if they

[121]See, for example, Moscow Domestic Service in Russian, August 6, 1964.
[122]Soviet European Service in German to Germany, September 30, 1958, Yestafeyev commentary.
[123]Khrushchev's letter of September 7 took this line as did many other commentaries. See, for example, Soviet European Service in English, September 9, 1958, Buranov commentary, Soviet North American Service, September 22, 1958, *Pravda* article by observer.
[124]Department of State, *American Foreign Policy, 1958,* p. 1157. See also pp. 1158, 1159.
[125]Secretary of State Dulles in his press conference on September 30 said that the Soviets are saying that they are prepared to back Chinese claims to the offshore islands and Formosa "to the hilt." He also revealed that "as far as we can tell, every plane, every piece of artillery, and practically all the ammunition that is being shot there today is of Soviet origin." *The New York Times* transcript of Dulles news conference, October 1, 1958, p. 8, answer 29. See also the Dulles remarks in his speech of September 25, 1958, *The New York Times,* September 26, 1958, p. 3.

can take Quemoy and Matsu by *armed assault* that will open the way for *them* to take Formosa and the Pescadores and, as *they* put it, *'expel'* the United States from the West Pacific and cause its Fleet to leave international waters and 'go home' I cannot dismiss these boastings as mere bluff.[126] [Emphasis added.]

Apparently, in order to rally support for a firm American stand, the President ignored the careful distinctions the Soviets had been making.[127] However, Washington apparently recognized the limits the Russians had placed on their involvement. One observer commented that it was "an article of faith" with the U.S. government that "Russia will not risk a world war over Quemoy and Matsu."[128] The government's sentiments at the time seemed to be reflected in unpublished portions of a speech drafted for Secretary Dulles. In recalling the Peking meeting of Mao and Khrushchev, the draft asserted, "it is, I am sure, not a fantasy of speculation that during that visit what is now occurring was planned."[129] It was then speculated that the Soviet government was trying to embroil Peking in a conflict with the United States because China was becoming too strong.[130] While the explanation was implausible, the assumption that Russia would not intervene was implicit in the remarks.

The President reacted to Khrushchev's first letter with restraint. The impact of the forceful message had been dampened by the release the same day of Mao's statement that he was "hopeful" that in Warsaw "talks might lead to some results,"[131] seemingly another indication of a lack of Sino-Soviet coordination. The American replies stressed that Khrushchev could control the situation if he wanted to and that Washington had no aggressive intentions.[132]

There may, however, have been some increased concern in Washington when a more threatening letter was received from Khrushchev on September 19. The government responded firmly by return-

[126]Department of State, *American Foreign Policy, 1958,* p. 1171. In another part of the letter the President referred to "the threat of Sino-Soviet armed aggression," p. 1172.

[127]The President's remarks to Senator Green may have motivated Khrushchev to call in reporters several days later and again state the limits of Soviet commitment. See page 251.

[128]*The Observer* (London) article by Philip Oeane, September 14, 1958, p. 1.

[129]September 25, 1958, draft of Secretary Dulles's speech to Boston Atlantic Assembly given on September 27, 1958, p. 17 of draft. The John Foster Dulles Papers, category 1B, Princeton University.

[130]Ibid. Similar explanations were given on page 28 of the draft. This line of reasoning did not appear in the address as actually presented on September 27, 1958.

[131]New China News Agency in English, September 8, 1958.

[132]*The New York Times,* September 14, 1958, p. 6. See also Secretary Dulles's similar remarks in his speech of September 25, *The New York Times,* September 26, 1958, p. 3.

ing the letter to the Soviets because of its abusive tone.[133] Editorial opinion, which had been critical of the administration's stand, expressed anger at Khrushchev's message and applauded the President's rejection of the message.[134] The belligerent Soviet letter appeared to give the executive a boost domestically. In spite of the more ominous and authoritative Russian declaratory support for Peking during this phase of the crisis, Washington, while demonstrating prudent concern, remained confident that Moscow did not intend to match words with deeds. The best evidence was the continuing absence of Soviet military maneuvers.

10.3 BRITISH POLICY

With rising domestic opposition, Washington desired greater support from its allies. But Her Majesty's Government, facing a more severe public reaction, appeared barely able to hold its previous position of implying some tacit support for the United States in any major showdown.

An outcry resulted from Randolph Churchill's comment, after visiting Prime Minister Macmillan, that Britain was not going "to let the United States down over Quemoy or Matsu."[135] The government immediately issued a formal disclaimer saying, "We have no commitment of any kind with the U.S. over the Far East situation."[136] But Randolph Churchill countered that nothing he had written conflicted "in principle" with the government's policy and that "The truth is that though we have no precise commitments we shall not betray our American allies if they should be involved in war. People who don't know this don't know anything."[137] This statement was probably an accurate assessment of Britain's position on any major war that might develop. But London was unlikely to provide military aid in a local war restricted to defense of the offshore islands.

To clarify its position, the British Foreign office declared on September 12 that

We have no obligation or commitment of any kind to take military action for the defense of Quemoy, Matsu, or Formosa. Our only ob-

[133]Department of State, *American Foreign Policy, 1958,* "US Rejection of Soviet Condemnation of American Policy in the China Area," September 20, 1958, p. 1163.

[134]See, for example, *The Washington Post* editorial "On Slamming Doors," September 22, 1958, p. A12, and *The New York Times* editorial "That Common Language," September 22, 1958, p. 30.

[135]He also stated that "Britain will stand by the United States in the Far East." *Evening Standard* article by Randolph Churchill, September 11, 1958.

[136]*The Times,* September 12, 1958, p. 10.

[137]*The Times,* September 15, 1958, p. 4.

ligations are those in accordance with the Charter of the United Nations. . . . The U.S. Government have neither sought nor received promises of British support in the event of war over the Chinese offshore islands.[138]

The statement also asserted that the issue should be settled by negotiations rather than by force. The implication was that the British would give the United States some diplomatic support. In a follow-up speech Prime Minister Macmillan emphasized that since the British were not "militarily involved" it ". . . puts all the greater obligation upon us to help in any way we can by private consultation and public action to secure a peaceful solution of these problems. All this was implicit in the Foreign Office statement of September 5, and is made clear beyond doubt by the statement today."[139]

The Labour Party, however, was not satisfied and issued a steady stream of statements criticizing the government for not clearly disavowing the American position. It argued that Britain should provide no support whatsoever, that the offshore islands ought to be evacuated, and that Formosa should be taken over by the United Nations.[140] The Conservatives were relatively silent, but there was evidently some concern expressed in private.[141] In replying to criticism, the Prime Minister stressed that public airing of "difficulties" would only play into Communists' hands.[142] Although his remarks implied that disagreements existed, he may well have been privately assuring the United States that Britain would rally to America's support in a showdown.

Public sentiment was decidedly against any British involvement over the offshore islands.[143] A Gallup survey reported that 82 per-

[138]*The Times,* September 13, 1958.

[139]*The Guardian,* September 13, 1958, p. 1.

[140]See, for example, *The Guardian,* September 9, 1958, p. 1, and September 26, 1958, p. 14; and *The Washington Post,* September 30, 1958. Labour leader Hugh Gatskill demanded, for example, in a public letter to Macmillan that the British government make its position clear. *The Times* article "Labor Backs Peking Claim to Quemoy," September 16, 1958, p. 8. At a Labour Party Conference the 1250 delegates approved unanimously a resolution declaring Britain "should neither take part in nor support a war to defend Quemoy." *The Washington Post,* October 4, 1958, p. A5.

[141]*The New York Times* article by Drew Middleton, September 24, 1958, p. 3.

[142]See his letter in reply to Gatskell's in *The Times,* September 16, 1958, p. 8. See also his communiqué issued following consultations with representatives of the British Trade Union Congress. *The Washington Post,* September 26, 1958, p. A8.

[143]A *Washington Post* reporter commented, "to anyone returning to Britain after a few weeks absence . . . the overwhelming criticism of the United States line is shocking." *The Washington Post* article "British Press Continues Intensive Criticism of U.S. Policy on Quemoy," September 23, 1958, p. A6.

cent of persons polled felt Britain should keep out of any fighting over Quemoy.[144] The poll, however, did not reflect attitudes toward an expanded conflict. Editorial writers were united in criticism of American policy, but there were varying opinions about Britain's obligation if war occurred. *The Times*, for example, while commenting that Britain should stay out of a "limited war," warned that London could not sit on the sidelines if the war spread.[145] *The Economist* noted that the British shared the American predicament: "Britain can never contract out of the alliance; we cannot really say, anywhere in the world, that we have no commitments to the United States."[146] However, most editorials concentrated on the folly of the American position and disavowed any British commitment.

In addition to the concerns shared by the general public, British commercial interests had practical reasons for not provoking China. Chinese retaliation for a pro-American position might mean loss of the important, but vulnerable, trade center of Hong Kong. At one point, the U.S. government evidently considered employing economic sanctions against China to counter the blockade of Quemoy. However, it was doubtful that the British, who were expecting a substantial trade increase with China following a reduction in the embargo list, would cooperate.[147]

During this period London again announced that its Far Eastern fleet would be expanded. The first aircraft carrier, however, would not arrive until early 1959.[148] While it postponed previous plans, the statement indicated Britain's continuing interest in the Far East. The delay was partly due to the strain of sustained naval operations in the vicinity of the Middle East.

The impact of British disenchantment with the American stand was increased because London's view was also shared in other allied capitals. One report claimed that criticism expressed at an off the record meeting in England between American and Western European officials had been an important factor in causing a shift in the U.S. position.[149] A survey taken in mid-September showed

[144]Seven percent answered, "Britain should get involved" and 11 percent said, "Don't Know." Although the poll was not released until October 24 it appears to substantiate the feelings expressed in press reports during this phase. Copy of poll supplied by Mr. George Gallup, Jr., in letter of July 6, 1968.

[145]*The Times* editorial "Persuasion," September 17, 1958.

[146]"All Aid Short of War," *The Economist,* September 20, 1958, p. 912.

[147]*The New York Times* article by Thomas F. Roman, October 2, 1958, p. 12.

[148]*The Washington Post,* October 1, 1958, p. A5.

[149]*The Washington Post* article by Marquis Childs, October 8, 1958.

"widespread distrust and scepticism among European governments about the premises of American action in the Formosa Strait."[150]

American leaders were questioned frequently about the negative European reaction. In his press conference on September 9, Secretary Dulles admitted that there was not a "united" stand but rejoined that he did not think Washington should require allies to agree with everything the United States did in an area of the world where it had "primary responsibility."[151] In a statement that indicated the difficulties of obtaining allied support in such situations, he said,

> . . . there cannot be an adequate discharge of our responsibilities if, in an area like this, where we have the treaty obligations, where we have the force, where others do not, that we just say we will not do anything unless all of some forty-five allies agree with us. That would not be a position which would admit of effective responsible action.[152]

The problem, of course, was that allied support, while desirable, was not obtainable. President Eisenhower admitted that he was "puzzled" by the reaction.[153] But in his letter of October 2, 1958, to Senator Green he asserted that the allies would give support in any major confrontation. He wrote, "Not only do I believe that our friends and allies would support the United States if hostilities should tragically, and against our will, be forced upon us, I believe that most of them would be appalled if the United States were spinelessly to retreat before the threat of Sino-Soviet armed aggression."[154] In the absence of a major war, however, support was limited to diplomatic maneuvering behind the scenes.

[150]Alstair Buchan, *Crisis Management* (Paris: The Atlantic Institute, 1966), p. 31. The author stated that the survey was conducted by the European offices of *The New York Times* on September 15, 1958.

[151]*The New York Times*, "State Department Transcript of Remarks Made by Dulles at his News Conference," September 10, 1958, p. 8, Question 37. He contrasted the "international situation" with the "internal domestic situation" which he claimed was "united."

[152]Ibid., Question 38. He indicated in his press conference on September 30 that there had been "very widespread general discussions" with "fifteen or twenty countries about the whole situation" but that no real effort to organize measures like trade sanctions had yet been made although such possibilities had been considered. *The New York Times,* October 1, 1958, p. 8, Question 24.

[153]This remark was made in the Eisenhower press conference of October 1, 1958. See, for example, *The Guardian* article "Allies 'Puzzle' Mr. Eisenhower," October 2, 1958, p. 9.

[154]Department of State, *American Foreign Policy, 1958,* pp. 1171, 1172. Text of letter from the President to the Chairman of the Senate Committee on Foreign Relations, dated October 2, 1958.

10.4 EVALUATION OF U.S. CAPABILITY

Although United States policy did not undergo a major shift during this period, Washington demonstrated an increasing willingness to negotiate a solution to the problem and clearly indicated it was not interested in supporting Nationalist aspirations toward the mainland. Changes in factors influencing U.S. capability provide some indication of why it was feasible to lean toward greater flexibility in the American position.

Because Soviet threats became stronger the United States probably was slightly more concerned about the possibility of Soviet intervention. Moscow put its prestige on the line in official statements. Although the Russians made a clear distinction between support in case of an unlikely United States attack on China and support for Chinese aspirations to conquer the Nationalist-held islands, the possibility remained that in an actual clash it would be difficult to determine the difference. Soviet contribution to any Chinese-initiated invasion would be strictly limited to moral support, but in the case of an attack on the mainland, Khrushchev threatened nuclear war. Although the credibility of the Soviet threats was questionable and they came in a slightly alleviated phase of the crisis, the United States could not ignore them. While it was still unlikely that the Soviets intended to intervene, the possibility had to be taken more seriously during this phase of the crisis.

On the other hand, the military situation improved considerably. After a shaky beginning with a week of frustrated attempts to land supplies on the beaches of Quemoy in the face of an effective Chinese bombardment, the blockade was surmounted by utilization of American escorts and amphibious vehicles. The Nationalists also began to assert command of the air over the Formosa Strait. By the end of September the immediate local military problems had been solved, the Seventh Fleet had been augmented to unprecedented size, and the Chinese continued to demonstrate a reluctance to mount an invasion. Under these conditions defense estimates of U.S. capability were substantially greater.

During this phase of the crisis domestic opposition to the administration's Quemoy policy began to be expressed publicly. The President was aware that there was division and little desire to take risks in order to maintain Nationalist possession of the offshore islands. The mounting dissent undoubtedly had some influence on American policy during this period. It was probably a major factor influencing the government to assume a more flexible public approach.

It is important to remember, however, that the shift in the U.S. position was more apparent than real. The position that evolved publicly in late September was not very different from that which had been taken in 1955, and it appeared to bring the public policy of the United States closer to what it was offering privately. It was apparently decided to feel the Chinese out secretly before informing the public of a more flexible position. A U.S. government admission that the islands should be demilitarized, for example, would have confused the credibility of the carefully developed case that Quemoy was related to defense of Formosa. It would have had an unfortunate domestic reaction on Formosa, and might have been interpreted as a sign of weakness by Peking since the blockade had barely been breached. This may have been a negotiating ploy by the United States, but undoubtedly the pressures being felt at the time had some bearing on the approach. The slight softening of the U.S. position in late September appeared only to have brought the private and public positions more closely into line. This was probably done for a variety of reasons. Since the Nationalists were demonstrating an increasing capability to cope with the local situation, there was less need for a firm American position. The possibility of a Chinese invasion was becoming increasingly remote. A more flexible declaratory position helped alleviate domestic criticism, added credibility to privately expressed negotiating positions in Warsaw and American professions of a desire to calm the crisis, and reflected Washington's misgivings about being drawn into a Nationalist scheme to reconquer the mainland.

If a war had come, the administration was probably correct to assume that the public would rally to the support of the government. But in the President's attempt to deter aggression by a firm stand, public dissent was a hindrance. It can be concluded that adverse domestic opinion had a greater influence during this period.

Although dependence on British backing was not a larger factor in comparison with domestic dissidence, Washington seemed to have a slightly greater need for London's support during this period. What the United States desired was moral and diplomatic bolstering rather than promises of military aid. The cumulative effect of domestic and international opinion tended to give the impression that there was little support for the U.S. position on Quemoy. Domestic critics pointed to the lack of allied support, and foreign critics underlined the domestic dissent in the United States against the policy. By not following the recommendations of the Labour Party to disavow their association with the United States in the Far

East, the British government helped the administration. The Chinese and Soviets could not be certain that the United Kingdom would not support the United States when put to the test. The indications were that London's backing in an all-out war would be firm.

During this period the American government felt mounting pressure to resolve the crisis. But it remained confident that the United States had the capability to cope with the situation. The improved military situation facilitated increased flexibility in the U.S. position toward the end of the phase.

11. ANALYSIS AND CONCLUSIONS

In the Quemoy crisis of 1958 the United States successfully confronted a difficult challenge in an extremely vulnerable location. Although its obligation to defend the offshore islands was uncertain, American support for the Nationalists was sufficient to discourage a Chinese invasion. Peking probably did not plan a direct assault. Its objective apparently was to apply enough pressure to force an evacuation. During the crisis there was danger of being drawn into war, possibility of Soviet intervention, a difficult military problem, severe domestic criticism, and minimal allied support. In addition, U.S. capabilities were limited to some extent by the preexisting involvement in the Middle East. In the latter part of the crisis, the U.S. declaratory position became increasingly flexible, but the basic stand remained firm. The Chinese gradually eased the siege.

11.1 CHANGES IN FACTORS DURING VARIOUS PHASES AND THEIR INFLUENCE ON CRISIS DECISIONS

There were a number of important factors influencing the U.S. decision to defend the offshore islands. By comparing relative changes in the major capability factors during the various phases it is easier to understand their relation to gradual shifts in declaratory policy and assessments of capability to cope with the crisis. (See Figure 11.1.) These factors, of course, were interdependent.

11.1.1 ESTIMATE OF SOVIET INTENTIONS TO INTERVENE

As the United States assessed the impending crisis the possibility of direct Soviet

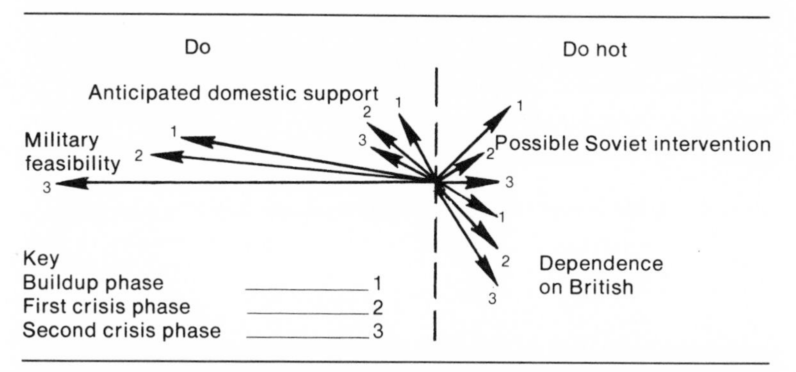

Figure 11.1 Relative effect of capability factors in each phase on decision to defend Quemoy against attack

backing of a Chinese invasion seemed remote, but a degree of uncertainty existed. During the first crisis phase the combination of an initially weak Soviet declaratory position and the absence of military forces resulted in much greater confidence that the Russians would not intervene. However, more authoritative and bellicose Soviet declarations of support for China in the second crisis phase probably slightly increased American concern about Soviet intentions. But throughout the crisis it was believed Khrushchev did not intend to assist Peking with Russian forces.

11.1.2 DEFENSE ESTIMATES OF U.S. CAPABILITY TO DEFEND QUEMOY Military experts approached the difficult problem of defense of the islands with some trepidation, but they were confident Quemoy could be held, by using tactical nuclear weapons if necessary. The failure of Peking to utilize its bomber potential during the first phase significantly improved military estimates. In the succeeding phase ability to cope with the situation became increasingly apparent. The Chinese failed to mount an invasion, successful resupply techniques were developed, and the Nationalists demonstrated they could control the air without American assistance. In addition, Seventh Fleet reinforcements had arrived, bringing considerable American power to the local area.

11.1.3 ESTIMATE OF CONGRESSIONAL AND PUBLIC SUPPORT Although some opposition was anticipated, the administration initially assumed that defense of Quemoy, under the conditions of the Formosa resolution, would meet with domestic approval. This prediction seemed justified during the first phase as the public adopted the government's "wait and see" attitude, and Congress appeared willing to follow the President's lead. Critics were, for the most part, silent while the American commitment was finalized, and they failed to capitalize on convincing arguments such as the dangers of using tactical nuclear weapons and the failure of the Chinese to employ their bomber force. However, in the second crisis phase following the clear delineation of the American policy, there was mounting opposition. Majority support apparently remained, but growing dissatisfaction probably encouraged the administration to seek a negotiated solution and present a more flexible interpretation of the policy.

11.1.4 DEPENDENCE ON BRITISH SUPPORT Support from Great Britain was desired but not essential to the defense of Quemoy. During the early phases there was little need; however, as the crisis dragged on, it became increasingly desirable for the administration to have some foreign approval to counter domestic and international opposition. But, as dependence on the British increased, the possibility decreased of obtaining more than behind-the-scenes diplomatic assistance. In response to stronger internal pressure, London increasingly clarified its neutral position publicly. The British government provided what moral and diplomatic support it could under the circumstances.

By examining the capability factors on a chart of the decision, their relative influence during various phases of the crisis becomes more apparent. (See Figure 11.1.) It is clearer why the administration felt it was capable of defending Quemoy. The length of a vector indicates its relative weight and the direction its effect on the decision. These estimates are, of course, highly speculative.

The administration had a number of strategic military, political, and psychological reasons for feeling that defense of Quemoy was important. An examination of the capability factors indicates that they were not a barrier to such a decision. In each phase the military estimate of ability to defend Quemoy appeared to merit the greatest weight of the four factors. The Soviet and domestic factors were next in overall importance. British support was of least significance. During the buildup phase estimates of military capability and domestic support outweighed prudent concern about Soviet intentions and dependence on unlikely British support. During the critical first crisis phase, the three most significant factors moved in the "Do" direction. Factors in the following phase were less favorable. An improvement in the military situation helped compensate for reduced domestic support, increased need for British backing, and promoted a slight negative change in the Soviet factor. The overall weight of the factors, however, supported the administration decision in all three phases. After adding the four factors for each phase, their relative weight in the "Do" direction appears as:

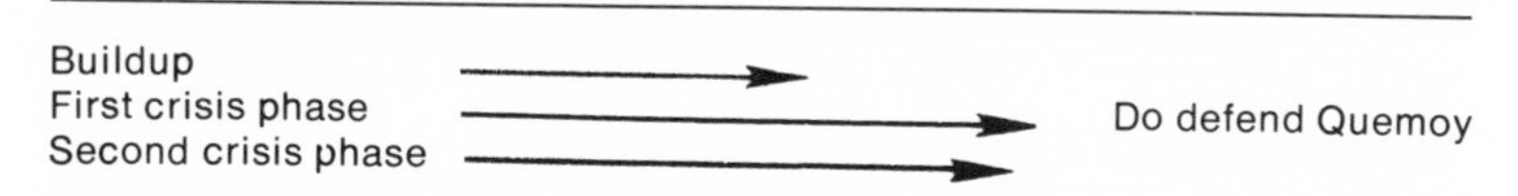

During the most critical phase of the crisis capability was highest, and in the succeeding phase it decreased slightly. This perhaps partially explains the government's cautious position during the buildup, its firm commitment near the end of the first crisis phase, and the more flexible declaratory policy in the second crisis period.

The decision to defend Formosa and the Pescadores was less difficult. Compared with the Quemoy situation, each capability factor was more favorable. Formosa was easier to defend militarily because of U.S. naval superiority and some 100 miles of open water. There was a clear treaty commitment approved by the Senate in addition to the Formosa resolution so that greater congressional and public backing could be anticipated. British support, while needed less, was more likely. The Soviets would have been more reluctant to encourage such an adventurous Chinese undertaking.

11.2 INFLUENCE OF THE PREEXISTING INVOLVEMENT IN THE MIDDLE EAST

It is difficult to assess the influence of the preexisting American involvement in Lebanon. The government undoubtedly had some reservations as it approached an additional cold war crisis. Failure of the United States to act decisively during the buildup phase of the Quemoy crisis could be attributed to preoccupation with Lebanon or a psychological reluctance to recognize a second problem until absolutely necessary. There seemed to be less of a tendency to deal boldly with the developing situation than there had been in the weeks before the Lebanon landings. American marine forces in the Mediterranean had been doubled and the Sixth Fleet augmented prior to the Middle East crisis. However, because of the many complicating factors, one cannot attribute too much to different approaches to the two solutions. By comparing capability factors affecting the Quemoy decisions with relative changes that might have occurred without a Middle East involvement, the influence of the prior commitment becomes clearer. Because the possibility of serious involvement in the Middle East decreased as the Quemoy crisis unfolded, the potential limitations of a second crisis were less keenly felt.

11.2.1 ESTIMATE OF SOVIET INTENTIONS TO INTERVENE It might be surmised that a heavy commitment of U.S. forces in the Middle East could trigger Russian aggression somewhere else in the world. Such a hypothesis might apply to some American engagements remote from Russian borders. But in this case the Soviets seemed to be genuinely concerned about the presence of Western troops close to their southern boundary. For a short time after the intense shelling of Quemoy began, Soviet propaganda continued to put primary emphasis on the Middle East situation. It even referred to the Far Eastern developments as an American-instigated diversion. Moscow may have welcomed a shift of attention away from the Middle East as a further strain on U.S. limited war forces. But the Soviets probably would have been slightly less opposed to an offshore islands probe with no U.S. military presence in Lebanon.

It may seem strange that Russia would place its Middle Eastern concerns above the interests of a Communist ally, but such a pragmatic Soviet approach already had many precedents in Sino-Soviet relations. The Russians also characteristically avoid more than one involvement at a time, particularly on different fronts. In addition, Quemoy's distance from the Soviet Union made it difficult to exert a direct Soviet influence.

The Lebanon landings added credibility to American shows of strength. Moscow could have little doubt that Washington would use force in certain circumstances. There was, nonetheless, an important qualifying distinction between the two situations. Lebanon was still recognized as an American sphere of influence. Intervention there was an acceptable precept of the cold war. An assault against China was not.

Russian failure to respond militarily in the Middle East increased American confidence that Khrushchev would not directly support a Quemoy invasion. Throughout the crisis, the careful phrasing and timing of Russian threats combined with military inactivity indicated that Moscow was not going to commit itself directly. The Russians probably would have responded similarly to a Quemoy crisis without a concurrent Middle East crisis. It is, however, speculated that Moscow was slightly less inclined to become involved in the Far East with U.S. troops in Lebanon.

11.2.2 DEFENSE ESTIMATES OF U.S. CAPABILITY TO DEFEND QUEMOY

Although the Lebanon experience increased confidence that there would be no Soviet military response, the involvement of U.S. forces in the Middle East slightly reduced American flexibility to meet a second challenge. Firmness in the Far East was a more acceptable strategy because the Lebanon crisis had passed the acute stage and appeared to be controllable without additional drain on other units. Because both conflicts remained limited, U.S. involvement in Lebanon did not have great influence on evaluations of military capability to cope with the Quemoy situation. But the United States would have been in a stronger position if there had been no prior commitment.

11.2.3 ESTIMATE OF CONGRESSIONAL AND PUBLIC SUPPORT Although the President's firm response to the Middle East crisis had widespread approval, some critics warned that the United States was beginning to commit and overextend itself around the world. This feeling was intensified by U.S. engagement in a second conflict. Criticism of the American global role became a rallying cry for those who disagreed with the Quemoy policy. The positive and negative influences of the Lebanon involvement tended to cancel each other. But as the

Quemoy crisis progressed, public sentiment seemed to swing from approbation of the Middle East response to increasing concern about the number of conflicts in which the United States might become engaged. It is speculated that Lebanon became a liability rather than an asset to the administration in trying to mobilize domestic support for its policy during the second crisis phase.

11.2.4 DEPENDENCE ON BRITISH SUPPORT The American commitment to Lebanon increased the importance of obtaining allied endorsement of an additional controversial involvement. Commitments to two trouble spots simultaneously increased the importance of cooperative effort. Although the United States did not need British military assistance in the Taiwan area, it was helpful to have a strong British supporting presence in the Mediterranean. Great Britain provided almost the full extent of its limited military resources in an effort to control the Mideast and Cyprus situations. This eased the American peace-keeping load, complicated the problem for the Soviets, and utilized British forces while avoiding the political complications associated with aiding the Nationalists. British political support in the Middle East crisis was also significant because joint military and diplomatic action helped mitigate domestic charges that the United States was the lonely policeman of the world. Criticism of the Quemoy policy in the United States greatly increased Washington's psychological need for international approval. Without a preexisting conflict the United States probably would have had less of a requirement for British political, diplomatic, and psychological support.

Predicted changes in factors with no previous involvement, although highly speculative, demonstrate the almost neglibible influence of the Lebanon crisis on the U.S. decision to defend Quemoy. (See Figure 11.2.) The domestic support factor was the only one whose relative weight varied during the phases of the Quemoy crisis owing to changing perceptions of the Middle East involvement. Comparing the sum of the factors in Figure 11.2 with and without the Lebanon crisis reveals only a slight increase in capability factors with no preexisting conflict.

With Mideast involvement ————→ Do defend Quemoy
Without Mideast involvement ————→

The prior commitment did not appear to influence significantly the capability to defend Quemoy. A full-scale engagement in the Middle East, of course, would have made a greater difference.

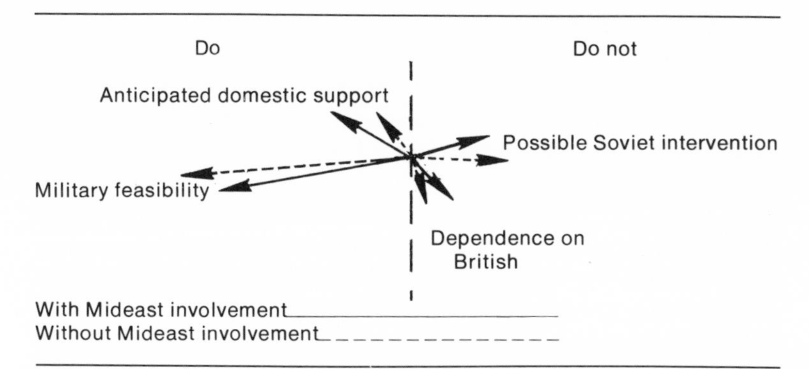

Figure 11.2 Effect of Middle East involvement on decision to defend Quemoy against attack

While this analysis has examined the influence of a first crisis on the handling of a second, it is also valuable to consider the reverse. The developing crisis in the Taiwan area did not seem to have a significant influence on the handling of the Lebanon situation. It probably intensified American and Soviet desires to resolve the conflict peacefully. While the Quemoy crisis increased the strain on American forces in the Middle East, troop strength was maintained there. On September 27, 1958, the U.S. government reported to the U.N. Secretary General that it intended to begin withdrawal of forces in the "near future" and that it hoped to have completed the evolution by the end of October.[1] While the United States may have had some increased desire to withdraw because of domestic criticism of the Quemoy involvement, there was no military necessity for the move. The last troops departed on October 24. By then the Formosa Strait military situation had become much more favorable. Although an attack carrier was dispatched from the Mediterranean to the Far East, it was rapidly replaced by a carrier from the Atlantic fleet.

The second crisis did appear to stimulate some criticism toward the first. Silent critics of the Lebanon policy grew more vociferous as they became convinced a series of U.S. involvements might occur. Dependence on allied support in the Middle East was greater because of a serious crisis in the Far East. However, there was little difficulty in obtaining British participation in the Middle East. While the Quemoy crisis slightly decreased capability to deal effectivly with Lebanon, it did not appear to have had an adverse influence on U.S. policy there.

[1]Department of State, *American Foreign Policy, Current Documents, 1958* (Washington, 1962), p. 1049. Memorandum of the U.S. government to the U.N. Secretary General, September 27, 1958, U.N. Document A/3934/Rev. 1/Annex 1.

11.3 EFFECTIVENESS OF NAVAL FORCES AS INSTRUMENTS OF AMERICAN POLICY

In evaluating the Quemoy crisis it could be concluded that the Seventh Fleet was the most significant factor preventing an escalation of the conflict. On the other hand, the U.S. naval buildup, while apparently decisive, actually may have been irrelevant if neither the Soviets nor the Chinese planned an assault on the offshore islands. Even with no U.S. military presence, an invasion of the islands might not have been attempted. The truth probably lies somewhere in between these contradictory assessments.

Faced with an intensive bombardment initiated by the Chinese, the United States could no longer sit anxiously on the sidelines and hope that it was merely a passing harassment. A Chinese probe required a response to make it clear that Washington would not allow the Nationalists to be forced off the islands by assault or siege. By concentrating a large force in the area and agreeing to escort Nationalist supply ships, the United States underlined its position. Deterrence of a probe had already failed, but a forceful American presence may have discouraged further aggression. Washington's response seized the initiative and presented Peking with a much more difficult problem. Because U.S. ships were interposed in the Formosa Strait, the impression was conveyed to Soviet and Chinese strategists that American obstacles would have to be removed before Formosa or the offshore islands could be invaded.

Soviet intentions were not clear. Their feelings toward the Chinese were ambivalent. Although Moscow wanted to improve relations with Peking, it was not willing to risk war with the United States. The Soviets were sincerely concerned about the possibility of a nuclear holocaust arising from limited clashes. Khrushchev apparently refused to provide direct support or to attempt to deter the United States from defending the Nationalists. Once U.S. resolve and local superiority had been demonstrated, it was clearer in Moscow and Peking that plans for assault, if there were any, would be extremely dangerous. The forceful American response probably strengthened the argument of Sino-Soviet leaders opposed to a Quemoy confrontation.[2]

The late arrival of American forces decreased the influence they might have exerted on the situation. During the buildup period when the Chinese still were contemplating their probe, the United

[2]It is not meant to imply that a major internal policy debate was in progress on this issue in the Soviet Union. Rather, it would appear that the Soviets were united in opposition to the adventure.

States did not make a bold demonstration of resolve. Theoretically, if ships had converged on the area prior to the intensive bombardment, Peking might have canceled its plans. It would have been evident that the United States would not allow the situation to remain an "internal affair." Once the shelling had begun, a cease-fire as soon as American warships came into view would have meant considerable loss of Chinese prestige.

United States reluctance to adopt such tactics reflected a practical limitation of secondary deterrence techniques. The U.S. government was not ready to commit itself to defense of the offshore islands. It was hoped that increasing tensions in the area would amount to no more than one of the numerous nuisances of the cold war. However, the buildup of Chinese air and troop strength in the area was a more ominous portent than the rising tempo of clashes in the Formosa Strait. It was apparently reasoned that American overreaction would aggravate and perhaps escalate the situation. Washington did not want to play into the hands of Mao, Khrushchev, or Chiang.

When the heavy combatants of the Seventh Fleet reached the Formosa Strait the danger of a Chinese bomber attack had lessened considerably. Major reinforcements did not arrive during the significant first crisis phase. By the time the principal augmenting forces reached the scene, Peking had already agreed to resume negotiations. Naval task forces had to be in the vicinity for rapid response. Ironically, in order to transfer ships expeditiously from the Mediterranean to the Taiwan area, it was necessary to obtain the approval of Egypt's Nasser, whose revolutionary activities had helped instigate the Lebanon crisis. Political and distance factors can restrict global naval operations. However, since deterrence is primarily psychological, the highly publicized commitment of additional ships was of significance. While not altering the immediate military balance, publishing orders symbolized American resolve to resist aggression.

The Seventh Fleet would have been more effective in support of a less ambiguous declaratory position, but the government was not ready politically to make a categorical commitment to defense of the offshore islands. The arrival of U.S. warships signaled to Communist capitals the probable American reaction. Seventh Fleet operations provided a positive response to the shelling of the offshore islands while allowing the American government to delay a final decision. The continuing buildup of forces during the second crisis phase, after a commitment had been made, underlined Washington's resolve, in spite of growing domestic and worldwide dissatisfaction with the American Quemoy policy.

Publicized fleet moves had some negative aspects. They heightened domestic concerns that the government would involve itself in war with China and triggered a Soviet propaganda response. Dispatching the Seventh Fleet put pressure on Moscow to defend its image as protector of the Communist camp, and provided a target for an anti-American campaign in the Third World.

At the same time the Soviet media reflected frustration and embarrassment because of Seventh Fleet operations. The Russians revealed their preoccupation with the fleet and an underlying respect for its power. Khrushchev indicated he understood the significance of fleet movements when he complained to President Eisenhower that "... in truth, by the direction of movement of the American naval fleet one can now judge almost without error to what place will be directed the spearhead of the next blackmail and provocations."[3] The Soviet leader asserted that naval movements did not make any sense against states with modern weapons and that "In the century of nuclear and rocket weapons of hitherto unheard of power and speed of action, these once threatening naval vessels are fit in essence, only for paying courtesy visits, giving salutes, and can still serve as targets for appropriate types of missiles."[4] Khrushchev evidently sincerely believed the day of the surface ship had passed, as reflected in the Russian naval construction program. But he was annoyed because the United States refused to share his view and was thus embarrassing the USSR.[5] Fleet operations obviously made an impression. While undoubtedly antagonizing the Soviets, the buildup of force made the power realities of the situation clearer. By the timing, restraint, and careful wording of official statements and the absence of military maneuvers, Moscow appeared to have recognized that the Seventh Fleet's presence had closed certain options to them. The American initiative meant that a Russian counterdemonstration would increase the risk of an inadvertent involvement. The naval maneuvers also provided Moscow with a convenient excuse for not aiding Peking's probe. The Soviets

[3]Tass in English to Europe, September 8, 1958, "Text of Khrushchev Letter to Eisenhower."

[4]Ibid.

[5]While Khrushchev's view predominated, it did not appear to be shared by all of the naval leaders. See, for example, the follow-up to Khrushchev's remarks in Captain Polyansioy, "The Big Stick of the American Aggressors," *Soviet Fleet,* October 3, 1958.

were not against the Chinese resolving an internal affair. They simply wanted to avoid risk of war with the United States.

The American buildup in the Formosa Strait may have had little effective deterrent value since the Chinese and Soviets were already aware of its capability. It is not inconceivable that Peking anticipated a strong American reaction but decided that a limited probe would serve its interests, perhaps to restore internal cohesion for initiation of the commune system. Moreover, Peking may have considered Quemoy to be impregnable, or at least not worth the heavy cost of direct assault even without American support of the Nationalists.

It is more likely that the primary objective of the probe was to regain territory that has historically been part of the mainland. The Nationalist-held islands were a sharp thorn in the Chinese side. But the formal American commitment to defend Quemoy had been deliberately couched in ambiguous and flexible language. Even though the Chinese scheme appeared to be limited, it was necessary for the United States to make its commitment clear by meaningful actions.

Convoying Nationalist supply ships increased the dangers of inadvertent involvement in a much larger conflict that could be triggered by design of Peking or Taipei or due to honest misunderstanding. However, in this situation no U.S. ships were hit, and the siege of the offshore islands was finally lifted. Some risk seemed to be required to make U.S. determination clear. The United States tried to contain the conflict with a strong show of strength. Paradoxically, the risk of escalation was increased by moving forces into the area.

By its cautious but firm support of the Nationalists, American prestige as a defender of its friends was enhanced. This was in sharp contrast to the Soviet image. Although Moscow may have cautioned against an invasion of Quemoy, and Peking perhaps never planned one, the American capability and subsequent demonstration of determination closed options that may have been considered open in the Communist capitals.

11.4 ADEQUACY OF CONVENTIONAL NAVAL FORCES TO MEET THE DEMANDS OF THE MULTICRISIS

Anticipatory warship maneuvers might have provided increased deterrence, but restraint during the buildup phase was a political decision and was not due to inadequacy of available forces. In fact, at a critical point in the Lebanon crisis, the attack carrier *Lexington* had been deployed from San Diego to "improve the readiness posture in the Western Pacific."[6] Considering the limited Russian and Chinese naval capability, it could even be argued that the United States was excessive in its augmentation of the Seventh Fleet. However, the attack carriers matched the number of operational mainland airfields in the vicinity of Taiwan. A sizable armada was also needed to protect the carriers from potential communist air and submarine attack.

As long as there was no fighting in the Middle East, American forces easily met the challenge.[7] The Quemoy requirements, however, would have been much more difficult to meet if ground forces rather than warplanes and ships had been the primary instruments of military power required in the Formosa Strait. The strain of keeping a major part of the Navy on station in two remote areas of the world would have been felt if Mideast tension had not continued to diminish. Two-thirds of the Navy's attack carriers were occupied with Lebanon and Quemoy as well as most mobile marine battalions.[8] However, naval forces in both regions were adequate for the duration of the two crises.

11.5 UNDERLYING QUESTIONS

The Quemoy crisis provided insight into a number of the underlying questions being considered.

11.5.1 ASSESSMENT OF THE VALUE OF ALLIANCES

The crisis illustrated some of the limits as well as the benefits of global partnerships. Washington was hopeful, but not expectant, of receiving London's support. However, British interests simply did not coincide with American concerns in the Far East. The British were vulnerable to Chinese pressure. As domestic criticism intensified, the United States sought allied approval of its policy. But Her Majesty's Government could barely keep from outright condemnation of the American policy owing to the severe internal reaction of the British public and political opposition. Nevertheless, there were benefits from London's actions in the Middle East where Anglo-American interests were almost identical. British forces helped free American Medi-

[6]The ship sailed from the United States on July 17, 1958. Admiral David L. McDonald, USN, "Carrier Employment Since 1950," US Naval Institute *Proceedings,* Vol. 90, No. 11 (November 1964), p. 29.

[7]However, major military requirements in the Middle East were not likely even in the case of fighting except in the remote case of the intervention of Soviet "volunteers."

[8]Of the Navy's fifteenth attack aircraft carriers, eight were involved directly with the crises and three were not available for full service. McDonald, "Carrier Employment Since 1950," p. 29.

terranean units to deal with the multicrisis. Not unexpectedly, the Quemoy situation demonstrated that the special relationship with Great Britain did not mean that moral and military backing would be forthcoming in conflicts where there was no mutually shared interest at stake.

The experience of dealing with the Nationalists also indicated the mixed blessings of alliances. Nationalist capability to cope with minimal U.S. assistance demonstrated the value of military assistance programs. Chinese Nationalists, rather than Americans, returned the fire from the mainland and commanded the air space over the strait. Although some doubts existed before the action began, Chiang's forces proved to be extremely capable in engagements with the Chinese. The defeat in the air caused a significant loss of Peking's prestige in the Far East. A strong local Nationalist force backed by a demonstration of American determination to combat an expansion of the conflict appeared to be an effective combination.

American emphasis on Nationalist self-help reflected a major complication in dealing with the ally. Chiang's ambitions went beyond U.S. interests. It was not certain that Taipei would accept an American solution to the offshore island problem any more than Peking. The Nationalists may have desired an escalation of the conflict. Chiang's insistence on maintaining large troop concentrations on the islands against American advice had made U.S. commitment to defense of Quemoy almost inevitable. Controlling the Nationalists was a major American consideration. Chiang was naturally unhappy in early stages of the crisis with American reluctance to take measures that might deeply involve the United States. In dealing with an ambitious and independent-minded ally, there were dangers along with the advantages. In spite of the leverage available to the United States in dealing with Chiang, the Republic of China, like Israel, was obviously not a dependent state.

The American decision to prevent loss of the offshore islands, vague and hesitating as it was at times during the crisis, indicated Chiang's considerable importance in American national security considerations. The obligations of the alliance worked both ways. In 1955 Washington wanted to avoid any commitment to the offshore islands, but the United States was not ready to give up its alliance with Chiang or the viability of his army. Thus, the United States made a commitment to defend the islands under certain conditions and assented to their fortification.

11.5.2 TYPES OF COMMITMENTS The built-in ambiguity of the Formosa resolution provided flexibility in responding to the Quemoy probe and in dealing with Chiang. It was not clear to Peking which offshore islands the United States would defend, if any. Therefore, the Chinese could not discount the possibility that Washington might defend every inch of Nationalist-held territory. On the other hand, if the commitment to Quemoy and Matsu had been explicit, the Chinese might not have attempted a probe at all, assuming that the bombardment was an attempt to gain control of the islands and not just a propaganda ploy to alleviate internal pressure. A formal U.S. commitment might have given them pause. It also would have eased domestic criticism in the United States if the obligation had been clear-cut, and not hinged on a presidential judgment. Whether the Formosa resolution should have included the offshore islands remains a moot question. Flexibility was probably advantageous in the 1958 crisis, but there were definite disadvantages.

11.5.3 RELATIONSHIP OF LOCAL CONFLICTS TO GLOBAL WAR Although the American limited war doctrine was still in a state of flux, Washington evidently felt it could confine the conflict to the local Taiwan area. Peking obviously had limited aspirations. American maneuvers may have increased the possibility of general war and therefore opened more dangerous options while closing others. Moscow's belief that local wars would inevitably end in a nuclear exchange increased its reluctance to become directly involved. Since the Soviet Union was not able to bring force to bear in the local area, Soviet intervention could have meant an expansion of the territory associated with the conflict as well as a further escalation. Moscow seemed to be seriously concerned that American imprudence would lead to war by design of Chiang or Mao or as a result of inadvertence. Unfounded rumors that Peking had been given nuclear weapons and that nuclear shells had been sent to Quemoy were not denied by the rival powers, apparently in order to heighten uncertainty. It is speculated, however, that it would have taken a deliberate massive American attack on the mainland before Moscow would have risked war. Therefore, in this situation the potential for global war seemed small.

11.5.4 RELEVANCE OF SHIFTS OF FORCES AS INDICATORS OF POLICY

Movements of forces removed some of the speculative element concerning the intentions of the naval powers. During the buildup phase American reluctance to become embroiled was obvious from a glance at the disposition of carrier and amphibious forces. On the day heavy shelling began, half of the Seventh Fleet carrier-cruiser force was docked in the Philippines, and the Marine Landing Force was on liberty in Singapore.

Before taking a firm declaratory position, the United States had indicated its determination by speeding task forces to the Taiwan area. Washington wanted the Chinese to see sonic sweeps of American jets on their radar scopes. The publicized augmentations of the Seventh Fleet could not be mistaken as mere precautionary measures. There was, however, some doubt in Chiang's mind because of initial American reluctance to provide direct support and the ambiguity of Washington's declaratory position. In evaluating the significance of the initial ship movements one might assume they had occurred with the President's approval. Actually, the Seventh Fleet was ordered to sail for Taiwan prior to the Navy's even receiving concurrence of the State Department.[9] However, announcement of augmentations several days later was a deliberate effort to demonstrate American determination. It was the President who apparently conceived the idea of moving a carrier from the Mediterranean as a further expression of American commitment. On September 4, 1958, the day that a stronger American declaratory policy was defined, U.S. warships began escorting Nationalist convoys. The movements of ships proved to be fairly valid indicators of U.S. policy.

By keeping their ships in port, the Russians made it clear there would be considerable advance notice prior to Soviet naval assistance being available in the area. While Russian aircraft could have reached the scene fairly quickly, naval support of an amphibious assault would have taken a number of days. Barring an unlikely resort to thermonuclear weapons or a counteraction in some other area of the world, Soviet verbal warnings lacked credibility.

The British apparently tried to imply by token movements of troops or units and announcements of eventual increases in the Far Eastern fleet that it still had an interest in Asia. But by keeping its ships well clear of the Formosa Strait, London also clearly signaled that it was not going to support the United States directly.

11.5.5 USEFULNESS OF THE UNITED NATIONS IN CRISIS SITUATIONS The United Nations served as a forum for American and Soviet exchanges concerning the crisis, but the organization appeared to have little capability for effective action to control a crisis involving conflicting interests of the superpowers and a defiant nonmember.

[9]This fact is reported in Capt. Edward F. Baldridge's article, "Lebanon and Quemoy—the Navy's Role," U.S. Naval Institute *Proceedings*, Vol. 87, No. 2 (February 1961), p. 98.

The United States "reserved the right" to bring the matter to the United Nations if the Warsaw talks failed.[10] But this appeared to be merely a gesture to allay world and domestic opinion. Secretary of State Dulles apparently saw little hope of a U.N. solution to the crisis. In editing a draft of the U.N. speech, he deleted the remark "there is still hope that the United Nations could exert a peaceful influence on the situation."[11] While there was some talk of a U.N. trusteeship as an eventual solution to the offshore islands problem, such a proposal was evidently never made in the Warsaw negotiations. This would have been too patently unacceptable to Peking and Taipei. Although the United Nations did not play a significant role in this crisis, it continued to be an important arena for discussion of the Middle Eastern situation.

11.5.6 LIMITS OF BIPARTISANSHIP The crisis also demonstrated limits to the spirit of bipartisanship in foreign policy. Although Majority Leader Lyndon Johnson and House Speaker Sam Rayburn remained silent, and former President Truman emphasized the need for support of the President in time of crisis, the Democratic members of the Foreign Relations Committee made a vigorous effort through individual statements to reverse the Quemoy policy in the second crisis phase. Senator Green's letter to the President was a strong dissent from the government's position. In view of the deep reservations of Democrats on the Foreign Relations Committee, their relative silence during the most critical phase may have reflected a sense of crisis loyalty. Quemoy is a particularly interesting case because Congress in 1955 had overwhelmingly authorized the President to make a judgment concerning the need to commit U.S. forces. The Formosa resolution still stood. If the Congress had been in session, a less speculative assessment of congressional consensus could be made. The Democrats appeared to be split rather than predominantly opposed. By the time a new Congress convened in 1959 there was no longer strong support for abandoning the Formosa resolution.

11.5.7 BUREAUCRATIC BIAS Within the government a variety of competing opinions were offered on how to deal effectively with the crisis. There were disagreements between the American military commander in the Taiwan area and the American ambassador to the Republic of China,[12] and the Secretary of State found much criti-

[10]*The Washington Post,* September 19, 1958, p. A8. "Remarks by Dulles, Gromyko at UN."

[11]Correction to September 11, 1958, draft of Secretary Dulles's U.N. General Assembly Speech. The John Foster Dulles Papers, Category 1B, Princeton University Library.

[12]Letter from Vice Admiral Roland N. Smoot, USN (Ret.), to Lt. Comdr. J. T. Howe, USN, dated March 7, 1969.

cism of his policy within his department. Military leaders were impatient with the tight restrictions placed on their counteraction, and on that issue they sided with Chiang.[13] Yet there was seemingly more suspicion within the U.S. military than in the Department of State that Chiang was trying to exploit the crisis to satisfy his own ambitions. It was the Secretary of Defense who cautioned the President, and there were marked differences in the assessments of U.S. military leaders on Taiwan and the Embassy on this point.[14] Among the military there seemed to be more of a tendency to regard the garrisoning of Quemoy as an implicit commitment of the United States to defense of the islands. American advisers had helped build the extensive island fortifications. Embassy and State Department personnel appeared to take a more legalistic and conservative approach to the American commitment to the offshore islands.

11.6 CONCLUSIONS

In spite of a preexisting involvement, the United States was able to cope successfully with the Quemoy confrontation. Without American forces firing a shot, a tenuous strategic position was held against a Chinese challenge. Evaluation of the capability demonstrated must be tempered by the limited scope of the Chinese probe and the diminished probability that the United States would have to fight in Lebanon by the time the Quemoy crisis intensified. The difficulties of meeting even this limited test exhibited the limitations and complications of a cold war confrontation.

Although the United States was capable of coping with the crisis during all its stages, analysis of the principal factors affecting capability revealed some weaknesses in the American position. The possibility of Soviet intervention was remote, but it had to be considered seriously. There were many reasons for Moscow's reluctance to support Peking. The Quemoy crisis seemed to demonstrate, however, that there were limits to Soviet commitments, that Russia would not necessarily respond to the plight of a prestigious ally, and that it was not interested in a showdown with the United States. Moscow was placed in a difficult strategic predicament because of overall American superiority in strategic weapons and its ability to concentrate force rapidly in the local area. The Middle

[13]Smoot, letter.

[14]A marked contrast existed between the opinions expressed in the letters of Adm. Smoot and an informed observer concerning the Quemoy crisis of 1958 to Lt. Comdr. J. T. Howe, USN, dated March 13, 1969, and the opinions expressed by Ambassador Everett F. Drumright in letter of March 7, 1969, to Lt. Comdr. J. T. Howe, USN, and by Mr. Joseph A. Yager in letter of March 11, 1969.

East experience had demonstrated an American capability and will to intervene in a local conflict even in the face of a threatening Soviet declaratory position. A logical Soviet counteraction to the Quemoy pressure might have been to threaten a vulnerable Western position like West Berlin. But the Soviets were particularly concerned about the possibilities of escalation of a local conflict. Moscow was not willing to risk world war to help the Chinese remove a "thorn" in their side. The Soviets apparently were not convinced that American policy was entirely rational or that the United States was a paper tiger, as the Chinese claimed.

Throughout the crisis American military leaders were confident that the United States had the capability to intervene effectively. This was perhaps the most important factor that made the defense of Quemoy a feasible policy. However, the situation could have been extremely difficult. China's sizable bomber force stayed grounded, thus narrowing the scope of American counteraction required. United States capability estimates were based on the possible use of tactical nuclear weapons. Employment of these weapons would have greatly complicated the crisis. Although the offshore islands were in a very unfavorable geographical position, American defense capability was enhanced by the fact that naval and air power were the primary military instruments needed as a backup for the Nationalists. Modern weapons could make a difference in this situation. Contemplation of an invasion of the mainland requiring massive troop strength would have given military estimates a gloomy cast. Nationalist command of the air was an unanticipated but crucial positive factor in the military-political equation. The United States emphasized Nationalist self-help. The solution of the immediate military problems allowed Washington to suggest a more flexible Quemoy policy based on control of the situation at a time when domestic and international pressures to back down had increased substantially.

Public opposition to the Quemoy policy developed slowly. It did not have much influence until after a clear commitment had been made and the most critical phase of the crisis had passed. One government advantage in the relatively late decision to help the Nationalists hold the islands was that opponents of the alternative had little on which to focus. Prolongation of the crisis provided an opportunity for public dissent to grow. If the crisis had been extended and increased in intensity, the signs of growing dissatisfaction might have created a serious complication for the administration. Even though considerable criticism was eventually expressed, it did not have an important effect on actual policy. It seemed to be a contributing factor in pressing the government to express a more flexible declaratory position, but the influence of public opinion was largely on the periphery of policy.

The crisis demonstrated that even with sufficient power for unilateral American action, it was important to have the support of allies. In addition to justifying American action internationally, the backing of friends would have helped dispel the unpopular domestic image of world policeman. The Quemoy stand was weakened by severely critical opinion in allied countries.

The prior involvement in the Middle East did not significantly restrict American response to a second crisis. While some reduced capability resulted from the Lebanon operation, that crisis was not the kind of draining experience that might have made the United States reluctant to take on an additional commitment. Examination of the two simultaneous situations revealed the global vulnerability resulting from the commitment of even small numbers of forces. The greater part of American limited war capability was tied down in two areas with practically no comparable Soviet expenditure. However, a favorable aspect of American pressure in the Middle East was that it probably slightly decreased Soviet inclination to become involved in a second crisis.

In facing the offshore island challenge, the United States did not appear to renege on an obligation. The United States did not do everything that Chiang desired, but it helped him hold a vulnerable strategic position and certainly lived up to any tacit obligation that might have existed. Known Nationalist ambitions caused the United States to be extremely reluctant about clarifying its commitment. Although American action seemed inevitable if the major offshore islands were in danger of falling, the government position remained fluid for almost two weeks. While providing more flexibility, American reluctance to commit itself undoubtedly increased Chiang's anxiety.

Dispatching naval forces to the area was intended to deter the Communists from invading the islands. While there are limitations to what can be attributed to the presence of the Seventh Fleet, it did close some options to Peking and Moscow. Fleet operations undoubtedly contributed to the success of the American stance. It made American determination apparent prior to a final decision to use force. Once the policy had been declared, it added credibility to the U.S. position. The Soviets appeared to have a heightened awareness that the combination of strategic superiority and rapid application of pressure could prove decisive in the missile age.

In the aftermath of the crisis the United States hardened its public position,[15] and domestic criticism died down as the tension eased. Although the Secretary of State claimed to have no plans for urging Chiang to reduce his military strength on the offshore islands,[16] the United States did attempt to persuade Chiang to reduce the garrison. Heavy artillery was offered as a *quid pro quo* for the reduction.[17] A modest reduction in troop strength was made, but Chiang Kai-shek has subsequently claimed to have "about the same number of troops . . . as there were at the time of the bombardment of 1958."[18] The U.S. government continued its policy toward the offshore islands. When faced with a buildup opposite Quemoy in June 1962, President John Kennedy, an outspoken critic of the offshore island policy in 1955 and 1958, invoked the Formosa resolution.[19]

Although the wisdom of the American policy toward the offshore islands is questionable, the 1958 stance was on the whole successful. The United States demonstrated a capability to deal effectively with a difficult crisis while coping with a limited preexisting involvement in another part of the globe.

[15]On October 24, 1958, Chiang and Dulles issued a joint statement at the conclusion of what must have been a difficult visit to Taiwan by the Secretary of State. The statement recognized that "under the present conditions the defense of the Quemoys, together with the Matsus, is closely related to the defense of Taiwan and Penghi [Pescadores]." *The New York Times*, October 24, 1958, p. 3.

[16]In his news conference on October 14, 1958, Secretary Dulles stated that "We have no plans whatsoever for urging him [President Chiang Kai-shek] to do that [to reduce the military strength of forces on Quemoy]," and "I don't think that [the thinning down of the Chinese Nationalist garrison on Quemoy] has anything to do with bargaining with the Chinese Communists." He said that steps could be taken to assure that the islands would not become a source of provocation, but he indicated that what he had in mind was the prevention of "commando raids" and the infiltration of agents from the Islands. U.S., Department of State, *American Foreign Policy—Current Documents, 1958* (Washington, D.C., 1962), pp. 1175–1177.

[17]Letter from Gen. Maxwell D. Taylor, USA (Ret.), to Lt. Comdr. J. T. Howe, USN, dated March 4, 1969.

[18]Interview with President Chiang Kai-shek and Mme. Chiang Kai-shek conducted on September 24, 1964, by Mr. Spencer Davis for the Dulles Oral History Project, Princeton University, p. 24.

[19]President Kennedy said in a press conference on June 27, 1962, "One possibility is that there might be aggressive action against the offshore islands of Matsu and Quemoy. In that event the policy of this country will be that established seven years ago under the Formosa resolution. The United States will take the action necessary to assure the defense of Formosa and the Pescadores." U.S., Department of State, *American Foreign Policy—Current Documents, 1962* (Washington, D.C., 1966), p. 1007.

IV THE TWO CRISES AND FUTURE TRENDS

12. COMPARISON

By examining the similarities and differences between the Middle East crisis of 1967 and the Quemoy crisis of 1958, comparing various factors affecting assessments of U.S. capability to take action, and studying the influence of a previous crisis in each case, the ability of the United States to cope with a multicrisis can be better understood.

12.1 SIMILARITIES AND DIFFERENCES

There were a number of interesting similarities and some important differences in the situations faced by the United States nearly a decade apart.[1] Both crises developed in remote and difficult geographical positions and were complicated by a variety of factors. The situations involved vulnerable and sensitive points in the U.S. security system. Such areas are, of course, inviting targets for probes.

In each case there may have been some Soviet encouragement for a carefully calculated increase in tension, but Moscow later appeared to have little control of either situation. Like the United States, the Soviet Union had to deal with strong-willed and aggressive allies. In many ways the problems for the superpowers in both crises were identical. Russian influence in dealing with the Arabs in 1967 and the Chinese in 1958 had definite limitations. Both Nasser and Mao apparently hoped to use Soviet power for their own ends. The United States, on its part, was deeply concerned that it might get dragged into a war by Chiang Kai-shek. Some government officials also may have felt that Tel Aviv was trying to promote a confrontation in 1967 in order to satisfy its national ambitions. But a legitimate concern for national survival appeared to be a more valid explanation for Israeli activities. In any case, the United States was not able to control Israel's movements.

In both 1958 and 1967 there was a remote possibility that a conflict between third parties would bring about a war between the two superpowers, a situation neither sought. Washington and Moscow rec-

[1] No attempt will be made to document all of them, but some of the more significant parallels and distinctions will be discussed. In making these general comparisons no attempt has been made to distinguish the changing attitudes which have been identified in Parts Two and Three. For example, in the sections that follow, the statement that Moscow lost control of Nasser should be clarified by giving the specific time. The assertion that Nasser tried to use Soviet power for his own ends should be qualified by the statement that the reverse was true until well into the crisis.

ognized the dangers and apparently tried to contain the conflicts. Uncertainty about the intentions of the enemy and direct antagonists seemed to exist in both capitals. Israel, Egypt, China, and the Republic of China were all in doubt about the plans of their patrons as well as their enemies.

In each conflict the nation Washington supported—either directly as with Nationalist China or indirectly as with Israel—demonstrated military capability in its own right. There was some concern about the Nationalists when the crisis began, but their armed forces proved themselves both in the air and in withstanding the Chinese siege, with only a slight assist from the United States. The outnumbered Israelis showed that as long as the Soviets were kept neutralized, Israel did not need outside military support.

Even though both crises developed during periods of concern about growing Soviet missile capability, the United States had an edge in strategic weapons. However, American general purpose forces were strained considerably in meeting two multicrises challenges. In the case of Lebanon, the situation was under control when the Quemoy crisis developed. Nevertheless, a large concentration of naval forces was still needed in both areas.[2] The Soviets, on the other hand, though expending resources to equip and supply their allies, did not have to commit Russian forces.

While it might be expected that U.S. allies would more readily take up the American cause in the event of Soviet probes in a multicrisis, both situations demonstrated the limitations of alliances when dealing with distant areas. In the Arab-Israeli conflict, economic considerations restricted British support for such a move as asserting international rights in the Straits of Tiran. British public opinion and government policy would not have supported direct intervention in Middle East fighting in 1967. In the case of Quemoy public opinion, commercial interests, and a genuine diplomatic difference between the governments on the issues restricted British assistance. The United Kingdom, a global ally of relatively long standing, proved to be very vulnerable in both situations.[3]

[2]The United States probably could have successfully coped with the military situation with fewer naval forces as long as the crisis was of short duration. But the most serious potential military threat was from Chinese airfields. Six attack carriers would not have seemed excessive if the Chinese had utilized their bomber force to attack Taiwan and U.S. ships.

[3]The British, of course, had no prior agreement in the case of Quemoy. Their policy was clearly opposed to that of the United States, and therefore their support could not be counted upon. In the case of the Middle East in 1967 the British appeared to dampen their original enthusiasm for forcing the Gulf of Aqaba blockade when they realized there might be serious economic repercussions for them.

Both of the earlier crises in Lebanon and Vietnam had some positive aspects. They demonstrated that the United States would go to considerable lengths in employing forces. Landing troops in Lebanon manifested a capacity and determination to intervene in the Third World rather than allow friendly governments to fall as a result of indirect subversion. The bombing of North Vietnam and sustained American resistance in the south again demonstrated U.S. resolve to the Soviets. Each situation was embarrassing for the Soviet Union.

Moscow's propaganda was so similar in the two cases that it easily could be interchanged without indicating any modification in the Soviet line. United States warships were depicted as the "big stick" of the "international gendarme" threatening the Soviet ally, and demands were made that the fleet return home. (See Table 12.1.) There was, however, a difference in the timing of the Soviet campaign. During the buildup phase of the 1967 Middle East crisis Moscow initiated a large propaganda attack on the U.S. Sixth Fleet. The intensive Quemoy propaganda campaign did not occur until the crisis phase began.

Moreover, statements of Soviet leaders did indicate a change in the Russian approach to U.S. naval forces. Khrushchev, obviously frustrated by American use of conventional sea power, was probably quite sincere when he asked President Eisenhower in 1958, "Does it not seem to you, Mr. President, that such transferring of military vessels now in one, now in another direction to a significant degree is now deprived of any sense, at least in the relations of states which have modern types of weapons at their disposal?"[4] Khrushchev's policy toward the Russian fleet and the tactics he employed reflected his conviction that conventional men-of-war were ineffective in the nuclear age. By contrast, when Premier Kosygin addressed the United Nations in June 1967, he referred to the fact that "powerful circles" had made "statements" and taken *"practical actions"* and asked, 'How else could one qualify the military demonstrations by the American Sixth Fleet off the coast of the Arab states . . . ?"[5] He did not question the effectiveness of this use of sea power, and, of course, Russia itself had already begun to make a greater use of naval forces. Media descriptions of U.S. fleets in 1958 as well as 1967 indicated an underlying respect for their capabilities.

[4]Premier N. Khrushchev, letter of September 7, 1958, to President Eisenhower.

[5]Alexi Kosygin, "Text of Kosygin address to General Assembly," *The New York Times,* June 20, 1967, p. 16. (Emphasis added.)

Table 12.1 Soviet Media Treatment of U.S. Fleets during 1958 Quemoy and 1967 Mideast Crises

1958	1967
1. THREAT TO SOVIET CLIENT:	
"Then add to this the guns of the U.S. naval vessels plying the Taiwan Straits and you will see what the picture in the Far East really looks like . . . in the meantime more U.S. warships and aircraft head for Chinese shores." Soviet North American Service, September 2, 1958[a]	"The U.S. Sixth Fleet is openly menacing the Arab peoples with its guns." Tass International Service, May 26, 1967[b]
2. U.S. FLEETS AS "BIG STICK" OF "INTERNATIONAL GENDARME":	
"The U.S. has assumed the functions of an international gendarme." *International Affairs*, October 1958[c]	"The return home of the 'floating gendarme' would surely improve the international situation in the Mediterranean." *International Affairs*, August 1967[d]
"It is trying to act as a self imposed supergendarme, threatening to club into submission those who disagree with its dictates." Soviet European Service, August 28, 1958[e]	". . . Washington was ready and threatening to swing its Mediterranean big stick." *International Affairs*, August 1967[f]
3. CALL FOR RETURN HOME OF U.S. FLEETS:	
"There can be no stable peace in the Far East until the American naval forces are withdrawn from the Taiwan Strait. . . ." N. S. Khrushchev, September 7, 1958[g]	"The time has come for the demand that the U.S. Sixth Fleet be withdrawn from the Mediterranean to ring out at full strength." Leonard Brezhnev, April 25, 1967[h]

[a] Moscow, Soviet North American Service in English, September 2, 1958, Yeniseyev commentary.
[b] Moscow, Tass International Service in English, May 26, 1967.
[c] Editorial, "The World Gendarme's Policy," *International Affairs*, No. 10 (Moscow: October 1958), p. 8.
[d] A. Kafman, "U.S. Big Stick in the Mediterranean," *International Affairs*, No. 8 (Moscow: August 1967), p. 75.
[e] Moscow, Soviet European Service in English, August 28, 1958, Petr Zarin commentary.
[f] Kafman, "U.S. Big Stick," p. 74.
[g] Tass in English to Europe, September 8, 1958. "Text of Khrushchev Note to Eisenhower of 7 September."
[h] *Pravda*, April 25, 1967; *Izvestia*, April 26, 1967; *CDSP*, Vol. XIX, No. 17.

While Soviet declaratory policy subsequently became stronger in both cases, there were marked similarities in expression of concern. For example, it was warned in 1958 that "The Soviet Union cannot remain inactive in the face of what is happening on the border or on the territory of its brave ally. The Soviet Union will not quietly watch the U.S. military preparations in the Pacific *whose waters also wash on Soviet shores.*"[6] (Emphasis added.) The 1967 version was almost identical in stating, "The Soviet Government keeps a close watch on the developments in the Near East. It proceeds from the fact that the maintenance of peace and security in the area *directly adjacent to the Soviet borders* meets the vital interests of the Soviet Union."[7] (Emphasis added.) There were, of course, some important differences in the circumstances under which these statements were issued. The 1958 *Pravda* article was published at the height of the crisis; the 1967 government statement was released during the buildup phase. The 1958 warning was directed at possible U.S. intervention; the 1967 pronouncement and subsequent warnings were more directed toward stopping Israel's action. The Soviet Union had a treaty commitment to China; it had only an implicit commitment to Egypt and Syria. But the Middle East was at least as important to Russian security interests in 1967.[8] The United States had a similar relationship with its allies, that is, a defensive treaty in the case of the Nationalists and a tacit understanding in the case of Israel.

There was also a difference in official American treatment of each of these situations during their buildup phases, although Washington did not make a strong stand in either case. The United States made few official comments on the Quemoy situation until intensive shelling began. Even then, more than a week passed before an official statement on the developments was made.[9] When faced with a potential Arab-Israeli war, the United States made its declaratory position clearer. However, in that case U.S. policy was one of studied neutrality, and the United States tried to avoid provocative military movements.

During the course of both crises the United States appeared to

[6]Tass in Russian to Europe, September 5, 1958. *Pravda* article by observer, "Military Adventure for U.S. Imperialists in Far East."

[7]Soviet government statement on the situation in the Middle East, Moscow Tass International Service in English, May 23, 1967. The reference to "vital interests" was, of course, an important difference.

[8]The Soviet Union does not characteristically refer to its vital interests casually. It did not, for example, refer to vital interests in similar statements associated with the Lebanon landings. This seems to reflect both changed power realities and the fact that Moscow no longer regards the Middle East as a Western sphere of influence.

[9]The letter from the Secretary of State to the Acting Chairman of the House Committee on Foreign Affairs on August 23, 1958, could be construed, however, to be a semiofficial statement on the situation.

weaken its public position slightly. However, Washington did not soften its Quemoy stand until well into the second crisis phase, after solving the local military problems and demonstrating preponderant power in the area. Subsequently, when the Quemoy crisis had subsided, a strong declaratory policy was resumed.

There is perhaps some truth in allegations that the U.S. government was preoccupied in both these situations because of a previous involvement. President Johnson appeared to have been engrossed with the Vietnam war, but he was not unaware of developments in the Middle East. As previously mentioned, the Secretary of State devoted more of his time to the Mideast situation than to Vietnam. In any case the situation received attention from the highest officials for at least two weeks prior to the outbreak of the fighting. In the Quemoy situation the President had even more warning and an opportunity to formulate a plan of action prior to the intensification of pressure.

12.2 COMPARISON OF FACTORS AFFECTING CAPABILITY

A better understanding of the differences and similarities in the two situations can be gained by comparing the influence of capability factors in each crisis. Such a comparison is, of course, extremely subjective and very difficult because of the totally different contexts of the two situations and the complex interrelationships of the factors. However, a general idea of the relative influence can be obtained by such an analysis.

12.2.1 SOVIET INTENTIONS TO INTERVENE The Soviets probably had no intention of intervening in either crisis. However, in the Arab-Israeli confrontation of 1967 there was greater uncertainty because of the presence of Soviet naval forces in the Mediterranean and because Soviet-supported regimes were being administered a shattering defeat. Although Russian warships could not have been particularly effective in changing the outcome of the desert war, they reflected direct Soviet interest and were an obstacle that the United States had to consider. However, the Soviet fleet in no way deterred the President from approving bold moves during the crisis. The tone of Moscow's statements in 1958, although carefully qualified, was slightly more threatening to the United States. The hot line warnings in 1967 concerned halting Israel's advance on Arab territory. In 1967 both the United States and the Soviet Union had a nearly invulnerable second-strike nuclear capability. Therefore, it was not likely that either would promote a confrontation with ballistic missiles. The Soviet philosophy toward limited and local war had become ambiguous and further complicated U.S. calculations. In 1958 the possibility of Soviet intervention, as viewed by American policy makers, was very remote. However, some key decision makers believed intervention was quite possible in the latter stages of the 1967 Middle East crisis. It was generally felt in both situations that the Soviet Union would avoid intervention in the face of resolute American action. Nonetheless, the possibility of Soviet intervention was greater in 1967.

12.2.2 DEFENSE ESTIMATES OF U.S. CAPABILITY Throughout the Quemoy crisis U.S. defense estimates indicated that any military problem concerning a challenge in the Formosa Strait could be circumvented. The number of military reinforcements sent into the area may have been an overreaction, but it is significant that a force of this strength was available. In 1958 some U.S. military leaders, as well as Chiang Kai-shek, had to be restrained. In 1967, however, the Joint Chiefs wanted to avoid military involvement in another limited war situation; a massive sustained buildup would have been a heavier strain.

Quemoy involved primarily the use of naval and air power. But effective intervention in the Middle East in 1967 might have necessitated landing troops. The Middle East, therefore, was a more difficult military problem for the United States in relation to its capabilities and other involvements. However, American power in the Mediterranean was strong enough to maintain a favorable balance vis-à-vis the Russians. Localized Soviet intervention by sea or air would have been difficult if challenged by U.S. forces. In 1958 the U.S. military establishment also had many shortcomings in capability, particularly for limited war contingencies. However, it had a greater capacity in relation to that of the Soviets in both strategic weapons and ability to project power to a distant area. There was also more political acceptance of using tactical nuclear weapons to make up for disparities. In 1958 the United States planned to use these weapons under certain circumstances; in 1967 it would have been extremely reluctant to do so. For a variety of reasons, defense estimates of capability to cope effectively were relatively lower in 1967.

12.2.3 ESTIMATES OF CONGRESSIONAL AND PUBLIC SUPPORT Significant public opposition to involvement existed during both crises. Policy choices were made in an atmosphere of domestic criticism of the global role of the United States. For example, Senator William Fulbright complained in 1958 that "If we go on as we are, soon—in the fashion of the cat on the hot tin roof—we shall be skipping from one crisis to another all over the globe, unable to get our footing anywhere."[10] In 1967 Senator Fulbright stated in strikingly similar language that "Having now experienced the frenetic mobility of the 1960s, the overheated activisim and the ubiquitous developments in the mounting sense of a global mission often referred to as the responsibilities of power, I now see merit that I formerly did not in occasional delay or inaction."[11] These sentiments had been less widely shared in 1958. Policy was made in 1967 with a deep sensitivity to preexisting dissension toward worldwide commitments and greater political pressures as well as a more convincing legal argument for the White House to seek congressional approval before involving American military forces. It is doubtful that Congress would have approved any act of direct military support for Israel unless that nation were in serious danger of being subjected to attack by Soviet forces. This attitude was especially relevant to unilateral precrisis initiatives. However, in the middle of the critical confrontation with the USSR, when minutes seemed important, sentiment against unilateral action was almost irrelevant to presidential decisions.

In the case of Quemoy, opinion opposed to the government's involvement was not a significant influence until after the major policy decisions had been made and publicized. The President had a mandate to use his judgment, and Congress adjourned as the shelling began. The President probably would have gotten support for action in defense of Quemoy if he had called Congress back into session, although such a judgment is highly speculative. The margin of approval, of course, would have been much smaller than it was when the Formosa resolution was passed in 1955. The Democrats were divided in 1958 on the Quemoy issue.

In both situations sentiment against involvement was offset by the determination of a key decision maker to persevere in spite of opposition. In 1958 Secretary Dulles was willing to stand up to opponents of his policy both inside and outside the State Department. Almost a decade later the personal conviction of President Johnson was that America had obligations to Israel.

In comparing the situations, however, there appeared to be less domestic support for American involvement in 1967.

[10]U.S., Senate, *Congressional Record*, 85th Cong., 2nd sess., vol. 104, part 13 (August 6, 1958), p. 16318. Fulbright speech, "On the Brink of Disaster."
[11]U.S., Senate, Committee on Foreign Relations, *U.S. Commitments to Foreign Powers*. 90th Cong., 1st sess. (Washington, 1967), pp. 2, 3. Opening Statement of Chairman J. W. Fulbright. Although this statement was made in August, it is representative of Senator Fulbright's attitude toward the American role in the world throughout 1967.

12.2.4 DEPENDENCE ON BRITISH SUPPORT There was also greater dependence on the British in dealing with the Arab-Israeli conflict in 1967. Although the United Kingdom was not assisting the United States in Vietnam, the presence of British carriers, both north and south of the Suez Canal, indicated to Moscow that it had to reckon with Washington and London. The Kremlin could not count on the United States being isolated politically, nor could it simply compare Soviet naval power with that of the Sixth Fleet. Augmented by U.K. warships, the U.S. Navy was considerably more powerful. The presence of relatively strong British forces in the region of Aden meant that units were available on short notice to test the Gulf of Aqaba blockade even against opposition by the Egyptian navy. For psychological reasons Washington needed British participation in any move to break the blockade. When London dampened its enthusiasm for an allied maritime force, it decreased the probability of the move.

British moral backing would have been useful in 1958, but Washington withstood critical opinion and took the action it felt was necessary. British forces did help stabilize the Lebanon-Jordan situation in 1958, and Anglo-American cooperation in the Middle East decreased the impact of international isolation during the offshore islands test. Washington was more encumbered during the buildup period of the 1967 crisis.

An appreciation of the estimated influence of the various factors in each situation can be gained by comparing them on a chart of one of the possible alternatives. (See Figure 12.1.) There are, of course, many other factors that enter into any comparison of this type. The

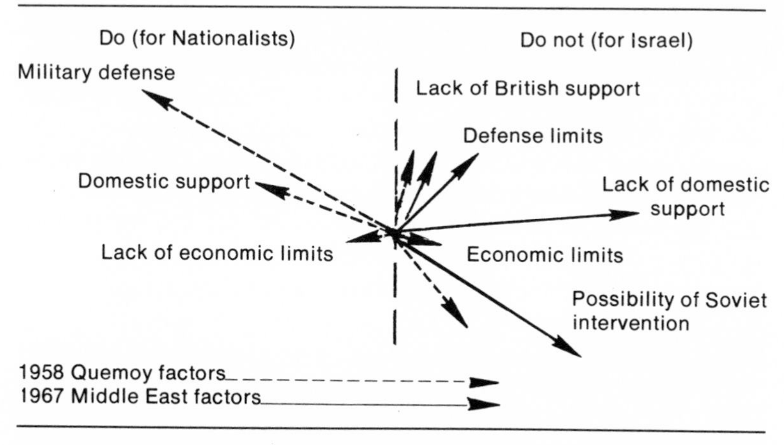

Figure 12.1 Comparison of effect of capability factors in each multicrisis on a show of military support with intent to use force if required

extent of commitment, the need for U.S. aid, and the context in which the decisions were formulated were completely different in each situation. However, the general trends show that capability factors were more favorable in one case than in the other. In 1958 the predominant capability factor was confident military estimates. In 1967 military limitations, lack of domestic support, and the possibility of Soviet intervention were significant factors, along with Middle Eastern political considerations, against any direct action. Capability is, of course, just one of the variables in the decision equation. Even with greater limitations in 1967 the United States was ready to respond to intervention of the Soviet Union.

12.3 INFLUENCE OF A PREEXISTING CRISIS SITUATION

There were a number of similarities in the influence of a prior involvement on the ability to cope effectively with a second crisis. It is in the degree of magnitude that differences can be observed between the two critical situations. If the United States had become involved in fighting in Lebanon, the negative influence of that involvement would have been greater. However, since the Quemoy crisis came shortly after the Lebanon landings, an isolationist reaction to U.S. engagement probably would not have developed domestically to the extent that it did in 1967 because of the arduous, seemingly endless struggle in Vietnam.

12.3.1 SOVIET INTENTIONS TO INTERVENE It is speculated that in both cases the prior involvement caused the Soviets to be less inclined to intervene. There were, of course, many more significant reasons for Moscow to avoid intervention than the existence of another crisis. Intervention may have been a slightly more inviting alternative in the Mideast in 1967 because the United States was more tied down in Vietnam and the relative U.S. military strength in the rest of the world had decreased. But it was the plight of Soviet clients that eventually raised the possibility of Russian intervention. Such actions, if taken, would have been aimed at Israel rather than the United States directly. With a clear expression of U.S. determination to respond to intervention, the Soviets seemed to refrain, although the important test of June 10, 1967, was not long enough to demonstrate Soviet reactions to U.S. determination.

12.3.2 DEFENSE ESTIMATES OF U.S. CAPABILITY Each preexisting crisis tended to make the military less anxious to take on another commitment, at least from a capabilities standpoint.[12] But the strain

[12] It may, however, have been considered important from a psychological point of view to show that U.S. involvement in another crisis did not preclude an American reaction.

of Vietnam was much greater. The ready power that could be committed to defend Quemoy was substantially larger.

12.3.3 ESTIMATE OF CONGRESSIONAL AND PUBLIC SUPPORT During both of these multicrisis situations the negative influence of a simultaneous involvement was felt. However, the positive effect of the Lebanon success had not worn off at the time crucial Quemoy decisions were made. On the other hand, in the case of Vietnam, the duration of that war had allowed dissident opinion to grow and consolidate. There were, of course, many other factors that contributed to the greater influence of opinion opposed to involvement during the buildup phase of the 1967 crisis.

Nevertheless, it is speculated that toward the end of the second phase of the crisis the percentage division of opinion on the Quemoy issue reached about the same numerical proportions as that which existed in 1967 concerning Vietnam. However, the impact of the two experiences was much different. The concerned public was substantially larger in 1967, and the intensity of feeling was greater. Domestic desire to avoid a second involvement was much stronger in the case of the Arab-Israeli conflict. Action in Lebanon was viewed as a success,[13] whereas Vietnam was a disappointing stalemate.

During the Arab-Israeli war there was less congressional criticism of the absence of a legal U.S. obligation to act but more stress on the need to avoid involvement in another remote area of the world. The criticism was rooted in frustration with the Vietnamese experience rather than the tenuous and questionable responsibility for Israel's welfare or careful assessment of American security interests.

12.3.4 DEPENDENCE ON BRITISH SUPPORT The world policeman image fostered by circumstances in Vietnam contributed to the greater need for allied military and psychological support in 1967. In both multicrises the value of the United Kingdom's contribution to global peace-keeping and deterrence of the USSR was demonstrated. In 1958 and 1967 Britain engaged in operations in other parts of the world which facilitated U.S. concentration of attention and resources on its other crisis problem.

The overall comparison indicates that the Vietnamese situation had a much greater limiting influence on capability of the United States to cope effectively with a second test. The Soviets had gained relatively in available military strength, U.S. defense capabil-

[13]The word "success" may be, in some senses, misleading since the coup in Iraq, for example, was a loss for the West. However, preventing further losses and stabilizing the situation in the Middle East for a number of years to come without a soldier being killed could be called a "success."

ity was lower in other regions of the world, Congress and the public were more reluctant to approve involvement, and support from the United Kingdom was more essential to the conduct of American foreign policy. If the Quemoy crisis had developed in 1967, there would have been less capability to intervene than existed in 1958.

12.4 COMPARISON OF THE EFFECTIVENESS OF NAVAL FORCES AS INSTRUMENTS OF AMERICAN POLICY

While it has been concluded that employment of naval forces closed options to the Soviet Union in both situations, it is difficult to measure and compare the relative degrees of effectiveness.[14] Since the possibility of Soviet intervention was greater in the 1967 crisis, it would seem to follow logically that U.S. forces were more effective vis-à-vis the Soviets in that confrontation. Whether Russia would have intervened if there had been no American forces in the Mediterranean or Formosa Strait in 1958 is highly speculative; however; there was a greater likelihood of Soviet intervention in 1967.

In evaluating effectiveness, more than just deterrence of possible Soviet intervention must be considered. In 1958 Peking as well as Moscow appeared to have been discouraged from acting. The strong American response to the initial shelling of Quemoy seemingly had a greater influence on Mao than the movement of ships to the Eastern Mediterranean had on Nasser.

The United States did not take the initiative in either buildup phase. It was the Soviets who augmented their weaker forces just prior to the June war. However, by the nature of the ships sent, this move appeared to be a low-risk political response rather than a military challenge to the Sixth Fleet. Policy makers in Washington and officers of the Sixth Fleet were not impressed. Nevertheless, in 1958 Russian ships were not deployed. This contrast did not necessarily indicate a lessening of Soviet respect for U.S. naval capability in the interim. Rather, it seemed to reflect different political objectives and increased Soviet naval capabilities.

The United States made a bolder and more ostentatious show of force during the Quemoy crisis; but in 1967 movements were also meant as a signal to Moscow that the United States intended to keep the Soviet Union out. In 1958 Washington wanted to deter a Chinese attack; in 1967 the United States also desired to prevent an assault on Israel by Egypt, but the task was complicated by the political problem of having friends on both sides of the Arab-Israeli dispute.

[14] There were so many other variables involved that it is difficult to differentiate the influence of naval moves from other interacting factors.

Washington tried to restrain both Taipei and Tel Aviv. American caution in the buildup period of each dispute was not based on fear of Soviet military capability. Rather, Washington felt such tactics would better prevent aggravation and escalation of the situation, avoid great power involvement, and keep from overly encouraging Israel and the Republic of China. As it turned out, neither China nor Egypt initiated an actual invasion. However, the maneuvers of the Seventh Fleet in the Formosa Strait probably were more of a deterrent than those of the Sixth Fleet in the Eastern Mediterranean in 1967.

In both situations, the fleet provided defense in depth. Emphasis was placed on the Israeli and Nationalist self-help. However, in 1958 it became virtually certain that American forces would be used if necessary to hold the offshore islands, with or without Soviet intervention. The situation was less definite for most of the 1967 crisis.

Although it might seem that the impressive buildup in 1958 was a more effective tactic than the relatively subtle and restrained style of 1967, such a conclusion is not necessarily valid. While it is quite possible that the United States would have employed the same approach to a hypothetical 1967 Quemoy crisis as it did in 1958, the Middle Eastern situation was much more complicated in 1967 than in 1958. The Lebanon landings would have been difficult to duplicate in 1967. Of course, Lebanon was a slightly simpler problem because the United States was answering the request of a "moderate" Arab nation. American peace-keeping efforts never got beyond the planning stage in 1967, but there were no efforts at all in the Formosa Strait until after heavy shelling had begun. Undoubtedly, the strong augmentation of forces in the Taiwan area had some influence in convincing the Chinese to calm the conflict. Even though important reinforcements did not reach the area until after China had agreed to talks, the commitment of additional warships was well advertised. In 1967 the U.S. presence seemingly had little influence on preventing heavy fighting. However, it may have kept the Soviets from trying to prolong the war by intervention or indirect aid. The maneuvers of the Sixth Fleet on June 6, 1967, may have influenced Moscow's position concerning Egypt. It is speculated that if the battle in Syria had continued on June 10, 1967, the movement of Sixth Fleet units toward the east probably would have caused cancellation of any Soviet intentions to intervene militarily. In that sense, U.S. warships played a restraining role by making American resolve clearer. Unless Moscow wanted a third world war, direct involvement would have been a risky adventure based on a remote hope that Washington was bluffing.

Although ship movements might have been utilized even more effectively, U.S. fleets played an important part in both crises. Comparing their degrees of effectiveness defies a simple explanation; the similarities in techniques employed are easier to discern. (See Table 12.2.)

Table 12.2 Similarities in Employment of Naval Forces in the Two Crises

Phase	Quemoy 1958	Mideast 1967	Intended Meanings
Buildup	Marine amphibious force on liberty in Singapore	Marine amphibious force on liberty in Malta	United States desire to play down crisis. No troop requirement anticipated
	Half carrier-cruiser force at Subic Bay, Philippines, 525 miles away; fleet ready but not in immediate vicinity	Carrier-cruiser force positioned near Crete, at least 450 miles from area of conflict; fleet ready but well clear	Ability to respond quickly with aircraft; attempt to encourage restraint; United States not looking for trouble
		Intrepid removal to Vietnam; antisubmarine warfare exercise rescheduled for Mediterranean; *Dyess* moved south of Suez	United States not anticipating offensive action; bolstering defenses
First Crisis	Seventh Fleet movement into Formosa Strait	Sixth Fleet movement to the east on second day and again on sixth day	United States intention to prevent outside interference and to defend allies if necessary
	United States refusal to convoy operations for thirteen days	Lack of U.S. provisions for direct help for Israel	United States reluctance to become involved prematurely
	Ordering of major augmenting force	No significant augmentation	Reinforcement of U.S. determination
Second Crisis	Arrival of augmenting forces	Orders prepared for augmenting forces on June 10	United States determination to sustain its presence; serious about protecting allies

12.5 COMPARISON OF ADEQUACY OF CONVENTIONAL NAVAL FORCES TO MEET THE DEMANDS OF THE MULTICRISIS

The conventional capabilities of the U.S. Navy in 1958 and 1967 were quite similar. There were fifteen attack carriers in commission during both periods. In comparing the adequacy of naval forces the question of *adequacy to do what* must again be raised. In 1958 there was a ready backup force that was utilized. But the challenge was of a different nature. In 1958 warships were employed to deter a heavy Chinese bomber attack and potential amphibious invasion. Interposed between the Chinese and their island objectives, the ships served as obstacles to further escalation of the war. In 1967 the paramount need was to deter the Soviet Union from acting. This, the existing force was apparently capable of doing. The fleet operating on the periphery could not interpose itself between the Israelis and Arabs, even if marine forces had been at full strength. It was believed in Washington that a strong American show of strength would only increase the chance of the outbreak of hostilities. As previously indicated, this consideration, rather than inadequacy of American military power, better explained the restrained posture of the Sixth Fleet throughout the buildup phase. The peace-keeping mission was directed toward only one part of the problem: elimination of the Israeli *casus belli* of free passage through the Straits of Tiran. While restrictions on available forces contributed to the delay of forceful action concerning the Gulf of Aqaba, the major limitations were political and psychological rather than military.

Shortages, reduced backup forces, and the experience of Vietnam partially contributed to Washington's restrained position in 1967. But in 1958 the United States was also cautious with comparatively fewer military limitations. It was only after intensive bombardment began that a major show of strength in the area was made. Again, international political considerations rather than inadequate military capabilities predominated. While relatively weaker in 1967 than during the Quemoy crisis, U.S. forces were adequate to meet the immediate challenges in the Middle East.

13. SOVIET NAVAL EXPANSION

13.1 INTRODUCTION

The Middle East crisis of 1967 added a dimension to U.S. problem solving in crisis situations that did not exist during the Quemoy conflict. For the first time, the United States had to contend with a Soviet naval presence.[1] Russia has attempted to neutralize the influence of the Sixth Fleet and has been developing a Soviet capability to intervene in Third World crises. Therefore, U.S. decision making has now become more complicated in conflicts limited to conventional weapons because of credible opposing nuclear deterrent forces.

At the peak of tension prior to the outbreak of hostilities in the Middle East the Soviets doubled their Mediterranean naval force. In the aftermath of the crisis, they again doubled the number of warships. Subsequent port visits to certain Arab countries have been used to imply a Soviet shield.

Because of the publicity centered on the 1967 Middle East crisis, Soviet capability in the Mediterranean has been regarded as a new phenomenon. Actually, Russian warships had visited Egyptian ports frequently long before the crisis, the Soviet Mediterranean task force had been in existence since 1964, and construction of a helicopter carrier had begun in 1963.[2] However, deployed Soviet naval strength has increased since the 1967 crisis. The June war brought into sharp focus the significance of a Russian naval presence.

The first augmentation of Soviet surface ships following the Middle East war began on June 18, 1967, when three cruisers, five destroyers, and two auxiliaries entered the Mediterranean.[3] Significantly, this was well after the military situation had been clarified.[4] Since that time the number of Russian warships has usually varied

[1] There was a confrontation of sorts in the largely manufactured Syrian situation of September and October 1957. See J. M. Mackintosh, *Strategy and Tactics of Soviet Foreign Policy* (New York: Oxford University Press, 1963), pp. 227, 228.

[2] Phil G. Goulding, Assistant Secretary of Defense, address to Pittsburgh World Affairs Council, December 8, 1967, Duquesne University, Pittsburgh, Pa., p. 11. The first public revelation, however, did not occur until about five months after the June war.

[3] *The New York Times*, June 19, 1967, p. 70. Although it was reported at the same time that ten vessels would be withdrawn, they did not represent the power of the ships being sent into the Mediterranean. Two minesweepers, four patrol boats, an icebreaker, and a cruiser were withdrawn.

[4] Political maneuvering was still in progress and the moves may have been associated with the Kosygin visit to the United Nations which occurred at that time.

between thirty and fifty. Moscow apparently intends to maintain a base level of about forty ships in the Mediterranean on a permanent basis.[5] It seems likely that augmentations were intended to restore some prestige with Arab allies. The Soviets were doing practically nothing for Cairo when it was receiving a crushing defeat. The port visits, which emulate the pattern of twenty years of Sixth Fleet operations, received tremendous publicity. A dozen ships visited Port Said and Alexandria on July 10, 1967,[6] in a move calculated to show strong support for the Arabs. The crews in Port Said were not granted liberty and evidently put on alert following PT boat clashes between the Arabs and Israelis shortly after their arrival.[7] The ships were said to be "ready to repel any aggression,"[8] and a Soviet embassy spokesman who was asked what the ships were doing in the war zone responded, "we are not quite on a picnic."[9] Since then Russian ships have been maintained almost continuously in Egyptian ports. Alexandria, Port Said, and the Syrian port of Latakia are practically Soviet naval bases.[10]

The presence of Soviet vessels in Egyptian ports at the time of the sinking of the destroyer *Eilat* complicated the problem of Israeli retaliation. The commander of allied forces in southern Europe commented,

> When Egyptian missiles from the harbour of Port Said sank the Israeli destroyer 'Eilat,' there were Soviet warships in the harbour. Therefore the Israelis could not strike back in that harbour. This shows that really a new situation has arisen in the Mediterranean, which greatly affects the political and the psychological factors.[11]

This is the reason the Israelis selected shelling of Egyptian refiner-

[5]Chief of Naval Operations, Admiral Thomas H. Moorer, USN, testified in October 1968 that a level of approximately forty ships is expected to be a "permanent deployment on their [the Russians] part." Testimony of Admiral Moorer in U.S., Congress, House, Special Subcommittee on Sea Power, Committee on Armed Services, *Status of Naval Ships,* 90th Cong., 2nd sess. (Washington, 1969), p. 150.

[6]This move was announced by the Soviet press, Moscow Tass International Service in English, July 9, 1967. The Soviets previously had only rarely announced movements of their ships. The Russian vessels included a missile cruiser, two destroyers, four assault ships, and tankers.

[7]Bombay Press Trust India in English, 1835 GMT, July 13, 1967 (radio broadcast). *The New York Times,* July 13, 1967, p. 1.

[8]Randolph S. Churchill and Winston S. Churchill, *The Six Day War* (Boston: Houghton Mifflin Co., 1967), p. 207. This statement reputedly was made by Adm. Molotsov, the Russian commander.

[9]Bombay Press Trust India in English, July 13, 1967.

[10]Transcript of German television interview with Adm. Horacio Rivero, USN, supplied by letter from Comdr. W. A. Cockell, USN, executive assistant to Admiral Rivero, to Lt. Comdr. J. T. Howe, USN, dated August 13, 1968.

[11]Interview between Adm. Horacio Rivero, CinC South, and German magazine *Der Spiegel,* May 1968. Transcript provided by Comdr. W. A. Cockell, USN, Executive Assistant to Adm. Rivero, in letter of August 13, 1968.

ies as their method of retaliation. Soviet forces were dramatically augmented at Port Said immediately after the Israeli shelling. Admiral Rivero subsequently observed that Soviet ships made Egyptian harbors "a sanctuary that cannot be attacked without involving a direct confrontation with the Soviets."[12]

Moscow has also shown great interest in the Red Sea and Indian Ocean areas. Since March 1968 a Soviet naval presence has been demonstrated with increasing frequency. There have been a number of reports of Soviet efforts to obtain the use of air and naval facilities in the area. The Russians helped build the ports of Hodeida in Yemen and Berbera in Somalia.[13] Reportedly, they have built airfields in Sudan and have use of a naval base at Port Sudan, and there are rumors that the Russian navy has been given permission to use the former Royal Navy base at Aden in southern Yemen as well as facilities on the island of Socotra which is strategically located at the entrance of the Gulf of Aden.[14] They are evidently seeking refueling facilities in East Pakistan and reportedly are interested in obtaining use of facilities in Singapore and on the island of Mauritius.[15] It has been claimed that by spacing the delivery of Soviet submarines to India and maintaining Soviet naval technicians, the Soviets are acquiring a *de facto* base in the Indian Ocean at Vishakhapatnam on the Bay of Bengal.[16] In addition speculation continues that the former French base at Mers el Kébir in Algeria will fall to the Soviets, giving them a base at the western end of the Mediterranean, but the Algerians have denied that this is a possibility.[17]

It is not certain either that the Soviets particularly want bases or

[12]Interview with Admiral H. J. Rivero, USN, in *Lo Speiccho*, February 11, 1969, transcript provided by Capt. J. J. Ness, USN, of Admiral Rivero's staff in letter dated April 2, 1969.

[13]*The Christian Science Monitor,* December 15, 1967, p. 6. J. K. Cooley said on July 2, 1968, "Facilities at Hodeida might be available if the Russians ever chose to put combat air units into the Red Sea Area." *The Christian Science Monitor,* July 2, 1968, p. 4. The Soviets are apparently in the process of obtaining base facilities there. James D. Atkinson, "Who Will Dominate the Strategic Indian Ocean Area in the 1970s?," *Navy Magazine* (September 1968). For one of the many reports of efforts in Somalia see Denes Warner, "Memo from the Indian Ocean," *Look* (July 15, 1969).

[14]This report is attributed to "indiscretions of sources in close contact with the Russians in Egypt." *Roma*, January 13, 1969. Information about Socotra is reported in "Russia: Toward a Global Reach," *Time*, Vol. 96, No. 14 (October 5, 1970).

[15]*The Christian Science Monitor* article "Soviet Refueling Deal," August 3, 1968.

[16]Editorial board, *The Asia Letter,* January 11, 1969.

[17]See *The Christian Science Monitor,* April 19, 1968. See also *The New York Times* article "French Leaving Algeria Base; No Soviet Move Expected Soon," January 28, 1968, p. 15.

that the nationalist-minded Third World countries are about to give them away. As the USSR Navy has become more self-sustaining, the operation of such facilities is of reduced military value. However, the bases do afford convenient footholds for further political subversion and penetration into the Third World areas and possible sites for airfields to make up for Russia's lack of attack aircraft carriers. The Soviet Union's interest in increasing its political influence in these regions of the world has been reflected in highly publicized visits of Russian warships to many countries including India, Somalia, Iran, Pakistan, Iraq, Yemen, Algeria, Tanzania, Libya, Ceylon, Cambodia, and even Cuba. The Russian navy has been assigned a growing role in Moscow's attempts to increase influence in the Third World. Among the advertised purposes of Soviet ship visits to thirty-eight countries in 1969 was "supporting the national liberation movement."[18] "The presence of Russian warships in the Mediterranean," according to the Russian Naval Chief of Staff, is "in fulfillment of our duty as internationalists to safeguard peace and the security of *all* peoples."[19]

13.2 RECENT DEVELOPMENT OF SOVIET NAVAL CAPABILITY FOR OPERATIONS IN THE THIRD WORLD

Although the Soviet surface fleet was downgraded during most of the Khrushchev era,[20] Russia simply shifted emphasis from massive building programs to improvements in quality. Today, in addition to developing a first class nuclear attack and missile submarine force, the Russians are building surface combatants with "modern armament, electronic, and propulsion systems."[21] One of the most significant developments has been the installation of surface-to-air

[18] *Izvestiya* article by Navy Political Directorate Chief Admiral V. Grishanov, "Always on the Move," July 26, 1970. p. 1. Moscow claimed the purpose of the first cruise of Soviet ships to India was to "further develop friendly relations" and to *"strengthen ties between armed forces."* (Emphasis added.) Captain 1st Rank V. Mitin, "A Cruise to Friends," Soviet Military Review, No. 10 (October 1968), pp. 12–14.

[19] (Emphasis added.) Admiral Sergheev explained that this purpose was "apart from answering the purposes of defence of Russian and the other socialist countries." Interview with Admiral Nikolas Sergheev in the Italian Communist newspaper *L'Unita*, February 13, 1969. See also Tass statement in *Pravda*, November 24, 1968, p. 4, *CDSP*, Vol. XX No. 47, p. 6, which said approximately the same thing.

[20] In Khrushchev's 1960 report to the Supreme Soviet he announced drastic cuts in conventional forces. He said concerning naval forces, "In the Navy . . . surface ships can no longer play the role they played in the past." *Pravda* and *Izvestia*, January 15, 1960. *CDSP*, Vol. XII, No. 2 (February 19, 1960), p. 10.

[21] U.S. Navy, *Answers to Questions Concerning the Soviet Navy*, pamphlet provided by the U.S. Sixth Fleet, cleared on November 1, 1967, p. 20.

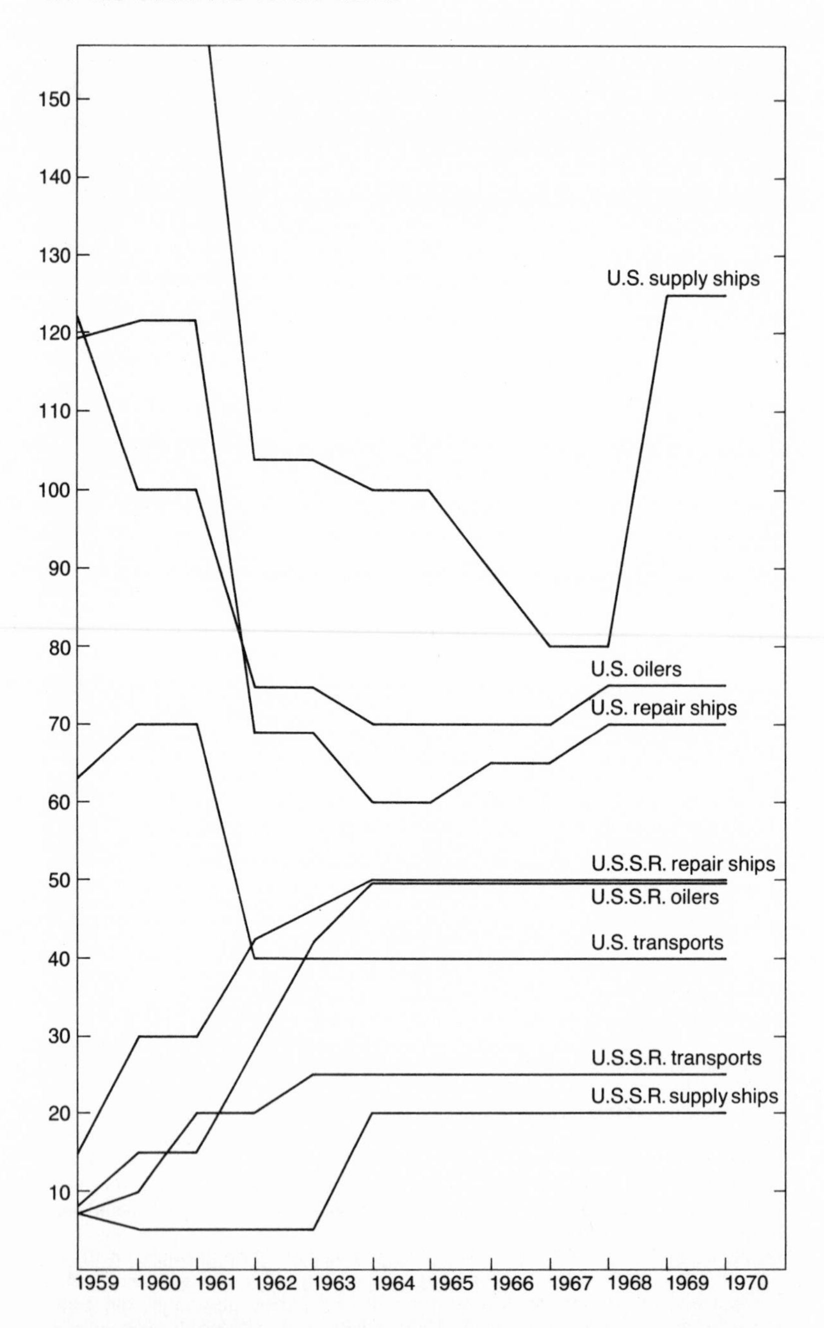

Figure 13.1 Comparison of number of repair ships, oilers, transports, and supply ships in American and Soviet navies from 1959 through 1970. Data from R. V. B. Blackman, *Jane's Fighting Ships* (London: Sampson Low, Marston and Co., Ltd., 1966), p. iv.

missiles and surface-to-surface missiles.[22] A new class of guided missile cruisers with helicopter hangars, surface and antiaircraft missiles, and antisubmarine weapons unveiled in 1967 is typical of Soviet emphasis on quality.[23] The antishipping missiles are estimated to have a range of at least 400 miles.[24]

Another significant change is the construction of ships necessary to project and sustain a fleet beyond Russian shores. A substantial increase in the numbers of oilers, repair ships, transports, and supply ships occurred between 1961 and 1964. (See Figure 13.1.) This increase in capability paralleled more highly publicized developments such as construction of a helicopter carrier and reactivation of the Marine Corps.

It prepared the way for stepped-up Russian naval operations beginning in 1964. The apparent leveling out of construction of these ship types may indicate that the Soviets do not presently plan to expand the size of the surface navy or the tempo of its operations. The USSR merchant fleet, however, which contains comparable ship types, continues to expand.

Great attention has been given to Russian construction of small aircraft carriers.[25] The first is not large enough for jet aircraft and apparently will be used in a dual role as a helicopter carrier in support of amphibious assault operations and as an antisubmarine warfare ship to counter Polaris submarines. During its first deployment to the Mediterranean in the fall of 1968 and subsequent operations, the *Moskva* has engaged primarily in antisubmarine training. The second helicopter carrier, *Leningrad,* has also engaged in extensive antisubmarine activities and has been described by the Soviets as an "antisubmarine cruiser."[26]

[22]There are some twenty cruisers and destroyers and sixty submarines fitted with surface-to-surface missiles. Remarks of Adm. Thomas H. Moorer, USN, Chief of Naval Operations before the American Bar Foundation, Chicago, Illinois, January 25, 1969, p. 3.

[23]A picture of the ship appeared in *U.S. News and World Report,* November 6, 1967, p. 14. There are estimated to be close to ten of these ships presently operational in the Soviet navy.

[24]Information supplied by Office of Naval Intelligence, *Status of Naval Ships,* p. 241.

[25]The information was first announced in reports of interviews with Admiral E. P. Holmes, USN, CinC Atlantic Fleet, and Vice Admiral W. E. Ellis, USN, Chief of Staff, U.S. Atlantic Fleet. The following accounts of the interviews provide slightly different information: *The New York Times* article by William Beecher, October 23, 1967, p. 1; *The Boston Globe* story by United Press International, October 23, 1967. The carrier was actually at sea in the spring of 1967. The ship is named *Moskva.*

[26]A description of the *Leningrad* trailing a submarine in the Mediterranean using helicopter "radio buoys" and ship's sonar is contained in *Red Star*

The Soviet counterpart is smaller than U.S. antisubmarine warfare carriers and is about the size of U.S. amphibious helicopter carriers.[27] It is estimated to carry twenty-five to thirty-five helicopters; thus it has the same capacity as U.S. helicopter carriers, designated LPH. In design concept, however, it more closely resembles the American LPD, or amphibious dock. This U.S. ship has a helicopter platform in the after section as does the Soviet ship, and it combines capabilities to transport and land troops either via helicopter or landing craft.[28] There is speculation that more Soviet vessels of this type are being constructed.[29] In addition to parallel developments of amphibious capability the very lengthy and detailed description of U.S. helicopter carriers in an article by Fleet Admiral Kasatonov[30] seems to be indicative of a Soviet special interest in the amphibious potential for this type of vessel even though this mission has not been emphasized during initial training.

Many authorities believe the Soviets will go on to build large attack carriers.[31] However, in February 1967 the Commander in Chief of the USSR Navy seemed to disavow any desire for carriers by saying that

> . . . the combat potential even of nuclear powered aircraft carriers is inferior to the strike potentials of submarine and air forces. Analyzing the development of the Soviet Navy as well as of the navies

article by Engr. Maj. A. Kontiyevskiy, "Contact," April 23, 1970, p. 4. The Soviets have described the "antisubmarine warfare cruiser" *Moskva* as a "mobile base for ASW [antisubmarine warfare] helicopters that locate submarines at a considerable distance from the ship." Tass International Service in English, April 14, 1970.

[27]United States attack carriers range from 42,000 to 85,000 tons; antisubmarine carriers from 40,000 to 42,000 tons; U.S. helicopter carriers from 18,000 to 33,000 tons; Soviet carriers are 18,000 tons; and U.S. amphibious landing ship docks are 17,150 tons.

[28]The Soviet carrier is 650 feet long. The only flight deck space is in the after half of the ship. American LPDs (of the Austin class) are 569 feet long and have a flight deck 219 feet in length. Goulding, address, pp. 11, 12. The ship has a surface-to-air missile system forward.

[29]*The New York Times* reported on February 14, 1968, that a third Soviet carrier was believed to be on the ways. Adm. Charles D. Griffin, Commander of NATO Forces in southern Europe said on February 14, 1968, that "a number of helicopter carriers are now under construction." *Navy Times*, February 14, 1968.

[30]Fleet Adm. V. Kasatonov, "Strategy of Aggression on the Sea," *Izvestia*, January 9, 1966.

[31]See, for example, Adm. Charles D. Griffin, "Now Russia Builds Up Power," p. 50; *Navy Times* review of *Jane's Fighting Ships 1967–68*, December 6, 1967, p. 33; Rivero transcript of *Der Spiegel* interview, May 1968. Admiral E. P. Holmes, USN, Commander of the Atlantic Fleet, said, "with their growing awareness of NATO strategy, it wouldn't surprise me a bit if they decided to have carriers for high performance aircraft." *The New York Times*, October 23, 1967, p. 1.

of other naval powers, we become more and more convinced that we have chosen the correct direction for the buildup of our navy.[32]

The Kremlin may not yet be ready to pay the heavy cost of modern jet carriers. For now at least, it is a serious Soviet shortcoming in comparison with U.S. naval strength. The Russians could, of course, equip their helicopter carriers with high-performance vertical-takeoff aircraft. It is estimated that the *Moskva* could accommodate up to forty of these warplanes.[33]

Russia's modern shore-based air arm, which includes naval aircraft with air-to-surface missiles, makes up for some of the deficiency in carrier air power, but it cannot support operations on all the "world ocean." Even in the Mediterranean, Moscow might have difficulty obtaining permission for overflights from countries that block their access.[34] However, if Russia gains control of airfields in the Mediterranean and Red Sea coastal regions, the present weakness will be diminished considerably. Reportedly, Soviet manned aircraft with Egyptian markings have been flying from Cairo airfields over elements of the Sixth Fleet.[35]

Another important trend is the construction of oceangoing landing ships. Vessels similar to the U.S. landing ship tank were first constructed in 1965 and commissioned in 1966. Pictures of these craft are now featured prominently in Soviet military publications, and

[32]Fleet Adm. S. Gorshkov, USSR, "Soviet Naval Art," *Soviet Military Review*, No. 7 (July 1967), p. 4. Reprinted from *Morskoi Sbornik*, No. 2 (February 1967).

[33]The Soviets apparently have operated vertical-takeoff aircraft but not from seaborne platforms. See the exchange on the possibility of this installation on Russian carriers in U.S., Congress, House, Committee on Armed Services, *Hearings on Military Posture An Act (S.3293)*, 90th Cong., 2nd sess. (Washington, 1968), pp. 8746–8748. Testimony of Dr. John Foster, Director of Defense Research and Engineering, May 2, 1968. A similar role for the Soviet multipurpose vessel was envisioned by Vice Adm. Turner F. Caldwell, Director of Antisubmarine warfare programs, Office of Chief of Naval Operations. *The New York Times*, October 9, 1968.

[34]This is, of course, a political problem similar to that faced by the United States when flying troops to Lebanon from Germany in 1958. There is no absolute guarantee that the Russians would not violate overflight rights in peacetime, and such restrictions would be of little practical inhibition in time of war. During the 1967 Middle East crisis Soviet planes flew over Yugoslavian airspace.

[35]*The New York Times* article by Hanson W. Baldwin, "Outlook in the Mideast," March 16, 1969, p. 24. Admiral Horacio Rivero, CinC Allied Forces Southern Europe, said on March 24, 1969, that "right now we have no proof of any Soviet air in the Mediterranean at all." However, because of the sophisticated equipment in Soviet built reconnaissance aircraft with Egyptian markings reconnoitering with NATO naval forces, he speculated that at least some of the crews have Soviet technicians. Interview of Admiral Rivero by Mr. Louis Flemming of *The Los Angeles Times*, March 24, 1969. Transcript supplied by Captain J. J. Nuss, USN, in letter of April 2, 1969.

there has been a marked increase in the total number of landing ships in the Soviet navy. The construction of transports, helicopter carriers, and landing ships is a significant indication that the Soviets are developing a new, modern amphibious capability.

The reactivation of the Russian Marine Corps, which is essential for a rapid show of force in world trouble spots, was an important clue that the Soviets were putting new emphasis on limited war capability. Initial hints that the Soviets had made the decision to reactivate an amphibious capability appeared in 1964.[36] The first pictures of Soviet marine units in action appeared in *Red Star* in connection with Navy Day 1964.[37] Specific reference to the Marine Corps was made in a speech in 1965.[38] On Navy Day 1966 there were many references to the Marines. "Highly mobile marine units" were said to be "developing on a *new* material basis"[39] and Admiral Gorshkov reported that "Marines are successfully mastering combat equipment, weapons, and tactics and are improving them in the course of their training." In addition, Fleet Admiral Kasatonov said, "our marines are now quite different from what they were in the war."[40] Marine capability is now a common theme in Soviet Navy Day speeches.[41]

Soviet amphibious capability is still relatively small and limited. However, the number of marines may be increasing rapidly. Estimates of 3000 men in 1966[42] doubled in 1967[43] and reached 15,000 in 1970.[44]

[36]*The Military Balance, 1964–1965* (London: Institute for Strategic Studies, 1964), p. 6. The decision to construct an amphibious carrier had, however, been made earlier.

[37]*Red Star,* July 24, 1964. T. W. Wolfe, *Trends in Soviet Thinking on Theater Warfare, Conventional Operations, and Limited War,* Rand Memo 4305-PR, December 1964 (Santa Monica: Rand Corporation, 1964), p. 104.

[38]Fleet Adm. S. Gorshkov, "Loyal Sons of the Homeland," *Pravda,* July 24, 1965, p. 2. *CDSP,* Vol. XVII, No. 30, p. 14.

[39](Emphasis added.) Moscow Tass International Service in English, July 30, 1966.

[40]Fleet Adm. V. Kasatonov, interview by *Trud* correspondent, Moscow Domestic Service in Russian, July 30, 1966.

[41]For example see, Fleet Adm. S. G. Gorshkov remarks at Navy Day celebrations in Leningrad, Moscow Domestic Service, July 30, 1967; Admiral Vinogradov talk, Moscow in Turkish to Turkey, July 29, 1967; interview with Vice Adm. G. M. Yegoroy, Deputy CinC USSR Navy in Moscow *Sovetskaya Rossiy*, July 30, 1967; Fleet Adm. V. A. Kasatonov, Moscow Domestic Service in Russian, July 29, 1967; *Red Star*, July 28, 1968, Fleet Admiral V. Kasatonov; *Rural Life,* July 29, 1968, Adm. S. M. Lobov.

[42]*The Military Balance 1966–1967* (London: Institute for Strategic Studies, 1966), p. 5.

[43]*The Military Balance 1967–1968* (London: Institute for Strategic Studies, 1967), p. 8.

[44]*The Military Balance 1970–1971* (London: Institute for Strategic Studies, 1970). p. 9. The estimate of the Institute for Strategic Studies as of July

The Russians are giving the new marines the image of an elite corps. Admiral Kasatonov said in 1966, "Our marines are courageous, and full of endurance, combining the habit of soldier, sailor, and scout. They wear a beautiful naval uniform with a black beret and short boots."[45] The appearance of these troops in the Fiftieth Anniversary Parade in Moscow in November 1967 dramatized their new place in military thinking. About 600 marines marched "at a modified goose step" and were dressed in black jackets trimmed with gold and wearing black berets.[46]

This new elite group has been provided modern amphibious equipment. As early as 1965 it was asserted that "the marines have been equipped with modern weapons." [47] In 1966 "modern floating technology, armored transport, tanks, and other means" were reputedly available.[48] And in July 1967 a Soviet admiral asserted that the " . . . naval infantry has special armament and various types of amphibious equipment. Landing ships with naval infantrymen can *surmount vast spaces of water* and quickly put the men ashore."[49] (Emphasis added.) Other speeches have stressed the "modern combat means" of marines.[50] A Soviet article in September 1963 contained a detailed description of the advantages helicopter techniques give the U.S. marines in amphibious operations, and it included a picture of twenty Soviet helicopters flying in formation.[51] In recent years there have been a number of pictures of Soviet amphibious training.[52] Although there may still be some question as to

1968 was 8000 marines. *The Military Balance 1968–1969* (London: Institute for Strategic Studies, 1968), p. 8.

[45]Kasatonov, Domestic Service, July 30, 1966.

[46]*The New York Times* article by Henry Kamm, November 8, 1967, p. 12, and *Philadelphia Bulletin* column by M. Whiteleather, November 15, 1967, p. 16. *Navy Times* article "Russians Seen Starting Amphibious Force," December 1967.

[47]Fleet Adm. S. G. Gorshkov, "Naval Might of Soviet Power," *Soviet Military Review,* No. 7 (July 1965), p. 6.

[48]Kasatonov, Domestic Service, July 30, 1966.

[49]Engr. Vice Adm. Kotov, Deputy Commander in Chief of the Navy, Moscow *Trud,* July 31, 1967, p. 1.

[50]Fleet Adm. S. G. Gorshkov, report of Leningrad celebrations, Moscow Domestic Service, July 30, 1967. Admiral Amelko, interview at Vladivostok Navy Day Review, Moscow Domestic Service in Russian, July 30, 1967. According to an article in July 1968 the new equipment includes "amphibious tanks, armored personnel carriers, and diverse radio-electronic equipment." Capt. 1st Rank F. Vodynin, "The Fighting Record of the Soviet Navy," *Soviet Military Review,* No. 7 (July 1968), p. 56.

[51]Capt. N. P. Vyunenko, "Soviet Amphibious Operations," *Soviet Naval Digest (Morskoi Sbornik)* (September 1963), translated by Col. L. J. Dulacki, USMC, *Marine Corps Gazette,* No. 49 (March 1965), pp. 29–33. Picture p. 32.

[52]Gorshkov, "Soviet Naval Art," p. 5. For other pictures of Soviet amphibious operations see Col. N. Taratorin, "Tanks Attack From Sea," *Soviet*

how large a capability the Soviets will develop, there can be no doubt that a modern marine arm has been created.

Essential to the development of mobile forces for limited naval warfare is the parallel creation of a frame of mind that allows their utilization. This failing rather than any significant physical defect appears to be one of the reasons why the world's second largest navy was impotent in the 1950s. It is only when forces are deployed on a long-term basis that defects in equipment are ironed out and the psychological outlook necessary for employment of forces is developed.

The call for an oceangoing philosophy was sounded as early as 1963 when the Commander in Chief of the Soviet navy stated, "In the past, our ships and naval aviation have operated primarily in off shore areas. . . . Now . . . we must be prepared through broad offensive operations to deliver crushing strikes against sea and ground targets of the imperialist *on any point of the world ocean*, and adjacent territories."[53] (Emphasis added.) Construction of the first carrier was begun at this time. The world ocean theme was mentioned frequently in subsequent Navy Day speeches,[54] with the claim by 1966 that an offensive capability had already been achieved. Fleet Admiral Gorshkov exclaimed in February 1966 that "the Naval flag of our fatherland is now flying in every latitude of the world ocean."[55] And Fleet Admiral Kasatonov stressed in July 1966 that the purpose of naval cruises was to "protect the national interests of the Soviet Union."[56] On Navy Day 1967 he claimed that

As a result of technical re-equipping, our navy has been able in recent years to *transfer to a qualitatively new type of combat train-*

Military Review No. 11 (November 1968), pp. 28–30, and this author's "Soviet Beachhead in the Third World," USNI *Proceedings,* Vol. 94, No. 10 (October 1968), pp. 60, 61.

[53]Fleet Adm. S. G. Gorshkov, Moscow *Kommunist Veorazhennyth Sil,* No. 13 (July 1963). He wrote in *Pravda* that "New submarines, aircraft, and surface ships with their powerful weapons have radically changed former concepts of the Navy's missions and of conditions and capabilities for executing them under strained situations. The Soviet Navy is an ocean fleet . . . ," *Pravda,* statement of Fleet Adm. Gorshkov, July 28, 1963.

[54]For example, Fleet Adm. V. Kasatonov, interview in Tass International Service in English, July 26, 1966; Admiral Panteleyev, Domestic Service in Russian, July 27, 1966; Adm. S. G. Gorshkov, report of *Pravda* interview, Tass International Service in Russian, July 30, 1967. See also *The Christian Science Monitor* article by Paul Wohl, "Moscow Boasts Navy Plies Every Ocean," August 12, 1968, p. 6.

[55]Fleet Adm. S. G. Gorshkov, "The Watch on the Sea," *Soviet Russia,* February 1, 1966.

[56]Kasatonov, Domestic Service, July 30, 1966. He went on to explain that, "At present our ships are undergoing naval training in parts of world ocean which earlier used to be considered the traditional preserve of the British and American navies."

ing, which was previously considered a zone of supremacy of the fleets of imperialist powers. Our ships can now be seen in the Atlantic and Pacific Oceans, in the tropic latitudes of the Indian Ocean, and in the severe Arctic.[57] [Emphasis added.]

He went on to explain the value of these deployments: "Long range cruises have become a genuine school of combat training of our military seamen, as well as a method of checking the quality and reliability of ship equipment."[58]

The marines have also been pictured as perfecting combat training. The interest in amphibious warfare reflected in earlier articles is now being put into practice. The "highly mobile" marines are described as ". . . successfully mastering military equipment, armaments, and the new tactics, and are perfecting their skills in battle training." [59] In their amphibious exercises they are using tactics similar to our own, although there apparently has been less emphasis on helicopter assaults. Soviet marines in landing craft participated in a highly publicized North Sea exercise in the summer of 1969[60] and widely publicized landing exercises in three areas in connection with Operation Ocean in 1970.[61] A philosophy is obviously being developed that will allow serious consideration of the possible employment of these forces to implement Russian policy. Significantly, in an August 1968 commentary Soviet Fleet Admiral Gorshkov included "the *deployment of navy planes*, various types of surface vessels, *marine units*" among those elements of the fleet capable of "*independent operations* as well as in joint operations with the other branches of the armed forces."[62] In the past the ma-

[57]Fleet Adm. V. Kasatonov, *Krasnaya Zvezda*, July 30, 1967, p. 1.

[58]Ibid. The Chief of Soviet Naval Communications commented in 1966, "Now, with the departure of the fleet for the ocean, communications are being subjected to a severe test." Vice Adm. G. Tolstolutsky, Chief of Naval Communications, "The Navy's Electronic Nerves," Moscow *Red Star*, July 27, 1966.

[59]Report of meeting with Fleet Adm. Kasatonov, Moscow Domestic Service in Russian, July 29, 1967. In 1966, Adm. Gorshkov said in a speech at the Central Theater of the Soviet army "Marines are successfully mastering combat equipment, weapons, and tactics, and are improving them in the course of their training." Moscow Domestic Service in Russian, July 30, 1966.

[60]Moscow Domestic Service in Russian, July 27, 1968. This exercise included Polish and East German troops.

[61]Exercises were conducted in the Barents, Black, and Baltic Seas. A description of the landing in the north in rough sea conditions is described in *Izvestia* article by Val Golsev, "Landing Forces Attack the Coast," April 30, 1970, p. 4.

[62](Emphasis added.) *Neues Deutschland* article by Soviet Admiral Sergey Gorshkov, August 3, 1968, p. 5. An article in 1970 mentioned "high-speed aircraft with operational radius of thousands of kilometers and linked 'landing ships' with those ships capable of fulfilling their tasks at any point in the world's oceans." *Izvestiya* article by Admiral Grishanov, July 26, 1970, p. 1.

rines have been depicted primarily as a coastal defense force operating in coordination with the Red army.

Operating days also reflect the emergence of the Soviet navy. In the first six months of 1967, warship operations were 400 percent greater than the comparable figure for all of 1963.[63] In 1966 there were more Soviet naval port visits and transits of warships on the high seas outside home waters than in any previous year.[64] Although the whole world had witnessed a new Soviet presence, the chief effort has been concentrated in the Mediterranean. In 1963 the numbers of ships deployed started to increase, and since 1964 a Soviet naval force has been maintained there. In 1966 the Soviet task force commander announced that from now on the presence of the Soviet fleet (called Eskadra by the Russians) in the Mediterranean would be "permanent."[65] Soviet ship operating days in the Mediterranean had increased in a three-year period by 600 percent and the monthly average of combatant ships in the Mediterranean by 1000 percent.[66] Soviet submarine operating days in the Mediterranean have increased by nearly 2000 percent.[67]

The deployment of amphibious ships is of more recent vintage. Although there were a few vessels in the Mediterranean at the time of the June war, the majority of the sightings of these ships have occurred following the crisis. As the Commander of the Atlantic Fleet said,

> An example of the extension of Soviet naval capability beyond the periphery of the Soviet Union is the recent appearance of a number of amphibious landing ships similar to American LSTs in the Mediterranean. In the past the Soviets had a few small landing craft that looked like they were built to operate in rivers and lakes. Now they have built a number of ocean going landing ships and deployed them well beyond their shores. This *signifies an awareness of what it takes to project force forward.*[68] [Emphasis added.]

[63]Letter from Ambassador Harland Cleveland, U.S. NATO Representative, to Lt. Comdr. J. T. Howe, USN, dated May 10, 1968.

[64]U.S. Navy, *Answers to Questions,* p. 7.

[65]Admiral Charles P. Griffin, "Now Russia Builds Up Power in the Mediterranean," *U.S. News and World Report,* Vol. LXIII, No. 24 (December 11, 1967), p. 51. See also U.S. Navy, *Answers to Questions,* p. 2. The editor of *Jane's Fighting Ships* noted in 1966, "The USSR now has a powerful permanent fleet in the Mediterranean for the first time in her history." R. V. B. Blackman, *Jane's Fighting Ships* (London: Sampson Low, Marston and Co., Ltd., 1966), p. IV.

[66]Griffin, "Now Russia Builds Up Power," p. 46. Ambassador Cleveland reported the increase of Soviet Mediterranean forces between 1963 and 1966 was "tenfold." Cleveland, letter.

[67]Cleveland, letter.

[68]Admiral E. P. Holmes, USN, as quoted in *The New York Times,* October 23, 1967.

The Soviets are maintaining one to four of the LSTs (called "Alligator Type") in the Mediterranean at all times as well as some smaller amphibious vessels. They may have as much as a battalion of marines on these ships.[69]

In addition to planning increased capabilities the Soviets have become more aggressive in their naval operations. Russian harassment of U.S. naval formations is not a new development, but the deliberate brushing of a U.S. destroyer in the Sea of Japan on two successive days in May 1967 in a kind of game of "chicken" was a very serious incident.[70] The appearance of a Soviet task force in the Sea of Japan following the *Pueblo* seizure was in many ways similar to the pattern established during the Middle East crisis. The Soviet task force arrived in the area after U.S. ships and was circumspect in its conduct. The Sea of Japan, like the Mediterranean, is a logical area for Soviet naval operations. It is probable that a USSR presence will be evident in future high-tension situations in that region and possibly others. In their global naval exercises of April and May 1970, involving all four Russian fleets and stretching into the Atlantic and Pacific Oceans as well as the Barents, Norwegian, North, Okhotsk, Japanese, Philippines, Mediterranean, Black, and Baltic Seas, the Soviets demonstrated an increasing capability to project modern naval forces to distant areas.

13.3 SOVIET MOTIVATION FOR DEPLOYMENT OF NAVAL FORCES FOR LIMITED WAR

In assessing the effect of Soviet naval expansion on American handling of multicrisis situations it is important to examine Moscow's motivation for deployment of these forces. Apparently a major Soviet goal is to achieve the mobility necessary to apply direct pressure in its campaign for influence in the Third World and to offset the considerable impact of the U.S. fleets. Russia seeks increased political and psychological influence, but it also has gained some military advantages. Moscow needs to be able to back words with deeds; it needs a credible bluff.[71] Russian lack of mobility and

[69]Rivero, interview, May 1968. A battalion is about 2000 men, which at that time was believed to be the approximate strength of marine forces in the Black Sea fleet.

[70]The press in recent years has had numerous accounts of these episodes. See, for example, *Christian Science Monitor*, "Soviet Ship Tricks Shown," December 18, 1967, p. 15. See also *The New York Times*, October 23, 1967, p. 12. For descriptions of deliberate collisions in the Pacific see *The New York Times*, May 12 to May 14, 1967. See also Section 2.2.

[71]By a credible bluff I mean one in which the forces on the scene are powerful enough to take effective action, and while not seeking action there is the implied will to use them if necessary.

restricted ability to maneuver was emphasized by the Lebanon and Quemoy crises of 1958. Combating American fleets by a campaign to reduce the number of U.S. bases[72] has not been a complete failure, but such tactics do not offer any hope of removing the American presence in the Third World. Indirect penetration has brought success, but has also been fraught with embarrassment—Cuba, Vietnam, and the 1967 Middle East crisis. Peking continues to advertise Moscow's failure to provide direct support as China competes with the Russians for influence in the Third World. In some measure Moscow's projection of military power into the Third World may be directed at Peking.

A number of experts accurately characterized the dilemma and indicated possible Kremlin solutions a few years ago. For example, Professor Uri Ra'anan said,

> Some of the military leaders apparently argued that since it was proving so difficult to insure that the 'national liberation movement' would avoid provoking the West, the attempt should be made to deter the West from reacting to such activities . . . that is from exploiting its regional military predominance for the purpose of suppressing local wars; in that case, the USSR could pursue its offensive in the 'third world' without having to worry about the consequences of Afro-Asian militancy. In this context, the West meant primarily the US Sixth and Seventh Fleets.[73]

A growing frustration with inability to influence matters in the Third World has been reflected in the Soviet literature. The idea of bluffing the American fleets has apparently now gained some favor and commitment of resources. The Soviets, of course, have not matched U.S. naval capability, but equality is not necessarily essential—particularly for the nation maintaining the initiative in Third World situations. The decision to build ships with a potential amphibious mission is an extremely important indication of how far the Soviets may go in perfecting this capability.[74] The time has

[72]Mackintosh, *Strategy and Tactics of Soviet Foreign Policy,* p. 332.

[73]Uri Ra'anan, "Tactics in the Third World: Contradictions and Dangers," *Survey,* Vol. 57 (October 1965), pp. 35, 36. See also Raymond L. Garthoff, *Soviet Military Policy* (New York: Praeger, 1966), p. 129.

[74]The following commentary from the *Economist* written after the Mideast crisis but before the announcement of carrier construction gives an excellent summary of the Soviet dilemma: "The combination of an offensive ideology with a defensive strategy is apt to produce such diplomatic defeats. To avoid more Cubas and Sinais, the Russians will have either to resist the temptation to take on commitments in the third world (which includes encouraging 'wars of liberation'), or else to acquire the military capacity this sort of policy calls for. This means building aircraft carriers and acquiring staging ports for airborne troops. *It will be a bad omen for East-West relations if there are signs that they have chosen the second way out of their dilemma.*" *The Economist,* June 24, 1967, reprinted in *Survival,* September 1967, The Institute for Strategic Studies, p. 283. (Emphasis added.)

evidently come for a change in Moscow's tactics for operations in the Third World. At the least, the need to have more options has been recognized.

While there are obvious advantages in being able to bring direct pressure to bear in areas where the Soviet Union has commitments and in increasing the credibility of pledges of assistance and threats of intimidation, there are also disadvantages. Soviet understanding of these has resulted in their inaction in the past. The relatively late development of modern mobile forces reflects Moscow's understanding of the very real hazards involved in a game of bluff with a stronger power rather than any technological or economic obstacles. Kremlin leaders, of course, also recognize the considerable investment of resources necessary to develop credible forces.

One danger of Russian naval operations is the increased possibility of a direct confrontation between the superpowers from which neither can withdraw. Although neither nation desires a world war, there is no guarantee that the Khrushchev philosophy of inevitable escalation of limited war between the United States and Russia is not correct. The result may be more wars by proxy, the Russians giving increased aid but not getting directly involved. Soviet caution in the 1967 Middle East crisis is a hopeful sign; it also underlines the other hazard of a naval presence. If a country has the means but does not come to the aid of its allies—whether it encouraged the conflict or not—that nation may lose a great deal of prestige. In the aftermath of the *Pueblo* seizure Moscow was again cautious. More than likely, the Soviets still have not totally committed themselves to a new course of action. Moscow's doctrine on direct intervention with their forces in the Third World remains ambiguous. It is clear, however, that Russia will have a greater range of choices in future situations and make its presence felt more directly in the Third World.

Moscow does not need a great many words to back up its material commitment to a military force for contingencies in neutral underdeveloped countries. The Soviet leaders, while voicing obvious frustration with the American naval presence, have been careful not to say what they would do with theirs. Soviet claims following the Middle East crisis lend some credence to the view that current Kremlin leaders, at least, do not intend to employ their naval strength rashly and that they continue to recognize the dangers. Russian action was described as having provided "all around support of the Arab countries" and to have once again demonstrated "firm determination to continue complete support for the just struggle of all the peoples" of the Third World."[75] The Soviet Union is pictured as having shown by "resolute acts" that "it wants to hold the aggressor and its patrons in check."[76] Premier Kosygin's speech to the United Nations in the aftermath of the crisis cautioned that "a seemingly small event, or so-called 'local wars,' may grow into big military conflicts."[77]

The Soviets appeared to recognize that their show of force should be accompanied by a soft declaratory policy in the Third World when they said in reference to Russian ships in the Mediterranean, ". . . the rise in prestige of the USSR in the Mediterranean countries is due not to them (Soviet naval forces), but to the Soviet policy of sincere friendship and equal co-operation with all countries in that area."[78] At the same time, it is now more frequently claimed that Russian warships are a political force in the Third World. Soviet vessels are said to be in the Mediterranean to guard "state interests in the area,"[79] to counter the "provocational activity of the U.S. Sixth Fleet,"[80] and to prevent threats to states that "have taken the path of political independence."[81]

The apparent aim of Soviet surface ship deployments is to neutralize the influence of the Sixth Fleet and provide leverage and political influence in the Third World. As yet, there is no indication that Kremlin strategists believe intervention could be successful in areas considered of vital interest to the United States. A September 1968 article in the *Soviet Military Review* seemed to put the role of Soviet forces in the Third World in proper perspective. The author stated that the "forms and methods of the liberation movement" to be utilized are those which "correspond most fully to the given situ-

[75]Professor V. Israelyan, "The October Revolution and Foreign Policy" *International Affairs,* No. 9 (September 1967), pp. 8, 9.
[76]Editorial, "Check the Israeli Aggression," *International Affairs,* No. 7 (July 1967), p. 4.
[77]He also pointed out that in conflicts "involving relatively small states not infrequently it is the big powers that are behind them," and that the events in the Middle East had "greatly complicated the already complex and dangerous international situation." *The New York Times,* "Text of Kosygin Address to General Assembly, June 20, 1967," p. 18.
[78]I. Belyalev and Y. Primakov, "Lessons of the 1967 Middle East Crisis," *International Affairs,* No. 3 (March 1968), p. 41.
[79]*Norodna Armiya,* February 20, 1968, article by Fleet Admiral S. G. Gorshkov.
[80]Moscow Tass International Service in English, November 26, 1968, V. Yermakov in *Pravda.*
[81]*Krasnaya Zvezda,* November 12, 1968, article by Vice Admiral N. Smirnov, p. 3. *CDSP,* Vol. XX, No. 47, p. 7.

ation."[82] In a significant passage, he cautioned:

Experience has demonstrated that such a strong and treacherous enemy as imperialism can be defeated only by counterposing to him, along with determination and selfless readiness for struggle, *sober political calculation, composure and self-control*. It is imperative to counterpose to this enemy such a strategy which draws on scientific analysis of the *balance of forces* with each country and in the *international arena*, such tactics, forms and methods of struggle which most fully take into account the specific conditions.[83] [Emphasis added.]

This is not a new approach to the national liberation movement. Rather, it is the reiteration of the standard line.[84] But it would seem to indicate clearly that Moscow will not use its naval capability in the face of American opposition. As Nasser's confidant, M. H. Haykal, realistically cautioned in August 1967, "it is also essential that our requirements must be within the Soviet Union's capabilities."[85]

The lesson for Washington seems obvious. Where there is American capability and will sufficient to create uncertainty in Soviet minds, Moscow will be cautious. The corollary is that risk of Soviet political and military intervention is increased significantly in areas where there is no corresponding American capability and committment. A Soviet warship visit in support of a political faction, for example, might prove effective.

The Russians are pleased with the British decision to reduce forces east of Suez, a policy that they describe as "forward looking."[86] They are not happy with the return of British warships to the Mediterranean,[87] and the creation of an "on call" NATO naval force

[82]Colonel V. Dolgopolov, "National Liberation and Armed Struggle," *Soviet Military Review,* No. 9 (September 1968), p. 48. See his article in the April 1969 issue, especially page 53, for a similar view.

[83]Col. V. Dolgopolov, "National Liberation and Armed Struggle" *Soviet Military Review,* No. 9 (September 1968), p. 50.

[84]For example, an editorial in the *World Marxist Review* in December 1960 asserted that "the peoples of the colonial countries win their independence both through armed struggle and by non-military methods, depending on the specific conditions in the country concerned."

[85]Cairo Radio, August 25, 1967. Translation given in *Survival,* Vol. IX, No. 11 (November 1967), p. 362. Haykal is editor of the Cairo newspaper *Al Ahram.*

[86]See review of book by Christopher Mayhew, *Britain's Role To-Morrow,* O. Orestov, in *International Affairs* (Moscow), No. 1, 1968, p. 105. They have, however, expressed concern that the withdrawal is not moving fast enough and may only be a cover for a buildup in the Persian Gulf, a move that would frustrate Soviet plans. See article by "Commentator," "Provocative Imperialist Rustle in the Persian Gulf," *International Affairs* (Moscow), No. 3 (March 1968), pp. 75, 76.

[87]In addition to denouncements in *Pravda,* it was reported by the Italian paper *Roma* that the Soviet ambassador in Cairo had vigorously tried to persuade Nasser to protest the British move. *Roma,* January 29, 1969.

in the region.[88] Russia would like to gain naval dominance of the strategic crossroads of the Middle East. Whether they will achieve it using a force modeled after the Sixth Fleet remains to be seen. The Soviets must operate in the presence of a stronger, more viable naval opponent, a problem that has not hampered the Sixth Fleet in the past two decades.

It has yet to be proved that demonstration of power by the Soviet Union will impress leaders of the national liberation movements. Russia may find itself hopelessly embroiled in the conflicting antagonisms of the Third World. Moscow's image building is also complicated by its current rivalry with Peking. The following commentary from Peking's *People's Daily* just prior to the June 1967 war underlines one of Soviet difficulties in reaping propaganda advantages by naval showmanship:

US imperialists recently dispatched a large number of warships to the Middle East region to intimidate the Arab people and support the Israeli aggressions. The Soviet revisionist clique also sent a number of warships to plow back and forth in the Mediterranean in the name of supporting the Arab countries to oppose Israeli aggression. When the United States and Soviet warships meet at sea, however, they greet one another warmly.

This can be called a normal 'strange phenomenon' because US imperialism supports Israel whereas the Soviets revisionist clique *pretends to support the Arab countries*. As far as the situation in the Middle East is concerned, their aim is identical. The sending of warships to the Middle East area by the US and the Soviet Union is in fact a joint action taken with an identical objective: this is part of their conspiracy to *dominate* the *world through U.S.-Soviet cooperation*.[89] [Emphasis added.]

In many ways, the present Soviet use of sea power is analogous to that of Germany before World War I.[90] Like the Germans, the Soviets are trying to act in the grand manner of a great naval power and attempting to offset the dominance that the United States has had on the world ocean since World War II. Much of Soviet success depends on the effectiveness of their bluff. Moscow has campaigned hard to make it uncomfortable for U.S. fleets. The Russians would like to see the American presence disappear from the Mediterranean and other areas, leaving the Soviet fleet to dominate the scene.

Moscow appears to have two major political objectives for deploying warships to the Mediterranean. It hopes to deter the United States from employing its fleet and thus effectively neutralize the

[88]See, for example, article by Yu Nelin, "NATO's New Fire-Brigade," No. 13 (March 1969), *International Affairs*, pp. 56–58, 64.
[89]Peking Domestic Service in Mandarin, June 2, 1967.
[90]Interview with Professor William E. Griffith conducted April 16, 1968.

American presence. Moscow also wants to gain leverage and prestige as the protector of certain nations of the region. Russians are telling their Arab audience that "the Mediterranean countries now well know that the hands of the Pentagon and NATO adventurers are tied."[91] Fleet Admiral Gorshkov has asserted that the presence of Soviet ships in the Mediterranean exerts a "sobering influence" on the Sixth Fleet and the Israelis.[92] They also have begun to boast that the Soviet navy in the Mediterranean surpasses the U.S. fleet and that the majority of American ships in the Mediterranean are of an "old type."[93] It would be a brilliant coup for Moscow if Washington were impressed by such claims. Russia has also asserted that its ships protect its friends. Admiral Sergheev, for example, said recently that "Russia cannot leave her friends—the Arab states—in the lurch in face of the danger of reinforcement of Israeli aggression."[94] Soviet vessels are intended to "guarantee" Moscow's conception of "peace and security" in the Third World,[95] but their success is by no means a foregone conclusion.

[91]Moscow in Arabic to Arab world, December 2, 1968, talk by Russian cruiser commander Boshakov. A Soviet broadcast in March 1970 attributed to a Cairo newspaper that the Soviet fleet "serves to constrain the naval power" of NATO and the U.S. Fleet. Moscow Radio Peace and Progress in Mandarin to China, March 26, 1970, Borisov commentary. Fleet Admiral Gorshkov wrote in 1970 that "the presence of our ships in these regions ties the imperialists' hands and deprives them of the opportunity to freely interfere in the peoples' internal affairs." *Pravda* article by Fleet Admiral S. Gorshkov, "The Motherland's Ocean Guard," July 26, 1970, p. 2.
[92]*Narodna Armiya* (Sopia) article "Over the Seas and Oceans," by Fleet Adm. S. Forshkov, May 5, 1970, pp. 1, 39. A similar statement was made in *Izvestia* article by Fleet Adm. S. Gorshkov, "Battles on the Seas," February 27, 1970. The Soviets have also emphasized that times have changed in the Mediterranean. For example, in Moscow Domestic Service in Russian, February 15, 1970, International Observers Roundtable. In bragging about the success of the 1970 "ocean" maneuvers, Fleet Admiral Gorshkov commented, "It is to be hoped they (our enemies) draw the appropriate conclusions for themselves, moderate their aggressive ardor, and show a greater sense of realism in their approach to solving international problems." *Pravda*, July 26, 1970, p. 2.
[93]Talk by Russian cruiser commander Boshakov.
[94]Interview with chief of Russian navy staff, Adm. Nikolai Sergheev, conducted on February 13, 1969, by the Italian newspaper *L'Unità* and appearing in the February 13, 1969, issue.
[95]Tass statement on the presence of the Soviet Fleet in the Mediterranean, *Pravda*, November 24, 1968, p. 4. Also *CDSP*, Vol. XX, No. 47, p. 6.

14. BRITISH WITHDRAWAL OF FORCES OUTSIDE EUROPE

14.1 INTRODUCTION

The Middle East crisis of 1967 brought into sharp focus the implications for the United States of Britain's intentions to withdraw her forces from outside Europe. The experience indicated the value of British capability to concentrate naval forces in an area south of the Suez Canal and to augment U.S. forces in the Mediterranean. It also emphasized the important role that the Royal Navy has been playing throughout the world as a stabilizing force. Although the United States would not necessarily have taken over these British missions, the simultaneous conflicts involving the small Royal Navy in the Middle East, Nigeria, Hong Kong, Singapore, Rhodesia, and Somalia had important implications for the United States. America has citizens, interests, and U.N. responsibilities in these areas too.

British assistance in 1958 was not without significance. By maintaining carrier task forces on either side of the Suez Canal, the United Kingdom played an important part in helping to stabilize the Middle East situation during the Quemoy crisis. A Russian probe in the region to relieve pressure in the Far East would have been counteracted by Anglo-American forces. London kept the Cyprus dispute between Turkey and Greece under control and sent a token force to Hong Kong in response to Chinese pressure there.

The Middle East crisis of 1967 provided a focus for renewed criticism of British plans for withdrawal from areas east of Suez. It was reputed to be one of the principal topics of discussion between President Johnson and British Prime Minister Harold Wilson on June 2, 1967, three days before the outbreak of the fighting.[1] Edward Heath, the leader of the Conservatives, said in the Middle East parliamentary debate of May 31, 1967, "I believe that Aden is now the weak link in the whole of the Government's policy in the Middle East and in trying to establish reasonable relations."[2] And Mr. Duncan Sandys remarked concerning the impending withdrawal from Aden, " . . . I assume that the Government will grab with both hands the excuse provided by the present crisis to rescind their foolish decision to withdraw our forces in January."[3] This exchange between the British defense secretary and the shadow defense sec-

[1]*The Times* article by Louise Heren, June 3, 1967, p. 1.
[2]*Hansard Parliamentary Debates,* 5th Series, Vol. 747, House of Commons, May 31, 1967, p. 115.
[3]Ibid., p. 153.

retary on June 1, 1967, was typical of the Labour Government's response to criticism of the Aden policy because of what was happening in the Middle East.

Mr. Denis Healey: There is no change in our plans to withdraw from the Aden base when Southern Arabia achieves independence and families are now coming home. We have now begun to run down our stocks.
Mr. Enoch Powell: Are you seriously saying that in the Government's view, the possibilities at the Northern end of the Red Sea is irrelevant to the presence of British forces in South Arabia?
Mr. Denis Healey: I say that a crisis in the middle of 1967 is not relevant to what we do in 1968.[4]

Mr. Heath also made the point that with Britain "in the process of withdrawing from certain Middle East commitments and the United States preoccupied in South-East Asia," Nasser might see this as the proper moment to "attempt to liquidate" Israel.[5]

The outbreak of hostilities brought further questions concerning the future of British forces.

Rear Admiral Morgan Giles: In view of the threat to our interests will you make an unequivocal statement that Britain will maintain an effective presence East of Suez for the foreseeable future?
Mr. Harold Wilson: We are considering that position. I can now take into account the views of the President of the US. We shall discuss the matter with Australia and New Zealand Governments in the next few weeks before making an announcement in the House.[6]

The announcement came on July 7, 1967, in a statement by the Foreign Office saying, ". . . the recent Arab-Israeli fighting does not in any way affect the principles and policies of the plans which we have put forward for independence for South Arabia on 9th January of next year."[7] The British have now taken that step and are speeding up others.[8] The objective is that "After the end of 1971 Britain will, with certain minor exceptions, maintain no military bases outside Europe and the Mediterranean."[9] But the withdrawal is not restricted to bases. The British will radically decrease the peacekeeping capability of their navy. It had been planned that "The

[4]*The Guardian,* June 1, 1967, p. 3.
[5]*Hansard Parliamentary Debates,* May 31, 1967, p. 117.
[6]*The Guardian,* "Commons Questions on the Middle East," June 6, 1967.
[7]Statement of George Thomson, Minister of State for Foreign Affairs, House of Commons, July 6, 1967, *Official Text,* British Information Service Doc. No. T.33, p. 12.
[8]Policy statement of Prime Minister in House of Commons, January 16, 1968, British Information Services, "Economic and Overseas Policy: Cuts in Public Expenditure," p. 2. See also *Statement on the Defence Estimates 1969,* presented to Parliament by the Secretary of State for Defence by Command of Her Majesty, February 1969, Cmnd. 3927 (London: Her Majesty's Stationery Office, 1969), pp. 4–6.
[9]Policy statement, January 16, 1968, Cmnd. 3927, p. 2.

British aircraft carrier force will be phased out as soon as withdrawals from Malaysia, Singapore, and the Persian Gulf have been completed. The rate of some new naval construction will be reduced."[10] The Conservative government, however, modified these plans slightly by stating in 1970 that a token force would be retained in Singapore and that an aircraft carrier will be maintained in the navy until late in the decade.

14.2 THE WITHDRAWAL

The withdrawal does not result from a lack of appreciation of the importance of a British presence outside of Europe. London simply feels it cannot support such forces economically. The government reasons that with a weak economic base it is worse than a paper tiger; it is in danger of financial chaos. As Prime Minister Wilson explained,

> . . . it is not only in our own interests but in those of our friends and allies for this country to strengthen its economic base quickly and decisively. There is *no military strength* whether for Britain or for our alliances *except on the basis of economic strength*, and it is on this basis that we best ensure the security of this country.[11] [Emphasis added.]

The 1969 defense estimate states the new British orientation succinctly, "The essential feature of our current defence policy is a readiness to recognise that *political and economic realities* reinforce the defence arguments for concentrating Britain's military role on Europe"[12] (Emphasis added.)

The dread of an economic drain such as the one Vietnam has caused in America is only part of the concern. Britain would need major U.S. assistance for any open-ended engagement of that magnitude in any case. The United Kingdom simply cannot finance more than a limited peace-keeping presence east of Suez. Deployed forces are "seriously over-stretched and in some respects dangerously under-equipped."[13]

In addition to the economic question, other criticisms have been made concerning the concept of maintaining such a presence. In a surprising switch of the Conservative Party in October 1965, the

[10] British government white paper on defense, February 22, 1968, British Information Services, Policy background paper, February 23, 1968, p. 6.

[11] Policy statement of Prime Minister in House of Commons, January 16, 1968, British Information Services, "Economic and Overseas Policy: Cuts in Public Expenditure," p. 2.

[12] *Statement on the Defence Estimates 1969,* p. 1.

[13] Edward Skloot, "Labour East of Suez," *Orbis,* Vol. 10, No. 3 (Fall 1966), p. 947.

shadow defense minister asserted that the presence of British troops east of Suez was "self defeating."[14] Labour M.P. Christopher Mayhew agreed with Enoch Powell's analysis that the presence was increasingly anachronistic and counterproductive as well as beyond British resources.[15]

In spite of this criticism from both parties, the importance of a U.K. presence was recognized. As the British defense review for 1966 stated, "Recent experience . . . has shown that our ability to give rapid help to friendly governments, with even small British forces, can prevent large scale catastrophies. In some parts of the world, the visible presence of British forces by itself is a deterrent to local conflict."[16] Some British leaders argued that deployed forces had strengthened the Commonwealth, excused a reduced presence in Europe, and achieved a special relationship with the United States.[17] The British have had a great advantage in the regions east of Suez because their presence is accepted. Many of the oil rich leaders of the Persian Gulf countries feel that a U.K. force is a "lesser evil than the social reaction threatened by feudal neighbors."[18] The prime ministers of Malaysia and Singapore welcomed a British presence but not an American one.[19] London still recognizes some responsibilities. In emphasizing that withdrawal from Aden did not mean abandonment of the Persian Gulf, a Foreign Office spokesman explained,

> In South Arabia and the Persian Gulf we have obligations which we cannot simply shrug away. We have responsibilities which we have to carry out. . . . The Gulf is a cockpit of territorial rivalries. . . . If the British Government were suddenly to withdraw we would leave behind us a dangerous vacuum which might well precipitate in another part of the Middle East a dangerous Great Power confrontation.[20]

Although the British withdrawal has been smooth and responsibly conducted, recent statements have played down what future role

[14]Walter Goldstein, statement of Enoch Powell as quoted in *The Dilemma of British Defense* (Columbus: Ohio State University Press, 1966), p. 27.
[15]Christopher Mayhew, *Britain's Role Tomorrow* (London: Hutchinson and Co., 1967), p. 102. See also Robert V. Roosa, "Where is Britain Heading," *Foreign Affairs,* Vol. 46, No. 3 (April 1968), p. 517, for a similar view.
[16]Rear Admiral Morgan Giles, "The Case for a British Presence East of Suez," Chapter 5 of *Brassey's Annual: The Armed Forces Year Book 1967* (New York: Praeger, 1967).
[17]Goldstein, *Dilemma of British Defense,* p. 27.
[18]Michael Howard, "Britain's Strategic Problem East of Suez," *International Affairs* (British), Vol. 42, No. 2 (April 1966), p. 180.
[19]Goldstein, *Dilemma of British Defense,* p. 64.
[20]Statement of George Thomson, Minister of State for Foreign Affairs, House of Commons, July 6, 1967, official text, British Information Services, Doc. No. T.33, p. 7.

Britain might be willing to play outside of Europe.[21]

There was another important argument for a British presence east of Suez. Some British spokesmen felt that U.S. public opinion would not support a large U.S. presence in Europe while the United Kingdom withdrew leaving vacuums to be filled. The feeling was that Great Britain could do a more effective job outside Europe and that an American presence in Europe was an essential shield.[22] Reginald Maulding predicted that such a withdrawal would leave the American position "politically" intolerable. After talking to persons in the United States he concluded that "American opinion would not allow the American government to continue alone the role of world policeman."[23] London recognized that it could not necessarily depend on Washington to take up the slack. But Britain's tenuous economic situation simply rendered discussions about the pros and cons of peace-keeping irrelevant. The British government does not feel it can afford such operations, and in the light of devaluation and the continuing deficit, there are few persons today who would argue with that economic analysis. There are, of course, many other factors related to London's decisions, not the least of which is domestic politics, but economic realities are the overriding impetus for accelerated withdrawal.

In 1965 pressure for contraction began to mount. At that time the Conservatives started to point out the dangers of the British presence east of Suez. The Prime Minister held fast, but in 1966 he made a "dramatic reversal."[24] Defence Minister Healey admitted that "some contraction in our overseas commitments was clearly necessary if we were to keep our economy healthy,"[25] but he implied that the exodus would not be sudden. However, in that year the decision not to build an aircraft carrier brought the resignation of the Minister of Defence for the Royal Navy and the First Sea Lord. Their feeling was that Britain could not meet existing commitments without constructing a new carrier. In 1967 it was announced that two aircraft carriers would continue in service until the

[21]Compare the *Supplementary Statement on Defence Policy 1967,* Cmnd. 3357, July 1967 (London: HMSO, 1967), pp. 4, 5; and *Statement on the Defence Estimates 1969,* pp. 5, 6.
[22]Giles, "Case for a British Presence," p. 50. See also L. W. Martin, *The Sea in Modern Strategy* (New York: Praeger, 1967), p. 172.
[23]Reginald Maulding, "The Real Threat to the West," *The Atlantic Community Quarterly,* Vol. 5, No. 3 (Fall 1967), p. 345.
[24]Neville Brown, "British Armies and the Switch Towards Europe," *International Affairs* (British), Vol. 43, No. 3 (July 1967), p. 470.
[25]*The New York Times,* February 27, 1966, p. 4E.

mid-1970s.[26] However, apparently now all but one carrier will be phased out when withdrawals from bases are completed.[27] The Royal Navy will then rely on the Royal Air Force for cover[28] and will thus have substantially decreased credibility and range as a conventional naval power.

The order for fifty high-performance aircraft from the United States, which had originally been substituted for construction of the aircraft carrier, has also been canceled.[29] Forces in the Mediterranean have been reduced substantially. The contingent of three or four small minesweepers that comprised the only Royal Navy force assigned to the Mediterranean in 1967 left Malta in April of 1969, ending a British presence that began in 1800. London plans to retain bases in Cyprus, but it is reducing forces there also.[30]

Although the global capability of the British navy has been greatly reduced, the trend of contraction in the Mediterranean may be reversed. The Royal Navy will operate primarily in the Atlantic,[31] but even before the Czechoslovakian invasion of 1968, London had assigned two frigates to the Mediterranean and announced its intention to add a guided missile destroyer in 1970.[32] In the aftermath of the Russian invasion, the British decided to maintain an aircraft carrier, assault ship, or commando ship in the Mediterranean almost continuously beginning in January 1969.[33] These deployments fit in with the European orientation of London's new defense policy.

The British still profess to have an interest in the areas from which they are departing and report making progress in arrangements with allies to preserve stability. London claims to have retained the capability to deploy forces rapidly overseas.[34] A joint five-power ex-

[26]*Supplementary Statement on Defence Policy 1967,* presented to Parliament by Secretary of State for Defence by Command of Her Majesty, July 1967, Cmnd. 3357 (London: HMSO, 1967), p. 7.

[27]British Information Services, Policy Background Paper, February 23, 1968, pp. 3, 6. *Statement on the Defence Estimates 1969*, p. 35. The H.M.S. *Ark Royal* will complete conversion to carry Phantom aircraft in 1970 and may be kept in commission until late in the decade.

[28]*Supplementary Statement on Defence Policy 1967,* p. 7.

[29]British government white paper on defence, February 22, 1968. British Information Services, policy background paper, Annex A, p. 6.

[30]Statement of Prime Minister in House of Commons on January 16, 1968, British Information Service, January 16, 1968, p. 2.

[31]British Information Services, Policy Background Paper, February 23, 1968, pp. 1, 2.

[32]*Supplementary Statement on Defence Policy 1968,* Cmnd. 3701, July 1968, p. 8.

[33]*Statement on the Defence Estimates 1969,* p. 11.

[34]Statement of Prime Minister in House of Commons on January 16, 1968, British Information Services, January 16, 1968, p. 2. See also *The Guardian*

ercise in the Far East conducted by Australia, New Zealand, Malaysia, and Singapore scheduled for 1970 raised some legitimate concern.[35] The Middle East crisis of 1967 is a case in point. With the Suez Canal closed, it would have taken a British task force sustaining a speed of twenty knots more than twenty days to reach Aden from England. And of course Aden is several days by boat from Aqaba. In the Quemoy crisis, the British force south of Suez was about thirteen days from the Taiwan area. The great distances involved demonstrate the importance of having naval forces reasonably close to the areas of possible conflict. As a partial solution to this problem there has been increased interest in regional defense arrangements for the Commonwealth. Australia and New Zealand, for example, have agreed to retain small forces in Malaysia and Singapore following the British withdrawal.[36] The October 1970 British decision to retain a small force in the Singapore area will provide an additional stabilizing factor.

14.3 SIGNIFICANCE OF BRITISH WITHDRAWAL ON U.S. HANDLING OF MULTICRISIS SITUATIONS

The Middle East crisis of 1967 demonstrated U.S. dependence on its British ally as well as some of the limitations of that alliance. Militarily, the buildup of U.K. naval strength in the area south of Suez added credibility to U.S. statements concerning the Gulf of Aqaba. The U.S. force in the Red Sea was equaled, at least numerically, by the Egyptian navy. It would have taken days for the United States to establish a stronger presence there if the Suez Canal had been impassable.

The augmentation of British warships in the Mediterranean, including an aircraft carrier and three frigates, matched the highly publicized Russian increase of naval forces during the buildup phase. Reliance on U.K. support was at least as much psychological as it was military. With domestic concern about overcommitment and the unfavorable international image of the United States it became essential to have London's backing for any peace-

article by Francis Boyd, "Britain 'Still Involved' East Defense," June 18, 1968, p. 12; *The Times* article by Fred Emery, "Big British Airlift to Malaysia," June 12, 1968, p. 8. *Statement on The Defence Estimates 1969*, pp. 5, 6.

[35]See, for example, *The Christian Science Monitor* article by Albert E. Norman, "Australia Reaffirms Viet Support for US," March 14, 1968.

[36]*The New York Times*, April 16, 1969, p. 12.

keeping act prior to the outbreak of the war. This dependence might have been greatly reduced if the Russians had attacked or if Israel were being demolished. However, in the absence of such eventualities, the need for an ally in any undertaking was paramount.

The British contributed less in the Quemoy situation than in the 1967 crisis. But if there had been no U.K. forces along the Middle East littoral in 1958, the United States would have been more reluctant to send forces from the Mediterranean to augment its Far Eastern fleet. The joint Anglo-American Middle Eastern endeavor had some psychological value in averting arguments that the United States alone was assuming the role of world policeman; without allied support in 1958 the United States still would have been able to act, but with more difficulty.

Military contraction of America's closest ally is particularly significant in meeting the challenges of multicrises. In such a period the United States is more militarily and psychologically vulnerable, and in assuming a second challenge, the aid of allies becomes increasingly important.

The withdrawal of the British from the Persian Gulf and Red Sea areas would be more tolerable for the United States if it were not for the indications that Soviet naval power will next expand to that region. The present Soviet leaders are less likely to embark on adventures in areas where clearly surpassed in regional military strength, but the step from the Mediterranean to south of Suez is a feasible objective for Moscow. American absence is more serious if the enemy gains the initiative by establishing a presence.

The limitations of dependence on allies were also demonstrated during the two crises. The British, who were much more vulnerable economically, became acutely aware of the consequences of a show of strength against the Arabs in 1967. However, there were plans for cooperative effort between the United States and Great Britain. Although there was less likelihood of British cooperation in the Quemoy area, it appeared clear, in 1958, that London would stand with Washington in a major showdown of world powers, even though it disagreed with U.S. policy.

Examined in the light of the Middle Eastern and Quemoy crises, British contraction means that the United States will have more difficulty meeting its worldwide commitments in the inevitable conflicts of the future. The stronger Royal Navy presence in the Mediterranean beginning in late 1969 improved the Western position. In view of the thrust of United Kingdom defense policy it is reasonable to assume that forces assigned to the Mediterranean will grow larger in the decade of the 1970s. The Mediterranean is the logical place for deployment of Britain's NATO oriented forces, but the Royal Navy will no longer be able to assemble a force as strong as that mustered during the 1967 crisis.

15. THE PROBLEMS IN THE 1970S

15.1 QUEMOY AND THE MIDDLE EAST IN RETROSPECT

The United States had sufficient capability to guard its vital interests in the 1967 Middle East and 1958 Quemoy crises. In each complex situation Washington persevered, and no American lives were lost in responding to challenges the United States had not sought. In both cases the nation aligned with Moscow failed to achieve its goals.

The United States approached both second crises with caution, but it did not renege on commitments to Tel Aviv and Taipei. America had no formal obligation to Israel, although the 1957 *aide-mémoire* implied a forceful U.S. defense of the right of free and innocent passage through the Gulf of Aqaba.[1] Washington's reluctance to test the blockade seemed to work in Israel's favor toward the end of the buildup period as Nasser increasingly committed himself to a showdown with Israel. In spite of Vietnam limitations, the President made it clear to Moscow that Soviet intervention risked U.S. counteraction. Israel could not reasonably have asked for more than the helpful American performance in the United Nations and in the Mediterranean during the six days of fighting.

Although Chiang was frustrated by American reluctance to commit itself outright to defense of the offshore islands in 1958, U.S. statements under the circumstances stretched the Formosa resolution to its limit. Taipei apparently felt at first that implied promises had been neglected. But it became clear that the United States was not going to allow the islands to fall. In the end, both Israel and Nationalist China were satisfied with the outcome of the crises.

Nevertheless, American options in the weeks before the 1967 war were somewhat limited by economic, political, and military considerations. Heavy involvement in Vietnam contributed to confining policy choices to the diplomatic arena and restraining initiatives while the crisis was developing. The American posture of studied neutrality prior to the June war, however, resulted primarily from political considerations associated with that region and not from capability limitations. When the fighting began, the United States withstood heavy Soviet pressure and supported a firm diplomatic stand with a strong military posture.

[1]However, it perhaps could be charged that the United States violated the understanding inscribed on that document by Secretary of State Dulles.

Options during the Quemoy crisis were not as restricted. This was at least partially attributable to the relatively less demanding preexisting involvement. A controversial policy was maintained in spite of the commitment of U.S. forces in another part of the globe. However, Washington may not have been able to duplicate its handling of the 1958 multicrisis in the year 1967. The United States was certainly not ready for a Lebanon-type situation in 1967 as well as Vietnam.

From examination of the two situations, insight has been gained concerning the influence of various capability factors.[2] Confidence in military capability is particularly important in considering precrisis initiatives. Reduced readiness narrows the range of U.S. policy choices, but greater capability does not necessarily lead to selection of an aggressive posture in the buildup period. During a short crisis relative power already available in the local area becomes more significant. As confidence increases in a successful military outcome, other negative aspects of maintaining a firm stand are offset to some extent.

Since domestic dissent grows slowly, it becomes significant during a prolonged crisis phase or when a preexisting atmosphere of negative opinion exists as a crisis develops. With such an environment, unilateral American initiatives during a buildup period are more difficult. On the other hand, in a fast-changing crisis phase domestic opinion has little impact on policy decisions. Similarly, after the United States is publicly committed to a course of action during a crisis, domestic pressure must be strong to influence a modification. When there is little internal support, the need for allied backing is intensified. The psychological dependence is especially acute when considering peace-keeping initiatives related to a second developing crisis.

Paradoxically, the Soviet Union, like the United States, also seems slightly less inclined to intervene in a second crisis situation involving superpower interests, although the evidence is more speculative. While American preoccupation in a previous involvement may tempt a Soviet probe in another vulnerable area, there appears to be little likelihood of actual Soviet military intervention.

[2]Because the cases had distinctly different characteristics, any generalizations tend to be an oversimplification. Those factors which in some measure limited policy choices were significant primarily in relation to certain alternatives at distinct periods of the crises. These comments pertaining to capability factors are not meant as rules but simply as observations based on a limited sample. In many instances the factors provided a meaningful contrast rather than indicating a similar effect.

In the Formosa Strait and the eastern Mediterranean, American naval forces proved to be effective instruments of foreign policy. They provided defense in depth for the Nationalists and Israelis. Fleet movements closed options to the Soviet Union and underlined American determination at times when the U.S. declaratory position was not clearly defined. The U.S. government "spoke softly and carried a big stick." Once American warships appeared on the scene in strength, Peking could not afford to chance an invasion of Quemoy or Formosa. In the 1967 crisis, movement of the Sixth Fleet toward the eastern Mediterranean indicated American interests would be protected.

Warship activity appeared to be an excellent indicator of Washington's intentions.[3] In 1967 fleet maneuvers, in keeping with U.S. policy, were deliberately restrained and aggressive only at the time of presumed Soviet threat. Highly publicized augmentations in 1958 demonstrated U.S. determination. In both cases, Soviet emphasis on naval activity as a true reflection of American intentions increased the significance of warship movements.

United States fleets were adequate to meet the demands of the two multicrises. Although American naval forces throughout the world were strained in order to meet Lebanon and Quemoy needs, sufficient power was available. Because of shortages of material and inexperienced personnel, the Sixth Fleet was in a reduced state of readiness in 1967. Still, it was capable of neutralizing Soviet naval forces in the Mediterranean. Options such as breaking the Gulf of Aqaba blockade and augmenting forces in the Mediterranean may have been less attractive because of the Vietnam strain, but overall fleet strength seemed to be sufficient to meet crisis challenges. In contemplating possible intervention, Moscow had to consider American superiority in land-based and carrier air power in the region as well as the relative U.S. advantage in strategic weapons.

It is only when the "ifs" and "might have beens" in the two situations are considered that a certain military vulnerability is exposed. If there had been resistance to the 1958 Lebanon landings, a strong sustained demonstration of force in the Pacific would have been more difficult. If Moscow in 1967 had sent major amphibious units, flown large troop contingents or bombers to Arab fields, or flooded the Mediterranean with submarines, relative Sixth Fleet superiority

[3]There were, however, instances, as described in earlier chapters, in which ship movements were first ordered on the initiative of local naval commanders.

would have been greatly reduced. As it was, U.S. intervention would have been difficult if American citizens had been threatened in Arab countries.

Both experiences demonstrated that a heavy U.S. military involvement may be required without comparable employment of Soviet forces. Therefore, merely matching Soviet capability does not appear to be a wise premise on which to estimate American requirements for general purpose forces. In 1958 U.S. forces were stretched thin meeting situations in which no Russian units were involved. While the United States operated under simultaneous strain in Vietnam and the Middle East, the USSR expended only a small naval task force and some military advisers.

On the other hand, the 1967 crisis seemed to show that an unaugmented Sixth Fleet at reduced strength was sufficient to decrease the possibility of Soviet intervention. The "conclusive" movements of a relatively stronger fleet signaled American resolve. Yet, if the United States had doubled its carrier force during the buildup period, the Soviet Union possibly would not have seriously contemplated intervention in Syria. United States determination and relative military advantage would have been clearer. However, the complex American problem was to play down the situation by not overly encouraging Israel or increasing Arab animosity while at the same time deterring the Soviet Union. The United States could neutralize the Soviet Union, but it had a reduced capacity to take the initiative.

In 1967 naval units not engaged in combat in Southeast Asia had been drawn down in terms of personnel and general readiness. Owing to heavy costs of the Vietnam war and political resistance to further spending, there was an understandable tendency to weaken forces in other parts of the world and a hesitancy to activate reserve components. United States success in the Middle East was due largely to the relative local superiority of Israel.

Nevertheless, backing provided by U.S. fleets combined with the capability of indigenous forces proved to be an effective combination. Israel and Nationalist China were able to assert military dominance in the local area. Assuming that it was in the U.S. interest in these cases to protect a friendly nation against an apparent threat, assistance to Taipei and Tel Aviv through arms aid programs seemingly reduced rather than increased the possiblity of direct U.S. involvement. Although there were provocations on both sides, it was not the country hopeful of U.S. backing that made the initial challenge. If Israel and the Republic of China had been incapable of defending themselves, the American dilemma of facing a second crisis would have increased significantly. If American jets had had to go into action in the Formosa Strait or over the Sinai, the situations would have been much more serious.

Therefore, it would seem wise to develop a regional self-defense capability for friendly nations considered vital to American security interests. United States forces could then provide defense in depth, which in today's terms means keeping the Soviet Union neutralized. The United States would need sufficient forces to develop a strong presence in local regions while maintaining overall strategic superiority.

The two crises demonstrated the potential psychological and military value of having the global support of major allies like Great Britain. United Kingdom military capability and cooperation provided added insurance for the United States. The buildup of British forces in the Near East in 1958 and 1967 improved the overall position of the West in relation to that of the Soviet Union. However, the American need was primarily for U.K. participation in peacekeeping operations, and no direct aid was forthcoming. A clash with the Soviet Union might well have escalated rapidly into a nuclear exchange. In considering multinational forces and assessing the strength of allies, it is apparent that the range of situations in which the interests of friendly nations coincide may be very narrow.

The cases examined also provided insights concerning American security commitments. None of the four cases—Israel, Vietnam, Lebanon, and Quemoy—involved a U.S. treaty. Only the Republic of China was among those forty-three nations with which the United States now has collective defense arrangements. It is not surprising that tests occur in areas where U.S. commitments are ambiguous. In such a situation, an enemy may logically conclude there is greater opportunity for success without triggering American counteraction. If the United States had been formally committed to the defense of Israel or Quemoy, the Soviets, Arabs, and Chinese might have been discouraged from making probes.

On the other hand, ambiguity in the cases studied had some advantages. A formal alliance with Israel would have raised the ire of moderate Arab friends of the United States and perhaps reduced U.S. options in dealing with the Middle East. A clarification of the commitment to the Nationalists might well have meant a rescinding of any obligation to defend the offshore islands. A sharply drawn defense perimeter may be misconstrued as an open invitation to the Chinese Communists to repeat their 1958 threats.

Rigid and inflexible commitments also may increase the danger of being drawn into a conflict by an enemy or ambitious ally. However, the opposite seemed to be true in these cases. With increased confidence in American assistance, Israel might have been willing to invest more time before going to war. With a strong American commitment to defend Quemoy, Chiang might have been less inclined to involve the United States in the offshore island resupply effort.

While it may have seemed to Moscow that close coordination existed between Washington and Tel Aviv in 1967 and between Washington and Taipei in 1958, the appearance was deceptive. Although apparently determined to prevent Israel's demise and loss of the offshore islands, the American government communicated with its friends in a formal and somewhat ambiguous manner. Israeli and Nationalist perceptions of American intentions appeared to contain a larger guess factor than is ideal for close working relationships in times of crisis. Washington's reticence is understandable. It strove to avoid encouraging a Nationalist or Israeli initiative. Tel Aviv, on its part, did not give the United States advance word of its attack on the Arabs and in the minds of some officials broke a promise. Taipei apparently tried to involve U.S. forces in supply operations in order to obtain an American guarantee for a fuzzy commitment. However, mutual trust and confidence that facilitate frank communication in time of danger are essential. Without such a relationship, within the framework of recognized limitations of respect for the different responsibilities and aspirations of independent nations, U.S. obligations are a much greater liability.

In both situations, informal assurances not on the public record may have initially raised expectations of friends beyond what the U.S. government considered to be its obligation. In 1967, U.S. decision makers were not even aware that Secretary Dulles had added some strong comments to the 1957 *aide-mémoire*. In 1958, Chiang may have felt he was being let down because of alleged U.S. promises concerning the offshore islands made during the 1955 Tachen Islands evacuation. Both of these informal assurances came back to haunt the United States.

The United States should reevaluate all its obligations, both tacit and explicit, to other nations. It would seem desirable to repledge and consistently demonstrate firm U.S. backing for allies with whom common security interests are shared. Ties that do not meet this criterion should be withdrawn from the list of U.S. defense commitments and assurances, with the recognition, however, that in a complex world not all requirements can be anticipated or necessarily spelled out in formal public documents. If a commitment has been clearly and constitutionally created, this country will be more likely to respond politically, psychologically, and economically to the full extent of its vast capacity. The primary U.S. problem in tapping its resources to meet existing international obligations appears to be psychological. It is believed that U.S. commitments can be made with the proper proportions of firmness, flexibility, and realism. A pragmatic and honest assessment of existing ones is needed.

Since these crises involved the interests of the superpowers, it is not surprising that United Nations machinery failed to maintain the peace. In the case of Quemoy, the United Nations served as a court of last appeal, although China was not a member. The United Nations provided a place for diplomatic exchanges and working out cease-fires during the 1967 Mideast problem; but it proved ineffective in preventing a war clearly in the making.

Perhaps more surprising is the fact that both cases appeared to be exceptions to the mythical rule of bipartisanship in foreign policy. During the Quemoy crisis, the Democrats of the Senate Foreign Relations Committee were sharply critical of the Republican administration's position. At the same time, some prominent Democrats supported the policy. In 1967, Congress was unified but only coincidentally in agreement with the administration's policy. The convergence of congressional opinion that the United States should not take unilateral action stemmed from diverse motivations. However, the divergence that did exist appeared to be based on the merits rather than party loyalty.

Definite differences of opinion existed between and within the various executive departments on how to approach the crises. There were divergent points of view in the White House and Congress in both situations and between the White House and the Defense and State Departments to varying degrees. In the case of Quemoy, for example, the local military commander and ambassador disagreed on a number of issues. In 1967 the State Department and the White House had different conceptions of the problem. Obviously foreign policy results from a complex mix of conflicting inputs that reflect the diversity of participants in policy selection. Even in a crisis situation there does not seem to be a unifying force that harmonizes these different elements into one concerted approach. During the fast-moving events of the June war, however, the effects of divergencies were minimized because decision making was centered in the White House basement where the President directed the proceedings.

In spite of many problems associated with both multicrises, American capability proved adequate, and the United States did not renege on its obligations.

15.2 THE PROBLEM IN THE 1970S AND POSSIBLE SOLUTIONS

In the 1970s the United States will continue to have major global interests and responsibilities. The arena of clashing American-Soviet interests is not likely to diminish in size. The psychological problem of dealing with a partial peace-partial war environment will remain.

With respect to the interrelated factors affecting capability, the forecast, although neither entirely predictable nor irreversible, is for a relative decrease in U.S. capability to cope with multicrises. Soviet intentions to intervene will be difficult to predict and complicated by changes and uncertainties in Moscow. Yet Russian capability to project military strength well beyond its borders continues to develop. This development, paralleled by forward movement in strategic missile programs, means that Moscow will have increased capability to use military force for political purposes beyond Eastern Europe.

If the United States maintains the existing relative strategic and tactical power advantage, military capability should continue to be a positive factor in most assessments of U.S. options in developing crises. However, the United States is cutting back its general purpose forces. Whether remaining strength will be adequate to meet the requirements of the 1970s depends on many factors. Nevertheless, relative U.S. military capability in places like the Mediterranean and the Sea of Japan is likely to be less than in the last decade.

The trend of U.S. domestic opinion is difficult to predict and clouded by the Vietnam conflict. However, there is growing pressure for a decrease in U.S. military commitments abroad and a probable tendency to weigh the cost of involvement in the most pessimistic terms. The executive will be more likely to seek congressional approval before committing U.S. forces.

Because of growing criticism of America's world role, international support and backing will be even more important in future crises. However, at the present time there seems to be less likelihood that assistance will be provided by America's traditional big power allies. Certainly, the decline of Great Britain is apparent.

The U.S. domestic outlook combined with inflation and resulting tight money policies has led to demands for cuts in defense spending. The defense budget was cut some $3 billion in fiscal year 1970, and future reductions are almost inevitable. In announcing reductions, Defense Secretary Melvin Laird said that "defense readiness would be weakened" and "our capability to meet current commitments would be reduced."[4] Thus, the economic base will affect worldwide readiness.

Unless there are radical changes in these trends, the United States will have less capability to deal with second crisis situations in the next decade. In the specific cases of Quemoy and the Middle East, U.S. political and military capabilities appear to be less than in 1958 or 1967. Even though Moscow would be reluctant to support a Chinese invasion, America has reduced military and psychological capability to defend the offshore islands. In the Mediterranean, American and Russian forces are now more evenly balanced, and increasing numbers of Soviet military advisers are entrenched in Syria and Egypt.

Focusing specifically on situations primarily involving sea power, the American problem is complicated by British contraction and Soviet expansion.

There is no reason to predict that in the 1970s ability to exert superior force along the Third World littoral will be less advantageous. Russia will gain substantial leverage and influence if the American presence is markedly reduced or eliminated in areas like the Mediterranean. The Soviet decision to copy the tactics of U.S. fleets has increased the need for having a counteracting American force available in potential local war situations.

Paradoxically, however, the impact that U.S. fleets once had on Russian strategy has decreased. Moscow's options are now less restricted because a U.S. naval presence can be somewhat offset and an additional element of uncertainty introduced into a crisis situation. By establishing a Russian presence, Moscow can now raise the stakes higher for U.S. commitment of forces like the Sixth Fleet and put teeth into usual crisis statements that the Soviet Union "cannot remain indifferent."

The United States is not likely again to enjoy the naval freedom of

[4]Testimony of Defense Secretary Melvin Laird in U.S., Congress, House, Subcommittee of the Committee on Appropriations, *Department of Defense Appropriations for 1970,* Part 7, 91st Cong., 1st sess. (Washington, 1969), p. 384.

action it was able to exploit so successfully during the multicrisis of 1958. The mere presence of Soviet ships, principally for propaganda and political advantage, was one of many factors contributing to a more restrained U.S. style in 1967. Washington does not want to give Moscow cause for intervention, counteraction, or the need to make some face-saving gesture. The hazards of a conflict resulting from inadvertence in high-tension situations are also greater.

But the risks, of course, are still two-way. The Soviet Union does not want a third world war and would probably suffer considerable loss of face before risking engagement against a more powerful foe. For this reason alone, the implications of reductions in relative strength available in future multicrisis situations must be carefully evaluated. Since World War II, the United States has not relied on parity. In crises along the world littoral it has taken advantage of local naval dominance backed by strong U.S. air and army forces worldwide and global strategic superiority. If Soviet naval power continues to increase, convincing American demonstrations of resolve will be more difficult to achieve.

The show of strength is obviously less effective as a peacekeeping tactic when counterpoised by a force representing diverse interests. This decline of effectiveness appears to have been demonstrated in June 1967 even when *both* superpowers desired that war between Israel and the Arabs be avoided. The restraining influence of the United States in the Third World may lessen. It is apparent that the Soviets have decided to alter their previous policy limited to economic and political penetration and combine a military presence as a third method of influencing Third World nations.

Although the chance of Russian marines landing on the coast of Africa or in the Middle East in a crisis to "preserve peace" is remote, the possibility of a Soviet political and military initiative has to be considered in future contingency planning. The Kremlin can be expected to evaluate the political effectiveness of training exercises, outside the Soviet Union, "courtesy visits," and "shows of force" scorned in the Khrushchev era. While the history of the Russian navy and its cautious approach to past crises indicate that an aggressive policy is not likely, Soviet naval strategy is apparently in a state of flux. However, there is no indication yet that Moscow will take the initiative in Third World crisis situations.

Even without an aggressive policy, the Russians could achieve a major gain if by deployment of modern vessels they could psychologically or militarily neutralize American forces. In 1967 the Soviet "Eskadra" slightly increased American uncertainty and restraint, but it did not significantly affect U.S. policy choices. In the future, however, neutralization could occur with a decrease in American political and military capability, an increase in Soviet strength, and a lack of American confidence in the considerable U.S. strategic and tactical power. The analogy of the Soviet navy versus the American to that of the Germans versus the British prior to World War I is valid. A land power is making a bid for some of the advantages of naval predominance.

Increased Soviet operations in the Mediterranean and the Sea of Japan will undoubtedly be followed by a greater presence in the Baltic, North and Red Seas, Persian Gulf, the Indian Ocean, and even the Western Hemisphere.

While Soviet employment of surface vessels will probably be carefully restricted, it is the anticipated response of the United States which is likely to be persuasive in Kremlin calculations. In 1967 the President did not hesitate to underline American determination with naval forces. The Soviet presence was not a significant deterrent. The United States had the advantages of superior strength and the will to use it.

Whether the United States will retain these two decisive elements affecting the political military employment of forces in future crises remains to be seen. In both categories U.S. capability appears to be decreasing. The question is whether naval strength will be adequate for the job it is likely to be called upon to do in the new decade. The obsolescence of many vessels of World War II vintage has been forecast for a number of years. But priorities of other programs and the natural desire to stretch the World War II investment as far as possible have resulted in a serious problem. Today 58 percent of U.S. combatant ships have been in service at least twenty years. Less than one percent of Soviet ships are as old as that.[5] The situation in 1971 will be as follows:[6]

Attack carriers 40% are 20 years or older
Antisubmarine carriers all 7 are 25 years or older
Destroyers and escorts 46% will be 20 years or older
Cruisers 90% will be 25 years or older

Two sizable reductions in naval ships in service in 1968 have been followed by a cut of more than 100 additional ships in 1969. Although primarily the result of budget requirements and mainte-

[5]U.S., Congress, House, Report of the Seapower Subcommittee of the Committee on Armed Services, *Status of Naval Ships,* 91st Cong., 1st sess., March 19, 1969 (Washington, 1969), p. 415.

[6]Taken from testimony of Admiral Thomas H. Moorer, USN, Chief of Naval Operations, in testimony before the Special Subcommittee on Sea Power of the Committee on Armed Services, U.S., Congress, House, *Status of Naval Ships,* 90th Cong., 2nd sess. (Washington, 1969), p. 133.

nance costs, they also are the result of decreasing capability of these ships. While the most modern ships have been employed off Vietnam, aging ships patrolling the Formosa Strait, for example, occasionally opened holes below the waterline from the vibration of shooting their guns in practice.

The outlook for reversing this trend is bleak. Even with a war in progress a major reduction of the armed services has begun. A further retrenchment of force levels will be a natural outgrowth of the Vietnamese war. With the increased costs of modernizing, the competition of domestic requirements for fiscal resources, and current political realities, it would appear that barring some new major threat these trends will continue. The Vietnam war has resulted in a marked increase in the tempo of naval operations further straining aging ships and a tendency to decrease non-Vietnam units so as to reduce the war cost. It has also created a political environment unfavorable to increased military investment.

The Vietnamese experience has also fostered an attitude toward contraction from worldwide involvements which has a direct bearing on the will of the United States to employ its armed strength. Moscow undoubtedly is delighted with announcements that the United States will withdraw more forces stationed abroad and reduce the number of forward bases. One of the reasons that the United States was relatively successful in the Middle East in June 1967 and effective in the Quemoy crisis of 1958 was the strong reputation of Sixth and Seventh Fleets in the minds of the Soviets and others. Movements during these crises were consistent, for the most part, with that image. However, the Soviets may have been surprised at subsequent U.S. failure to react forcefully to incidents like the seizure of the *Pueblo*. It seems reasonable to forecast future tests of American will. In the aftermath of the Vietnam experience, Washington's tendency may be to overlook a great deal before becoming involved and approach new challenges with great caution.

During the 1967 Middle East crisis the United States had a marginal naval capability to deal with the situation. Since that time, Soviet naval strength in the Mediterranean has doubled. The trends of Soviet expansion—the development of the means and a gradual evolution from a conservative military doctrine, British contraction from world power status, and the reduction of American capability indicate that the United States will be less able militarily to cope effectively with future multicrisis situations involving the Middle East, the Formosa Strait, and other areas of the globe.

But the most serious decrease in capability that may result is psychological. From closely examining Soviet policy in these two cases and subsequent employment of naval power, it is apparent that while the Russians are opportunistic, they are also cautious. As long as the United States has a credible force and it is clear that vital U.S. interests are involved, the chance of Soviet counteraction is remote. Russia is engaged in *low-risk* opportunism. Soviet literature, peacetime movements, and crisis actions demonstrate this. Russia apparently will try to capitalize on its naval armadas but not at the risk of a showdown with the United States at sea. Moscow's campaign is directed at making Washington believe that U.S. fleets have been neutralized. But the United States still holds the edge militarily and psychologically. It is particularly in the latter category that American credibility must be maintained.

A number of approaches have been proposed for meeting the naval challenge of the new decade. Among the possible alternatives are plans to develop NATO naval forces for the Atlantic and Mediterranean, finance a British peace-keeping force, develop regional forces, and rely primarily on American naval strength. From an American point of view the organization of standing NATO task forces is an ideal method for overcoming the political, psychological, and economic strains of Atlantic obligations and meeting the Soviet challenge in the Mediterranean. As former U.S. NATO Ambassador Harland Cleveland has written,

> In general, we have come to believe that cooperation is the better (if not the only) alternative; we are simply too big and too much involved in the affairs of the world to 'go it alone' very far or very effectively anymore. And this is why we are talking with our allies about a NATO response to the Soviet Mediterranean buildup.[7]

The idea of a NATO maritime task force for the Mediterranean was proposed following the June war, but the concept was not approved by the NATO ministers until January 1969. This points up one of the many difficulties in developing an effective collective force. It was the Soviet invasion of Czechoslovakia that triggered enough concern about the Soviet threat in the Mediterranean to obtain approval for such a scheme. It is necessary for NATO members, especially the nations of southern Europe, to have a perception of threat that is comparable to that of the United States in order for the force to be successful. It is not likely that this will occur consistently.

One need only look at the animosities between Turkey and Greece to anticipate some of the problems in formulating a concert of power in the area. Italy, the United States, and Britain, as presently

[7]Letter from Ambassador Harland Cleveland, U.S. Permanent Representative on the North Atlantic Council, to Lt. Comdr. J. T. Howe, USN, dated May 10, 1968.

conceived, will provide the nucleus of the Mediterranean force with Greece and Turkey assigning units from time to time. Since this is a NATO force, it is not likely to solve many of the other peace-keeping needs for the United States in the Mediterranean area. Activation of the force in times of tension will require the consent of participating countries as well as the approval of all other members. For this reason it does not appear to be a concept of very great political effectiveness. While it can serve as a symbol of NATO unity in peacetime, that function is somewhat redundant since there has been a rather extensive program of NATO naval exercises in the Mediterranean for some time. If the force could be mobilized in times of increasing Soviet threat in the Mediterranean, it would be a useful concept. However, whether such a concept will work out on a practical basis remains to be seen. As presently envisaged it is an *on-call* group to conduct port visits and participate in exercises. It is not an "intervention force."[8]

In any case, there is little hope that such a flotilla would reduce American peace-keeping operations in non-NATO areas of the Mediterranean. The Middle East crisis of 1967 provided an excellent example of the kinds of difficulties that can arise. Not only were there greater limitations on Britain's ability to act in that region, but the United States and United Kingdom together were able to arouse only minimal interest on the part of other maritime nations in guaranteeing innocent passage through the Gulf of Aqaba.

The development of a permanent standing NATO naval force for the Atlantic has reached the operational stage. Its initial composition consisted of single ships of the frigate type contributed by the Netherlands, Norway, the United Kingdom, and the United States. A German ship joined the force in March 1968, and Canadian and Portuguese ships have operated periodically with the group. While planners foresee no "insoluble" peace-keeping problems,[9] it would appear that there are also some fairly obvious limitations home governments would place on the employment of this force. Serious differences of opinion on utilization could negate many of the gains from its development.

However, there are some unifying benefits for the Atlantic alliance from the creation of these forces, as well as domestic and interna-

[8]Transcript of interview between Admiral Horacio Rivero, CinC, Allied Forces Southern Europe and the Italian newspaper *Lo Specchio* conducted on February 11, 1969, p. 3.

[9]Lt. Col. Thomas Soberick, USA, Staff of Supreme Allied Commander Atlantic, commented "we foresee no insoluble problems should a peace-keeping role for the force arise." Letter to Lt. Comdr. J. T. Howe, USN, dated March 4, 1968.

tional political advantages. If an Atlantic NATO naval unit could be counted on, the need for U.S. warships in the Atlantic and Mediterranean might be lessened. However, there would probably be many circumstances in which such a force simply would not be available to serve the interests of the United States in these areas. If there were open warfare between the United States and the USSR, NATO ships would obviously become involved, but no preexisting multinational flotillas would be necessary for this type of guarantee. It is in the political crises of the cold war where such an organization would be most useful but seems least likely to be available.

Another method of increasing U.S. strength in the Mediterranean would be to seek a trade-off between U.S. contributions to the troop strength in Europe and the naval forces in the Mediterranean and Indian Ocean regions. Although American army reductions would have to be gradual in order to surmount the considerable political repercussions and to allow other NATO countries to replace these forces, this might be a feasible way to reduce the adverse gold flow and alleviate some of the Vietnam strain on existing forces. Enough American troops would have to be maintained to convince Moscow that NATO was no less vunerable and that the implied guarantee that the U.S. must use nuclear weapons to defend its forces remained.[10] On the other hand, even if such a reallocation of U.S. contributions were workable with NATO allies, the dependency of Mediterranean forces on U.S. troops in Europe for following through on an initial commitment would have to be overcome. In Lebanon for example U.S. army troops were flown from Europe to reinforce the small marine contingent initially landed.

It has been suggested that one solution might be to strengthen Anglo-American ties and specifically to help finance a British peacekeeping force with U.S. funds.[11] Others argue that such a scheme would be self-defeating in the long run.[12]

[10]Nuclear weapons become more important when a limited-war situation becomes difficult to meet with conventional forces. If the United States becomes outclassed at sea, as it felt it was on land in Europe versus the Red Army for many years, then the need to employ at least tactical nuclear weapons to overcome deficiencies in strength will become greater. However, public and world opinion and increasing Soviet strategic and tactical nuclear capabilities would be powerful deterrents to the employment of such weapons.

[11]See, for example, George Fielding Eliot, "Alliance Diplomacy in Limited Wars," U.S. Naval Institute *Proceedings*, Vol. 93, No. 4 (April 1967), p. 56. Of course, the presence of U.S. forces has greater impact than a comparable British demonstration because behind American units is the total U.S. power.

[12]See, for example, George W. Ball, *The Discipline of Power* (Boston: Little, Brown and Company, 1968), pp. 94, 95.

Reputedly, Kuwait has offered to help offset the cost of the British presence in order to retain its stabilizing influence in the Persian Gulf. But while Britain is willing to assign some military advisers, London is obviously determined to contract from that region. Another approach would be to make a greater effort to try to solve Britain's economic problems. Some British military writers favor the idea of an international task force.[13] But beyond an American and British bilateral venture the possibility of developing an effective multinational force for worldwide operations still appears to be remote.

There is increasing hope for developing regional arrangements to try to stabilize Third World areas. A Persian Gulf force headed by Iran, a Southeast Asian force under the leadership of Australia, an Asian force led by Japan, and a buildup of Indian naval strength all are in early stages of development. Although these regional groupings will be subject to a number of political difficulties in obtaining cooperative effort, they have many advantages. Efforts of this type should reduce some of the instability resulting from the withdrawal of the British. But in the type of global confrontation considered in this study, it is the forces of the United States and the Soviet Union that count. A regional peace-keeping force cannot be expected to standup to the Soviet Union unless it has some visible American backing.

The United States should continue to try to obtain greater cooperation from its NATO allies. But since practically all plans for joint efforts would have to be backed by an American ability to act unilaterally, it would perhaps be cheapest and most satisfactory for the United States to maintain the necessary capability with its own naval forces.

The most feasible approach would be a combination of all these methods, recognizing the distinct limitations in each case. The development of regional peace-keeping forces, existence of NATO naval groups, and retention of American strength at least at its present level may provide an adequate solution in the near future. Certainly, the British should be encouraged to retain an attack carrier in their navy during the 1970s.

The American naval need is not for attaining greater numerical strength in ships but rather for keeping pace in terms of propulsion

[13]See Vice Adm. B. B. Schofield, RN (Ret.) "Sentinels at the Bridge," U.S. Naval Institute *Proceedings*, Vol. 93, No. 10 (October 1967), p. 53. And Rear Admiral Morgan Giles, "The Case for a British Presence East of Suez," Chapter 5 of *Brassey's Annual: The Armed Forces Year Book 1967* (New York: Praeger, 1967), p. 50.

and weapons systems with Soviet counterparts.[14] Actually, the increased capability of a modern warship reduces the numbers required versus older versions. Since the United States has greater worldwide responsibilities than the Soviet Union, American fleets have a much larger area to cover. As defensive or reaction forces, their job is complicated. Therefore, U.S. ships must be modern and capable of sustained operations.

In regions of vital security interest to the United States, the advantages of maintaining a naval presence appear to far outweigh the disadvantages. But the forces should be credible enough to convince the potential enemy that the United States cannot be bluffed and to make U.S. intentions clear. In regions of less vital concern, it would appear that periodic visits rather than a permanent presence is more within the capabilities of the United States.

Although the U.S. Sixth Fleet is presently of adequate strength, there are some specific steps that should be taken to bolster it. Following the Middle East crisis it was reported that an antisubmarine carrier force would be stationed in the Mediterranean at all times.[15] During the Arab-Israeli war, the Soviet submarine forces represented the major threat to the Sixth Fleet. Although an antisubmarine group was finally deployed to the Mediterranean, it arrived in the aftermath of the war. The force has subsequently withdrawn and is presently not being maintained in the Mediterranean because of the requirements of Vietnam and other areas of the world.[16] It would increase Sixth Fleet credibility to assign such a force permanently to the Mediterranean. The marine battalion there should also be kept at full strength and given a helicopter lift capability.

There is, of course, no guarantee that having forces at full strength will overcome the political, economic, and psychological resistance to further involvement that an extended conflict like Vietnam appears to have produced. The combination of adequate strategic and tactical American strength to deter Soviet intervention and local national forces that have a strong defensive capability relative to their neighbors appears to have many advantages. It should reduce the need for direct American involvement in local

[14]In considering Soviet capability one must consider a variety of possible situations and commitments. The areas where the Soviets can make use of land-based air forces are more suited to credible Soviet threat. In some cases, as in Quemoy, naval power is used versus land and air forces.

[15]*The Christian Science Monitor,* February 26, 1968, p. 1.

[16]Letter from Admiral L. R. Geis, USN, to Lt. Comdr. J. T. Howe, USN, dated April 9, 1969. These are among the type of ships hardest hit by recent force reductions.

conflicts and the cost of maintaining large numbers of conventional forces around the world. Other than in Latin America, where U.S. protection is more easily provided, most of the nations with which the United States has formal defense commitments are relatively strong. It is in informal and tacit commitments that the United States has associated itself with some relatively weak nations. Although there are many complications in each arrangement, it would seem advisable that along with clarifying its commitments, the United States must also assist in the military and economic strengthening of those nations considered to be essential allies.

In facing its international obligations, efforts to forge closer ties with allies should continue. The United States must uphold legitimate commitments that reflect its interests and are within the total capacity of this nation and its reliable allies to meet. Greater efforts must be made to close the awareness gap between the government and the attentive public concerning American interests and commitments. In a dynamic world of change, the necessity for specific obligations should be reviewed regularly. The government then must work to achieve the kind of atmosphere that allows the tapping of the full potential of this nation to meet international obligations.

In light of Soviet naval expansion, British withdrawal, and the obvious strain of the Vietnam war, it would appear prudent to maintain viable American strength throughout the world and particularly in the Mediterranean. It is hard to understand how the United States can cut back its forces and realistically expect to meet existing commitments. If the political, psychological, and military trends continue and a genuine gap between American capabilities and commitments develops, policy alternatives in future multicrisis situations may be significantly restricted. Because of existing national interests and responsibilities, such a limitation does not appear to be tolerable.

APPENDIX A

STATEMENTS BY PRESIDENT DWIGHT D. EISENHOWER AND SECRETARY OF STATE JOHN FOSTER DULLES CONCERNING THE QUEMOY CRISIS OF 1958

A.1 ON THE U.S. POSITION CONCERNING THE DEFENSE OF QUEMOY AND MATSU

1

We have no commitment of any kind, sort, or description, expressed or implied, which binds the United States to anything except the defense of Formosa and the Pescadores.

I repeat—again and again and again—that our only commitment is to defend Formosa and the Pescadores and if there were no challenge to Formosa and the Pescadores, then there wouldn't be any question as far as we are concerned of fighting in that area.

John Foster Dulles
April 5, 1955[a]

2

. . . we have recognized that the securing and protecting of Quemoy and Matsu have increasingly become related to the defense of Taiwan. This is indeed also recognized by the Chinese Communists.

. . . the President is authorized by joint resolution of the Congress to employ the armed forces of the United States for the securing and protection of related positions such as Quemoy and Matsu.

John Foster Dulles
September 4, 1958[b]

3

Therefore, it is quite clear, and I think had been *made clear from the beginning* of this affair, that the offshore *islands are not to be defended as such by the United States*. If they are to be involved in what is in effect an attack upon areas which we are bound to de-

[a]Department of State, *American Foreign Policy, 1950–1955,* p. 2495. Dulles News conference of April 5, 1955. (Emphasis added.)
[b]*The New York Times,* "Text of Dulles Statement on the Far East," September 5, 1958, p. 2.

fend, namely Taiwan and the Penghus, then we will meet the attack at that point. But we cannot just say that we will defend, come what may, under any and all circumstances, an area which is beyond that to which we are committed by the treaty. This can be done only if there is an actual relationship between the two at the time in question. I think that was made very clear at the time of the adoption of the resolution. I made it clear in my press conferences back in 1955 and it is the same situation today as it was at that time.

. . . what is at stake there is not just two pieces of real estate, Quemoy and Matsu. Obviously, if *that was all that was involved there would be no basis for action on the part of the United States*. What is involved there is the whole position . . . of the free world in the Western Pacific and the vital interests of the United States are involved.

John Foster Dulles
September 9, 1958[c]

4
Now, I assure you that no American boy will be asked by me to fight *just* for Quemoy.

Dwight D. Eisenhower
September 11, 1958[d]

5
When all the factors, moral and material, are taken into account, it may well be that the defense of these different areas cannot be achieved piecemeal but that their defense may not be divisible . . . and President Eisenhower has in relation to those islands made clear that United States forces may be used more actively if the Chinese Communists push further a military effort which they themselves proclaim has Formosa as its goal.

John Foster Dulles
September 25, 1958[e]

We don't intend to have a war just on account of Quemoy and Matsu. If that was all there was to it, there wouldn't be any problem.

. . . if the United States believed that these islands could be aban-

[c] *The New York Times* transcript of Dulles news conference, September 10, 1958, p. 8. (Emphasis added.)
[d] Department of State, *American Foreign Policy, 1958*, p. 1159. (Emphasis added by speaker.)
[e] *The New York Times* text of Dulles speech, September 26, 1958, p. 3.

doned without its having any adverse impact upon the potential defense of Formosa and the treaty area, we would not be thinking of using forces there. It's because there is that relationship under present conditions, conditions primarily of the Communist making, that there is the tie in there.

... we do not *have any legal commitment to defend the offshore islands*. We do not want to make any such commitment. We do not have it today.

John Foster Dulles
September 30, 1958[f]

6

... fundamentally anyone can see that the two islands as of themselves, as two pieces of territory, are not greatly vital to Formosa. But of course the *Chinese Nationalists* hold that if you give way to that, you have given way to exposing us to attack, and that is a different thing, from just concluding that two pieces of territory are the vital issue.

Dwight D. Eisenhower
October 1, 1958[g]

Neither you nor any other American need feel that the United States will be involved in military hostilities *merely in defense of Quemoy or Matsu.*

Certainly there is always the possibility that it may in certain contingencies, after taking account of all relevant facts, become necessary or appropriate for the defense of Formosa and the Pescadores also to take measures to secure and protect the related positions of Quemoy and Matsu.

Dwight D. Eisenhower
October 2, 1958[h]

A.2 ON THE RELATIONSHIP BETWEEN DEFENSE OF THE OFFSHORE ISLANDS AND DEFENSE OF TAIWAN

1

... is authorized to employ the Armed Forces of the United States as he deems necessary for the specific purpose of *securing and*

[f] *The New York Times* transcript of news conference, October 1, 1958, p. 8. (Emphasis added.)

[g] Department of State, *American Foreign Policy, 1958,* p. 1170. (Emphasis added.)

[h] Ibid., pp. 1170, 1171. Letter to Chairman of the Senate Committee on Foreign Relations. (Emphasis added.)

protecting Formosa and the Pescadores against armed attack, this authority to include the *securing and protection* of such related positions and territories of that area now in friendly hands and the taking of such other *measures as he judges to be required or appropriate in assuring the defense of Formosa and the Pescadores*.

Joint Congressional Resolution
January 29, 1955[a]

2
As you know, these islands have been continuously in the hands of the Republic of China, and over the last four years the *ties between these islands and Formosa have become closer and their interdependence has increased*.

John Foster Dulles
August 23, 1958[b]

3
Well, they have this *increased importance*: what we call the Nationalist Chinese have now deployed about a third of their forces to certain of these islands west of the Pescadores, and that makes a *closer interlocking between the defense systems of the islands with Formosa* than was the case before that. Before that, I think, they were largely thought of as outposts, strongly held, but nevertheless outposts.

Dwight D. Eisenhower
August 27, 1958[c]

4
The President would not, however, hesitate to make such a finding if he judged that the circumstances made this necessary to accomplish the purposes of the Joint Resolution. In this connection we have recognized that the *securing and protecting of Quemoy and Matsu have increasingly become related to the defense of Taiwan*.

John Foster Dulles
September 4, 1958[d]

[a]*Mutual Defense Treaty with the Republic of China,* pp. 11, 12. (Emphasis added.)
[b]Department of State, *American Foreign Policy, 1958,* p. 1144. Letter from the Secretary of State to the Acting Chairman of the House Committee on Foreign Affairs, August 23, 1958. (Emphasis added.)
[c]Department of State, *American Foreign Policy, 1958,* p. 1144. (Emphasis added.)
[d]*The New York Times,* "Text of Dulles Statement on the Far East," September 5, 1958, p. 2. (Emphasis added.)

5
Question: Mr. Secretary, in view of the fact that the Chinese Communists' radio, in talking about Quemoy and Formosa makes no distinction separating Quemoy from the eventual plan to liberate Formosa, if there were to be an attack say today, would you think that everything added up to a decision to go ahead and help defend Quemoy on the ground that it is essential to the defense of Formosa?
Answer: I think you can guess the answer to that if you read the statement of September 4.

John Foster Dulles
September 9, 1958[e]

6
They frankly say that their present military effort is part of a program to conquer Formosa. It is as certain as can be that the shooting which the Chinese Communists started on August 23rd had as its purposes not just the taking of Quemoy.
Today, the Chinese Communists announce, repeatedly and officially, that their military operations against Quemoy are preliminary to attack on Formosa. So *it is clear that the Formosa Straits resolution of 1955 applies to the present situation.*

Dwight D. Eisenhower
September 11, 1958[f]

7
Now there is a *very close relationship* between Formosa and these offshore islands, and that is attested to not only by the Republic of China but it is asserted by the Chinese Communists themselves.

John Foster Dulles
September 25, 1958[g]

8
It is because there is that relationship, under present conditions,

[e]*The New York Times* transcript of Dulles news conference, September 10, 1958, p. 8.
[f]Department of State, *American Foreign Policy, 1958,* pp. 1157, 1159. Speech to nation of September 11, 1958. (Emphasis added.)
[g]*The New York Times* text of Dulles speech, September 26, 1958, p. 3. (Emphasis added.)

conditions primarily of the Communists' making, that there is the tie in there.

John Foster Dulles
September 30, 1958[h]

9

Now, the best evidence on this particular issue, as of now, is that the Communists themselves, while calling it a civil war, have stated that their effort is not confined . . . to Quemoys and Matsus, and not only to Formosa but to driving the United States forces out of the Western Pacific. . . .

Dwight D. Eisenhower
October 1, 1958[i]

10

The Chinese and Soviet Communist leaders assert, and have reason to believe, that if they can take Quemoy and Matsu by armed assault, that will open the way for them to take Formosa and the Pescadores and, as they put it, "expel" the United States from the West Pacific and cause its Fleet to leave international waters and "go home." I cannot dismiss these boastings as mere bluff. Certainly there is always the possibility that it may in certain contingencies, after taking account of all relevant facts, become necessary or appropriate for the defense of Formosa and the Pescadores also to take measures to secure and protect the related positions of Quemoy and Matsu.

Dwight D. Eisenhower
October 2, 1958[j]

A.3 ON THE PERMANENCY OF A COMMUNIST REGIME AND THE POSSIBILITY OF A NATIONALIST RETURN

1

It is true that there is no reason to believe that the Chinese Communist regime is on the verge of collapse, but there is equally no reason to accept its present rule on mainland China as permanent. The

[h] *The New York Times* transcript of news conference, October 1, 1958, p. 8.
[i] Department of State, *American Foreign Policy, 1958,* p. 1170. Press conference.
[j] Ibid., p. 1171. Letter to Chairman of the Senate Committee on Foreign Relations.

United States holds the view that Communism's role in China is not permanent and that it one day will pass.

State Department Statement of Policy
August 8, 1958[a]

2
We do not consider that the Chinese Communists' hold upon the mainland is to be accepted as a permanent fact of life and one of those inevitable things which we all have to accept and give way to. . . . I believe that it is inevitable, sooner or later, that . . . desire for personal freedom will manifest itself.

John Foster Dulles
September 9, 1958[b]

3
But it is agreed between us that the use of force by either of the parties in the area 'will be a matter of joint agreement. . . .' Pursuant to this arrangement there has been no aggressive or offensive use of force by the US or by the Republic of China against Communist China.

John Foster Dulles
September 25, 1958[c]

4
I think it all depends upon on what happens on the mainland. I don't think that just by their own steam they are going to get there. If you had on the mainland a sort of unrest and revolt, like, for example, what broke out in Hungary, then the presence of a free China with considerable power a few miles away could be a very important element in the situations.

So I wouldn't want to exclude any possibility of a situation developing on the mainland of China or on parts of the mainland of China which might lead to reunification of some sort between mainland China and the free Government of China, the Republic of China now on Formosa. I do not exclude it.

No. There is no commitment of any kind to aid in that.

John Foster Dulles
September 30, 1958[d]

[a] *The New York Times,* August 10, 1958, p. 30.
[b] *The New York Times* transcript of Dulles news conference, September 10, 1958, p. 8.
[c] *The New York Times* text of Dulles speech, September 26, 1958, p. 3.
[d] *The New York Times* transcript of news conference, October 1, 1958, p. 8.

A.4 ON WHAT ACTIONS THE UNITED STATES MIGHT BE WILLING TO TAKE IF CHINA RENOUNCED FORCE

1

Question: Mr. Secretary, could the United States give the Chinese Communists assurances in any such discussions that the Chinese Nationalists would not engage in force?

Answer: I think that the treaty arrangements which we have with the Republic of China make it quite clear that it is in our *mutual contemplation that force shall not be used.* The whole character of that treaty is *defensive.* That is underlined throughout the treaty itself and in the concurrent understandings that were arrived at in that connection. . . .

John Foster Dulles
August 2, 1955[a]

2

I recall that in the extended negotiations which the representatives of the United States and Chinese Communist regime conducted at Geneva between 1955 and 1958, a sustained effort was made by the United States to secure with particular reference to the Taiwan area, a declaration of *mutual and reciprocal renunciation of force,* except in self-defense, which however, would be without prejudice to the pursuit of policies by peaceful means. The Chinese Communists rejected any such declaration. We believe, however, that such a course constitutes the only civilized and acceptable procedure.

John Foster Dulles
September 4, 1958[b]

3

. . . if there were an effective, dependable renunciation of force, that it would be certainly a very constructive new element in the situation which might have further consequences.

. . . But I don't want to attempt to say what those consequences would be because they involve the rights and interests of an ally.

. . . But I think the matter can perhaps be dealt with in a more spe-

[a] U.S., Department of State, *American Foreign Policy, 1950–1955, Basic Documents, Vol. II* (Washington, 1957), p. 2508. News conference of August 2, 1955. (Emphasis added.)

[b] *The New York Times,* "Text of Dulles Statement on the Far East," September 5, 1958, p. 2. (Emphasis added.)

cific way rather than in abstract generalities. . . .

John Foster Dulles
September 9, 1958[c]

4
There are measures that can be taken to assure that these offshore islands will not be a thorn in the side of peace.

Dwight D. Eisenhower
September 11, 1958[d]

5
But so far as we are concerned, we would find acceptable any arrangement which on the one hand did not involve surrender to force or the threat of force and on the other hand eliminated from the situation features that could reasonably be regarded as provocative, or which, to use President Eisenhower's phrase, were "a thorn on the side of peace."

John Foster Dulles
September 25, 1958[e]

6
If there were a cease-fire in the area which seemed to be reasonably dependable, I think it would be foolish to keep those large forces on these islands . . . if there were a cease-fire it would be our judgment, military judgment, even, that it would not be wise or prudent to keep them there . . . we have assumed that the *renunciation of force should be reciprocal if it occurs*, and that it would be obviously quite impractical and quite wrong to ask the Chinese Communists to abandon use of force if they were being attacked by the Chinese Nationalists.

We obviously believe that if there was a renunciation of force, it *should be a renunciation on both sides*. We could not expect a unilateral renunciation of force. It should be on the basis of and conditioned upon reciprocity.

John Foster Dulles
September 30, 1958[f]

[c]*The New York Times* transcript of Dulles news conference, September 10, 1958, p. 8.
[d]Department of State, *American Foreign Policy, 1958,* p. 1160.
[e]*The New York Times* text of Dulles speech, September 26, 1958, p. 3. *The New York Times* account was taken from a radio broadcast. The press release used the expression "a thorn in the side of peace."
[f]*The New York Times* transcript of news conference, October 1, 1958, p. 8. (Emphasis added.)

A.5 ON WHETHER THE UNITED STATES ENCOURAGED TROOP BUILDUP ON QUEMOY

1

Question: After the passage of the Formosa Resolution did this country do anything to encourage the Chinese Nationalists to build up their forces on the Quemoys in a formal or an informal way?

Answer: I think not. My distinct impression is that the decision to build up the defensive strength on Quemoy and Matsu was taken by the Chinese Nationalist Republic, the Republic of China, and that that was not urged or encouraged by the United States.

Question: Mr. Secretary, do you think it was wise to have stood by while the buildup occurred on these islands?

Answer: Yes, I think it was.

. . . The attempt by the United States to impose its will in that respect upon the Republic of China would have had very unfortunate consequences.

John Foster Dulles
September 9, 1958[a]

2

Now, of course, these offshore islands do not constitute an ideal defensive position. The *United States has not been blind to the fact, nor have we been unconcerned about it*. But there are other facts also to which we cannot be blind.

John Foster Dulles
September 25, 1958[b]

3

If there were a cease-fire in the area which seemed to be reasonably dependable, I think it would be foolish to keep these large forces on these islands. We though that *it was rather foolish to put them there. . . .*

The United States did not feel that it was sound to make the major commitment of force to those areas that the Chinese Government wished to make. In view, however, of the very strong views of the Republic of China, we were *acquiescent* in that. We did not attempt to veto it. The result is, I might say, one of acquiescence on the part

[a]*The New York Times* transcript of Dulles news conference, September 10, 1958, p. 8.
[b]*The New York Times* text of Dulles speech, September 26, 1958, p. 3.

of the United States *not of approval*. Nor did we attempt to veto it after having used persuasion.

John Foster Dulles
September 30, 1958[c]

4

Now, you mentioned the question of it would be foolish for them keeping large forces there for a long time. I believe, as a soldier, that was not a good thing to do, to have all these troops there. But, remember, we have differences with our allies all over the world.

Dwight D. Eisenhower
October 1, 1958[d]

[c]*The New York Times* transcript of news conference, October 1, 1958, p. 8.
[d]Department of State, *American Foreign Policy, 1958,* p. 1169.

APPENDIX B

SELECTED INTERVIEWS

B.1 INTERVIEW WITH AN OFFICIAL FAMILIAR WITH POLICY DURING QUEMOY CRISIS OF 1958, CONDUCTED JANUARY 31, 1969

1

Question: Were we confident of our military capability to defend the major offshore islands throughout the Quemoy crisis?

Answer: Yes, and particularly so if we used our nuclear power. The military situation was always under control. We were of course relieved when the Chinese did not try to employ their large bomber force. If the Chinese had been willing to accept heavy attrition their bombers could have been a threat to the Nationalist positions and the Seventh Fleet. One big indication of Chinese military inadequacy was the failure of their fighter aircraft against the Nationalists. We were surprised and shocked by the ease with which the Nationalists demonstrated their superiority. We wondered whether the Chinese were putting first-class pilots in the area. Their pilots seemed to lack experience and they appeared to freeze in combat. We never saw how there could be a successful attack from the sea mounted by the Chinese. They simply could not meet the shipping requirements.

Question: Not even to invade Quemoy? A few miles off the mainland?

Answer: Even there they would have had great difficulty. They would have had a most difficult time taking Quemoy as long as there was resistance.

Question: Did we lose confidence at any point in our ability to resupply the islands?

Answer: No. We knew it would take a little ingenuity, but we were confident we could overcome the problem. We were certain about our ability to overcome the problem ultimately, but we had to try various methods. The islands were well stocked so there was no immediate problem.

2

Question: At what point did we decide that the offshore islands must be defended or was that our policy all along?

Answer: We had a solid commitment to Formosa all along but not necessarily to defense of the offshore islands. However, you could argue that our hands were tied in a sense when Chiang put such a large portion of his troops in the islands. It would have been most difficult for him to defend Formosa if he had lost the troops on the offshore islands.

3

Question: President Eisenhower has written that he was told Chiang's refusal to evacuate the islands "was a reflection of his hope of promoting a fight between the United States and the Chinese Communists as a prelude to a Chinese Nationalist invasion of the mainland." Why did this feeling exist?
Answer: Chiang had professed a desire to return to the mainland. He could not hope to invade without U.S. support. His motivation was not entirely Machiavellian. He evidently felt it was essential to the morale of his people. Some felt he would like to see us get involved militarily. His refusal to reduce his garrisons on the islands appeared to reflect Chiang's desire to get us embroiled. He appeared even willing to go down as a nation rather than surrender the islands. We were not for his throwing away the islands but disagreed with the proportion of his forces that had been put there.
Question: President Eisenhower's remarks indicate that this was a change of opinion on the part of the Defense Department. Was this assessment of Chiang a new insight or was the thought simply articulated in the president's mind for the first time on the 11th?
Answer: I don't believe there was any great significance to the timing. There had been discussions of the pros and cons in the Quemoy situation on a daily basis.

4

Question: President Eisenhower has also written that "even more remarkable, the Defense Department now seemed willing to shift its position . . . the Joint Chiefs now felt the Quemoy and Matsu islands should be vacated (or lightly manned as outposts only). What position was the Joint Chiefs of Staff shifting from?
Answer: The Joint Chiefs of Staff were never very enthusiastic about defending the islands. I'm having difficulty recalling a particular shift. As I remember there was not any sharp shift. The bombardment may have caused them to focus more closely on the problem and to distinguish what geographical positions in the area were really important from a defense standpoint.

5

Question: We apparently offered to demilitarize the islands in

stages at one of the first Warsaw negotiations with the Communist Chinese. Were we softening our position in response to domestic or military pressure?
Answer: I don't recall that the discussions at Warsaw were particularly significant. At no point did we think that we were softening our position. If anything we thought we were hardening it. We naturally didn't like domestic criticism of our policy from people who did not understand the significance of defending Quemoy. No administration does. But this sort of pressure never reached the point where we were not able to do what we thought we had to do.

6
Question: What was our estimate of Soviet intentions to aid the Chinese?
Answer: We didn't think that they would.
Question: Did we think that the Chinese had been given a nuclear capability by the Soviets?
Answer: No. What worried us was their very substantial bomber fleet. We didn't think the Soviets would trust foreigners with atomic weapons.

7
Question: Did we ever really feel that the Chinese were going to try to take the islands by force?
Answer: We thought they might. We felt in their initial heavy bombardment that they were trying to immobilize the defense force. Actually the bombardments were fairly ineffective and casualties were light. We had to believe that they hoped to storm the defense force. But it would have taken an immense force to assault Quemoy. We thought in the early part of the crisis that they might try if they wanted to utilize their whole bomber fleet in support.

8
Question: To what extent was our approach to the Quemoy situation influenced by our experiences in Lebanon and the existing involvement in the Middle East?
Answer: We felt Quemoy was just another testing point of the resolution of the United States. We felt no limitations because of Lebanon. At that time it looked as if we would not become involved in a direct confrontation. There was not much activity in Lebanon since the Soviets were not coming in. Of course, we had to consider the implications of two crises in such a short time and what we would do if there were a half dozen.

9
Question: Was there a sense of an easing of the crisis when the Chinese accepted resumption of talks in Warsaw on September 6?
Answer: It made no particular impact on me. When China did not commit its bomber force we knew they weren't going to bother us much. This was the significant turning point for us.

10
Question: Why did we not make a show of strength in the Taiwan Straits area in the weeks prior to August 23 when we suspected that trouble was developing?
Answer: We didn't have any real assurance that the threat was anything more than a nuisance. Within 48 hours of commencement of the shelling we had F104s flying up and down the straits. It was difficult to believe the Communists would carry it very far. We didn't want to be extravagant in our show of force or use more power than we anticipated would be necessary.

11
Question: Were there any economic factors that would have prevented our fighting a limited war if we had been challenged or sustaining our show of strength for a lengthy period in the area?
Answer: Nothing economic appeared to be a limiting factor. Of course if there had been an all out fight with the Communists no one knew how severe the strain would be. You don't know how far you're going to have to go when you get into these things. You hope it will be limited. We would have had to organize additional transportation. We had substantial backup of materiel and aircraft in the Far East (Okinawa, etc.). We didn't think that we were short of forces, bombers, etc. We weren't thinking of a mass Army going into China or a contest on land. It is hard to answer the question. But generally speaking economic considerations were not a major concern.

12
Question: Would tactical nuclear weapons have been necessary in order to defend the offshore islands?
Answer: Yes, they would have been necessary if we had to deny the Chinese use of close in air fields.

13
Question: There were reports in the press at the time stressing that we still had a strategic superiority vis-à-vis the Soviets. Were these

published for the benefit of the Soviets in light of the approaching crisis? Did we have any doubts about our strategic superiority vis-à-vis the Soviets?

Answer: We did not have any doubts at the time about our overall superiority with bombers, missiles and carriers. Congress was making some hay out of the missile gap business but we never had any doubt about our strategic superiority. We did talk rather consistently about it to make sure that the Russians understood this.

B.2 INTERVIEW WITH AN INFORMED WHITE HOUSE SOURCE CONCERNING MIDDLE EAST CRISIS OF 1967, CONDUCTED MARCH 6, 1969

1

Question: President Johnson reputedly told Foreign Minister Eban on May 26, 1967, that he would have to obtain Congressional approval prior to using U.S. forces to test the Aqaba blockade or providing direct military support for Israel. Is this correct?

Answer: I was not at the meeting. However, an hour before the visit we were presented with a document which had a number of notes written on it in Dulles's hand indicating if there was a violation the United States could be counted upon to help out. Rostow tried to find out in the State Department if it was genuine—or at least whether we had a copy. It has been said that Johnson deliberately made Eban wait to see him, but actually Johnson was stalling him. A copy was finally found in the U.S. files which was quite a strong assertion of what the United States would do. As far as what the President told Eban about Congress, what has been written is probably based on hearsay. I doubt if the President made a flat statement to Eban. He was trying to keep Israel from going to war. Johnson tried to hold them back.

Question: Were the Dulles notes additions to the published *aide-mémoire* from Secretary Dulles to Israeli Ambassador to the United States Abba Eban of February 1957?

Answer: Yes.

2

Question: The President also apparently asked Israel to wait two weeks prior to taking action. Is this correct?

Answer: It was something like that. He asked them to wait for some period of time. He was trying to hold them off. I saw the President later that evening on another matter. He asked me "What do you think is going to happen?" I told him they *[Israel]* are going to hit them. He replied, "Yes, they are going to hit them." He made no other comment.

3

Question: Did we really make an effort to get together a group of nations to test the blockade of Aqaba?

Answer: Yes. We made a real effort to put one together, but we had trouble getting any takers.

Question: The idea of testing the blockade seems to have been abandoned in the days just prior to the war. Is this correct?

Answer: We were still trying to organize a multinational force. The real problem was that we couldn't raise any takers. There was a side squabble over whether Israel was going to be allowed to participate. Someone at State first said they wouldn't and then after a lot of noise on the hill we denied that we had said it couldn't sign the declaration and participate.

Question: Then, would Israel have been allowed to sign and participate?

Answer: Yes.

Question: Did we think the blockade-busting idea would be a success?

Answer: There were a number of problems. First of all, we didn't have the power. We had nothing there until we ran the *Intrepid* through the canal. The *Intrepid* at least gave us some air if we were going to force the blockade.

Question: But didn't we have to get Nasser's approval to use the Suez Canal? Didn't we have to give him some sort of guarantee that the *Intrepid* would not be used against him?

Answer: No. I am quite certain we had no agreement with Nasser.

Question: Was the lack of carrier power a serious factor when considering the blockade?

Answer: Yes, it was. You have to have some air power. That whole area south of Suez was a power vacuum. I never thought the blockade idea would have much success. I was very skeptical about it.

Question: Why?

Answer: Because I didn't think we'd get any customers.

Question: Why were we so insistent on a multilateral force?

Answer: Because of the war in Vietnam.

Question: What about the British? Were they willing to join us?

Answer: The British attitude was of the nature, "If everyone else is willing to sign, then you can count on us."

4

Question: Were we confident prior to the fighting of Soviet intentions not to intervene?

Answer: No. We were not confident. What the Soviets did would depend, we thought, on how things went. They might have intervened if Israel took over Syria. They at least planted some stories to this effect—that they would not permit Syria to be taken over. We had some conflicting indications of what the Soviets might be up to, and the most disconcerting sign seemed to be that they hadn't necessarily agreed among themselves what to do.

Question: Did we feel they were sincerely trying to restrain the Arabs?

Answer: This is a tough question. One of the big troublemakers was the Russian ambassador in Cairo. He was anything but restrained. It seemed quite likely that the Soviet man on the spot in Egypt was not plugged in to what the Kremlin was trying to do. We received conflicting readings. My guess is that their staff work was as good as ours. Our Joint Chiefs of Staff had predicted if fighting broke out Israel would win within three days. The President, reluctant to accept military estimates because of the Vietnamese experience, sent it out to two other places. The other organizations came up with essentially the same estimate. I think the Russians were as smart as we were and their military did not want to see a war since they knew Egypt would be defeated. On the other hand, I believe some of the ideologues were urging that the Arabs should let the Israelis have it. After the war began and the Soviets began making threatening noises concerning intervention to assist the Arabs we made it clear over the hot line that we were not going to look in relaxed fashion at their intervention. We moved the Sixth Fleet towards the Eastern Mediterranean to make this clear to the Soviets.

Question: How did the augmentation of Soviet forces affect our confidence in their professed desire for restraint?

Answer: It decreased our confidence.

5

Question: It has been said that the United States and Soviets agreed prior to the crisis not to intervene. Is this overstating our understanding with the Soviets?

Answer: Yes.

6

Question: There were reports on May 21 that the United States had sent messages to the Soviet Union urging it to use its influence to dampen down the crisis. Did we initiate this type of message this early in the crisis?

Answer: We went to the Soviets and told them to call off their boys.

7

Question: In considering various alternatives prior to the June war, how influential was our involvement in Vietnam? Would our policy have been different without a war in Vietnam?

Answer: I don't think it had the slightest influence. We were not paralyzed as *The New York Times* and others said. The Israelis didn't need ground troops. We had air and naval power available. From a political viewpoint you could say that our penchant for multilateral forces stemmed from the Vietnam experience. It is true that Washington is a one-crisis town. The State Department is always prepared for the last crisis, and it seems impossible for the top policy makers to focus on more than one problem at a time. From this standpoint you could probably say that Vietnam made an impact.

8

Question: How large a factor was the balance of payments situation in American consideration of alternatives?

Answer: I don't think it was raised once in the upper echelons. I doubt if Rusk, the Rostows, or Johnson raised it at all.

9

Question: If Israel were being defeated do you feel the United States would have intervened?

Answer: Yes.

Question: If there had been direct Soviet support would we have been even more likely to intervene?

Answer: Yes. Even more so.

Question: Had a tentative decision been made to intervene if necessary?

Answer: The only decision was made in the mind or heart of the President. He never stated one. But he loved the people of Israel. There was never the slightest doubt that he would have gone in there if Israel had needed American forces.

Question: Was it felt that domestic opinion would have supported such an action?

Answer: Probably, as long as he was successful. Public opinion was sympathetic to Israel, but one poll indicated that about 50 percent of the people just didn't care. But this wasn't the big problem, because if we had had to go in it would have been a serious eyeball to eyeball confrontation with the Soviets. It wouldn't be just a case of helping Israel. Israel could take care of the Arabs. It would have been much more serious than Vietnam.

Question: Was the President's attachment for Israel motivated by political considerations?
Answer: If you mean the influence of Jewish voters I don't think so. Johnson was a political man, but he had a deep personal attachment to Israel.
Question: Was this conveyed to Israel, that is, that we would help them if necessary?
Answer: In a way the President was trying to disguise his feelings because he didn't want them to jump to conclusions. He wanted to restrain them. He remarked at one point to Ambassador Harman that the U.S. people couldn't just give Israel a blank check. Harman got on the phone and soon Jewish leaders all over the country were calling the President. This annoyed the President.

10
Question: Was a stronger statement of support for Israel and a firmer show of force considered by the administration?
Answer: Some people were advocating a stronger stand. But the main feeling was that Israel was not in real trouble unless the Soviets came in. They weren't worried about being able to handle the Arabs.

11
Question: Did the United States do all that Israel expected?
Answer: Absolutely. Deputy Premier Allon's speech not too long ago was a good indication. It praised President Johnson's handling of the crisis as one of his greatest acts. I went to Johnson and urged him to tell the whole story of how much he had done. But the President rejected this with an emphatic "No!" on my memo. He wanted to do business with the Russians over missiles and he didn't see any point in rubbing their nose into their Middle East failures. He felt there was nothing to gain from gloating.
Question: Could we have done more to head off a war?
Answer: Yes. I think we should have laid our cards on the table. We should have made an alliance with Israel.

12
Question: Was the Soviet naval presence a significant limitation in considering various alternatives?
Answer: No. Their fleet was no bigger than the Italian fleet. The main importance was symbolic. If we had gotten into it militarily the local capability would have been fairly insignificant.

13
Question: Reputedly, there was a Rusk-McNamara memorandum on an approach to the crisis which outlined three phases: (1) peace making efforts through the United Nations, (2) Declaration of Maritime Powers, (3) use of warships to test the blockade if the other measures failed. Did such a memo exist and was this our general approach?
Answer: This was the way the scenario was phased, but the clock ran out on 2 and 3 and I was a nonstarter. Rusk and McNamara were the key men, but I never saw a formal memo.

14
Question: It has been written that the President was upset by the announcement on June 5 that the U.S. was "neutral in thought, word, and deed." Is this correct?
Answer: I have never seen him more upset. I informed him of the comment and the President told the Secretary of State to go to Congress immediately and clarify our position. Secretary Rusk announced that while the United States was not a belligerent it was not indifferent.

APPENDIX C

BIBLIOGRAPHY

C.1 INTRODUCTION

In developing this book a large number of interviews, as well as an extensive correspondence, were conducted with persons familiar with the crisis situations and other topics addressed. A listing of interviews and correspondence of particular importance is given in Sections C.2.1 and C.2.2, respectively. Invaluable materials were also received from the organizations listed in Section C.2.3. In many cases subject files were researched and a wealth of information provided.

The following libraries were utilized: Edwin Ginn Library of the Fletcher School of Law and Diplomacy; Tufts University Library; Widener, Lamont, and Center for International Affairs Libraries of Harvard University; Library of the Center for International Studies, Massachusetts Institute of Technology; Library of the U.S. Naval War College, Newport, Rhode Island; World Peace Foundation Library, Boston, Massachusetts; and Princeton University Library.

The John Foster Dulles Papers located at Princeton University were studied along with the Dulles Oral History Project. The files of the International Communism Project managed by Professor W. E. Griffith at the Massachusetts Institute of Technology were used extensively, and special papers made available by Professor W. Y. Elliott at Harvard University were perused.

Because more than 1000 newspaper articles and foreign radio broadcasts were particularly relevant to this study, no attempt has been made to document them in the bibliography. The following newspapers were examined for the periods August 1—October 26, 1958, and May 22—June 10, 1967: *The New York Times, The Times* (London), *The Sunday Times* (London), and *The Guardian* (Manchester). *The Washington Post* for the periods August 15—October 10, 1958, and June 1–10, 1967 was also studied. *The Observer* (London) was researched for the period July 1—October 1, 1958. Selective examination of *The New York Times* and *The Christian Science Monitor* was accomplished for periods before and after the dates indicated. Moreover, available Soviet and selected Chinese broadcast information and Tass releases were examined for the periods August 2—October 10, 1958, May 4—June 10, 1967, as well as the *Current Digest of the Soviet Press* and other Soviet and Chinese newspaper translations.

In addition, examination of *The New York Times, Current Digest of the Soviet Press*, and Soviet broadcast information during the period June 20—July 31, 1958, related to the Lebanon landings; the periods August 2—August 16, 1964, February 4—February 15, 1965, and February 23—March 6, 1967, and May 4—May 18, 1967, relating to naval activity during the war in Vietnam; and January 22—February 10, 1968, relating to the *Pueblo* crisis, has provided valuable background information. The same sources were utilized in analysis of Soviet naval expansion.

Particularly useful material has been listed in the more detailed selected bibliography that follows.

C.2 SOURCES

C.2.1 INTERVIEWS OF PARTICULAR INTEREST

Bartlett, Ruhl J., Professor of Diplomatic History, Fletcher School of Law and Diplomacy, Tufts University, conducted March 12, 1968, and July 25, 1968.

Carroll, George A., special assistant to Vice President Hubert H. Humphrey, conducted December 6, 1968.*

Chiang Kai-shek, President of the Republic of China, and Madame Chiang Kai-shek, conducted on September 24, 1964, by Mr. Spencer Davis of The Dulles Oral History Project. During this interview President Chiang discussed the Quemoy crises of 1955 and 1958. The original approved copy is on file with Princeton University.

Cole, Allen B., Professor of East Asian Affairs, Fletcher School of Law and Diplomacy, Tufts University, conducted July 30, 1968, and October 18, 1968.

Cooney, Commander D. M., USN, Public Affairs Officer, U.S. Atlantic Fleet, conducted by telephone on April 21, 1969.

Eisenhower, Dwight D., President of the United States during the Quemoy crises of 1955 and 1958, conducted on July 28, 1964, by Dr. P. A. Crowl of The Dulles Oral History Project. President Eisenhower commented extensively, during this interview, on both Quemoy crises. The approved transcript is on file at Princeton University Library.

Elliott, William Y., Leroy B. Williams Professor of History and Political Science, Emeritus, Harvard University, and University Professor, The American University, conducted July 23, 1958.

Griffith, William E., Professor of Soviet Diplomacy, Fletcher School of Law and Diplomacy, Tufts University, conducted April 16, 1968, and January 3, 1969.

Gross, Leo, Professor of International Law, Fletcher School of Law and Diplomacy, Tufts University, conducted April 17, 1968.

Gullion, Edmund A., Dean, Fletcher School of Law and Diplomacy, Tufts University, conducted July 31, 1968.

Humphrey, Don D., William L. Clayton Professor of International Economic Affairs, Fletcher School of Law and Diplomacy, Tufts University, conducted April 16, 1968.

*Asterisks denote material on file at the Fletcher School of Law and Diplomacy, Tufts University.

Macomber, William B., Jr., Assistant Secretary for Congressional Relations, Department of State, conducted June 12 and 19, 1966, by The Dulles Oral History Project The approved transcript is on file at the Princeton University Library.

Mangrum, Lt. General Richard C., USMC (Ret.), Assistant Commandant of the Marine Corps, conducted October 16, 1967, and September 2, 1968.

Merrill, Captain Ralph F., USN, Chief of Staff, Commander Service Force Sixth Fleet, conducted October 4, 1968.

Moceri, James, Visiting Associate Professor of Public Diplomacy, Fletcher School of Law and Diplomacy, Tufts University, Acting Public Affairs Officer, USIS Taiwan, during Quemoy crisis of 1958.*

Nixon, Vice President Richard M., now President of the United States, conducted on March 5, 1965, by Dr. R. D. Challener of The Dulles Oral History Project. Vice President Nixon comments on Secretary Dulles's handling of the Quemoy crises and the internal and external dissent during the period of the crises. The approved transcript is on file at the Princeton University Library.

Ra'anan, Uri, Professor of International Politics, Fletcher School of Law and Diplomacy, Tufts University, conducted numerous times in 1968 and 1969.

Rivero, Admiral Horacio, USN, Commander in Chief, Allied Forces Southern Europe, conducted in March, May, July, and August 1968 and February and March 1969. These interviews were conducted by representatives of the Italian, German, and U.S. media, and transcripts were provided by Cdr. W. A. Cockell, USN, Executive Assistant to Admiral Rivero, in a letter of August 13, 1968, and Captain J. J. Ness, USN, Executive Assistant to Admiral Rivero, in letter of April 2, 1969.

Roosevelt, Kermit, Middle East expert, conducted February 20, 1969.*

Secretary Dean Rusk, Secretary of State, conducted April 9, 1969.

Shulman, Professor Marshall D., Director of Columbia University's Institute on Communist Affairs, conducted April 12, 1968.

Wolfe, Dr. Thomas W., Senior Staff member of The Rand Corporation and member of faculty of Institute of Sino-Soviet Studies, George Washington University, conducted December 9, 1968.

Wylie, Rear Admiral J. C., Jr., Deputy Commander in Chief U.S. Naval Forces Europe, during 1967 Middle East Crisis, conducted December 22, 1967.*

Informed observer concerning the Quemoy crisis of 1958, conducted April 16, 1969.

Member of the Staff of the Chief of Naval Operations, conducted by telephone on April 7, 1968.

An official familiar with policy during the Quemoy crisis of 1958. (Appendix B.1.)

Informed White House source concerning Middle East crisis of 1967. (Appendix B.2.)

State Department officer familiar with the handling of the Arab-Israeli crisis of 1967, conducted December 10, 1968.*

Senior Israel Foreign Ministry Official, conducted October 24, 1968.*

C.2.2 LETTERS OF PARTICULAR INTEREST

Bartch, Carl E., Deputy Director, Office of News, Department of State, dated December 4, 1968.

Bowie, Professor Robert R., Director of Center for International Affairs, Harvard University, dated August 16, 1968.

Bundy, McGeorge, President, The Ford Foundation, dated April 3, 1968.*

Burke, Admiral Arleigh A., USN (Ret.), former Chief of Naval Operations, dated March 15, 1968, and July 9, 1968.*

Cleveland, Ambassador Harland, United States Permanent Representative on the North Atlantic Council, dated May 10, 1968.*

Cockell, Commander W. A., Executive Assistant to Admiral Horacio Rivero, Commander, Allied Forces Southern Europe, dated August 13, 1968, and March 22, 1969.

Cooney, Commander D. M., USN, Public Affairs Officer, U.S. Atlantic Fleet, dated April 17, 1969.

Cutler, Frederick, Chief, International Investments Section, Balance of Payments Division, U.S. Department of Commerce, dated July 24, 1968.

Drumright, Everett F., Ambassador to the Republic of China, dated March 7, 1969.*

Edmonds, R., Defence Secretariat Division, Ministry of Defence, Great Britain, dated March 11, 1969.

Eller, Rear Admiral E. M., USN (Ret.), Director of Naval History, dated March 6, 1968, and July 17, 1968.

Felt, Admiral Harry D., USN (Ret.), Commander in Chief, Pacific, dated July 16, 1968.*

Gallup, George, Jr., President, American Institute of Public Opinion, dated July 6, 1968, and July 18, 1968.

Geis, Rear Admiral Laurence R., USN, Commander, U.S. Sixth Fleet Carrier Task Force, dated April 7, 1969, and April 16, 1969.*

Griffin, Admiral Charles D., USN, Commander in Chief, Allied Forces Southern Europe, dated May 2, 1968.*

Hamilton, Lt. Comdr. L. D., USN, Acting Public Affairs Officer, CinC, U.S. Pacific Fleet, dated March 27, 1969.

Hurewitz, Professor J. C., Middle East Institute, Columbia University, dated April 30, 1968, and July 24, 1968.*

Hyland, Admiral John J., USN, Commander in Chief, U.S. Pacific Fleet, dated April 12, 1968.

Javits, Jacob K., U.S. Senator from State of New York, dated November 25, 1968.*

Klein, Helen, Assistant to Louis Harris, dated June 2, 1968, and July 19, 1968.

Kivette, Vice Admiral Frederick N., USN (Ret.), Commander, U.S. Seventh Fleet, dated March 5, 1968.

Lloyd Jones, R. A., Defence Secretariat Division, Ministry of Defence, Great Britain, dated February 26, 1968, April 9, 1968, and August 22, 1968.

Mangrum, Lt. General Richard C., USMC (Ret.), Assistant Commandant Marine Corps, dated November 20, 1967, April 6, 1968, and August 8, 1968.*

Mansfield, Senator Mike, Majority Leader, dated February 22, 1968, and July 17, 1968.*

Manson, Captain Frank A., Chief of Public Information, NATO Headquarters of the Supreme Allied Commander Atlantic, dated February 21, 1968.

Moose, Richard M., White House staff, dated March 1, 1968.*

McCloskey, Robert J., Deputy Assistant Secretary for Public Affairs, Department of State, dated March 6, 1968.*

McCain, Admiral John S., Jr., USN, Commander in Chief, U.S. Naval Forces Europe, dated March 11, 1968.*

Nuss, Captain J. J., USN, Special Assistant to Commander Allied Forces Southern Europe, dated April 2, 1969.

Owen, Henry, Chairman Policy Planning Council, Department of State, dated July 17, 1968.

Reston, James, Associate Editor, *The New York Times,* dated March 13, 1968.

Robertson, Walter Spencer, Assistant Secretary of State for Far Eastern Affairs, dated December 12, 1968.*

Rodgers, Captain George, USN, Public Affairs Officer, Commander U.S. Sixth Fleet Staff, dated March 30, 1968.

Saunders, Harold H., Staff, National Security Council, dated July 17, 1968.*

Smoot, Vice Admiral Roland N., USN (Ret.), Commander, U.S. Taiwan Defense Command, dated March 1, 1969.*

Soberick, Lt. Col. Thomas, USA, Deputy Chief of Public Information, NATO Headquarters of the Supreme Allied Commander Atlantic, dated March 4, 1968, and July 19, 1968.

Talley, Rear Admiral George C., Jr., USN, Deputy Director, Strategic Plans and Policy Division, Office of the Chief of Naval Operations, received April 10, 1969.*

Taylor, General Maxwell D., USA (Ret.), Chief of Staff of the Army, dated March 4, 1969.*

Tillman, Seth, Special Consultant, Senate Committee on Foreign Relations, dated March 4, 1969.

Yager, Joseph A., former Economic Counselor, U.S. Embassy Taiwan, dated March 7, 1969.*

Wylie, Rear Admiral J. C., USN, Deputy Commander, U.S. Naval Forces Europe, dated December 7, 1967.*

Letter from an informed observer concerning the Quemoy crisis of 1958, dated March 13, 1969.*

Letter from an informed observer concerning the Middle East crisis of 1967, December 15, 1969.

C.2.3 ORGANIZATIONS

MILITARY AND DIPLOMATIC

Headquarters, Allied Forces Southern Europe.

Office of the United States Permanent Representative on the North Atlantic Council, Brussels, Belgium.

Headquarters of the Supreme Allied Commander Atlantic, North Atlantic Treaty Organization.

Staff, Commander in Chief, U.S. Atlantic Fleet.

Staff, Commander in Chief, U.S. Pacific Fleet.

Staff, Commander in Chief, U.S. Sixth Fleet.

Staff, Commander in Chief, U.S. Seventh Fleet.

U.S. Naval War College, Newport, Rhode Island.

Office of Information, Department of the Navy.

Office of Naval History, Department of the Navy.

Office of the Director of Military Assistance, Department of Defense.

Policy Planning Council, Department of State.

Office of News, Department of State.

Office of Historical Policy Research, Department of State.

CONGRESSIONAL

U.S., Congress, House, Committee on Appropriations.

U.S., Congress, House, Committee on Armed Services.

U.S., Congress, Senate, Committee on Foreign Relations.

U.S., Congress, Senate, Committee on Armed Services.

Office of Senator John Stennis.

Office of Senator Jacob K. Javits.

PUBLIC

The American Institute of Public Opinion.

Louis Harris Associates, Inc.

National Opinion Research Center.

ECONOMIC

U.S., Department of Commerce, Balance of Payments Division.

Council of Economic Advisers.

FOREIGN

British Ministry of Defense.

British Information Service.

Israel Information Service.

OTHER

White House Office.

Kermit Roosevelt and Associates.

C.2.4 THE JOHN FOSTER DULLES PAPERS (PRINCETON UNIVERSITY)

Various drafts of the following speeches: before the United Nations General Assembly, September 18, 1958; before the Far East America Council, September 25, 1958; before the Boston Atlantic Assembly, September 27, 1958.

Transcript of background briefing given to newsmen on September 4, 1958, by Secretary Dulles at Newport, Rhode Island. No official transcript released.

Remarks by Secretary Dulles before participants of Foreign Service Senior Officer Course (off the record), September 29, 1958.

Rome-Taipei trip file of Secretary Dulles, October 1958.

C.2.5 SPEECHES

Cleveland, Harland, U.S. Ambassador to NATO. "How To Make Peace with the Russians," 1968 Cardinal O'Hara memorial lecture. University of Notre Dame, South Bend, Indiana, March 13, 1968.

Fulbright, J. W., Senator. "The War In Vietnam." Address of October 11, 1967, copy provided by Senator Fulbright.

Gullion, Edmund A., Dean, Fletcher School of Law and Diplomacy. "U.S. Foreign Policy; Goals and Tactics." Lecture delivered at U.S. Naval War College, Newport, Rhode Island, January 11, 1968.

Goulding, Phil G., Assistant Secretary of Defense (Public Affairs). Address at luncheon meeting of Pittsburgh World Affairs Council, Duquesne University, Pittsburgh, Pennsylvania, December 8, 1967.

Griffin, Charles D., Admiral, USN. Remarks at the Navy League Convention, Madrid, Spain, November 14, 1967.

Groverman, William H., Rear Adm., USN. Speech to the Commonwealth Club of California, November 17, 1967.

Javits, Jacob K., Senator. "Confrontation In the Middle East." Remarks of February 29, 1968, copy provided by Senator Javits.

Kilmarx, Robert T. "Nuclear Balance." Address delivered at U.S. Civil Defense Conference, Milwaukee, Wisconsin, October 30, 1968.

Kintner, William R. "U.S. Overseas Defense Commitments Now and in the 1970s." Foreign Policy Research Institute, University of Pennsylvania, June 1968.

Lemnitzer, Lyman L., General. Remarks upon inauguration of MARIRMED, Naples, Italy, November 21, 1968.

Moorer, Thomas A., Admiral, USN. Speech by the Supreme Allied Commander Atlantic on the occasion of the change of command ceremonies, Norfolk, Virginia, June 17, 1967.

———, Chief of Naval Operations. Address at the National Security Industrial Association 24th Annual Dinner, September 28, 1967, Washington, D.C.

———. Remarks before the American Bar Foundation, Chicago, Illinois, January 25, 1969.

McCain, John S., Jr., Admiral, USN. Presentation entitled "Expanding Scope of Seapower," provided by U.S. Navy Department Office of Information.

———. "Russia Looks to the Sea." Address at Edward R. Murrow World Affairs Forum, Overseas Press Club, New York City, January 23, 1968.

Nitze, Paul H., Jr., Secretary of the Navy. Luncheon remarks, Azalea Festival, Norfolk, Virginia, April 21, 1966.

Stoessinger, John G. "The Middle East and Vietnam, Two Crises at the Same Time," address delivered at Tufts University, April 17, 1968.

C.2.6 PAMPHLETS

BY INDIVIDUALS

Buchan, Alastair. *Crisis Management.* Paris, France: The Atlantic Institute, 1966.

Burke, Arleigh, Admiral, USN (Ret.). *The Naval Stature of the United States of America in World Affairs.* Unpublished, provided by Admiral Burke.

Crane, Robert D., ed. *Soviet Nuclear Strategy,* 2nd printing. Washington, D.C.: The Center for Strategic Studies, February 1965.

Dinerstein, Herbert S. *The Revolution in Soviet Strategic Thinking, Rand Memo: 927.* Santa Monica: Rand Corporation.

Gasteyger, Curt. *Conflict and Tension in the Mediterranean.* Adelphi Papers, No. 51 (September 1968). London: Institute of Strategic Studies, 1968.

Howard, Michael, and Hunter, Robert. *Israel and the Arab World: The Crisis of 1967.* Adelphi Papers, No. 4 (October 1967). London: Institute for Strategic Studies, 1967.

Jacoby, Neil H. *An Evaluation of U.S. Economic Aid to Free China, 1951–1965.* A.I.D. Discussion No. 11. Washington, 1966.

King, James F., Jr. "Collective Defense: The Military Commitment," *Military Policy Papers.* Washington: The Washington Center of Foreign Policy Research, December 1958.

Lenczowski, George, ed. *United States Interests in the Middle East.* Washington: American Enterprise Institute for Public Policy Research, October 1968.

Menger, Constantine C. *Military Aspects of International Relations in the Developing Areas.* Rand Paper P-3480. Santa Monica: Rand Corporation, December 1966.

Nitze, Paul H. "Brinkmanship and the Averting of War," *Military Policy Papers.* Washington: The Washington Center of Foreign Policy Research, December 1958.

———. "Symmetry and Intensity of Great Power Involvement in Limited Wars," *Military Policy Papers.* Washington: The Washington Center of Foreign Policy Research, December 1958.

Vinaike, Harold M. *U.S. Policy Toward China.* Center for Study of U.S. Foreign Policy, Occasional Paper No. 1, Department of Political Science, University of Cincinnati, 1961.

Wolfe, Thomas W. *Impact of Khrushchev's Downfall on Soviet Military Policy and Detente.* Rand Paper P-3010. Santa Monica: Rand Corporation, November 1964.

———. *Problems of Soviet Defense Policy Under the New Regime.* Rand Paper P-3098. Santa Monica: Rand Corporation, March 1965.

———. *Some Recent Signs of Reaction Against Prevailing Soviet Doctrinal Emphasis on Missiles.* Rand Paper P-2929. Santa Monica: Rand Corporation, June 1964.

———. *Soviet Military Policy Under Khrushchev's Successors.* Rand Paper P-3193. Santa Monica: Rand Corporation, August 1965.

———. *The Soviet Military Science: Institutional and Defense Policy Considerations.* Rand Memo 4913-PR. Santa Monica: Rand Corporation, June 1966.

———. *The Soviet Union and the Sino-Soviet Dispute.* Rand Paper P-3203. Santa Monica: Rand Corporation, August 1965.

———. *Trends in Soviet Thinking on Theater Warfare, Conventional Operations, and Limited War.* Rand Memo RM 4305-PR. Santa Monica: Rand Corporation, December 1964.

Yarmolinsky, Adam. *U.S. Military Power and Foreign Policy.* Chicago: University of Chicago Press, 1967.

Young, Kenneth T. *Diplomacy and Power in Washington—Peking Dealings: 1953–1967.* Chicago: University of Chicago Press, 1967.

BY ORGANIZATIONS

The Defense of Quemoy and the Free World. Taipei: Asian Peoples' Anti-Communist League, 1959.

Economic Impact of the Vietnam War. Special Report No. 5. Washington: Center for Strategic Studies, June 1967.

The Military Balance, 1959. London: Institute for Strategic Studies, 1959.

The Military Balance, 1964–1965, 1966–1967, 1967–1968, 1968–1969, 1969–1970. London: Institute for Strategic Studies, 1964, 1966, 1967, 1968, 1969.

The Sputnik Decade. Proceedings of the 19th Student Conference on U.S.

Affairs, December 6–9, 1967. West Point: United States Military Academy, 1967.

C.2.7 U.S. GOVERNMENT MATERIALS

SENATE

U.S., Congress, Senate, Subcommittee on National Security and International Operations of the Committee on Government Operations, *The Atlantic Alliance, Parts 1–6*, 89th Cong., 2nd sess. Washington, 1966.

U.S., Congress, Senate, Committee on Armed Services and the Subcommittee on Department of Defense of the Committee on Appropriations, *Military Procurement Authorizations for Fiscal Year 1968,* 90th Cong., 1st sess. Washington, 1967.

U.S., Congress, Senate, Committee on Armed Services, *Authorization for Military Procurement, Research and Development, Fiscal Year 1969, and Reserve Strength,* 90th Cong., 2nd sess. Washington, 1968.

U.S., Congress, Senate, Committee on Foreign Relations, *U.S. Commitments to Foreign Powers,* 90th Cong., 1st sess. Washington, 1967.

U.S., Congress, Senate, Committee on Foreign Relations, *National Commitments,* Report No. 797, 90th Cong., 1st sess. Washington, November 1967.

U.S., Congress, Senate, Preparedness Investigating Subcommittee of the Committee on Armed Services, *Worldwide Military Commitments, Parts 1, 2,* 89th Cong., 2nd sess. Washington: Part 1, 1966; Part 2, 1967.

U.S., Congress, Senate, Subcommittee on Separation of Powers of the Committee on the Judiciary, *Separation of Powers,* 90th Cong., 1st sess. Washington, 1967.

U.S., Congress, Senate, *Russia's Burgeoning Maritime Strength,* Staff Study for the Committee on the Judiciary, 90th Cong., 1st sess. Washington, 1964.

U.S., Congress, Senate, Committee on Foreign Relations, *Mutual Defense Treaty with the Republic of China,* 84th Cong., 1st sess., Executive Report No. 2. Washington, 1955.

U.S., Congress, Senate, Committee on Foreign Relations, *Review of Foreign Policy, 1958,* 85th Cong., 2nd sess. Washington, 1958.

U.S., Congress, Senate, Committee on Foreign Relations, *United States Foreign Policy,* Asia, 86th Cong., 1st sess., study by Conlon Associates, November 1959. Washington, 1959.

U.S., Congress, Senate, Committee on Foreign Relations, *Mutual Security Act of 1958,* 85th Cong., 2nd sess. Washington, 1958.

U.S., Congress, Senate, Committee on Foreign Relations, *Mutual Security Act of 1959,* Parts 1, 11, 86th Cong., 1st sess. Washington, 1959.

U.S., Congress, Senate, Subcommittee of Committee on Foreign Relations, *Disarmament and Foreign Policy,* 86th Cong., 1st sess. Washington, 1959.

U.S., Congress, Senate, Combined Subcommittee of Foreign Relations and Armed Services Committees, *U.S. Troops in Europe,* 90th Cong., 1st sess. Washington, 1967.

U.S., Congress, Senate, Committee on Foreign Relations, *Conflicts Between United States Capabilities and Foreign Commitments*. 90th Cong., 1st sess., Washington, 1967.

U.S., Congress, Senate, Committee on Foreign Relations, *A Select Chronology and Background Documents Relating to the Middle East.* Washington, 1963.

U.S., Senate, Committee on Foreign Relations, *The Rim of Asia,* report of

Senator Mike Mansfield, September 1967, 90th Cong., 1st sess. Washington, 1967.

U.S., Senate, Committee on Foreign Relations, *The Far East and The Middle East,* report of Senator John Sparkman, 86th Cong., 2nd sess., November 30, 1960. Washington, 1960.

U.S., Congress, Senate, Preparedness Investigating Subcommittee of The Committee on Armed Services, *Inquiry into Satellite and Missile Programs, Part 1,* 85th Cong., 1st and 2nd sess. Washington, 1958.

U.S., Congress, Senate, Subcommittee of the Committee on Appropriations, *Department of Defense Appropriations, 1959,* 85th Cong., 2nd sess. Washington, 1958.

U.S., Congress, Joint Economic Committee, *Economic Effect of Vietnam Spending,* Vol. 1 "Statements of Witnesses and Supporting Materials." Vol. 2 "The Military Impact on the American Economy: Now and After Vietnam," 90th Cong., 1st sess. Washington, 1967.

HOUSE

U.S., Congress, House, Subcommittee of the Committee on Appropriations, *Department of Defense Appropriations for 1969,* 90th Cong., 2nd sess. Washington, 1968.

U.S., Congress, House, *United States Defense Policies in 1957,* House Document No. 436, 85th Cong., 2nd sess., written by Charles H. Donnelly, January 10, 1958. Washington, 1958.

U.S., Congress, House, *United States Defense Policies in 1958,* House Document No. 227, 86th Cong., 1st sess., July 10, 1959. Washington, 1959.

U.S., Congress, House, Committee on Foreign Affairs, *Mutual Security Act of 1958,* 85th Cong., 2nd sess. Washington, 1958.

U.S., Congress, House, Committee on Armed Services, *Hearings on Military Posture and An Act (S.3293),* 90th Cong., 2nd sess. Washington, 1968.

U.S., Congress, House, Committee on Armed Services, *The Changing Strategic Naval Balance USSR vs. U.S.A.,* 90th Cong., 2nd sess., December 1968. Washington, 1968.

U.S., Congress, House, Special Subcommittee on Sea Power of the Committee on Armed Services, *Status of Naval Ships,* No. 4 (January 1969), No. 5 (March 19, 1969), 91st Cong., 1st sess. Washington, 1969.

U.S., Congress, House, Special Subcommittee on National Defense Posture of the Committee on Armed Services, *Review of the Vietnam Conflict and Its Impact on U.S. Military Commitments Abroad,* 90th Cong., 2nd sess., report of August 24, 1968. Washington, 1968.

CONGRESSIONAL RECORD

U.S., *Congressional Record,* 84th Cong., 1st sess., vol. 101, part 1 (January 26, 1955).

U.S., *Congressional Record,* 85th Cong., 2nd sess., vol. 104, part 9 (June 20, 1958); part 13 (August 6, 1958); part 15 (August 21, 1958).

U.S., *Congressional Record,* 90th Cong., 1st sess., vol. 113 (March 22, 1967); No. 52 (April 10, 1967); No. 79 (May 19, 1967); No. 80 (May 22, 1967); No. 81 (May 23, 1967); No. 86 (June 1, 1967); No. 87 (June 5, 1967); No. 105 (July 10, 1967); No. 125 (August 9, 1967); No. 201 (December 8, 1967); No. 203 (December 12, 1967); No. 204 (December 13, 1967).

COUNCIL OF ECONOMIC ADVISORS

U.S., *Economic Report of the President and The Annual Report of the Coun-*

cil of Economic Advisers, February 1968. Washington, 1968.

DEPARTMENT OF COMMERCE

U.S., Department of Commerce, *Statistical Abstract of the United States, 1967,* 88th edition. Washington, 1967.

DEPARTMENT OF STATE

U.S., Department of State, *American Foreign Policy 1950–1955,* Vols. 1 and 11. Washington, 1957.

U.S., Department of State, *American Foreign Policy, Current Documents, 1958.* Washington, 1962.

U.S., Department of State, *American Foreign Policy Current Documents 1962.* Washington, 1966.

U.S., Department of State, *The Communist Threat in the Taiwan Area,* Far Eastern Series No. 76. Washington: September 1958.

U.S., Department of State, *The Republic of China,* Far Eastern Series No. 81 (October 1958). Washington, 1959.

U.S., Department of State *Bulletin,* "Statement by President on Signing Joint Resolution," Vol. XXXII (February 7, 1955).

U.S., Department of State *Bulletin,* "Foundations of Peace," address by Secretary John F. Dulles on August 18 (September 8, 1958), pp. 373–377.

U.S., Department of State *Bulletin,* "US Policy on Non Recognition of Communist China," August 11, 1958 (September 8, 1958), pp. 385–390.

U.S., Department of State *Bulletin,* "Address of Secretary Rusk on May 18th," Vol. LVI, No. 1459 (June 12, 1967), pp. 874–879.

U.S., Department of State *Bulletin,* "Statement of President Johnson on May 23, 1967," Vol. LVI, No. 1459 (June 12, 1967), p. 891.

U.S., Department of State *Bulletin,* "Statement of June 6 Before the United Nations by U.S. Representative A. J. Goldberg," Vol. LVI, No. 1461 (June 26, 1967), pp. 935, 936.

U.S., Department of State *Bulletin,* "News Briefing at the White House, June 6, 1967," Vol. LVI, No. 1461 (June 26, 1967), pp. 949–951.

U.S., Department of State *Bulletin,* "Principles for Peace in the Middle East," address by President Johnson, Vol. LVII, No. 1463 (July 10, 1967), pp. 31–34.

U.S., Department of State *Bulletin* article by Eugene V. Rostow, "The Middle East Crisis and Beyond," Vol. LVIII, No. 1489 (January 8, 1968), pp. 41–48.

U.S., Department of State *Bulletin,* "Secretary Rusk and Secretary of Defense McNamara Discuss Vietnam and Korea on 'Meet the Press,'" Vol. LVIII, No. 1496 (February 26, 1968), p. 271.

U.S., Department of State, *Foreign Policy Briefs,* "Rusk on Spheres!" Vol. XVIII, No. 8 (October 7, 1968).

NAVY

U.S., Navy, *Answers to Questions Concerning the Soviet Navy,* No. 8769, cleared November 1, 1967, pp. 1–39. [Good coverage of status of Soviet navy at the time.]

U.S., Navy, *Facts About the United States Sixth Fleet in the Mediterranean,* Public Information Office, Commander Sixth Fleet, May 7, 1958.

U.S., Navy, *Growth and Expanding Operations of the Soviet Navy,* Chief of Information Notice No. 5721 of December 27, 1965.

U.S., Navy, *NATO's Standing Naval Force Atlantic,* fact sheet provided by Staff, Supreme Allied Commander Atlantic.

U.S., Navy, *The New Four Ocean Challenge,* Office of Information, Navy Department. Washington, 1964.

U.S., Navy, *Standing Naval Force Atlantic,* information sheets provided by Supreme Allied Commander Atlantic.

U.S., Navy, Summary of Proceedings of U.S. Navy Court of Inquiry convened June 10, 1967, attack on U.S.S. *Liberty* Unclassified testimony of commanding officer of U.S.S. *Liberty,* supplied by letter from U.S. Navy Department, Office of Information.

U.S., Navy, *The United States Sixth Fleet,* Public Affairs Officer, Commander Sixth Fleet, January 1967.

U.S., Navy, *The United States Seventh Fleet,* pamphlet supplied by U.S. Navy Department, Office of Information.

U.S., Navy, *The United States Navy Keeping the Peace,* Naval History Division, Library of Congress No. 66-61705 (Washington: U.S. Government Printing Office, 1966).

C.2.8 SPECIAL MATERIALS

American Institute of Public Opinion. "Results of British Gallup Poll," October 23, 1958. Copy of release supplied by Mr. George Gallup, Jr., July 6, 1968.

Barnes, Susan, Eglis, Arsene, and Gilliam, Olivia. *Soviet News Media and the Middle East Crisis.* Radio Liberty Research Paper, No. 16, 1967. Covers period from May 17 to June 25, 1967. [Thorough and accurate in most instances.]

Barnett, Robert W. *Quemoy: The Use and Consequences of Nuclear Deterrence.* Unpublished paper, Center for International Affairs, Harvard University, March 1960.

Burke, Arleigh, Adm. USN (Ret.). *The Naval Stature of the United States of America In World Affairs.* Unpublished booklet supplied by Adm. Burke in letter of March 15, 1968.

Duevel, Christian. "Soviet Censorship Tones Down Militancy of Marshall Grechko's Speech." Radio Liberty Research Report CRD 385/67, Munich, July 11, 1967.

Elliott, William Y. Unpublished paper on "The Peaceful Uses of Nuclear Energy," copy made available by Professor Elliott.

Ermach, Fritz. "Recent Soviet Military Doctrine." Radio Liberty Research Paper, March 24, 1965.

Gallup, George. "Johnson Wins Vote of Confidence on Handling of Middle East Crisis." Release supplied by American Institute of Public Opinion, June 12, 1967.

———. "Americans Think Arabs, Israelis Should Decide Own Peace Plans." Release supplied by American Institute of Public Opinion, July 9, 1967.

———. "Overwhelming Public Support for UN Handling Quemoy Crisis." Release supplied by Mr. George Gallup, Jr., President, American Institute of Public Opinion, September 25, 1958.

Goedhart, Frans, Rapporteur of the Committee on Defence Questions and Armaments of the Western European Union. *Defence of the Mediterranean and the NATO Southern Flank.* Preliminary draft report, A/P 4076, Paris, October 30, 1967, pp. 1–49.

Harrigan, Anthony. "Soviet Goals in the Middle East." *Washington Report,* WR 67-17, April 24, 1967.

Long, John. "A Note on Soviet Navy Day, 1966." D.I.B. No. 2304, August 11, 1966.

———. "Marshal Sokolovsky and General Cherednechenko Speak Out Again." D.I.B. No. 2234, April 28, 1966.

———. "Soviet Navy Day in Retrospect." D.I.B. No. 2050, August 2, 1965.

———. "USSR Shifts Its Position Once Again on a Middle East Settlement." Radio Liberty dispatch, October 3, 1967.

Riollot, Jean. "The Middle East Crisis: The Soviet Role and Soviet Media Reactions Since the Outbreak of Hostilities." Radio Liberty dispatch, July 28, 1967.

———. "The Middle East Crisis: The Soviet Role and Soviet Media Reactions Prior to the Outbreak of Hostilities." Radio Liberty dispatch, June 19, 1967.

Morris, Willie. *How the Arab/Israel War of June, 1967 Happened.* Unpublished paper, Center for International Affairs, Harvard University, November 1967.

Wiggins, James Russell. "Notes on Conversations Between J. R. Wiggins and John Foster Dulles." Notes on file at Princeton University Library.

C.2.9 UNITED NATIONS DOCUMENTS

U.N., Security Council, *Report of the Security Council,* July 10, 1966–July 15, 1967, official records, 22nd sess., Supplement No. 2. New York: United Nations, 1967.

U.N., Security Council, Provisional Record of 1346th Meeting, June 3, 1967, Document S/PV 1346.

———, Provisional Record of 1348th Meeting, June 6, 1967, Document S/PV 1348.

———, Provisional Record of 1354th Meeting, June 10, 1967, Document No. 1354.

———, Provisional Record of 1355th Meeting, June 10, 1967, Document No. 1355.

———, Provisional Record of 1356th Meeting, June 10, 1967, Document No. S/PV 1356.

U.N., Security Council, "Report by the Secretary General," Document S/7896 of May 19, 1967.

U.N., Security Council, "Report by the Secretary General," Document S/7906 of May 26, 1967.

C.2.10 BRITISH DOCUMENTS (Supplied by British Information Services)

Text of speech by George Brown, Secretary of State for Foreign Affairs, opening the debate in the House of Commons on the Middle East on May 31, 1967, Doc. No. T.23, June 1, 1967.

Text of speech by Prime Minister Harold Wilson closing the debate in the House of Commons on the Middle East on May 31, 1967, Doc. No. T.24, June 1, 1967.

Text of statement to the House of Commons in reply to Parliamentary questions by Prime Minister Harold Wilson, June 6, 1967, Doc. No. T.26, June 6, 1967.

Text of statement by George Brown, Foreign Secretary, in the House of Commons, on June 7, 1967, Doc. No. T.24 of June 7, 1967.

Text of speech by George Brown, Secretary of State for Foreign Affairs opening the 1529th session of the General Assembly of the United Nations in New York, June 21, 1967, Doc. No. T.30, June 21, 1967.

Text of statement by Mr. George Thomson, Minister of State for Foreign Affairs, opening the debate on the Middle East in the House of Commons on July 6, 1967, Doc. No. T.33, July 7, 1967.

"Economic and Overseas Policy: Cuts in Public Expenditure," Policy Statements, January 16, 1968.

"Defence Estimates 1968/69," policy background paper, February 23, 1968.

"Defence: Supplementary Statement," policy background paper, July 11, 1968.

"Defence Estimates 1969/70," policy background paper, February 25, 1969.

Defence Outline of Future Policy, presented by the Minister of Defence to Parliament by Command of Her Majesty, April 1957, Cmnd. 124. London: HMSO, 1957.

Supplementary Statement on Defence Policy 1967, presented to Parliament by the Secretary of State for Defence, July 1967, Cmnd. 3357. London: HMSO, 1967.

Supplementary Statement on Defence Policy 1968, presented to Parliament by the Secretary of State for Defence, July 1968, Cmnd. 3701. London: HMSO, 1968.

Statement on the Defence Estimates 1969, presented to Parliament by the Secretary of Defence, February 1969, Cmnd. 3927. London: HMSO, 1969.

C.2.11 PERIODICALS, OTHER THAN SOVIET AND CHINESE

SIGNED ARTICLES

Alexander, Hunter, Lt. USNR. Review of *The Soviet Navy* by Vice Adm. Vasility Danilovich Yakovlev. US Naval Institute *Proceedings,* Vol. 93, No. 4 (April 1967), p. 123.

Alsop, Stewart. "The Story Behind Quemoy: How We Drifted Close to War." *The Saturday Evening Post*, Vol. 231, No. 24 (December 13, 1958), pp. 26, 27, 86–88.

Anderson, George W., Jr., Adm., USN (Ret.). "Soviet Sea Power: 'Modern, Strong, Second Only to U.S.' " *U.S. News and World Report*, Vol. LXVI, No. 3 (January 20, 1969), pp. 51–54.

Ascoli, Max. "For a Formosa Settlement." *The Reporter*, Vol. 19, No. 6 (October 16, 1958), pp. 10–17.

———. "Central High and Quemoy—an Editorial." *The Reporter,* Vol. 19, No. 4 (September 18, 1958), pp. 12, 13.

———. "This Talk of Munich—An Editorial." *The Reporter,* Vol. 19, No. 5 (October 2, 1958), p. 10.

Ashurst, Albert J., Comdr. "The Formosa Resolution, 1954–1955, 1958." *Naval War College Review*, Vol. XX, No. 7 (February 1961), pp. 94–100.

Baldwin, Hanson W. "How The Military Rate McNamara's Performance." *The Reporter,* Vol. 38, No. 8 (April 18, 1968), pp. 15–18.

———. "Limited War." *The Atlantic*, Vol. 203, No. 5 (May 1959), pp. 35–44.

———. "Red Flag Over the Seven Seas." *The Atlantic Monthly,* Vol. 214, No. 3 (September 1964), pp. 37–43.

Bates, Richard W., Comdr., USN. "Communist Party Control in the Soviet Navy." Naval War College *Review*, Vol. XX, No. 3 (October 1967), pp. 3–42.

Brandon, Henry. "The Struggle for Power." *The Saturday Review* (August 12, 1967), p. 11.

Brown, Neville. "British Arms and the Switch Towards Europe." *International Affairs,* Vol. 43, No. 3 (July 1967), pp. 468–482.

Buchan, Alastair, Director of Institute for Strategic Studies. "The Great Contingency." *Encounter,* Vol. XXIX, No. 2 (August 1967), pp. 3–6.

Cattell, David T. "Soviet Foreign Policy." *Current History,* Vol. 49, No. 290 (October 1965).

Cleveland, Harland. "The Real Deterrent." *Survival,* Vol. IX, No. 12 (December 1967), pp. 378–383, 386.

Clubb, Edmund O. "Chiang's Shadow Over Warsaw." *The Reporter,* Vol. 13, No. 5 (October 2, 1958), pp. 16, 17.

Crankshaw, Edward. "Khrushchev and China." *The Atlantic,* Vol. 207, No. 5 (May 1961), pp. 43–47.

Davy, John, and Wilson, Andrew. "Secret World War of the Antennae." *Atlas,* Vol. 15, No. 3 (March 1968), pp. 17–19.

Dorn, Jurgen. "Red Flag at Sea—A Super Power American Style." Translated from *Rheinlscher Merkur* (Cologne), *Atlas,* Vol. 16, No. 1 (July 1968), pp. 27, 28.

Draper, Theodore. "Israel and World Politics." *Commentary,* Vol. 44, No. 2 (August 1967), pp. 19–48.

Dutt, R. P. "Britain's Crisis of Neocolonialism." *International Affairs* (January 1968), pp. 16–21.

Eliot, George Fielding. "Alliance Diplomacy in Limited Wars." U.S. Naval Institute *Proceedings,* Vol. 93, No. 4 (April 1967), pp. 52–57.

———. "Will the Soviets Provoke a War At Sea?" *The American Legion Magazine* (November 1966), pp. 10–15, 40–42.

Elon, Amos. "Letter from the Sinai Front." *Commentary,* Vol. 44, No. 2 (August 1967), pp. 60–68.

Erickson, John. "Detente, Deterence and 'Military Superiority', a Soviet Dilemma." *The World Today* (August 1965), pp. 337–345.

———. "The Fly in Outer Space: The Soviet Union and the Anti-ballistic Missile." *The World Today,* Vol. 23, No. 3 (March 1967), p. 107.

Galay, N. "The Limits of the Soviet Potential." *Bulletin, Institute for the Study of the USSR,* Vol. XII, No. 5 (May 1965), pp. 26–31.

———. "The Soviet Armed Forces on the Threshold of a New Era." *Bulletin, Institute for the Study of the USSR,* Vol. XII, No. 4 (April 1965), pp. 15–20.

Garthoff, Raymond L. "Sea Power in Soviet Strategy." U.S. Naval Institute *Proceedings,* Vol. 84, No. 2 (February 1958), pp. 85–93.

Gasteyger, Curt. "Modern Warfare and Soviet Strategy." *Survey,* No. 57 (October 1965), pp. 46–55.

———. "Moscow and the Mediterranean." *Foreign Affairs,* Vol. 46, No. 4 (July 1968), pp. 676–687.

Griffin, Charles D., Adm., USN. "Now Russia Builds Up Power in the Mediterranean." *US News and World Report,* Vol. LXIII, No. 24 (December 11, 1967).

Griffith, William E. "Containing Communism East and West." *The Atlantic Monthly,* Vol. 215, No. 5 (May 1965), pp. 71–75.

———. "World Communism Divided." *Headline Series,* No. 166 (August 1964).

Gross, Leo. "Passage Through the Suez Canal of Israel-Bound Cargo and Israel Ships." *American Journal of International Law,* Vol. 51, No. 3 (July 1957), pp. 530–568.

Halperin, Morton H. "The Gaither Committee and the Policy Process." *World Politics,* Vol. XIII, No. 3 (April 1961), pp. 360–384.

Halperin, Morton H., and Tsou, Tang. "United States Policy Toward the Offshore Islands." *Public Policy,* Vol. XV (1966), pp. 119–138, Center for International Affairs, Harvard University, Reprint Series.

Hanning, Hugh. "Britain East of Suez—Facts and Figures." *International Affairs,* Vol. 42, No. 2 (April 1966), pp. 253–260.

Haykal, Muhammad Hasanayn. "Arab Soviet Friendship." Cairo Radio, August 25, 1967, reprinted in *Survival,* Vol. IX, No. 11 (November 1967), pp. 358–362.

Hessler, William H. "The Seventh Fleet is Ready." *The Reporter,* Vol. 24, No. 12 (June 8, 1961), pp. 30, 31.

Horrigan, Frederick J. "Problems and Conflicts in Asia." *Naval War College Review,* Vol. XX, No. 7 (February 1968), pp. 27–34.

Howard, Michael. "Britain's Strategy Problem East of Suez." *International Affairs,* Vol. 42, No. 2 (April 1966), p. 180.

Howe, Jonathan T., Lt. Comdr., USN. "Soviet Beachhead in the Third World." U.S. Naval Institute *Proceedings,* Vol. 94, No. 10 (October 1968), pp. 60–67.

Hsieh, Alice Langley. "Sino-Soviet Nuclear Dialogue." Reprinted in *Survival,* Vol. 6, No. 5 (September–October 1964), pp. 228–239.

Hudson, G. F. "Mao, Marx, and Moscow." *Foreign Affairs,* Vol. No 37, No. 4 (July 1959), pp. 561–570.

Irish, Marion D. "Public Opinion and American Foreign Policy: The Quemoy Crisis of 1958." *The Political Quarterly,* Vol. 31, No. 2 (April–June 1960), pp. 151–162.

Jacobs, Walter Darnell. "Soviet Views of Wars of National Liberation." *Military Review,* Vol. XLVII, No. 10 (October 1967), pp. 59–66.

Johnson, Max S., Lt. Gen., USA (Ret.). "U.S. Stake in the Mid East." *US News and World Report,* Vol. LXIII, No. 25 (June 19, 1967), p. 77.

Kerr, Malcolm. "Coming to Terms with Nasser." *International Affairs,* Vol. 43, No. 1 (January 1967), pp. 65–84.

Kirkpatrick, Lyman B. "The Sino-Soviet Split." *Naval War College Review,* Vol. XX, No. 6 (January 1968), pp. 44–54.

Kosygin, Aleksei. "A Rare Private Interview." *Life*, Vol. 64, No. 5 (February 2, 1967), pp. 21–32B.

Laqueur, Walter. "Israel, the Arabs and World Opinion." *Commentary,* Vol. 44, No. 2 (August 1967), pp. 49–59.

Lederer, Walter, and Cutler, Frederick K. "International Investments of the United States in 1966." *Survey of Current Business* (September 1967), pp. 39–52.

Lewis, Bernard. "The Consequences of Defeat." *Foreign Affairs,* Vol. 46, No. 2 (January 1968), pp. 321–335.

Lewis, John Wilson. "Quemoy and American China Policy." *Asian Survey,* Vol. 2, No. 1 (March 1962), pp. 12–19.

Lowenthal, Richard. "America's Asian Commitment." *Encounter,* Vol. XXV, No. 4 (October 1965), pp. 53–59.

Mackintosh, Malcolm. "The Military Aspects of the Sino-Soviet Dispute." *Bulletin of the Atomic Scientists,* Vol. XXI, No. 8 (October 1965), pp. 14–17.

Martin, Robert P. "With The Seventh Fleet." *US News and World Report,* Vol. XLV, No. 12 (September 19, 1958), pp. 31–33.

Maulding, Reginald. "The Real Threat to the West." *The Atlantic Community Quarterly,* Vol. 5, No. 3 (Fall 1967), pp. 344–346.

Meister, J. "Soviet Seapower Amphibious Assault." *Military Review* Vol. XXXVIII, No. 9 (December 1958), pp. 107–109.

Millar, T. B. "Control of the Indian Ocean." *Survival,* Vol. IX, No. 10 (October 1967), pp. 323–326.

Monroe, Elizabeth. "British Bases in the Middle East." *International Affairs,* Vol. 42, No. 1 (June 1966), pp. 24–34.

Morison, David. "Russia, Israel, and the Arabs." *Mizan,* Vol. 9, No. 3 (May–June, 1967), pp. 91–107.

Mosley, Philip E. "The Kremlin and the Third World." *Foreign Affairs,* Vol. 46, No. 1 (October 1967), pp. 64–77.

Mostert, Noel. "High Stakes Southeast of Suez." *The Reporter,* Vol. 38, No. 5 (March 7, 1968), pp. 17–20.

Murphy, F. M., Capt., USN. "The Soviet Navy in the Mediterranean." U.S. Naval Institute *Proceedings,* Vol. 93, No. 3 (March 1967), pp. 65–79.

MacFarquhar, Roderick. "China Goes It Alone." *The Atlantic Monthly,* Vol. 215, No. 4 (April 1965), pp. 69–75.

McClelland, Charles A. "Decisional Opportunity and Political Controversy, The Quemoy Case." *Journal of Conflict Resolution,* Vol. VI, No. 3 (September 1962), pp. 201–213.

McClintock, Robert. "The American Landings in Lebanon." U.S. Naval Institute *Proceedings* Vol. 88, No. 10 (October 1967), pp. 65–79.

McDonald, David L., Adm., USN. "Carrier Employment Since 1950." U.S. Naval Institute *Proceedings,* Vol. 90, No. 11 (November 1964), pp. 26–33.

McLane, Charles H. "The Moscow-Peking Alliance: The First Decade." *Current History,* Vol. 37, No. 220 (December 1959), pp. 326–332.

———. "USSR Policy in Asia." *Current History,* Vol. 49, No. 290 (October 1965), 214–220, 241.

McNamara, Robert S. "American ABM Deployment." *Survival,* Vol. IX, No. 11 (November 1967), pp. 342–346.

Parry, Albert. "Soviet Aid to Vietnam." *The Reporter,* Vol. 36, No. 1 (January 12, 1967), pp. 28–33.

Pesce, Livio. "Why Europe Fears the Russian Navy." translation from *Epoca* (Milan), *Atlas,* Vol. 16, No. 1 (July 1968), pp. 29, 30, 63, 64.

Phillips, Thomas R., Brig. Gen., USA (Ret.). "The Military Worth of Quemoy." *The Reporter,* Vol. 19, No. 5 (October 2, 1958), pp. 14, 15.

Ra'anan, Uri. "Challenge to the West." *The New Leader* (September 9, 1968), pp. 9–11.

———. "Moscow and the Third World." *Problems of Communism* (January–February, 1965).

———. "Moscow and the Third World, Contradictions and Dangers." *Survey,* No. 57 (October 1965), pp. 26–37.

Roberts, Chalmers M. "Caught in a Trap of Our Own Making." *The Reporter,* Vol. 19, No. 5 (October 2, 1958), pp. 11–13.

Roosa, Robert V. "Where is Britain Heading?" *Foreign Affairs,* Vol. 46, No. 3 (April 1968), pp. 503–518.

Schofield, B. B., Vice Adm., Royal Navy (Ret.). "Alliance Diplomacy in Limited Wars." U.S. Naval Institute *Proceedings,* Vol. 93, No. 10 (October 1967), p. 102.

———. "Sentinels at the Bridge." U.S. Naval Institute *Proceedings,* Vol. 93, No. 10 (October 1967), pp. 49–53.

Seaton-Watson, Hugh. "The Khrushchev Era." *Survey,* No. 58 (January 1966) pp. 187–195.

Shor, Franc. "Life Under Shell Fire on Quemoy." *The National Geographic Magazine,* Vol. CXV, No. 3 (March 1959), pp. 415–438.

———. "Pacific Fleet: Force for Peace." *The National Geographic Magazine,* Vol. CXVI, No. 3 (September 1959), pp. 283–333.

Shulman, Marshal D. "American Militancy: The Soviet View." *Survival,* Vol. IX, No. 2 (February 1967), pp. 63–67.

Sidey, Hugh. "The Presidency: Over the Hot Line—The Middle East," *Life,* Vol. 62, No. 24 (June 16, 1967), p. 24.

Skloot, Edward. "Labour East of Suez." *Orbis*, Vol. 10, No. 3 (Fall 1966), pp. 947–957.

Sterling, Claire. "The Soviet Fleet in the Mediterranean." *The Reporter,* Vol. 37, No. 10 (December 14, 1967), pp. 14–18.

Thomas, John R. "Limited Nuclear War in Soviet Strategic Thinking." *Orbis* (Spring 1966), reprint.

———. "Soviet Behavior in the Quemoy Crisis of 1958." *Orbis*, Vol. VI, No. 1 (Spring 1962), pp. 38–64.

Tsou, Tang. "Mao's Limited War in the Taiwan Strait." *Orbis,* Vol. III, No. 3 (Fall 1959), pp. 332–350.

———. "The Quemoy Imbroglio: Chiang Kai Shek and the United States." *The Western Political Quarterly,* Vol. XII, No. 4 (December 1959), pp. 1075–1077.

Velie, Lester. "The Week the Hot Line Burned." *Reader's Digest* (August 1968), pp. 37–44.

Warner, Denis. "The Forgotten People of Taiwan." *The Reporter,* Vol. 19, No. 7 (October 30, 1958).

Watt, D. C. "The Arab Summit Conference and After." *The World Today,* Vol. 23, No. 10 (October 1967), pp. 443–450.

———. "The Decision to Withdraw from the Gulf." *The Political Quarterly,* Vol. 39, No. 3 (July–September, 1968), pp. 310–321.

Weiner, Herbert. "The Ebbing of Euphoria." *The Reporter*, Vol. 37, No. 8 (November 16, 1967), pp. 16–19.

Werth, Alexander. "Year of Jubilee: The USSR at Fifty." *The Nation,* Vol. 205, No. 14 (October 30, 1967), pp. 424–430.

Windsor, Philip. "The Middle East and the World Balance." *The World Today,* Vol. 23, No. 7 (July 1967), pp. 279–285.

Wohlsetter, Albert. "The Delicate Balance of Terror." *Foreign Affairs,* Vol. 37, No. 2 (January 1959).

Wolfe, Bertram B. "Communist Ideology and Soviet Foreign Policy." *Foreign Affairs,* Vol. 42, No. 3 (April 1964), pp. 475–486.

Wolfe, Thomas W. "Military Policy a Soviet Dilemma." *Current History,* Vol. 49, No. 290 (October 1965), pp. 201–207, 238–240, 245.

———. "Russia's Forces Go Mobile." *Interplay,* Vol. 1, No. 8 (March 1968), pp. 28, 33–37.

———. "Shifts in Soviet Strategic Thought." *Foreign Affairs,* Vol. 42, No. 3 (April 1968), pp. 475–486.

———. "Soviet Military Policy at the Fifty Year Mark." *Current History* (October 1967), pp. 209–216.

Yost, Charles W. "How the Arab-Israeli War Began." *Foreign Affairs,* Vol. 46, No. 2 (January 1968), pp. 304–320.

THE ATLANTIC COMMUNITY

"British Statements on Defense Policy." *The Atlantic Community Quarterly,* Vol. 5, No. 3 (Fall 1967), pp. 457–462.

THE ECONOMIST

"All Aid Short of War." *The Economist* (September 20, 1958), pp. 911, 912.

"Bears Can't Fly." *The Economist* (June 24, 1967), reprinted in *Survival,* September 1967, pp. 282–283.

"Can Nasser Make Peace?" *The Economist*, Vol. CCXXIII, Nos. 6–58 (June 3, 1967), pp. 994–995.

"The Economic Fall Out of the War." *The Economist,* Vol. CCXXIV, No. 6459 (June 10, 1967), pp. 1104, 1105.

"Egypt Had Done Its Homework." *The Economist,* Vol. CCXXIII, No. 6458 (June 3, 1967), pp. 1008, 1107.

"Islands of Doubt." *The Economist* (September 20, 1958), pp. 935, 936.

"Ivan's Breakthrough." *The Economist,* Vol. CCXXIII, No. 6458 (January 14, 1966), pp. 139, 140.

"Moscow Picks Up the Pieces." *The Economist,* Vol. CCXXIV, No. 6460 (June 17, 1967).

"Nasser Does It." *The Economist,* Vol. CCXXIII, No. 6457 (May 27, 1967), pp. 879–880.

"Offshore Squeeze." *The Economist* (September 6, 1958), p. 750.

"Quemoy Again." *The Economist* (August 23, 1958), pp. 582–584.

"Quemoy and Moscow." *The Economist* (September 13, 1958), pp. 817, 818.

"The Russians' Game." *The Economist,* Vol. CCXXIII, No. 6457 (May 27, 1967), pp. 881–887.

"Siege and Seat." *The Economist* (September 27, 1958), p. 1003.

"The Small World of LBJ." *The Economist,* Vol. CCXXIII, No. 6458 (June 3, 1967), pp. 993, 994.

"Sterling." *The Economist*, Vol. CCXXIV, No. 6459 (June 10, 1967), pp. 1144, 1145.

"Suez Still Matters." *The Economist,* Vol. CCXXIII, No. 6458 (June 3, 1967), pp. 1034, 35.

"Taking It Out On the Oil Companies." *The Economist,* Vol. CCXXIV, No. 6460 (June 24, 1967), pp. 1368, 1369.

"Those Sterling Islands." *The Economist,* Vol. CCXXII, No. 6440 (January 28, 1967), pp. 336, 337.

"Two More Views." *The Economist,* Vol. CCXXIV, No. 6459 (June 10, 1967), p. 1144.

"Waiting for a Middle Eastern Bang." *The Economist,* Vol. CCXXIII, No. 6456 (May 20, 1967), p. 779.

"The War Revivalists." *The Economist,* Vol. CCXXIII, No. 6457 (May 27, 1967), p. 879–880.

"We'll Do It Again." *The Economist,* Vol. CCXXIII, No. 6457 (May 27, 1967), p. 899.

"We're Ready for You." *The Economist,* Vol. CCXXIII, No. 6457 (May 27, 1967).

"What Happens Next Time." *The Economist,* CCXXIV, No. 6458 (June 10, 1967), pp. 1133, 1134.

"Why U Thant Felt He Had to Get Out." *The Economist,* Vol. CCXXIII, No. 6457 (May 27, 1967), p. 896, 899.

MIZAN

"The USSR and the Middle East Arab States in 1965." *Mizan,* Vol. 7, No. 4 (April 1965), pp. 1–13.

LE NOUVEL OBSERVATEUR

"Pourquoi Moscou a lâché Nasser, *Le Nouvel Observateur*, No. 135 (June 14–June 20, 1967).

NATO NEWSLETTER

"STANAVFORLANT: NATO's First Standing Naval Force" (photostory). *NATO Letter,* Vol. 16, No. 4 (April 1968), pp. 14–19.

THE NEW REPUBLIC

"Robertson's Adventure." *The New Republic,* Vol. 139, No. 10, issue 2286 (September 8, 1958), p. 5.

NEWSWEEK

Newsweek, Vol. LXIX, No. 25 (June 19, 1967), p. 36.

SURVEY OF BRITISH AND COMMONWEALTH AFFAIRS

"The Middle East Crisis." *Survey of British and Commonwealth Affairs,* British Information Services, Vol. I, No. 12 (June 9, 1967), pp. 613–625.

SURVIVAL

"NATO Strategy-Soviet View." Reprint from *Red Star* of April 26, 1968. *Survival,* Vol. X, No. 8 (August 1968), pp. 256–258.

TIME

"Dulles at Newport," The Nation, *Time,* Vol. LXXII, No. 11 (September 15, 1958), pp. 3, 14.

"Power Play on the Oceans." *Time,* Vol. 91, No. 8 (February 23, 1968), pp. 23–28.

"Remember Korean Negotiations." *U.S. News and World Report,* Vol. LXIV, No. 4 (January 22, 1968), p. 33.

"Rough Week in the Strait." *Time,* Vol. LXXII, No. 12 (September 22, 1958), pp. 22–24.

U.S. NEWS AND WORLD REPORT

"Aim of Russia's Growing Naval Might." *U.S. News and World Report,* Vol. LXIII, No. 19 (November 6, 1967), p. 14.

"Alaska: Biggest in Oil, Too?" *U.S. News and World Report,* Vol. LXV, No. 5 (July 29, 1968), p. 8.

"As It Looks At The Front: Only US Can Save Quemoy." *U.S. News and World Report,* Vol. XLV, No. 13 (September 26, 1958), p. 4.

"Facts About Truce Talks." *U.S. News and World Report,* Vol. LXIV, No. 4 (January 22, 1968), pp. 29, 30.

"Lessons of the Liberty—Weak Spots in U.S. Defenses." *U.S. News and World Report,* Vol. LXV, No. 4 (July 22, 1968), p. 7.

"If War Comes, Will US Have Enough Goods." *U.S. News and World Report,* Vol. XLV, No. 4 (July 25, 1958), pp. 96, 97.

"Nixon's Views in a Nutshell." *U.S. News and World Report,* Vol. LXIV, No. 11 (March 11, 1968), p. 44.

"The Story of Britain's Decline and Fall." *U.S. News and World Report,* Vol. LXIV, No. 7 (February 12, 1968), pp. 64, 65.

"Troubles for Israel in Hostile Middle East." *U.S. News and World Report,* Vol. LXII, No. 16 (April 17, 1967).

"US Fleet: Peace Keeper in the Mediterranean." *U.S. News and World Report,* Vol. 56 (March 16, 1964), p. 42.

"War in Asia: Reds Push to The Edge." *U.S. News and World Report,* Vol. XLV, No. 11 (September 12, 1958), pp. 33, 34.

"War in The Far East." *U.S. News and World Report,* Vol. XLV, No. 8 (August 22, 1958), pp. 33–35.

"What US Is Ready to Do in the Shooting Around Formosa." *U.S. News and World Report,* Vol. XLV, No. 11 (September 12, 1958), pp. 71–73.

"Will It Be War in Asia." *U.S. News and World Report,* Vol. XLV, No. 10 (September 5, 1958), pp. 29, 30.

"Will US Avoid War in Far East." *U.S. News and World Report,* Vol. XLV, No. 12 (September 19, 1958), pp. 29, 30.

THE WORLD TODAY

"The USSR and The Arab Israeli Conflict." *The World Today,* Vol. 23, No. 7, (July 1967), pp. 271–275.

THE YUVA NEWSLETTER

The Yuva Newsletter, Vol. IV, No. 4 (July 1965), pp. 1–6.

C.2.12 SOVIET PERIODICALS

SIGNED ARTICLES

Akimov, A. "US and British Armed Forces and the Middle East Crisis." *International Affairs,* No. 8 (August 1967), pp. 104–106.

Alexandrov, O. "Israel's Aggression." *Soviet Military Review*, No. 7 (July 1967), p. 57.

Alexandrov, V. "Great Task Ahead." *International Affairs,* No. 11 (November 1958), pp. 19–25.

Andreasyan, R. "New Aspects of Middle East Countries' Oil Policy." *International Affairs*, No. 9 (September 1968), pp. 28–36.

Andreyev, A. A. "Bonds of Brotherhood." *New Times*, No. 39 (September 1958), pp. 2, 3.

Astakhov, S. "More About the Secret Springs of the Israeli Aggression." *International Affairs,* No. 10 (October 1967), pp. 33–40.

Baryshnikov, V. "Background to the Taiwan Crisis." *New Times,* No. 38 (September 1958), pp. 26–28.

Belashchenko, T., Capt. 2nd Rank. "Following the Road of Aggressive War." *Soviet Military Review,* No. 6 (June 1965), pp. 44–46.

Belskaya, A. "Will They Finally Learn?" *New Times,* No. 42 (October 1958), pp. 7–9.

Belyaev, I. "Ways of Ending the Middle East Crisis." *International Affairs,* No. 10 (October 1968), pp. 25–28.

Belyaev, I., and Primakov, Y. "Lessons of the 1967 Middle East Crisis." *International Affairs,* No. 3 (March 1968), pp. 40–46.

Berzynesky, Lev. "The Mediterranean Knot." *New Times,* No. 28 (July 12, 1967), p. 9.

Blishchenko, I. "International Law and the Middle East Crisis." *International Affairs,* No. 1 (January 1969), pp. 29–35.

Bochkaryov, Y. "The Faces Behind the Aggressor." *New Times,* No. 25 (June 21, 1967).

Bulatov, M., Colonel. "U.S. Bridgehead in Spain." *Soviet Military Review,* No. 2 (February 1969), pp. 52–54.

Bykov, O. "Atlantic Policy of the USA and European Security." *International Affairs,* No. 9 (September 1967), pp. 37–45.

Chernov, V. "Background to the Pueblo Affair." *New Times,* No. 5 (February 7, 1968), pp. 2–5.

Dmitriev, B. "Anxiety Over America's Future." *International Affairs* (January 1968), pp. 93, 94.

———. "Hot Spots on the Globe." *Soviet Military Review,* No. 1 (January 1965), pp. 48, 49.

Dolgopolov, V., Col. "Wars of Liberation: Fact and Fiction." *Soviet Military Review,* No. 3 (March 1966), pp. 49, 50.

Dolgopolov, Y. "National Liberation Wars in the Present Epoch." *International Affairs,* No. 2 (February 1962), p. 21.

Domogatskikh, M. "In China Today." *New Times,* No. 41 (October 1958), pp. 24–26.

Doronin, A. "Unity and Solidarity in Face of Aggression." *Soviet Military Review,* No. 9 (September 1966), p. 56.

Fedorenko, N. T. "Perfidity and Aggression." *New Times,* No. 26 (June 28, 1967), pp. 3–7.

Gerasimov, G. "Pentagon in 1967." *International Affairs,* No. 7 (July 1967), pp. 40–44.

Glozov, V., Col. "The Evolution of U.S. Military Doctrine." *Soviet Military Review,* No. 11 (November 1965), pp. 56, 57.

———. "The New 'Local War' Conceptions." *New Times,* No. 48 (December 2, 1964), pp. 6–8.

Gorshkov, S. G., Fleet Adm., CinC USSR Navy. "Naval Might of Soviet Power." *Soviet Military Review,* No. 7 (July 1965), pp. 3–6.

———. "Soviet Naval Art." *Soviet Military Review,* No. 7 (July 1967), pp. 1–6. Reprinted in abridged form from Morskoy-Sbornik No. 2 (February 1967).

Isakov, I. S. "Crimea and Taiwan—Object Lessons of History." *New Times,* No. 39 (September 1958), pp. 9–12.

Israelyan, V., Prof. "The October Revolution and Foreign Policy." *International Affairs,* No. 9 (September 1967), pp. 4–9.

Istomin, V. "A Sea of Sorrow." *New Times,* No. 44 (October 1958), pp. 11, 12.

Ivanov, K. "Israel, Zionism and International Imperialism." *International Affairs,* No. 6 (June 1968), pp. 13–21.

Kafman, A. "U.S. Big Stick in the Mediterranean." *International Affairs,* No. 8 (August 1967), pp. 71–75.

Kasatonov, V. A., Fleet Adm. "The XVth Congress of the VLKSM and The Tasks of the Fleet." *Morskoi-Sbornik,* No. 8 (August 1966), pp. 3–11.

Khrushchev, N. S. "N. S. Khrushchev replies to Questions Sent to Him by Murilo Manoquinde Souze, The Brazilian Journalist." *International Affairs,* No. 11 (November 1958), pp. 3–5.

———. "Message to D. D. Eisenhower." *New Times,* No. 30 (July 1958), pp. 7–9.

Kolodkin, A. "Piracy and International Law." *International Affairs,* No. 10 (October 1967), pp. 75–78.

Kondratkov, T., Lt. Col. "The Substance of War." *Soviet Military Review,* No. 6 (June 1968), pp. 11–13.

Korotrov, G. "Seato: A Threat to Asia." *Soviet Military Review,* No. 1 (July 1966), pp. 50–52.

Korotkov, V. "War: Its Flashes and Torch-bearers." *International Affairs,* No. 9 (September 1964), pp. 83–84.

Krymov, A. "The Nine Victorious Years." *International Affairs,* No. 10 (October 1958), pp. 20–25.

Kudryavtsev, V. "The Middle East Knot." *International Affairs,* No. 9 (September 1967), pp. 29–34.

Kushnir, Alexander. "Truth About Israel's Aggression." *Soviet Military Review,* No. 8 (August 1967), pp. 56, 57.

Kuzin, N., Major. "U.S. Navy and 'Flexible Response' Strategy." *Soviet Military Review,* No. 5 (May 1966), pp. 55–59.

Kuzmiv, P. "Collecting Intelligence on the Situation at Sea." *Morskoy Sbornik,* No. 11 (November 1966), pp. 20–28.

Kuz'mn, P., Capt. 1st Rank. "Collecting Intelligence on the Situation at Sea." *Morskoy Sbornik,* No. 11 (November 1966), pp. 20–28.

Laurischev, A. "The Soviet Union and The Developing Countries." *International Affairs,* No. 1 (January 1968), pp. 59–65.

Lavrov, Vladimir. "Behind the Israeli Aggressor." *New Times,* No. 27 (July 5, 1967), pp. 6–8.

Markov, M. "Taiwan and America's Aggressive Plans." *International Affairs,* No. 12 (December 1958), pp. 20–27.

Marushkin, B. "Ideological Crisis of U.S. Foreign Policy." *International Affairs,* No. 11 (November 1966), pp. 68–73.

Matsolenko, V., Col. "The 'Small War' Theory at the Service of the Imperialists." *Soviet Military Review,* No. 4 (April 1966), pp. 53–55. Review of book, *Big Lie About Small Wars* by Mochalov, V.

Mikuson, I. "Crisis in the United States and Its Political Reflection." *International Affairs,* No. 10 (October 1958), pp. 52–59.

Millstein, M., and Slobodinko, A. "Limited War—Weapon of Unlimited Aggression." *New Times,* No. 40 (October 1958), pp. 13–15.

Mitin, V., Captain 1st Rank. "A Cruise to Friends." *Soviet Military Review,* No. 10 (October 1968), pp. 12–14.

Mochalov, V., Col. "Concerning the 'Theory of Limited Wars.' " *Soviet Military Review,* No. 2 (February 1965), pp. 40–43.

Morsin, Yu, Capt. 1st Rank. "From Gunboat to Aircraft Carrier Diplomacy." *Soviet Military Review,* No. 11 (November 1965), pp. 54, 55.

Nelin, Yu. "NATO's New Fire-Brigade." *International Affairs,* No. 13 (March 1969), pp. 56–58, 64.

Nevsky, Gerald A. "Modern Armaments and Problems of Strategy." *World Marxist Review,* Vol. 6, No. 3 (March 1963), pp. 28–34.

Nevzorov, P. O., Maj. Gen. of Aviation. *Morskoy Sbornik,* No. 9 (September 1964).

Novoseltoev, E., and Khomutov, N. "Soviet Relations With Leading Capitalist Countries." *International Affairs,* No. 3 (March 1968), pp. 68–74.

Osokin, S., Capt. 2nd Rank. "The Mediterranean Is Not for the Yankees." *Soviet Military Review,* No. 10 (October 1965), pp. 46, 47.

———. "East of Suez." *Soviet Military Review,* No. 9 (September 1966), pp. 51–53.

Paramonov, V. "Enclaves of Aggression." *International Affairs,* No. 11 (November 1966), pp. 38–43.

Pchelkin, I. P., Capt. 1st Rank, and Volgin, I. F., Capt. 2nd Rank. "Unfortunate Flaws in a Necessary Book." *Morskoy Sbornik,* No. 11 (November 1966), pp. 90–93.

Penzin, K., Capt. 1st Rank. "The Changing Methods and Forms of Warfare at Sea." *Soviet Military Review,* No. 3 (March 1967), pp. 18–21.

Perov, V. "The Situation in Indonesia," *International Affairs,* No. 5 (May 1958), pp. 42–45.

Petrov, M. "Pentagon's Shadow Over Asia." *Soviet Military Review,* No. 10 (October 1966), pp. 51–52.

Polyansky, V. "Off the Shores Not Their Own." *Soviet Military Review,* No. 9 (September 1965), pp. 45–47.

Primakov, Y. "Behind the Scenes of the Israeli Gamble." *International Affairs,* No. 7 (July 1967), pp. 58–61.

Raratorin, N., Col. "Tanks Attack from Sea." *Soviet Military Review,* No. 11 (November 1968), pp. 28–30.

Rodionov, K. R., Rear Adm. Reserve. "The Regime of the Black Sea Straits." *Morskoy Sbornik,* No. 11 (November 1966), pp. 26–30.

Rzheshevsky, O., Lt. Col. "Focus on the Leathernecks." *Soviet Military Review,* No. 10 (October 1965), p. 50.

———. "Garthoff vs. Garthoff." *Soviet Military Review,* No. 9 (September 1967), pp. 55–57.

Sanin, A. "U.S. Bases in the Far East and South East Asia." *International Affairs,* No. 8 (August 1964), pp. 109–111.

Saprykov, V. "The Doctrine of Globalism in Action." *Soviet Military Review,* No. 12 (December 1965), pp. 44, 45.

Sedin, L. "Absurdities of American Policy." *New Times,* No. 38 (September 1958), pp. 12–14.

———. "The Arab Peoples' Just Cause." *International Affairs,* No. 8 (August 1967), pp. 23–29.

———. "Britain: Secret of Her Success." *New Times,* No. 23 (June 7—Moscow edition June 2), p. 18, 19.

Seiful-Mulyukov. "Washington's Middle East Strategy." *New Times*, No. 23 (June 12, 1968), pp. 8–10.

Seleznoyova, Y. "Developing States and International Relations." *International Affairs,* No. 5 (May 1968), pp. 67–73.

Shevchenko, A., Maj. General. "Defensive Alliance of Socialist Countries." *Soviet Military Review,* No. 5 (May 1968), pp. 9–12.

Shishkov, Y. "New Stage in International-Imperialist Contradictions." *International Affairs,* No. 3 (March 1967), pp. 55–63.

Sokolovsky, V. "On the Soviet Military Doctrine." *Soviet Military Review,* No. 4 (April 1965), pp. 6–9.

Spartak, Beglov. "What Is Behind the Special Relationship." *International Affairs,* No. 3 (March 1968), pp. 34–39.

Talenskii, N., Maj. Gen. "Modern War: Its Character and Consequences." *International Affairs,* No. 10 (October 1960), p. 36.

Teplinsky, B. "U.S. Military Programme." *International Affairs,* No. 8 (August 1967), pp. 46–51.

Tuganova, G. E. "The Foreign Policy of the Developing Countries." *International Affairs,* No. 5 (May 1967), pp. 62–65.

Tyushevich, S., Col. "Balance of Forces in Armed Struggle." *Soviet Military Review,* No. 4 (April 1968), pp. 12–15.

Ukraintsev, Valdimir. "Tool of Provocations and Aggressions." *Soviet Military Review,* No. 8 (August 1967), p. 58.

Usvatov, A. "U.S. Seventh Fleet—Menace to Asia." *New Times,* No. 33 (August 1964), pp. 16–17.

Vladimirov, Y., and Olenev, Y. "Fruits of Political Adventurism." *International Affairs,* No. 3 (March 1968), pp. 27–33.

Vodynin, F., Capt. 1st Rank. "The Fighting Record of the Soviet Navy." *Soviet Military Review,* No. 7 (July 1968), pp. 54–56.

Volsky, D. "Vanguard of the Third World." *New Times,* No. 9 (March 1967), pp. 4–6.

Vyunenko, N. P., Capt. "Soviet Amphibious Operations." *Morskoi Sbornik,* No. 9 (September 1963), translated by Dulacki, Leo J., Col., USMC, in *Marine Corps Gazette,* No. 49 (March 1965), pp. 29–33.

Yeremeyev, L. "The U.S. Seventh Fleet." *International Affairs,* No. 7 (July 1964), pp. 113, 114.

Yermahov, I. "Aggressive U. S. Navalism: Its Sources, Theory and Practice." *International Affairs,* No. 1 (January 1965), pp. 60–67.

Yermashov, I. "China's Road to Victory." *New Times,* No. 39 (September 1958), pp. 3–5.

———. "Oligarchy of the Big." *New Times,* No. 42 (October 1958), pp. 3–5.

Yudin, U., and Vanich, I. "Indirect Aggression—A Weapon of the Imperialist Powers." *International Affairs,* No. 11 (November 1958), pp. 38–40.

Zavyalov, V., Lt. Col. "Flexible Response Strategy: Theory and Practice." *Soviet Military Review,* No. 5 (May 1965), pp. 50–53.

Zhukov, Y. "The American Decade Myth and International Relations." *International Affairs,* No. 9 (September 1967), pp. 66–74.

———. "The National Liberation Movement and Peaceful Co-Existence." *Soviet Military Review,* No. 10 (October 1965), pp. 7–9.

UNSIGNED ARTICLES

"Aggression Against the Arab World." *New Times,* No. 24 (June 14, 1967), pp. 1–3.

"Big Stick." *New Times*, No. 40 (October 1958), p. 19.

"Check the Israeli Aggressor." *International Affairs,* No. 7 (July 1967), pp. 4–5.

"China's Revolution." *New Times,* No. 39 (September 1958), p. 1.

"The Fight Goes On." *New Times,* No. 27 (July 5, 1967), pp. 3–5.

"Indonesia, A New Plot." *International Affairs,* No. 8 (August 1958), pp. 97–99.

"Main Stages in Soviet Foreign Policy." *International Affairs,* No. 1 (January 1968), pp. 52–56.

"The Middle East Situations." *New Times,* No. 23 (June 7, 1967), p. 3.

"No Time Must Be Lost." *New Times,* No. 41 (October 1958), p. 2.

"The Peking Meeting." *New Times*, No. 32 (August 1958), pp. 1, 2.

"Perilous Venture of the American Aggressors." *International Affairs,* No. 4 (April 1968), pp. 3–6.

"Policy in Asia." *International Affairs,* No. 10 (October 1958), pp. 99–105.

"Provocative Imperialist Bustle In the Persian Gulf." *International Affairs,* No. 3 (March 1968), pp. 75, 76.

"Purely Internal Matter." *New Times,* No. 42 (October 1958), p. 1.

"Recklessness or Provocation." *New Times,* No. 39 (September 1958), p. 17.

"Risky Game." *New Times,* No. 40 (October 1958), pp. 2, 3.

"Time to End the Provocations." *New Times,* No. 37 (September 1968), pp. 1, 2.

"The War Machine of Imperialism Today." *International Affairs*, No. 3 (March 1968), pp. 104–106.

"U.S. and British Naval Forces." *New Times*, No. 23 (June 7, 1967—Russian edition of June 2), p. 3.

"With Pride and Confidence." *New Times,* No. 12, (March 1967), pp. 1, 2.

"World Events September 1958." *New Times,* No. 37 (September 1958), p. 32.

"The World's Gendarme's Policy." *International Affairs,* No. 10 (October 1958), pp. 8–13.

C.2.13 CHINESE PERIODICALS

(All articles from *Peking Review*)

SIGNED

Chao-Li, Yu. "The Forces of the New Are Bound to Defeat the Forces of Decay." Vol. I, No. 25 (August 19, 1958), pp. 8–11.

Chen, Yi. "Statement of Foreign Minister Chen Yi Refuting Dulles' Speech at UN." Vol. I, No. 30 (September 23, 1958), pp. 5, 6.

Chou En-lai. "Premier Chou En-Lai's Statement on the Situation in the Taiwan Straits Area." Vol. I, No. 28 (September 9, 1958), pp. 15, 16.

Mao Tse-tung. "Chairman Mao Speaks on Current Situation." Vol. I, No. 29 (September 16, 1958), pp. 4, 5.

Yung, Kiu Tse. "A Major Step to Protect China's Sovereign Right." Vol. I, No. 29 (September 16, 1958), pp. 11–13.

UNSIGNED

"Chinese Government's Statement on Sino-American Ambassadorial Talks Issued June 30, 1958." Vol. I, No. 19 (July 8, 1958), pp. 21, 22.

"650 Million Ready to Smash US Aggression." Vol. I, No. 29 (September 16, 1958), pp. 6–8.

"The Powerful Voices of Peace," editorial. Vol. I, No. 24 (August 12, 1958), p. 3.

"A shopworn U. S. Tune." Vol. I, No. 25 (August 19, 1958), pp. 6, 7.

"Statement by the Spokesman of the Chinese Government," September 1, 1963. Vol. VI, No. 36 (September 6, 1963), pp. 7–16.

"Taiwan and The Coastal Islands Will Be Liberated." Vol. I, No. 29 (September 16, 1958), pp. 19, 20.

"The US Aggressors Have Put Nooses Round Their Own Necks." Vol. I, No. 29 (September 16, 1958), pp. 9–11.

"US Forces in Singapore—Threat to Asian Peace." Vol. I, No. 26 (August 26, 1958), p. 19.

"US Intensifies Tension in Taiwan Straits." Vol. I, No. 27 (September 7, 1958), p. 4.

"US Must Halt Immediately." Vol. I, No. 29 (September 16, 1958), p. 3.

"US Must Stop Kindling the Flames of War—Right Now." Vol. I, No. 30 (September 23, 1958), pp. 8, 9.

C.2.14 BOOKS

Adams, Sherman. *Firsthand Report.* New York: Harper and Bros., 1961.

Bailey, Thomas A. *The Art of Diplomacy: The American Experience.* New York: Appleton-Century-Crofts, 1968.

Baldwin, Hanson W. "Strategic Background." Chapter 5 of *The Soviet Navy,* M. G. Saunders, Comdr. RN ed. New York: Praeger, 1958.

Ball, George W. *The Discipline of Power.* Boston: Little, Brown and Co., 1968.

Barclay, C. N., Brig. Gen. "East of Suez: A Suggested Western Strategy." Chapter 4 of *Brassey's Annual: The Armed Forces Year Book 1967.* New York: Praeger, 1967.

Bartlett, Ruhl. *Policy and Power: Two Centuries of American Foreign Relations.* New York: Hill and Wang, 1963.

Beal, John Robinson. *John Foster Dulles: 1888–1959.* New York: Harper and Bros., 1959.

Blackman, Raymond V. B., ed. *Jane's Fighting Ships 1959–1960, 1960–1961, 1961–1962, 1962–1963, 1963–1964, 1966–1967, 1967–1968, 1968–1969, 1969–1970.* London: Sampson Low, Marston and Co., 1959, 1960, 1961, 1962, 1963, 1966, 1967, 1968, 1969.

Blum, Robert. *The United States and China in World Affairs.* A. Doak Barnett, ed. New York: McGraw-Hill Book Co., 1966.

Brackman, Arnold C. *Indonesian Communism.* New York: Praeger, 1963.

Brodie, Bernard. *Escalation and the Nuclear Option.* Princeton: Princeton University Press, 1966.

Brzezinski, Zbigniew K. *The Soviet Bloc.* Rev. ed. Cambridge: Harvard University Press, 1967.

Buchan, Alstair, ed. *China and the Peace of Asia.* London: Chatto and Windus, Institute for Strategic Studies, 1965.

Campbell, John C. *Defense of the Middle East.* New York: Harper and Bros., Council on Foreign Relations, 1958.

Churchill, Randolph S. and Winston S. *The Six Day War.* Boston: Houghton Mifflin Co., 1967.

Clemens, Walter C., Jr. *The Arms Race and Sino-Soviet Relations.* Stanford: Hoover Institute, 1968.

Crankshaw, Edward. *The New Cold War, Moscow v. Pekin.* Baltimore: Penguin Books, 1963.

Dallin, David J. *Soviet Foreign Policy After Stalin.* New York: Lippincott, 1961.

De Conde, Alexander. *A History of American Foreign Policy.* New York: Charles Scribner's Sons, 1963.

Dinerstein, Herbert S. *Intervention Against Communism.* Baltimore: The Johns Hopkins Press, 1967.

———. "The United States and the Soviet Union: Standoff or Confrontation." Chapter in *The Military-Technical Revolution: Its Impact on Strategy and Foreign Policy,* John Erickson, ed. New York: Praeger, 1966.

———. *War and the Soviet Union.* Rev. ed. New York: Praeger, 1962.

Donovan, Robert J., and the staff of *The Los Angeles Times. Israel's Fight for Survival.* New York: New American Library, 1967.

Draper, Theodore. *Israel and World Politics.* New York: The Viking Press, 1968.

Drummond, Roscoe, and Coblentz, Gaston. *Duel at the Brink.* Garden City, N.Y.: Doubleday and Co., 1960.

Eisenhower, Dwight D. *Mandate for Change, 1953–1956.* Garden City, N.Y.: Doubleday and Co., 1963.

———. *Public Papers of the Presidents of the United States, 1958.* Washington: Government Printing Office, 1959.

———. *Waging Peace 1956–1961.* Garden City, N.Y.: Doubleday and Co., 1965.

Eliot, George Fielding. *Victory Without War 1958–1961.* Annapolis, Md.: U.S. Naval Institute, 1958.

Eller, E. M., Rear Adm. USN. "Implications of Soviet Sea Power." Chapter 15 of *The Soviet Navy,* M. G. Saunders, Comdr. RN, ed. New York: Praeger, 1958.

Ferguson, Gilbert W. Chapter 2 of *Brassey's Annual: The Armed Forces Yearbook 1967.* New York: Praeger, 1967.

Field, James A., Jr. *History of United States Naval Operations Korea.* Washington: Government Printing Office, 1962.

Fleming, D. F. *The Cold War and Its Origins,* Vol. Two, 1950–1960. Garden City, N.Y.: Doubleday and Co., 1961.

Ford, Harold P. "Sino-Soviet Politico-Military Problems, 1957–1960." Chapter 6 of *Sino-Soviet Military Relations,* R. L. Garthoff, ed. New York: Praeger, 1966.

Fulbright, J. William. *The Arrogance of Power.* New York: Random House, 1966.

———. *The Vietnam Hearings.* New York: Random House, 1966.

Garthoff, Raymond L. "Military Power in Soviet Policy." Chapter in the *Military-Technical Revolution: Its Impact on Strategy and Foreign Policy,* John Erickson, ed. New York: Praeger, 1966.

———. "Military Power in Soviet Policy." Chapter in the *Military-Technical Revolution: Its Impact on Strategy and Foreign Policy,* John Erickson, ed. New York: Praeger, 1966.

———. *Sino-Soviet Military Relations.* New York: Praeger, 1966.

———. *The Soviet Image of Future War.* Washington: Public Affairs Press, 1959.

———. *Soviet Strategy in the Nuclear Age.* Rev. ed. New York: Praeger, 1962.

———. *Soviet Military Policy.* New York: Praeger, 1966.

Gerson, Louis L. *The American Secretaries of State and Their Diplomacy,* Vol. XVII, John Foster Dulles. New York: Cooper Square Publishers, 1967.

Gervasi, Frank. *The Case for Israel.* New York: The Viking Press, 1967.

Giles, Morgan, Rear Adm., RN. "The Case for A British Presence East of Suez." Chapter 5 of *Brassey's Annual: The Armed Forces Year Book 1967.* New York: Praeger, 1967.

Goldstein, Walter. *The Dilemma of British Defense.* Athens: Ohio University Press, 1966.

Greene, Fred. *U.S. Policy and the Security of Asia.* New York: McGraw-Hill Book Co., 1968.

Griffith, William E. "Communist Polycentrism and the Underdeveloped Areas." Chapter in *New Nations in a Divided World,* Kurt London, ed. New York: Praeger, 1963.

———. *Sino-Soviet Relations 1964–1965.* Cambridge: The M.I.T. Press, 1967.

———. *The Sino-Soviet Rift.* Cambridge: The M.I.T. Press, 1964.

Gullion, Edmund A., ed. *Uses of the Seas.* Englewood Cliffs, N.J.: Prentice-Hall, Inc., 1968.

Hadelen, Wilhelm. "The Ships of the Soviet Navy." Chapter 7 of *The Soviet Navy,* M. G. Saunders, ed. New York: Praeger, 1958.

Halperin, Morton H. *China and the Bomb.* New York: Praeger, 1965.

(Hansard) Parliamentary Debates, Volumes 536, 548, 594, 747, House of Commons. London: HMSO, 1955, 1956, 1958, 1967.

Herrick, Robert W. "Soviet Naval Strategy." Chapter in *The Military Technological Revolution: Its Impact on Strategy and Foreign Policy,* John Erickson, ed. New York: Praeger, 1966.

Herrick, Robert Waring, Comdr., USN (Ret.). *Soviet Naval Strategy.* Annapolis: U.S. Naval Institute, 1968.

Hilsman, Roger. *To Move a Nation.* Garden City, N.Y.: Doubleday and Co., 1967.

Hoffmann, Stanley. *Gulliver's Troubles.* New York: McGraw-Hill Book Co., 1968.

Horelick, Arnold L., and Rush, Myron. *Strategic Power and Soviet Foreign Policy.* Chicago: University of Chicago Press, 1966.

Hudson, G. F. Introduction of *The Sino-Soviet Dispute.* New York: Praeger, 1961.

Hughes, John Emmet. *The Ordeal of Power.* New York: Atheneum, 1963.

Huntington, Samuel P. *The Common Defense.* New York: Columbia University Press, 1961.

Hsieh, Alice Langley. *Communist China's Strategy in the Nuclear Era.* Englewood Cliffs, N.J.: Prentice-Hall, 1962.

Jacobson, Harold Karan, and Stein, Eric. *Diplomats, Scientists, and Politicians.* Ann Arbor: The University of Michigan Press, 1966.

Kaplan, Lawrence S. *Recent American Foreign Policy: Conflicting Interpretations.* Homewood, Ill.: The Dorsey Press, 1968.

Kaufman, William W. *The McNamara Strategy.* New York: Harper and Row, 1964.

Kintner, William R., and Scott, Harriet East. *The Nuclear Revolution in Soviet Military Affairs.* Norman: University of Oklahoma Press, 1968.

Kissinger, Henry A. "NATO: Evolution or Decline." Chapter in *The US and The Atlantic Community.* Austin: University of Texas Press, 1967.

———, ed. *Problems of National Strategy.* New York: Praeger, 1965.

Kolkowicz, Roman. *The Soviet Military and The Communist Party.* Princeton: Princeton University Press, 1967.

Kowalewski, Jan. "The Geopolitical Aspects of Soviet Imperialism." Chapter 14 in *The Soviet Navy,* M. G. Saunders, ed. New York: Praeger, 1958.

Laqueur, Walter Z. *The Road to Jerusalem.* New York: Macmillan, 1968.

———. *The Soviet Union and the Middle East.* New York: Praeger, 1959.

Linden, Carl A. *Khrushchev and the Soviet Leadership, 1957–1964.* Baltimore: The Johns Hopkins Press, 1966.

McIntryre, William R. "Report on Limited War" in *Editorial Research Reports,* Vol. II, 1958, July 23, 1958, pp. 549–568.

McKean, Dayton David. *Party and Pressure Politics.* Boston: Houghton Mifflin Co., 1949.

Mackintosh, J. Malcolm. "The Soviet General's View of China in the 1960s." Chapter 10 of *Sino-Soviet Military Relations.* New York: Praeger, 1966.

———. *Strategy and Tactics of Soviet Foreign Policy.* New York: Oxford University Press, 1963.

Marshall, Charles Burton. *The Cold War: A Concise History.* New York: Franklin Watts, Inc., 1965.

Martin, L. W. *The Sea In Modern Strategy.* New York: Praeger, 1967.

Mayhew, Christopher. *Britain's Role Tomorrow.* London: Hutchinson, 1967.

Moore, James E. "The Military Effectiveness of NATO." Chapter in *NATO In Quest of Cohension,* Karl H. Cerny, and Henry W. Briefs, eds. New York: Praeger, 1965.

Morley, Derek W. "Technology and Weapons." Chapter 10 of *The Soviet Navy,* M. G. Saunders, ed. New York: Praeger, 1958.

Mosely, Philip E. *The Kremlin and World Politics.* New York: Random House, 1960.

Moulton, J. L., Maj. Gen. "British Defence Policy 1968." Chapter in *Brassey's Annual, The Armed Forces Yearbook, 1968.* New York: Praeger, 1968.

———. "The Israel-Arab War June, 1967." Chapter 1 of *Brassey's Annual: The Armed Forces Yearbook 1967.* New York: Praeger, 1967.

Nicholl, A. D., Rear Adm., RN. "Geography and Strategy." Chapter 12 of

The Soviet Navy, M. G. Saunders, ed. New York: Praeger, 1958.

Osgood, Robert Endicott. *Limited War, the Challenge to American Strategy.* Chicago: University of Chicago Press, 1957.

Perkins, Dexter. *The Diplomacy of A New Age.* Bloomington: Indiana University Press, 1967.

Ra'anan, Uri. "Problems of a Communist Foreign Policy." Chapter 8 of *The USSR After 50 years: Promise and Reality.* New York: Knopf, 1967.

———. "The USSR in the Near East: A Decade of Vicissitudes." Chapter 17 of *Modernizations of the Arab World,* J. H. Thompson and R. D. Reischauer, eds. Princeton: D. Van Nostrand Co., 1966.

Rankin, Karl Lott. *China Assignment.* Seattle: University of Washington Press, 1964.

Rubinstein, Alvin Z. *The Foreign Policy of the Soviet Union.* 2nd ed. New York: Random House, 1966.

Saunders, M. G., Comdr., RN. Introduction to *The Soviet Navy*. New York: Praeger, 1958.

Schelling, Thomas C. *Arms and Influence.* New Haven: Yale University Press, 1966.

Schofield, B. B. *British Sea Power.* London: B. T. Batsford, 1967.

Shulman, Marshall D. *Beyond the Cold War.* New Haven: Yale University Press, 1966.

———. *Stalin's Foreign Policy Reappraised.* Cambridge: Harvard University Press, 1963.

Sokolovskii, V. D. *Soviet Military Strategy,* translated by Herbert S. Dinerstein, Leon Goure, Thomas W. Wolfe, Moscow: Military Publishing House of the USSR. Translation published by Rand Corporation. Englewood Cliffs, N.J.: Prentice-Hall, 1963.

Sorensen, Theodore C. *Kennedy*. New York: Harper and Row, 1965.

Stebbins, Richard B. *The US in World Affairs, 1958,* Council of Foreign Relations. New York: Harper and Bros., 1959.

Steel, Ronald. *Pax Americana*. New York: The Viking Press, 1967.

Steele, T. *The American People and China*. New York: McGraw-Hill Book Co., 1966.

Stevenson, William. *Strike Zion*. New York: Bantam, 1967.

Stock, Ernest. *Israel on the Road to Sinai, 1949–1956, with a Sequel on the Six Day War, 1967*. Ithaca: Cornell University Press, 1967.

Thomas, John R. "The Limits of Alliance: The Quemoy Crisis of 1958." Chapter 7 of *Sino-Soviet Military Relations,* Raymond L. Garthoff, ed. New York: Praeger, 1966.

Thursfield, H. G., Rear Adm., RN, ed. *Brassey's Annual: The Armed Forces Year Book, 1958*. New York: Macmillan, 1958.

———. *Brassey's Annual: The Armed Forces Year Book, 1959*. New York: Macmillan, 1959.

Toshikazu, Ohmal, Capt. "The New Position of Japan in the General Strategic Picture of the Far East." in Chapter 13 "On the Perimeter." *The Soviet Navy*, Saunders, Cdr. M. T., RN, ed. New York: Praeger, 1958.

Truman, Harry S. *Years of Trial and Hope, 1946–1952*. Garden City, N.Y.: Doubleday and Co., 1956.

Tsou, Tang. *The Embroilment Over Quemoy: Mao, Chiang and Dulles.* Salt Lake City: University of Utah Press, 1958.

Ulam, Adam B. *Expansion & Coexistence, The History of Soviet Foreign Policy, 1917–67.* New York: Praeger, 1968.

Warburg, James P. *Crosscurrents in the Middle East.* New York: Atheneum, 1968.

Watson, Hugh Seaton *The East European Revolution.* London: Methuen and Co., 1950.

Weintal, Edward, and Bartlett, Charles. *Facing The Brink.* New York: Charles Scribner's Sons, 1967.

Wolfe, Thomas W. *Soviet Strategy at the Crossroads.* Cambridge: Harvard University Press, 1964.

———. "Trends in Soviet Thinking on Theater Warfare and Limited War." Chapter in *The Military-Technical Revolution: Its Impact on Strategy and Foreign Policy,* John Erickson, ed. New York: Praeger, 1966.

Young, Kenneth T. *Negotiating with the Chinese Communists: The United States Experience, 1953–1967.* New York: McGraw-Hill Book Co., 1968.

Zagoria, Donald S. *The Sino-Soviet Conflict 1956–1961.* Princeton: Princeton University Press, 1962.

———. *Vietnam Triangle.* New York: Pegasus, 1967.

INDEX